10 ACTUAL, OFFICIAL RECENT LSAT PREPTESTS

Official LSAT PrepTests 41–50

Published by
Cambridge LSAT
225 W. Verdugo Ave., #302
Burbank, CA 91502

Author: Morley Tatro

Manufactured in the United States
September 2010

ISBN-10: 1-4538-2069-8
ISBN-13: 978-1-4538-2069-8

Official LSAT content delivered instantly to your computer!

www.cambridgelsat.com

Full-Length Tests   **Individual Sections**   **Drilling Problem Sets**   **Prep Books**   **Explanations**   **Bundles**

If you're preparing for the LSAT (Law School Admission Test), chances are you understand the importance of this crucial admission test. In order to perform at your highest potential, quality preparation is critical. With so many prep courses and guides on the market, it's easy to become confused. The key to preparation is consistent and effective use of real LSAT questions. Until recently, it has been very difficult to acquire real LSAT questions in various groupings. Short of shelling out the money for an expensive prep course, you would have to go through the time-consuming process of breaking up PrepTests into question/game/passage types. Cambridge LSAT has the answer. We have done all that for you, so that you can allocate your time effectively. In addition to being broken down by type, our question/game/passage groupings are each presented in order of increasing difficulty, so that you can start with the most manageable content and progress through the most difficult material the LSAT has to offer. The site also features a number of useful free resources, including a test tracking spreadsheet, a Logic Games tracker, advice, an LSAT FAQ, tutor listings, Logic Games practice, prep book excerpts/recommendations, and June 2007 LSAT explanations. Stop by today and download the materials you need.

Why Cambridge LSAT?
o   You can print clean copies when needed to redo problems
o   No need to wait for books in the mail or go to the bookstore
o   Eliminates the cost of shipping
o   No need to tear out pages should you need to separate particular problems into groups
o   Gives you immediate access to real test content
o   You can purchase questions in whatever grouping fits your study plan
o   You can acquire tests/questions that are hard to find and/or out-of-print

Have a question, comment, or concern? E-mail us at info@cambridgelsat.com.

Available at www.cambridgelsat.com/bookstore/

LSAT Logic Games Drilling Workbooks, Volumes 1, 2, and 3

LSAT Logical Reasoning Drilling Workbooks, Volumes 1, 2, and 3

LSAT Reading Comprehension Drilling Workbooks, Volumes 1, 2, and 3

10 Actual, Official LSAT PrepTests (Out-of-Print, Recent, and More Recent)

LSAT Endurance Training, Volumes 1, 2, and Extreme Edition

LSAT Logic Games Repetition Workbooks, Volumes 1, 2, and 3

LSAT Logic Games Solutions Manual

The Big Fat Genius Guide to LSAT Logic Games

LSAT Logical Reasoning Strategy Guide Workbook

Ultimate LSAT Prep Package

TABLE OF CONTENTS

INTRODUCTION

About the LSAT

The LSAT, or Law School Admission Test, is a half-day standardized test which is used to compare candidates for admission to most law schools in the United States and Canada. The test consists of four scored multiple-choice sections, one unscored multiple-choice section, and one unscored Writing Sample. The test is administered four times each year, once in each of four months: February, June, September or October, and December. As of 2001, the February administrations have been undisclosed, which means that they are not released to the test takers, nor are they released as PrepTests.

The following table illustrates the structure of the test:

Section Type	Time	Scored?	Questions
Logical Reasoning	35 minutes	Yes	24-26
Logical Reasoning	35 minutes	Yes	24-26
Logic Games (Analytical Reasoning)	35 minutes	Yes	22-24
Reading Comprehension	35 minutes	Yes	26-28
Experimental (one of the above types)	35 minutes	No	22-28
Writing Sample	35 minutes	No	NA

Keep in mind that, with the exception of the Writing Sample, which is always given as the sixth section, these sections can appear in any order. In previous years, the experimental section was consistently among the first three sections; however, recent test administrations have broken with this tradition. The first three sections are completed consecutively without any breaks. There is a 10 to 15 minute break in between the third and fourth sections. The fourth and fifth sections are completed consecutively, and then the test booklets are collected. Once you have completed the Writing Sample, the test day is over.

LSAT PrepTests

In June of 1991, the modern format of the LSAT was unveiled and administered for the first time. LSAT PrepTests are previously-administered actual LSATs dating from that initial administration which have been released for the purpose of preparation. Including the three February tests in LSAC's The Official LSAT SuperPrep, there are over 70 available LSAT PrepTests. With so much official content available, there's no compelling reason to practice with anything but real questions. This book contains PrepTests numbered 41 through 50, each in its entirety. These tests were administered from October of 2003 through September of 2006. With the exception of PrepTest 18, the tests are numbered in the order in which they were administered. For a complete list of available PrepTests and their respective administration dates, visit **www.cambridgelsat.com/resources/data/preptest-numbers-dates/**. LSAC does not release the unscored experimental sections; the questions are subsequently used on scored sections. Thus, each LSAT PrepTest contains four multiple-choice sections.

Logical Reasoning

Each LSAT features two scored Logical Reasoning sections, each of which contains between 24 and 26 questions. Logical Reasoning questions ask you to critically dissect arguments and fact sets and make inferences from the statements, collectively referred to as the stimulus. Stimuli with argumentation can be followed by any one of the following question types: Main Conclusion, Flaw, Parallel (Reasoning), Parallel (Flaw), Necessary Assumption, Sufficient Assumption, Strengthen, Weaken, Evaluate, Principle (Identify), Principle (Apply), etc. Stimuli without argumentation, typically presented as factual information, tend to be followed by one of the following question types: Must Be True, Most Strongly Supported, Paradox, etc. A thorough understanding of formal logic principles, especially sufficient and necessary conditions, is helpful in answering the most difficult Logical Reasoning questions.

Logic Games (Analytical Reasoning)

The Logic Games, or Analytical Reasoning section, is typically the most intimidating section for people starting out with their preparation. For most, taking a timed Logic Games section without any prior prep work in this area results in incomplete and inaccurate performance. LSAT Logic Games test your ability to deductively examine a framework of relationships and determine what must be true, what could be true, what is not necessarily true, and what cannot be true. Each Analytical Reasoning section consists of exactly four games, or puzzles, and each game is followed by between five and eight questions. Logic Games tend to hinge on at least one of three recurring themes: ordering, grouping, and assignment.

Reading Comprehension

The Reading Comprehension section of the test is generally the most familiar of the three scored section types. Consequently, it can be the most difficult of the three section types in which to make gains. Each Reading Comprehension section features four passages, each followed by between five and eight questions. Since the June 2007 administration (available as a free PrepTest at **www.lsac.org**), every Reading Comprehension section has featured one set of comparative passages in place of one of the single passages. Since none of the PrepTests in this book contain comparative reading passages, we highly recommend that you purchase some of the most recent tests, either individually through **www.cambridgelsat.com**, or by picking up a copy of 10 More Actual, Official Recent LSAT PrepTests or 10 Very Recent Actual, Official LSAT PrepTests. The questions test your command of both global ideas and fine details presented in the passages. Reading Comprehension questions routinely inquire about authors' views, outside views, main points, definitions, passage structures, argumentative functions, and general inferences.

The Experimental Section

LSAC uses a process called equating to ensure that the same score across different test administrations means the same thing. In other words, a 160 on one test should indicate the same

INTRODUCTION

level of performance as a 160 on another test. In order to equate the tests, LSAC includes an unscored experimental section with each administration. Multiple experimental sections are used during each administration so that LSAC can pretest a lot of questions. Prior to ever appearing on a scored section of an LSAT, each individual question has undergone extensive testing. In this way, LSAC can control the difficulty levels of the individual scored sections to a high degree of accuracy. The experimental section is always one of the three multiple-choice section types (Logical Reasoning, Logic Games, or Reading Comprehension). There is little use in trying to figure out which section is experimental, and attempting to do so could have a detrimental effect on your score.

The Writing Sample

Since most law school exams involve writing under timed pressure, the LSAT includes a timed Writing Sample, administered as the sixth section of the test. It is unscored. However, each law school to which you apply will receive a copy of your Writing Sample. Thus, it is important that you at least exert some effort in framing an appropriate argument for the topic at hand. The writing prompt is given in the form of a decision prompt. A scenario will be presented, followed by two distinct courses of action. Your job is to persuasively argue one of the two choices. There is no "right" or "wrong" answer; each side will have both positives and negatives. Make sure to write legibly, and back up your position clearly and concisely.

Timed Practice

The time constraints are one of the biggest challenges of the LSAT, and as such, it is important to include regular timed practice in your prep regimen as the date of your actual test approaches. This book is designed so that you can practice under timed conditions with some of the most recent LSAT PrepTests. You can use this book to take either individual sections of tests or full-length, timed tests. Visit **www.cambridgelsat.com/resources/spreadsheets/test-tracking-spreadsheet/** to pick up a free copy of our test tracking spreadsheet. You can use it to score PrepTests 48–50, and it will help you identify particular areas to focus on in your subsequent prep work. If you need to print additional answer sheets, visit **www.cambridgelsat.com/resources/free-downloads/answer-sheets-etc/**.

The Fundamentals

While timed practice is necessary, it is generally not sufficient to reach your maximum potential on the exam. Taking test after test without learning and integrating effective problem-solving strategies is akin to taking algebra tests before learning proper addition, subtraction, multiplication, and division techniques. The logical thinking tested by the LSAT is foreign to the majority of beginning students and it takes time, practice, and patience to assimilate. To master the concepts routinely tested by the LSAT, we recommend that you also purchase at least one reputable strategy guide and problem sets for drilling the different question types. Our website features both downloadable and paperback products which address these critical prep components. Should you have any questions regarding recommended materials, send an e-mail to **info@cambridgelsat.com**.

PREPTEST 41
OCTOBER 2003
FORM 3LSS58

SECTION I

Time—35 minutes

25 Questions

<u>Directions:</u> The questions in this section are based on the reasoning contained in brief statements or passages. For some questions, more than one of the choices could conceivably answer the question. However, you are to choose the <u>best</u> answer; that is, the response that most accurately and completely answers the question. You should not make assumptions that are by commonsense standards implausible, superfluous, or incompatible with the passage. After you have chosen the best answer, blacken the corresponding space on your answer sheet.

1. Because the statement "all gray rabbits are rabbits" is true, it follows by analogy that the statement "all suspected criminals are criminals" is also true.

The reasoning above is flawed because it fails to recognize that

(A) the relationship between being a criminal and being a rabbit is not of the same kind as that between being suspected and being gray

(B) the relationship between being suspected and being a rabbit is not of the same kind as that between being gray and being a criminal

(C) the relationship between being a gray rabbit and being a rabbit is not of the same kind as that between being a suspected criminal and being a criminal

(D) not all rabbits are gray

(E) not all criminals are suspected

2. A study of plaque buildup on teeth used three randomly assigned groups of people who brushed their teeth twice a day for a year. People in Group 1 used the same toothbrush all year. People in Group 2 used the same toothbrush all year but sterilized it each month. People in Group 3 used a new, sterile toothbrush each month. At the end of the year, people in Groups 1 and 2 had the same amount of plaque buildup as each other, while people in Group 3 had less plaque buildup.

Which one of the following, if true, most helps to explain the relative amounts of plaque buildup found in the three groups?

(A) The buildup of plaque on teeth, which brushing twice a day helps to prevent, is accelerated by the growth of bacteria on toothbrushes that remained unsterilized for more than a month.

(B) The stiffness of the bristles on new toothbrushes, which the mechanical action of brushing destroys after several months, inhibits the buildup of plaque.

(C) The people who did the study measured the amount of plaque buildup by a new method not usually employed by dentists.

(D) Before they joined the study, some of the people in Group 3 had been in the habit of brushing their teeth only once a day.

(E) The people in Group 2 and Group 3 brushed their teeth as vigorously as did the people in Group 1.

3. Xavier: Demand by tourists in Nepal for inexpensive *thangka* paintings has resulted in the proliferation of inferior *thangkas* containing symbolic inaccuracies—a sure sign of a dying art form. Nepal should prohibit sales of *thangkas* to tourists, for such a prohibition will induce artists to create *thangkas* that meet traditional standards.

Yvette: An art form without dedicated young artists will decay and die. If tourists were forbidden to buy *thangkas*, young artists would cease making *thangkas* and concentrate instead on an art form tourists can buy.

Yvette responds to Xavier by

(A) denying the existence of the problem that Xavier's proposal is designed to ameliorate

(B) challenging the integrity of Xavier's sources of information

(C) arguing that Xavier's proposal, if implemented, would result in the very consequences it is meant to prevent

(D) using an analogy to draw a conclusion that is inconsistent with the conclusion drawn by Xavier

(E) showing that the evidence presented by Xavier has no bearing on the point at issue

GO ON TO THE NEXT PAGE.

4. Industry experts expect improvements in job safety training to lead to safer work environments. A recent survey indicated, however, that for manufacturers who improved job safety training during the 1980s, the number of on-the-job accidents tended to increase in the months immediately following the changes in the training programs.

Which one of the following, if true, most helps to resolve the apparent discrepancy in the passage above?

(A) A similar survey found that the number of on-the-job accidents remained constant after job safety training in the transportation sector was improved.

(B) Manufacturers tend to improve their job safety training only when they are increasing the size of their workforce.

(C) Manufacturers tend to improve job safety training only after they have noticed that the number of on-the-job accidents has increased.

(D) It is likely that the increase in the number of on-the-job accidents experienced by many companies was not merely a random fluctuation.

(E) Significant safety measures, such as protective equipment and government safety inspections, were in place well before the improvements in job safety training.

5. Statistician: Two major studies found no causal link between medical procedure X and disorder Y, but these studies are flawed. One study looked at 1,000 people who had undergone procedure X and the other study looked at 1,100 people who had undergone procedure X. But because disorder Y occurs in only .02 percent of the population, researchers would need to include many more than 1,100 people in a study to detect even a doubling of the rate of disorder Y.

Which one of the following most accurately expresses the main conclusion of the statistician's argument?

(A) Contrary to the findings of two major studies, there is reason to think that procedure X causes disorder Y.

(B) Two studies that discovered no causal link between procedure X and disorder Y are unsound.

(C) Researchers should conduct more-extensive studies of procedure X to determine whether the procedure is causally linked with disorder Y.

(D) The two studies cited did not reach a conclusion as to whether disorder Y results from procedure X.

(E) Despite the opinions of many medical experts, it has not been established that there is a causal link between procedure X and disorder Y.

6. Patti: Most parents are eager for their preschoolers to learn as much as possible. However, instead of providing general opportunities for their children to learn, parents often direct their children's learning to their own personal concerns. Because children have a natural curiosity and thirst for knowledge, they learn an enormous amount simply through growing and adapting to the world. Therefore, this type of directed learning is unlikely to improve a child's preschool education.

Which one of the following is an assumption on which Patti's argument depends?

(A) Parents who use the type of directed learning in question have been exposed to misguided psychological theories about children.

(B) Children will have difficulty adapting to the world without the unique help and guidance of their parents.

(C) The type of directed learning in question is likely to enhance the general opportunities for children to learn.

(D) The type of directed learning in question is not a necessary part of the process of growing and adapting to the world.

(E) General opportunities to learn are not typical of the early years of formal education.

GO ON TO THE NEXT PAGE.

7. Two things are true of all immoral actions. First, if they are performed in public, they offend public sensibilities. Second, they are accompanied by feelings of guilt.

If all of the statements above are true, then which one of the following must be false?

(A) Some immoral actions that are not performed in public are not accompanied by feelings of guilt.

(B) Immoral actions are wrong solely by virtue of being accompanied by feelings of guilt.

(C) Some actions that offend public sensibilities if they are performed in public are not accompanied by feelings of guilt.

(D) Some actions that are accompanied by feelings of guilt are not immoral, even if they frequently offend public sensibilities.

(E) Every action performed in public that is accompanied by feelings of guilt is immoral.

8. Vervet monkeys use different alarm calls to warn each other of nearby predators, depending on whether the danger comes from land or from the air.

Which one of the following, if true, contributes most to an explanation of the behavior of vervet monkeys described above?

(A) By varying the pitch of its alarm call, a vervet monkey can indicate the number of predators approaching.

(B) Different land-based predators are responsible for different numbers of vervet monkey deaths.

(C) No predators that pose a danger to vervet monkeys can attack both from land and from the air.

(D) Vervet monkeys avoid land-based predators by climbing trees but avoid predation from the air by diving into foliage.

(E) Certain land-based predators feed only on vervet monkeys, whereas every predator that attacks vervet monkeys from the air feeds on many different animals.

9. Technological improvements will enable food production to increase as populations increase. However, increases in food production will be negligible unless societies become more centralized so that all factors contributing to the production of food can be better coordinated. But, historically, the more centralized a society was, the greater the percentage of its people who perished if and when it collapsed. Thus, increasing the centralization of societies in an effort to increase food production via better technology will merely exacerbate the disasters associated with societal collapse.

The statements above, if true, most strongly support which one of the following?

(A) The more centralized a society is, the greater its need for increased food production.

(B) Not every problem associated with the collapse of a centralized society would be prevented by technological improvements.

(C) The rate at which the world's population is growing will continue to increase indefinitely.

(D) The production of food can be increased only by improved technology.

(E) Societies have become more centralized as technology has improved.

10. In an experiment, scientists changed a single gene in cloned flies of a certain species. These cloned flies lacked the eye cells that give flies ultraviolet vision, even though cloned siblings with unaltered, otherwise identical genes had normal vision. Thus, scientists have shown that flies of this species lacking ultraviolet vision must have some damage to this gene.

Which one of the following is an assumption required by the argument?

(A) The relationship between genes and vision in flies is well understood.

(B) No other gene in the flies in the experiment is required for the formation of the ultraviolet vision cells.

(C) Ultraviolet vision is a trait found in all species of flies.

(D) The gene change had no effect on the flies other than the lack of ultraviolet vision cells.

(E) Ultraviolet vision is an environmentally influenced trait in the species of flies in the experiment.

GO ON TO THE NEXT PAGE.

11. In the recent election, a country's voters overwhelmingly chose Adler over Burke. Voters knew that Burke offered more effective strategies for dealing with most of the country's problems. Moreover, Burke has a long public record of successful government service that testifies to competence and commitment. It was well known, however, that Burke's environmental policy coincided with the interests of the country's most dangerous polluter, whereas Adler proposed a policy of strict environmental regulation.

Which one of the following is most strongly supported by the information above?

(A) Throughout their respective political careers, Adler has been more committed to taking measures to protect the country's environment than Burke has been.

(B) Voters realized that their country's natural resources are rapidly being depleted.

(C) The concern of the country's voters for the environment played an important role in Adler's election.

(D) Offering effective strategies for dealing with a country's problems is more important in winning an election than having a long record of successful government service.

(E) In every respect other than environmental policy, Burke would have served the country better than Adler will.

12. Poor nutrition is at the root of the violent behavior of many young offenders. Researchers observed that in a certain institution for young offenders, the violent inmates among them consistently chose, from the food available, those items that were low in nutrients. In a subsequent experiment, some of the violent inmates were placed on a diet high in nutrients. There was a steady improvement in their behavior over the four months of the experiment. These results confirm the link between poor nutrition and violent behavior.

Which one of the following, if true, most strengthens the argument?

(A) Some of the violent inmates who took part in the experiment had committed a large number of violent crimes.

(B) Dietary changes are easier and cheaper to implement than any other type of reform program in institutions for young offenders.

(C) Many young offenders have reported that they had consumed a low-nutrient food sometime in the days before they committed a violent crime.

(D) A further study investigated young offenders who chose a high-nutrient diet on their own and found that many of them were nonviolent.

(E) The violent inmates in the institution who were not placed on a high-nutrient diet did not show an improvement in behavior.

13. Robin: When a region's economy is faltering, many people lose their jobs. As a result, spending on consumer goods declines, leading in turn to more lost jobs and a worsening of the economy. Eventually, the economy becomes so bad that prices collapse; the lower prices encourage people to increase spending on consumer goods, and this higher spending results in economic improvement.

Terry: People cannot increase their spending if they have no jobs and no money for anything other than basic necessities, so price collapses cannot lead to economic improvement.

Which one of the following, if true, most undermines Terry's objection to Robin's analysis?

(A) Companies hire more workers after the economy starts to improve again, and many newly hired workers then make long-deferred purchases.

(B) Even when economic conditions are worsening, consumers realize that the economy will eventually improve.

(C) Even people who do not lose their jobs spend less in bad economic times and thus have savings available to spend when prices collapse.

(D) People who have lost their jobs must continue to buy some basic goods such as food, even during bad economic times.

(E) The prices of some consumer goods remain stable, even during a general price collapse.

GO ON TO THE NEXT PAGE.

14. Laila: Though lying may be unacceptable in most cases, there are exceptions: when lying brings about more good than harm, lying is morally permissible.

Which one of the following judgments conforms most closely to the principle stated by Laila?

(A) It is morally permissible for Marcus to lie to his parents about where he is going for the evening as long as what he is going to do is not itself a bad thing to do.

(B) It is morally permissible for Lane to lie to the police about the whereabouts of a friend even if Lane suspects the friend has committed a crime.

(C) It is morally permissible to lie about anything that affects only yourself.

(D) It is morally permissible for Debra to lie to keep Thomas from being unhappy as long as the lie helps Thomas and does no harm.

(E) It is morally permissible to lie to innocent people if the lie will cause those people to make a choice that will benefit them but may harm others.

15. If all works of art evoke intense feelings, and this sculpture is a work of art, then it follows that this sculpture evokes intense feelings. But this sculpture does not evoke intense feelings at all. So either this sculpture is not a work of art, or not all works of art evoke intense feelings.

Which one of the following arguments is most similar in its pattern of reasoning to the argument above?

(A) If all classes are canceled, and the biology lab is a class, then it follows that the biology lab is canceled. But the biology lab is not a class. So the biology lab is not canceled, or some classes are not canceled.

(B) If all medical research is significant, and this research is medical, then it follows that this research is significant. But this research is actually of no significance. So not all medical research is significant, and this research is not medical.

(C) If all vitamins are safe in large doses, and beta-carotene is a vitamin, then it follows that beta-carotene is safe in large doses. But beta-carotene is not safe in large doses. So not all vitamins are safe in large doses, or beta-carotene is not a vitamin.

(D) If all sciences rely heavily on mathematics, and clinical psychology is a science, then it follows that clinical psychology relies heavily on mathematics. But clinical psychology does not rely heavily on mathematics. So clinical psychology is not a science.

(E) If all classes are canceled today, then it follows that today is a holiday and the library is closed. But today is not a holiday. So some classes are not canceled, or the library is open.

16. With decreased production this year in many rice-growing countries, prices of the grain on world markets have increased. Analysts blame this increase on the fact that only a small percentage of world production is sold commercially, with government growers controlling most of the rest, distributing it for local consumption. With so little rice being traded freely, even slight changes in production can significantly affect the amount of rice available on world markets.

Which one of the following, if true, would most call into question the analysts' explanation of the price increase?

(A) Rice-importing countries reduce purchases of rice when the price increases dramatically.

(B) In times of decreased rice production, governments store more of the rice they control and reduce their local distribution of rice.

(C) In times of decreased rice production, governments export some of the rice originally intended for local distribution to countries with free grain markets.

(D) Governments that distribute the rice crop for local consumption purchase the grain commercially in the event of production shortfalls.

(E) During reduced rice harvests, rice-importing countries import other kinds of crops, although this fails to compensate for decreased rice imports.

GO ON TO THE NEXT PAGE.

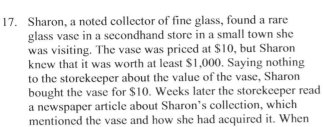

17. Sharon, a noted collector of fine glass, found a rare glass vase in a secondhand store in a small town she was visiting. The vase was priced at $10, but Sharon knew that it was worth at least $1,000. Saying nothing to the storekeeper about the value of the vase, Sharon bought the vase for $10. Weeks later the storekeeper read a newspaper article about Sharon's collection, which mentioned the vase and how she had acquired it. When the irate storekeeper later accused Sharon of taking advantage of him, Sharon replied that she had done nothing wrong.

Which one of the following principles, if established, most helps to justify Sharon's position?

(A) A seller is not obligated to inform a buyer of anything about the merchandise that the seller offers for sale except for the demanded price.

(B) It is the responsibility of the seller, not the buyer, to make sure that the amount of money a buyer gives a seller in exchange for merchandise matches the amount that the seller demands for that merchandise.

(C) A buyer's sole obligation to a seller is to pay in full the price that the seller demands for a piece of merchandise that the buyer acquires from the seller.

(D) It is the responsibility of the buyer, not the seller, to ascertain that the quality of a piece of merchandise satisfies the buyer's standards.

(E) The obligations that follow from any social relationship between two people who are well acquainted override any obligations that follow from an economic relationship between the two.

18. Health officials now recommend that people reduce their intake of foods that are high in cholesterol, such as red meat. The recent decline in the total consumption of beef indicates that many people are following this recommendation. But restaurants specializing in steak are flourishing despite an overall decline in the restaurant industry. So clearly there still are a lot of people completely ignoring the health recommendation.

The argument is vulnerable to criticism on which one of the following grounds?

(A) It neglects to consider whether restaurants that specialize in steak try to attract customers by offering steak dinners at low prices.

(B) It assumes without warrant that people who eat steak at steak restaurants do not need to reduce their intake of foods that are high in cholesterol.

(C) It presupposes that the popularity of restaurants that specialize in steaks is a result of a decrease in the price of beef.

(D) It mistakes the correlation of the decline in beef consumption and the decline in the restaurant industry for a causal relation.

(E) It fails to consider whether the people who patronize steak restaurants have heeded the health officials by reducing their cholesterol intake in their at-home diets.

19. Film critic: There has been a recent spate of so-called "documentary" films purporting to give the "true story" of one historical event or another. But most of these films have been inaccurate and filled with wild speculations, usually about conspiracies. The filmmakers defend their works by claiming that freedom of speech entitles them to express their views. Although that claim is true, it does not support the conclusion that anyone ought to pay attention to the absurd views expressed in the films.

To which one of the following principles does the film critic's commentary most closely conform?

(A) Although filmmakers are entitled to express absurd views, they are not justified in doing so.

(B) Everyone ought to ignore films containing wild speculations about conspiracies.

(C) Freedom of speech sometimes makes the expression of absurd views necessary.

(D) Freedom of speech does not entitle filmmakers to present inaccurate speculations as truth.

(E) Views that people are entitled to express need not be views to which anyone is obliged to pay attention.

GO ON TO THE NEXT PAGE.

20. The people most likely to watch a televised debate between political candidates are the most committed members of the electorate and thus the most likely to have already made up their minds about whom to support. Furthermore, following a debate, uncommitted viewers are generally undecided about who won the debate. Hence, winning a televised debate does little to bolster one's chances of winning an election.

The reasoning in the argument is most vulnerable to criticism because the argument fails to consider the possibility that

(A) watching an exciting debate makes people more likely to vote in an election
(B) the voting behavior of people who do not watch a televised debate is influenced by reports about the debate
(C) there are differences of opinion about what constitutes winning or losing a debate
(D) people's voting behavior may be influenced in unpredictable ways by comments made by the participants in a televised debate
(E) people who are committed to a particular candidate will vote even if their candidate is perceived as having lost a televised debate

21. Many successful graphic designers began their careers after years of formal training, although a significant number learned their trade more informally on the job. But no designer ever became successful who ignored the wishes of a client.

If all of the statements above are true, which one of the following must also be true?

(A) All graphic designers who are unsuccessful have ignored the wishes of a client.
(B) Not all formally trained graphic designers ignore clients' wishes.
(C) The more attentive a graphic designer is to a client's wishes, the more likely the designer is to be successful.
(D) No graphic designers who learn their trade on the job will ignore clients' wishes.
(E) The most successful graphic designers learn their trade on the job.

22. If violations of any of a society's explicit rules routinely go unpunished, then that society's people will be left without moral guidance. Because people who lack moral guidance will act in many different ways, chaos results. Thus, a society ought never to allow any of its explicit rules to be broken with impunity.

The reasoning in the argument is most vulnerable to criticism on the grounds that the argument

(A) takes for granted that a society will avoid chaos as long as none of its explicit rules are routinely violated with impunity
(B) fails to consider that the violated rules might have been made to prevent problems that would not arise even if the rules were removed
(C) infers, from the claim that the violation of some particular rules will lead to chaos, that the violation of any rule will lead to chaos
(D) confuses the routine nonpunishment of violations of a rule with sometimes not punishing violations of the rule
(E) takes for granted that all of a society's explicit rules result in equally serious consequences when broken

23. Perception cannot be a relationship between a conscious being and a material object that causes that being to have beliefs about that object. For there are many imperceptible material objects about which we have beliefs.

Which one of the following is most closely parallel in its flawed reasoning to the flawed reasoning in the argument above?

(A) Art cannot be an artifact created by someone with the express purpose of causing an aesthetic reaction in its audience. For we often have aesthetic reactions to artifacts that are not art.
(B) Liberty cannot be the obligation of other people not to prevent one from doing as one wishes. For no matter what one tries to do some people will try to prevent it.
(C) Preparation cannot be action directed toward fulfilling needs and solving problems before they arise. For there are problems so severe that no amount of preparation will help.
(D) Happiness cannot be the state of mind in which pleasure both qualitatively and quantitatively predominates over pain. For we simply cannot compare pain and pleasure qualitatively.
(E) Physics cannot be the science that investigates the ultimate principles of nature. For human beings are finite, and the ultimate principles cannot be understood by finite beings.

GO ON TO THE NEXT PAGE.

24. Ethicist: In general it is wrong to use medical treatments and procedures of an experimental nature without the patient's consent, because the patient has a right to reject or accept a treatment on the basis of full information about all the available options. But knowledge of the best treatment for emergency conditions can be gained only if consent to experimental practices is sometimes bypassed in medical emergencies. So some restricted nonconsensual medical research should be allowed.

Which one of the following is an assumption required by the ethicist's argument?

(A) Doctors often do not know what is best for their own patients in emergency situations.

(B) If patients knew that experimental treatments were being used in medical emergencies, it could adversely affect the outcome of that research.

(C) Nonconsensual medical research should be allowed only if the research is highly likely to yield results that will benefit the patient.

(D) In cases where the best treatment option is unknown, a patient ceases to have the right to know the treatment plan and the alternatives.

(E) The right of patients to informed consent is outweighed in at least some medical emergencies by the possible benefits of research conducted without their consent.

25. Gas station owner: Increased fuel efficiency reduces air pollution and dependence on imported oil, which has led some people to suggest that automobile manufacturers should make cars smaller to increase their fuel efficiency. But smaller cars are more likely to be seriously damaged in collisions and provide less protection for their occupants. Greater fuel efficiency is not worth the added risk to human lives; therefore, manufacturers should not seek to increase fuel efficiency.

The reasoning in the gas station owner's argument is flawed because the argument

(A) presumes, without providing justification, that it would be impossible to reduce the likelihood of dangerous accidents for small cars

(B) concludes, on the basis of the claim that one means to an end is unacceptable, that the end should not be pursued

(C) draws a conclusion about what should be done from premises all of which are about factual matters only

(D) presupposes the truth of what it sets out to prove

(E) presumes, without providing justification, that increasing fuel efficiency is the only way to reduce air pollution

S T O P
IF YOU FINISH BEFORE TIME IS CALLED, YOU MAY CHECK YOUR WORK ON THIS SECTION ONLY.
DO NOT WORK ON ANY OTHER SECTION IN THE TEST.

SECTION II
Time—35 minutes
24 Questions

Directions: Each group of questions in this section is based on a set of conditions. In answering some of the questions, it may be useful to draw a rough diagram. Choose the response that most accurately and completely answers each question and blacken the corresponding space on your answer sheet.

Questions 1–7

A closet contains exactly six hangers—1, 2, 3, 4, 5, and 6—hanging, in that order, from left to right. It also contains exactly six dresses—one gauze, one linen, one polyester, one rayon, one silk, and one wool—a different dress on each of the hangers, in an order satisfying the following conditions:

The gauze dress is on a lower-numbered hanger than the polyester dress.
The rayon dress is on hanger 1 or hanger 6.
Either the wool dress or the silk dress is on hanger 3.
The linen dress hangs immediately to the right of the silk dress.

1. Which one of the following could be an accurate matching of the hangers to the fabrics of the dresses that hang on them?

(A) 1: wool; 2: gauze; 3: silk; 4: linen; 5: polyester; 6: rayon
(B) 1: rayon; 2: wool; 3: gauze; 4: silk; 5: linen; 6: polyester
(C) 1: polyester; 2: gauze; 3: wool; 4: silk; 5: linen; 6: rayon
(D) 1: linen; 2: silk; 3: wool; 4: gauze; 5: polyester; 6: rayon
(E) 1: gauze; 2: rayon; 3: silk; 4: linen; 5: wool; 6: polyester

2. If both the silk dress and the gauze dress are on odd-numbered hangers, then which one of the following could be true?

(A) The polyester dress is on hanger 1.
(B) The wool dress is on hanger 2.
(C) The polyester dress is on hanger 4.
(D) The linen dress is on hanger 5.
(E) The wool dress is on hanger 6.

3. If the silk dress is on an even-numbered hanger, which one of the following could be on the hanger immediately to its left?

(A) the gauze dress
(B) the linen dress
(C) the polyester dress
(D) the rayon dress
(E) the wool dress

4. If the polyester dress is on hanger 2, then which one of the following must be true?

(A) The silk dress is on hanger 1.
(B) The wool dress is on hanger 3.
(C) The linen dress is on hanger 4.
(D) The linen dress is on hanger 5.
(E) The rayon dress is on hanger 6.

5. Which one of the following CANNOT be true?

(A) The linen dress hangs immediately next to the gauze dress.
(B) The polyester dress hangs immediately to the right of the rayon dress.
(C) The rayon dress hangs immediately to the left of the wool dress.
(D) The silk dress is on a lower-numbered hanger than the gauze dress.
(E) The wool dress is on a higher-numbered hanger than the rayon dress.

6. Which one of the following CANNOT hang immediately next to the rayon dress?

(A) the gauze dress
(B) the linen dress
(C) the polyester dress
(D) the silk dress
(E) the wool dress

7. Assume that the original condition that the linen dress hangs immediately to the right of the silk dress is replaced by the condition that the wool dress hangs immediately to the right of the silk dress. If all the other initial conditions remain in effect, which one of the following must be false?

(A) The linen dress is on hanger 1.
(B) The gauze dress is on hanger 2.
(C) The wool dress is on hanger 4.
(D) The silk dress is on hanger 5.
(E) The polyester dress is on hanger 6.

GO ON TO THE NEXT PAGE.

Questions 8–12

At a children's festival, exactly four songs are performed, each exactly once: "Night's All Right," "Question Man," "Rhino Rock," and "Sammy." The songs are performed consecutively, each on a different one of exactly four instruments: flute, guitar, harmonica, or keyboard. The songs are performed in accordance with the following:

The first song performed is not performed on the flute.
If "Sammy" is performed on the keyboard, then "Rhino Rock" is performed on the harmonica.
If "Question Man" is performed on the keyboard, then "Night's All Right" is performed on the flute.
The song performed on the keyboard immediately follows "Rhino Rock" and immediately precedes "Night's All Right."

8. Which one of the following could be an accurate matching of the four songs performed at the festival with the instruments on which they are performed, listed in order from the first song performed to the last?

    (A)   "Night's All Right": guitar; "Question Man": keyboard; "Sammy": guitar; "Rhino Rock": flute
    (B)   "Question Man": guitar; "Rhino Rock": harmonica; "Sammy": keyboard; "Night's All Right": flute
    (C)   "Rhino Rock": flute; "Question Man": keyboard; "Night's All Right": harmonica; "Sammy": guitar
    (D)   "Sammy": harmonica; "Night's All Right": guitar; "Question Man": keyboard; "Rhino Rock": flute
    (E)   "Sammy": harmonica; "Rhino Rock": guitar; "Question Man": flute; "Night's All Right": keyboard

9. Which one of the following could be true?

    (A)   "Question Man" immediately follows the song performed on the keyboard.
    (B)   "Night's All Right" immediately precedes the song performed on the keyboard.
    (C)   "Question Man" immediately precedes the song performed on the guitar.
    (D)   "Rhino Rock" immediately precedes the song performed on the harmonica.
    (E)   "Sammy" immediately precedes the song performed on the guitar.

10. Which one of the following CANNOT be true of the song performed on the flute?

    (A)   It immediately precedes "Question Man."
    (B)   It immediately follows "Question Man."
    (C)   It immediately precedes "Rhino Rock."
    (D)   It immediately follows "Night's All Right."
    (E)   It immediately follows "Sammy."

11. If "Rhino Rock" is the second song performed at the festival, then which one of the following could be true?

    (A)   The first song performed is performed on the keyboard.
    (B)   The third song performed is performed on the guitar.
    (C)   The third song performed is performed on the flute.
    (D)   "Night's All Right" is performed on the guitar.
    (E)   "Rhino Rock" is performed on the guitar.

12. If "Question Man" is the third song performed at the festival, then each of the following could be true EXCEPT:

    (A)   "Question Man" is performed on the guitar.
    (B)   "Question Man" is performed on the keyboard.
    (C)   "Rhino Rock" is performed on the guitar.
    (D)   "Sammy" is performed on the guitar.
    (E)   "Sammy" is performed on the harmonica.

GO ON TO THE NEXT PAGE.

Questions 13–17

Each of the seven members of the board of directors—
Guzman, Hawking, Lepp, Miyauchi, Upchurch, Wharton,
and Zhu—serves on exactly one of two committees—the
finance committee or the incentives committee. Only board
members serve on these committees. Committee membership
is consistent with the following conditions:

If Guzman serves on the finance committee, then Hawking
serves on the incentives committee.
If Lepp serves on the finance committee, then Miyauchi
and Upchurch both serve on the incentives committee.
Wharton serves on a different committee from the one on
which Zhu serves.
Upchurch serves on a different committee from the one on
which Guzman serves.
If Zhu serves on the finance committee, so does Hawking.

13. Which one of the following could be a complete and
accurate list of the members of the finance committee?

(A)   Guzman, Hawking, Miyauchi, Wharton
(B)   Guzman, Lepp, Zhu
(C)   Hawking, Miyauchi, Zhu
(D)   Hawking, Upchurch, Wharton, Zhu
(E)   Miyauchi, Upchurch, Wharton

14. Which one of the following pairs of board members
CANNOT both serve on the incentives committee?

(A)   Guzman and Hawking
(B)   Guzman and Wharton
(C)   Hawking and Wharton
(D)   Miyauchi and Upchurch
(E)   Miyauchi and Wharton

15. What is the maximum number of members on the finance
committee?

(A)   two
(B)   three
(C)   four
(D)   five
(E)   six

16. If Miyauchi and Wharton both serve on the finance
committee, then which one of the following could be
true?

(A)   Guzman and Lepp both serve on the finance
committee.
(B)   Guzman and Upchurch both serve on the
incentives committee.
(C)   Hawking and Zhu both serve on the finance
committee.
(D)   Lepp and Upchurch both serve on the incentives
committee.
(E)   Zhu and Upchurch both serve on the finance
committee.

17. If Guzman serves on the incentives committee, then
which one of the following must be true?

(A)   Hawking serves on the finance committee.
(B)   Lepp serves on the incentives committee.
(C)   Miyauchi serves on the finance committee.
(D)   Wharton serves on the incentives committee.
(E)   Zhu serves on the finance committee.

GO ON TO THE NEXT PAGE.

Questions 18–24

Eight people—Fiona, George, Harriet, Ingrid, Karl, Manuel, Olivia, and Peter—are sitting, evenly spaced, around a circular picnic table. Any two of them are said to be sitting directly across from one another if and only if there are exactly three other people sitting between them, counting in either direction around the table. The following conditions apply:

Fiona sits directly across from George.

Harriet sits immediately next to neither Fiona nor Karl.

Ingrid sits immediately next to, and immediately clockwise from, Olivia.

18. Which one of the following could be the order in which four of the people are seated, with no one else seated between them, counting clockwise around the table?

(A)   George, Peter, Karl, Fiona
(B)   Harriet, Olivia, Ingrid, Karl
(C)   Ingrid, Fiona, Peter, Manuel
(D)   Olivia, Manuel, Karl, George
(E)   Peter, Harriet, Karl, Fiona

19. If Harriet and Olivia each sits immediately next to George, then which one of the following could be the two people each of whom sits immediately next to Peter?

(A)   Fiona and Karl
(B)   Fiona and Olivia
(C)   Harriet and Ingrid
(D)   Harriet and Karl
(E)   Karl and Manuel

20. If George does not sit immediately next to Harriet, then which one of the following could be the two people each of whom sits immediately next to Manuel?

(A)   Fiona and Harriet
(B)   Fiona and Peter
(C)   George and Karl
(D)   George and Peter
(E)   Harriet and Peter

21. If Manuel sits immediately next to Olivia, then which one of the following people must sit immediately next to Fiona?

(A)   Harriet
(B)   Ingrid
(C)   Karl
(D)   Manuel
(E)   Peter

22. What is the minimum possible number of people sitting between Ingrid and Manuel, counting clockwise from Ingrid around the table?

(A)   zero
(B)   one
(C)   two
(D)   three
(E)   four

23. If Karl sits directly across from Ingrid, then each of the following people could sit immediately next to Olivia EXCEPT:

(A)   Fiona
(B)   George
(C)   Harriet
(D)   Manuel
(E)   Peter

24. If Karl sits directly across from Harriet, then what is the minimum possible number of people sitting between George and Karl, counting clockwise from George to Karl?

(A)   zero
(B)   one
(C)   two
(D)   three
(E)   four

S T O P
IF YOU FINISH BEFORE TIME IS CALLED, YOU MAY CHECK YOUR WORK ON THIS SECTION ONLY.
DO NOT WORK ON ANY OTHER SECTION IN THE TEST.

SECTION III
Time—35 minutes
26 Questions

Directions: The questions in this section are based on the reasoning contained in brief statements or passages. For some questions, more than one of the choices could conceivably answer the question. However, you are to choose the best answer; that is, the response that most accurately and completely answers the question. You should not make assumptions that are by commonsense standards implausible, superfluous, or incompatible with the passage. After you have chosen the best answer, blacken the corresponding space on your answer sheet.

1. The water of Lake Laberge, in Canada, currently contains high levels of the pesticide toxaphene. Authorities are puzzled because toxaphene was banned in North America in the early 1980s and now is used only in a few other parts of the world.

   Which one of the following, if true, does most to explain why the water of Lake Laberge currently contains high levels of toxaphene?

   (A) Levels of pesticides in the environment often continue to be high for decades after their use ends.
   (B) Lake Laberge's water contains high levels of other pesticides besides toxaphene.
   (C) Toxic chemicals usually do not travel large distances in the atmosphere.
   (D) North American manufacturers opposed banning toxaphene.
   (E) Toxic chemicals become more readily detectable once they enter organisms the size of fish.

2. Although Samantha likes both oolong and green tea, none of her friends likes both. However, all of her friends like black tea.

   If the statements above are true, each of the following could be true EXCEPT:

   (A) Samantha likes black tea.
   (B) None of Samantha's friends likes green tea.
   (C) Samantha's friends like exactly the same kinds of tea as each other.
   (D) One of Samantha's friends likes neither oolong nor green tea.
   (E) One of Samantha's friends likes all the kinds of teas that Samantha likes.

3. Because it permits a slower and more natural rhythm of life, living in the country is supposed to be more healthy and relaxed than living in the city. But surveys show that people living in the country become ill as often and as seriously as people living in the city, and that they experience an equal amount of stress.

   The statements above, if true, provide the most support for which one of the following?

   (A) Living in the country is neither healthier nor more relaxing than living in the city.
   (B) Living in the country does not in fact permit a slower and more natural rhythm of life than living in the city.
   (C) People whose rhythm of life is slow and natural recover quickly from illness.
   (D) Despite what people believe, a natural rhythm of life is unhealthy.
   (E) The amount of stress a person experiences depends on that person's rhythm of life.

4. Industrialist: Environmentalists contend that emissions from our factory pose a health risk to those living downwind. The only testimony presented in support of this contention comes from residents of the communities surrounding the factory. But only a trained scientist can determine whether or not these emissions are dangerous, and none of the residents are scientists. Hence our factory's emissions present no health risk.

   The reasoning in the industrialist's argument is flawed because the argument

   (A) impugns the motives of the residents rather than assessing the reasons for their contention
   (B) does not consider the safety of emissions from other sources in the area
   (C) presents no testimony from scientists that the emissions are safe
   (D) fails to discuss the benefits of the factory to the surrounding community
   (E) equivocates between two different notions of the term "health risk"

GO ON TO THE NEXT PAGE.

5. In the city of Glasgow, Scotland, trade doubled between 1750, when the first bank opened there, and 1765, when government regulations on banking were first implemented in Scotland.

Each of the following, if true, could contribute to an explanation of the doubling described above EXCEPT:

(A) The technological revolution that started in the early eighteenth century in England resulted in increased trade between England and Scotland.

(B) Reductions in tariffs on foreign goods in 1752 led to an increase in imports to Glasgow.

(C) The establishment of banking in Glasgow encouraged the use of paper money, which made financial transactions more efficient.

(D) Improvements in Scottish roads between 1750 and 1758 facilitated trade between Glasgow and the rest of Scotland.

(E) The initial government regulation of Scottish banks stimulated Glasgow's economy.

6. Some argue that laws are instituted at least in part to help establish a particular moral fabric in society. But the primary function of law is surely to help order society so that its institutions, organizations, and citizenry can work together harmoniously, regardless of any further moral aims of the law. Indeed, the highest courts have on occasion treated moral beliefs based on conscience or religious faith as grounds for making exceptions in the application of laws.

The statements above, if true, most strongly support which one of the following?

(A) The manner in which laws are applied sometimes takes into account the beliefs of the people governed by those laws.

(B) The law has as one of its functions the ordering of society but is devoid of moral aims.

(C) Actions based on religious belief or on moral conviction tend to receive the protection of the highest courts.

(D) The way a society is ordered by law should not reflect any moral convictions about the way society ought to be ordered.

(E) The best way to promote cooperation among a society's institutions, organizations, and citizenry is to institute order in that society by means of law.

7. In Western economies, more energy is used to operate buildings than to operate transportation. Much of the decline in energy consumption since the oil crisis of 1973 is due to more efficient use of energy in homes and offices. New building technologies, which make lighting, heating, and ventilation systems more efficient, have cut billions of dollars from energy bills in the West. Since energy savings from these efficiencies save several billion dollars per year today, we can conclude that 50 to 100 years from now they will save more than $200 billion per year (calculated in current dollars).

On which one of the following assumptions does the argument rely?

(A) Technology used to make buildings energy efficient will not become prohibitively expensive over the next century.

(B) Another oil crisis will occur in the next 50 to 100 years.

(C) Buildings will gradually become a less important consumer of energy than transportation.

(D) Energy bills in the West will be $200 billion lower in the next 50 to 100 years.

(E) Energy-efficient technologies based on new scientific principles will be introduced in the next 50 to 100 years.

GO ON TO THE NEXT PAGE.

8. Travel writer: A vacationer should choose an airline that has had an accident in the past 5 years. Though this may seem counterintuitive, studies show that the average airline has 1 accident every 5 years. So if an airline has had no accident during the past 5 years, the chances that the airline will have a crash are increased.

The flawed reasoning in the travel writer's argument is most similar to that in which one of the following arguments?

(A) A tossed coin has come up heads 100 times in a row. It is therefore reasonable to believe that the coin is not fair, and thus that it is more likely to come up heads than tails when it is flipped again.

(B) If there are 10 adult male baboons in a troop, the chance of an average adult male baboon ascending to dominance in any given year is 1 in 10. Thus, if an adult male baboon has been in the troop more than 10 years and has never ascended to dominance, then the chance of his doing so is now better than 1 in 10.

(C) On a given day, an average resident's chance of being involved in a traffic accident in a certain city is 1 in 10,000. Therefore, the chance of Marty, a 5-year-old resident, being involved in a traffic accident in the city on any given day is also 1 in 10,000.

(D) The average adolescent who works full-time in a certain country makes about 76 cents for every dollar that an adult who works full-time there makes. Therefore, since in this country the average adolescent who works part-time makes less than the average adolescent who works full-time, the average adolescent who works part-time makes less than 76 cents for every dollar made by an employed adult.

(E) Though until recently this chess grandmaster had responded to opening move X with move Y half of the time, in the current tournament he has responded to move X with move Y 90 percent of the time. Thus, in the next game of the current tournament, he is 90 percent likely to respond to move X with move Y.

9. Phoebe: There have been many reported sightings of strange glowing lights, but a number of these sightings have a straightforward, natural explanation. They occurred clustered in time and location around the epicenters of three earthquakes, and so were almost certainly earthquake lights, a form of ball lightning caused by stresses in the ground.

Quincy: I am skeptical that the association between the lights and the earthquakes is anything more than a coincidence. The theory that ground stresses related to earthquakes can cause any kind of lightning is extremely speculative.

In responding to Phoebe, Quincy

(A) takes a correlation to be a causal relation
(B) challenges the accuracy of the data about sightings that Phoebe takes for granted
(C) criticizes Phoebe's explanation as unsubstantiated
(D) offers an explanation of the glowing lights different from Phoebe's
(E) accuses Phoebe of introducing irrelevant information

10. Those who have the ability to fully concentrate are always of above-average intelligence. Also, being successfully trained in speed-reading will usually be accompanied by an increased ability to concentrate.

If the statements above are true, then each of the following could be true EXCEPT:

(A) Some people can speed-read, and are able to fully concentrate, but are of below-average intelligence.
(B) All people who can speed-read are of above-average intelligence.
(C) Many people of above-average intelligence are unable to fully concentrate.
(D) Some people with little ability to concentrate are of below-average intelligence, but can speed-read.
(E) All people who can speed-read are able to concentrate to some extent.

GO ON TO THE NEXT PAGE.

11. In order to maintain a high standard of living, a nation must maintain a functioning infrastructure. Major investment in the improvement of its infrastructure will, over time, reward a nation with a corresponding rise in its standard of living. Hence a nation whose standard of living is on the rise can be safely assumed to be a nation that has invested heavily in improving its infrastructure.

The reasoning in the argument is flawed because the argument fails to take into account that

(A) a nation that fails to invest in its infrastructure need not experience any resulting decline in its standard of living

(B) many nations are unable to make the needed investments in infrastructure

(C) the rise in a nation's standard of living that is prompted by investment in its infrastructure may take a long time to occur

(D) a rise in a nation's standard of living need not be the result of major investments in its infrastructure

(E) nations often experience short-term crises that require that resources be diverted to purposes other than the maintenance and improvement of infrastructure

12. Yang: Yeast has long been known to be a leaven, that is, a substance used in baking to make breads rise. Since biblical evidence ties the use of leavens to events dating back to 1200 B.C., we can infer that yeast was already known to be a leaven at that time.

Campisi: I find your inference unconvincing; several leavens other than yeast could have been known in 1200 B.C.

Campisi counters Yang's argument by

(A) suggesting that an alternative set of evidence better supports Yang's conclusion

(B) questioning the truth of a presumption underlying Yang's argument

(C) denying the truth of Yang's conclusion without considering the reason given for that conclusion

(D) pointing out that the premises of Yang's argument more strongly support a contrary conclusion

(E) calling into question the truth of the evidence presented in Yang's argument

13. Researcher: People with certain personality disorders have more theta brain waves than those without such disorders. But my data show that the amount of one's theta brain waves increases while watching TV. So watching too much TV increases one's risk of developing personality disorders.

A questionable aspect of the reasoning above is that it

(A) uses the phrase "personality disorders" ambiguously

(B) fails to define the phrase "theta brain waves"

(C) takes correlation to imply a causal connection

(D) draws a conclusion from an unrepresentative sample of data

(E) infers that watching TV is a consequence of a personality disorder

14. The authorship of the *Iliad* and the *Odyssey* has long been debated. Some traditional evidence suggests that Homer created both works, or at least large portions of them, but there is equally forceful evidence that he had nothing to do with either. Since there is no overwhelming evidence for either claim, we ought to accept the verdict of tradition that Homer is the principal author of both works.

Which one of the following most accurately expresses the principle underlying the argumentation above?

(A) If there is no overwhelming evidence for or against a hypothesis, then one should suspend judgment as to its truth.

(B) If a hypothesis goes against tradition, one should not accept the hypothesis without overwhelming evidence.

(C) If there is no overwhelming evidence for or against a hypothesis, one should believe it.

(D) One should accept the authority of tradition only if one has nontraditional evidence for the traditional hypothesis.

(E) One should defer to the authority of tradition if two or more hypotheses conflict with it.

GO ON TO THE NEXT PAGE.

15. Midlevel managers at large corporations are unlikely to suggest reductions in staff in their own departments even when these departments are obviously overstaffed.

Each of the following, if true, supports the claim above EXCEPT:

(A) The compensation paid to midlevel managers is greater when they supervise more workers.
(B) Midlevel managers have less work to do when their departments are overstaffed.
(C) Staff morale and productivity often suffer when workers are laid off.
(D) Departmental workloads at most large corporations increase and decrease significantly and unpredictably.
(E) Many large corporations allow managers to offer early retirement as a means of reducing staff.

16. Editorialist: Some people propose that, to raise revenues and encourage conservation, our country's taxes on oil, gasoline, and coal should be increased. Such a tax increase, however, would do more harm than good. By raising energy costs, the tax increase would decrease our competitiveness with other countries. Many families would be unfairly burdened with higher transportation costs. Finally, by reducing the demand for energy, the tax increase would reduce the number of energy production jobs.

Each of the following, if true, would weaken the editorialist's argument EXCEPT:

(A) The editorialist's country's budget deficit will decrease if the energy tax increase is implemented, thus benefiting the economy.
(B) Higher gasoline prices tend to lead to a cleaner environment, because people do less nonessential driving.
(C) The proposed tax increase would be larger for some energy sources than for others.
(D) Higher gasoline prices will encourage people to carpool, which will reduce individual transportation costs.
(E) The government would use the increase in tax revenue to create many more jobs than would be lost in the energy production sector.

17. Reporter: A team of scientists has recently devised a new test that for the first time accurately diagnoses autism in children as young as 18 months old. When used to evaluate 16,000 children at their 18-month checkup, the test correctly diagnosed all 10 children later confirmed to be autistic, though it also wrongly identified 2 children as autistic. Autistic children can therefore now benefit much earlier in life than before from the treatments already available.

Which one of the following is an assumption on which the reporter's argument depends?

(A) No test intended for diagnosing autism at such an early age existed before the new test was devised.
(B) A diagnostic test that sometimes falsely gives a positive diagnosis can still provide a reasonable basis for treatment decisions.
(C) The new test can be used to evaluate all children, regardless of the level of development of their verbal skills.
(D) Those children incorrectly identified as autistic will not be adversely affected by treatments aimed at helping autistic children.
(E) There was no reliable evidence that autism could affect children so young until the advent of the new test.

GO ON TO THE NEXT PAGE.

18. Tallulah: The columnist attributes the decline of interest in novels to consumerism, technology, and the laziness of people who prefer watching television to reading a novel. However, in reaching this conclusion, the columnist has overlooked important evidence. It is surely relevant that contemporary fiction is frequently of poor quality—indeed, much of it is meaningless and depressing—whereas many good newspapers, magazines, professional journals, and books of other types are currently available.

Which one of the following most accurately expresses the main conclusion of Tallulah's argument?

(A) Contemporary fiction is unpopular because it is meaningless, depressing, and of poor overall quality.

(B) The columnist's claim that novels are being displaced by consumerism, technology, and television is false.

(C) The view expressed by the columnist was formed without considering all of the pertinent evidence.

(D) People read as much as they used to, but most of the works they now read are not novels.

(E) A large number of high-quality newspapers, magazines, professional journals, and nonfiction books are currently published.

19. Renting cars from dealerships is less expensive than renting cars from national rental firms. But to take advantage of dealership rates, tourists must determine which local dealerships offer rentals, and then pay for long taxi rides between the airport and those dealerships. So renting from dealerships rather than national rental firms is generally more worthwhile for local residents than for tourists.

Each of the following, if true, strengthens the argument EXCEPT:

(A) To encourage future business, many car dealerships drop off and pick up rental cars for local residents at no charge.

(B) Tourists renting cars from national rental firms almost never need to pay for taxi rides to or from the airport.

(C) Travel agents generally are unable to inform tourists of which local car dealerships offer rentals.

(D) Many local residents know of local car dealerships that offer low-priced rentals.

(E) For local residents, taxi rides to car dealerships from their homes or workplaces are usually no less expensive than taxi rides to national rental firms.

20. On some hot days the smog in Hillview reaches unsafe levels, and on some hot days the wind blows into Hillview from the east. Therefore, on some days when the wind blows into Hillview from the east, the smog in Hillview reaches unsafe levels.

The reasoning in the argument is flawed in that the argument

(A) mistakes a condition that sometimes accompanies unsafe levels of smog for a condition that necessarily accompanies unsafe levels of smog

(B) fails to recognize that one set might have some members in common with each of two others even though those two other sets have no members in common with each other

(C) uses the key term "unsafe" in one sense in a premise and in another sense in the conclusion

(D) contains a premise that is implausible unless the conclusion is presumed to be true

(E) infers a particular causal relation from a correlation that could be explained in a variety of other ways

GO ON TO THE NEXT PAGE.

21. Labor representative: Social historians have shown
    conclusively that if workers strike when the
    working conditions at their jobs are poor, those
    conditions usually significantly improve after
    five years. Although workers in this industry are
    familiar with this fact, they nonetheless refuse to
    strike even though their working conditions are
    poor.

    Which one of the following, if true, most helps to
    resolve the apparent discrepancy described by the labor
    representative?

    (A)   Until recently it was widely believed that strikes
          do not generally improve working conditions.
    (B)   Most factories in this industry change ownership
          every two years.
    (C)   Working conditions in many other industries are
          worse than conditions in this industry.
    (D)   Workers typically plan to work in this industry
          only three years.
    (E)   Wages in this industry have increased each year.

22. Paleontologists recently discovered teeth from several
    woolly mammoths on an isolated Arctic island where no
    mammoth fossils had previously been found. The teeth
    were 25 percent smaller on average than adult mammoth
    teeth that have been found elsewhere, but they are clearly
    adult mammoth teeth. Therefore, provided that the teeth
    are representative of their respective populations, woolly
    mammoths that lived on the island were smaller on
    average than those that lived elsewhere.

    Which one of the following, if assumed, would allow the
    conclusion to be properly drawn?

    (A)   Neither tooth size nor overall body size is
          completely uniform among adult members of
          most species, including woolly mammoths.
    (B)   The tooth wear that naturally occurs in many
          animals over the course of their adult years did
          not result in a significant change in tooth size
          among adult woolly mammoths as they aged.
    (C)   Unusually small mammoth teeth found at
          locations other than the island have always been
          those of juvenile mammoths rather than adult
          mammoths.
    (D)   Tooth size among adult woolly mammoths was
          always directly proportional to the overall size
          of those mammoths.
    (E)   Woolly mammoths of the kind that lived on the
          island had the same number and variety of teeth
          as mammoths that lived elsewhere had.

23. Diplomat: Every major war in the last 200 years has
    been preceded by a short, sharp increase in
    the acquisition of weapons by the nations that
    subsequently became participants in those
    conflicts. Clearly, therefore, arms control
    agreements will preserve peace.

    Of the following, which one most accurately describes a
    reasoning flaw in the diplomat's argument?

    (A)   The argument infers, merely from the claim
          that events of one type have for a long time
          consistently preceded events of a second type,
          that an event of the second type will not occur
          unless an event of the first type occurs.
    (B)   The argument reasons that, simply because
          weapons are used in war, a rapid, dramatic
          increase in the acquisition of weapons will
          always lead to war.
    (C)   The argument draws a conclusion that simply
          restates a claim presented in support of that
          conclusion.
    (D)   The argument fails to consider that a short,
          sharp increase in the acquisition of weapons
          by a nation may be a response to the increased
          armament of neighboring nations.
    (E)   The argument fails to consider that some of
          the minor wars that have occurred in the last
          200 years may have been preceded by rapid
          increases in the acquisition of weapons by the
          nations that subsequently became participants in
          those wars.

GO ON TO THE NEXT PAGE.

24. Newscaster: In order for the public to participate in a meaningful way in the current public policy debate, one requirement is that the issues be stated in terms the public can understand. The mayor's speech has just stated these issues in such terms, so now the public at least might be able to participate in a meaningful way in the current public policy debate.

Which one of the following most closely parallels the newscaster's argument in its reasoning?

(A) One must know Russian if one is to read Dostoyevski's original text of *Crime and Punishment*. Rachel has never learned Russian; therefore she cannot read the original text of *Crime and Punishment*.

(B) In order to reach one's goals, one must be able to consider these goals carefully. Laura has reached her goals, so she must have been able to consider those goals carefully.

(C) One cannot confuse the majority of one's students if one wants to be a good teacher. Hugo wants to be a good teacher; therefore, he might be able to avoid confusing the majority of his students.

(D) In order to discover the meaning of certain seldom-used words, one must use a good dictionary. Paul has used a good dictionary, so Paul must have discovered the meaning of those words.

(E) One must at least have warm clothing if one is to survive in a very cold climate. Jerome has obtained warm clothing; therefore, he might be able to survive in a very cold climate.

25. Most serious students are happy students, and most serious students go to graduate school. Furthermore, all students who go to graduate school are overworked.

Which one of the following can be properly inferred from the statements above?

(A) Most overworked students are happy students.
(B) Some happy students are overworked.
(C) All overworked students are serious students.
(D) Some unhappy students go to graduate school.
(E) All serious students are overworked.

26. Editorialist: Some people argue that highway speed limits should be increased to reflect the actual average speeds of highway drivers, which are currently 10 to 20 percent higher than posted speed limits. Any such increase would greatly decrease highway safety, however; as past experience teaches, higher average highway speeds would result, since even though most drivers who currently violate posted speed limits would obey higher ones, almost all drivers who obey current speed limits would likely increase their speed.

Which one of the following, if true, most seriously weakens the editorialist's argument?

(A) Some drivers who obey current speed limits would not change their speeds after the introduction of the new speed limits.

(B) Uniformity of speeds among vehicles is more important for highway safety than is a low average highway speed.

(C) Most drivers who drive 10 to 20 percent faster than current speed limits have never been involved in a highway accident.

(D) Some drivers who violate current speed limits would also violate higher speed limits.

(E) Most drivers who violate current speed limits determine their speeds by what they believe to be safe in the situation.

S T O P
IF YOU FINISH BEFORE TIME IS CALLED, YOU MAY CHECK YOUR WORK ON THIS SECTION ONLY.
DO NOT WORK ON ANY OTHER SECTION IN THE TEST.

SECTION IV
Time—35 minutes
26 Questions

Directions: Each set of questions in this section is based on a single passage or a pair of passages. The questions are to be answered on the basis of what is stated or implied in the passage or pair of passages. For some of the questions, more than one of the choices could conceivably answer the question. However, you are to choose the best answer; that is, the response that most accurately and completely answers the question, and blacken the corresponding space on your answer sheet.

In a recent court case, a copy-shop owner was accused of violating copyright law when, in the preparation of "course packs"—materials photocopied from books and journals and packaged as readings for
(5) particular university courses—he copied materials without obtaining permission from or paying sufficient fees to the publishers. As the owner of five small copy shops serving several educational institutions in the area, he argued, as have others in the photocopy
(10) business, that the current process for obtaining permissions is time-consuming, cumbersome, and expensive. He also maintained that course packs, which are ubiquitous in higher education, allow professors to assign important readings in books and journals too
(15) costly for students to be expected to purchase individually. While the use of copyrighted material for teaching purposes is typically protected by certain provisions of copyright law, this case was unique in that the copying of course packs was done by a copy
(20) shop and at a profit.

Copyright law outlines several factors involved in determining whether the use of copyrighted material is protected, including: whether it is for commercial or nonprofit purposes; the nature of the copyrighted work;
(25) the length and importance of the excerpt used in relation to the entire work; and the effect of its use on the work's potential market value. In bringing suit, the publishers held that other copy-shop owners would cease paying permission fees, causing the potential
(30) value of the copyrighted works of scholarship to diminish. Nonetheless, the court decided that this reasoning did not demonstrate that course packs would have a sufficiently adverse effect on the current or potential market of the copyrighted works or on the
(35) value of the copyrighted works themselves. The court instead ruled that since the copies were for educational purposes, the fact that the copy-shop owner had profited from making the course packs did not prevent him from receiving protection under the law.
(40) According to the court, the owner had not exploited copyrighted material because his fee was not based on the content of the works he copied; he charged by the page, regardless of whether the content was copyrighted.
(45) In the court's view, the business of producing and selling course packs is more properly seen as the exploitation of professional copying technologies and a result of the inability of academic parties to reproduce printed materials efficiently, not the exploitation of
(50) these copyrighted materials themselves. The court held

that copyright laws do not prohibit professors and students, who may make copies for themselves, from using the photoreproduction services of a third party in order to obtain those same copies at lesser cost.

1. Which one of the following most accurately states the main point of the passage?

(A) A court recently ruled that a copy shop that makes course packs does not illegally exploit copyrighted materials but rather it legally exploits the efficiency of professional photocopying technology.

(B) A court recently ruled that course packs are protected by copyright law because their price is based solely on the number of pages in each pack.

(C) A court recently ruled that the determining factors governing the copyrights of material used in course packs are how the material is to be used, the nature of the material itself, and the length of the copied excerpts.

(D) A recent court ruling limits the rights of publishers to seek suit against copy shops that make course packs from copyrighted material.

(E) Exceptions to copyright law are made when copyrighted material is used for educational purposes and no party makes a substantial profit from the material.

GO ON TO THE NEXT PAGE.

2. In lines 23–27, the author lists several of the factors used to determine whether copyrighted material is protected by law primarily to

   (A) demonstrate why the copy-shop owner was exempt from copyright law in this case
   (B) explain the charges the publishers brought against the copy-shop owner
   (C) illustrate a major flaw in the publishers' reasoning
   (D) defend the right to use copyrighted materials for educational purposes
   (E) provide the legal context for the arguments presented in the case

3. The copy-shop owner as described in the passage would be most likely to agree with which one of the following statements?

   (A) The potential market value of a copyrighted work should be calculated to include the impact on sales due to the use of the work in course packs.
   (B) Publishers are always opposed to the preparation and sale of course packs.
   (C) More copy shops would likely seek permissions from publishers if the process for obtaining permissions were not so cumbersome and expensive.
   (D) Certain provisions of copyright law need to be rewritten to apply to all possible situations.
   (E) Copy shops make more of a profit from the preparation and sale of course packs than from other materials.

4. The information in the passage provides the most support for which one of the following statements about copyright law?

   (A) Copyright law can be one of the most complex areas of any legal system.
   (B) Courts have been inconsistent in their interpretations of certain provisions of copyright law.
   (C) The number of the kinds of materials granted protection under copyright law is steadily decreasing.
   (D) New practices can compel the courts to refine how copyright law is applied.
   (E) Copyright law is primarily concerned with making published materials available for educational use.

5. Which one of the following describes a role most similar to that of professors in the passage who use copy shops to produce course packs?

   (A) An artisan generates a legible copy of an old headstone engraving by using charcoal on newsprint and frames and sells high-quality photocopies of it at a crafts market.
   (B) A choir director tapes a selection of another well-known choir's best pieces and sends it to a recording studio to be reproduced in a sellable package for use by members of her choir.
   (C) A grocer makes several kinds of sandwiches that sell for less than similar sandwiches from a nearby upscale café.
   (D) A professional graphic artist prints reproductions of several well-known paintings at an exhibit to sell at the museum's gift shop.
   (E) A souvenir store in the center of a city sells miniature bronze renditions of a famous bronze sculpture that the city is noted for displaying.

6. Which one of the following, if true, would have most strengthened the publishers' position in this case?

   (A) Course packs for courses that usually have large enrollments had produced a larger profit for the copy-shop owner.
   (B) The copy-shop owner had actively solicited professors' orders for course packs.
   (C) The revenue generated by the copy shop's sale of course packs had risen significantly within the past few years.
   (D) Many area bookstores had reported a marked decrease in the sales of books used for producing course packs.
   (E) The publishers had enlisted the support of the authors to verify their claims that the copy-shop owner had not obtained permission.

GO ON TO THE NEXT PAGE.

Countee Cullen (Countee Leroy Porter, 1903–1946) was one of the foremost poets of the Harlem Renaissance, the movement of African American writers, musicians, and artists centered in the
(5) Harlem section of New York City during the 1920s. Beginning with his university years, Cullen strove to establish himself as an author of romantic poetry on abstract, universal topics such as love and death. Believing poetry should consist of "lofty thoughts
(10) beautifully expressed," Cullen preferred controlled poetic forms. He used European forms such as sonnets and devices such as quatrains, couplets, and conventional rhyme, and he frequently employed classical allusions and Christian religious imagery,
(15) which were most likely the product both of his university education and of his upbringing as the adopted son of a Methodist Episcopal reverend.

Some literary critics have praised Cullen's skill at writing European-style verse, finding, for example, in
(20) "The Ballad of the Brown Girl" an artful use of diction and a rhythm and sonority that allow him to capture the atmosphere typical of the English ballad form of past centuries. Others have found Cullen's use of European verse forms and techniques unsuited to treating
(25) political or racial themes, such as the themes in "Uncle Jim," in which a young man is told by his uncle of the different experiences of African Americans and whites in United States society, or "Incident," which relates the experience of an eight-year-old child who hears a
(30) racial slur. One such critic has complained that Cullen's persona as expressed in his work sometimes seems to vacillate between aesthete and spokesperson for racial issues. But Cullen himself rejected this dichotomy, maintaining that his interest in romantic
(35) poetry was quite compatible with his concern over racial issues. He drew a distinction between poetry of solely political intent and his own work, which he believed reflected his identity as an African American. As the heartfelt expression of his personality
(40) accomplished by means of careful attention to his chosen craft, his work could not help but do so.

Explicit references to racial matters do in fact decline in Cullen's later work, but not because he felt any less passionately about these matters. Rather,
(45) Cullen increasingly focused on the religious dimension of his poetry. In "The Black Christ," in which the poet imagines the death and resurrection of a rural African American, and "Heritage," which expresses the tension between the poet's identification with Christian
(50) traditions and his desire to stay close to his African heritage, Cullen's thoughts on race were subsumed within what he conceived of as broader and more urgent questions about the suffering and redemption of the soul. Nonetheless, Cullen never abandoned his
(55) commitment to the importance of racial issues, reflecting on one occasion that he felt "actuated by a strong sense of race consciousness" that "grows upon me, I find, as I grow older."

7. Which one of the following most accurately states the main point of the passage?

(A) While much of Cullen's poetry deals with racial issues, in his later work he became less concerned with racial matters and increasingly interested in writing poetry with a religious dimension.

(B) While Cullen used European verse forms and his later poems increasingly addressed religious themes, his poetry never abandoned a concern for racial issues.

(C) Though Cullen used European verse forms, he acknowledged that these forms were not very well suited to treating political or racial themes.

(D) Despite the success of Cullen's poetry at dealing with racial issues, Cullen's primary goal was to re-create the atmosphere that characterized the English ballad.

(E) The religious dimension throughout Cullen's poetry complemented his focus on racial issues by providing the context within which these issues could be understood.

8. Given the information in the passage, which one of the following most closely exemplifies Cullen's conception of poetry?

(A) a sonnet written with careful attention to the conventions of the form to re-create the atmosphere of sixteenth-century English poetry

(B) a sonnet written with deliberate disregard for the conventions of the form to illustrate the perils of political change

(C) a sonnet written to explore the aesthetic impact of radical innovations in diction, rhythm, and sonority

(D) a sonnet written with great stylistic freedom to express the emotional upheaval associated with romantic love

(E) a sonnet written with careful attention to the conventions of the form expressing feelings about the inevitability of death

GO ON TO THE NEXT PAGE.

9. Which one of the following is NOT identified by the author of the passage as characteristic of Cullen's poetry?

(A) It often deals with abstract, universal subject matter.

(B) It often employs rhyme, classical allusions, and religious imagery.

(C) It avoids traditional poetic forms in favor of formal experimentation.

(D) It sometimes deals explicitly with racial issues.

(E) It eventually subsumed racial issues into a discussion of religious issues.

10. The passage suggests which one of the following about Cullen's use of controlled poetic forms?

(A) Cullen used controlled poetic forms because he believed they provided the best means to beautiful poetic expression.

(B) Cullen's interest in religious themes naturally led him to use controlled poetic forms.

(C) Only the most controlled poetic forms allowed Cullen to address racial issues in his poems.

(D) Cullen had rejected the less controlled poetic forms he was exposed to prior to his university years.

(E) Less controlled poetic forms are better suited to poetry that addresses racial or political issues.

11. The references to specific poems in the second paragraph are most likely intended to

(A) contrast some of Cullen's more successful poems with some of his less successful ones

(B) serve as illustrations of Cullen's poetry relevant to the critics' claims

(C) demonstrate that Cullen's poetic persona vacillates from poem to poem

(D) summarize the scope of Cullen's treatment of racial issues in his poetry

(E) illustrate the themes Cullen used in expressing his concern about racial matters

12. Based on the passage, the literary critics mentioned in line 18 would be most likely to hold which one of the following views of Cullen's poetry?

(A) It demonstrates that European verse forms can be successfully adapted to different contexts.

(B) It is most notable for the ways in which its content reflects Cullen's upbringing and education.

(C) It is more successful when it does not attempt to capture the atmosphere of previous poetic styles.

(D) Its reliance on European verse forms is best suited to dealing with racial concerns.

(E) Its focus is divided between aesthetic and racial concerns.

13. Which one of the following most accurately describes the organization of the passage?

(A) Biographical information about Cullen is outlined, his artistic development is traced through several of his poems, and a critical evaluation of his later work is offered.

(B) Biographical information about Cullen is outlined, criticism of his use of European verse forms is presented, and the success of this use is evaluated.

(C) Biographical information about Cullen is outlined, his approach to writing poetry is described, and the relationship between his poetry and his life is discussed.

(D) Cullen's approach to poetry is described, certain poems are characterized as his most notable, and a claim about the religious focus of his work is made.

(E) Cullen's approach to poetry is described, differing opinions about the success of his poetry are presented, and thematic developments in his later work are discussed.

GO ON TO THE NEXT PAGE.

The following passage was written in the mid-1990s.

The demand for electricity in certain countries has been projected recently to grow by 50 percent by the year 2010. Unfortunately, the increased use of fossil fuels to generate this electricity may ultimately damage
(5) human and environmental health. For example, emissions of air pollutants in these countries are expected to double over the next 25 years, even if energy is used efficiently, so that local urban air quality will likely deteriorate. Renewable sources of
(10) electricity, such as solar radiation, wind, and waterpower, are possible solutions to the problems caused by increasing demand for electricity. Unlike fossil fuels, renewable energy sources are available in virtually all geographic regions, and they allow
(15) electricity production without dangerous environmental pollutants. Additionally, these sources can usually be located closer to consumers than can plants that use fossil fuels, thus reducing transmission and distribution costs. Technologies for the successful long-term
(20) exploitation of these resources, however, are not always implemented successfully.

In rural Brazil, for example, millions of citizens do not have electricity, and the lack of necessary infrastructure has limited efforts to provide it. In 1992,
(25) an energy agency from the United States developed a joint project with two Brazilian states to install 800 household solar electrical systems and train local personnel to service them. Under the project's terms, local utilities install, maintain, and own the systems,
(30) and collect fees from users. Backers hoped the project would attract enough private investment for substantial expansion throughout Brazil. But the project directors rejected the relatively high bids of local Brazilian companies to produce the solar collectors and thus
(35) missed an opportunity to stimulate local production. Consequently, a short-term savings in start-up costs precluded the long-term benefits deriving from the development of local production capacity and technological skill, which eventually would have led to
(40) independence from costly foreign expertise. As a result, participating utilities can generate only enough income to cover operating and maintenance costs, which makes further investment and expansion unlikely. Thus, the movement toward a sustainable,
(45) rural electricity system in Brazil remains stalled.

But some efforts have avoided these pitfalls. In the mid-1980s, a Danish energy agency helped agencies in India build three modern wind turbine plants and gradually develop local technical capacity. Local
(50) participants were trained in planning, operation, maintenance, and construction of turbines. Indian firms subsequently began manufacturing turbines and, as more locally manufactured equipment became available, Indian utilities were able to increase their use
(55) of wind energy profitably. The success of these small projects spurred enthusiasm; Indian utilities were soon ordering more equipment and private investment in wind energy surged. Because the Danish agency, unlike its U.S. counterpart, recognized the importance
(60) of local involvement at all levels, the project has a good chance of remaining competitive and profitable for the long run.

14. Which one of the following most accurately expresses the main point of the passage?

(A) While some later efforts to implement renewable energy systems have been plagued and eventually halted by economic conflicts, early renewable energy projects relying more heavily on local involvement enjoyed a larger degree of success.

(B) Investors in renewable energy projects should consider not only financial factors but also the potential gains in human and environmental health from using this technology—gains that are not always readily measurable.

(C) Renewable energy sources represent a promising means for addressing many countries' energy demands and environmental concerns, but the necessary technologies can be implemented most effectively in countries that have continuing access to foreign investment or expertise.

(D) Though renewable energy sources represent a promising means for meeting the rising energy demands of certain countries, the exploitation of these resources is unlikely to succeed unless long-term, local participation at all levels is seen as integral to renewable energy projects.

(E) Certain types of renewable energy sources, such as wind-generated electricity systems, are more likely to be successful than other types, but continued investment and experimentation are necessary to establish which renewable energy projects will succeed.

15. Based on the information in the passage, with which one of the following statements regarding solar electrical systems would the author be most likely to agree?

(A) Despite previous difficulties, these systems can be implemented profitably in many countries.

(B) Though these systems do not produce pollutants, they must be seen as an impractical substitute for fossil-fuel systems.

(C) These systems would be more effectively employed in densely populated areas than in rural areas.

(D) These systems are more costly to install, operate, and maintain than are wind-energy systems.

(E) Until the long-term functioning of these systems is demonstrated, they cannot be considered a viable type of energy technology.

GO ON TO THE NEXT PAGE.

16. The author mentions which one of the following in the passage?

   (A)   a specific example of an energy-generating system that relies on fossil fuels

   (B)   an example of a project that successfully utilized the local manufacture of equipment

   (C)   an example of the added transmission costs incurred by a specific fossil-fuel energy plant

   (D)   the approximate size of a community that can be served by a modern wind turbine plant

   (E)   the approximate number of years it takes to develop local technical capacity to generate energy from renewable sources

17. The author's attitude toward the directors of the Brazil project can most accurately be described as

   (A)   disapproving of their heavy dependence on private investment

   (B)   surprise at their lack of faith in the quality of local technological expertise

   (C)   critical of their lack of foresight in overemphasizing the importance of reducing short-term costs

   (D)   outrage at their favoring profit over humanitarian goals

   (E)   doubtful of their desire to implement a successful solar electrical system in Brazil

18. In the passage, the author is primarily concerned with

   (A)   summarizing the reasons why renewable energy resources should be used and explaining why certain promising technologies cannot be implemented profitably

   (B)   arguing for the advantages of renewable energy resources and illustrating with examples what factors will favor their successful implementation

   (C)   illustrating the advantages of adopting renewable energy resources by summarizing how they have been implemented in the past

   (D)   comparing and contrasting two types of renewable energy technology and giving examples of the benefits and drawbacks of each

   (E)   discussing two types of renewable energy resources and analyzing why one is more easily implemented than the other

19. The author's discussion in lines 5–9 is intended primarily to

   (A)   substantiate the claim that the demand for electricity will climb 50 percent by the year 2010

   (B)   undermine the claim that efficient energy use is an effective means of addressing environmental problems caused by increased energy demand

   (C)   specify the time frame within which it will be necessary to develop renewable energy technology

   (D)   offer evidence for the claim that fossil fuels are a problematic source of electricity

   (E)   foreshadow a claim concerning the need for localized involvement in environmentally sound technological development

20. Which one of the following, if true, would most call into question the author's assertion in the last sentence of the passage?

   (A)   The profitability of the India project was due primarily to temporary subsidies from the Indian government.

   (B)   The Danish energy agency invested more funds in the India project than the U.S. agency invested in the Brazil project.

   (C)   Indian firms are not required to limit user fees charged to consumers.

   (D)   Environmental pollutants are produced in the manufacture of some equipment used in wind turbines.

   (E)   New technology is poised to decrease sharply the level of pollutants produced by fossil-fuel plants.

GO ON TO THE NEXT PAGE.

Although philanthropy—the volunteering of private resources for humanitarian purposes—reached its apex in England in the late nineteenth century, modern commentators have articulated two major
(5) criticisms of the philanthropy that was a mainstay of England's middle-class Victorian society. The earlier criticism is that such philanthropy was even by the later nineteenth century obsolete, since industrialism had already created social problems that were beyond the
(10) scope of small, private voluntary efforts. Indeed, these problems required substantial legislative action by the state. Unemployment, for example, was not the result of a failure of diligence on the part of workers or a failure of compassion on the part of employers, nor
(15) could it be solved by well-wishing philanthropists.

The more recent charge holds that Victorian philanthropy was by its very nature a self-serving exercise carried out by philanthropists at the expense of those whom they were ostensibly serving. In this view,
(20) philanthropy was a means of flaunting one's power and position in a society that placed great emphasis on status, or even a means of cultivating social connections that could lead to economic rewards. Further, if philanthropy is seen as serving the interests
(25) of individual philanthropists, so it may be seen as serving the interests of their class. According to this "social control" thesis, philanthropists, in professing to help the poor, were encouraging in them such values as prudence, thrift, and temperance, values perhaps
(30) worthy in themselves but also designed to create more productive members of the labor force. Philanthropy, in short, was a means of controlling the labor force and ensuring the continued dominance of the management class.

(35) Modern critics of Victorian philanthropy often use the words "amateurish" or "inadequate" to describe Victorian philanthropy, as though Victorian charity can only be understood as an antecedent to the era of state-sponsored, professionally administered charity. This
(40) assumption is typical of the "Whig fallacy": the tendency to read the past as an inferior prelude to an enlightened present. If most Victorians resisted state control and expended their resources on private, voluntary philanthropies, it could only be, the argument
(45) goes, because of their commitment to a vested interest, or because the administrative apparatus of the state was incapable of coping with the economic and social needs of the time.

This version of history patronizes the Victorians,
(50) who were in fact well aware of their vulnerability to charges of condescension and complacency, but were equally well aware of the potential dangers of state-managed charity. They were perhaps condescending to the poor, but—to use an un-Victorian metaphor—they
(55) put their money where their mouths were, and gave of their careers and lives as well.

21. Which one of the following best summarizes the main idea of the passage?

(A) While the motives of individual practitioners have been questioned by modern commentators, Victorian philanthropy successfully dealt with the social ills of nineteenth-century England.

(B) Philanthropy, inadequate to deal with the massive social and economic problems of the twentieth century, has slowly been replaced by state-sponsored charity.

(C) The practice of reading the past as a prelude to an enlightened present has fostered revisionist views of many institutions, among them Victorian philanthropy.

(D) Although modern commentators have perceived Victorian philanthropy as either inadequate or self-serving, the theoretical bias behind these criticisms leads to an incorrect interpretation of history.

(E) Victorian philanthropists, aware of public resentment of their self-congratulatory attitude, used devious methods to camouflage their self-serving motives.

GO ON TO THE NEXT PAGE.

22. According to the passage, which one of the following is true of both modern criticisms made about Victorian philanthropy?

(A) Both criticisms attribute dishonorable motives to those privileged individuals who engaged in private philanthropy.
(B) Both criticisms presuppose that the social rewards of charitable activity outweighed the economic benefits.
(C) Both criticisms underemphasize the complacency and condescension demonstrated by the Victorians.
(D) Both criticisms suggest that government involvement was necessary to cure social ills.
(E) Both criticisms take for granted the futility of efforts by private individuals to enhance their social status by means of philanthropy.

23. Which one of the following best describes the attitude of the author of the passage toward the "Whig" interpretation of Victorian philanthropy?

(A) strong disagreement
(B) mild skepticism
(C) cynical amusement
(D) bland indifference
(E) unqualified support

24. Which one of the following best describes the primary purpose of the passage?

(A) providing an extended definition of a key term
(B) defending the work of an influential group of theorists
(C) narrating the chronological development of a widespread practice
(D) examining modern evaluations of a historical phenomenon
(E) analyzing a specific dilemma faced by workers of the past

25. It can be inferred from the passage that a social control theorist would be most likely to agree with which one of the following statements concerning the motives of Victorian philanthropists?

(A) Victorian philanthropists were driven more by the desire for high social status than by the hope of economic gain.
(B) Victorian philanthropists encouraged such values as thrift and temperance in order to instill in the working class the same acquisitiveness that characterized the management class.
(C) Though basically well-intentioned, Victorian philanthropists faced problems that were far beyond the scope of private charitable organizations.
(D) By raising the living standards of the poor, Victorian philanthropists also sought to improve the intellectual status of the poor.
(E) Victorian philanthropists see philanthropy as a means to an end rather than as an end in itself.

26. Which one of the following best describes the organization of the passage?

(A) Two related positions are discussed, then both are subjected to the same criticism.
(B) Two opposing theories are outlined, then a synthesis between the two is proposed.
(C) A position is stated, and two differing evaluations of it are given.
(D) Three examples of the same logical inconsistency are given.
(E) A theory is outlined, and two supporting examples are given.

STOP
IF YOU FINISH BEFORE TIME IS CALLED, YOU MAY CHECK YOUR WORK ON THIS SECTION ONLY.
DO NOT WORK ON ANY OTHER SECTION IN THE TEST.

ACKNOWLEDGMENTS

Acknowledgment is made to the following sources from which material has been adapted for use in this test booklet:

"Autism: Early Detection." ©1996 by Sussex Publishers Inc.

Black Writers. ©1994 by Gale Research.

Keith Lee Kozloff, "Rethinking Development Assistance for Renewable Electricity Sources." ©1995 by the Helen Dwight Reid Educational Foundation.

Denise K. Magner, "Appeals Court Rules against Publishers in 'Course Packs' Case." ©1996 by The Chronicle of Higher Education, Inc.

Wait for the supervisor's instructions before you open the page to the topic.
Please print and sign your name and write the date in the designated spaces below.

Time: 35 Minutes

General Directions

You will have 35 minutes in which to plan and write an essay on the topic inside. Read the topic and the accompanying directions carefully. You will probably find it best to spend a few minutes considering the topic and organizing your thoughts before you begin writing. In your essay, be sure to develop your ideas fully, leaving time, if possible, to review what you have written. **Do not write on a topic other than the one specified. Writing on a topic of your own choice is not acceptable.**

No special knowledge is required or expected for this writing exercise. Law schools are interested in the reasoning, clarity, organization, language usage, and writing mechanics displayed in your essay. How well you write is more important than how much you write.

Confine your essay to the blocked, lined area on the front and back of the separate Writing Sample Response Sheet. Only that area will be reproduced for law schools. Be sure that your writing is legible.

Both this topic sheet and your response sheet must be turned over to the testing staff before you leave the room.

Topic Code	Print Your Full Name Here		
	Last	First	M.I.

Date	Sign Your Name Here
/ /	

Scratch Paper
Do not write your essay in this space.

LSAT® Writing Sample Topic

> Directions: The scenario presented below describes two choices, either one of which can be supported on the basis of the information given. Your essay should consider both choices and argue for one over the other, based on the two specified criteria and the facts provided. There is no "right" or "wrong" choice: a reasonable argument can be made for either.

A scholarly professional association must select a site for its annual four-day conference. The association has narrowed its choices to either the city of Phillipsburgh or the Rancho Mesa Hotel. Write an argument in favor of one of the sites over the other based on the following criteria:

- The association wants the conference to be as well attended as possible.
- The association also wants to persuade conference attendees to remain in the hotel for talks and organized events such as dinners.

Phillipsburgh is traditionally a very popular destination for travelers. It offers many fine restaurants, theaters, museums, and opportunities for shopping and sight-seeing. While conferences held in Phillipsburgh in the past were well attended, past experience also shows that, because of the many attractions of Phillipsburgh, many conference events are under-attended. However, one of the most celebrated scholars in the field has indicated an interest in speaking and attending conference events if the conference is held in Phillipsburgh. Expense is a concern: several hotels offer conference rates, but the rates are still high enough that graduate students and most young scholars may be priced out of the conference if it is held in Phillipsburgh.

The Rancho Mesa is a luxury resort hotel located in an isolated high desert setting, and it is highly rated by many travel guidebooks. In the past, the association has sometimes found it difficult to attract large numbers of attendees to isolated resort settings, but it has also found that members who travel to conferences in such settings are apt to attend more conference events. To attract the association's patronage, Rancho Mesa is offering a large discount to association members, making the room rates quite reasonable. As attractions for its guests, the hotel offers activities such as swimming, hiking, and horseback riding. The hotel also offers excellent food and large group dining facilities that the association can use for its dinner events, and meals are included in the room rate. Unfortunately, since Rancho Mesa is far from any travel hub, getting to the hotel is time consuming and usually costly.

Scratch Paper
Do not write your essay in this space.

Writing Sample Response Sheet

DO NOT WRITE IN THIS SPACE

**Begin your essay in the lined area below.
Continue on the back if you need more space.**

COMPUTING YOUR SCORE

Directions:

1. Use the Answer Key on the next page to check your answers.

2. Use the Scoring Worksheet below to compute your raw score.

3. Use the Score Conversion Chart to convert your raw score into the 120-180 scale.

Scoring Worksheet

1. Enter the number of questions you answered correctly in each section.

	Number Correct
SECTION I	_____
SECTION II	_____
SECTION III	_____
SECTION IV...............	_____

2. Enter the sum here: _____

   This is your Raw Score.

Conversion Chart
For Converting Raw Score to the 120-180 LSAT Scaled Score
LSAT Form 3LSS58

Reported Score	Raw Score Lowest	Raw Score Highest
180	99	101
179	98	98
178	97	97
177	96	96
176	95	95
175	94	94
174	93	93
173	—*	—*
172	92	92
171	90	91
170	89	89
169	88	88
168	87	87
167	86	86
166	84	85
165	83	83
164	81	82
163	80	80
162	78	79
161	77	77
160	75	76
159	73	74
158	72	72
157	70	71
156	68	69
155	67	67
154	65	66
153	63	64
152	61	62
151	60	60
150	58	59
149	56	57
148	54	55
147	53	53
146	51	52
145	49	50
144	48	48
143	46	47
142	44	45
141	43	43
140	41	42
139	39	40
138	38	38
137	36	37
136	35	35
135	33	34
134	32	32
133	30	31
132	29	29
131	27	28
130	26	26
129	24	25
128	23	23
127	22	22
126	20	21
125	19	19
124	18	18
123	16	17
122	15	15
121	14	14
120	0	13

*There is no raw score that will produce this scaled score for this form.

ANSWER KEY

SECTION I

1.	C	8.	D	15.	C	22.	D
2.	B	9.	B	16.	C	23.	A
3.	C	10.	B	17.	C	24.	E
4.	B	11.	C	18.	E	25.	B
5.	B	12.	E	19.	E		
6.	D	13.	C	20.	B		
7.	A	14.	D	21.	B		

SECTION II

1.	A	8.	B	15.	C	22.	A
2.	B	9.	E	16.	D	23.	B
3.	E	10.	C	17.	B	24.	C
4.	E	11.	E	18.	C		
5.	B	12.	A	19.	D		
6.	D	13.	E	20.	A		
7.	D	14.	C	21.	C		

SECTION III

1.	A	8.	B	15.	E	22.	D
2.	E	9.	C	16.	C	23.	A
3.	A	10.	A	17.	B	24.	E
4.	C	11.	D	18.	C	25.	B
5.	E	12.	B	19.	E	26.	B
6.	A	13.	C	20.	B		
7.	A	14.	B	21.	D		

SECTION IV

1.	A	8.	E	15.	A	22.	D
2.	E	9.	C	16.	B	23.	A
3.	C	10.	A	17.	C	24.	D
4.	D	11.	B	18.	B	25.	E
5.	B	12.	A	19.	D	26.	A
6.	D	13.	E	20.	A		
7.	B	14.	D	21.	D		

PREPTEST 42
DECEMBER 2003
FORM 3LSS57

SECTION I
Time—35 minutes
23 Questions

Directions: Each group of questions in this section is based on a set of conditions. In answering some of the questions, it may be useful to draw a rough diagram. Choose the response that most accurately and completely answers each question and blacken the corresponding space on your answer sheet.

Questions 1–5

A panel of five scientists will be formed. The panelists will be selected from among three botanists—F, G, and H—three chemists—K, L, and M—and three zoologists—P, Q, and R. Selection is governed by the following conditions:

The panel must include at least one scientist of each of the three types.

If more than one botanist is selected, then at most one zoologist is selected.

F and K cannot both be selected.

K and M cannot both be selected.

If M is selected, both P and R must be selected.

1. Which one of the following is an acceptable selection of scientists for the panel?

    (A)   F, G, K, P, Q
    (B)   G, H, K, L, M
    (C)   G, H, K, L, R
    (D)   H, K, M, P, R
    (E)   H, L, M, P, Q

2. If M is the only chemist selected for the panel, which one of the following must be true?

    (A)   F and G are both selected.
    (B)   G and H are both selected.
    (C)   H and P are both selected.
    (D)   F, G, and H are all selected.
    (E)   P, Q, and R are all selected.

3. If four of the scientists selected are F, L, Q, and R, which one of the following must be the fifth scientist selected?

    (A)   G
    (B)   H
    (C)   K
    (D)   M
    (E)   P

4. If P is the only zoologist selected, which one of the following must be true?

    (A)   If K is selected, G cannot be selected.
    (B)   If L is selected, F cannot be selected.
    (C)   If exactly one chemist is selected, it must be K.
    (D)   If exactly two chemists are selected, F cannot be selected.
    (E)   If exactly two chemists are selected, G cannot be selected.

5. If both G and H are among the scientists selected, then the panel must include either

    (A)   F or else K
    (B)   F or else M
    (C)   K or else M
    (D)   M or else Q
    (E)   P or else Q

GO ON TO THE NEXT PAGE.

Questions 6–12

A loading dock consists of exactly six bays numbered 1 through 6 consecutively from one side of the dock to the other. Each bay is holding a different one of exactly six types of cargo—fuel, grain, livestock, machinery, produce, or textiles. The following apply:

The bay holding grain has a higher number than the bay holding livestock.

The bay holding livestock has a higher number than the bay holding textiles.

The bay holding produce has a higher number than the bay holding fuel.

The bay holding textiles is next to the bay holding produce.

6. Which one of the following lists could accurately identify the cargo held in each of the loading dock's first three bays, listed in order from bay 1 to bay 3?

   (A) fuel, machinery, textiles
   (B) grain, machinery, fuel
   (C) machinery, livestock, fuel
   (D) machinery, textiles, fuel
   (E) machinery, textiles, produce

7. Which one of the following CANNOT be the type of cargo held in bay 4?

   (A) grain
   (B) livestock
   (C) machinery
   (D) produce
   (E) textiles

8. If there is exactly one bay between the bay holding machinery and the bay holding grain, then for exactly how many of the six bays is the type of cargo that bay is holding completely determined?

   (A) two
   (B) three
   (C) four
   (D) five
   (E) six

9. Which one of the following could be the bay holding livestock?

   (A) bay 1
   (B) bay 2
   (C) bay 3
   (D) bay 5
   (E) bay 6

10. Which one of the following must be false?

   (A) The bay holding fuel is next to the bay holding machinery.
   (B) The bay holding grain is next to the bay holding machinery.
   (C) The bay holding livestock is next to the bay holding fuel.
   (D) The bay holding produce is next to the bay holding livestock.
   (E) The bay holding textiles is next to the bay holding fuel.

11. If the bay holding produce is next to the bay holding livestock, then each of the following could be true EXCEPT:

   (A) Bay 2 is holding fuel.
   (B) Bay 4 is holding produce.
   (C) Bay 4 is holding textiles.
   (D) Bay 5 is holding grain.
   (E) Bay 5 is holding machinery.

12. If bay 4 is holding produce, then for exactly how many of the six bays is the type of cargo that bay is holding completely determined?

   (A) two
   (B) three
   (C) four
   (D) five
   (E) six

GO ON TO THE NEXT PAGE.

Questions 13–18

A bakery makes exactly three kinds of cookie—oatmeal, peanut butter, and sugar. Exactly three batches of each kind of cookie are made each week (Monday through Friday) and each batch is made, from start to finish, on a single day. The following conditions apply:

No two batches of the same kind of cookie are made on the same day.

At least one batch of cookies is made on Monday.

The second batch of oatmeal cookies is made on the same day as the first batch of peanut butter cookies.

The second batch of sugar cookies is made on Thursday.

13. Which one of the following could be a complete and accurate list of the days on which the batches of each kind of cookie are made?

(A) oatmeal: Monday, Wednesday, Thursday
peanut butter: Wednesday, Thursday, Friday
sugar: Monday, Thursday, Friday

(B) oatmeal: Monday, Tuesday, Thursday
peanut butter: Tuesday, Wednesday, Thursday
sugar: Monday, Wednesday, Thursday

(C) oatmeal: Tuesday, Wednesday, Thursday
peanut butter: Wednesday, Thursday, Friday
sugar: Tuesday, Thursday, Friday

(D) oatmeal: Monday, Tuesday, Thursday
peanut butter: Monday, Wednesday, Thursday
sugar: Monday, Thursday, Friday

(E) oatmeal: Monday, Thursday, Friday
peanut butter: Tuesday, Wednesday, Thursday
sugar: Monday, Thursday, Friday

14. How many of the days, Monday through Friday, are such that at most two batches of cookies could be made on that day?

(A) one
(B) two
(C) three
(D) four
(E) five

15. If the first batch of peanut butter cookies is made on Tuesday, then each of the following could be true EXCEPT:

(A) Two different kinds of cookie have their first batch made on Monday.

(B) Two different kinds of cookie have their first batch made on Tuesday.

(C) Two different kinds of cookie have their second batch made on Wednesday.

(D) Two different kinds of cookie have their second batch made on Thursday.

(E) Two different kinds of cookie have their third batch made on Friday.

16. If no batch of cookies is made on Wednesday, then which one of the following must be true?

(A) Exactly three batches of cookies are made on Tuesday.

(B) Exactly three batches of cookies are made on Friday.

(C) At least two batches of cookies are made on Monday.

(D) At least two batches of cookies are made on Thursday.

(E) Fewer batches of cookies are made on Monday than on Tuesday.

17. If the number of batches made on Friday is exactly one, then which one of the following could be true?

(A) The first batch of sugar cookies is made on Monday.

(B) The first batch of oatmeal cookies is made on Tuesday.

(C) The third batch of oatmeal cookies is made on Friday.

(D) The first batch of peanut butter cookies is made on Wednesday.

(E) The second batch of peanut butter cookies is made on Tuesday.

18. If one kind of cookie's first batch is made on the same day as another kind of cookie's third batch, then which one of the following could be false?

(A) At least one batch of cookies is made on each of the five days.

(B) At least two batches of cookies are made on Wednesday.

(C) Exactly one batch of cookies is made on Monday.

(D) Exactly two batches of cookies are made on Tuesday.

(E) Exactly one batch of cookies is made on Friday.

GO ON TO THE NEXT PAGE.

Questions 19–23

For the school paper, five students—Jiang, Kramer, Lopez, Megregian, and O'Neill—each review one or more of exactly three plays: *Sunset*, *Tamerlane*, and *Undulation*, but do not review any other plays. The following conditions must apply:

Kramer and Lopez each review fewer of the plays than Megregian.

Neither Lopez nor Megregian reviews any play Jiang reviews.

Kramer and O'Neill both review *Tamerlane*.

Exactly two of the students review exactly the same play or plays as each other.

19. Which one of the following could be an accurate and complete list of the students who review only *Sunset*?

   (A) Lopez
   (B) O'Neill
   (C) Jiang, Lopez
   (D) Kramer, O'Neill
   (E) Lopez, Megregian

20. Which one of the following must be true?

   (A) Jiang reviews more of the plays than Lopez does.
   (B) Megregian reviews more of the plays than Jiang does.
   (C) Megregian reviews more of the plays than O'Neill does.
   (D) O'Neill reviews more of the plays than Jiang does.
   (E) O'Neill reviews more of the plays than Kramer does.

21. If exactly three of the students review *Undulation*, which one of the following could be true?

   (A) Megregian does not review *Undulation*.
   (B) O'Neill does not review *Undulation*.
   (C) Jiang reviews *Undulation*.
   (D) Lopez reviews *Tamerlane*.
   (E) O'Neill reviews *Sunset*.

22. Which one of the following could be an accurate and complete list of the students who review *Tamerlane*?

   (A) Jiang, Kramer
   (B) Kramer, O'Neill
   (C) Kramer, Lopez, O'Neill
   (D) Kramer, Megregian, O'Neill
   (E) Lopez, Megregian, O'Neill

23. If Jiang does not review *Tamerlane*, then which one of the following must be true?

   (A) Jiang reviews *Sunset*.
   (B) Lopez reviews *Undulation*.
   (C) Megregian reviews *Sunset*.
   (D) Megregian reviews *Tamerlane*.
   (E) O'Neill reviews *Undulation*.

STOP
IF YOU FINISH BEFORE TIME IS CALLED, YOU MAY CHECK YOUR WORK ON THIS SECTION ONLY.
DO NOT WORK ON ANY OTHER SECTION IN THE TEST.

SECTION II

Time—35 minutes

26 Questions

Directions: The questions in this section are based on the reasoning contained in brief statements or passages. For some questions, more than one of the choices could conceivably answer the question. However, you are to choose the best answer; that is, the response that most accurately and completely answers the question. You should not make assumptions that are by commonsense standards implausible, superfluous, or incompatible with the passage. After you have chosen the best answer, blacken the corresponding space on your answer sheet.

1. Carl is clearly an incompetent detective. He has solved a smaller percentage of the cases assigned to him in the last 3 years—only 1 out of 25—than any other detective on the police force.

   Which one of the following, if true, most seriously weakens the argument above?

   (A) Because the police chief regards Carl as the most capable detective, she assigns him only the most difficult cases, ones that others have failed to solve.
   (B) Before he became a detective, Carl was a neighborhood police officer and was highly respected by the residents of the neighborhood he patrolled.
   (C) Detectives on the police force on which Carl serves are provided with extensive resources, including the use of a large computer database, to help them solve crimes.
   (D) Carl was previously a detective in a police department in another city, and in the 4 years he spent there, he solved only 1 out of 30 crimes.
   (E) Many of the officers in the police department in which Carl serves were hired or promoted within the last 5 years.

2. It is well documented that people have positive responses to some words, such as "kind" and "wonderful," and negative responses to others, such as "evil" and "nausea." Recently, psychological experiments have revealed that people also have positive or negative responses to many nonsense words. This shows that people's responses to words are conditioned not only by what the words mean, but also by how they sound.

   The claim that people have positive or negative responses to many nonsense words plays which one of the following roles in the argument?

   (A) It is a premise offered in support of the conclusion that people have either a positive or a negative response to any word.
   (B) It is a conclusion for which the only support provided is the claim that people's responses to words are conditioned both by what the words mean and by how they sound.
   (C) It is a generalization partially supported by the claim that meaningful words can trigger positive or negative responses in people.
   (D) It is a premise offered in support of the conclusion that people's responses to words are engendered not only by what the words mean, but also by how they sound.
   (E) It is a conclusion supported by the claim that people's responses under experimental conditions are essentially different from their responses in ordinary situations.

GO ON TO THE NEXT PAGE.

3. People with high blood pressure are generally more nervous and anxious than are people who do not have high blood pressure. This fact shows that this particular combination of personality traits—the so-called hypertensive personality—is likely to cause a person with these traits to develop high blood pressure.

The reasoning in the argument is most vulnerable to criticism on the ground that the argument

(A) fails to define the term "hypertensive personality"
(B) presupposes that people have permanent personality traits
(C) simply restates the claim that there is a "hypertensive personality" without providing evidence to support that claim
(D) takes a correlation between personality traits and high blood pressure as proof that the traits cause high blood pressure
(E) focuses on nervousness and anxiety only, ignoring other personality traits that people with high blood pressure might have

4. In his book, published in 1892, Grey used the same metaphor that Jordan used in her book, which was published in 1885. The metaphor is so unusual that there is little chance that two different people independently created it. Therefore, it is highly likely that Grey read Jordan's book.

Which one of the following, if true, most weakens the argument?

(A) A text that was probably known to both Jordan and Grey was published in 1860 and also contained the same unusual metaphor.
(B) The passage in Grey's book that employs the unusual metaphor expresses an idea that bears little relation to any ideas expressed in Jordan's book.
(C) Both Grey's book and Jordan's book were written for the same audience.
(D) Jordan used the same metaphor in a work that she wrote in 1894 and published in 1895.
(E) According to most scholars, Grey was generally a more inventive writer than Jordan and developed many original metaphors.

5. Medical specialists report that patients with back muscle injuries who receive a combination of drugs and physical therapy do only as well as those who receive physical therapy alone. Yet the specialists state that drugs are a necessary part of the treatment of all patients who receive them for back muscle injuries.

Which one of the following, if true, most helps to reconcile the medical specialists' two claims?

(A) Medical specialists treat all patients who have serious back muscle injuries with either physical therapy alone or a combination of drugs and physical therapy.
(B) Medical specialists who prescribe these treatments make accurate judgments about who needs both drugs and physical therapy and who needs physical therapy alone.
(C) Some back muscle injuries have been completely healed by a combination of drugs and physical therapy.
(D) Some back muscle injuries that have been aggravated by improper attempts at physical therapy, such as home massage, have been successfully treated with drugs.
(E) Patients with injuries to other muscles show more improvement when treated with both drugs and physical therapy than when treated with physical therapy alone.

6. Commentator: In many countries the influence of fringe movements is increasing. The great centrifugal engine of modern culture turns faster and faster, spinning off fashions, ideologies, religions, artistic movements, economic theories, cults, and dogmas in fabulous profusion. Hence, modern culture threatens the national identities that now exist in the world.

Which one of the following statements, if true, most seriously weakens the commentator's argument?

(A) New national identities are often forged out of conflicts among diverse groups.
(B) A stable national identity is typically a composite of a staggering number of subcultures.
(C) The rate of cultural change in most countries will soon change drastically.
(D) It is preferable to have a pluralistic rather than a monolithic national culture.
(E) A culture with a solidified national identity tends to have more social problems than one without such an identity.

GO ON TO THE NEXT PAGE.

7. Packaging is vital to a product's commercial success. For example, the maker of a popular drink introduced a "new, improved" version which succeeded in blind taste tests. However, customers did not buy the product when marketed, mainly because the can, almost identical to that used for the earlier version of the beverage, made consumers expect that the new product would share certain features of the old, an expectation not satisfied by the new product.

Which one of the following is most strongly supported by the information above?

(A) Proper product packaging is more important than the quality of the product.

(B) Products generally succeed in the market if they are packaged in a manner that accurately reflects their nature.

(C) Changing the packaging of a product will not improve the product's sales unless the product is also changed.

(D) To succeed in the market, a new product should not be packaged in a way that creates expectations that it does not meet.

(E) An improved version of an existing product will sell better than the earlier version unless the improved version is packaged like the earlier one.

8. Larew: People in the lowest income quintile had a much higher percentage increase in average income over the last ten years than did those in the highest quintile. So their economic prosperity increased relative to the highest quintile's.

Mendota: I disagree. The average income for the lowest quintile may have increased by a greater percentage, but the absolute amount of the increase in average income was surely greater for the highest quintile.

Larew and Mendota disagree about whether

(A) change in the economic prosperity of the lowest income quintile relative to the highest is accurately measured by comparing their percentage changes in average income

(B) change in the economic prosperity of the lowest income quintile is more accurately measured in terms relative to the highest income quintile than in terms relative only to the lowest income quintile

(C) changes in the average income of people in the lowest quintile should ever be compared to changes in the average income of people in the highest quintile

(D) there were any improvements at all in the economic situation of those in the lowest income quintile during the ten years being considered

(E) the average income of people in the lowest quintile increased by a greater percentage over the last decade than did that of people in the highest quintile

9. Challenge can be an important source of self-knowledge, since those who pay attention to how they react, both emotionally and physically, to challenge can gain useful insights into their own weaknesses.

Which one of the following most closely conforms to the principle above?

(A) A concert pianist should not have an entirely negative view of a memory lapse during a difficult performance. By understanding why the memory lapse occurred, the pianist can better prepare for future performances.

(B) A salesperson should understand that the commission earned is not the only reward of making a sale. Salespeople should also take satisfaction from the fact that successful sales reflect well on their personalities.

(C) Compassion is valuable not only for the wonderful feelings it brings, but also for the opportunities it affords to enrich the lives of other people.

(D) While some of the value of competition comes from the pleasure of winning, the primary reward of competition is competition itself.

(E) Even people who dread public speaking should accept invitations to speak before large groups. People will admire their courage and they will experience the fulfillment of having attempted something that is difficult for them.

10. In some countries, national planners have attempted to address the problems resulting from increasing urbanization by reducing migration from rural areas. But some economists have suggested an alternative approach. These economists assert that planners could solve these problems effectively by trading goods or services produced by a predominantly urban population in order to obtain the agricultural products that were previously produced domestically.

Which one of the following, if true, would provide the most support for the economists' assertion?

(A) Government subsidies to urban manufacturers can ease the problems caused by the migration of people from rural to urban areas.

(B) All problems that have economic causes must have economic solutions.

(C) A scarcity of agricultural products is a central element of many problems created by urbanization.

(D) Problems associated with migration to cities from rural areas are primarily due to trade imbalances between countries.

(E) Free trade policies can exacerbate the problems caused by increasing urbanization.

GO ON TO THE NEXT PAGE.

11. Inez: The book we are reading, *The Nature of Matter*, is
       mistitled. A title should summarize the content
       of the whole book, but nearly half of this book is
       devoted to discussing a different, albeit closely
       related subject: energy.

    Antonio: I do not think that the author erred; according to
       modern physics, matter and energy are two facets
       of the same phenomenon.

    Which one of the following is most strongly supported by
    the conversation above?

    (A)   Inez believes that the book should be called *The
          Nature of Energy*.
    (B)   Antonio believes that there are no differences
          between matter and energy.
    (C)   Inez and Antonio disagree on whether matter and
          energy are related.
    (D)   Inez and Antonio disagree about the overall value
          of the book.
    (E)   Inez believes that the book's title should not
          mention matter without mentioning energy.

12. Politician: Those economists who claim that consumer
       price increases have averaged less than 3 percent
       over the last year are mistaken. They clearly have
       not shopped anywhere recently. Gasoline is up
       10 percent over the last year; my auto insurance,
       12 percent; newspapers, 15 percent; propane, 13
       percent; bread, 50 percent.

    The reasoning in the politician's argument is most
    vulnerable to criticism on the grounds that the argument

    (A)   impugns the character of the economists rather
          than addressing their arguments
    (B)   fails to show that the economists mentioned are
          not experts in the area of consumer prices
    (C)   mistakenly infers that something is not true from
          the claim that it has not been shown to be so
    (D)   uses evidence drawn from a small sample that
          may well be unrepresentative
    (E)   attempts to persuade by making an emotional
          appeal

13. Sherrie: Scientists now agree that nicotine in tobacco is
       addictive inasmuch as smokers who try to stop
       smoking suffer withdrawal symptoms. For this
       reason alone, tobacco should be treated the same
       way as other dangerous drugs. Governments
       worldwide have a duty to restrict the manufacture
       and sale of tobacco.

    Fran: By your own admission, "addictive" is broad
       enough to include other commonly consumed
       products, such as coffee and soft drinks containing
       caffeine. But of course the manufacture and sale
       of these products should not be restricted.

    The dialogue above lends the most support to the claim
    that Sherrie and Fran disagree with each other about
    which one of the following statements?

    (A)   The manufacture and sale of all drugs should be
          regulated by governments.
    (B)   Coffee and soft drinks that contain caffeine
          should not be regulated by governments.
    (C)   Agreement by scientists that a substance is
          addictive justifies government restrictions on
          products containing that substance.
    (D)   Scientists are not proper authorities with respect
          to the question of whether a given substance is
          addictive.
    (E)   Scientists and governments have a duty to
          cooperate in regulating drugs to protect the
          public health.

14. In 1963, a young macaque monkey was observed
    venturing into a hot spring to retrieve food which had
    fallen in. Soon, other macaques began to enter the
    spring, and over a few years this behavior was adopted
    by the entire troop. Prior to 1963, no macaques had
    ever been observed in the hot spring; by 1990, the troop
    was regularly spending time there during the winters.
    Thus, these macaques are able to adopt and pass on new
    patterns of social behavior, and are not complete captives
    of their genetic heritage.

    Which one of the following is an assumption required by
    the argument above?

    (A)   Mutations in the genetic heritage of a certain
          variety of macaques can occur over a time span
          as short as a few years or decades.
    (B)   New patterns of behavior that emerge in macaque
          populations over the course of a few years
          or decades are not necessarily genetically
          predetermined.
    (C)   Only when behaviors become typical among
          an animal population can we conclude that a
          genetic alteration has occurred in that variety or
          species.
    (D)   The social behaviors of macaques are completely
          independent of their genetic heritage.
    (E)   The macaques' new pattern of behavior will
          persist over several generations.

GO ON TO THE NEXT PAGE.

15. Technological innovation rarely serves the interests of society as a whole. This can be seen from the fact that those responsible for technological advances are almost without exception motivated by considerations of personal gain rather than societal benefit in that they strive to develop commercially viable technology.

The argument is most vulnerable to criticism on the grounds that it

(A) contains a premise that cannot possibly be true
(B) takes for granted that technology beneficial to society as a whole cannot be commercially viable
(C) fails to consider the possibility that actions motivated by a desire for personal gain often do not result in personal gain
(D) takes for granted that an action is unlikely to produce a certain outcome unless it is motivated by a desire to produce that outcome
(E) draws a conclusion about the practical consequences of people's actions on the basis of theoretical views about what people should or should not do

16. There are two kinds of horror stories: those that describe a mad scientist's experiments and those that describe a monstrous beast. In some horror stories about monstrous beasts, the monster symbolizes a psychological disturbance in the protagonist. Horror stories about mad scientists, on the other hand, typically express the author's feeling that scientific knowledge alone is not enough to guide human endeavor. However, despite these differences, both kinds of horror stories share two features: they describe violations of the laws of nature and they are intended to produce dread in the reader.

If the statements above are true, which one of the following would also have to be true?

(A) All descriptions of monstrous beasts describe violations of the laws of nature.
(B) Any story that describes a violation of a law of nature is intended to invoke dread in the reader.
(C) Horror stories of any kind usually describe characters who are psychologically disturbed.
(D) Most stories about mad scientists express the author's antiscientific views.
(E) Some stories that employ symbolism describe violations of the laws of nature.

17. Politician: Some of my opponents have argued on theoretical grounds in favor of reducing social spending. Instead of arguing that there is excessive public expenditure on social programs, my opponents should focus on the main cause of deficit spending: the fact that government is bloated with bureaucrats and self-aggrandizing politicians. It is unwarranted, therefore, to reduce social expenditure.

A reasoning flaw in the politician's argument is that the argument

(A) does not address the arguments advanced by the politician's opponents
(B) makes an attack on the character of opponents
(C) takes for granted that deficit spending has just one cause
(D) portrays opponents' views as more extreme than they really are
(E) fails to make clear what counts as excessive spending

18. While it is true that bees' vision is well suited to the task of identifying flowers by their colors, it is probable that flowers developed in response to the type of vision that bees have, rather than bees' vision developing in response to flower color.

Which one of the following, if true, most strongly supports the statement above?

(A) Many insects that have vision very similar to that of bees do not depend on perceiving an object's color.
(B) Some flowers rely on insects other than bees.
(C) The number of different species of flowers is greater than the number of different species of bees.
(D) Many nonflowering plants rely on bees.
(E) Present-day bees rely exclusively on flowers for their food.

GO ON TO THE NEXT PAGE.

19. Professor: It has been argued that freedom of thought is a precondition for intellectual progress, because freedom of thought allows thinkers to pursue their ideas, regardless of whom these ideas offend, in whatever direction they lead. However, it is clear that one must mine the full implications of interrelated ideas to make intellectual progress, and for this, thinkers need intellectual discipline. Therefore, this argument for freedom of thought fails.

The conclusion drawn by the professor follows logically if which one of the following is assumed?

(A) Thinkers who limit their line of thought to a particular orthodoxy are hindered in their intellectual progress.

(B) Thinkers can mine the full implications of interrelated ideas only in the context of a society that values intellectual progress.

(C) In societies that protect freedom of thought, thinkers invariably lack intellectual discipline.

(D) Freedom of thought engenders creativity, which aids the discovery of truth.

(E) Without intellectual discipline, thinkers can have no freedom of thought.

20. People who have specialized knowledge about a scientific or technical issue are systematically excluded from juries for trials where that issue is relevant. Thus, trial by jury is not a fair means of settling disputes involving such issues.

Which one of the following, if true, most seriously weakens the argument?

(A) The more complicated the issue being litigated, the less likely it is that a juror without specialized knowledge of the field involved will be able to comprehend the testimony being given.

(B) The more a juror knows about a particular scientific or technical issue involved in a trial, the more likely it is that the juror will be prejudiced in favor of one of the litigating parties before the trial begins.

(C) Appointing an impartial arbitrator is not a fair means of settling disputes involving scientific or technical issues, because arbitrators tend to favor settlements in which both parties compromise on the issues.

(D) Experts who give testimony on scientific or technical issues tend to hedge their conclusions by discussing the possibility of error.

(E) Expert witnesses in specialized fields often command fees that are so high that many people involved in litigation cannot afford their services.

21. If one has evidence that an act will benefit other people and performs that act to benefit them, then one will generally succeed in benefiting them.

Which one of the following best illustrates the proposition above?

(A) A country's leaders realized that fostering diplomatic ties with antagonistic nations reduces the chances of war with those nations. Because those leaders worried that war would harm their chances of being reelected, they engaged in diplomatic discussions with a hostile country, and the two countries avoided a confrontation.

(B) A government study concluded that a proposed bureaucratic procedure would allow people to register their cars without waiting in line. The government adopted the procedure for this reason, and, as with most bureaucratic procedures, it was not successful.

(C) Betsy overheard a heating contractor say that regularly changing the filter in a furnace helps to keep the furnace efficient. So Betsy has regularly changed the furnace filter in her daughter's house. As a result, the furnace has never required maintenance due to becoming clogged with dust or dirt.

(D) Sejal learned in a psychology class that the best way to help someone overcome an addiction is to confront that person. So she confronted her friend Bob, who was struggling with a chemical dependency.

(E) Zachary hoped that psychotherapy could help his parents overcome their marital difficulties. He persuaded his parents to call a psychotherapist, and eventually their problems were resolved.

GO ON TO THE NEXT PAGE.

22. Radio airplay restrictions are nationally imposed regulations. The City Club has compiled a guide to all nationally imposed regulations except those related to taxation or to labor law. Radio airplay restrictions are related neither to taxation nor to labor law, so the City Club's guide covers radio airplay restrictions.

Which one of the following exhibits a pattern of reasoning most similar to that exhibited by the argument above?

(A) All prepackaged desserts pose a risk of tooth decay. The Nutrition Foundation recommends avoiding all prepackaged desserts that are not high in vitamins or protein. Many prepackaged snack foods are low in vitamins or protein, so the Nutrition Foundation recommends avoiding prepackaged snack foods as well.

(B) Coreopsis is a perennial. The Garden Club awards a prize each year for each perennial except those that are shrubs or not native to North America. Coreopsis is native to North America and is not a shrub. So the Garden Club awards a prize each year for coreopsis.

(C) The Windsor Coalition is an example of a community organizing to discourage overdevelopment. The Neighborhood Association is in favor of this sort of community organizing, except when it poses a threat to regional economic growth. Therefore, the Neighborhood Association is in favor of the Windsor Coalition.

(D) Compact discs are a kind of data storage device. Leotol Corporation does not produce data storage devices that use analog storage methods. Compact discs do not use analog storage methods, so it follows that Leotol Corporation produces compact discs.

(E) Traffic laws are a type of government regulation. The association supports traffic laws that are in the public interest, even if they have not been shown to reduce the accident rate. Thus, the association should support all government regulations that are in the public interest.

23. Physics professor: Some scientists claim that superheated plasma in which electrical resistance fails is a factor in causing so-called "ball lightning." If this were so, then such lightning would emit intense light and, since plasma has gaslike properties, would rise in the air. However, the instances of ball lightning that I observed were of low intensity and floated horizontally before vanishing. Thus, superheated plasma with failed electrical resistance is never a factor in causing ball lightning.

The physics professor's conclusion follows logically if which one of the following is assumed?

(A) Superheated plasma in which electrical resistance fails does not cause types of lightning other than ball lightning.

(B) The phenomena observed by the physics professor were each observed by at least one other person.

(C) Ball lightning can occur as the result of several different factors.

(D) Superheating of gaslike substances causes bright light to be emitted.

(E) All types of ball lightning have the same cause.

GO ON TO THE NEXT PAGE.

24. Advertisement: Our oat bran cereal is the only one that has printed right on its package all of its claimed health benefits. And really health-conscious consumers have demonstrated that these health claims are true by buying our cereal since they would not have bought our cereal unless the claims were true. How do we know these consumers are really health-conscious? No really health-conscious consumer would buy food in a package that did not have accurate information about the food's health benefits printed on it.

Which one of the following employs a flawed argumentative strategy that is most closely parallel to the flawed argumentative strategy in the advertisement above?

(A) Greeting one's coworkers must be a polite thing to do, because people who are considered polite always greet their coworkers. The proof that these people really are polite is that they are consistently polite in their daily lives.

(B) This card game must be intellectually challenging, because it is played by highly intelligent people, who play only intellectually challenging card games. In fact, these players' intelligence is demonstrated by the fact that they play this game.

(C) When coffee is being chosen, Brand Z is the coffee chosen by people with highly developed taste in coffee. These people showed their highly developed taste in coffee by correctly distinguishing eight brands of coffee from each other in a taste test.

(D) That jacket must have been made for a very short person, because only very short people were able to fit into it. We know that they were very short because we saw them before they tried on the jacket.

(E) This painting is a poor imitation, because only people with poor eyesight mistook it for the original. That these people have poor eyesight is demonstrated by the fact that they also mistook a vase of flowers in the painting for a peacock.

25. A study of 86 patients, all of whom suffered from disease T and received the same standard medical treatment, divided the patients into 2 equal groups. One group's members all attended weekly support group meetings, but no one from the other group attended support group meetings. After 10 years, 41 patients from each group had died. Clearly, support group meetings do not help patients with disease T live longer.

Which one of the following statements, if true, most seriously weakens the argument?

(A) Of the 4 patients who survived more than 10 years, the 2 who had attended weekly support group meetings lived longer than the 2 who had not.

(B) For many diseases, attending weekly support group meetings is part of the standard medical treatment.

(C) The members of the group that attended weekly support group meetings lived 2 years longer, on average, than the members of the other group.

(D) Some physicians have argued that attending weekly support group meetings gives patients less faith in the standard treatment for disease T.

(E) Everyone in the group whose members attended weekly support group meetings reported after 1 year that those meetings had helped them to cope with the disease.

26. Astronomer: I have asserted that our solar system does not contain enough meteoroids and other cosmic debris to have caused the extensive cratering on the far side of the moon. My opponents have repeatedly failed to demonstrate the falsity of this thesis. Their evidence is simply inconclusive; thus they should admit that my thesis is correct.

The reasoning in the astronomer's argument is flawed because this argument

(A) criticizes the astronomer's opponents rather than their arguments

(B) infers the truth of the astronomer's thesis from the mere claim that it has not been proven false

(C) ignores the possibility that alternative explanations may exist for the cratering

(D) presumes that the astronomer's thesis should not be subject to rational discussion and criticism

(E) fails to precisely define the key word "meteoroids"

STOP
IF YOU FINISH BEFORE TIME IS CALLED, YOU MAY CHECK YOUR WORK ON THIS SECTION ONLY.
DO NOT WORK ON ANY OTHER SECTION IN THE TEST.

SECTION III
Time—35 minutes
26 Questions

Directions: Each set of questions in this section is based on a single passage or a pair of passages. The questions are to be answered on the basis of what is stated or implied in the passage or pair of passages. For some of the questions, more than one of the choices could conceivably answer the question. However, you are to choose the best answer; that is, the response that most accurately and completely answers the question, and blacken the corresponding space on your answer sheet.

Most of what has been written about Thurgood Marshall, a former United States Supreme Court justice who served from 1967 to 1991, has just focused on his judicial record and on the ideological content of his
(5) earlier achievements as a lawyer pursuing civil rights issues in the courts. But when Marshall's career is viewed from a technical perspective, his work with the NAACP (National Association for the Advancement of Colored People) reveals a strategic and methodological
(10) legacy to the field of public interest law. Though the NAACP, under Marshall's direction, was not the first legal organization in the U.S. to be driven by a political and social agenda, he and the NAACP developed innovations that forever changed the landscape of
(15) public interest law: during the 1940s and 1950s, in their campaign against state-sanctioned racial segregation, Marshall and the NAACP, instead of simply pursuing cases as the opportunity arose, set up a predetermined legal campaign that was meticulously
(20) crafted and carefully coordinated.

One aspect of this campaign, the test case strategy, involved sponsoring litigation of tactically chosen cases at the trial court level with careful evaluation of the precedential nuances and potential impact of each
(25) decision. This allowed Marshall to try out different approaches and discover which was the best to be used. An essential element in the success of this tactic was the explicit recognition that in a public interest legal campaign, choosing the right plaintiff can mean the
(30) difference between success and failure. Marshall carefully selected cases with sympathetic litigants, whose public appeal, credibility, and commitment to the NAACP's goals were unsurpassed.

In addition, Marshall used sociological and
(35) psychological statistics—presented in expert testimony, for example, about the psychological impact of enforced segregation—as a means of transforming constitutional law by persuading the courts that certain discriminatory laws produced public harms in violation
(40) of constitutional principles. This tactic, while often effective, has been criticized by some legal scholars as a pragmatic attempt to give judges nonlegal material with which to fill gaps in their justifications for decisions where the purely legal principles appear
(45) inconclusive.

Since the time of Marshall's work with the NAACP, the number of public interest law firms in the U.S. has grown substantially, and they have widely adopted his combination of strategies for litigation,
(50) devoting them to various public purposes. These strategies have been used, for example, in consumer advocacy campaigns and, more recently, by politically conservative public interest lawyers seeking to achieve, through litigation, changes in the law that they have not
(55) been able to accomplish in the legislature. If we focus on the particular content of Marshall's goals and successes, it might seem surprising that his work has influenced the quest for such divergent political objectives, but the techniques that he honed—
(60) originally considered to be a radical departure from accepted conventions—have become the norm for U.S. public interest litigation today.

1. Which one of the following most accurately expresses the main point of the passage?

(A) In his role as a lawyer for the NAACP, Marshall developed a number of strategies for litigation which, while often controversial, proved to be highly successful in arguing against certain discriminatory laws.

(B) The litigation strategies that Marshall devised in pursuit of the NAACP's civil rights goals during the 1940s and 1950s constituted significant innovations that have since been adopted as standard tactics for public interest lawyers.

(C) Although commentary on Marshall has often focused only on a single ideological aspect of his accomplishments, a reinvestigation of his record as a judge reveals its influence on current divergent political objectives.

(D) In his work with the NAACP during the 1940s and 1950s, Marshall adopted a set of tactics that were previously considered a radical departure from accepted practice, but which he adapted in such a way that they eventually became accepted conventions in the field of law.

(E) Contrary to the impression commonly given by commentary on Marshall, his contributions to the work of the NAACP have had more of a lasting impact than his achievements as a U.S. Supreme Court justice.

GO ON TO THE NEXT PAGE.

2. Which one of the following most accurately describes two main functions of the first sentence of the passage?

   (A) It disputes a claim that has often been accepted and summarizes Marshall's achievements.

   (B) It establishes the passage's main topic and indicates the controversial nature of Marshall's ideologies.

   (C) It introduces two aspects of Marshall's career and outlines the historical significance of both.

   (D) It identifies Marshall's better-known achievements and suggests that commentary has neglected certain other achievements.

   (E) It provides a new perspective on Marshall's achievements and corrects a historical inaccuracy.

3. Which one of the following pairs of tactics used by an environmental-advocacy public interest law firm is most closely analogous to the strategies that Marshall utilized during his work with the NAACP?

   (A) a decision to pursue a pollution case based on its potential legal implications for a large class of related cases; and testimony by a noted medical authority whose data support the claim that the pollution in question causes widespread medical problems

   (B) acceptance of a pollution case based on the practical urgency of its expected impact on the environment if a ruling in favor of the plaintiff is rendered; and assignment of the case to the most widely known members of the firm

   (C) preference for pursuing a series of cases that are to be tried in courts having a record of decisions that are favorable to environmental interests; and taking these cases to judges who strictly uphold constitutional principles

   (D) acceptance of a pollution damage case based primarily on the potential plaintiff's needs; and careful orchestration of pretrial publicity designed to acquaint the public with the relevant issues

   (E) thorough and painstaking research of precedents relating to a current pollution case; and consultations with lawyers for the defense regarding a pretrial settlement

4. It can be most reasonably inferred from the passage that the author views the test case strategy developed by Marshall as

   (A) arbitrary
   (B) inflexible
   (C) unprecedented
   (D) necessary
   (E) subjective

5. The passage provides the most support for which one of the following statements?

   (A) The ideological motivations for Marshall's work with the NAACP changed during his tenure on the U.S. Supreme Court.

   (B) Marshall declined to pursue some cases that were in keeping with the NAACP's goals but whose plaintiffs' likely impression on the public he deemed to be unfavorable.

   (C) Marshall's tactics were initially opposed by some other members of the NAACP who favored a more traditional approach.

   (D) Marshall relied more on expert testimony in lower courts, whose judges were more likely than higher court judges to give weight to statistical evidence.

   (E) Marshall's colleagues at the NAACP subsequently revised his methods and extended their applications to areas of law and politics beyond those for which they were designed.

6. Based on the passage, it can be most reasonably inferred that the author would agree with which one of the following statements?

   (A) In light of a reconsideration of Marshall's career, it seems that commentary has undervalued both his innovations in litigation strategy and his accomplishments on the U.S. Supreme Court.

   (B) The most controversial of Marshall's methods was, somewhat paradoxically, the most unequivocally successful part of his overall campaign with the NAACP.

   (C) Lawyers representing private interests had previously used sociological evidence in court cases.

   (D) In response to Marshall's successes in NAACP litigations, the first public interest law firms were established, and they represented a radical change from previous types of U.S. law firms.

   (E) Marshall's techniques lend themselves to being used even for purposes that Marshall might not have intended.

7. According to the passage, some legal scholars have criticized which one of the following?

   (A) the ideology Marshall used to support his goals
   (B) recent public interest campaigns
   (C) the use of Marshall's techniques by politically conservative lawyers
   (D) the use of psychological statistics in court cases
   (E) the set of criteria for selecting public interest litigants

GO ON TO THE NEXT PAGE.

The painter Roy Lichtenstein helped to define pop art—the movement that incorporated commonplace objects and commercial-art techniques into paintings—by paraphrasing the style of comic books in his work.
(5) His merger of a popular genre with the forms and intentions of fine art generated a complex result: while poking fun at the pretensions of the art world, Lichtenstein's work also managed to convey a seriousness of theme that enabled it to transcend mere
(10) parody.

That Lichtenstein's images were fine art was at first difficult to see, because, with their word balloons and highly stylized figures, they looked like nothing more than the comic book panels from which they were
(15) copied. Standard art history holds that pop art emerged as an impersonal alternative to the histrionics of abstract expressionism, a movement in which painters conveyed their private attitudes and emotions using nonrepresentational techniques. The truth is that by the
(20) time pop art first appeared in the early 1960s, abstract expressionism had already lost much of its force. Pop art painters weren't quarreling with the powerful early abstract expressionist work of the late 1940s but with a second generation of abstract expressionists whose
(25) work seemed airy, high-minded, and overly lyrical. Pop art paintings were full of simple black lines and large areas of primary color. Lichtenstein's work was part of a general rebellion against the fading emotional power of abstract expressionism, rather than an aloof
(30) attempt to ignore it.

But if rebellion against previous art by means of the careful imitation of a popular genre were all that characterized Lichtenstein's work, it would possess only the reflective power that parodies have in relation
(35) to their subjects. Beneath its cartoonish methods, his work displayed an impulse toward realism, an urge to say that what was missing from contemporary painting was the depiction of contemporary life. The stilted romances and war stories portrayed in the comic books
(40) on which he based his canvases, the stylized automobiles, hot dogs, and table lamps that appeared in his pictures, were reflections of the culture Lichtenstein inhabited. But, in contrast to some pop art, Lichtenstein's work exuded not a jaded cynicism about
(45) consumer culture, but a kind of deliberate naivete, intended as a response to the excess of sophistication he observed not only in the later abstract expressionists but in some other pop artists. With the comics—typically the domain of youth and innocence—as his
(50) reference point, a nostalgia fills his paintings that gives them, for all their surface bravado, an inner sweetness. His persistent use of comic-art conventions demonstrates a faith in reconciliation, not only between cartoons and fine art, but between parody and true
(55) feeling.

8. Which one of the following most accurately states the main point of the passage?

(A) Lichtenstein's use of comic book elements in his paintings, considered simply a parodic reaction to the high-mindedness of later abstract expressionism, is also an attempt to re-create the emotionally powerful work of earlier abstract expressionists.

(B) Lichtenstein's use of comic book elements is not solely a parodic reaction to the high-mindedness of later abstract expressionism but also demonstrates an attempt to achieve realistic and nostalgic effects simultaneously in his paintings.

(C) Lichtenstein's use of comic book elements obscures the emotional complexity contained in his paintings, a situation that has prevented his work from being recognized as fine art in the expressionist tradition.

(D) Lichtenstein's use of comic book elements appears to mark his paintings as parodic reactions to the whole of abstract expressionism when they are instead a rebellion against the high-mindedness of the later abstract expressionists.

(E) Lichtenstein's use of comic book elements in his paintings, though a response to the excessive sophistication of the art world, is itself highly sophisticated in that it manages to reconcile pop art and fine art.

9. Which one of the following best captures the author's attitude toward Lichtenstein's work?

(A) enthusiasm for its more rebellious aspects
(B) respect for its successful parody of youth and innocence
(C) pleasure in its blatant rejection of abstract expressionism
(D) admiration for its subtle critique of contemporary culture
(E) appreciation for its ability to incorporate both realism and naivete

GO ON TO THE NEXT PAGE.

10. The author most likely lists some of the themes and objects influencing and appearing in Lichtenstein's paintings (lines 38–43) primarily to

    (A) show that the paintings depict aspects of contemporary life
    (B) support the claim that Lichtenstein's work was parodic in intent
    (C) contrast Lichtenstein's approach to art with that of abstract expressionism
    (D) suggest the emotions that lie at the heart of Lichtenstein's work
    (E) endorse Lichtenstein's attitude toward consumer culture

11. Based on the passage, which one of the following would be an example of pop art that is most in keeping with the spirit of Lichtenstein's work?

    (A) a painting that uses realistic techniques to represent several simple objects arranged on a table
    (B) a painting that parodies human figures by depicting them as stick figures
    (C) a painting that conveys its creator's inner turmoil through the use of bold lines and primary colors
    (D) a painting that employs vague shapes and images to make a statement about consumer culture
    (E) a painting that depicts products as they appear in magazine advertisements to comment on society's values

12. Which one of the following, if true, would most challenge the author's characterization of Lichtenstein?

    (A) Lichtenstein frequently attended exhibitions by abstract expressionist painters in the 1960s.
    (B) Lichtenstein praised a contemporary abstract expressionist in the 1960s for producing an atypically emotional painting.
    (C) Lichtenstein praised an early abstract expressionist for producing emotional paintings.
    (D) Lichtenstein criticized a pop artist in the 1960s for producing emotional paintings.
    (E) Lichtenstein criticized a pop artist in the 1960s for producing paintings void of emotion.

13. The primary purpose of the passage is most likely to

    (A) express curiosity about an artist's work
    (B) clarify the motivation behind an artist's work
    (C) contrast two opposing theories about an artist's work
    (D) describe the evolution of an artist's work
    (E) refute a previous overestimation of an artist's work

14. Based on the passage, which one of the following does the author appear to believe about the rebellious aspect of Lichtenstein's work?

    (A) It was directed less against abstract expressionism exclusively than against overly sophisticated art.
    (B) It was directed less against later abstract expressionism than against commercial art.
    (C) It was directed less against later abstract expressionism exclusively than against abstract expressionism in general.
    (D) It was an objection to the consumerism of the culture.
    (E) It was an objection to the simplicity of line and color used by pop artists.

15. Based on the passage, which one of the following can most reasonably be inferred about abstract expressionism?

    (A) Over time, it moved from abstraction to realism.
    (B) Over time, it moved from intensity to lyricism.
    (C) Over time, it moved from intellectualism to emotionalism.
    (D) Over time, it moved from obscurity to clarity.
    (E) Over time, it moved from density to sparseness.

GO ON TO THE NEXT PAGE.

Because the market system enables entrepreneurs and investors who develop new technology to reap financial rewards from their risk of capital, it may seem that the primary result of this activity is that some
(5) people who have spare capital accumulate more. But in spite of the fact that the profits derived from various technological developments have accrued to relatively few people, the developments themselves have served overall as a remarkable democratizing force. In fact,
(10) under the regime of the market, the gap in benefits accruing to different groups of people has been narrowed in the long term.

This tendency can be seen in various well-known technological developments. For example, before the
(15) printing press was introduced centuries ago, few people had access to written materials, much less to scribes and private secretaries to produce and transcribe documents. Since printed materials have become widely available, however, people without special
(20) position or resources—and in numbers once thought impossible—can take literacy and the use of printed texts for granted. With the distribution of books and periodicals in public libraries, this process has been extended to the point where people in general can have
(25) essentially equal access to a vast range of texts that would once have been available only to a very few. A more recent technological development extends this process beyond printed documents. A child in school with access to a personal computer and modem—
(30) which is becoming fairly common in technologically advanced societies—has computing power and database access equal to that of the best-connected scientists and engineers at top-level labs of just fifteen years ago, a time when relatively few people had
(35) personal access to any computing power. Or consider the uses of technology for leisure. In previous centuries only a few people with abundant resources had the ability and time to hire professional entertainment, and to have contact through travel and written
(40) communication—both of which were prohibitively expensive—with distant people. But now broadcast technology is widely available, and so almost anyone can have an entertainment cornucopia unimagined in earlier times. Similarly, the development of
(45) inexpensive mail distribution and telephone connections and, more recently, the establishment of the even more efficient medium of electronic mail have greatly extended the power of distant communication.

This kind of gradual diffusion of benefits across
(50) society is not an accident of these particular technological developments, but rather the result of a general tendency of the market system. Entrepreneurs and investors often are unable to maximize financial success without expanding their market, and this
(55) involves structuring their prices to the consumers so as to make their technologies genuinely accessible to an ever-larger share of the population. In other words, because market competition drives prices down, it tends to diffuse access to new technology across
(60) society as a result.

16. Which one of the following does the passage identify as being a result of a technological development?

(A) burgeoning scientific research
(B) educational uses of broadcasting
(C) widespread exchange of political ideas
(D) faster means of travel
(E) increased access to databases

17. As used in the passage, the word "democratizing" (line 9) most nearly means equalizing which one of the following?

(A) distribution of tangible and intangible goods
(B) opportunity to create new technology
(C) accumulation of financial assets in investments
(D) participation in the regulation of society through either public or private institutions
(E) generally acknowledged social status in a community

18. Which one of the following most accurately represents the primary function of the reference to maximization of financial success (lines 52–54)?

(A) It forms part of the author's summary of the benefits that have resulted from the technological developments described in the preceding paragraph.
(B) It serves as the author's logical conclusion from data presented in the preceding paragraph regarding the social consequences of technological development.
(C) It forms part of a speculative hypothesis that the author presents for its interest in relation to the main topic rather than as part of an argument.
(D) It serves as part of a causal explanation that reinforces the thesis in the first paragraph regarding the benefits of technological development.
(E) It forms part of the author's concession that certain factors complicate the argument presented in the first two paragraphs.

GO ON TO THE NEXT PAGE.

19. It can be most reasonably inferred from the passage that the author would agree with which one of the following statements?

   (A)   The profits derived from computer technology have accrued to fewer people than have the profits derived from any other technological development.
   (B)   Often the desire of some people for profits motivates changes that are beneficial for large numbers of other people.
   (C)   National boundaries are rarely barriers to the democratizing spread of technology.
   (D)   Typically, investment in technology is riskier than many other sorts of investment.
   (E)   Greater geographical mobility of populations has contributed to the profits of entrepreneurs and investors in technology.

20. From the passage it can be most reasonably inferred that the author would agree with which one of the following statements?

   (A)   The democratizing influence of technology generally contributes to technological obsolescence.
   (B)   Wholly unregulated economies are probably the fastest in producing an equalization of social status.
   (C)   Expanded access to printed texts across a population has historically led to an increase in literacy in that population.
   (D)   The invention of the telephone has had a greater democratizing influence on society than has the invention of the printing press.
   (E)   Near equality of financial assets among people is a realistic goal for market economies.

GO ON TO THE NEXT PAGE.

Neurobiologists once believed that the workings of the brain were guided exclusively by electrical signals; according to this theory, communication between neurons (brain cells) is possible because electrical
(5) impulses travel from one neuron to the next by literally leaping across the synapses (gaps between neurons). But many neurobiologists puzzled over how this leaping across synapses might be achieved, and as early as 1904 some speculated that electrical impulses
(10) are transmitted between neurons chemically rather than electrically. According to this alternative theory, the excited neuron secretes a chemical called a neurotransmitter that binds with its corresponding receptor molecule in the receiving neuron. This binding
(15) of the neurotransmitter renders the neuron permeable to ions, and as the ions move into the receiving neuron they generate an electrical impulse that runs through the cell; the electrical impulse is thereby transmitted to the receiving neuron.
(20)   This theory has gradually won acceptance in the scientific community, but for a long time little was known about the mechanism by which neurotransmitters manage to render the receiving neuron permeable to ions. In fact, some scientists
(25) remained skeptical of the theory because they had trouble imagining how the binding of a chemical to a receptor at the cell surface could influence the flow of ions through the cell membrane. Recently, however, researchers have gathered enough evidence for a
(30) convincing explanation: that the structure of receptors plays the pivotal role in mediating the conversion of chemical signals into electrical activity.
    The new evidence shows that receptors for neurotransmitters contain both a neurotransmitter
(35) binding site and a separate region that functions as a channel for ions; attachment of the neurotransmitter to the binding site causes the receptor to change shape and so results in the opening of its channel component. Several types of receptors have been isolated that
(40) conform to this structure, among them the receptors for acetylcholine, gamma-aminobutyric acid (GABA), glycine, and serotonin. These receptors display enough similarities to constitute a family, known collectively as neurotransmitter-gated ion channels.
(45)   It has also been discovered that each of the receptors in this family comes in several varieties so that, for example, a GABA receptor in one part of the brain has slightly different properties than a GABA receptor in another part of the brain. This discovery is
(50) medically significant because it raises the possibility of the highly selective treatment of certain brain disorders. As the precise effect on behavior of every variety of each neurotransmitter-gated ion channel is deciphered, pharmacologists may be able to design
(55) drugs targeted to specific receptors on defined categories of neurons that will selectively impede or enhance these effects. Such drugs could potentially help ameliorate any number of debilitating conditions, including mood disorders, tissue damage associated
(60) with stroke, or Alzheimer's disease.

21. Which one of the following most completely and accurately states the main point of the passage?

(A)   Evidence shows that the workings of the brain are guided, not by electrical signals, but by chemicals, and that subtle differences among the receptors for these chemicals may permit the selective treatment of certain brain disorders.

(B)   Evidence shows that the workings of the brain are guided, not by electrical signals, but by chemicals, and that enough similarities exist among these chemicals to allow scientists to classify them as a family.

(C)   Evidence shows that electrical impulses are transmitted between neurons chemically rather than electrically, and that enough similarities exist among these chemicals to allow scientists to classify them as a family.

(D)   Evidence shows that electrical impulses are transmitted between neurons chemically rather than electrically, and that subtle differences among the receptors for these chemicals may permit the selective treatment of certain brain disorders.

(E)   Evidence shows that receptor molecules in the brain differ subtly from one another, and that these differences can be exploited to treat certain brain disorders through the use of drugs that selectively affect particular parts of the brain.

22. Based on the passage, the author's attitude toward the discovery presented in the last paragraph is most accurately described as

(A)   certainty that its possible benefits will be realized
(B)   optimism about its potential applications
(C)   apprehension about the possibility of its misuse
(D)   concern that its benefits are easily exaggerated
(E)   skepticism toward its assumptions about the brain

23. Each of the following statements is affirmed by the passage EXCEPT:

(A)   The secretion of certain chemicals plays a role in neuron communication.
(B)   The flow of ions through neurons plays a role in neuron communication.
(C)   The binding of neurotransmitters to receptors plays a role in neuron communication.
(D)   The structure of receptors on neuron surfaces plays a role in neuron communication.
(E)   The size of neurotransmitter binding sites on receptors plays a role in neuron communication.

GO ON TO THE NEXT PAGE.

24. The author most likely uses the phrase "defined categories of neurons" in lines 55–56 in order to refer to neurons that

    (A) possess channels for ions
    (B) respond to drug treatment
    (C) contain receptor molecules
    (D) influence particular brain functions
    (E) react to binding by neurotransmitters

25. Which one of the following most accurately describes the organization of the passage?

    (A) explanation of a theory; presentation of evidence in support of the theory; presentation of evidence in opposition to the theory; argument in favor of rejecting the theory; discussion of the implications of rejecting the theory
    (B) explanation of a theory; presentation of evidence in support of the theory; explanation of an alternative theory; presentation of information to support the alternative theory; discussion of an experiment that can help determine which theory is correct
    (C) explanation of a theory; description of an obstacle to the theory's general acceptance; presentation of an explanation that helps the theory overcome the obstacle; discussion of a further implication of the theory
    (D) explanation of a theory; description of an obstacle to the theory's general acceptance; argument that the obstacle is insurmountable and that the theory should be rejected; discussion of the implications of rejecting the theory
    (E) explanation of a theory; description of how the theory came to win scientific acceptance; presentation of new information that challenges the theory; modification of the theory to accommodate the new information; discussion of an implication of the modification

26. The primary purpose of the passage is most likely to

    (A) propose a new theory about the workings of the brain
    (B) introduce evidence that challenges a widely accepted theory about the workings of the brain
    (C) describe the approach scientists use when studying the workings of the brain
    (D) discuss new support for a widely accepted theory about the workings of the brain
    (E) illustrate the practical utility of scientific research into the workings of the brain

S T O P
IF YOU FINISH BEFORE TIME IS CALLED, YOU MAY CHECK YOUR WORK ON THIS SECTION ONLY.
DO NOT WORK ON ANY OTHER SECTION IN THE TEST.

SECTION IV
Time—35 minutes
26 Questions

Directions: The questions in this section are based on the reasoning contained in brief statements or passages. For some questions, more than one of the choices could conceivably answer the question. However, you are to choose the best answer; that is, the response that most accurately and completely answers the question. You should not make assumptions that are by commonsense standards implausible, superfluous, or incompatible with the passage. After you have chosen the best answer, blacken the corresponding space on your answer sheet.

1. Many newborn babies have a yellowish tinge to their skin because their blood contains a high level of the pigment bilirubin. One group of doctors treats newborns to reduce high levels of bilirubin, since bilirubin, if it enters the brain, might cause the tetanus that sometimes occurs in newborns. However, a second group of doctors argues for allowing bilirubin levels in newborn babies to remain high, since the brain's own natural defenses normally prevent bilirubin from entering.

   Which one of the following, if true, most helps to support the position of the second group of doctors?

   (A) The treatment that most effectively reduces high levels of bilirubin in newborns has no known negative side effects.
   (B) Some diseases that occur in newborns can weaken the brain's natural defenses and allow bilirubin to enter.
   (C) In newborns the pigment bilirubin, like other pigments, occurs not only in the blood but also in fluids involved in digestion.
   (D) Bilirubin neutralizes certain potentially damaging substances to which newborns are exposed at birth.
   (E) Among doctors who recommend treating newborns to reduce high levels of bilirubin, there is general agreement about what levels should be considered excessively high.

2. Economist: Some sociologists argue that because capitalism intrinsically involves competition, it weakens the ties between the people of a community. Although this may formerly have been true, modern capitalism requires that there be large corporations. Thus, modern capitalism promotes, rather than weakens, communal ties.

   Which one of the following is an assumption on which the economist's argument depends?

   (A) Few economic systems are more successful than modern capitalism in fostering communal ties between citizens.
   (B) Modern capitalism is designed primarily to distribute goods and services, not to create communal ties between people.
   (C) Corporations that compete with each other must develop some ties to each other in order to reach agreement on the rules of the competition.
   (D) Having large corporations in a modern capitalist system promotes the strength of communal ties.
   (E) An economic system that does not encourage large corporations will be less successful economically than one that does.

GO ON TO THE NEXT PAGE.

3. Teacher: Participating in organized competitive athletics may increase a child's strength and coordination. As critics point out, however, it also instills in those children who are not already well developed in these respects a feeling of inferiority that never really disappears. Yet, since research has shown that adults with feelings of inferiority become more successful than those free of such anxieties, funding for children's athletic programs should not be eliminated.

Which one of the following most accurately describes the role played in the teacher's argument by the assertion that participating in organized competitive athletics may increase a child's strength and coordination?

(A) It is mentioned as one possible reason for adopting a policy for which the teacher suggests an additional reason.

(B) It is a claim that the teacher attempts to refute with counterarguments.

(C) It is a hypothesis for which the teacher offers additional evidence.

(D) It is cited as an insufficient reason for eliminating funding for children's athletic programs.

(E) It is cited as an objection that has been raised to the position that the teacher is supporting.

4. Columnist: Donating items to charity may be a sign of generosity, but any generosity it may demonstrate is rarely a permanent virtue, since most donors make donations only intermittently.

Which one of the following most accurately describes a flaw in the columnist's argument?

(A) The argument takes for granted that truly generous people are the most virtuous.

(B) The argument attacks the character of those whose values are different from those of the columnist.

(C) The argument takes for granted that a character trait is present only when manifested.

(D) The argument generalizes from too small a sample of cases.

(E) The argument takes for granted that most people donate out of generosity.

5. Researchers have found that, hours after birth, infants are able to distinguish faces from other images. Infants stare at drawings of faces for longer periods of time than they do at blank ovals or drawings in which facial features are scrambled.

Which one of the following, if true, most helps to explain the ability of newborn infants described above?

(A) Certain abilities of facial pattern recognition are innate in humans, rather than learned.

(B) The longer an infant stares at an object, the more interesting the infant finds that object.

(C) Infants learn to associate human faces with the necessities of comfort and nourishment.

(D) The less an infant stares at an object, the weaker the preference the infant has for that object.

(E) Infants learn to associate the sound of human voices with the images of human faces.

6. Violent crime in this town is becoming a serious problem. Compared to last year, local law enforcement agencies have responded to 17 percent more calls involving violent crimes, showing that the average citizen of this town is more likely than ever to become a victim of a violent crime.

Which one of the following, if true, most seriously weakens the argument?

(A) The town's overall crime rate appears to have risen slightly this year compared to the same period last year.

(B) In general, persons under the age of 65 are less likely to be victims of violent crimes than persons over the age of 65.

(C) As a result of the town's community outreach programs, more people than ever are willing to report violent crimes to the proper authorities.

(D) In response to worries about violent crime, the town has recently opened a community center providing supervised activities for teenagers.

(E) Community officials have shown that a relatively small number of repeat offenders commit the majority of violent crimes in the town.

GO ON TO THE NEXT PAGE.

7. Two different dates have been offered as the approximate end point of the last ice age in North America. The first date was established by testing insect fragments found in samples of sediments to determine when warmth-adapted open-ground beetles replaced cold-adapted arctic beetles. The second date was established by testing pollen grains in those same samples to determine when ice masses yielded to spruce forests. The first date is more than 500 years earlier than the second.

The statements above, if true, most strongly support which one of the following conclusions about the last ice age and its aftermath in North America?

(A) Toward the end of the ice age, warmth-adapted open-ground beetles ceased to inhabit areas where the predominant tree cover consisted of spruce forests.

(B) Among those sediments deposited toward the end of the ice age, those found to contain cold-adapted arctic beetle fragments can also be expected to contain spruce-pollen grains.

(C) Ice masses continued to advance through North America for several hundred years after the end of the ice age.

(D) The species of cold-adapted arctic beetle that inhabited areas covered by ice masses died out toward the end of the last ice age.

(E) Toward the end of the ice age, warmth-adapted open-ground beetles colonized the new terrain opened to them faster than soil changes and seed dispersion established new spruce forests.

8. When presented with the evidence against him, Ellison freely admitted to engaging in illegal transactions using company facilities. However, the company obtained the evidence by illegally recording Ellison's conversations. Therefore, although the company may demand that he immediately cease, it cannot justifiably take any punitive measures against him.

Which one of the following judgments best illustrates the principle illustrated by the argument above?

(A) After Price confessed to having stolen money from Long over a period of several years, Long began stealing from Price. Despite Price's guilt, Long was not justified in taking illegal action against him.

(B) Shakila's secretary has admitted that he is illegally receiving cable television without paying for it. Shakila would not be justified in reporting him, though, since she once did the same thing.

(C) After Takashi told Sarah's parents that he had seen her at the movies on Tuesday, Sarah confessed to sneaking out that day. On Monday, however, Takashi had violated the local curfew for minors. Hence Sarah's parents cannot justifiably punish her in this case.

(D) After a conservation officer discovered them, Kuttner admitted that he had set the illegal animal traps on his land. But, because she was trespassing at the time, the conservation officer cannot justifiably punish Kuttner in this case.

(E) Ramirez was forced by the discovery of new evidence to admit that she lied about her role in managing the chief of staff's financial affairs. Nevertheless, the board of directors cannot justifiably take action against Ramirez, because in past instances it has pardoned others guilty of similar improprieties.

GO ON TO THE NEXT PAGE.

9. In a recent study, each member of two groups of people, Group A (composed of persons sixty-five to seventy-five years old) and Group B (composed of college students), was required to make a telephone call to a certain number at a specified time. The time when each call was initiated was recorded electronically. Group A proved far better at remembering to make a telephone call precisely at a specified time than did Group B. There were fourteen lapses in Group B but only one lapse in Group A. Clearly, at least one type of memory does not suffer as a person ages.

Which one of the following, if all of them are true, is LEAST helpful in establishing that the conclusion above is properly drawn?

(A) There was the same number of people in each group.

(B) The same group of researchers answered the calls made by the callers in both study groups.

(C) Among the college students there were no persons more than forty years old.

(D) Both groups had unrestricted access to telephones for making the required calls.

(E) The members of the two groups received their instructions approximately the same amount of time before they were to make their telephone calls.

10. Prediction, the hallmark of the natural sciences, appears to have been made possible by reducing phenomena to mathematical expressions. Some social scientists also want the power to predict accurately and assume they ought to perform the same reduction. But this would be a mistake; it would neglect data that are not easily mathematized and thereby would only distort the social phenomena.

Which one of the following most accurately expresses the main conclusion of the argument?

(A) The social sciences do not have as much predictive power as the natural sciences.

(B) Mathematics plays a more important role in the natural sciences than it does in the social sciences.

(C) There is a need in the social sciences to improve the ability to predict.

(D) Phenomena in the social sciences should not be reduced to mathematical formulas.

(E) Prediction is responsible for the success of the natural sciences.

11. Studies have shown that the more high-stress points a bridge has, the more likely it is to fracture eventually. This might lead one to expect fractures to develop at high-stress points. Surprisingly, however, fractures develop not at high-stress points but elsewhere on the bridge.

Which one of the following, if true, contributes most to an explanation of why bridges fracture elsewhere than at high-stress points?

(A) In many structures other than bridges, such as ship hulls and airplane bodies, fractures do not develop at high-stress points.

(B) Fractures do not develop at high-stress points, because bridges are reinforced at those points; however, stress is transferred to other points on the bridge where it causes fractures.

(C) In many structures, the process of fracturing often causes high-stress points to develop.

(D) Structures with no high-stress points can nonetheless have a high probability of fracturing.

(E) Improper bridge construction, e.g., low-quality welding or the use of inferior steel, often leads both to the development of high-stress points and to an increased probability of fracturing.

12. Many people say that the press should not pry into the personal lives of private individuals. But the press has the right to publish any story of interest to the public unless that story is libelous. So, if a story about a private individual is not libelous, the press has an obligation to publish it, for such information is clearly of interest to the public.

The argument's reasoning is vulnerable to criticism on the grounds that the argument presumes, without giving warrant, that

(A) the press can publish nonlibelous stories about private individuals without prying into their personal lives

(B) one's having a right to do something entails one's having an obligation to do it

(C) the publishing of information about the personal lives of private individuals cannot be libelous

(D) if one has an obligation to do something then one has a right to do it

(E) the press's right to publish always outweighs the individual's right not to be libeled

GO ON TO THE NEXT PAGE.

13. Consumer advocate: A recent study concluded that top-loading washing machines are superior overall to front-loaders. But front-loaders have the controls and access in front. This is more convenient for wheelchair users, some of whom find it highly inconvenient to remove laundry from top-loaders. So for some consumers front-loaders are superior.

Which one of the following is an assumption upon which the consumer advocate's argument depends?

(A) For some consumers the convenience of front-loaders outweighs the advantages of top-loaders in assessing which is superior.

(B) Washing machines of a given type should be compared only with washing machines of that type.

(C) Convenience is the only important factor in determining which type of washing machine is superior.

(D) Retrieving clothes from a top-loader is convenient for people who do not use wheelchairs.

(E) Retrieving clothes from front-loaders is inconvenient for people who are not wheelchair users.

14. Over 90 percent of the human brain currently serves no purpose, as is evident from the fact that many people with significant brain damage show no discernible adverse effects. So once humans begin to tap into this tremendous source of creativity and innovation, many problems that today seem insurmountable will be within our ability to solve.

Which one of the following most accurately describes a flaw in the argument?

(A) The argument presumes, without providing justification, that the effects of brain damage are always easily detectable.

(B) The argument presumes, without providing justification, that the only reason that any problem remains unsolved is a lack of creativity and innovation.

(C) The argument infers that certain parts of the brain do nothing merely on the basis of the assertion that we do not know what they do.

(D) The argument infers that problems will be solved merely on the basis of the claim that they will be within our ability to solve.

(E) The argument presumes, without providing justification, that the currently unused parts of the brain are a potential source of tremendous creativity and innovation.

15. Some scientists have expressed reservations about quantum theory because of its counterintuitive consequences. But despite rigorous attempts to show that quantum theory's predictions were inaccurate, they were shown to be accurate within the generally accepted statistical margin of error. These results, which have not been equaled by quantum theory's competitors, warrant acceptance of quantum theory.

Which one of the following principles most helps to justify the reasoning above?

(A) A scientific theory should be accepted if it has fewer counterintuitive consequences than do its competitors.

(B) A scientific theory should be accepted if it has been subjected to serious attempts to disprove it and has withstood all of them.

(C) The consequences of a scientific theory should not be considered counterintuitive if the theory's predictions have been found to be accurate.

(D) A theory should not be rejected until it has been subjected to serious attempts to disprove it.

(E) A theory should be accepted only if its predictions have not been disproved by experiment.

16. Psychologist: The obligation to express gratitude cannot be fulfilled anonymously. However much society may have changed over the centuries, human psychology is still driven primarily by personal interaction. Thus, the important social function of positively reinforcing those behaviors that have beneficial consequences for others can be served only if the benefactor knows the source of the gratitude.

Which one of the following most accurately describes the role played in the psychologist's argument by the claim that the obligation to express gratitude cannot be fulfilled anonymously?

(A) It is an illustration of a premise that is used to support the argument's conclusion.

(B) It is used to counter a consideration that might be taken to undermine the argument's conclusion.

(C) It is used to support indirectly a claim that the argument in turn uses to support directly the conclusion.

(D) It is used to identify the social benefit with which the argument is concerned.

(E) It is the conclusion that the argument is intended to support.

GO ON TO THE NEXT PAGE.

17. Curator: Our museum displays only twentieth-century works, which are either on loan from private collectors or in the museum's permanent collection. Prints of all of the latter works are available in the museum store. The museum store also sells prints of some works that are not part of the museum's permanent collection, such as Hopper's *Nighthawks*.

If the curator's statements are true, which one of the following must be true?

(A) Every print in the museum store is of a work that is either on loan to the museum from a private collector or part of the museum's permanent collection.

(B) Every print that is sold in the museum store is a copy of a twentieth-century work.

(C) There are prints in the museum store of every work that is displayed in the museum and not on loan from a private collector.

(D) Hopper's *Nighthawks* is both a twentieth-century work and a work on loan to the museum from a private collector.

(E) Hopper's *Nighthawks* is not displayed in the museum.

18. Nutritionist: Because humans have evolved very little since the development of agriculture, it is clear that humans are still biologically adapted to a diet of wild foods, consisting mainly of raw fruits and vegetables, nuts and seeds, lean meat, and seafood. Straying from this diet has often resulted in chronic illness and other physical problems. Thus, the more our diet consists of wild foods, the healthier we will be.

The claim that humans are still biologically adapted to a diet of wild foods plays which one of the following roles in the nutritionist's argument?

(A) It is a conclusion for which the only support offered is the claim that straying from a diet of wild foods has often resulted in chronic illness and other physical problems.

(B) It is a premise for which no justification is provided, but which is used to support the argument's main conclusion.

(C) It is a phenomenon for which the main conclusion of the nutritionist's argument is cited as an explanation.

(D) It is an intermediate conclusion for which one claim is offered as support, and which is used in turn to support the argument's main conclusion.

(E) It is a premise offered in support of the claim that humans have evolved very little since the development of agriculture.

19. Editorialist: Some people argue that we have an obligation not to cut down trees. However, there can be no obligation to an entity unless that entity has a corresponding right. So if we have an obligation toward trees, then trees have rights. But trees are not the sort of things that can have rights. Therefore, we have no obligation not to cut down trees.

The editorialist's argument depends on assuming which one of the following?

(A) If an entity has a right to certain treatment, we have an obligation to treat it that way.

(B) Any entity that has rights also has obligations.

(C) Only conscious entities are the sort of things that can have rights.

(D) Avoiding cutting down trees is not an obligation owed to some entity other than trees.

(E) One does not always have the right to cut down the trees on one's own property.

20. A recent study suggests that consuming three glasses of wine daily substantially decreases the risk of stroke. Critics of the study, defending earlier research recommending one glass of wine daily, claim that binge drinkers (who drink once a week or less, but drink three or more drinks when they do drink) are the people most likely to drink three glasses of wine in one day and are more likely to die from sudden heart attacks than are other drinkers. According to these critics, drinking three glasses of wine daily would not benefit health overall, since the decrease in the risk of stroke associated with that level of consumption is negated by its associated increased risk of sudden heart attack.

The critics' argument is most vulnerable to criticism on the grounds that it

(A) inappropriately attributes the consequences of binge drinking to persons whose regular consumption of wine is three glasses a day

(B) confuses the risk of sudden alcohol-induced heart attacks with other health risks

(C) presumes, without providing justification, that there is no significant difference between wine and other alcoholic beverages in terms of health benefits and risks

(D) fails to address specifically the reduction in risk of stroke conferred by the level of consumption in the recent study

(E) overlooks the difference between strokes that result in death and less severe strokes

GO ON TO THE NEXT PAGE.

21. Scientist: Isaac Newton's *Principia*, the seventeenth-century work that served as the cornerstone of physics for over two centuries, could at first be understood by only a handful of people, but a basic understanding of Newton's ideas eventually spread throughout the world. This shows that the barriers to communication between scientists and the public are not impermeable. Thus recent scientific research, most of which also can be described only in language that seems esoteric to most contemporary readers, may also become part of everyone's intellectual heritage.

Which one of the following most accurately describes the role played in the scientist's argument by the claim that recent scientific research can often be described only in language that seems esoteric to most contemporary readers?

(A) It is raised as a potential objection to the argument's main conclusion, but its truth is called into doubt by the preceding statements.

(B) It is a premise that supports the argument's main conclusion by suggesting that the results of recent scientific research are only superficially different from claims made in Newton's *Principia*.

(C) It is cited as further evidence for the conclusion that the barriers to communication between scientists and the public are not impermeable.

(D) It is a claim that serves mainly to help establish the relevance of the preceding statements to the argument's final conclusion.

(E) It serves to cast doubt on an alleged similarity between Newton's *Principia* and recent scientific research.

22. Only a minority of those who engage in political action do so out of a sense of social justice. Therefore, some people who have a sense of social justice do not engage in political action.

Which one of the following uses flawed reasoning most similar to that used in the argument above?

(A) Most scholars are not motivated by a desire to win prestigious academic prizes. Thus, some of those who want to win prestigious academic prizes are not scholars.

(B) Only foolish politicians disregard the wishes of most voters. Thus, most voters deserve to be represented by foolish politicians.

(C) Some corporations only feign a concern for the environment when they advertise a product as environmentally friendly. Thus, no corporation has a genuine concern for the environment.

(D) Some parents show no interest in the curricula used in the schools that their children attend. Thus, some of the decisions regarding school curricula should be made without regard for the wishes of the children's parents.

(E) Only a small percentage of the profits that companies make are directly attributable to good management decisions. Thus, even companies that are managed badly will usually turn a profit.

23. Columnist: Even if the primary purpose of university education is to make students employable, such education should emphasize the liberal arts rather than the more narrow kind of technical training that prepares one for a particular sort of job. This is because the reasoning skills one acquires from a liberal arts education allow one to adapt to new intellectual challenges and thus to perform jobs for which one has received no specialized training.

Which one of the following, if true, most strengthens the columnist's argument?

(A) It is better for people to have good educations than good jobs.

(B) Many people with narrow technical training manage to find jobs.

(C) Having a series of different jobs is more interesting than having only one job.

(D) Having a general understanding of life is more important than possessing practical skills.

(E) Technical training does not help students acquire reasoning skills.

GO ON TO THE NEXT PAGE.

24. Provinces and states with stringent car safety requirements, including required use of seat belts and annual safety inspections, have on average higher rates of accidents per kilometer driven than do provinces and states with less stringent requirements. Nevertheless, most highway safety experts agree that more stringent requirements do reduce accident rates.

Which one of the following, if true, most helps to reconcile the safety experts' belief with the apparently contrary evidence described above?

(A) Annual safety inspections ensure that car tires are replaced before they grow old.

(B) Drivers often become overconfident after their cars have passed a thorough safety inspection.

(C) The roads in provinces and states with stringent car safety requirements are far more congested and therefore dangerous than in other provinces and states.

(D) Psychological studies show that drivers who regularly wear seat belts often come to think of themselves as serious drivers, which for a few people discourages reckless driving.

(E) Provinces and states with stringent car safety requirements have, on average, many more kilometers of roads than do other provinces and states.

25. It is difficult to grow cacti in a humid climate. It is difficult to raise orange trees in a cold climate. In most parts of a certain country, it is either easy to grow cacti or easy to raise orange trees.

If the statements above are true, which one of the following must be false?

(A) Half of the country is both humid and cold.

(B) Most of the country is hot.

(C) Some parts of the country are neither cold nor humid.

(D) It is not possible to raise cacti in the country.

(E) Most parts of the country are humid.

26. Essayist: Common sense, which is always progressing, is nothing but a collection of theories that have been tested over time and found useful. When alternative theories that prove even more useful are developed, they gradually take the place of theories already embodied in common sense. This causes common sense to progress, but, because it absorbs new theories slowly, it always contains some obsolete theories.

If all of the essayist's statements are true, then which one of the following must be true?

(A) At least some new theories that have not yet been found to be more useful than any theory currently part of common sense will never be absorbed into the body of common sense.

(B) Of the useful theories within the body of common sense, the older ones are generally less useful than the newer ones.

(C) The frequency with which new theories are generated prevents their rapid absorption into the body of common sense.

(D) Each theory within the body of common sense is eventually replaced with a new theory that is more useful.

(E) At least some theories that have been tested over time and found useful are less useful than some other theories that have not been fully absorbed into the body of common sense.

S T O P

IF YOU FINISH BEFORE TIME IS CALLED, YOU MAY CHECK YOUR WORK ON THIS SECTION ONLY.
DO NOT WORK ON ANY OTHER SECTION IN THE TEST.

ACKNOWLEDGMENTS

Acknowledgment is made to the following sources from which material has been adapted for use in this test booklet:

Jean-Pierre Changeux, "Chemical Signaling in the Brain." ©November 1993 by Scientific American, Inc.

Adam Gopnik, "The Wise Innocent." ©1993 by The New Yorker Magazine, Inc.

Stephen Weinberg, "Life in the Universe." ©October 1994 by Scientific American, Inc.

**Wait for the supervisor's instructions before you open the page to the topic.
Please print and sign your name and write the date in the designated spaces below.**

Time: 35 Minutes

General Directions

You will have 35 minutes in which to plan and write an essay on the topic inside. Read the topic and the accompanying directions carefully. You will probably find it best to spend a few minutes considering the topic and organizing your thoughts before you begin writing. In your essay, be sure to develop your ideas fully, leaving time, if possible, to review what you have written. **Do not write on a topic other than the one specified. Writing on a topic of your own choice is not acceptable.**

No special knowledge is required or expected for this writing exercise. Law schools are interested in the reasoning, clarity, organization, language usage, and writing mechanics displayed in your essay. How well you write is more important than how much you write.

Confine your essay to the blocked, lined area on the front and back of the separate Writing Sample Response Sheet. Only that area will be reproduced for law schools. Be sure that your writing is legible.

Both this topic sheet and your response sheet must be turned over to the testing staff before you leave the room.

Topic Code	Print Your Full Name Here		
	Last	First	M.I.

Date	Sign Your Name Here
/ /	

Scratch Paper
Do not write your essay in this space.

LSAT® Writing Sample Topic

Directions: The scenario presented below describes two choices, either one of which can be supported on the basis of the information given. Your essay should consider both choices and argue for one over the other, based on the two specified criteria and the facts provided. There is no "right" or "wrong" choice: a reasonable argument can be made for either.

The executors of the estate of a late, famous author recently found the manuscript of an unfinished novel among the author's papers. They must decide whether to publish the manuscript or donate it to a university library. In order to avoid unfortunate comparisons between a heavily edited published version and the original manuscript, they will not do both. Write an argument for choosing one option over the other based on the following considerations:

- The executors want to preserve the author's reputation as a literary genius.
- The executors want to maximize interest in the author's work among both scholars and the public.

Critics who have read the manuscript agree that the work is intriguingly experimental but that it is not among the author's best. If the novel is to be published, it will require heavy editing to make it seem complete. Its style differs greatly from that of the author's most popular novels, so it is unclear how well the novel will sell. Most of the author's other novels stayed on the bestseller list for months after publication, but it has been more than a decade since her last work was published. The publisher promises a large printing, wide distribution, and an aggressive marketing campaign. If the work is published, the executors will sell the original manuscript to a private collector who would not allow it to be copied or viewed by scholars.

Scholars have voiced a strong preference for access to the unedited manuscript. One prominent scholar has expressed dismay at the publisher's intention to alter the original manuscript in order to make the novel marketable. If donated, the manuscript will become part of a permanent display in the university's library, which is open to the public. Individual copies will be made available for a nominal fee to scholars and any others upon request. The donation of the manuscript to the university would likely revive waning scholarly interest in the author and lead to a new wave of commentaries by literary critics and biographers. Past commentaries on the author's life and work have sold well even beyond academic circles.

Scratch Paper
Do not write your essay in this space.

Writing Sample Response Sheet

DO NOT WRITE IN THIS SPACE

Begin your essay in the lined area below.
Continue on the back if you need more space.

COMPUTING YOUR SCORE

Directions:

1. Use the Answer Key on the next page to check your answers.

2. Use the Scoring Worksheet below to compute your raw score.

3. Use the Score Conversion Chart to convert your raw score into the 120-180 scale.

Scoring Worksheet

1. Enter the number of questions you answered correctly in each section.

	Number Correct
SECTION I	_____
SECTION II	_____
SECTION III	_____
SECTION IV..............	_____

2. Enter the sum here: _____

   This is your Raw Score.

Conversion Chart
For Converting Raw Score to the 120-180 LSAT Scaled Score
LSAT Form 3LSS57

Reported Score	Raw Score Lowest	Raw Score Highest
180	99	101
179	—*	—*
178	98	98
177	97	97
176	96	96
175	95	95
174	94	94
173	—*	—*
172	92	93
171	91	91
170	90	90
169	89	89
168	87	88
167	86	86
166	85	85
165	83	84
164	81	82
163	80	80
162	78	79
161	76	77
160	75	75
159	73	74
158	71	72
157	69	70
156	67	68
155	66	66
154	64	65
153	62	63
152	60	61
151	58	59
150	56	57
149	55	55
148	53	54
147	51	52
146	49	50
145	48	48
144	46	47
143	44	45
142	43	43
141	41	42
140	39	40
139	38	38
138	36	37
137	35	35
136	33	34
135	32	32
134	30	31
133	29	29
132	28	28
131	26	27
130	25	25
129	24	24
128	23	23
127	22	22
126	21	21
125	20	20
124	19	19
123	18	18
122	17	17
121	16	16
120	0	15

*There is no raw score that will produce this scaled score for this form.

ANSWER KEY

SECTION I

1.	C	8.	C	15.	C	22.	D
2.	E	9.	D	16.	D	23.	D
3.	E	10.	C	17.	A		
4.	D	11.	C	18.	E		
5.	A	12.	C	19.	A		
6.	A	13.	A	20.	B		
7.	A	14.	A	21.	E		

SECTION II

1.	A	8.	A	15.	D	22.	B
2.	D	9.	A	16.	E	23.	E
3.	D	10.	C	17.	A	24.	B
4.	A	11.	E	18.	A	25.	C
5.	B	12.	D	19.	C	26.	B
6.	B	13.	C	20.	B		
7.	D	14.	B	21.	C		

SECTION III

1.	B	8.	B	15.	B	22.	B
2.	D	9.	E	16.	E	23.	E
3.	A	10.	A	17.	A	24.	D
4.	C	11.	E	18.	D	25.	C
5.	B	12.	D	19.	B	26.	D
6.	E	13.	B	20.	C		
7.	D	14.	A	21.	D		

SECTION IV

1.	D	8.	D	15.	B	22.	A
2.	D	9.	B	16.	E	23.	E
3.	A	10.	D	17.	C	24.	C
4.	C	11.	B	18.	D	25.	A
5.	A	12.	B	19.	D	26.	E
6.	C	13.	A	20.	A		
7.	E	14.	E	21.	D		

PREPTEST 43
JUNE 2004
FORM 5LSN67

SECTION I

Time—35 minutes

28 Questions

<u>Directions:</u> Each set of questions in this section is based on a single passage or a pair of passages. The questions are to be answered on the basis of what is <u>stated</u> or <u>implied</u> in the passage or pair of passages. For some of the questions, more than one of the choices could conceivably answer the question. However, you are to choose the <u>best</u> answer; that is, the response that most accurately and completely answers the question, and blacken the corresponding space on your answer sheet.

The accumulation of scientific knowledge regarding the environmental impact of oil well drilling in North America has tended to lag behind the actual drilling of oil wells. Most attempts to
(5) regulate the industry have relied on hindsight: the need for regulation becomes apparent only after undesirable events occur. The problems associated with oil wells' potential contamination of groundwater—fresh water within the earth that
(10) supplies wells and springs—provide a case in point.

When commercial drilling for oil began in North America in the mid-nineteenth century, regulations reflected the industry's concern for the purity of the wells' oil. In 1893, for example, regulations were
(15) enacted specifying well construction requirements to protect oil and gas reserves from contamination by fresh water. Thousands of wells were drilled in such a way as to protect the oil, but no thought was given to the possibility that the groundwater itself might need
(20) protection until many drinking-water wells near the oil well sites began to produce unpotable, oil-contaminated water.

The reason for this contamination was that groundwater is usually found in porous and
(25) permeable geologic formations near the earth's surface, whereas petroleum and unpotable saline water reservoirs are generally found in similar formations but at greater depths. Drilling a well creates a conduit connecting all the formations that it
(30) has penetrated. Consequently, without appropriate safeguards, wells that penetrate both groundwater and oil or saline water formations inevitably contaminate the groundwater. Initial attempts to prevent this contamination consisted of sealing off the
(35) groundwater formations with some form of protective barrier to prevent the oil flowing up the well from entering or mixing with the natural groundwater reservoir. This method, which is still in use today, initially involved using hollow trees to seal off the
(40) groundwater formations; now, however, large metal pipe casings, set in place with cement, are used.

Regulations currently govern the kinds of casing and cement that can be used in these practices; however, the hazards of insufficient knowledge
(45) persist. For example, the long-term stability of this

way of protecting groundwater is unknown. The protective barrier may fail due to corrosion of the casing by certain fluids flowing up the well, or because of dissolution of the cement by these fluids.
(50) The effects of groundwater bacteria, traffic vibrations, and changing groundwater chemistry are likewise unassessed. Further, there is no guarantee that wells drilled in compliance with existing regulations will not expose a need for research in additional areas: on
(55) the west coast of North America, a major disaster recently occurred because a well's location was based on a poor understanding of the area's subsurface geology. Because the well was drilled in a channel accessing the ocean, not only was the area's
(60) groundwater completely contaminated, but widespread coastal contamination also occurred, prompting international concern over oil exploration and initiating further attempts to refine regulations.

1. Which one of the following most accurately states the main point of the passage?

(A) Although now recognized as undesirable, occasional groundwater contamination by oil and unpotable saline water is considered to be inevitable wherever drilling for oil occurs.

(B) Widespread coastal contamination caused by oil well drilling in North America has prompted international concern over oil exploration.

(C) Hindsight has been the only reliable means available to regulation writers responsible for devising adequate safeguard regulations to prevent environmental contamination associated with oil well drilling.

(D) The risk of environmental contamination associated with oil well drilling continues to exist because safeguard regulations are often based on hindsight and less-than-sufficient scientific information.

(E) Groundwater contamination associated with oil well drilling is due in part to regulations designed to protect the oil from contamination by groundwater and not the groundwater from contamination by oil.

GO ON TO THE NEXT PAGE.

2. The passage states which one of the following about underground oil reservoirs?

    (A) They are usually located in areas whose subsurface geology is poorly understood.
    (B) They are generally less common in coastal regions.
    (C) They are usually located in geologic formations similar to those in which gas is found.
    (D) They are often contaminated by fresh or saline water.
    (E) They are generally found at greater depths than groundwater formations.

3. The author's attitude regarding oil well drilling regulations can most accurately be described as

    (A) cynical that future regulatory reform will occur without international concern
    (B) satisfied that existing regulations are adequate to prevent unwarranted tradeoffs between resource collection and environmental protection
    (C) concerned that regulatory reform will not progress until significant undesirable events occur
    (D) optimistic that current scientific research will spur regulatory reform
    (E) confident that regulations will eventually be based on accurate geologic understandings

4. The author uses the phrase "the hazards of insufficient knowledge" (line 44) primarily in order to refer to the risks resulting from

    (A) a lack of understanding regarding the dangers to human health posed by groundwater contamination
    (B) a failure to comprehend the possible consequences of drilling in complex geologic systems
    (C) poorly tested methods for verifying the safety of newly developed technologies
    (D) an inadequate appreciation for the difficulties of enacting and enforcing environmental regulations
    (E) a rudimentary understanding of the materials used in manufacturing metal pipe casings

5. Based on the information in the passage, if a prospective oil well drilled near a large city encounters a large groundwater formation and a small saline water formation, but no oil, which one of the following statements is most likely to be true?

    (A) Groundwater contamination is unlikely because the well did not strike oil and hence will not be put in operation.
    (B) Danger to human health due to groundwater contamination is unlikely because large cities generally have more than one source of drinking water.
    (C) Groundwater contamination is likely unless the well is plugged and abandoned.
    (D) Groundwater contamination is unlikely because the groundwater formation's large size will safely dilute any saline water that enters it.
    (E) The risk of groundwater contamination can be reduced if casing is set properly and monitored routinely for breakdown.

GO ON TO THE NEXT PAGE.

In many bilingual communities of Puerto Rican Americans living in the mainland United States, people use both English and Spanish in a single conversation, alternating between them smoothly and
(5) frequently even within the same sentence. This practice—called code-switching—is common in bilingual populations. While there are some cases that cannot currently be explained, in the vast majority of cases subtle factors, either situational or rhetorical,
(10) explain the use of code-switching.

Linguists say that most code-switching among Puerto Rican Americans is sensitive to the social contexts, which researchers refer to as domains, in which conversations take place. The main
(15) conversational factors influencing the occurrence of code-switching are setting, participants, and topic. When these go together naturally they are said to be congruent; a set of three such congruent factors constitutes a conversational situation. Linguists
(20) studying the choice between Spanish and English among a group of Puerto Rican American high school students classified their conversational situations into five domains: family, friendship, religion, education, and employment. To test the effects of these domains
(25) on code-switching, researchers developed a list of hypothetical situations made up of two of the three congruent factors, or of two incongruent factors, approximating an interaction in one of the five domains. The researchers asked the students to
(30) determine the third factor and to choose which mix of language—on a continuum from all English to all Spanish—they would use in that situation. When given two congruent factors, the students easily supplied the third congruent factor and strongly
(35) agreed among themselves about which mix they would use. For instance, for the factors of participants "parent and child" and the topic "how to be a good son or daughter," the congruent setting chosen was "home" and the language mix chosen was Spanish
(40) only. In contrast, incongruent factors such as the participants "priest and parishioner" and the setting "beach" yielded less agreement on the third factor of topic and on language choice.

But situational factors do not account for all
(45) code-switching; it occurs even when the domain would lead one not to expect it. In these cases, one language tends to be the primary one, while the other is used only sparingly to achieve certain rhetorical effects. Often the switches are so subtle that the
(50) speakers themselves are not aware of them. This was the case with a study of a family of Puerto Rican Americans in another community. Family members believed they used only English at home, but their taped conversations occasionally contained some
(55) Spanish, with no change in situational factors. When asked what the presence of Spanish signified, they commented that it was used to express certain attitudes such as intimacy or humor more emphatically.

6. Which one of the following most accurately expresses the main point of the passage?

(A) The lives of Puerto Rican Americans are affected in various ways by code-switching.

(B) It is not always possible to explain why code-switching occurs in conversations among Puerto Rican Americans.

(C) Rhetorical factors can explain more instances of code-switching among Puerto Rican Americans than can situational factors.

(D) Studies of bilingual communities of Puerto Rican Americans have caused linguists to revise many of their beliefs about code-switching.

(E) Most code-switching among Puerto Rican Americans can be explained by subtle situational and rhetorical factors.

7. In lines 56–59, the author mentions the family members' explanation of their use of Spanish primarily in order to

(A) report evidence supporting the conclusion that the family's code-switching had a rhetorical basis

(B) show that reasons for code-switching differ from one community to another

(C) supply evidence that seems to conflict with the researchers' conclusions about why the family engaged in code-switching

(D) refute the argument that situational factors explain most code-switching

(E) explain how it could be that the family members failed to notice their use of Spanish

8. Which one of the following questions is NOT characterized by the passage as a question to which linguists sought answers in their code-switching studies involving high school students?

(A) Where do the students involved in the study think that a parent and child are likely to be when they are talking about how to be a good son or daughter?

(B) What language or mix of languages do the students involved in the study think that a parent and child would be likely to use when they are talking at home about how to be a good son or daughter?

(C) What language or mix of languages do the students involved in the study think that a priest and a parishioner would be likely to use if they were conversing on a beach?

(D) What topic do the students involved in the study think that a parent and child would be most likely to discuss when they are speaking Spanish?

(E) What topic do the students involved in the study think that a priest and parishioner would be likely to discuss on a beach?

GO ON TO THE NEXT PAGE.

9. The primary function of the third paragraph of the passage is to

(A) consider a general explanation for the phenomenon of code-switching that is different from the one discussed in the preceding paragraphs

(B) resolve an apparent conflict between two explanations for code-switching that were discussed in the preceding paragraphs

(C) show that there are instances of code-switching that are not explained by the factors discussed in the previous paragraph

(D) report some of the patterns of code-switching observed among a family of Puerto Rican Americans in another community

(E) show that some instances of code-switching are unconscious

10. Based on the passage, which one of the following is best explained as rhetorically determined code-switching?

(A) A speaker who does not know certain words in the primary language of a conversation occasionally has recourse to familiar words in another language.

(B) A person translating a text from one language into another leaves certain words in the original language because the author of the text invented those words.

(C) For the purpose of improved selling strategies, a businessperson who primarily uses one language sometimes conducts business in a second language that is preferred by some people in the community.

(D) A speaker who primarily uses one language switches to another language because it sounds more expressive.

(E) A speaker who primarily uses one language occasionally switches to another language in order to maintain fluency in the secondary language.

11. It can be inferred from the passage that the author would most likely agree with which one of the following statements?

(A) Research revealing that speakers are sometimes unaware of code-switching casts doubt on the results of a prior study involving high school students.

(B) Relevant research conducted prior to the linguists' work with high school students would lead one to expect different answers from those the students actually gave.

(C) Research conducted prior to the study of a family of Puerto Rican Americans was thought by most researchers to explain code-switching in all except the most unusual or nonstandard contexts.

(D) Research suggests that people engaged in code-switching are usually unaware of which situational factors might influence their choice of language or languages.

(E) Research suggests that the family of Puerto Rican Americans does not use code-switching in conversations held at home except for occasional rhetorical effect.

12. Which one of the following does the passage offer as evidence that code-switching cannot be entirely explained by situational factors?

(A) Linguists have observed that bilingual high school students do not agree among themselves as to what mix of languages they would use in the presence of incongruent situational factors.

(B) Code-switching sometimes occurs in conversations whose situational factors would be expected to involve the use of a single language.

(C) Bilingual people often switch smoothly between two languages even when there is no change in the situational context in which the conversation takes place.

(D) Puerto Rican Americans sometimes use Spanish only sparingly and for rhetorical effect in the presence of situational factors that would lead one to expect Spanish to be the primary language.

(E) Speakers who engage in code-switching are often unaware of the situational factors influencing their choices of which language or mix of languages to speak.

13. Which one of the following, if true, would most cast doubt on the author's interpretation of the study involving the family discussed in the third paragraph?

(A) In a previous twelve-month study involving the same family in their home, their conversations were entirely in English except when situational factors changed significantly.

(B) In a subsequent twelve-month study involving the same family, a particular set of situational factors occurred repeatedly without any accompanying instances of code-switching.

(C) In a subsequent twelve-month study involving the same family, it was noted that intimacy and humor were occasionally expressed through the use of English expressions.

(D) When asked about the significance of their use of Spanish, the family members replied in English rather than Spanish.

(E) Prior to their discussions with the researchers, the family members did not describe their occasional use of Spanish as serving to emphasize humor or intimacy.

GO ON TO THE NEXT PAGE.

Reader-response theory, a type of literary theory that arose in reaction to formalist literary criticism, has endeavored to shift the emphasis in the interpretation of literature from the text itself to the
(5) contributions of readers to the meaning of a text. According to literary critics who endorse reader-response theory, the literary text alone renders no meaning; it acquires meaning only when encountered by individual readers, who always bring varying
(10) presuppositions and ways of reading to bear on the text, giving rise to the possibility—even probability—of varying interpretations. This brand of criticism has met opposition from the formalists, who study the text alone and argue that reader-response theory can
(15) encourage and even validate fragmented views of a work, rather than the unified view acquired by examining only the content of the text. However, since no theory has a monopoly on divining meaning from a text, the formalists' view appears
(20) unnecessarily narrow.

The proponents of formalism argue that their approach is firmly grounded in rational, objective principles, while reader-response theory lacks standards and verges on absolute subjectivity. After
(25) all, these proponents argue, no author can create a work that is packed with countless meanings. The meaning of a work of literature, the formalists would argue, may be obscure and somewhat arcane; yet, however hidden it may be, the author's intended
(30) meaning is legible within the work, and it is the critic's responsibility to search closely for this meaning. However, while a literary work is indeed encoded in various signs and symbols that must be translated for the work to be understood and
(35) appreciated, it is not a map. Any complicated literary work will invariably raise more questions than it answers. What is needed is a method that enables the critic to discern and make use of the rich stock of meanings created in encounters between texts and
(40) readers.

Emphasizing the varied presuppositions and perceptions that readers bring to the interpretations of a text can uncover hitherto unnoticed dimensions of the text. In fact, many important works have received
(45) varying interpretations throughout their existence, suggesting that reader-based interpretations similar to those described by reader-response theory had been operating long before the theory's principles were articulated. And while in some cases critics' textual
(50) interpretations based on reader-response theory have unfairly burdened literature of the past with contemporary ideologies, legitimate additional insights and understandings continue to emerge years after an ostensibly definitive interpretation of a major
(55) work has been articulated. By regarding a reader's

personal interpretation of literary works as not only valid but also useful in understanding the works, reader-response theory legitimizes a wide range of perspectives on these works and thereby reinforces
(60) the notion of them as fluid and lively forms of discourse that can continue to support new interpretations long after their original composition.

14. Which one of the following most accurately describes the author's attitude toward formalism as expressed in the passage?

(A) scholarly neutrality
(B) grudging respect
(C) thoughtless disregard
(D) cautious ambivalence
(E) reasoned dismissal

15. Which one of the following persons displays an approach that most strongly suggests sympathy with the principles of reader-response theory?

(A) a translator who translates a poem from Spanish to English word for word so that its original meaning is not distorted
(B) a music critic who insists that early music can be truly appreciated only when it is played on original instruments of the period
(C) a reviewer who finds in the works of a novelist certain unifying themes that reveal the novelist's personal concerns and preoccupations
(D) a folk artist who uses conventional cultural symbols and motifs as a way of conveying commonly understood meanings
(E) a director who sets a play by Shakespeare in nineteenth-century Japan to give a new perspective on the work

16. With which one of the following statements would the author of the passage be most likely to agree?

(A) Any literary theory should be seen ultimately as limiting, since contradictory interpretations of texts are inevitable.
(B) A purpose of a literary theory is to broaden and enhance the understanding that can be gained from a work.
(C) A literary theory should provide valid and strictly objective methods for interpreting texts.
(D) The purpose of a literary theory is to make clear the intended meaning of the author of a work.
(E) Since no literary theory has a monopoly on meaning, a reader should avoid using theories to interpret literature.

GO ON TO THE NEXT PAGE.

17. The passage states that reader-response theory legitimizes which one of the following?

   (A)   a wide range of perspectives on works of literature

   (B)   contemporary ideology as a basis for criticism

   (C)   encoding the meaning of a literary work in signs and symbols

   (D)   finding the meaning of a work in its text alone

   (E)   belief that an author's intended meaning in a work is discoverable

18. Which one of the following most accurately describes the author's purpose in referring to literature of the past as being "unfairly burdened" (line 51) in some cases?

   (A)   to reinforce the notion that reader-based interpretations of texts invariably raise more questions than they can answer

   (B)   to confirm the longevity of interpretations similar to reader-based interpretations of texts

   (C)   to point out a fundamental flaw that the author believes makes reader-response theory untenable

   (D)   to concede a minor weakness in reader-response theory that the author believes is outweighed by its benefits

   (E)   to suggest that reader-response theory can occasionally encourage fragmented views of a work

19. Which one of the following, if true, most weakens the author's argument concerning reader-response theory?

   (A)   Reader-response theory is reflected in interpretations that have been given throughout history and that bring additional insight to literary study.

   (B)   Reader-response theory legitimizes conflicting interpretations that collectively diminish the understanding of a work.

   (C)   Reader-response theory fails to provide a unified view of the meaning of a literary work.

   (D)   Reader-response theory claims that a text cannot have meaning without a reader.

   (E)   Reader-response theory recognizes meanings in a text that were never intended by the author.

20. The author's reference to "various signs and symbols" (line 33) functions primarily to

   (A)   stress the intricacy and complexity of good literature

   (B)   grant that a reader must be guided by the text to some degree

   (C)   imply that no theory alone can fully explain a work of literature

   (D)   illustrate how a literary work differs from a map

   (E)   show that an inflexible standard of interpretation provides constant accuracy

21. Which one of the following can most reasonably be inferred from the information in the passage?

   (A)   Formalists believe that responsible critics who focus on the text alone will tend to find the same or similar meanings in a literary work.

   (B)   Critical approaches similar to those described by formalism had been used to interpret texts long before the theory was articulated as such.

   (C)   Formalists would not find any meaning in a text whose author did not intend it to have any one particular meaning.

   (D)   A literary work from the past can rarely be read properly using reader-response theory when the subtleties of the work's social-historical context are not available.

   (E)   Formalism is much older and has more adherents than reader-response theory.

GO ON TO THE NEXT PAGE.

Faculty researchers, particularly in scientific, engineering, and medical programs, often produce scientific discoveries and invent products or processes that have potential commercial value. Many
(5) institutions have invested heavily in the administrative infrastructure to develop and exploit these discoveries, and they expect to prosper both by an increased level of research support and by the royalties from licensing those discoveries having
(10) patentable commercial applications. However, although faculty themselves are unlikely to become entrepreneurs, an increasing number of highly valued researchers will be sought and sponsored by research corporations or have consulting contracts with
(15) commercial firms. One study of such entrepreneurship concluded that "if universities do not provide the flexibility needed to venture into business, faculty will be tempted to go to those institutions that are responsive to their commercialized desires." There is
(20) therefore a need to consider the different intellectual property policies that govern the commercial exploitation of faculty inventions in order to determine which would provide the appropriate level of flexibility.
(25) In a recent study of faculty rights, Patricia Chew has suggested a fourfold classification of institutional policies. A supramaximalist institution stakes out the broadest claim possible, asserting ownership not only of all intellectual property produced by faculty in the
(30) course of their employment while using university resources, but also for any inventions or patent rights from faculty activities, even those involving research sponsored by nonuniversity funders. A maximalist institution allows faculty ownership of inventions that
(35) do not arise either "in the course of the faculty's employment [or] from the faculty's use of university resources." This approach, although not as all-encompassing as that of the supramaximalist university, can affect virtually all of a faculty
(40) member's intellectual production. A resource-provider institution asserts a claim to faculty's intellectual product in those cases where "significant use" of university time and facilities is employed. Of course, what constitutes significant use of resources is a
(45) matter of institutional judgment.
As Chew notes, in these policies "faculty rights, including the sharing of royalties, are the result of university benevolence and generosity. [However, this] presumption is contrary to the common law,
(50) which provides that faculty own their inventions." Others have pointed to this anomaly and, indeed, to the uncertain legal and historical basis upon which the ownership of intellectual property rests. Although these issues remain unsettled, and though universities
(55) may be overreaching due to faculty's limited

knowledge of their rights, most major institutions behave in the ways that maximize university ownership and profit participation.
But there is a fourth way, one that seems to be
(60) free from these particular issues. Faculty-oriented institutions assume that researchers own their own intellectual products and the rights to exploit them commercially, except in the development of public health inventions or if there is previously specified
(65) "substantial university involvement." At these institutions industry practice is effectively reversed, with the university benefiting in far fewer circumstances.

22. Which one of the following most accurately summarizes the main point of the passage?

(A) While institutions expect to prosper from increased research support and royalties from patentable products resulting from faculty inventions, if they do not establish clear-cut policies governing ownership of these inventions, they run the risk of losing faculty to research corporations or commercial consulting contracts.

(B) The fourfold classification of institutional policies governing exploitation of faculty inventions is sufficient to categorize the variety of steps institutions are taking to ensure that faculty inventors will not be lured away by commercial firms or research corporations.

(C) To prevent the loss of faculty to commercial firms or research corporations, institutions will have to abandon their insistence on retaining maximum ownership of and profit from faculty inventions and adopt the common-law presumption that faculty alone own their inventions.

(D) While the policies of most institutions governing exploitation of faculty inventions seek to maximize university ownership of and profit from these inventions, another policy offers faculty greater flexibility to pursue their commercial interests by regarding faculty as the owners of their intellectual products.

(E) Most institutional policies governing exploitation of faculty inventions are indefensible because they run counter to common-law notions of ownership and copyright, but they usually go unchallenged because few faculty members are aware of what other options might be available to them.

GO ON TO THE NEXT PAGE.

23. Which one of the following most accurately characterizes the author's view regarding the institutional intellectual property policies of most universities?

(A) The policies are in keeping with the institution's financial interests.

(B) The policies are antithetical to the mission of a university.

(C) The policies do not have a significant impact on the research of faculty.

(D) The policies are invariably harmful to the motivation of faculty attempting to pursue research projects.

(E) The policies are illegal and possibly immoral.

24. Which one of the following institutions would NOT be covered by the fourfold classification proposed by Chew?

(A) an institution in which faculty own the right to some inventions they create outside the institution

(B) an institution in which faculty own all their inventions, regardless of any circumstances, but grant the institution the right to collect a portion of their royalties

(C) an institution in which all inventions developed by faculty with institutional resources become the property of the institution

(D) an institution in which all faculty inventions related to public health become the property of the institution

(E) an institution in which some faculty inventions created with institutional resources remain the property of the faculty member

25. The passage suggests that the type of institution in which employees are likely to have the most uncertainty about who owns their intellectual products is the

(A) commercial firm
(B) supramaximalist university
(C) maximalist university
(D) resource-provider university
(E) faculty-oriented university

26. According to the passage, what distinguishes a resource-provider institution from the other types of institutions identified by Chew is its

(A) vagueness on the issue of what constitutes university as opposed to nonuniversity resources

(B) insistence on reaping substantial financial benefit from faculty inventions while still providing faculty with unlimited flexibility

(C) inversion of the usual practices regarding exploitation of faculty inventions in order to give faculty greater flexibility

(D) insistence on ownership of faculty inventions developed outside the institution in order to maximize financial benefit to the university

(E) reliance on the extent of use of institutional resources as the sole criterion in determining ownership of faculty inventions

27. The author of the passage most likely quotes one study of entrepreneurship in lines 16–19 primarily in order to

(A) explain why institutions may wish to develop intellectual property policies that are responsive to certain faculty needs

(B) draw a contrast between the worlds of academia and business that will be explored in detail later in the passage

(C) defend the intellectual property rights of faculty inventors against encroachment by the institutions that employ them

(D) describe the previous research that led Chew to study institutional policies governing ownership of faculty inventions

(E) demonstrate that some faculty inventors would be better off working for commercial firms

28. The passage suggests each of the following EXCEPT:

(A) Supramaximalist institutions run the greatest risk of losing faculty to jobs in institutions more responsive to the inventor's financial interests.

(B) A faculty-oriented institution will make no claim of ownership to a faculty invention that is unrelated to public health and created without university involvement.

(C) Faculty at maximalist institutions rarely produce inventions outside the institution without using the institution's resources.

(D) There is little practical difference between the policies of supramaximalist and maximalist institutions.

(E) The degree of ownership claimed by a resource-provider institution of the work of its faculty will not vary from case to case.

STOP

IF YOU FINISH BEFORE TIME IS CALLED, YOU MAY CHECK YOUR WORK ON THIS SECTION ONLY.
DO NOT WORK ON ANY OTHER SECTION IN THE TEST.

SECTION II

Time—35 minutes

25 Questions

Directions: The questions in this section are based on the reasoning contained in brief statements or passages. For some questions, more than one of the choices could conceivably answer the question. However, you are to choose the best answer; that is, the response that most accurately and completely answers the question. You should not make assumptions that are by commonsense standards implausible, superfluous, or incompatible with the passage. After you have chosen the best answer, blacken the corresponding space on your answer sheet.

1. Pettengill: Bebop jazz musicians showed their distaste for jazz classics by taking great liberties with them, as though the songs could be made interesting only through radical reshaping.

   Romney: Only compelling, versatile songs can stand such radical reshaping. Bebop musicians recognized this, and their revolutionary approach to the jazz classics enabled them to discover previously unknown depths in the music.

   Pettengill and Romney disagree over whether

   (A) bebop jazz was radically different from the jazz music that preceded it
   (B) bebop jazz was an improvement on the jazz classics that preceded it
   (C) bebop musicians showed appreciation for jazz classics in radically reshaping them
   (D) jazz music requires musicians to adhere closely to the original version in order to be widely popular
   (E) bebop musicians were influenced by the more conservative styles of their predecessors

2. Essayist: Earth is a living organism, composed of other organisms much as animals are composed of cells, not merely a thing upon which creatures live. This hypothesis is supported by the fact that, like all organisms, Earth can be said to have a metabolism and to regulate its temperature, humidity, and other characteristics, divorced from the influences of its surroundings. Of course, Earth does not literally breathe, but neither do insects (they have no lungs), though they respire successfully.

   The assertion that insects do not literally breathe plays which one of the following roles in the essayist's argument?

   (A) a reason for not rejecting Earth's status as an organism on the basis of its not breathing
   (B) a reason for rejecting as false the belief that Earth is a living organism
   (C) an illustration of the general claim that to be an organism, a creature must have a metabolism
   (D) an example of a type of organism whose status, like Earth's, is unclear
   (E) an illustration of a type of organism out of which Earth is composed

3. Cognitive psychologist: In a recent survey, citizens of Country F were asked to state which one of the following two scenarios they would prefer: (1) Country F is the world economic leader, with a gross national product (GNP) of $100 billion, and Country G is second, with a GNP of $90 billion; or (2) Country G is the economic leader, with a GNP of $120 billion, and Country F is second, with a GNP of $110 billion. Despite the fact that, under scenario 2, Country F would have a higher GNP than under scenario 1, the majority of respondents stated that they preferred scenario 1.

   Which one of the following, if true, would most help to explain the survey results described by the cognitive psychologist?

   (A) Most citizens of Country F believe their country has a higher economic growth rate than Country G.
   (B) Most citizens of Country F want their country to have a GNP higher than $120 billion.
   (C) Most citizens of Country F believe that their personal welfare is unconnected to GNP.
   (D) Most citizens of Country F believe GNP is a poor measure of a nation's economic health.
   (E) Most citizens of Country F want their country to be more economically powerful than Country G.

GO ON TO THE NEXT PAGE.

4. A study claims that the average temperature on Earth has permanently increased, because the average temperature each year for the last five years has been higher than any previous yearly average on record. However, periods of up to ten years of average temperatures that have consistently been record highs are often merely part of the random fluctuations in temperature that are always occurring.

Which one of the following is most strongly supported by the information above?

(A) All large increases in average temperature on record have occurred in ten-year periods.

(B) Five successive years of increasing annual average temperature does not always signify a permanent increase in temperature.

(C) Record high temperatures can be expected on Earth for another five years.

(D) Random fluctuations in Earth's average temperature typically last less than ten years.

(E) The average temperature on Earth never increases except in cases of random temperature fluctuation.

5. Shipping Coordinator: If we send your shipment by air express, it will arrive tomorrow morning. If we send your shipment via ground carrier, it will arrive either tomorrow or the next day. Ground carrier is less expensive than air express, so which do you prefer?

Customer: If I don't choose air express, then I will not receive my shipment tomorrow, so I clearly have no choice but to spend the extra money and have it sent via air express.

The customer's response can best be explained on the assumption that she has misinterpreted the shipping coordinator to mean which one of the following?

(A) Ground carrier is as reliable a shipping method as air express.

(B) If the shipment is sent by air express, it will arrive tomorrow.

(C) Ground carrier is not more expensive than air express.

(D) Unless the shipment is sent by air express, it will not arrive tomorrow.

(E) The greater the shipping cost, the faster the shipment will arrive.

6. Therapists who treat violent criminals cannot both respect their clients' right to confidentiality and be sincerely concerned for the welfare of victims of future violent crimes. Reporting a client's unreported crimes violates the client's trust, but remaining silent leaves the dangerous client out of prison, free to commit more crimes.

Which one of the following, if true, most weakens the argument?

(A) Most therapists who treat violent criminals are assigned this task by a judicial body.

(B) Criminals are no more likely to receive therapy in prison than they are out of prison.

(C) Victims of future violent crimes also have a right to confidentiality should they need therapy.

(D) The right of victims of violent crimes to compensation is as important as the right of criminals in therapy to confidentiality.

(E) A therapist who has gained a violent criminal's trust can persuade that criminal not to commit repeat offenses.

GO ON TO THE NEXT PAGE.

7. Failure to rotate crops depletes the soil's nutrients gradually unless other preventive measures are taken. If the soil's nutrients are completely depleted, additional crops cannot be grown unless fertilizer is applied to the soil. All other things being equal, if vegetables are grown in soil that has had fertilizer applied rather than being grown in non-fertilized soil, they are more vulnerable to pests and, as a consequence, must be treated with larger amounts of pesticides. The more pesticides used on vegetables, the greater the health risks to humans from eating those vegetables.

Suppose there were some vegetables that were grown in soil to which fertilizer had never been applied. On the basis of the passage, which one of the following would have to be true regarding those vegetables?

(A) The soil in which the vegetables were grown may have been completely depleted of nutrients because of an earlier failure to rotate crops.

(B) It is not possible that the vegetables were grown in soil in which crops had been rotated.

(C) The vegetables were grown in soil that had not been completely depleted of nutrients but not necessarily soil in which crops had been rotated.

(D) Whatever the health risks to humans from eating the vegetables, these risks would not be attributable to the use of pesticides on them.

(E) The health risks to humans from eating the vegetables were no less than the health risks to humans from eating the same kinds of vegetables treated with pesticides.

8. Criminologist: Increasing the current prison term for robbery will result in no significant effect in discouraging people from committing robbery.

Each of the following, if true, supports the criminologist's claim EXCEPT:

(A) Many people who rob are motivated primarily by thrill-seeking and risk-taking.

(B) An increase in the prison term for embezzlement did not change the rate at which that crime was committed.

(C) Prison terms for robbery have generally decreased in length recently.

(D) Most people committing robbery believe that they will not get caught.

(E) Most people committing robbery have no idea what the average sentence for robbery is.

9. Activist: As electronic monitoring of employees grows more commonplace and invasive, we hear more and more attempted justifications of this practice by employers. Surveillance, they explain, keeps employees honest, efficient, and polite to customers. Such explanations are obviously self-serving, and so should not be taken to justify these unwarranted invasions of privacy.

A questionable technique used in the activist's argument is to

(A) attack an argument different from that actually offered by the employers

(B) presume that employees are never dishonest, inefficient, or rude

(C) insist that modern business practices meet moral standards far higher than those accepted in the past

(D) attack employers' motives instead of addressing their arguments

(E) make a generalization based on a sample that there is reason to believe is biased

10. When students receive negative criticism generated by computer programs, they are less likely to respond positively than when the critic is a human. Since the acceptance of criticism requires that one respond positively to it, students are more likely to learn from criticism by humans than from criticism by computers.

Which one of the following is an assumption on which the argument depends?

(A) Students are more likely to learn from criticism that they accept than from criticism they do not accept.

(B) Unlike human critics, computers are incapable of showing compassion.

(C) Students always know whether their critics are computers or humans.

(D) Criticism generated by computers is likely to be less favorable than that produced by human critics in response to the same work.

(E) Criticism generated by computers is likely to be no more or less favorable than that produced by human critics in response to the same work.

GO ON TO THE NEXT PAGE.

11. After examining the options, the budget committee discovered that QI's office-phone system would be inexpensive enough to be within the cost limit that had been set for the committee. However, Corelink's system must also be inexpensive enough to be within the limit, since it is even less expensive than QI's system.

The reasoning in the argument above is most closely paralleled by that in which one of the following?

(A) Marissa is just tall enough that she can touch the ceiling when she jumps as high as she can, and since Jeff is taller than Marissa, he too must be able to touch the ceiling when he jumps.

(B) By reducing the number of cigarettes she smoked per day, Kate was able to run five miles, and since Lana smokes fewer cigarettes per day than Kate now does, she too must be able to run five miles.

(C) John's blood-alcohol level was far above the legal limit for driving, so even if it turns out that Paul's blood-alcohol level was lower than John's, it too must have been above the legal limit.

(D) This chocolate is not quite dark enough for it to be the kind that Luis really likes, but that chocolate over there is darker, so it might be just right.

(E) Health Dairy's sharp cheddar cheese is low enough in fat to meet the labeling standard for "low fat" cheddar cheese, and since its mild cheddar cheese is even lower in fat, it too must meet the labeling standard.

12. Essayist: People once believed that Earth was at the center of the universe, and that, therefore, Earth and its inhabitants were important. We now know that Earth revolves around a star at the outskirts of a spiral arm of one of countless galaxies. Therefore, people's old belief that Earth and its inhabitants were important was false.

A flaw in the essayist's argument is that the argument

(A) presumes, without providing justification, that only true statements can have good reasons to be believed

(B) neglects to consider that a statement that was believed for questionable reasons may nevertheless have been true

(C) fails to consider that there can be no reason for disbelieving a true statement

(D) overlooks the fact that people's perception of their importance changed from century to century

(E) neglects the fact that people's perception of their importance varies from culture to culture

13. Davis: The only relevant factor in determining appropriate compensation for property damage or theft is the value the property loses due to damage or the value of the property stolen; the harm to the victim is directly proportional to the pertinent value.

Higuchi: I disagree. More than one factor must be considered: A victim who recovers the use of personal property after two years is owed more than a victim who recovers its use after only one year.

Davis's and Higuchi's statements most strongly support the view that they would disagree with each other about which one of the following?

(A) It is possible to consistently and reliably determine the amount of compensation owed to someone whose property was damaged or stolen.

(B) Some victims are owed increased compensation because of the greater dollar value of the damage done to their property.

(C) Victims who are deprived of their property are owed compensation in proportion to the harm they have suffered.

(D) Some victims are owed increased compensation because of the greater amount of time they are deprived of the use of their property.

(E) The compensation owed to victims should be determined on a case-by-case basis rather than by some general rule.

14. Resident: Residents of this locale should not consider their loss of farming as a way of life to be a tragedy. When this area was a rural area it was economically depressed, but it is now a growing bastion of high-tech industry with high-wage jobs, and supports over 20 times the number of jobs it did then.

Which one of the following, if true, does the most to justify the conclusion of the resident's argument?

(A) Farming is becoming increasingly efficient, with the result that fewer farms are required to produce the same amount of food.

(B) The development of high-tech industry is more valuable to national security than is farming.

(C) Residents of this locale do not value a rural way of life more than they value economic prosperity.

(D) Many residents of this locale have annual incomes that are twice what they were when the locale was primarily agricultural.

(E) The loss of a family farm is often perceived as tragic even when no financial hardship results.

GO ON TO THE NEXT PAGE.

15. Kendrick: Governments that try to prevent cigarettes from being advertised are justified in doing so, since such advertisements encourage people to engage in an unhealthy practice. But cigarette advertisements should remain legal since advertisements for fatty foods are legal, even though those advertisements also encourage people to engage in unhealthy practices.

Which one of the following, if true, most helps to resolve the apparent conflict between Kendrick's statements?

(A) Any advertisement that encourages people to engage in an unhealthy practice should be made illegal, even though the legality of some such advertisements is currently uncontroversial.

(B) The advertisement of fattening foods, unlike that of cigarettes, should not be prevented, because fattening foods, unlike cigarettes, are not addictive.

(C) Most advertisements should be legal, although advertisers are always morally responsible for ensuring that their advertisements do not encourage people to engage in unhealthy practices.

(D) Governments should try to prevent the advertisement of cigarettes by means of financial disincentives rather than by legal prohibition.

(E) Governments should place restrictions on cigarette advertisements so as to keep them from encouraging people to engage in unhealthy practices, but should not try to prevent such advertisements.

16. Environmentalist: Many people prefer to live in regions of natural beauty. Such regions often experience an influx of new residents, and a growing population encourages businesses to relocate to those regions. Thus, governmentally mandated environmental protection in regions of natural beauty can help those regions' economies overall, even if such protection harms some older local industries.

Which one of the following is an assumption on which the environmentalist's argument depends?

(A) Regions of natural beauty typically are beautiful enough to attract new residents only until governmentally mandated environmental protection that damages local industries is imposed.

(B) The economies of most regions of natural beauty are not based primarily on local industries that would be harmed by governmentally mandated environmental protection.

(C) If governmentally mandated environmental protection helps a region's economy, it does so primarily by encouraging people to move into that region.

(D) Voluntary environmental protection usually does not help a region's economy to the degree that governmentally mandated protection does.

(E) A factor harmful to some older local industries in a region need not discourage other businesses from relocating to that region.

GO ON TO THE NEXT PAGE.

17. No small countries and no countries in the southern hemisphere have permanent seats on the United Nations Security Council. Each of the five countries with a permanent seat on the Security Council is in favor of increased international peacekeeping efforts and a greater role for the United Nations in moderating regional disputes. However, some countries that are in favor of increased international peacekeeping efforts are firmly against increased spending on refugees by the United Nations.

If the statements above are true, which one of the following must also be true?

(A) Some small countries do not want the United Nations to increase its spending on refugees.

(B) Some countries in the southern hemisphere are not in favor of increased international peacekeeping efforts.

(C) Some countries that have permanent seats on the United Nations Security Council are against increased spending on refugees by the United Nations.

(D) Some small countries are in favor of a greater role for the United Nations in moderating regional disputes.

(E) Some countries that are in favor of a greater role for the United Nations in moderating regional disputes are not located in the southern hemisphere.

18. Editorial: It is clear that what is called "health education" is usually propaganda rather than education. Propaganda and education are never the same thing. The former is nothing but an attempt to influence behavior through the repetition of simplistic slogans, whereas the latter never involves such a method. Though education does attempt to influence behavior, it does so by offering information in all its complexity, leaving it up to the individual to decide how to act on that information. Sadly, however, propaganda is much more successful than education.

The conclusion drawn by the editorial follows logically if it is assumed that what is called "health education" usually

(A) does not leave it up to the individual to decide how to act on information

(B) does not offer information in all its complexity

(C) does not involve the repetition of simplistic slogans

(D) attempts to influence behavior solely by repeating simplistic slogans

(E) is very successful in influencing people's behavior

19. Marc: The fact that the people of our country look back on the past with a great deal of nostalgia demonstrates that they regret the recent revolution.

Robert: They are not nostalgic for the recent past, but for the distant past, which the prerevolutionary regime despised; this indicates that although they are troubled, they do not regret the revolution.

Their dialogue provides the most support for the claim that Marc and Robert agree that the people of their country

(A) tend to underrate past problems when the country faces troubling times

(B) are looking to the past for solutions to the country's current problems

(C) are likely to repeat former mistakes if they look to the country's past for solutions to current problems

(D) are concerned about the country's current situation and this is evidenced by their nostalgia

(E) tend to be most nostalgic for the things that are the farthest in their past

20. Social critic: One of the most important ways in which a society socializes children is by making them feel ashamed of their immoral behavior. But in many people this shame results in deep feelings of guilt and self-loathing that can be a severe hardship. Thus, moral socialization has had a net effect of increasing the total amount of suffering.

The social critic's argument is most vulnerable to criticism on the grounds that it

(A) overlooks the possibility that the purported source of a problem could be modified to avoid that problem without being eliminated altogether

(B) fails to address adequately the possibility that one phenomenon may causally contribute to the occurrence of another, even though the two phenomena do not always occur together

(C) presumes, without providing justification, that a phenomenon that supposedly increases the total amount of suffering in a society should therefore be changed or eliminated, regardless of its beneficial consequences

(D) takes for granted that a behavior that sometimes leads to a certain phenomenon cannot also significantly reduce the overall occurrence of that phenomenon

(E) presumes, without providing justification, that if many people have a negative psychological reaction to a phenomenon, then no one can have a positive reaction to that phenomenon

GO ON TO THE NEXT PAGE.

21. Curator: A magazine recently ran a very misleading story on the reaction of local residents to our controversial art exhibit. They quoted the responses of three residents, all of whom expressed a sense of moral outrage. These quotations were intended to suggest that most local residents oppose the exhibit; the story failed to mention, however, the fact that the three residents are all close friends.

Which one of the following principles most helps to justify the curator's argumentation?

(A)   It is misleading to present the opinions of people with no special expertise on a subject as though they were experts.

(B)   It is misleading to present the opinions of people on only one side of an issue when the population is likely to be evenly divided on that issue.

(C)   It is misleading to present the opinions of a few people as evidence of what the majority thinks unless the opinions they express are widely held.

(D)   It is misleading to present testimony from close friends and thereby imply that they must agree with each other.

(E)   It is misleading to present the opinions of a potentially nonrepresentative sample of people as if they represent public opinion.

22. All parrots can learn to speak a few words and phrases. Not all parrots have equally pleasant dispositions, though some of those native to Australia can be counted on for a sweet temper. Almost any parrot, however, will show tremendous affection for an owner who raised the bird from a chick by hand-feeding it.

If the statements above are true, then which one of the following must be true?

(A)   Some parrots that can learn to speak are sweet tempered.

(B)   If a parrot is not native to Australia, then it will be sweet tempered only if it is hand-fed as a chick.

(C)   The sweetest-tempered parrots are those native to Australia.

(D)   Australia is the only place where one can find birds that can both learn to speak and be relied on for a sweet temper.

(E)   All species of pet birds that are native to Australia can be counted on for a sweet temper.

23. Toxicologist: Recent research has shown that dioxin causes cancer in rats. Although similar research has never been done on humans, and probably never will be, the use of dioxin should be completely banned.

That dioxin causes cancer in rats figures in the argument in which one of the following ways?

(A)   It is presented as the hazard that the researcher is concerned with preventing.

(B)   It is presented as a benefit of not acting on the recommendation in the conclusion.

(C)   It is presented as evidence for the claim that similar research will never be done on humans.

(D)   It is presented as a finding that motivates the course of action advocated in the conclusion.

(E)   It is presented as evidence for the claim that similar research has never been done on humans.

GO ON TO THE NEXT PAGE.

24. Politician: The law should not require people to wear seat belts in cars. People are allowed to ride motorcycles without seat belts, and riding a motorcycle even while wearing a seat belt would be more dangerous than riding in a car without wearing one.

Which one of the following arguments is most similar in its flawed reasoning to the politician's argument?

(A) Marielle and Pat should allow their children to have snacks between meals. They currently allow their children to have a large dessert after dinner, and allowing them to have snacks between meals instead would improve their nutrition.

(B) Any corporation should allow its employees to take time off when they are under too much stress to concentrate on their work. Some corporations allow any employee with a bad cold to take time off, and even a healthy employee under stress may be less productive than an unstressed employee with a bad cold.

(C) Amusement parks should allow people to stand while riding roller coasters. It is legal for people to stand at the edges of high cliffs, and even sitting at the edge of a high cliff is more likely to result in a fatal fall than standing while riding a roller coaster.

(D) It should be illegal for anyone to smoke in a public place, for it certainly should be illegal to pollute public drinking water, and smoking even in the privacy of one's home can be more harmful to the health of others than polluting their water would be.

(E) Vanessa should be allowed to let her dog run around in the park without a leash. She already lets the dog roam around her yard without a leash, and the park differs from her yard only in size.

25. Burying beetles do whatever they can to minimize the size of their competitors' broods without adversely affecting their own. This is why they routinely destroy each other's eggs when two or more beetles inhabit the same breeding location. Yet, after the eggs hatch, the adults treat all of the larvae equally, sharing in the care of the entire population.

Which one of the following, if true, most helps to explain burying beetles' apparently contradictory behavior?

(A) Burying beetles whose eggs hatch before their competitors' are more likely to have large broods than are burying beetles whose eggs hatch later.

(B) The cooperation among adult burying beetles ensures that the greatest possible number of larvae survive.

(C) Burying beetles are unable to discriminate between their own larvae and the larvae of other burying beetles.

(D) Many of the natural enemies of burying beetles can be repelled only if burying beetles cooperate in defending the breeding site.

(E) Most breeding sites for burying beetles can accommodate only a limited number of larvae.

STOP

IF YOU FINISH BEFORE TIME IS CALLED, YOU MAY CHECK YOUR WORK ON THIS SECTION ONLY.
DO NOT WORK ON ANY OTHER SECTION IN THE TEST.

SECTION III
Time—35 minutes
26 Questions

Directions: The questions in this section are based on the reasoning contained in brief statements or passages. For some questions, more than one of the choices could conceivably answer the question. However, you are to choose the best answer; that is, the response that most accurately and completely answers the question. You should not make assumptions that are by commonsense standards implausible, superfluous, or incompatible with the passage. After you have chosen the best answer, blacken the corresponding space on your answer sheet.

1. The development of new inventions is promoted by the granting of patent rights, which restrict the right of anyone but the patent holders to profit from these inventions for a specified period. Without patent rights, anyone could simply copy another's invention; consequently, inventors would have no financial incentive for investing the time and energy required to develop new products. Thus, it is important to continue to grant patent rights, or else no one will engage in original development and consequently no new inventions will be forthcoming.

    Which one of the following is an assumption on which the argument depends?

    (A) Financial reward is the only incentive that will be effective in motivating people to develop new inventions.
    (B) When an inventor sells patent rights to a manufacturer, the manufacturer makes less total profit on the invention than the inventor does.
    (C) Any costs incurred by a typical inventor in applying for patent rights are insignificant in comparison to the financial benefit of holding the patent rights.
    (D) Patent rights should be granted only if an inventor's product is not similar to another invention already covered by patent rights.
    (E) The length of a patent right is usually proportional to the costs involved in inventing the product.

2. The Fenwicks returned home from a trip to find two broken bottles on their kitchen floor. There was no sign of forced entry and nothing in the house appeared to have been taken. Although the Fenwicks have a pet cat that had free run of the house while they were away, the Fenwicks hypothesized that they had left a back door unlocked and that neighborhood children had entered through it, attempted to raid the kitchen, and left after breaking the bottles.

    Each of the following, if true, helps to support the Fenwicks' hypothesis EXCEPT:

    (A) A neighbor thought he had seen the Fenwicks' back door closing while the Fenwicks were away.
    (B) When the Fenwicks returned home, they found children's footprints on the back porch that had not been there before their trip.
    (C) The two bottles that the Fenwicks found broken on their kitchen floor had been in the refrigerator when the Fenwicks left on vacation.
    (D) There have been several recent burglaries in the Fenwicks' neighborhood in which neighborhood children were suspected.
    (E) The Fenwicks returned home from their trip later than they had planned.

GO ON TO THE NEXT PAGE.

3. In an experiment, tennis players who were told that their performance would be used to assess only the quality of their rackets performed much better than an equally skilled group of tennis players who were told that their tennis-playing talent would be measured.

The situation described above most closely conforms to which one of the following propositions?

(A) People do less well on a task if they have been told that they will be closely watched while doing it.

(B) People execute a task more proficiently when they do not believe their abilities are being judged.

(C) People perform a task more proficiently when they have confidence in their abilities.

(D) People who assess their talents accurately generally perform near their actual level of proficiency.

(E) People who think that a superior performance will please those who are testing them generally try harder.

4. Sydonie: Parents differ in their beliefs about the rules to which their children should be subject. So any disciplinary structure in schools is bound to create resentment because it will contradict some parental approaches to raising children.

Stephanie: Your conclusion is incorrect; educational research shows that when parents list the things that they most want their children's schools to provide, good discipline is always high on the list.

Stephanie's argument is most vulnerable to criticism on the grounds that

(A) it focuses on educational research rather than educational practice

(B) it addresses a more general issue than that addressed in Sydonie's argument

(C) it does not counter Sydonie's suggestion that parents have diverse ideas of what constitutes good discipline

(D) the phrase "high on the list" is not specific enough to give useful information about what parents desire from a school

(E) it fails to discuss educators' attitudes toward discipline in schools

5. Art critic: The aesthetic value of a work of art lies in its ability to impart a stimulating character to the audience's experience of the work.

Which one of the following judgments most closely conforms with the principle cited above?

(A) This painting is aesthetically deficient because it is an exact copy of a painting done 30 years ago.

(B) This symphony is beautiful because, even though it does not excite the audience, it is competently performed.

(C) This sculpted four-inch cube is beautiful because it is carved from material which, although much like marble, is very rare.

(D) This painting is aesthetically valuable because it was painted by a highly controversial artist.

(E) This poem is aesthetically deficient because it has little impact on its audience.

6. Antonia: The stock market is the best place to invest your money these days; although it is often volatile, it provides the opportunity to make a large profit quickly.

Maria: I agree that the stock market provides the opportunity to make large profits quickly, but one is just as likely to take a huge loss. I think it is better to invest in savings bonds, which provide a constant, reliable income over many years.

Antonia's and Maria's statements provide the most support for holding that they disagree about whether

(A) the stock market is often volatile but provides the opportunity to make a large profit quickly

(B) savings bonds can provide a large return on one's investment

(C) the stock market provides the opportunity for an investor to make a constant, reliable income over many years

(D) it is safer to invest in savings bonds than to invest in the stock market

(E) it is preferable to pick an investment offering a reliable income over a riskier opportunity to make a large profit quickly

GO ON TO THE NEXT PAGE.

7. Very little is known about prehistoric hominid cave dwellers. However, a recent study of skeletons of these hominids has revealed an important clue about their daily activities: skeletal fractures present are most like the type and distribution of fractures sustained by rodeo riders. Therefore, it is likely that these cave dwellers engaged in activities similar to rodeo riders—chasing and tackling animals.

Which one of the following principles, if valid, most helps to justify the argumentation above?

(A) The primary source of clues about the lives of prehistoric hominids is their skeletal remains.
(B) The most important aspect of prehistoric life to be studied is how food was obtained.
(C) If direct evidence as to the cause of a phenomenon is available, then indirect evidence should not be sought.
(D) If there is a similarity between two effects, then there is probably a similarity between their causes.
(E) The frequency with which a hazardous activity is performed is proportional to the frequency of injuries resulting from that activity.

8. Studies suggest that, for the vast majority of people who have normal blood pressure, any amount of sodium greater than that required by the body is simply excreted and does not significantly raise blood pressure. So only persons who have high blood pressure and whose bodies are incapable of safely processing excess sodium need to restrict their sodium intake.

Which one of the following, if true, would most seriously weaken the argument?

(A) High blood pressure is more harmful than was previously believed.
(B) High blood pressure is sometimes exacerbated by intake of more sodium than the body requires.
(C) Excess sodium intake over time often destroys the body's ability to process excess sodium.
(D) Every human being has a physiological need for at least some sodium.
(E) Any sodium not used by the body will increase blood pressure unless it is excreted.

9. Most lecturers who are effective teachers are eccentric, but some noneccentric lecturers are very effective teachers. In addition, every effective teacher is a good communicator.

Which one of the following statements follows logically from the statements above?

(A) Some good communicators are eccentric.
(B) All good communicators are effective teachers.
(C) Some lecturers who are not effective teachers are not eccentric.
(D) Most lecturers who are good communicators are eccentric.
(E) Some noneccentric lecturers are effective teachers but are not good communicators.

10. Recently, photons and neutrinos emitted by a distant supernova, an explosion of a star, reached Earth at virtually the same time. This finding supports Einstein's claim that gravity is a property of space itself, in the sense that a body exerts gravitational pull by curving the space around it. The simultaneous arrival of the photons and neutrinos is evidence that the space through which they traveled was curved.

Which one of the following, if true, would most strengthen the reasoning above?

(A) Einstein predicted that photons and neutrinos emitted by any one supernova would reach Earth simultaneously.
(B) If gravity is not a property of space itself, then photons and neutrinos emitted simultaneously by a distant event will reach Earth at different times.
(C) Photons and neutrinos emitted by distant events would be undetectable on Earth if Einstein's claim that gravity is a property of space itself were correct.
(D) Photons and neutrinos were the only kinds of particles that reached Earth from the supernova.
(E) Prior to the simultaneous arrival of photons and neutrinos from the supernova, there was no empirical evidence for Einstein's claim that gravity is a property of space itself.

GO ON TO THE NEXT PAGE.

11. Geneticist: Billions of dollars are spent each year on high-profile experiments that attempt to link particular human genes with particular personality traits. Though such experiments seem to promise a new understanding of human nature, they have few practical consequences. Meanwhile, more mundane and practical genetic projects—for example, those that look for natural ways to make edible plants hardier or more nutritious—are grossly underfunded. Thus, funding for human gene research should be reduced while funding for other genetic research should be increased.

Which one of the following principles, if valid, most helps to justify the geneticist's reasoning?

(A) Experiments that have the potential to help the whole human race are more worthwhile than those that help only a small number of people.

(B) Experiments that focus on the genetics of plants are more practical than those that focus on the genetics of human nature.

(C) Experiments that help prevent malnutrition are more worthwhile than those that help prevent merely undesirable personality traits.

(D) Experiments that have modest but practical goals are more worthwhile than those that have impressive goals but few practical consequences.

(E) Experiments that get little media attention and are not widely supported by the public are more valuable than are those that get much media coverage and have wide public support.

12. Some argue that because attaining governmental power in democracies requires building majority coalitions, it is a necessary evil that policymakers do not adhere rigorously to principle when dealing with important issues, but rather shift policies as they try to please different constituents at different times. But it is precisely this behavior that allows a democracy to adapt more easily to serve public interests, and thus it is more a benefit than an evil.

Which one of the following is an assumption required by the argument?

(A) Government policymakers cannot retain power if they ignore any of the various factions of their original winning coalition.

(B) Democracies are more likely than nondemocratic forms of government to have policymakers who understand the complexity of governmental issues.

(C) In the formulation of government policy, the advantage conferred by adaptability to diverse or fluctuating public interests outweighs the detriment associated with a lack of strict fidelity to principle.

(D) In dealing with an important issue, policymakers in a democracy appeal to a principle in dealing with an issue only when that principle has majority support.

(E) Democracies appear to be more flexible than nondemocratic forms of government, but are not actually so.

GO ON TO THE NEXT PAGE.

3

13. Up until about 2 billion years ago, the sun was 30 percent dimmer than it is now. If the sun were that dim now, our oceans would be completely frozen. According to fossil evidence, however, life and liquid water were both present as early as 3.8 billion years ago.

Which one of the following, if true, most helps to resolve the apparent discrepancy described above?

(A) Our atmosphere currently holds in significantly less heat than it did 3.8 billion years ago.

(B) The liquid water present 3.8 billion years ago later froze, only to melt again about 2 billion years ago.

(C) A significant source of heat other than the sun contributed to the melting of ice sheets approximately 2 billion years ago.

(D) Evidence suggests that certain regions of ocean remained frozen until much more recently than 2 billion years ago.

(E) When large portions of the globe are ice-covered, more of the sun's heat is reflected and not absorbed by the earth than when only the poles are ice-covered.

14. Social critic: The operas composed by Bizet and Verdi are nineteenth-century European creations, reflecting the attitudes and values in France and Italy at the end of that century. Several recent studies impugn these operas on the grounds that they reinforce in our society many stereotypes about women. But only a small minority of contemporary North Americans, namely opera lovers, have had any significant exposure to these works.

Which one of the following most accurately expresses the conclusion that the social critic's argument, as it is stated above, is structured to establish?

(A) Bizet and Verdi constructed images of women that have significantly influenced contemporary stereotypes.

(B) Nineteenth-century French and Italian images of women are quite different from contemporary North American images of women.

(C) The operas of Bizet and Verdi have not significantly contributed to stereotypical images of women in contemporary North America.

(D) Opera is not an important factor shaping social attitudes in contemporary North America.

(E) People cannot be influenced by things they are not directly exposed to.

15. In 1975, a province reduced its personal income tax rate by 2 percent for most taxpayers. In 1976, the personal income tax rate for those taxpayers was again reduced by 2 percent. Despite the decreases in the personal income tax rate, the total amount of money collected from personal income taxes remained constant from 1974 to 1975 and rose substantially in 1976.

Each of the following, if true, could help to resolve the apparent discrepancy described above EXCEPT:

(A) The years 1975 and 1976 were ones in which the province's economy was especially prosperous.

(B) The definition of "personal income" used by the province was widened during 1975 to include income received from personal investments.

(C) The personal income tax rate for the wealthiest individuals in the province rose during 1975 and 1976.

(D) The province's total revenue from all taxes increased during both 1975 and 1976.

(E) A large number of people from other provinces moved to the province during 1975 and 1976.

16. Everything that is commonplace and ordinary fails to catch our attention, so there are things that fail to catch our attention but that are miracles of nature.

The conclusion of the argument follows logically if which one of the following is assumed?

(A) Only miracles of nature fail to be ordinary and commonplace.

(B) Some things that are ordinary and commonplace are miracles of nature.

(C) Some things that are commonplace and ordinary fail to catch our attention.

(D) Everything that fails to catch our attention is commonplace and ordinary.

(E) Only extraordinary or unusual things catch our attention.

GO ON TO THE NEXT PAGE.

17. If one of the effects of a genetic mutation makes a substantial contribution to the survival of the species, then, and only then, will that mutation be favored in natural selection. This process is subject to one proviso, namely that the traits that were not favored, yet were carried along by a trait that was favored, must not be so negative as to annul the benefits of having the new, favored trait.

If the statements above are true, each of the following could be true EXCEPT:

(A) A species possesses a trait whose effects are all neutral for the survival of that species.
(B) All the effects of some genetic mutations contribute substantially to the survival of a species.
(C) A species possesses a trait that reduces the species' survival potential.
(D) A genetic mutation that carries along several negative traits is favored in natural selection.
(E) A genetic mutation whose effects are all neutral to a species is favored in natural selection.

18. In a highly publicized kidnapping case in Ontario, the judge barred all media and spectators from the courtroom. Her decision was based on the judgment that the public interest would not be served by allowing spectators. A local citizen argued, "They pleaded with the public to help find the victim; they pleaded with the public to provide tips; they aroused the public interest, then they claimed that allowing us to attend would not serve the public interest. These actions are inconsistent."

The reasoning in the local citizen's argument is flawed because this argument

(A) generalizes from an atypical case
(B) trades on an ambiguity with respect to the term "public interest"
(C) overlooks the fact that the judge might not be the one who made the plea to the public for help
(D) attempts to support its conclusion by making sensationalistic appeals
(E) presumes that the public's right to know is obviously more important than the defendant's right to a fair trial

19. Today's farmers plant only a handful of different strains of a given crop. Crops lack the diversity that they had only a few generations ago. Hence, a disease that strikes only a few strains of crops, and that would have had only minor impact on the food supply in the past, would devastate it today.

Which one of the following, if true, would most weaken the argument?

(A) In the past, crop diseases would often devastate food supplies throughout entire regions.
(B) Affected crops can quickly be replaced from seed banks that store many strains of those crops.
(C) Some of the less popular seed strains that were used in the past were more resistant to many diseases than are the strains popular today.
(D) Humans today have more variety in their diets than in the past, but still rely heavily on cereal crops like rice and wheat.
(E) Today's crops are much less vulnerable to damage from insects or encroachment by weeds than were crops of a few generations ago.

20. Interviewer: A certain company released a model of computer whose microprocessor design was flawed, making that computer liable to process information incorrectly. How did this happen?

Industry spokesperson: Given the huge number of circuits in the microprocessor of any modern computer, not every circuit can be manually checked before a computer model that contains the microprocessor is released.

Interviewer: Then what guarantee do we have that new microprocessors will not be similarly flawed?

Industry spokesperson: There is no chance of further microprocessor design flaws, since all microprocessors are now entirely computer-designed.

The industry spokesperson's argument is most vulnerable to criticism on the grounds that it

(A) presumes, without providing justification, that the microprocessor quality-control procedures of the company mentioned are not representative of those followed throughout the industry
(B) ignores the possibility that a microprocessor can have a flaw other than a design flaw
(C) overlooks the possibility that a new computer model is liable to malfunction for reasons other than a microprocessor flaw
(D) treats a single instance of a microprocessor design flaw as evidence that there will be many such flaws
(E) takes for granted, despite evidence to the contrary, that some computers are not liable to error

GO ON TO THE NEXT PAGE.

21. Each of the many people who participated in the town's annual spring cleanup received a community recognition certificate. Because the spring cleanup took place at the same time as the downtown arts fair, we know that there are at least some spring cleanup participants who are not active in the town's artistic circles.

If the statements above are true, which one of the following must be true?

(A) Some of the persons who are active in the town's artistic circles received community recognition certificates.

(B) Not all of those who received community recognition certificates are active in the town's artistic circles.

(C) No participants in the downtown arts fair received community recognition certificates.

(D) No person who received a community recognition certificate has not participated in the spring cleanup.

(E) Persons who are active in the town's artistic circles are not concerned with the town's environment.

22. Taking advanced mathematics courses should increase a student's grade point average, for, as numerous studies have shown, students who have taken one or more advanced mathematics courses are far more likely to have high grade point averages than students who have not taken such courses.

The flawed pattern of reasoning in the argument above is most similar to that in which one of the following?

(A) Fur color is in large measure hereditary, for, as many studies have shown, black cats are more likely than others to have black kittens, and orange cats are more likely to have orange kittens.

(B) Water can cause intoxication. After all, imbibing scotch and water, whiskey and water, bourbon and water, gin and water, and vodka and water all cause intoxication.

(C) Eating a diet consisting primarily of fats and carbohydrates may cause weight gain in some people. Studies have shown that many overweight people eat such diets.

(D) Buying running shoes should increase the frequency with which a person exercises, since those who buy two or more pairs of running shoes each year tend to exercise more often than those who buy at most one pair.

(E) Reading to children at an early age should inspire them to read on their own later, since studies have shown that children who have not been read to are less likely to develop an interest in reading than children who have been read to.

23. Each of many different human hormones can by itself raise the concentration of glucose in the blood. The reason for this is probably a metabolic quirk of the brain. To see this, consider that although most human cells can produce energy from fats and proteins, brain cells can use only glucose. Thus, if blood glucose levels fall too low, brain cells will rapidly starve, leading to unconsciousness and death.

Which one of the following most accurately expresses the main conclusion of the argument above?

(A) Each of many different human hormones can by itself raise blood glucose levels.

(B) The reason that many different hormones can each independently raise blood glucose levels is probably a metabolic quirk of the brain.

(C) Although most human cells can produce energy from fats and proteins, brain cells can produce energy only from glucose.

(D) If blood glucose levels fall too low, then brain cells starve, resulting in loss of consciousness and death.

(E) The reason brain cells starve if deprived of glucose is that they can produce energy only from glucose.

24. Human resources director: While only some recent university graduates consider work environment an important factor in choosing a job, they all consider salary an important factor. Further, whereas the only workers who consider stress level an important factor in choosing a job are a few veteran employees, every recent university graduate considers vacation policy an important factor.

If all of the statements of the human resources director are true, then which one of the following must be true?

(A) All people who consider work environment an important factor in choosing a job also consider salary an important factor.

(B) At least some people who consider work environment an important factor in choosing a job consider vacation policy an important factor as well.

(C) At least some veteran employees do not consider work environment an important factor in choosing a job.

(D) All people who consider vacation policy an important factor in choosing a job also consider salary an important factor.

(E) No one for whom salary is an important factor in choosing a job also considers stress level an important factor.

GO ON TO THE NEXT PAGE.

25. Wealth is not a good thing, for good things cause no harm at all, yet wealth is often harmful to people.

   Which one of the following arguments is most similar in its pattern of reasoning to the argument above?

   (A)   Alex loves to golf, and no one in the chess club loves to golf. It follows that Alex is not in the chess club.
   (B)   Isabella must be a contented baby. She smiles a great deal and hardly ever cries, like all happy people.
   (C)   Growth in industry is not a good thing for our town. Although the economy might improve, the pollution would be unbearable.
   (D)   Sarah's dog is not a dachshund, for he hunts very well, and most dachshunds hunt poorly.
   (E)   There is usually more traffic at this time of day, unless it is a holiday. But since today is not a holiday, it is surprising that there is so little traffic.

26. In the aftermath of the Cold War, international relations between Cold War allies became more difficult. Leaders of previously allied nations were required to conduct tactful economic negotiations in order not to arouse tensions that had previously been overlooked.

   The situation described above conforms most closely to which one of the following propositions?

   (A)   International economic competition is a greater cause of tension than is international military competition.
   (B)   Bonds between allies are stronger when they derive from fear of a common enemy than when they derive from common economic goals.
   (C)   When there is a military commitment between countries, fundamental agreement between them on economic matters is more easily reached.
   (D)   Economic matters are considered unimportant during periods of actual or threatened war.
   (E)   A common enemy contributes to a strengthened bond between nations, enabling them to ignore economic tensions that would otherwise be problematic.

S T O P
IF YOU FINISH BEFORE TIME IS CALLED, YOU MAY CHECK YOUR WORK ON THIS SECTION ONLY.
DO NOT WORK ON ANY OTHER SECTION IN THE TEST.

SECTION IV
Time—35 minutes
22 Questions

Directions: Each group of questions in this section is based on a set of conditions. In answering some of the questions, it may be useful to draw a rough diagram. Choose the response that most accurately and completely answers each question and blacken the corresponding space on your answer sheet.

Questions 1–5

There are exactly six groups in this year's Civic Parade: firefighters, gymnasts, jugglers, musicians, puppeteers, and veterans. Each group marches as a unit; the groups are ordered from first, at the front of the parade, to sixth, at the back. The following conditions apply:

   At least two groups march behind the puppeteers but ahead of the musicians.
   Exactly one group marches behind the firefighters but ahead of the veterans.
   The gymnasts are the first, third, or fifth group.

1. Which one of the following could be an accurate list of the groups in the Civic Parade in order from first to last?

   (A)   firefighters, puppeteers, veterans, musicians, gymnasts, jugglers
   (B)   gymnasts, puppeteers, jugglers, musicians, firefighters, veterans
   (C)   veterans, puppeteers, firefighters, gymnasts, jugglers, musicians
   (D)   jugglers, puppeteers, gymnasts, firefighters, musicians, veterans
   (E)   musicians, veterans, jugglers, firefighters, gymnasts, puppeteers

2. If the gymnasts march immediately ahead of the veterans, then which one of the following could be the fourth group?

   (A)   gymnasts
   (B)   jugglers
   (C)   musicians
   (D)   puppeteers
   (E)   veterans

3. If the veterans march immediately behind the puppeteers, then which one of the following could be the second group?

   (A)   firefighters
   (B)   gymnasts
   (C)   jugglers
   (D)   musicians
   (E)   veterans

4. If the jugglers are the fifth group, then which one of the following must be true?

   (A)   The puppeteers are the first group.
   (B)   The firefighters are the first group.
   (C)   The veterans are the second group.
   (D)   The gymnasts are the third group.
   (E)   The musicians are the sixth group.

5. Which one of the following groups CANNOT march immediately behind the gymnasts?

   (A)   firefighters
   (B)   jugglers
   (C)   musicians
   (D)   puppeteers
   (E)   veterans

GO ON TO THE NEXT PAGE.

Questions 6–12

A rowing team uses a boat with exactly six seats arranged in single file and numbered sequentially 1 through 6, from the front of the boat to the back. Six athletes—Lee, Miller, Ovitz, Singh, Valerio, and Zita—each row at exactly one of the seats. The following restrictions must apply:

Miller rows closer to the front than Singh.
Singh rows closer to the front than both Lee and Valerio.
Valerio and Zita each row closer to the front than Ovitz.

6. Which one of the following could be an accurate matching of athletes to seats?

(A) Miller: seat 1; Valerio: seat 5; Lee: seat 6
(B) Singh: seat 3; Valerio: seat 4; Zita: seat 5
(C) Miller: seat 1; Valerio: seat 3; Lee: seat 6
(D) Lee: seat 3; Valerio: seat 4; Ovitz: seat 5
(E) Zita: seat 2; Valerio: seat 3; Ovitz: seat 6

7. If Valerio rows at seat 5, then which one of the following must be true?

(A) Miller rows at seat 1.
(B) Singh rows at seat 2.
(C) Zita rows at seat 3.
(D) Lee rows at seat 4.
(E) Ovitz rows at seat 6.

8. If Lee rows at seat 3, then each of the following could be true EXCEPT:

(A) Zita rows immediately behind Valerio.
(B) Ovitz rows immediately behind Valerio.
(C) Ovitz rows immediately behind Zita.
(D) Valerio rows immediately behind Lee.
(E) Singh rows immediately behind Zita.

9. Which one of the following CANNOT be true?

(A) Ovitz rows closer to the front than Singh.
(B) Zita rows closer to the front than Miller.
(C) Lee rows closer to the front than Valerio.
(D) Singh rows closer to the front than Zita.
(E) Valerio rows closer to the front than Lee.

10. Exactly how many different seats could be the seat occupied by Zita?

(A) two
(B) three
(C) four
(D) five
(E) six

11. If Valerio rows closer to the front than Zita, then which one of the following must be true?

(A) Miller rows immediately in front of Singh.
(B) Lee rows immediately in front of Valerio.
(C) Zita rows immediately in front of Ovitz.
(D) Singh rows immediately in front of Lee.
(E) Singh rows immediately in front of Valerio.

12. Suppose the restriction that Miller rows closer to the front than Singh is replaced by the restriction that Singh rows closer to the front than Miller. If the other two restrictions remain in effect, then each of the following could be an accurate matching of athletes to seats EXCEPT:

(A) Singh: seat 1; Zita: seat 2; Miller: seat 6
(B) Singh: seat 1; Valerio: seat 3; Ovitz: seat 5
(C) Singh: seat 3; Lee: seat 4; Valerio: seat 5
(D) Valerio: seat 3; Miller: seat 4; Lee: seat 5
(E) Valerio: seat 4; Miller: seat 5; Ovitz: seat 6

GO ON TO THE NEXT PAGE.

Questions 13–17

Exactly six of an artist's paintings, entitled *Quarterion, Redemption, Sipapu, Tesseract, Vale,* and *Zelkova,* are sold at auction. Three of the paintings are sold to a museum, and three are sold to a private collector. Two of the paintings are from the artist's first (earliest) period, two are from her second period, and two are from her third (most recent) period. The private collector and the museum each buy one painting from each period. The following conditions hold:

    Sipapu, which is sold to the private collector, is from an earlier period than *Zelkova,* which is sold to the museum.
    Quarterion is not from an earlier period than *Tesseract.*
    Vale is from the artist's second period.

13. Which one of the following could be an accurate list of the paintings bought by the museum and the private collector, listed in order of the paintings' periods, from first to third?

    (A)   museum: *Quarterion, Vale, Zelkova*
            private collector: *Redemption, Sipapu, Tesseract*
    (B)   museum: *Redemption, Zelkova, Quarterion*
            private collector: *Sipapu, Vale, Tesseract*
    (C)   museum: *Sipapu, Zelkova, Quarterion*
            private collector: *Tesseract, Vale, Redemption*
    (D)   museum: *Tesseract, Quarterion, Zelkova*
            private collector: *Sipapu, Redemption, Vale*
    (E)   museum: *Zelkova, Tesseract, Redemption*
            private collector: *Sipapu, Vale, Quarterion*

14. If *Sipapu* is from the artist's second period, which one of the following could be two of the three paintings bought by the private collector?

    (A)   *Quarterion* and *Zelkova*
    (B)   *Redemption* and *Tesseract*
    (C)   *Redemption* and *Vale*
    (D)   *Redemption* and *Zelkova*
    (E)   *Tesseract* and *Zelkova*

15. Which one of the following is a complete and accurate list of the paintings, any one of which could be the painting from the artist's first period that is sold to the private collector?

    (A)   *Quarterion, Redemption*
    (B)   *Redemption, Sipapu*
    (C)   *Quarterion, Sipapu, Tesseract*
    (D)   *Quarterion, Redemption, Sipapu, Tesseract*
    (E)   *Redemption, Sipapu, Tesseract, Zelkova*

16. If *Sipapu* is from the artist's second period, then which one of the following paintings could be from the period immediately preceding *Quarterion*'s period and be sold to the same buyer as *Quarterion*?

    (A)   *Redemption*
    (B)   *Sipapu*
    (C)   *Tesseract*
    (D)   *Vale*
    (E)   *Zelkova*

17. If *Zelkova* is sold to the same buyer as *Tesseract* and is from the period immediately preceding *Tesseract*'s period, then which one of the following must be true?

    (A)   *Quarterion* is sold to the museum.
    (B)   *Quarterion* is from the artist's third period.
    (C)   *Redemption* is sold to the private collector.
    (D)   *Redemption* is from the artist's third period.
    (E)   *Redemption* is sold to the same buyer as *Vale*.

GO ON TO THE NEXT PAGE.

Questions 18–22

Each of exactly six lunch trucks sells a different one of six kinds of food: falafel, hot dogs, ice cream, pitas, salad, or tacos. Each truck serves one or more of exactly three office buildings: X, Y, or Z. The following conditions apply:

The falafel truck, the hot dog truck, and exactly one other truck each serve Y.

The falafel truck serves exactly two of the office buildings.

The ice cream truck serves more of the office buildings than the salad truck.

The taco truck does not serve Y.

The falafel truck does not serve any office building that the pita truck serves.

The taco truck serves two office buildings that are also served by the ice cream truck.

18. Which one of the following could be a complete and accurate list of each of the office buildings that the falafel truck serves?

(A)   X
(B)   X, Z
(C)   X, Y, Z
(D)   Y, Z
(E)   Z

19. For which one of the following pairs of trucks must it be the case that at least one of the office buildings is served by both of the trucks?

(A)   the hot dog truck and the pita truck
(B)   the hot dog truck and the taco truck
(C)   the ice cream truck and the pita truck
(D)   the ice cream truck and the salad truck
(E)   the salad truck and the taco truck

20. If the ice cream truck serves fewer of the office buildings than the hot dog truck, then which one of the following is a pair of lunch trucks that must serve exactly the same buildings as each other?

(A)   the falafel truck and the hot dog truck
(B)   the falafel truck and the salad truck
(C)   the ice cream truck and the pita truck
(D)   the ice cream truck and the salad truck
(E)   the ice cream truck and the taco truck

21. Which one of the following could be a complete and accurate list of the lunch trucks, each of which serves all three of the office buildings?

(A)   the hot dog truck, the ice cream truck
(B)   the hot dog truck, the salad truck
(C)   the ice cream truck, the taco truck
(D)   the hot dog truck, the ice cream truck, the pita truck
(E)   the ice cream truck, the pita truck, the salad truck

22. Which one of the following lunch trucks CANNOT serve both X and Z?

(A)   the hot dog truck
(B)   the ice cream truck
(C)   the pita truck
(D)   the salad truck
(E)   the taco truck

STOP
IF YOU FINISH BEFORE TIME IS CALLED, YOU MAY CHECK YOUR WORK ON THIS SECTION ONLY.
DO NOT WORK ON ANY OTHER SECTION IN THE TEST.

ACKNOWLEDGMENTS

Acknowledgment is made to the following sources from which material has been adapted for use in this test booklet:

Wilfred L. Guerin et al., *A Handbook of Critical Approaches to Literature.* ©1966, 1979 by Wilfred L. Guerin, Earle Labor, Lee Morgan, and John R. Willingham.

Miwa Nishimura, "Japanese/English Code-Switching: Syntax and Pragmatics." ©1995 by Miwa Nishimura.

Michael A. Olivas, "The Political Economy of Immigration, Intellectual Property, and Racial Harassment: Case Studies of the Implementation of Legal Change on Campus." ©1992 by the Ohio State University Press.

Wait for the supervisor's instructions before you open the page to the topic.
Please print and sign your name and write the date in the designated spaces below.

Time: 35 Minutes

General Directions

You will have 35 minutes in which to plan and write an essay on the topic inside. Read the topic and the accompanying directions carefully. You will probably find it best to spend a few minutes considering the topic and organizing your thoughts before you begin writing. In your essay, be sure to develop your ideas fully, leaving time, if possible, to review what you have written. **Do not write on a topic other than the one specified. Writing on a topic of your own choice is not acceptable.**

No special knowledge is required or expected for this writing exercise. Law schools are interested in the reasoning, clarity, organization, language usage, and writing mechanics displayed in your essay. How well you write is more important than how much you write.

Confine your essay to the blocked, lined area on the front and back of the separate Writing Sample Response Sheet. Only that area will be reproduced for law schools. Be sure that your writing is legible.

Both this topic sheet and your response sheet must be turned over to the testing staff before you leave the room.

Topic Code

Date
/ /

Print Your Full Name Here		
Last	First	M.I.

Sign Your Name Here

Scratch Paper
Do not write your essay in this space.

LSAT® Writing Sample Topic

Directions: The scenario presented below describes two choices, either one of which can be supported on the basis of the information given. Your essay should consider both choices and argue for one over the other, based on the two specified criteria and the facts provided. There is no "right" or "wrong" choice: a reasonable argument can be made for either.

Alma owns a small art gallery that is situated in the middle of a busy commercial district. She is considering two different approaches to adding to the inventory of pieces she offers for sale. Write an essay in which you argue for one plan over the other, keeping in mind the following goals:

- Alma would like to specialize in locally produced artwork.
- The new items should attract new customers.

In the first plan, Alma would introduce a line of metalwork sculptures, made available through a regional consortium of artists, to fill a gap in her inventory for small, affordable gift items. Initially, the items would bring in new business from existing foot traffic and from those browsing or shopping during the lunch hour. Should these pieces do well, she would then bring in additional small-scale artwork in the hopes of establishing herself more firmly in the market for smaller pieces. Although Alma would be able to cater to a wider customer base, she would have competition from several stores in the area that also offer small gift items, although none specializes in the original artwork of local artists.

In the second plan, Alma would take advantage of an opportunity to become the sole representative for the artwork in the estate of a deceased painter whose works are now being valued at ever increasing amounts. The painter lived most of his life in the area, but his later works, making up most of the paintings in the estate, were actually painted elsewhere. By becoming the sole representative for the painter's work, she would acquire a limited collection of paintings for which there is a well-established niche market. The art gallery presently has only a small number of very expensive pieces, but attracting this small, specialized clientele would give Alma an established audience for other high-end works she might acquire in the future.

WP-L028-A

Scratch Paper
Do not write your essay in this space.

Writing Sample Response Sheet

DO NOT WRITE
IN THIS SPACE

Begin your essay in the lined area below.
Continue on the back if you need more space.

COMPUTING YOUR SCORE

Directions:

1. Use the Answer Key on the next page to check your answers.

2. Use the Scoring Worksheet below to compute your raw score.

3. Use the Score Conversion Chart to convert your raw score into the 120-180 scale.

Scoring Worksheet

1. Enter the number of questions you answered correctly in each section.

   Number Correct

   SECTION I .... _____
   SECTION II .... _____
   SECTION III .... _____
   SECTION IV .... _____

2. Enter the sum here: _____
   This is your Raw Score.

Conversion Chart
For Converting Raw Score to the 120-180 LSAT Scaled Score
LSAT Form 5LSN67

Reported Score	Raw Score Lowest	Raw Score Highest
180	99	101
179	98	98
178	97	97
177	96	96
176	95	95
175	94	94
174	93	93
173	92	92
172	91	91
171	90	90
170	89	89
169	88	88
168	86	87
167	85	85
166	84	84
165	82	83
164	81	81
163	79	80
162	78	78
161	76	77
160	75	75
159	73	74
158	71	72
157	70	70
156	68	69
155	67	67
154	65	66
153	63	64
152	62	62
151	60	61
150	58	59
149	57	57
148	55	56
147	53	54
146	51	52
145	50	50
144	48	49
143	46	47
142	45	45
141	43	44
140	42	42
139	40	41
138	38	39
137	37	37
136	35	36
135	34	34
134	33	33
133	31	32
132	30	30
131	28	29
130	27	27
129	26	26
128	25	25
127	23	24
126	22	22
125	21	21
124	20	20
123	18	19
122	17	17
121	16	16
120	0	15

ANSWER KEY

SECTION I

1.	D	8.	D	15.	E	22.	D
2.	E	9.	C	16.	B	23.	A
3.	C	10.	D	17.	A	24.	B
4.	B	11.	E	18.	D	25.	D
5.	E	12.	B	19.	B	26.	E
6.	E	13.	A	20.	B	27.	A
7.	A	14.	E	21.	A	28.	E

SECTION II

1.	C	8.	C	15.	D	22.	A
2.	A	9.	D	16.	E	23.	D
3.	E	10.	A	17.	E	24.	C
4.	B	11.	E	18.	D	25.	C
5.	D	12.	B	19.	D		
6.	E	13.	D	20.	D		
7.	C	14.	C	21.	E		

SECTION III

1.	A	8.	C	15.	D	22.	D
2.	E	9.	A	16.	B	23.	B
3.	B	10.	B	17.	E	24.	B
4.	C	11.	D	18.	B	25.	A
5.	E	12.	C	19.	B	26.	E
6.	E	13.	A	20.	E		
7.	D	14.	C	21.	B		

SECTION IV

1.	D	8.	E	15.	D	22.	C
2.	E	9.	A	16.	B		
3.	A	10.	D	17.	B		
4.	E	11.	A	18.	D		
5.	B	12.	C	19.	C		
6.	C	13.	B	20.	E		
7.	E	14.	B	21.	A		

PREPTEST 44

OCTOBER 2004
FORM G-4LSN61

SECTION I

Time—35 minutes

27 Questions

<u>Directions:</u> Each set of questions in this section is based on a single passage or a pair of passages. The questions are to be answered on the basis of what is <u>stated</u> or <u>implied</u> in the passage or pair of passages. For some of the questions, more than one of the choices could conceivably answer the question. However, you are to choose the <u>best</u> answer; that is, the response that most accurately and completely answers the question, and blacken the corresponding space on your answer sheet.

The Canadian Auto Workers' (CAW) Legal Services Plan, designed to give active and retired autoworkers and their families access to totally prepaid or partially reimbursed legal services, has
(5) been in operation since late 1985. Plan members have the option of using either the plan's staff lawyers, whose services are fully covered by the cost of membership in the plan, or an outside lawyer. Outside lawyers, in turn, can either sign up with the plan as a
(10) "cooperating lawyer" and accept the CAW's fee schedule as payment in full, or they can charge a higher fee and collect the balance from the client. Autoworkers appear to have embraced the notion of prepaid legal services: 45 percent of eligible union
(15) members were enrolled in the plan by 1988. Moreover, the idea of prepaid legal services has been spreading in Canada. A department store is even offering a plan to holders of its credit card.

While many plan members seem to be happy to
(20) get reduced-cost legal help, many lawyers are concerned about the plan's effect on their profession, especially its impact on prices for legal services. Some point out that even though most lawyers have not joined the plan as cooperating lawyers, legal fees
(25) in the cities in which the CAW plan operates have been depressed, in some cases to an unprofitable level. The directors of the plan, however, claim that both clients and lawyers benefit from their arrangement. For while the clients get ready access to
(30) reduced-price services, lawyers get professional contact with people who would not otherwise be using legal services, which helps generate even more business for their firms. Experience shows, the directors say, that if people are referred to a firm and
(35) receive excellent service, the firm will get three to four other referrals who are not plan subscribers and who would therefore pay the firm's standard rate.

But it is unlikely that increased use of such plans will result in long-term client satisfaction or in a
(40) substantial increase in profits for law firms. Since lawyers with established reputations and client bases can benefit little, if at all, from participation, the plans function largely as marketing devices for lawyers who have yet to establish themselves. While
(45) many of these lawyers are no doubt very able and conscientious, they will tend to have less expertise and to provide less satisfaction to clients. At the same time, the downward pressure on fees will mean that the full-fee referrals that proponents say will come
(50) through plan participation may not make up for a

firm's investment in providing services at low plan rates. And since lowered fees provide little incentive for lawyers to devote more than minimal effort to cases, a "volume discount" approach toward the
(55) practice of law will mean less time devoted to complex cases and a general lowering of quality for clients.

1. Which one of the following most accurately expresses the main point of the passage?

(A) In the short term, prepaid legal plans such as the CAW Legal Services Plan appear to be beneficial to both lawyers and clients, but in the long run lawyers will profit at the expense of clients.

(B) The CAW Legal Services Plan and other similar plans represent a controversial, but probably effective, way of bringing down the cost of legal services to clients and increasing lawyers' clientele.

(C) The use of prepaid legal plans such as that of the CAW should be rejected in favor of a more equitable means of making legal services more generally affordable.

(D) In spite of widespread consumer support for legal plans such as that offered by the CAW, lawyers generally criticize such plans, mainly because of their potential financial impact on the legal profession.

(E) Although they have so far attracted many subscribers, it is doubtful whether the CAW Legal Services Plan and other similar prepaid plans will benefit lawyers and clients in the long run.

2. The primary purpose of the passage is to

(A) compare and contrast legal plans with the traditional way of paying for legal services

(B) explain the growing popularity of legal plans

(C) trace the effect of legal plans on prices of legal services

(D) caution that increased use of legal plans is potentially harmful to the legal profession and to clients

(E) advocate reforms to legal plans as presently constituted

GO ON TO THE NEXT PAGE.

3. Which one of the following does the author predict will be a consequence of increased use of legal plans?

(A) results that are largely at odds with those predicted by lawyers who criticize the plans

(B) a lowering of the rates such plans charge their members

(C) forced participation of lawyers who can benefit little from association with the plans

(D) an eventual increase in profits for lawyers from client usage of the plans

(E) a reduction in the time lawyers devote to complex cases

4. Which one of the following sequences most accurately and completely corresponds to the presentation of the material in the passage?

(A) a description of a recently implemented set of procedures and policies; a summary of the results of that implementation; a proposal of refinements in those policies and procedures

(B) an evaluation of a recent phenomenon; a comparison of that phenomenon with related past phenomena; an expression of the author's approval of that phenomenon

(C) a presentation of a proposal; a discussion of the prospects for implementing that proposal; a recommendation by the author that the proposal be rejected

(D) a description of an innovation; a report of reasoning against and reasoning favoring that innovation; argumentation by the author concerning that innovation

(E) an explanation of a recent occurrence; an evaluation of the practical value of that occurrence; a presentation of further data regarding that occurrence

5. The passage most strongly suggests that, according to proponents of prepaid legal plans, cooperating lawyers benefit from taking clients at lower fees in which one of the following ways?

(A) Lawyers can expect to gain expertise in a wide variety of legal services by availing themselves of the access to diverse clientele that plan participation affords.

(B) Experienced cooperating lawyers are likely to enjoy the higher profits of long-term, complex cases, for which new lawyers are not suited.

(C) Lower rates of profit will be offset by a higher volume of clients and new business through word-of-mouth recommendations.

(D) Lower fees tend to attract clients away from established, nonparticipating law firms.

(E) With all legal fees moving downward to match the plans' schedules, the profession will respond to market forces.

6. According to the passage, which one of the following is true of CAW Legal Services Plan members?

(A) They can enjoy benefits beyond the use of the services of the plan's staff lawyers.

(B) So far, they generally believe the quality of services they receive from the plan's staff lawyers is as high as that provided by other lawyers.

(C) Most of them consult lawyers only for relatively simple and routine matters.

(D) They must pay a fee above the cost of membership for the services of an outside lawyer.

(E) They do not include only active and retired autoworkers and their families.

7. Which one of the following most accurately represents the primary function of the author's mention of marketing devices (line 43)?

(A) It points to an aspect of legal plans that the author believes will be detrimental to the quality of legal services.

(B) It is identified by the author as one of the primary ways in which plan administrators believe themselves to be contributing materially to the legal profession in return for lawyers' participation.

(C) It identifies what the author considers to be one of the few unequivocal benefits that legal plans can provide.

(D) It is reported as part of several arguments that the author attributes to established lawyers who oppose plan participation.

(E) It describes one of the chief burdens of lawyers who have yet to establish themselves and offers an explanation of their advocacy of legal plans.

GO ON TO THE NEXT PAGE.

In the field of historiography—the writing of history based on a critical examination of authentic primary information sources—one area that has recently attracted attention focuses on the responses

(5) of explorers and settlers to new landscapes in order to provide insights into the transformations the landscape itself has undergone as a result of settlement. In this endeavor historiographers examining the history of the Pacific Coast of the

(10) United States have traditionally depended on the records left by European American explorers of the nineteenth century who, as commissioned agents of the U.S. government, were instructed to report thoroughly their findings in writing.

(15)　　　But in furthering this investigation some historiographers have recently recognized the need to expand their definition of what a source is. They maintain that the sources traditionally accepted as documenting the history of the Pacific Coast have too

(20) often omitted the response of Asian settlers to this territory. In part this is due to the dearth of written records left by Asian settlers; in contrast to the commissioned agents, most of the people who first came to western North America from Asia during this

(25) same period did not focus on developing a self-conscious written record of their involvement with the landscape. But because a full study of a culture's historical relationship to its land cannot confine itself to a narrow record of experience, these

(30) historiographers have begun to recognize the value of other kinds of evidence, such as the actions of Asian settlers.

　　　As a case in point, the role of Chinese settlers in expanding agriculture throughout the Pacific Coast

(35) territory is integral to the history of the region. Without access to the better land, Chinese settlers looked for agricultural potential in this generally arid region where other settlers did not. For example, where settlers of European descent looked at willows

(40) and saw only useless, untillable swamp, Chinese settlers saw fresh water, fertile soil, and the potential for bringing water to more arid areas via irrigation. Where other settlers who looked at certain weeds, such as wild mustard, generally saw a nuisance,

(45) Chinese settlers saw abundant raw material for valuable spices from a plant naturally suited to the local soil and climate.

　　　Given their role in the labor force shaping this territory in the nineteenth century, the Chinese settlers

(50) offered more than just a new view of the land. Their vision was reinforced by specialized skills involving swamp reclamation and irrigation systems, which helped lay the foundation for the now well-known and prosperous agribusiness of the region. That

(55) 80 percent of the area's cropland is now irrigated and that the region is currently the top producer of many specialty crops cannot be fully understood by historiographers without attention to the input of Chinese settlers as reconstructed from their

(60) interactions with that landscape.

8. Which one of the following most accurately states the main point of the passage?

(A)　The history of settlement along the Pacific Coast of the U.S., as understood by most historiographers, is confirmed by evidence reconstructed from the actions of Asian settlers.

(B)　Asian settlers on the Pacific Coast of the U.S. left a record of their experiences that traditional historiographers believed to be irrelevant.

(C)　To understand Asian settlers' impact on the history of the Pacific Coast of the U.S., historiographers have had to recognize the value of nontraditional kinds of historiographic evidence.

(D)　Spurred by new findings regarding Asian settlement on the Pacific Coast of the U.S., historiographers have begun to debate the methodological foundations of historiography.

(E)　By examining only written information, historiography as it is traditionally practiced has produced inaccurate historical accounts.

9. Which one of the following most accurately describes the author's primary purpose in discussing Chinese settlers in the third paragraph?

(A)　to suggest that Chinese settlers followed typical settlement patterns in this region during the nineteenth century

(B)　to argue that little written evidence of Chinese settlers' practices survives

(C)　to provide examples illustrating the unique view Asian settlers had of the land

(D)　to demonstrate that the history of settlement in the region has become a point of contention among historiographers

(E)　to claim that the historical record provided by the actions of Asian settlers is inconsistent with history as derived from traditional sources

10. The passage states that the primary traditional historiographic sources of information about the history of the Pacific Coast of the U.S. have which one of the following characteristics?

(A)　They were written both before and after Asian settlers arrived in the area.

(B)　They include accounts by Native Americans in the area.

(C)　They are primarily concerned with potential agricultural uses of the land.

(D)　They focus primarily on the presence of water sources in the region.

(E)　They are accounts left by European American explorers.

GO ON TO THE NEXT PAGE.

11. The author would most likely disagree with which one of the following statements?

    (A) Examining the actions not only of Asian settlers but of other cultural groups of the Pacific Coast of the U.S. is necessary to a full understanding of the impact of settlement on the landscape there.

    (B) The significance of certain actions to the writing of history may be recognized by one group of historiographers but not another.

    (C) Recognizing the actions of Asian settlers adds to but does not complete the writing of the history of the Pacific Coast of the U.S.

    (D) By recognizing as evidence the actions of people, historiographers expand the definition of what a source is.

    (E) The expanded definition of a source will probably not be relevant to studies of regions that have no significant immigration of non-Europeans.

12. According to the passage, each of the following was an aspect of Chinese settlers' initial interactions with the landscape of the Pacific Coast of the U.S. EXCEPT:

    (A) new ideas for utilizing local plants
    (B) a new view of the land
    (C) specialized agricultural skills
    (D) knowledge of agribusiness practices
    (E) knowledge of irrigation systems

13. Which one of the following can most reasonably be inferred from the passage?

    (A) Most Chinese settlers came to the Pacific Coast of the U.S. because the climate was similar to that with which they were familiar.

    (B) Chinese agricultural methods in the nineteenth century included knowledge of swamp reclamation.

    (C) Settlers of European descent used wild mustard seed as a spice.

    (D) Because of the abundance of written sources available, it is not worthwhile to examine the actions of European settlers.

    (E) What written records were left by Asian settlers were neglected and consequently lost to scholarly research.

14. Which one of the following, if true, would most help to strengthen the author's main claim in the last sentence of the passage?

    (A) Market research of agribusinesses owned by descendants of Chinese settlers shows that the market for the region's specialty crops has grown substantially faster than the market for any other crops in the last decade.

    (B) Nineteenth-century surveying records indicate that the lands now cultivated by specialty crop businesses owned by descendants of Chinese settlers were formerly swamp lands.

    (C) Research by university agricultural science departments proves that the formerly arid lands now cultivated by large agribusinesses contain extremely fertile soil when they are sufficiently irrigated.

    (D) A technological history tracing the development of irrigation systems in the region reveals that their efficiency has increased steadily since the nineteenth century.

    (E) Weather records compiled over the previous century demonstrate that the weather patterns in the region are well-suited to growing certain specialty crops as long as they are irrigated.

GO ON TO THE NEXT PAGE.

The survival of nerve cells, as well as their performance of some specialized functions, is regulated by chemicals known as neurotrophic factors, which are produced in the bodies of animals,
(5) including humans. Rita Levi-Montalcini's discovery in the 1950s of the first of these agents, a hormonelike substance now known as NGF, was a crucial development in the history of biochemistry, which led to Levi-Montalcini sharing the Nobel Prize
(10) for medicine in 1986.

In the mid-1940s, Levi-Montalcini had begun by hypothesizing that many of the immature nerve cells produced in the development of an organism are normally programmed to die. In order to confirm this
(15) theory, she conducted research that in 1949 found that, when embryos are in the process of forming their nervous systems, they produce many more nerve cells than are finally required, the number that survives eventually adjusting itself to the volume of
(20) tissue to be supplied with nerves. A further phase of the experimentation, which led to Levi-Montalcini's identification of the substance that controls this process, began with her observation that the development of nerves in chick embryos could be
(25) stimulated by implanting a certain variety of mouse tumor in the embryos. She theorized that a chemical produced by the tumors was responsible for the observed nerve growth. To investigate this hypothesis, she used the then new technique of tissue culture, by
(30) which specific types of body cells can be made to grow outside the organism from which they are derived. Within twenty-four hours, her tissue cultures of chick embryo extracts developed dense halos of nerve tissue near the places in the culture where she
(35) had added the mouse tumor. Further research identified a specific substance contributed by the mouse tumors that was responsible for the effects Levi-Montalcini had observed: a protein that she named "nerve growth factor" (NGF).
(40) NGF was the first of many cell-growth factors to be found in the bodies of animals. Through Levi-Montalcini's work and other subsequent research, it has been determined that this substance is present in many tissues and biological fluids, and that it is
(45) especially concentrated in some organs. In developing organisms, nerve cells apparently receive this growth factor locally from the cells of muscles or other organs to which they will form connections for transmission of nerve impulses, and sometimes from
(50) supporting cells intermingled with the nerve tissue. NGF seems to play two roles, serving initially to direct the developing nerve processes toward the correct, specific "target" cells with which they must connect, and later being necessary for the continued
(55) survival of those nerve cells. During some periods of their development, the types of nerve cells that are affected by NGF—primarily cells outside the brain and spinal cord—die if the factor is not present or if they encounter anti-NGF antibodies.

15. Which one of the following most accurately expresses the main point of the passage?

(A) Levi-Montalcini's discovery of neurotrophic factors as a result of research carried out in the 1940s was a major contribution to our understanding of the role of naturally occurring chemicals, especially NGF, in the development of chick embryos.

(B) Levi-Montalcini's discovery of NGF, a neurotrophic factor that stimulates the development of some types of nerve tissue and whose presence or absence in surrounding cells helps determine whether particular nerve cells will survive, was a pivotal development in biochemistry.

(C) NGF, which is necessary for the survival and proper functioning of nerve cells, was discovered by Levi-Montalcini in a series of experiments using the technique of tissue culture, which she devised in the 1940s.

(D) Partly as a result of Levi-Montalcini's research, it has been found that NGF and other neurotrophic factors are produced only by tissues to which nerves are already connected and that the presence of these factors is necessary for the health and proper functioning of nervous systems.

(E) NGF, a chemical that was discovered by Levi-Montalcini, directs the growth of nerve cells toward the cells with which they must connect and ensures the survival of those nerve cells throughout the life of the organism except when the organism produces anti-NGF antibodies.

16. Based on the passage, the author would be most likely to believe that Levi-Montalcini's discovery of NGF is noteworthy primarily because it

(A) paved the way for more specific knowledge of the processes governing the development of the nervous system

(B) demonstrated that a then new laboratory technique could yield important and unanticipated experimental results

(C) confirmed the hypothesis that many of a developing organism's immature nerve cells are normally programmed to die

(D) indicated that this substance stimulates observable biochemical reactions in the tissues of different species

(E) identified a specific substance, produced by mouse tumors, that can be used to stimulate nerve cell growth

GO ON TO THE NEXT PAGE.

17. The primary function of the third paragraph of the passage in relation to the second paragraph is to

(A) indicate that conclusions referred to in the second paragraph, though essentially correct, require further verification

(B) indicate that conclusions referred to in the second paragraph have been undermined by subsequently obtained evidence

(C) indicate ways in which conclusions referred to in the second paragraph have been further corroborated and refined

(D) describe subsequent discoveries of substances analogous to the substance discussed in the second paragraph

(E) indicate that experimental procedures discussed in the second paragraph have been supplanted by more precise techniques described in the third paragraph

18. Information in the passage most strongly supports which one of the following?

(A) Nerve cells in excess of those that are needed by the organism in which they develop eventually produce anti-NGF antibodies to suppress the effects of NGF.

(B) Nerve cells that grow in the absence of NGF are less numerous than, but qualitatively identical to, those that grow in the presence of NGF.

(C) Few of the nerve cells that connect with target cells toward which NGF directs them are needed by the organism in which they develop.

(D) Some of the nerve cells that grow in the presence of NGF are eventually converted to other types of living tissue by neurotrophic factors.

(E) Some of the nerve cells that grow in an embryo do not connect with any particular target cells.

19. The passage describes a specific experiment that tested which one of the following hypotheses?

(A) A certain kind of mouse tumor produces a chemical that stimulates the growth of nerve cells.

(B) Developing embryos initially grow many more nerve cells than they will eventually require.

(C) In addition to NGF, there are several other important neurotrophic factors regulating cell survival and function.

(D) Certain organs contain NGF in concentrations much higher than in the surrounding tissue.

(E) Certain nerve cells are supplied with NGF by the muscle cells to which they are connected.

20. Which one of the following is most strongly supported by the information in the passage?

(A) Some of the effects that the author describes as occurring in Levi-Montalcini's culture of chick embryo extract were due to neurotrophic factors other than NGF.

(B) Although NGF was the first neurotrophic factor to be identified, some other such factors are now more thoroughly understood.

(C) In her research in the 1940s and 1950s, Levi-Montalcini identified other neurotrophic factors in addition to NGF.

(D) Some neurotrophic factors other than NGF perform functions that are not specifically identified in the passage.

(E) The effects of NGF that Levi-Montalcini noted in her chick embryo experiment are also caused by other neurotrophic factors not discussed in the passage.

GO ON TO THE NEXT PAGE.

The proponents of the Modern Movement in architecture considered that, compared with the historical styles that it replaced, Modernist architecture more accurately reflected the functional
(5) spirit of twentieth-century technology and was better suited to the newest building methods. It is ironic, then, that the Movement fostered an ideology of design that proved to be at odds with the way buildings were really built.
(10)   The tenacious adherence of Modernist architects and critics to this ideology was in part responsible for the Movement's decline. Originating in the 1920s as a marginal, almost bohemian art movement, the Modern Movement was never very popular with the public,
(15) but this very lack of popular support produced in Modernist architects a high-minded sense of mission—not content merely to interpret the needs of the client, these architects now sought to persuade, to educate, and, if necessary, to dictate. By 1945 the
(20) tenets of the Movement had come to dominate mainstream architecture, and by the early 1950s, to dominate architectural criticism—architects whose work seemed not to advance the evolution of the Modern Movement tended to be dismissed by
(25) proponents of Modernism. On the other hand, when architects were identified as innovators—as was the case with Otto Wagner, or the young Frank Lloyd Wright—attention was drawn to only those features of their work that were "Modern"; other aspects were
(30) conveniently ignored.
        The decline of the Modern Movement later in the twentieth century occurred partly as a result of Modernist architects' ignorance of building methods, and partly because Modernist architects were
(35) reluctant to admit that their concerns were chiefly aesthetic. Moreover, the building industry was evolving in a direction Modernists had not anticipated: it was more specialized and the process of construction was much more fragmented than in
(40) the past. Up until the twentieth century, construction had been carried out by a relatively small number of tradespeople, but as the building industry evolved, buildings came to be built by many specialized subcontractors working independently. The architect's
(45) design not only had to accommodate a sequence of independent operations, but now had to reflect the allowable degree of inaccuracy of the different trades. However, one of the chief construction ideals of the Modern Movement was to "honestly" expose
(50) structural materials such as steel and concrete. To do this and still produce a visually acceptable interior called for an unrealistically high level of craftsmanship. Exposure of a building's internal structural elements, if it could be achieved at all,
(55) could only be accomplished at considerable cost—

hence the well-founded reputation of Modern architecture as prohibitively expensive.
        As Postmodern architects recognized, the need to expose structural elements imposed unnecessary
(60) limitations on building design. The unwillingness of architects of the Modern Movement to abandon their ideals contributed to the decline of interest in the Modern Movement.

21. Which one of the following most accurately summarizes the main idea of the passage?

(A)   The Modern Movement declined because its proponents were overly ideological and did not take into account the facts of building construction.
(B)   Rationality was the theoretical basis for the development of the Modern Movement in architecture.
(C)   Changes in architectural design introduced by the Modern Movement inspired the development of modern construction methods.
(D)   The theoretical bases of the Modern Movement in architecture originated in changes in building construction methods.
(E)   Proponents of the Modern Movement in architecture rejected earlier architectural styles because such styles were not functional.

22. Which one of the following is most similar to the relationship described in the passage between the new methods of the building industry and pre-twentieth-century construction?

(A)   Clothing produced on an assembly line is less precisely tailored than clothing produced by a single garment maker.
(B)   Handwoven fabric is more beautiful than fabric produced by machine.
(C)   Lenses ground on a machine are less useful than lenses ground by hand.
(D)   Form letters produced by a word processor elicit fewer responses than letters typed individually on a typewriter.
(E)   Furniture produced in a factory is less fashionable than handcrafted furniture.

23. With respect to the proponents of the Modern Movement, the author of the passage can best be described as

(A)   forbearing
(B)   defensive
(C)   unimpressed
(D)   exasperated
(E)   indifferent

GO ON TO THE NEXT PAGE.

24. It can be inferred that the author of the passage believes which one of the following about Modern Movement architects' ideal of exposing structural materials?

(A) The repudiation of the ideal by some of these architects undermined its validity.

(B) The ideal was rarely achieved because of its lack of popular appeal.

(C) The ideal was unrealistic because most builders were unwilling to attempt it.

(D) The ideal originated in the work of Otto Wagner and Frank Lloyd Wright.

(E) The ideal arose from aesthetic rather than practical concerns.

25. Which one of the following, in its context in the passage, most clearly reveals the attitude of the author toward the proponents of the Modern Movement?

(A) "functional spirit" (lines 4–5)

(B) "tended" (line 24)

(C) "innovators" (line 26)

(D) "conveniently" (line 30)

(E) "degree of inaccuracy" (line 47)

26. The author of the passage mentions Otto Wagner and the young Frank Lloyd Wright (lines 27–28) primarily as examples of

(A) innovative architects whose work was not immediately appreciated by the public

(B) architects whom proponents of the Modern Movement claimed represented the movement

(C) architects whose work helped to popularize the Modern Movement

(D) architects who generally attempted to interpret the needs of their clients, rather than dictating to them

(E) architects whose early work seemed to architects of the Modern Movement to be at odds with the principles of Modernism

27. The author of the passage is primarily concerned with

(A) analyzing the failure of a movement

(B) predicting the future course of a movement

(C) correcting a misunderstanding about a movement

(D) anticipating possible criticism of a movement

(E) contrasting incompatible viewpoints about a movement

STOP
IF YOU FINISH BEFORE TIME IS CALLED, YOU MAY CHECK YOUR WORK ON THIS SECTION ONLY.
DO NOT WORK ON ANY OTHER SECTION IN THE TEST.

SECTION II
Time—35 minutes
25 Questions

Directions: The questions in this section are based on the reasoning contained in brief statements or passages. For some questions, more than one of the choices could conceivably answer the question. However, you are to choose the best answer; that is, the response that most accurately and completely answers the question. You should not make assumptions that are by commonsense standards implausible, superfluous, or incompatible with the passage. After you have chosen the best answer, blacken the corresponding space on your answer sheet.

1. The tidal range at a particular location is the difference in height between high tide and low tide. Tidal studies have shown that one of the greatest tidal ranges in the world is found in the Bay of Fundy and reaches more than seventeen meters. Since the only forces involved in inducing the tides are the sun's and moon's gravity, the magnitudes of tidal ranges also must be explained entirely by gravitational forces.

Which one of the following most accurately describes a flaw in the reasoning above?

(A) It gives only one example of a tidal range.
(B) It fails to consider that the size of a tidal range could be affected by the conditions in which gravitational forces act.
(C) It does not consider the possibility that low tides are measured in a different way than are high tides.
(D) It presumes, without providing warrant, that most activity within the world's oceans is a result of an interplay of gravitational forces.
(E) It does not differentiate between the tidal effect of the sun and the tidal effect of the moon.

2. Cardiologist: Coronary bypass surgery is commonly performed on patients suffering from coronary artery disease when certain other therapies would be as effective. Besides being relatively inexpensive, these other therapies pose less risk to the patient since they are less intrusive. Bypass surgery is especially debatable for single-vessel disease.

The cardiologist's statements, if true, most strongly support which one of the following?

(A) Bypass surgery is riskier than all alternative therapies.
(B) Needless bypass surgery is more common today than previously.
(C) Bypass surgery should be performed when more than one vessel is diseased.
(D) Bypass surgery is an especially expensive therapy when used to treat single-vessel disease.
(E) Sometimes there are equally effective alternatives to bypass surgery that involve less risk.

3. In the past, combining children of different ages in one classroom was usually a failure; it resulted in confused younger children, who were given inadequate attention and instruction, and bored older ones, who had to sit through previously learned lessons. Recently, however, the practice has been revived with excellent results. Mixed-age classrooms today are stimulating to older children and enable younger children to learn much more efficiently than in standard classrooms.

Which one of the following, if true, most helps to resolve the apparent discrepancy in the passage?

(A) On average, mixed-age classrooms today are somewhat larger in enrollment than were the ones of the past.
(B) Mixed-age classrooms of the past were better equipped than are those of today.
(C) Today's mixed-age classrooms, unlike those of the past, emphasize group projects that are engaging to students of different ages.
(D) Today's mixed-age classrooms have students of a greater range of ages than did those of the past.
(E) Few of the teachers who are reviving mixed-age classrooms today were students in mixed-age classrooms when they were young.

GO ON TO THE NEXT PAGE.

4. The top 50 centimeters of soil on Tiliga Island contain bones from the native birds eaten by the islanders since the first human immigration to the island 3,000 years ago. A comparison of this top layer with the underlying 150 centimeters of soil—accumulated over 80,000 years—reveals that before humans arrived on Tiliga, a much larger and more diverse population of birds lived there. Thus, the arrival of humans dramatically decreased the population and diversity of birds on Tiliga.

Which one of the following statements, if true, most seriously weakens the argument?

(A) The bird species known to have been eaten by the islanders had few natural predators on Tiliga.

(B) Many of the bird species that disappeared from Tiliga did not disappear from other, similar, uninhabited islands until much later.

(C) The arrival of a species of microbe, carried by some birds but deadly to many others, immediately preceded the first human immigration to Tiliga.

(D) Bones from bird species known to have been eaten by the islanders were found in the underlying 150 centimeters of soil.

(E) The birds that lived on Tiliga prior to the first human immigration generally did not fly well.

5. The corpus callosum—the thick band of nerve fibers connecting the brain's two hemispheres—of a musician is on average larger than that of a nonmusician. The differences in the size of corpora callosa are particularly striking when adult musicians who began training around the age of seven are compared to adult nonmusicians. Therefore, musical training, particularly when it begins at a young age, causes certain anatomic brain changes.

Which one of the following is an assumption on which the argument depends?

(A) The corpora callosa of musicians, before they started training, do not tend to be larger than those of nonmusicians of the same age.

(B) Musical training late in life does not cause anatomic changes to the brain.

(C) For any two musicians whose training began around the age of seven, their corpora callosa are approximately the same size.

(D) All musicians have larger corpora callosa than do any nonmusicians.

(E) Adult nonmusicians did not participate in activities when they were children that would have stimulated any growth of the corpus callosum.

6. Chai: The use of the word "tree" to denote both deciduous and coniferous plant forms, while acceptable as a lay term, is scientifically inadequate; it masks the fact that the two plant types have utterly different lineages.

Dodd: But the common name highlights the crucial fact that both are composed of the same material and have very similar structures; so it is acceptable as a scientific term.

The conversation provides the strongest grounds for holding that Chai and Dodd disagree over whether

(A) it is advisable to use ordinary terms as names for biological forms in scientific discourse

(B) using the same term for two biological forms with different lineages can be scientifically acceptable

(C) both deciduous and coniferous plant forms evolved from simpler biological forms

(D) it is important that the lay terms for plant forms reflect the current scientific theories about them

(E) biological forms with similar structures can have different lineages

7. Increases in the occurrence of hearing loss among teenagers are due in part to their listening to loud music through stereo headphones. So a group of concerned parents is recommending that headphone manufacturers include in their product lines stereo headphones that automatically turn off when a dangerous level of loudness is reached. It is clear that adoption of this recommendation would not significantly reduce the occurrence of hearing loss in teenagers, however, since almost all stereo headphones that teenagers use are bought by the teenagers themselves.

Which one of the following, if true, provides the most support for the argument?

(A) Loud music is most dangerous to hearing when it is played through stereo headphones.

(B) No other cause of hearing loss in teenagers is as damaging as their listening to loud music through stereo headphones.

(C) Parents of teenagers generally do not themselves listen to loud music through stereo headphones.

(D) Teenagers who now listen to music at dangerously loud levels choose to do so despite their awareness of the risks involved.

(E) A few headphone manufacturers already plan to market stereo headphones that automatically turn off when a dangerous level of loudness is reached.

8. Most plants have developed chemical defenses against parasites. The average plant contains about 40 natural pesticides—chemical compounds toxic to bacteria, fungi, and other parasites. Humans ingest these natural pesticides without harm every day. Therefore, the additional threat posed by synthetic pesticides sprayed on crop plants by humans is minimal.

Each of the following, if true, weakens the argument EXCEPT:

(A) Humans have been consuming natural plant pesticides for millennia and have had time to adapt to them.

(B) The concentrations of natural pesticides in plants are typically much lower than the concentrations of synthetic pesticides in sprayed crop plants.

(C) Natural plant pesticides are typically less potent than synthetic pesticides, whose toxicity is highly concentrated.

(D) Natural plant pesticides generally serve only as defenses against specific parasites, whereas synthetic pesticides are often harmful to a wide variety of organisms.

(E) The synthetic pesticides sprayed on crop plants by humans usually have chemical structures similar to those of the natural pesticides produced by the plants.

9. In addition to the labor and materials used to make wine, the reputation of the vineyard where the grapes originate plays a role in determining the price of the finished wine. Therefore, an expensive wine is not always a good wine.

Which one of the following is an assumption on which the argument depends?

(A) The price of a bottle of wine should be a reflection of the wine's quality.

(B) Price is never an accurate indication of the quality of a bottle of wine.

(C) The reputation of a vineyard does not always indicate the quality of its wines.

(D) The reputation of a vineyard generally plays a greater role than the quality of its grapes in determining its wines' prices.

(E) Wines produced by lesser-known vineyards generally are priced to reflect accurately the wines' quality.

10. Before their larvae hatch, each parental pair of *Nicrophorus* beetles buries the carcass of a small vertebrate nearby. For several days after the larvae hatch, both beetles feed their voracious larvae from the carcass, which is entirely consumed within a week. Since both parents help with feeding, larvae should benefit from both parents' presence; however, removing one parent before the hatching results in larvae that grow both larger and heavier than they otherwise would be.

Which one of the following, if true, best helps to explain why removing one parent resulted in larger, heavier larvae?

(A) Two beetles can find and bury a larger carcass than can a single beetle.

(B) Both parents use the carcass as their own food supply for as long as they stay with the larvae.

(C) Beetle parents usually take turns feeding their larvae, so that there is always one provider available and one at rest.

(D) After a week, the larvae are capable of finding other sources of food and feeding themselves.

(E) Two parents can defend the carcass from attack by other insects better than a single parent can.

11. For many centuries it was believed that only classical Euclidean geometry could provide a correct way of mathematically representing the universe. Nevertheless, scientists have come to believe that a representation of the universe employing non-Euclidean geometry is much more useful in developing certain areas of scientific theory. In fact, such a representation underlies the cosmological theory that is now most widely accepted by scientists as accurate.

Which one of the following is most strongly supported by the statements above?

(A) Scientists who use Euclidean geometry are likely to believe that progress in mathematical theory results in progress in natural science.

(B) Scientists generally do not now believe that classical Euclidean geometry is uniquely capable of giving a correct mathematical representation of the universe.

(C) Non-Euclidean geometry is a more complete way of representing the universe than is Euclidean geometry.

(D) An accurate scientific theory cannot be developed without the discovery of a uniquely correct way of mathematically representing the universe.

(E) The usefulness of a mathematical theory is now considered by scientists to be more important than its mathematical correctness.

GO ON TO THE NEXT PAGE.

12. Experts hired to testify in court need to know how to make convincing presentations. Such experts are evaluated by juries in terms of their ability to present the steps by which they arrived at their conclusions clearly and confidently. As a result, some less expert authorities who are skilled at producing convincing testimony are asked to testify rather than highly knowledgeable but less persuasive experts.

Which one of the following most closely conforms to the principle illustrated by the passage above?

(A) Successful politicians are not always the ones who best understand how to help their country. Some lack insight into important political issues but are highly skilled at conducting an election campaign.

(B) Trial lawyers often use the techniques employed by actors to influence the emotions of jurors. Many lawyers have studied drama expressly for the purpose of improving their courtroom skills.

(C) The opera singer with the best voice is the appropriate choice even for minor roles, despite the fact that an audience may be more affected by a singer with greater dramatic ability but a lesser voice.

(D) It is often best to try to train children with gentle reinforcement of desired behavior, rather than by simply telling them what to do and what not to do. This results in children who behave because they want to, not because they feel compelled.

(E) Job applicants are usually hired because their skills and training best meet a recognized set of qualifications. Only rarely is a prospective employer convinced to tailor a position to suit the skills of a particular applicant.

13. The solution to any environmental problem that is not the result of government mismanagement can only lie in major changes in consumer habits. But major changes in consumer habits will occur only if such changes are economically enticing. As a result, few serious ecological problems will be solved unless the solutions are made economically enticing.

The conclusion drawn in the argument above follows logically if which one of the following is assumed?

(A) Few serious ecological problems are the result of government mismanagement.

(B) No environmental problems that stem from government mismanagement have solutions that are economically feasible.

(C) Major changes in consumer habits can be made economically enticing.

(D) Most environmental problems that are not the result of government mismanagement are major ecological problems.

(E) Few serious ecological problems can be solved by major changes in consumer habits.

14. The economy is doing badly. First, the real estate slump has been with us for some time. Second, car sales are at their lowest in years. Of course, had either one or the other phenomenon failed to occur, this would be consistent with the economy as a whole being healthy. But, their occurrence together makes it quite probable that my conclusion is correct.

Which one of the following inferences is most strongly supported by the information above?

(A) If car sales are at their lowest in years, then it is likely that the economy is doing badly.

(B) If the economy is doing badly, then either the real estate market or the car sales market is not healthy.

(C) If the real estate market is healthy, then it is likely that the economy as a whole is healthy.

(D) If the economy is in a healthy state, then it is unlikely that the real estate and car sales markets are both in a slump.

(E) The bad condition of the economy implies that both the real estate and the car sales markets are doing badly.

GO ON TO THE NEXT PAGE.

15. According to current geological theory, the melting of ice at the end of the Ice Age significantly reduced the weight pressing on parts of the earth's crust. As a result, lasting cracks in the earth's crust appeared in some of those parts under the stress of pressure from below. At the end of the Ice Age Sweden was racked by severe earthquakes. Therefore, it is likely that the melting of the ice contributed to these earthquakes.

Which one of the following, if true, most strengthens the argument above?

(A) The earth's crust tends to crack whenever there is a sudden change in the pressures affecting it.

(B) There are various areas in Northern Europe that show cracks in the earth's crust.

(C) Evidence of severe earthquakes around the time of the end of the Ice Age can be found in parts of northern Canada.

(D) Severe earthquakes are generally caused by cracking of the earth's crust near the earthquake site.

(E) Asteroid impacts, which did occur at the end of the Ice Age, generally cause severe earthquakes.

16. Sociologist: Some economists hold that unregulated markets should accompany democratic sovereignty because they let people vote with their money. But this view ignores the crucial distinction between the private consumer and the public citizen. In the marketplace the question is, "What do I want?" At the voting booth the question is always, "What do we want?" Hence, supporters of political democracy can also support marketplace regulation.

Which one of the following most accurately expresses the conclusion drawn by the sociologist?

(A) Voters think of themselves as members of a community, rather than as isolated individuals.

(B) Unregulated markets are incompatible with democratic sovereignty.

(C) Where there is democratic sovereignty there should be unregulated markets.

(D) Private consumers are primarily concerned with their own self-interest.

(E) Opposition to unregulated markets is consistent with support for democracy.

17. The tiny hummingbird weighs little, but its egg is 15 percent of the adult hummingbird's weight. The volume and weight of an adult goose are much greater than those of a hummingbird, but a goose's egg is only about 4 percent of its own weight. An adult ostrich, much larger and heavier than a goose, lays an egg that is only 1.6 percent of its own weight.

Which one of the following propositions is best illustrated by the statements above?

(A) The eggs of different bird species vary widely in their ratio of volume to weight.

(B) The smaller and lighter the average adult members of a bird species are, the larger and heavier the eggs of that species are.

(C) The ratio of egg weight of a species to body weight of an adult member of that species is smaller for larger birds than for smaller ones.

(D) The size of birds' eggs varies greatly from species to species but has little effect on the volume and weight of the adult bird.

(E) Bird species vary more in egg size than they do in average body size and weight.

18. Bram Stoker's 1897 novel *Dracula* portrayed vampires— the "undead" who roam at night to suck the blood of living people—as able to turn into bats. As a result of the pervasive influence of this novel, many people now assume that a vampire's being able to turn into a bat is an essential part of vampire myths. However, this assumption is false, for vampire myths existed in Europe long before Stoker's book.

Which one of the following is an assumption on which the argument depends?

(A) At least one of the European vampire myths that predated Stoker's book did not portray vampires as strictly nocturnal.

(B) Vampire myths in Central and South America, where real vampire bats are found, portray vampires as able to turn into bats.

(C) Vampire myths did not exist outside Europe before the publication of Stoker's *Dracula*.

(D) At least one of the European vampire myths that predated Stoker's book did not portray vampires as able to turn into bats.

(E) At the time he wrote *Dracula*, Stoker was familiar with earlier European vampire myths.

GO ON TO THE NEXT PAGE.

19. It is unlikely that the world will ever be free of disease. Most diseases are caused by very prolific microorganisms whose response to the pressures medicines exert on them is predictable: they quickly evolve immunities to those medicines while maintaining their power to infect and even kill humans.

Which one of the following most accurately describes the role played in the argument by the claim that it is unlikely that the world will ever be free of disease?

(A) It is a conclusion that is claimed to follow from the premise that microorganisms are too numerous for medicines to eliminate entirely.

(B) It is a conclusion for which a description of the responses of microorganisms to the medicines designed to cure the diseases they cause is offered as support.

(C) It is a premise offered in support of the claim that most disease-causing microorganisms are able to evolve immunities to medicines while retaining their ability to infect humans.

(D) It is a generalization used to predict the response of microorganisms to the medicines humans use to kill them.

(E) It is a conclusion that is claimed to follow from the premise that most microorganisms are immune to medicines designed to kill them.

20. Scientist: My research indicates that children who engage in impulsive behavior similar to adult thrill-seeking behavior are twice as likely as other children to have a gene variant that increases sensitivity to dopamine. From this, I conclude that there is a causal relationship between this gene variant and an inclination toward thrill-seeking behavior.

Which one of the following, if true, most calls into question the scientist's argument?

(A) Many impulsive adults are not unusually sensitive to dopamine.

(B) It is not possible to reliably distinguish impulsive behavior from other behavior.

(C) Children are often described by adults as engaging in thrill-seeking behavior simply because they act impulsively.

(D) Many people exhibit behavioral tendencies as adults that they did not exhibit as children.

(E) The gene variant studied by the scientist is correlated with other types of behavior in addition to thrill-seeking behavior.

21. It is highly likely that Claudette is a classical pianist. Like most classical pianists, Claudette recognizes many of Clara Schumann's works. The vast majority of people who are not classical pianists do not. In fact, many people who are not classical pianists have not even heard of Clara Schumann.

The reasoning in the argument above is flawed in that it

(A) ignores the possibility that Claudette is more familiar with the works of other composers of music for piano

(B) presumes, without providing justification, that people who have not heard of Clara Schumann do not recognize her works

(C) presumes, without providing justification, that classical pianists cannot also play other musical instruments

(D) relies for its plausibility on the vagueness of the term "classical"

(E) ignores the possibility that the majority of people who recognize many of Clara Schumann's works are not classical pianists

GO ON TO THE NEXT PAGE.

22. All the evidence so far gathered fits both Dr. Grippen's theory and Professor Heissmann's. However, the predictions that these theories make about the result of the planned experiment cannot both be true. Therefore, the result of this experiment will confirm one of these theories at the expense of the other.

The argument above exhibits an erroneous pattern of reasoning most similar to that exhibited by which one of the following?

(A) David and Jane both think they know how to distinguish beech trees from elms, but when they look at trees together they often disagree. Therefore, at least one of them must have an erroneous method.

(B) Although David thinks the tree they saw was a beech, Jane thinks it was an elm. Jane's description of the tree's features is consistent with her opinion, so this description must be inconsistent with David's view.

(C) David and Jane have been equally good at identifying trees so far. But David says this one is an elm, whereas Jane is unsure. Therefore, if this tree turns out to be an elm, we'll know David is better.

(D) David thinks that there are more beeches than elms in this forest. Jane thinks he is wrong. The section of forest we examined was small, but examination of the whole forest would either confirm David's view or disprove it.

(E) David thinks this tree is a beech. Jane thinks it is an elm. Maria, unlike David or Jane, is expert at tree identification, so when Maria gives her opinion it will verify either David's or Jane's opinion.

23. Columnist: The relief from the drudgery of physical labor that much modern technology affords its users renders them dependent on this technology, and, more importantly, on the elaborate energy systems required to run it. This leads to a loss of self-sufficiency. Clearly, then, in addition to undermining life's charm, much modern technology diminishes the overall well-being of its users.

Which one of the following is an assumption required by the columnist's argument?

(A) Physical labor is essential to a fulfilling life.
(B) Self-sufficiency contributes to a person's well-being.
(C) People are not free if they must depend on anything other than their own capacities.
(D) Anything causing a loss in life's charm is unjustifiable unless this loss is compensated by some gain.
(E) Technology inherently limits the well-being of its users.

GO ON TO THE NEXT PAGE.

24. Psychologist: Some psychologists mistakenly argue that because dreams result from electrical discharges in the brain, they must be understood purely in terms of their physiological function. They conclude, against Freud, that dreams reveal nothing about the character of the dreamer. But since dream content varies enormously, then even if electrical discharges provide the terms of the physiological explanation of dreams, they cannot completely explain the phenomenon of dreaming.

The claim that dream content varies enormously plays which one of the following roles in the argument?

(A) It is used to support the anti-Freudian conclusion that some psychologists draw concerning dreams.

(B) It is used to support the explicitly stated conclusion that a fully satisfactory account of dreams must allow for the possibility of their revealing significant information about the dreamer.

(C) It is used to suggest that neither Freud's theory nor the theory of anti-Freudian psychologists can completely explain the phenomenon of dreaming.

(D) It is used to illustrate the difficulty of providing a complete explanation of the phenomenon of dreaming.

(E) It is used to undermine a claim that some psychologists use to argue against a view of Freud's.

25. The first bicycle, the Draisienne, was invented in 1817. A brief fad ensued, after which bicycles practically disappeared until the 1860s. Why was this? New technology is accepted only when it coheres with the values of a society. Hence some change in values must have occurred between 1817 and the 1860s.

The reasoning in the argument is flawed because the argument

(A) presumes, without giving justification, that fads are never indicative of genuine acceptance

(B) fails to recognize that the reappearance of bicycles in the 1860s may have indicated genuine acceptance of them

(C) offers no support for the claim that the Draisienne was the first true bicycle

(D) poses a question that has little relevance to the argument's conclusion

(E) ignores, without giving justification, alternative possible explanations of the initial failure of bicycles

STOP
IF YOU FINISH BEFORE TIME IS CALLED, YOU MAY CHECK YOUR WORK ON THIS SECTION ONLY.
DO NOT WORK ON ANY OTHER SECTION IN THE TEST.

SECTION III
Time—35 minutes
22 Questions

Directions: Each group of questions in this section is based on a set of conditions. In answering some of the questions, it may be useful to draw a rough diagram. Choose the response that most accurately and completely answers each question and blacken the corresponding space on your answer sheet.

Questions 1–6

In the course of one month Garibaldi has exactly seven different meetings. Each of her meetings is with exactly one of five foreign dignitaries: Fuentes, Matsuba, Rhee, Soleimani, or Tbahi. The following constraints govern Garibaldi's meetings:
    She has exactly three meetings with Fuentes, and exactly one with each of the other dignitaries.
    She does not have any meetings in a row with Fuentes.
    Her meeting with Soleimani is the very next one after her meeting with Tbahi.
    Neither the first nor last of her meetings is with Matsuba.

1. Which one of the following could be the sequence of the meetings Garibaldi has with the dignitaries?

    (A)   Fuentes, Rhee, Tbahi, Soleimani, Fuentes, Matsuba, Rhee
    (B)   Fuentes, Tbahi, Soleimani, Matsuba, Fuentes, Fuentes, Rhee
    (C)   Fuentes, Rhee, Fuentes, Matsuba, Fuentes, Tbahi, Soleimani
    (D)   Fuentes, Tbahi, Matsuba, Fuentes, Soleimani, Rhee, Fuentes
    (E)   Fuentes, Tbahi, Soleimani, Fuentes, Rhee, Fuentes, Matsuba

2. If Garibaldi's last meeting is with Rhee, then which one of the following could be true?

    (A)   Garibaldi's second meeting is with Soleimani.
    (B)   Garibaldi's third meeting is with Matsuba.
    (C)   Garibaldi's fourth meeting is with Soleimani.
    (D)   Garibaldi's fifth meeting is with Matsuba.
    (E)   Garibaldi's sixth meeting is with Soleimani.

3. If Garibaldi's second meeting is with Fuentes, then which one of the following is a complete and accurate list of the dignitaries with any one of whom Garibaldi's fourth meeting could be?

    (A)   Fuentes, Soleimani, Rhee
    (B)   Matsuba, Rhee, Tbahi
    (C)   Matsuba, Soleimani
    (D)   Rhee, Tbahi
    (E)   Fuentes, Soleimani

4. If Garibaldi's meeting with Rhee is the very next one after Garibaldi's meeting with Soleimani, then which one of the following must be true?

    (A)   Garibaldi's third meeting is with Fuentes.
    (B)   Garibaldi's fourth meeting is with Rhee.
    (C)   Garibaldi's fifth meeting is with Fuentes.
    (D)   Garibaldi's sixth meeting is with Rhee.
    (E)   Garibaldi's seventh meeting is with Fuentes.

5. If Garibaldi's first meeting is with Tbahi, then Garibaldi's meeting with Rhee could be the

    (A)   second meeting
    (B)   third meeting
    (C)   fifth meeting
    (D)   sixth meeting
    (E)   seventh meeting

6. If Garibaldi's meeting with Matsuba is the very next meeting after Garibaldi's meeting with Rhee, then with which one of the following dignitaries must Garibaldi's fourth meeting be?

    (A)   Fuentes
    (B)   Matsuba
    (C)   Rhee
    (D)   Soleimani
    (E)   Tbahi

GO ON TO THE NEXT PAGE.

Questions 7–12

During a certain week, an animal shelter places exactly six dogs—a greyhound, a husky, a keeshond, a Labrador retriever, a poodle, and a schnauzer—with new owners. Two are placed on Monday, two on Tuesday, and the remaining two on Wednesday, consistent with the following conditions:

The Labrador retriever is placed on the same day as the poodle.

The greyhound is not placed on the same day as the husky.

If the keeshond is placed on Monday, the greyhound is placed on Tuesday.

If the schnauzer is placed on Wednesday, the husky is placed on Tuesday.

7. Which one of the following could be a complete and accurate matching of dogs to the days on which they are placed?

(A) Monday: greyhound, Labrador retriever
Tuesday: husky, poodle
Wednesday: keeshond, schnauzer

(B) Monday: greyhound, keeshond
Tuesday: Labrador retriever, poodle
Wednesday: husky, schnauzer

(C) Monday: keeshond, schnauzer
Tuesday: greyhound, husky
Wednesday: Labrador retriever, poodle

(D) Monday: Labrador retriever, poodle
Tuesday: greyhound, keeshond
Wednesday: husky, schnauzer

(E) Monday: Labrador retriever, poodle
Tuesday: husky, keeshond
Wednesday: greyhound, schnauzer

8. Which one of the following must be true?

(A) The keeshond is not placed on the same day as the greyhound.

(B) The keeshond is not placed on the same day as the schnauzer.

(C) The schnauzer is not placed on the same day as the husky.

(D) The greyhound is placed on the same day as the schnauzer.

(E) The husky is placed on the same day as the keeshond.

9. If the poodle is placed on Tuesday, then which one of the following could be true?

(A) The greyhound is placed on Monday.
(B) The keeshond is placed on Monday.
(C) The Labrador retriever is placed on Monday.
(D) The husky is placed on Tuesday.
(E) The schnauzer is placed on Wednesday.

10. If the greyhound is placed on the same day as the keeshond, then which one of the following must be true?

(A) The husky is placed on Monday.
(B) The Labrador retriever is placed on Monday.
(C) The keeshond is placed on Tuesday.
(D) The poodle is not placed on Wednesday.
(E) The schnauzer is not placed on Wednesday.

11. If the husky is placed the day before the schnauzer, then which one of the following CANNOT be true?

(A) The husky is placed on Monday.
(B) The keeshond is placed on Monday.
(C) The greyhound is placed on Tuesday.
(D) The poodle is placed on Tuesday.
(E) The poodle is placed on Wednesday.

12. If the greyhound is placed the day before the poodle, then which one of the following CANNOT be placed on Tuesday?

(A) the husky
(B) the keeshond
(C) the Labrador retriever
(D) the poodle
(E) the schnauzer

GO ON TO THE NEXT PAGE.

Questions 13–17

A tour group plans to visit exactly five archaeological sites. Each site was discovered by exactly one of the following archaeologists—Ferrara, Gallagher, Oliphant—and each dates from the eighth, ninth, or tenth century (A.D.). The tour must satisfy the following conditions:

The site visited second dates from the ninth century.
Neither the site visited fourth nor the site visited fifth was discovered by Oliphant.
Exactly one of the sites was discovered by Gallagher, and it dates from the tenth century.
If a site dates from the eighth century, it was discovered by Oliphant.
The site visited third dates from a more recent century than does either the site visited first or that visited fourth.

13. Which one of the following could be an accurate list of the discoverers of the five sites, listed in the order in which the sites are visited?

   (A)   Oliphant, Oliphant, Gallagher, Oliphant, Ferrara
   (B)   Gallagher, Oliphant, Ferrara, Ferrara, Ferrara
   (C)   Oliphant, Gallagher, Oliphant, Ferrara, Ferrara
   (D)   Oliphant, Oliphant, Gallagher, Ferrara, Gallagher
   (E)   Ferrara, Oliphant, Gallagher, Ferrara, Ferrara

14. If exactly one of the five sites the tour group visits dates from the tenth century, then which one of the following CANNOT be a site that was discovered by Ferrara?

   (A)   the site visited first
   (B)   the site visited second
   (C)   the site visited third
   (D)   the site visited fourth
   (E)   the site visited fifth

15. Which one of the following could be a site that dates from the eighth century?

   (A)   the site visited first
   (B)   the site visited second
   (C)   the site visited third
   (D)   the site visited fourth
   (E)   the site visited fifth

16. Which one of the following is a complete and accurate list of the sites each of which CANNOT be the site discovered by Gallagher?

   (A)   third, fourth, fifth
   (B)   second, third, fourth
   (C)   first, fourth, fifth
   (D)   first, second, fifth
   (E)   first, second, fourth

17. The tour group could visit at most how many sites that were discovered by Ferrara?

   (A)   one
   (B)   two
   (C)   three
   (D)   four
   (E)   five

GO ON TO THE NEXT PAGE.

Questions 18–22

Each day of a five-day workweek (Monday through Friday), Anastasia parks for the entire day in exactly one of three downtown parking lots—X, Y, and Z. One of the lots costs $10 for the day, another costs $12, and the other costs $15. Anastasia parks in each of the three lots at least once during her workweek. The following conditions must apply:

On Thursday, Anastasia parks in the $15 lot.
Lot X costs more than lot Z.
The lot Anastasia parks in on Wednesday costs more than the one she parks in on Friday.
Anastasia parks in lot Z on more days of the workweek than she parks in lot X.

18. Which one of the following could be a complete and accurate list of which lot Anastasia parks in each day, listed in order from Monday through Friday?

(A) Y, Z, X, Y, Z
(B) Y, Z, Z, Y, X
(C) Z, Z, X, X, Y
(D) Z, Z, X, X, Z
(E) Z, Z, X, Z, Y

19. Anastasia CANNOT park in the $15 lot on which one of the following days?

(A) Monday
(B) Tuesday
(C) Wednesday
(D) Thursday
(E) Friday

20. If lot Z is the $12 lot, then on which one of the following days must Anastasia park in lot Y?

(A) Monday
(B) Tuesday
(C) Wednesday
(D) Thursday
(E) Friday

21. Anastasia CANNOT park in lot Z on which one of the following days?

(A) Monday
(B) Tuesday
(C) Wednesday
(D) Thursday
(E) Friday

22. Which one of the following could be a complete and accurate list of the days on which Anastasia parks in the $10 lot?

(A) Monday
(B) Tuesday
(C) Monday, Tuesday
(D) Monday, Wednesday
(E) Monday, Thursday

S T O P
IF YOU FINISH BEFORE TIME IS CALLED, YOU MAY CHECK YOUR WORK ON THIS SECTION ONLY.
DO NOT WORK ON ANY OTHER SECTION IN THE TEST.

SECTION IV
Time—35 minutes
26 Questions

Directions: The questions in this section are based on the reasoning contained in brief statements or passages. For some questions, more than one of the choices could conceivably answer the question. However, you are to choose the best answer; that is, the response that most accurately and completely answers the question. You should not make assumptions that are by commonsense standards implausible, superfluous, or incompatible with the passage. After you have chosen the best answer, blacken the corresponding space on your answer sheet.

1. Jones fell unconscious on the job and it was suspected that he had swallowed a certain chemical, so he was rushed to the local hospital's emergency room. In making her diagnosis, the emergency-room physician knew that if Jones had swallowed the chemical, a deficiency in the content of a mineral in his blood would result. She also knew that deficiency in the mineral causes inflammation of the skin. Since Jones's skin was not inflamed when he was admitted to the emergency room, the physician concluded that Jones had not swallowed the chemical.

    Which one of the following, if true, would undermine the physician's conclusion?

    (A) Jones did not know that the chemical was dangerous.
    (B) Jones had suffered inflammation of the skin in the past.
    (C) It takes 48 hours for the chemical to bring about deficiency of the mineral in the blood.
    (D) Jones often worked with the chemical.
    (E) Deficiency in minerals other than the mineral in question can cause inflammation of the skin.

2. Pacifist: It is immoral to do anything that causes harm to another person. But, since using force causes harm to another person, it is also immoral to threaten to use force, even when such a threat is made in self-defense.

    Which one of the following principles, if valid, would most help to justify the pacifist's reasoning?

    (A) Given the potential harm caused by the use of force, the line between use of force in self-defense and the aggressive use of force is always vague.
    (B) It is immoral to threaten to do what it is immoral to do.
    (C) It is immoral to do anything that causes more harm than good.
    (D) Whether a threat made in self-defense is immoral depends on the circumstances.
    (E) It is immoral to carry out a threat if making the threat is itself immoral.

3. Beginning in the 1950s, popular music was revolutionized by the electrification of musical instruments, which has enabled musicians to play with increased volume. Because individual musicians can play with increased volume, the average number of musicians per band has decreased. Nevertheless, electrification has increased rather than decreased the overall number of musicians who play popular music professionally.

    Which one of the following is most strongly supported by the statements above, if those statements are true?

    (A) The number of amateur musicians who play popular music has decreased.
    (B) Most professional musicians are able to play both electric and nonelectric instruments.
    (C) The number of professional musicians in some bands has increased.
    (D) The total number of professional bands has increased as a result of electrification.
    (E) Many professional musicians play in more than one band.

4. Statistics indicating a sudden increase in the incidence of a problem often merely reflect a heightened awareness of the problem or a greater ability to record its occurrence. Hence we should be wary of proposals for radical solutions to problems when those proposals are a reaction to new statistical data.

    The argumentation conforms most closely to which one of the following principles?

    (A) A better cognizance of a problem does not warrant the undertaking of a radical solution to the problem.
    (B) Attempts to stop the occurrence of a problem should be preceded by a determination that the problem actually exists.
    (C) Proposals for radical solutions to problems should be based on statistical data alone.
    (D) Statistical data should not be manipulated to make a radical solution to a problem seem more justified than it actually is.
    (E) Radical solutions to problems can cause other problems and end up doing more harm than good.

GO ON TO THE NEXT PAGE.

5. Barr: The National Tea Association cites tea's recent visibility in advertising and magazine articles as evidence of tea's increasing popularity. However, a neutral polling company, the Survey Group, has tracked tea sales at numerous stores for the last 20 years and has found no change in the amount of tea sold. We can thus conclude that tea is no more popular now than it ever was.

Which one of the following, if true, most seriously weakens Barr's argument?

(A) The National Tea Association has announced that it plans to carry out its own retail survey in the next year.

(B) A survey by an unrelated polling organization shows that the public is generally receptive to the idea of trying new types of tea.

(C) The Survey Group is funded by a consortium of consumer advocacy groups.

(D) The stores from which the Survey Group collected information about tea sales are all located in the same small region of the country.

(E) Tea has been the subject of an expensive and efficient advertising campaign funded, in part, by the National Tea Association.

6. Doctors urge people to reduce their cholesterol levels through dietary changes. But moderate dietary changes often do not work to lower cholesterol levels. One may need, therefore, to make more dramatic changes, such as switching to a vegetarian diet.

The statement that moderate dietary changes often do not work to lower cholesterol levels plays which one of the following roles in the argument?

(A) It is presented to counter doctors' suggestions that cholesterol levels can be reduced through dietary changes.

(B) It is a premise offered in support of the claim that vegetarian diets are more healthful than any diets containing meat.

(C) It is a premise offered in support of the claim that reducing cholesterol levels may require greater than moderate dietary changes.

(D) It is offered as an explanation of the success of vegetarian diets in reducing cholesterol levels.

(E) It is a conclusion for which the claim that dramatic changes in one's diet are sometimes required to reduce cholesterol levels is offered as support.

7. Since empathy is essential for people to be willing to follow moral codes that sometimes require them to ignore their own welfare to help others, civilized society could not exist without empathy.

Which one of the following is an assumption required by the argument?

(A) Civilized society can exist only if there are people who are willing to at least sometimes ignore their own welfare to help others.

(B) Failure to empathize with other people usually leads to actions detrimental to civilized society.

(C) If everyone in a society is sometimes willing to ignore his or her own welfare to help others, that society will be civilized.

(D) Moral codes that include the requirement that people disregard their own welfare in order to help others have arisen within some civilized societies.

(E) People who feel empathy tend to ignore their own welfare for the sake of others.

8. Insurgent political parties that are profoundly dissatisfied with the dominant party's reign and justificatory ideology always produce factions whose views and aims differ as greatly from each other's as they do from the dominant party's. Although these factions ignore their own disagreements for the sake of defeating the dominant party, their disagreements inevitably come forward upon victory. Therefore, _____.

Which one of the following is the most logical completion of the argument?

(A) no victorious insurgent party ever manages to stay in power for as long as the party it displaces did

(B) a victorious insurgent party must address the disagreements between its factions if it is to stay in power

(C) the heretofore insurgent party will not always promulgate a new ideology to justify its own policies, once it is victorious

(D) a victorious insurgent party always faces opposition from the party it recently ousted

(E) it is impossible for the different factions of a victorious insurgent party to effect the compromises necessary to keep the new party in power

GO ON TO THE NEXT PAGE.

9. Manager: When Sullivan was passed over for promotion, people said that the deciding factor was his being much older than the competition. But this is clearly not the case. Several recent promotions have been given to people older than Sullivan.

The manager's argument is most vulnerable to criticism because it fails to consider the possibility that

(A)   Sullivan was well qualified for the promotion
(B)   age is only one of a number of factors that kept Sullivan from being promoted
(C)   people often associate age with experience and good judgment
(D)   the people older than Sullivan who were promoted had no younger competitors
(E)   Sullivan's employer tries to keep deliberations involving promotion decisions confidential

10. Council member P: Alarmists are those who see an instance of pollution and exaggerate its significance into a major character fault of society. Such alarmists fail to distinguish the incident and the behavior that caused it from the disposition of people not to pollute.

Council member Q: To think that there is a lot of pollution based on the discovery of a serious single instance of pollution is simply an application of the widely accepted principle that actions tend to follow the path of least resistance, and it is surely easier to pollute than not to pollute.

Council members P and Q disagree over whether

(A)   pollution should be considered a problem
(B)   actions tend to follow the path of least resistance
(C)   people are responsible for pollution
(D)   people can change their behavior and not pollute
(E)   people are inclined to pollute

11. It is easy to see that the board of directors of the construction company is full of corruption and should be replaced. There are many instances of bribery by various persons on the staff of board member Wagston that are a matter of public record. These bribes perniciously influenced the awarding of government contracts.

The argument's reasoning is most vulnerable to criticism on the grounds that

(A)   the argument fails to show that corruption is not limited to Wagston's staff
(B)   the argument fails to show that Wagston's staff engaged in any bribery other than bribery of government officials
(C)   the argument fails to specify the relation between bribery and corruption
(D)   the argument presumes without giving justification that all of Wagston's staff have engaged in corruption
(E)   the argument attempts to deflect attention away from substantive issues by attacking the character of the board

12. Coffee and tea contain methylxanthines, which cause temporary increases in the natural production of vasopressin, a hormone produced by the pituitary gland. Vasopressin causes clumping of blood cells, and the clumping is more pronounced in women than in men. This is probably the explanation of the fact that women face as much as a tenfold higher risk than men do of complications following angioplasty, a technique used to clear clogged arteries.

Which one of the following statements is most strongly supported by the information above?

(A)   Men, but not women, should be given methylxanthines prior to undergoing angioplasty.
(B)   In spite of the risks, angioplasty is the only effective treatment for clogged arteries.
(C)   Women probably drink more coffee and tea, on average, than do men.
(D)   Prior to undergoing angioplasty, women should avoid coffee and tea.
(E)   Angioplasty should not be used to treat clogged arteries.

GO ON TO THE NEXT PAGE.

13. Whether a machine performs its intended function is plain for all to see, but recognition of excellence in art requires a rare subtlety of perception. So whereas engineers usually maintain their composure when their work is being evaluated, artists tend to become anxious under such circumstances.

The reasoning above conforms most closely to which one of the following propositions?

(A) People who have an interest in working as artists are no more likely to have especially anxious personalities than are people who have an interest in working as engineers.

(B) The value of a machine is independent of the feelings of those who create it, while the value of an artwork is not.

(C) Evaluation of the work of engineers should be based on a different set of standards than is evaluation of the work of artists.

(D) People who create things whose success can be easily ascertained worry less about others' opinions of their work than do people who create things whose value cannot be easily ascertained.

(E) Someone who creates a work that cannot be easily evaluated tends to be less confident about its value than are those who evaluate it.

14. Scientists hypothesize that a particular type of fat known as "P-fat" is required for the development of eyesight. Researchers were led to this hypothesis by observing that babies who are fed formulas low in P-fat tend to have worse eyesight than babies fed mother's milk, which is high in P-fat. It has also been shown that babies that are five to six weeks premature tend to have worse eyesight than babies carried to term.

Which one of the following, if true, most supports the scientists' hypothesis?

(A) Adults whose diets lack P-fat tend to have worse eyesight than those whose diets are high in P-fat.

(B) A fetus typically receives high levels of P-fat from the mother during only the last four weeks of pregnancy.

(C) Babies whose mothers have poor eyesight do not tend to have poor eyesight themselves.

(D) Babies generally prefer mother's milk to formulas low in P-fat.

(E) The eyesight of a fetus develops during the last trimester of pregnancy.

15. Artists have different ways of producing contours and hatching, and analysis of these stylistic features can help to distinguish works by a famous artist both from forgeries and from works genuinely by other artists. Indeed, this analysis has shown that many of the drawings formerly attributed to Michelangelo are actually by the artist Giulio Clovio, Michelangelo's contemporary.

If the statements above are true, then which one of the following must also be true?

(A) Contours and hatching are the main features that distinguish the drawing styles of different artists.

(B) Many of the drawings formerly attributed to Michelangelo are actually forgeries.

(C) No forgery can perfectly duplicate the contour and hatching styles of a famous artist.

(D) The contour and hatching styles used to identify the drawings of Clovio cited can be shown to be features of all Clovio's works.

(E) There is an analyzable difference between Clovio's contour and hatching styles and those of Michelangelo.

16. Moralist: Immoral actions are those that harm other people. But since such actions eventually harm those who perform them, those who act immorally do so only through ignorance of some of their actions' consequences rather than through a character defect.

Which one of the following is an assumption required by the moralist's argument?

(A) People ignorant of their actions' consequences cannot be held morally responsible for those consequences.

(B) An action harms those who perform it only if it also eventually harms others.

(C) Only someone with a character defect would knowingly perform actions that eventually harm others.

(D) Those who, in acting immorally, eventually harm themselves do not intend that harm.

(E) None of those who knowingly harm themselves lack character defects.

GO ON TO THE NEXT PAGE.

17. Climatologists believe they know why Earth has undergone a regular sequence of ice ages beginning around 800,000 years ago. Calculations show that Earth's orbit around the Sun has fluctuations that coincide with the ice-age cycles. The climatologists hypothesize that when the fluctuations occur, Earth passes through clouds of cosmic dust that enters the atmosphere; the cosmic dust thereby dims the Sun, resulting in an ice age. They concede, however, that though cosmic dust clouds are common, the clouds would have to be particularly dense in order to have this effect.

Each of the following, if true, would lend support to the climatologists' hypothesis EXCEPT:

(A) Earth did not pass through clouds of cosmic dust earlier than 800,000 years ago.
(B) Two large asteroids collided 800,000 years ago, producing a tremendous amount of dense cosmic dust that continues to orbit the Sun.
(C) Earth's average temperature drops slightly shortly after volcanic eruptions spew large amounts of dust into Earth's atmosphere.
(D) Large bits of cosmic rock periodically enter Earth's atmosphere, raising large amounts of dust from Earth's surface.
(E) Rare trace elements known to be prevalent in cosmic debris have been discovered in layers of sediment whose ages correspond very closely to the occurrence of ice ages.

18. Philosopher: The rational pursuit of happiness is quite different from always doing what one most strongly desires to do. This is because the rational pursuit of happiness must include consideration of long-term consequences, whereas our desires are usually focused on the short term. Moreover, desires are sometimes compulsions, and while ordinary desires result in at least momentary happiness when their goals are attained, compulsions strongly drive a person to pursue goals that offer no happiness even when reached.

If all of the philosopher's statements are true, each of the following could be true EXCEPT:

(A) The majority of people do not have compulsions.
(B) Attaining the goal of any desire results in momentary happiness.
(C) Most people do not pursue happiness rationally.
(D) Most people want more than their own personal happiness.
(E) All actions have long-term consequences.

19. Political scientist: All governments worthy of respect allow their citizens to dissent from governmental policies. No government worthy of respect leaves minorities unprotected. Thus any government that protects minorities permits criticism of its policies.

The flawed pattern of reasoning in which one of the following most closely parallels that in the political scientist's argument?

(A) Politicians are admirable if they put the interests of those they serve above their own interests. So politicians who sometimes ignore the interests of their own constituents in favor of the nation as a whole deserve admiration, for they are putting the interests of those they serve above their own.
(B) All jazz musicians are capable of improvising and no jazz musician is incapable of reading music. Therefore all musicians who can read music can improvise.
(C) Ecosystems with cool, dry climates are populated by large mammals. No ecosystems populated by large mammals have abundant and varied plant life. Thus ecosystems that do not have cool, dry climates have abundant and varied plant life.
(D) Some intellectuals are not socially active, and no intellectual is a professional athlete. Therefore any professional athlete is socially active.
(E) First-person narratives reveal the thoughts of the narrator but conceal those of the other characters. Some third-person narratives reveal the motives of every character. Thus books that rely on making all characters' motives apparent should be written in the third person.

GO ON TO THE NEXT PAGE.

20. Advertisement: Each of the Economic Merit Prize winners from the past 25 years is covered by the Acme retirement plan. Since the winners of the nation's most prestigious award for economists have thus clearly recognized that the Acme plan offers them a financially secure future, it is probably a good plan for anyone with retirement needs similar to theirs.

The advertisement's argumentation is most vulnerable to criticism on which one of the following grounds?

(A) It ignores the possibility that the majority of Economic Merit Prize winners from previous years used a retirement plan other than the Acme plan.

(B) It fails to address adequately the possibility that any of several retirement plans would be good enough for, and offer a financially secure future to, Economic Merit Prize winners.

(C) It appeals to the fact that supposed experts have endorsed the argument's main conclusion, rather than appealing to direct evidence for that conclusion.

(D) It takes for granted that some winners of the Economic Merit Prize have deliberately selected the Acme retirement plan, rather than having had it chosen for them by their employers.

(E) It presumes, without providing justification, that each of the Economic Merit Prize winners has retirement plan needs that are identical to the advertisement's intended audience's retirement plan needs.

21. A small car offers less protection in an accident than a large car does, but since a smaller car is more maneuverable, it is better to drive a small car because then accidents will be less likely.

Which one of the following arguments employs reasoning most similar to that employed by the argument above?

(A) An artist's best work is generally that done in the time before the artist becomes very well known. When artists grow famous and are diverted from artistic creation by demands for public appearances, their artistic work suffers. So artists' achieving great fame can diminish their artistic reputations.

(B) It is best to insist that a child spend at least some time every day reading indoors. Even though it may cause the child some unhappiness to have to stay indoors when others are outside playing, the child can benefit from the time by learning to enjoy books and becoming prepared for lifelong learning.

(C) For this work, vehicles built of lightweight materials are more practical than vehicles built of heavy materials. This is so because while lighter vehicles do not last as long as heavier vehicles, they are cheaper to replace.

(D) Although it is important to limit the amount of sugar and fat in one's diet, it would be a mistake to try to follow a diet totally lacking in sugar and fat. It is better to consume sugar and fat in moderation, for then the cravings that lead to uncontrolled binges will be prevented.

(E) A person who exercises vigorously every day has less body fat than an average person to draw upon in the event of a wasting illness. But one should still endeavor to exercise vigorously every day, because doing so significantly decreases the chances of contracting a wasting illness.

GO ON TO THE NEXT PAGE.

22. Trainer: Research shows that when dogs are neutered in early puppyhood, their leg bones usually do not develop properly. Improper bone development leads in turn to problems with arthritis as dogs grow older. Thus, if you want to protect your dog from arthritis you should not neuter your dog until it is full-grown.

Of the following, which one is a criticism to which the reasoning in the trainer's argument is most vulnerable?

(A) It fails to state exactly what percentage of dogs neutered in early puppyhood experience improper bone development.

(B) It fails to explain the connection between improper bone development and arthritis.

(C) It fails to address the effects of neutering in middle or late puppyhood.

(D) It fails to consider the possibility that the benefits of neutering a dog early might outweigh the risk of arthritis.

(E) It fails to consider the possibility that dogs with properly developed bones can develop arthritis.

23. Political scientist: One of the most interesting dilemmas in contemporary democratic politics concerns the regulation of political campaign spending. People certainly should be free, within broad limits, to spend their money as they choose. On the other hand, candidates who can vastly outspend all rivals have an unfair advantage in publicizing their platforms. Democratic governments have a strong obligation to ensure that all voices have an equal chance to be heard, but governments should not subsidize expensive campaigns for each candidate. The resolution of the dilemma, therefore, is clear: _____.

Which one of the following most logically completes the political scientist's argument?

(A) only candidates with significant campaign resources should be permitted to run for public office

(B) an upper limit on the political campaign spending of each candidate is warranted

(C) government subsidization of all political campaigns at a low percentage of their total cost is warranted

(D) all wealthy persons should be prohibited from spending their own money on political campaigns

(E) each candidate should be allowed to spend as much money on a political campaign as any other candidate chooses to spend

24. Some people have maintained that private ownership of the means of production ultimately destroys any society that sanctions it. This may be true of a less technologically advanced society that must share its economic resources to survive. But since only private ownership of the means of production permits individuals to test new technologies without the majority's consent, a technologically advanced society will actually endanger its survival if the means of production become public property.

The proposition that private ownership of the means of production ultimately destroys any society that sanctions it plays which one of the following roles in the argument above?

(A) It is a generalization that the argument suggests is no more applicable to less technologically advanced societies than to more technologically advanced societies.

(B) It is a hypothesis for whose widespread acceptance the argument offers an explanation.

(C) It is a general hypothesis that the argument suggests is inapplicable to societies more dependent for survival upon the introduction of new technologies than upon the sharing of resources.

(D) It is a contention about the consequences of an economic arrangement that the argument claims is incompatible with the needs of any society.

(E) It is a generalization about societies that according to the argument is true for any society in which the majority of its citizens does not impede the introduction of new technologies.

GO ON TO THE NEXT PAGE.

25. A certain medication that is frequently prescribed to lower a patient's cholesterol level is generally effective. A recent study of 1,000 subjects ranging widely in age indicates, however, that the cholesterol level of someone taking the medication is typically 12 to 15 percent higher than the average for that person's age group.

Which one of the following, if true, most helps to explain how both of the claims made above could be true?

(A) A recently developed cholesterol-lowering medication is more effective than the medication described above.

(B) Another medication is prescribed to treat high cholesterol just as often as the medication described above is.

(C) In most cases, people with high cholesterol levels are not treated with drug therapy but are put on restrictive low-cholesterol diets.

(D) The medication described above is usually prescribed only for people whose cholesterol level is at least 30 percent above the average for their age group.

(E) Within the population as a whole, approximately the same number of people have relatively high cholesterol levels as have relatively low cholesterol levels.

26. Political theorist: For all of its members to be strong in foreign policy, an alliance of countries must respond aggressively to problems. An alliance will do so only if every member of the alliance perceives the problems as grave. But the European Union countries will not all perceive a problem as grave unless they all agree that it threatens their alliance's economy. Thus, not all of the member countries of the European Union will be strong in foreign policy.

The conclusion drawn above follows logically if which one of the following is assumed?

(A) Countries that refuse to join alliances generally respond more aggressively to problems than do countries that do join alliances.

(B) Countries become less aggressive in foreign policy if greater wealth leads them to think that they have more to lose by responding to problems aggressively.

(C) Problems that appear to some member countries of the European Union to threaten the alliance's economy will not appear so to others.

(D) European Union member countries that fail to perceive the economic relevance of problems are generally weak in foreign policy.

(E) Alliances that are economically beneficial for a given country are not necessarily beneficial with regard to foreign policy.

STOP
IF YOU FINISH BEFORE TIME IS CALLED, YOU MAY CHECK YOUR WORK ON THIS SECTION ONLY.
DO NOT WORK ON ANY OTHER SECTION IN THE TEST.

ACKNOWLEDGMENTS

Acknowledgment is made to the following sources from which material has been adapted for use in this test booklet:

Marsha Kideckel, "Pre-Paid Legal Plans: Legal Help for Less or Less Help?" ©October 1989 by Canadian Lawyer.

Patty Limerick, "American Landscape Discovered from the West." ©1992 by the Journal of American History.

Wait for the supervisor's instructions before you open the page to the topic.
Please print and sign your name and write the date in the designated spaces below.

Time: 35 Minutes

General Directions

You will have 35 minutes in which to plan and write an essay on the topic inside. Read the topic and the accompanying directions carefully. You will probably find it best to spend a few minutes considering the topic and organizing your thoughts before you begin writing. In your essay, be sure to develop your ideas fully, leaving time, if possible, to review what you have written. **Do not write on a topic other than the one specified. Writing on a topic of your own choice is not acceptable.**

No special knowledge is required or expected for this writing exercise. Law schools are interested in the reasoning, clarity, organization, language usage, and writing mechanics displayed in your essay. How well you write is more important than how much you write.

Confine your essay to the blocked, lined area on the front and back of the separate Writing Sample Response Sheet. Only that area will be reproduced for law schools. Be sure that your writing is legible.

Both this topic sheet and your response sheet must be turned over to the testing staff before you leave the room.

Topic Code	Print Your Full Name Here		
	Last	First	M.I.

Date	Sign Your Name Here
/ /	

Scratch Paper
Do not write your essay in this space.

LSAT® Writing Sample Topic

Directions: The scenario presented below describes two choices, either one of which can be supported on the basis of the information given. Your essay should consider both choices and argue for one over the other, based on the two specified criteria and the facts provided. There is no "right" or "wrong" choice: a reasonable argument can be made for either.

The program manager of a public television station intends to purchase a documentary program on diabetes and has narrowed the choice down to two programs. Write an argument for purchasing one program over the other, taking into account the following:

- The program manager wants to increase youth awareness of diabetes by engaging a younger audience.
- The program manager wants to air a well-researched and accurate depiction of the challenges of living with diabetes.

"What's Up, Doc?" tells the story of 19-year-old Carlene, a popular rap artist. A physician who worked with Carlene is interviewed, but the documentary focuses primarily on Carlene, her family, and the musicians who work with her. The discussion centers on how Carlene has dealt with her diabetes since it was diagnosed at the age of 14. Carlene explains the innovative and interesting ways she found to integrate the daily monitoring and control of the disease into her very demanding schedule. The program touches on risk factors, warning signs, complications, and self-care skills for managing diabetes. Carlene ends the program by directing a plea to teenagers to learn about the symptoms of diabetes and become more aware of the disease.

"Living with Diabetes" is an investigation of teenagers with diabetes in four different high schools across the country narrated by Andre Smith, a well-known, prizewinning health reporter. Smith interviews a number of students with the disease, along with school administrators and teachers, about the effect of diabetes on the students' lives. He visits local hospitals and counseling centers to interview doctors and psychologists, who outline the various physical and psychological effects of diabetes. The camera also takes viewers to the Diabetes Research Institute's information outreach program, where visitors meet researchers and learn what they are doing to find a cure for the disease. Included in the program are detailed descriptions of treatment options available and their costs, as well as advice about prevention and testing. WP-L024-A

Scratch Paper
Do not write your essay in this space.

LAST NAME (Print)

L

FIRST NAME (Print)

LAST 4 DIGITS OF SOCIAL SECURITY/SOCIAL INSURANCE NO.

MI

TEST CENTER NO.

SIGNATURE _____

M M D D Y Y
TEST DATE

LSAC ACCOUNT NO.

TOPIC CODE

Writing Sample Response Sheet

DO NOT WRITE IN THIS SPACE

Begin your essay in the lined area below.
Continue on the back if you need more space.

COMPUTING YOUR SCORE

Directions:

1. Use the Answer Key on the next page to check your answers.

2. Use the Scoring Worksheet below to compute your raw score.

3. Use the Score Conversion Chart to convert your raw score into the 120-180 scale.

Scoring Worksheet

1. Enter the number of questions you answered correctly in each section.

	Number Correct
SECTION I	_____
SECTION II	_____
SECTION III	_____
SECTION IV	_____

2. Enter the sum here: _____

   This is your Raw Score.

Conversion Chart
For Converting Raw Score to the 120-180 LSAT Scaled Score
LSAT Form G-4LSN61

Reported Score	Raw Score Lowest	Raw Score Highest
180	98	100
179	—*	—*
178	97	97
177	96	96
176	95	95
175	—*	—*
174	94	94
173	93	93
172	92	92
171	91	91
170	90	90
169	89	89
168	88	88
167	87	87
166	85	86
165	84	84
164	82	83
163	81	81
162	80	80
161	78	79
160	76	77
159	75	75
158	73	74
157	72	72
156	70	71
155	68	69
154	67	67
153	65	66
152	63	64
151	61	62
150	60	60
149	58	59
148	56	57
147	54	55
146	53	53
145	51	52
144	49	50
143	47	48
142	46	46
141	44	45
140	42	43
139	41	41
138	39	40
137	37	38
136	36	36
135	34	35
134	32	33
133	31	31
132	29	30
131	28	28
130	26	27
129	25	25
128	23	24
127	22	22
126	20	21
125	19	19
124	17	18
123	16	16
122	15	15
121	14	14
120	0	13

*There is no raw score that will produce this scaled score for this form.

ANSWER KEY

SECTION I

1.	E	8.	C	15.	B	22.	A
2.	D	9.	C	16.	A	23.	C
3.	E	10.	E	17.	C	24.	E
4.	D	11.	E	18.	E	25.	D
5.	C	12.	D	19.	A	26.	B
6.	A	13.	B	20.	D	27.	A
7.	A	14.	B	21.	A		

SECTION II

1.	B	8.	E	15.	D	22.	E
2.	E	9.	C	16.	E	23.	B
3.	C	10.	B	17.	C	24.	E
4.	C	11.	B	18.	D	25.	E
5.	A	12.	A	19.	B		
6.	B	13.	A	20.	B		
7.	D	14.	D	21.	E		

SECTION III

1.	C	8.	B	15.	A	22.	C
2.	D	9.	A	16.	E		
3.	E	10.	E	17.	D		
4.	E	11.	D	18.	A		
5.	D	12.	A	19.	E		
6.	A	13.	E	20.	E		
7.	E	14.	C	21.	D		

SECTION IV

1.	C	8.	B	15.	E	22.	C
2.	B	9.	D	16.	D	23.	B
3.	D	10.	E	17.	D	24.	C
4.	A	11.	A	18.	B	25.	D
5.	D	12.	D	19.	B	26.	C
6.	C	13.	D	20.	D		
7.	A	14.	B	21.	E		

PREPTEST 45
DECEMBER 2004
FORM 5LSN64

SECTION I
Time—35 minutes
26 Questions

<u>Directions:</u> The questions in this section are based on the reasoning contained in brief statements or passages. For some questions, more than one of the choices could conceivably answer the question. However, you are to choose the <u>best</u> answer; that is, the response that most accurately and completely answers the question. You should not make assumptions that are by commonsense standards implausible, superfluous, or incompatible with the passage. After you have chosen the best answer, blacken the corresponding space on your answer sheet.

1. The obsession of economists with consumption as a measure of economic well-being has prevented us from understanding the true nature of economic well-being. We get very little satisfaction out of the fact that our clothing wears out, our automobiles depreciate, and the gasoline in our tanks burns up and must be replaced.

   The author is arguing that

   (A) economic well-being cannot be defined solely in terms of consumption
   (B) satisfaction is possible without consumption
   (C) valid measures of consumption cannot be devised
   (D) modern products are designed for early obsolescence
   (E) satisfaction can provide an adequate quantitative measure of economic well-being

2. Commentator: Many people argue that the release of chlorofluorocarbons into the atmosphere is harming humans by damaging the ozone layer, thus allowing increased amounts of ultraviolet radiation to reach Earth. But 300,000 years ago a supernova greatly damaged the ozone layer, with no significant effect on our earliest ancestors. Because the supernova's disruption was much greater than the estimated effect of chlorofluorocarbons today, there is no reason to think that these chemicals in the atmosphere harm humans in this way.

   Which one of the following, if true, would most seriously weaken the commentator's argument?

   (A) Extraterrestrial influences on the ozone layer tend to occur less often than terrestrial ones.
   (B) Natural events, such as the eruption of volcanoes, continue to damage the ozone layer today.
   (C) Our earliest ancestors possessed genetic characteristics making them more resistant than we are to the harmful effects of ultraviolet radiation.
   (D) The ozone layer regenerates at a slow rate, barring counteractive processes.
   (E) Scientists have discovered that genetic changes occurred in our ancestors during the period in which the supernova affected Earth.

3. A reason Larson cannot do the assignment is that she has an unavoidable scheduling conflict. On the other hand, a reason Franks cannot do the assignment is that he does not quite have the assertiveness the task requires. So, the task must be assigned to Parker, the only supervisor in the shipping department other than Larson and Franks.

   The argument depends on assuming which one of the following?

   (A) Larson has the assertiveness the task requires.
   (B) The task cannot be assigned to anyone other than a supervisor in the shipping department.
   (C) Franks would be assigned the task if Franks had the assertiveness the task requires.
   (D) The task cannot be assigned to anyone who has any kind of scheduling conflict.
   (E) No one who is not a supervisor in the shipping department has the assertiveness this task requires.

GO ON TO THE NEXT PAGE.

4. Columnist: Analysts argue that as baby boomers reach the age of 50, they will begin seriously planning for retirement. This will lead them to switch from being primarily consumers to being savers. Thus, these analysts conclude, more money will flow into the stock market, resulting in continued gains in stock prices. Analysts would stand to gain if this were true, but they are being overly optimistic. As consumption decreases, so will corporate earnings; therefore high stock prices will not be justified, and thus boomers' money will more likely flow into investments other than stocks.

The columnist's argument does which one of the following?

(A) attempts to undermine the analysts' argument by questioning the truth of its premises
(B) attempts to undermine the analysts' argument by suggesting that the analysts present it for self-serving reasons
(C) attempts to undermine the analysts' argument by drawing an alternative conclusion from the analysts' premises
(D) argues that the analysts' conclusion is basically right, but suggests that it is somewhat too optimistic
(E) argues in favor of the analysts' conclusion, but does so on the basis of a different body of evidence

5. Item Removed From Scoring.

6. Maria: Popular music is bad art because it greatly exaggerates the role love plays in everyday life and thereby fails to represent reality accurately.

Theo: Popular music is not supposed to reflect reality; it performs other artistic functions, such as providing consoling fantasies and helping people create some romance in their often difficult lives. You should understand popular music before you condemn it.

The dialogue provides the most support for the claim that Maria and Theo disagree over whether

(A) most good art creates consoling illusions
(B) some bad art exaggerates the role love plays in everyday life
(C) art should always represent reality as it could be, not as it is
(D) art need not represent reality accurately to be good art
(E) popular music should not be considered to be an art form

7. An artificial hormone has recently been developed that increases milk production in cows. Its development has prompted some lawmakers to propose that milk labels should be required to provide information to consumers about what artificial substances were used in milk production. This proposal should not be implemented: just imagine trying to list every synthetic fertilizer used to grow the grass and grain the cows ate, or every fungicide used to keep the grain from spoiling!

The argument proceeds by

(A) proposing an alternative course of action for achieving the objectives of the proposal being argued against
(B) raising considerations in order to show that the proposal being argued against, if strictly implemented, would lead to absurd consequences
(C) using specific examples in order to show that an alternative to the proposal being argued against would better achieve the ends to which the original proposal was directed
(D) introducing a case analogous to the one under consideration to show that a general implementation of the proposal being argued against would be impossible
(E) questioning the motivation of those who made the proposal being argued against

GO ON TO THE NEXT PAGE.

8. Trust, which cannot be sustained in the absence of mutual respect, is essential to any long-lasting relationship, personal or professional. However, personal relationships, such as marriage or friendship, additionally require natural affinity. If a personal relationship is to endure, it must be supported by the twin pillars of mutual respect and affinity.

If the statements above are true, then which one of the following must also be true?

(A) A friendship supported solely by trust and mutual respect will not be long-lasting.

(B) In the context of any professional relationship, mutual respect presupposes trust.

(C) If a personal relationship is supported by mutual respect and affinity, it will last a long time.

(D) Personal relationships, such as marriage or friendship, are longer-lasting than professional relationships.

(E) Basing a marriage on a natural affinity will ensure that it will endure.

9. The use of phrases like "as so-and-so said" or "as the saying goes" suggests that the quote that follows has just been illustrated. Such phrases are inappropriately used when an apparent counterexample has just been given.

Which one of the following contains an inappropriate usage of a phrase, according to the principle stated above?

(A) Fatima was a mathematician who often thought about unsolved problems of mathematics, although it was unpleasant to be reminded that most would probably remain unsolved in her lifetime. As the saying goes, "Strange how much you've got to know before you know how little you know."

(B) Harold's friends were surprised when he revealed that he had left his wallet at home and asked that someone lend him money. But he had done the same thing many times before. As Halliard said, "The force of selfishness is as inevitable and as calculable as the force of gravitation."

(C) The best model of vacuum cleaner was the most expensive on the market, but it would have made Roger unhappy to purchase it. For although he never wanted anything but the best, he was also quite frugal, and would never have forgiven himself for spending the money. As the saying goes, "A penny saved is a penny earned."

(D) Sharon loved cats, but her husband was allergic to them. Still, he was occasionally willing to accompany her to cat shows. As the saying goes, "Shared lives mean shared loves."

(E) Raoul spent a year planning and preparing for a fantastic ski trip. He enjoyed his ski trip greatly until he broke his leg and had to spend two weeks in the hospital. As the saying goes, "All's well that ends well."

GO ON TO THE NEXT PAGE.

10. Rachel: Though contemporary artists are pleased to be free of the constraints that bound their predecessors, this freedom has caused a decline in the quality of art. Great art can be produced only when artists struggle to express themselves within externally imposed boundaries.

James: People have always been critical of the art of their own time. They forget all but the greatest art from past eras. Since inferior contemporary artworks have not yet been forgotten, people today mistakenly think that contemporary art is generally inferior to earlier art.

On the basis of their statements, Rachel and James are committed to disagreeing with each other about whether

(A) contemporary art is of lower quality than earlier art
(B) contemporary artists are bound by the same constraints as their predecessors
(C) great art is produced only when an artist struggles against limitations
(D) inferior art from past eras is generally forgotten
(E) one can correctly assess the quality of art only if it was produced in past eras

11. The average cost of groceries will rise again next month. Consequently, butter and eggs can be expected to cost more next month.

The flawed reasoning in the argument above most closely parallels the reasoning in which one of the following?

(A) The price of gasoline has been rising each month for the past year. Therefore, we can expect to pay more for gasoline next month.
(B) Either the government will reduce taxes or the economy will fall into a recession. The government is unlikely to reduce taxes. Therefore, the economy will fall into a recession.
(C) The average amount of time spent by people younger than 20 in watching television has recently risen rapidly. Therefore, the amount of time fourth graders spend watching television must have risen recently.
(D) Since sugar is a major ingredient in ice cream, the price of ice cream increases whenever the price of sugar increases. The price of sugar is expected to increase next month. Therefore, the price of ice cream can be expected to increase next month.
(E) Real estate prices go down when the population of those from 20 to 30 years old declines, and the number in that age group will decrease over the next decade. Therefore, real estate prices will go down over that period.

12. Biologists have noted reproductive abnormalities in fish that are immediately downstream of paper mills. One possible cause is dioxin, which paper mills release daily and which can alter the concentration of hormones in fish. However, dioxin is unlikely to be the cause, since the fish recover normal hormone concentrations relatively quickly during occasional mill shutdowns and dioxin decomposes very slowly in the environment.

Which one of the following statements, if true, most seriously weakens the argument?

(A) Some of the studies that show that fish recover quickly during shutdowns were funded by paper manufacturers.
(B) The rate at which dioxin decomposes varies depending on the conditions to which it is exposed.
(C) Normal river currents carry the dioxin present in the river far downstream in a few hours.
(D) Some of the fish did not recover rapidly from the physiological changes that were induced by the changes in hormone concentrations.
(E) The connection between hormone concentrations and reproductive abnormalities is not thoroughly understood.

13. If the play were successful, it would be adapted as a movie or revived at the Decade Festival. But it is not successful. We must, regrettably, conclude that it will neither become a movie nor be revived at the Decade Festival.

The argument's reasoning is flawed because the argument

(A) fails to draw the conclusion that the play will not both be adapted as a movie and be revived at the Decade Festival, rather than that it will do neither
(B) fails to explain in exactly what way the play is unsuccessful
(C) equates the play's aesthetic worth with its commercial success
(D) presumes, without providing justification, that there are no further avenues for the play other than adaptation as a movie or revival at the Decade Festival
(E) fails to recognize that the play's not satisfying one sufficient condition does not preclude its satisfying a different sufficient condition for adaptation as a movie or revival at the Decade Festival

GO ON TO THE NEXT PAGE.

14. Physician: In order to investigate diseases caused by hormonal imbalances, a certain researcher wants to study, among others, 200 children whose pituitary glands fail to produce typical amounts of Human Growth Hormone (HGH). The study would involve administering a synthetic version of HGH to the children over a two-year period. But medical research should be permitted only if it is likely to reveal important information about a medical condition and is known to pose only a minimal risk to the subjects. The researcher's proposed study should be prohibited.

Which one of the following, if true, would most help to justify the physician's argumentation?

- (A) The resources expended on the HGH study could be spent instead on research likely to lead to treatments for medical conditions more serious than diseases stemming from hormonal imbalances.
- (B) About 10,000 children have already been given synthetic HGH without obvious side effects.
- (C) Obtaining informed consent from children is impossible, because they are not yet mature enough to understand complex medical issues.
- (D) Although hormonal imbalances can cause disease, the imbalances themselves do not constitute a medical condition.
- (E) The long-term effects of synthetic HGH have never been tested and are unknown.

15. At the request of Grove Park residents, speed bumps were installed on all streets in their neighborhood. However, although through traffic does cause noise and congestion in Grove Park, this remedy is blatantly unfair. The neighborhood is not a private community, and its streets were built with public funds, and thus all drivers have the right to use them whenever they please.

The reasoning in the argument is most vulnerable to criticism on the grounds that it

- (A) ignores the possibility that speed bumps may not reduce the speeds at which drivers drive through the neighborhood
- (B) neglects the possibility that drivers frequently drive through the neighborhood at high speeds
- (C) provides no evidence that drivers have complained about the new speed bumps in the neighborhood
- (D) contains the tacit assumption that residents of neighborhoods should have the right to restrict traffic through their communities
- (E) presumes, without providing justification, that speed bumps do prevent drivers from using the roads on which the bumps are found

16. Literary critic: Often the heirs of a successful writer decide to publish the manuscripts and the letters the dead writer left behind, regardless of the merit of the work. However, many writers have manuscripts that they judge to be unworthy of publication and with which they would not like to be publicly associated even after they die. Hence a successful writer who decides not to publish a recently completed manuscript should destroy it immediately.

Which one of the following statements, if true, most calls into question the soundness of the literary critic's advice?

- (A) Some writers whose work becomes both popular and respected after they die received no literary recognition during their lifetimes.
- (B) Writers who achieve a certain degree of fame can expect that some of their personal correspondence will become publicly available after they die.
- (C) Most successful writers' judgments of their recently completed work is unnecessarily harsh and is often later revised.
- (D) Many posthumously published books would have been published by the author had the author lived.
- (E) Some heirs of successful writers do not consider themselves qualified to judge the merits of a literary work.

17. In practice the government will have the last word on what an individual's rights are, because its police will do what its officials and courts say. But that does not mean that the government's view is necessarily the correct view; anyone who thinks it is must believe that persons have only such moral rights as the government chooses to grant, which means that they have no moral rights at all.

Which one of the following most accurately expresses the conclusion of the argument?

- (A) Individuals have no rights at all unless the government says that they do.
- (B) What government officials and courts say an individual's rights are may not be correct.
- (C) Individuals have rights unless the government says that they do not.
- (D) The police always agree with government officials and the courts about what an individual's rights are.
- (E) One should always try to uphold one's individual rights against the government's view of what those rights are.

GO ON TO THE NEXT PAGE.

18. There is evidence to suggest that our cave-dwelling ancestors polished many of their flints to a degree far surpassing what was necessary for hunting purposes. It seems, therefore, that early humans possessed an aesthetic sense.

Which one of the following statements, if true, most seriously weakens the argument?

(A) Most flints used by our cave-dwelling ancestors were not highly polished.
(B) The caves in which the highly polished flints were found are unadorned by cave paintings.
(C) There is evidence that these highly polished flints were used for display in religious ceremonies.
(D) Flints were often used by early humans for everyday chores other than hunting.
(E) Any benefits that an aesthetic sense would have given to cave-dwelling humans are poorly understood.

19. Columnist: Much of North America and western Europe is more heavily forested and has less acid rain and better air quality now than five decades ago. Though this may be due largely to policies advocated by environmentalists, it nonetheless lends credibility to the claims of people who reject predictions of imminent ecological doom and argue that environmental policies that excessively restrict the use of natural resources may diminish the wealth necessary to adopt and sustain the policies that brought about these improvements.

Which one of the following, if true, most strengthens the columnist's reasoning?

(A) Nations sustain their wealth largely through industrial use of the natural resources found within their boundaries.
(B) The more advanced the technology used in a nation's industries, the greater is that nation's ability to devote a portion of its resources to social programs.
(C) A majority of ecological disasters arise from causes that are beyond human control.
(D) If a compromise between the proponents of economic growth and the environmentalists had been enacted rather than the current policies, the environment would have seen significantly less improvement.
(E) The concern demonstrated by a nation for the health and integrity of its natural ecosystems leads to an increase in that nation's wealth.

20. Reviewer: Many historians claim, in their own treatment of subject matter, to be as little affected as any natural scientist by moral or aesthetic preconceptions. But we clearly cannot accept these proclamations of objectivity, for it is easy to find instances of false historical explanations embodying the ideological and other prejudices of their authors.

The reviewer's reasoning is most vulnerable to criticism on the grounds that it

(A) takes for granted that the model of objectivity offered by the natural sciences should apply in other fields
(B) offers evidence that undermines rather than supports the conclusion it reaches
(C) fails to recognize that many historians employ methodologies that are intended to uncover and compensate for prejudices
(D) takes for granted that some historical work that embodies prejudices is written by historians who purport to be objective
(E) fails to recognize that not all historical explanations embodying ideologies are false

21. Although the geological record contains some hints of major meteor impacts preceding mass extinctions, there were many extinctions that did not follow any known major meteor impacts. Likewise, there are many records of major meteor impacts that do not seem to have been followed by mass extinctions. Thus the geological record suggests that there is no consistent causal link between major meteor impacts and mass extinctions.

Which one of the following assumptions enables the argument's conclusion to be properly inferred?

(A) If there were a consistent causal link between major meteor impacts and mass extinctions, then all major meteor impacts would be followed by mass extinctions.
(B) Major meteor impacts and mass extinctions cannot be consistently causally linked unless many mass extinctions have followed major meteor impacts.
(C) Of the mass extinctions that did not follow any known major meteor impacts, few if any followed major meteor impacts of which the geological record contains no hints.
(D) If there is no consistent causal link between major meteor impacts and mass extinctions, then not all mass extinctions could have followed major meteor impacts.
(E) There could be a consistent causal link between major meteor impacts and mass extinctions even if not every major meteor impact has been followed by a mass extinction.

GO ON TO THE NEXT PAGE.

22. When uncontrollable factors such as lack of rain cause farmers' wheat crops to fail, fertilizer and seed dealers, as well as truckers and mechanics, lose business, and fuel suppliers are unable to sell enough diesel fuel to make a profit.

Which one of the following claims follows logically from the information above?

(A) If several of the businesses that sell to farmers do not prosper, it is because farming itself is not prospering.

(B) If rainfall is below average, those businesses that profit from farmers' purchases tend to lose money.

(C) Farmers are not responsible for the consequences of a wheat crop's failing if wheat growth has been affected by lack of rain.

(D) A country's dependence on agriculture can lead to major economic crises.

(E) The consequences of a drought are not restricted to the drought's impact on farm productivity.

23. For each action we perform, we can know only some of its consequences. Thus the view that in no situation can we know what action is morally right would be true if an action's being morally right were the same as the action's having the best consequences.

The conclusion follows logically if which one of the following is assumed?

(A) On some occasions we can come to learn that it is morally wrong to perform a certain action.

(B) On some occasions we can know what action is morally right.

(C) Knowing that an action has the best consequences requires knowing all the consequences of that action.

(D) Only the immediate consequences of our actions are relevant in determining whether they are morally right.

(E) An action may be morally right for one particular person without being morally right for all people.

24. In criminal proceedings, defense attorneys occasionally attempt to establish that a suspect was not present at the commission of a crime by comparing the suspect's DNA to the DNA of blood or hair samples taken from the scene of the crime. Although every person's DNA is unique, DNA tests often fail to distinguish among DNA samples taken from distinct individuals. Hence, it is a mistake to exonerate a suspect simply because that person's DNA did not match the DNA samples taken from the scene of the crime.

Which one of the following is an error in the reasoning above?

(A) It assumes without warrant that the use of physical evidence in identifying suspects is never mistaken.

(B) It confuses a test that incorrectly identifies DNA samples as coming from the same person with a test that incorrectly shows as coming from different persons samples that come from a single person.

(C) It generalizes about the reliability of all methods used to identify those involved in the commission of a crime on the basis of results that pertain to only a few such methods.

(D) It relies on experimental data derived from DNA testing that have not been shown to hold under nonexperimental conditions.

(E) It fails to demonstrate that physical evidence taken from the scene of a crime is the only sort of evidence that should be admitted in criminal court proceedings.

GO ON TO THE NEXT PAGE.

25. Some visitors to the park engage in practices that seriously harm the animals. Surely, no one who knew that these practices seriously harm the animals would engage in them. So it must be concluded that some of the visitors do not know that these practices seriously harm the animals.

The pattern of reasoning exhibited by which one of the following arguments is most similar to that exhibited by the argument above?

(A)   Some of the people who worked on the failed project will be fired. Everyone in this department played an important part in that project. Therefore some people in this department will be fired.

(B)   Some of the people who signed the petition were among the mayor's supporters. Yet the mayor denounced everyone who signed the petition. Hence the mayor denounced some of her own supporters.

(C)   Some of the people polled live outside the city limits. However, no one who can vote in city elections lives outside the city. Therefore some of the people polled cannot vote in the upcoming city election.

(D)   All of the five original planners are responsible for this problem. Yet none of the original planners will admit responsibility for the problem. Thus some of the people responsible for the problem will not admit responsibility.

(E)   Some members of the Liberal Party are in favor of the proposed ordinance. But all members of the city council are opposed to the proposed ordinance. Hence some members of the city council are not Liberals.

26. Rapid population growth can be disastrous for a small city. Ideally there should be at least one municipal employee for every hundred residents; when too many people move in at once, city services responsible for utilities and permits are quickly overloaded. Most city budgets do not allow for the immediate hiring of new staff.

Which one of the following, if true, most strengthens the argument?

(A)   During budget shortages, small cities tend to place a high priority on basic municipal services while cutting back on less essential services.

(B)   New residents of any city bring with them new ideas about how a city should be run.

(C)   Some large cities can absorb rapid population growth more readily than many small cities can.

(D)   A low unemployment rate is one of the main reasons that new residents move to a city.

(E)   New residents of most small cities do not start paying city taxes for at least a year.

S T O P
IF YOU FINISH BEFORE TIME IS CALLED, YOU MAY CHECK YOUR WORK ON THIS SECTION ONLY.
DO NOT WORK ON ANY OTHER SECTION IN THE TEST.

SECTION II

Time—35 minutes

27 Questions

Directions: Each set of questions in this section is based on a single passage or a pair of passages. The questions are to be answered on the basis of what is <u>stated</u> or <u>implied</u> in the passage or pair of passages. For some of the questions, more than one of the choices could conceivably answer the question. However, you are to choose the <u>best</u> answer; that is, the response that most accurately and completely answers the question, and blacken the corresponding space on your answer sheet.

A number of natural disasters in recent years—
such as earthquakes, major storms, and floods—that
have affected large populations of people have forced
relief agencies, communities, and entire nations to
(5)   reevaluate the ways in which they respond in the
aftermaths of such disasters. They believe that
traditional ways of dealing with disasters have proved
ineffective on several occasions and, in some cases,
have been destructive rather than helpful to the
(10) communities hit by these sudden and unexpected
crises. Traditionally, relief has been based on the
premise that aid in postdisaster situations is most
effective if given in the immediate aftermath of an
event. A high priority also has been placed on the
(15) quantity of aid materials, programs, and personnel, in
the belief that the negative impact of a disaster can
be counteracted by a large and rapid infusion of aid.
       Critics claim that such an approach often creates
a new set of difficulties for already hard-hit
(20) communities. Teams of uninvited experts and
personnel—all of whom need food and shelter—as
well as uncoordinated shipments of goods and the
establishment of programs inappropriate to local
needs can quickly lead to a secondary "disaster" as
(25) already strained local infrastructures break down
under the pressure of this large influx of resources. In
some instances, tons of food have disappeared into
local markets for resale, and, with inadequate
accounting procedures, billions of dollars in aid
(30) money have gone unaccounted for.
       To develop a more effective approach, experts
recommend shifting the focus to the long term. A
response that produces lasting benefit, these experts
claim, requires that community members define the
(35) form and method of aid that are most appropriate to
their needs. Grassroots dialogue designed to facilitate
preparedness should be encouraged in disaster-prone
communities long before the onset of a crisis, so that
in a disaster's immediate aftermath, relief agencies
(40) can rely on members of affected communities to take
the lead. The practical effect of this approach is that
aid takes the form of a response to the stated desires
of those affected rather than an immediate, though
less informed, action on their behalf.
(45)   Though this proposal appears sound, its success
depends on how an important constituency,
namely donors, will respond. Historically,
donors—individuals, corporations, foundations, and
governmental bodies—have been most likely to
(50) respond only in the immediate aftermath of a crisis.

However, communities affected by disasters typically
have several long-term needs such as the rebuilding
of houses and roads, and thus the months and years
after a disaster are also crucial. Donors that
(55) incorporate dialogue with members of affected
communities into their relief plans could foster
strategies that more efficiently utilize immediate aid
as well as provide for the difficulties facing
communities in the years after a disaster.

1. Which one of the following most accurately expresses the
    main point of the passage?

    (A)   The most useful response to a natural disaster is
          one in which relief agencies allow victims to
          dictate the type of aid they receive, which will
          most likely result in the allocation of long-term
          rather than immediate aid.

    (B)   The quantity of aid given after a natural disaster
          reflects the desires of donors more than the
          needs of recipients, and in some cases great
          quantities of aid are destructive rather than
          helpful.

    (C)   Aid that focuses on long-term needs is difficult
          to organize because, by its very definition,
          it requires that relief agencies focus on
          constructing an adequate dialogue among
          recipients, providers, and donors.

    (D)   Disaster relief efforts have been marked by
          inefficiencies that attest to the need for donors
          and relief agencies to communicate with
          affected communities concerning how best to
          meet not only their short-term but also their
          long-term needs.

    (E)   Though the years after a disaster are crucial
          for communities affected by disasters, the
          days and weeks immediately after a disaster
          are what capture the attention of donors, thus
          forcing relief agencies into the role of mediators
          between the two extremes.

GO ON TO THE NEXT PAGE.

2. Which one of the following examples best illustrates the type of disaster response recommended by the experts mentioned in the third paragraph?

(A) After a flood, local officials reject three more expensive proposals before finally accepting a contractor's plan to control a local river with a dam.

(B) Following a plan developed several years ago by a relief agency in consultation with donors and community members, the relief agency provides temporary shelter immediately after a flood and later helps rebuild houses destroyed by the flood.

(C) Immediately after a flood, several different relief agencies, each acting independently, send large shipments of goods to the affected community along with teams of highly motivated but untrained volunteers to coordinate the distribution of these goods.

(D) At the request of its donors, a private relief agency delays providing any assistance to victims of a flood until after the agency conducts a thorough study of the types of aid most likely to help the affected community in the long run.

(E) After a flood, government officials persuade local companies to increase their corporate giving levels and to direct more aid to the surrounding community.

3. The author of the passage would be most likely to agree with which one of the following statements?

(A) Disaster relief plans are appropriate only for disaster-prone communities.

(B) When communities affected by disasters have articulated their long-term needs, donors typically have been responsive to those needs.

(C) Donors would likely provide more disaster relief aid if they had confidence that it would be used more effectively than aid currently is.

(D) It is not the amount of aid but rather the way this aid is managed that is the source of current problems in disaster relief.

(E) Few communities affected by disasters experience a crucial need for short-term aid.

4. The author discusses donors in the final paragraph primarily in order to

(A) point to an influential group of people who have resisted changes to traditional disaster response efforts

(B) demonstrate that the needs of donors and aid recipients contrast profoundly on the issue of disaster response

(C) show that implementing an effective disaster relief program requires a new approach on the part of donors as well as relief agencies

(D) illustrate that relief agencies and donors share similar views on the goals of disaster response but disagree on the proper response methods

(E) concede that the reformation of disaster relief programs, while necessary, is unlikely to take place because of the disagreements among donors

5. It can be inferred from the passage that the author would be most likely to view a shift toward a more long-term perspective in disaster relief efforts as which one of the following?

(A) a development that would benefit affected communities as well as aid providers who have a shared interest in relief efforts that are effective and well managed

(B) a change that would help communities meet their future needs more effectively but would inevitably result in a detrimental reduction of short-term aid like food and medicine

(C) an approach that would enable aid recipients to meet their long-term needs but which would not address the mismanagement that hampers short-term relief efforts

(D) a movement that, while well intentioned, will likely be undermined by the unwillingness of donors to accept new methods of delivering aid

(E) the beginning of a trend in which aid recipients play a major role after a disaster and donors play a minor role, reversing the structure of traditional aid programs

6. Which one of the following inferences about natural disasters and relief efforts is most strongly supported by the passage?

(A) Although inefficiencies have long been present in international disaster relief programs, they have been aggravated in recent years by increased demands on relief agencies' limited resources.

(B) Local communities had expressed little interest in taking responsibility for their own preparedness prior to the most recent years, thus leaving donors and relief agencies unaware of potential problems.

(C) Numerous relief efforts in the years prior to the most recent provided such vast quantities of aid that most needs were met despite evidence of inefficiency and mismanagement, and few recipient communities questioned traditional disaster response methods.

(D) Members of communities affected by disasters have long argued that they should set the agenda for relief efforts, but relief agencies have only recently come to recognize the validity of their arguments.

(E) A number of wasteful relief efforts in the most recent years provided dramatic illustrations of aid programs that were implemented by donors and agencies with little accountability to populations affected by disasters.

GO ON TO THE NEXT PAGE.

The moral precepts embodied in the Hippocratic oath, which physicians standardly affirm upon beginning medical practice, have long been considered the immutable bedrock of medical ethics,

(5) binding physicians in a moral community that reaches across temporal, cultural, and national barriers. Until very recently the promises expressed in that oath—for example to act primarily for the benefit and not the harm of patients and to conform to various standards

(10) of professional conduct including the preservation of patients' confidences—even seemed impervious to the powerful scientific and societal forces challenging it. Critics argue that the oath is outdated; its fixed moral rules, they say, are incompatible with more flexible

(15) modern ideas about ethics. It also encourages doctors to adopt an authoritarian stance that depreciates the privacy and autonomy of the patient. Furthermore, its emphasis on the individual patient without regard for the wider social context frustrates the physician's

(20) emerging role as gatekeeper in managed care plans and impedes competitive market forces, which, some critics believe, should determine the quality, price, and distribution of health care as they do those of other commodities. The oath is also faulted for its

(25) omissions: its failure to mention such vital contemporary issues as human experimentation and the relationships of physicians to other health professionals. Some respected opponents even cite historical doubts about the oath's origin and

(30) authorship, presenting evidence that it was formulated by a small group of reformist physicians in ancient Greece and that for centuries it was not uniformly accepted by medical practitioners.

This historical issue may be dismissed at the

(35) outset as irrelevant to the oath's current appropriateness. Regardless of the specific origin of its text—which, admittedly, is at best uncertain—those in each generation who critically appraise its content and judge it to express valid

(40) principles of medical ethics become, in a more meaningful sense, its authors. More importantly, even the more substantive, morally based arguments concerning contemporary values and newly relevant issues cannot negate the patients' need for assurance

(45) that physicians will pursue appropriate goals in treatment in accordance with generally acceptable standards of professionalism. To fulfill that need, the core value of beneficence—which does not actually conflict with most reformers' purposes—should be

(50) retained, with adaptations at the oath's periphery by some combination of revision, supplementation, and modern interpretation. In fact, there is already a tradition of peripheral reinterpretation of traditional wording; for example, the oath's vaguely and

(55) archaically worded proscription against "cutting for the stone" may once have served to forbid surgery, but with today's safer and more effective surgical techniques it is understood to function as a promise to practice within the confines of one's expertise,

(60) which remains a necessary safeguard for patients' safety and well-being.

7. Which one of the following most accurately states the main point of the passage?

(A) The Hippocratic oath ought to be reevaluated carefully, with special regard to the role of the physician, to make certain that its fundamental moral rules still apply today.

(B) Despite recent criticisms of the Hippocratic oath, some version of it that will continue to assure patients of physicians' professionalism and beneficent treatment ought to be retained.

(C) Codes of ethics developed for one society at a particular point in history may lose some specific application in later societies but can retain a useful fundamental moral purpose.

(D) Even the criticisms of the Hippocratic oath based on contemporary values and newly relevant medical issues cannot negate patients' need for assurance.

(E) Modern ideas about ethics, especially medical ethics, obviate the need for and appropriateness of a single code of medical ethics like the Hippocratic oath.

8. Which one of the following most accurately describes the organization of the material presented in the passage?

(A) A general principle is described, criticisms of the principle are made, and modifications of the principle are made in light of these criticisms.

(B) A set of criticisms is put forward, and possible replies to those criticisms are considered and dismissed.

(C) The history of a certain code of conduct is discussed, criticisms of the code are mentioned and partially endorsed, and the code is modified as a response.

(D) A general principle is formulated, a partial defense of that principle is presented, and criticisms of the principle are discussed and rejected.

(E) The tradition surrounding a certain code of conduct is discussed, criticisms of that code are mentioned, and a general defense of the code is presented.

GO ON TO THE NEXT PAGE.

9. The passage cites which one of the following as a value at the heart of the Hippocratic oath that should present no difficulty to most reformers?

   (A) creation of a community of physicians from all eras, nations, and cultures
   (B) constant improvement and advancement of medical science
   (C) provision of medical care to all individuals regardless of ability to pay
   (D) physician action for the benefit of patients
   (E) observance of established moral rules even in the face of challenging societal forces

10. The author's primary purpose in the passage is to

   (A) affirm society's continuing need for a code embodying certain principles
   (B) chastise critics within the medical community who support reinterpretation of a code embodying certain principles
   (C) argue that historical doubts about the origin of a certain code are irrelevant to its interpretation
   (D) outline the pros and cons of revising a code embodying certain principles
   (E) propose a revision of a code embodying certain principles that will increase the code's applicability to modern times

11. Based on information in the passage, it can be inferred that which one of the following sentences could most logically be added to the passage as a concluding sentence?

   (A) The fact that such reinterpretations are so easy, however, suggests that our rejection of the historical issue was perhaps premature.
   (B) Yet, where such piecemeal reinterpretation is not possible, revisions to even the core value of the oath may be necessary.
   (C) It is thus simply a failure of the imagination, and not any changes in the medical profession or society in general, that has motivated critics of the Hippocratic oath.
   (D) Because of this tradition of reinterpretation of the Hippocratic oath, therefore, modern ideas about medical ethics must be much more flexible than they have been in the past.
   (E) Despite many new challenges facing the medical profession, therefore, there is no real need for wholesale revision of the Hippocratic oath.

12. Each of the following is mentioned in the passage as a criticism of the Hippocratic oath EXCEPT:

   (A) The oath encourages authoritarianism on the part of physicians.
   (B) The version of the oath in use today is not identical to the oath formulated in ancient Greece.
   (C) The oath fails to address modern medical dilemmas that could not have been foreseen in ancient Greece.
   (D) The oath's absolutism is incompatible with contemporary views of morality.
   (E) The oath's emphasis on the individual patient is often not compatible with a market-driven medical industry.

13. Which one of the following can most accurately be used to describe the author's attitude toward critics of the Hippocratic oath?

   (A) enthusiastic support
   (B) bemused dismissal
   (C) reasoned disagreement
   (D) strict neutrality
   (E) guarded agreement

14. Which one of the following would be most suitable as a title for this passage if it were to appear as an editorial piece?

   (A) "The Ancients versus the Moderns: Conflicting Ideas About Medical Ethics"
   (B) "Hypocritical Oafs: Why `Managed Care' Proponents are Seeking to Repeal an Ancient Code"
   (C) "Genetic Fallacy in the Age of Gene-Splicing: Why the Origins of the Hippocratic Oath Don't Matter"
   (D) "The Dead Hand of Hippocrates: Breaking the Hold of Ancient Ideas on Modern Medicine"
   (E) "Prescription for the Hippocratic Oath: Facelift or Major Surgery?"

GO ON TO THE NEXT PAGE.

A lichen consists of a fungus living in symbiosis (i.e., a mutually beneficial relationship) with an alga. Although most branches of the complex evolutionary family tree of fungi have been well established, the
(5) evolutionary origins of lichen-forming fungi have been a mystery. But a new DNA study has revealed the relationship of lichen-forming fungi to several previously known branches of the fungus family tree. The study reveals that, far from being oddities,
(10) lichen-forming fungi are close relatives of such common fungi as brewer's yeast, morel mushrooms, and the fungus that causes Dutch elm disease. This accounts for the visible similarity of certain lichens to more recognizable fungi such as mushrooms.

(15) In general, fungi present complications for the researcher. Fungi are usually parasitic or symbiotic, and researchers are often unsure whether they are examining fungal DNA or that of the associated organism. But lichen-forming fungi are especially
(20) difficult to study. They have few distinguishing characteristics of shape or structure, and they are unusually difficult to isolate from their partner algae, with which they have a particularly delicate symbiosis. In some cases the alga is wedged between
(25) layers of fungal tissue; in others, the fungus grows through the alga's cell walls in order to take nourishment, and the tissues of the two organisms are entirely enmeshed and inseparable. As a result, lichen-forming fungi have long been difficult to
(30) classify definitively within the fungus family. By default they were thus considered a separate grouping of fungi with an unknown evolutionary origin. But, using new analytical tools that allow them to isolate the DNA of fungi in parasitic or symbiotic
(35) relationships, researchers were able to establish the DNA sequence in a certain gene found in 75 species of fungi, including 10 species of lichen-forming fungi. Based on these analyses, the researchers found 5 branches on the fungus family tree to which
(40) varieties of lichen-forming fungi belong. Furthermore, the researchers stress that it is likely that as more types of lichen-forming fungi are analyzed, they will be found to belong to still more branches of the fungus family tree.

(45) One implication of the new research is that it provides evidence to help overturn the long-standing evolutionary assumption that parasitic interactions inevitably evolve over time to a greater benignity and eventually to symbiosis so that the parasites will not
(50) destroy their hosts. The addition of lichen-forming fungi to positions along branches of the fungus family tree indicates that this assumption does not hold for fungi. Fungi both harmful and benign can now be found both early and late in fungus
(55) evolutionary history. Given the new layout of the fungus family tree resulting from the lichen study, it appears that fungi can evolve toward mutualism and then just as easily turn back again toward parasitism.

15. Which one of the following most accurately states the main point of the passage?

(A) New research suggests that fungi are not only parasitic but also symbiotic organisms.
(B) New research has revealed that lichen-forming fungi constitute a distinct species of fungus.
(C) New research into the evolutionary origins of lichen-forming fungi reveals them to be closely related to various species of algae.
(D) New research has isolated the DNA of lichen-forming fungi and uncovered their relationship to the fungus family tree.
(E) New research into the fungal component of lichens explains the visible similarities between lichens and fungi by means of their common evolutionary origins.

16. Which one of the following most accurately describes the author's purpose in the last paragraph of the passage?

(A) to suggest that new research overturns the assumption that lichen-forming fungi are primarily symbiotic, rather than parasitic, organisms
(B) to show that findings based on new research regarding fungus classification have implications that affect a long-standing assumption of evolutionary science
(C) to explain the fundamental purposes of fungus classification in order to position this classification within the broader field of evolutionary science
(D) to demonstrate that a fundamental assumption of evolutionary science is verified by new research regarding fungus classification
(E) to explain how symbiotic relationships can evolve into purely parasitic ones

GO ON TO THE NEXT PAGE.

17. Which one of the following most accurately describes the organization of the passage?

(A) explanation of the difficulty of classifying lichens; description of the DNA sequence of lichen-forming fungi; summary of the implications of this description

(B) definition of lichens; discussion of new discoveries concerning lichens' evolutionary history; application of these findings in support of an evolutionary theory

(C) definition of lichens; discussion of the difficulty in classifying their fungal components; resolution of this difficulty and implications of the resulting research

(D) discussion of the symbiotic relationship that constitutes lichens; discussion of how new research can distinguish parasitic from symbiotic fungi; implications of this research

(E) explanation of the symbiotic nature of lichens; discussion of the problems this poses for genetic researchers; delineation of the implications these problems have for evolutionary theory

18. According to the passage, the elimination of which one of the following obstacles enabled scientists to identify the evolutionary origins of lichen-forming fungi?

(A) The DNA of lichen-forming fungi was not easy to separate from that of their associated algae.

(B) Lichen-forming fungi are difficult to distinguish from several common fungi with which they are closely related.

(C) Lichen-forming fungi were grouped separately from other fungi on the fungus family tree.

(D) Lichen-forming fungi are far less common than more recognizable fungi such as mushrooms.

(E) The DNA of lichen-forming fungi is significantly more complex than that of other fungi.

19. Which one of the following, if true, most weakens the author's criticism of the assumption that parasitic interactions generally evolve toward symbiosis?

(A) Evolutionary theorists now postulate that symbiotic interactions generally evolve toward greater parasitism, rather than vice versa.

(B) The evolutionary tree of fungi is somewhat more complex than that of similarly parasitic or symbiotic organisms.

(C) The DNA of fungi involved in symbiotic interactions is far more difficult to isolate than that of fungi involved in parasitic interactions.

(D) The placement of lichen-forming fungi as a separate group on the fungus family tree masked the fact that parasitic fungi sometimes evolved much later than symbiotic ones.

(E) Branches of the fungus family tree that have evolved from symbiosis to parasitism usually die out shortly thereafter.

GO ON TO THE NEXT PAGE.

The following passage was written in the late 1980s.

The struggle to obtain legal recognition of aboriginal rights is a difficult one, and even if a right is written into the law there is no guarantee that the future will not bring changes to the law that
(5) undermine the right. For this reason, the federal government of Canada in 1982 extended constitutional protection to those aboriginal rights already recognized under the law. This protection was extended to the Indian, Inuit, and Métis peoples, the
(10) three groups generally thought to comprise the aboriginal population in Canada. But this decision has placed on provincial courts the enormous burden of interpreting and translating the necessarily general constitutional language into specific rulings. The
(15) result has been inconsistent recognition and establishment of aboriginal rights, despite the continued efforts of aboriginal peoples to raise issues concerning their rights.

Aboriginal rights in Canada are defined by the
(20) constitution as aboriginal peoples' rights to ownership of land and its resources, the inherent right of aboriginal societies to self-government, and the right to legal recognition of indigenous customs. But difficulties arise in applying these broadly conceived
(25) rights. For example, while it might appear straightforward to affirm legal recognition of indigenous customs, the exact legal meaning of "indigenous" is extremely difficult to interpret. The intent of the constitutional protection is to recognize
(30) only long-standing traditional customs, not those of recent origin; provincial courts therefore require aboriginal peoples to provide legal documentation that any customs they seek to protect were practiced sufficiently long ago—a criterion defined in practice
(35) to mean prior to the establishment of British sovereignty over the specific territory. However, this requirement makes it difficult for aboriginal societies, which often relied on oral tradition rather than written records, to support their claims.
(40) Furthermore, even if aboriginal peoples are successful in convincing the courts that specific rights should be recognized, it is frequently difficult to determine exactly what these rights amount to. Consider aboriginal land claims. Even when
(45) aboriginal ownership of specific lands is fully established, there remains the problem of interpreting the meaning of that "ownership." In a 1984 case in Ontario, an aboriginal group claimed that its property rights should be interpreted as full ownership in the
(50) contemporary sense of private property, which allows for the sale of the land or its resources. But the provincial court instead ruled that the law had previously recognized only the aboriginal right to use the land and therefore granted property rights so
(55) minimal as to allow only the bare survival of the community. Here, the provincial court's ruling was excessively conservative in its assessment of the current law. Regrettably, it appears that this group will not be successful unless it is able to move its
(60) case from the provincial courts into the Supreme Court of Canada, which will be, one hopes, more insistent upon a satisfactory application of the constitutional reforms.

20. Which one of the following most accurately states the main point of the passage?

(A) The overly conservative rulings of Canada's provincial courts have been a barrier to constitutional reforms intended to protect aboriginal rights.

(B) The overwhelming burden placed on provincial courts of interpreting constitutional language in Canada has halted efforts by aboriginal peoples to gain full ownership of land.

(C) Constitutional language aimed at protecting aboriginal rights in Canada has so far left the protection of these rights uncertain due to the difficult task of interpreting this language.

(D) Constitutional reforms meant to protect aboriginal rights in Canada have in fact been used by some provincial courts to limit these rights.

(E) Efforts by aboriginal rights advocates to uphold constitutional reforms in Canada may be more successful if heard by the Supreme Court rather than by the provincial courts.

21. Which one of the following most accurately describes the author's main purpose in lines 11–14 of the passage?

(A) to demonstrate that the decisions of the provincial courts rarely conform to the goals of the constitutional reforms

(B) to locate the source of a systemic problem in protecting aboriginal rights in Canada

(C) to identify the specific source of problems in enacting constitutional reforms in Canada

(D) to describe one aspect of the process by which constitutional reforms are enacted in Canada

(E) to criticize the use of general language in the Canadian constitution

GO ON TO THE NEXT PAGE.

22. The passage explicitly states that which one of the following was intended as a consequence of the constitutional protection of aboriginal rights?

   (A)   definition of the type of property rights that apply to aboriginal societies

   (B)   establishment of the Supreme Court of Canada as the arbiter of aboriginal rights

   (C)   recognition of traditional customs but not those of recent origin

   (D)   clarification of which groups comprise the aboriginal population in Canada

   (E)   creation of local governments for aboriginal communities

23. The passage provides the most evidence for the claim that the author has a negative attitude toward which one of the following?

   (A)   the 1982 constitutional reforms' burdening the provincial courts with the task of interpretation

   (B)   the difficulties in interpreting such terms as "indigenous" and "ownership"

   (C)   the criterion used to determine which customs are too recent to merit constitutional protection

   (D)   the requirement that aboriginal peoples provide documentation for traditional customs

   (E)   the definition of ownership imposed by the provincial court in 1984

24. The passage provides evidence to suggest that the author would be most likely to assent to which one of the following proposals?

   (A)   Aboriginal peoples in Canada should not be answerable to the federal laws of Canada.

   (B)   Oral tradition should sometimes be considered legal documentation of certain indigenous customs.

   (C)   Aboriginal communities should be granted full protection of all of their customs.

   (D)   Provincial courts should be given no authority to decide cases involving questions of aboriginal rights.

   (E)   The language of the Canadian constitution should more carefully delineate the instances to which reforms apply.

25. Which one of the following, if true, would lend the most credence to the author's statement in lines 56–58?

   (A)   Other Ontario courts had previously interpreted "use" to include sale of the land or its resources.

   (B)   The ruling created thousands of jobs by opening the land in question to logging by a timber corporation.

   (C)   Previous court decisions in Ontario have distinguished the right to use land from the right to sell it.

   (D)   The ruling prompted aboriginal groups in other provinces to pursue land claims in those courts.

   (E)   Prior to the decision in question, the provincial court had not heard a case concerning the constitutional reforms.

26. Based on the information in the passage, the author would be most likely to agree with which one of the following statements about the 1984 case in Ontario?

   (A)   The court's ruling directly contravened the language of the constitutional reforms protecting aboriginal land ownership rights in the full modern sense.

   (B)   The Supreme Court remains the best hope for the recognition of full aboriginal property rights because provincial courts are not authorized to rule on the definition of property rights.

   (C)   If there had been clear documentary evidence that the group had occupied the land before the establishment of British sovereignty, the court would probably have upheld the aboriginal claims.

   (D)   The unsatisfactory ruling in the case was the result of pressure from conservative politicians and other conservative interests.

   (E)   The court correctly understood the intent of the constitutional reforms, but it failed to apply them correctly because it misconstrued their relation to existing law.

27. The passage as a whole can most accurately be described as

   (A)   an argument stressing the need for advocates of certain rights to adopt certain strategies

   (B)   a comprehensive study of efforts to guarantee the protection of certain rights

   (C)   an examination of problems associated with efforts to protect certain rights

   (D)   an argument favoring the need for revising the definition of certain rights

   (E)   an attempt to correct misunderstandings regarding the protection of certain rights

S T O P

IF YOU FINISH BEFORE TIME IS CALLED, YOU MAY CHECK YOUR WORK ON THIS SECTION ONLY.
DO NOT WORK ON ANY OTHER SECTION IN THE TEST.

SECTION III
Time—35 minutes
22 Questions

Directions: Each group of questions in this section is based on a set of conditions. In answering some of the questions, it may be useful to draw a rough diagram. Choose the response that most accurately and completely answers each question and blacken the corresponding space on your answer sheet.

Questions 1–6

On one afternoon, Patterson meets individually with each of exactly five clients—Reilly, Sanchez, Tang, Upton, and Yansky—and also goes to the gym by herself for a workout. Patterson's workout and her five meetings each start at either 1:00, 2:00, 3:00, 4:00, 5:00, or 6:00. The following conditions must apply:
    Patterson meets with Sanchez at some time before her workout.
    Patterson meets with Tang at some time after her workout.
    Patterson meets with Yansky either immediately before or immediately after her workout.
    Patterson meets with Upton at some time before she meets with Reilly.

1. Which one of the following could be an acceptable schedule of Patterson's workout and meetings, in order from 1:00 to 6:00?

    (A)   Yansky, workout, Upton, Reilly, Sanchez, Tang
    (B)   Upton, Tang, Sanchez, Yansky, workout, Reilly
    (C)   Upton, Reilly, Sanchez, workout, Tang, Yansky
    (D)   Sanchez, Yansky, workout, Reilly, Tang, Upton
    (E)   Sanchez, Upton, workout, Yansky, Tang, Reilly

2. How many of the clients are there, any one of whom could meet with Patterson at 1:00?

    (A)   one
    (B)   two
    (C)   three
    (D)   four
    (E)   five

3. Patterson CANNOT meet with Upton at which one of the following times?

    (A)   1:00
    (B)   2:00
    (C)   3:00
    (D)   4:00
    (E)   5:00

4. If Patterson meets with Sanchez the hour before she meets with Yansky, then each of the following could be true EXCEPT:

    (A)   Patterson meets with Reilly at 2:00.
    (B)   Patterson meets with Yansky at 3:00.
    (C)   Patterson meets with Tang at 4:00.
    (D)   Patterson meets with Yansky at 5:00.
    (E)   Patterson meets with Tang at 6:00.

5. If Patterson meets with Tang at 4:00, then which one of the following must be true?

    (A)   Patterson meets with Reilly at 5:00.
    (B)   Patterson meets with Upton at 5:00.
    (C)   Patterson meets with Yansky at 2:00.
    (D)   Patterson meets with Yansky at 3:00.
    (E)   Patterson's workout is at 2:00.

6. Which one of the following could be the order of Patterson's meetings, from earliest to latest?

    (A)   Upton, Yansky, Sanchez, Reilly, Tang
    (B)   Upton, Reilly, Sanchez, Tang, Yansky
    (C)   Sanchez, Yansky, Reilly, Tang, Upton
    (D)   Sanchez, Upton, Tang, Yansky, Reilly
    (E)   Sanchez, Upton, Reilly, Yansky, Tang

GO ON TO THE NEXT PAGE.

Questions 7–12

Exactly six people—Lulu, Nam, Ofelia, Pachai, Santiago, and Tyrone—are the only contestants in a chess tournament. The tournament consists of four games, played one after the other. Exactly two people play in each game, and each person plays in at least one game. The following conditions must apply:

Tyrone does not play in the first or third game.
Lulu plays in the last game.
Nam plays in only one game and it is not against Pachai.
Santiago plays in exactly two games, one just before and one just after the only game that Ofelia plays in.

7. Which one of the following could be an accurate list of the contestants who play in each of the four games?

   (A) first game: Pachai, Santiago; second game: Ofelia, Tyrone; third game: Pachai, Santiago; fourth game: Lulu, Nam
   (B) first game: Lulu, Nam; second game: Pachai, Santiago; third game: Ofelia, Tyrone; fourth game: Lulu, Santiago
   (C) first game: Pachai, Santiago; second game: Lulu, Tyrone; third game: Nam, Ofelia; fourth game: Lulu, Nam
   (D) first game: Nam, Santiago; second game: Nam, Ofelia; third game: Pachai, Santiago; fourth game: Lulu, Tyrone
   (E) first game: Lulu, Nam; second game: Santiago, Tyrone; third game: Lulu, Ofelia; fourth game: Pachai, Santiago

8. Which one of the following contestants could play in two consecutive games?

   (A) Lulu
   (B) Nam
   (C) Ofelia
   (D) Santiago
   (E) Tyrone

9. If Tyrone plays in the fourth game, then which one of the following could be true?

   (A) Nam plays in the second game.
   (B) Ofelia plays in the third game.
   (C) Santiago plays in the second game.
   (D) Nam plays a game against Lulu.
   (E) Pachai plays a game against Lulu.

10. Which one of the following could be true?

   (A) Pachai plays against Lulu in the first game.
   (B) Pachai plays against Nam in the second game.
   (C) Santiago plays against Ofelia in the second game.
   (D) Pachai plays against Lulu in the third game.
   (E) Nam plays against Santiago in the fourth game.

11. Which one of the following is a complete and accurate list of the contestants who CANNOT play against Tyrone in any game?

   (A) Lulu, Pachai
   (B) Nam, Ofelia
   (C) Nam, Pachai
   (D) Nam, Santiago
   (E) Ofelia, Pachai

12. If Ofelia plays in the third game, which one of the following must be true?

   (A) Lulu plays in the third game.
   (B) Nam plays in the third game.
   (C) Pachai plays in the first game.
   (D) Pachai plays in the third game.
   (E) Tyrone plays in the second game.

GO ON TO THE NEXT PAGE.

Questions 13–17

An album contains photographs picturing seven friends: Raimundo, Selma, Ty, Umiko, Wendy, Yakira, Zack. The friends appear either alone or in groups with one another, in accordance with the following:

Wendy appears in every photograph that Selma appears in.
Selma appears in every photograph that Umiko appears in.
Raimundo appears in every photograph that Yakira does not appear in.
Neither Ty nor Raimundo appears in any photograph that Wendy appears in.

13. Which one of the following could be a complete and accurate list of the friends who appear together in a photograph?

(A) Raimundo, Selma, Ty, Wendy
(B) Raimundo, Ty, Yakira, Zack
(C) Raimundo, Wendy, Yakira, Zack
(D) Selma, Ty, Umiko, Yakira
(E) Selma, Ty, Umiko, Zack

14. If Ty and Zack appear together in a photograph, then which one of the following must be true?

(A) Selma also appears in the photograph.
(B) Yakira also appears in the photograph.
(C) Wendy also appears in the photograph.
(D) Raimundo does not appear in the photograph.
(E) Umiko does not appear in the photograph.

15. What is the maximum number of friends who could appear in a photograph that Yakira does not appear in?

(A) six
(B) five
(C) four
(D) three
(E) two

16. If Umiko and Zack appear together in a photograph, then exactly how many of the other friends must also appear in that photograph?

(A) four
(B) three
(C) two
(D) one
(E) zero

17. If exactly three friends appear together in a photograph, then each of the following could be true EXCEPT:

(A) Selma and Zack both appear in the photograph.
(B) Ty and Yakira both appear in the photograph.
(C) Wendy and Selma both appear in the photograph.
(D) Yakira and Zack both appear in the photograph.
(E) Zack and Raimundo both appear in the photograph.

GO ON TO THE NEXT PAGE.

Questions 18–22

The Export Alliance consists of exactly three nations: Nation X, Nation Y, and Nation Z. Each nation in the Alliance exports exactly two of the following five crops: oranges, rice, soybeans, tea, and wheat. Each of these crops is exported by at least one of the nations in the Alliance. The following conditions hold:

    None of the nations exports both wheat and oranges.
    Nation X exports soybeans if, but only if, Nation Y does also.
    If Nation Y exports rice, then Nations X and Z both export tea.
    Nation Y does not export any crop that Nation Z exports.

18. Which one of the following could be an accurate list, for each of the nations, of the crops it exports?

    (A)   Nation X: oranges, rice; Nation Y: oranges, tea; Nation Z: soybeans, wheat
    (B)   Nation X: oranges, tea; Nation Y: oranges, rice; Nation Z: soybeans, wheat
    (C)   Nation X: oranges, wheat; Nation Y: oranges, tea; Nation Z: rice, soybeans
    (D)   Nation X: rice, wheat; Nation Y: oranges, tea; Nation Z: oranges, soybeans
    (E)   Nation X: soybeans, rice; Nation Y: oranges, tea; Nation Z: soybeans, wheat

19. If Nation X exports soybeans and tea, then which one of the following could be true?

    (A)   Nation Y exports oranges.
    (B)   Nation Y exports rice.
    (C)   Nation Y exports tea.
    (D)   Nation Z exports soybeans.
    (E)   Nation Z exports tea.

20. If Nation Z exports tea and wheat, then which one of the following must be true?

    (A)   Nation X exports oranges.
    (B)   Nation X exports tea.
    (C)   Nation X exports wheat.
    (D)   Nation Y exports rice.
    (E)   Nation Y exports soybeans.

21. It CANNOT be the case that both Nation X and Nation Z export which one of the following crops?

    (A)   oranges
    (B)   rice
    (C)   soybeans
    (D)   tea
    (E)   wheat

22. Which one of the following pairs CANNOT be the two crops that Nation Y exports?

    (A)   oranges and rice
    (B)   oranges and soybeans
    (C)   rice and tea
    (D)   rice and wheat
    (E)   soybeans and wheat

STOP
IF YOU FINISH BEFORE TIME IS CALLED, YOU MAY CHECK YOUR WORK ON THIS SECTION ONLY.
DO NOT WORK ON ANY OTHER SECTION IN THE TEST.

SECTION IV
Time—35 minutes
25 Questions

Directions: The questions in this section are based on the reasoning contained in brief statements or passages. For some questions, more than one of the choices could conceivably answer the question. However, you are to choose the best answer; that is, the response that most accurately and completely answers the question. You should not make assumptions that are by commonsense standards implausible, superfluous, or incompatible with the passage. After you have chosen the best answer, blacken the corresponding space on your answer sheet.

1. Mayor McKinney's policies have often been criticized on the grounds that they benefit only wealthy city residents, but that is not a fair evaluation. Some of McKinney's policies have clearly benefited the city's less affluent residents. McKinney actively supported last year's proposal to lower the city's high property taxes. Because of this tax decrease, more development is taking place in the city, helping to end the housing shortage and stabilize the rents in the city.

Which one of the following most accurately expresses the main conclusion of the argument?

(A) It is impossible to tell whether McKinney is more committed to the interests of the wealthy than to those of the poor.
(B) McKinney's policies have often been criticized for benefiting only wealthy city residents.
(C) The decrease in property taxes that McKinney supported caused more development to take place in the city.
(D) The criticism that McKinney's policies benefit only the wealthy is unjustified.
(E) McKinney's efforts helped end the housing shortage and stabilize the rents in the city.

2. A factory spokesperson argued that the factory should not be required to clean up the water in the nearby wetlands, maintaining that although wastewater from the factory polluted the wetlands over the past several years, the factory is not to blame for this, since the disposal of the factory's wastewater is handled entirely by an independent contractor.

Which one of the following arguments most closely conforms to the principle underlying the reasoning in the spokesperson's argument?

(A) A recent survey revealed that over two-thirds of the teachers in the district are permitted to teach classes on subjects in which they have received no formal training. Thus parents of students in the district should check the qualifications of their children's teachers.
(B) I object to the policy of making parents responsible for the offenses of their older adolescent children. After all, these adolescents have minds of their own and freely choose to act as they do, often in ways that do not reflect the wishes of their parents.
(C) The students are justified in their objection to the reading assignment. Many of the topics concern material that is not covered in class, and students should not be required to do such reading in order to do well in the course.
(D) The most recent appointee to the prize committee should not be permitted to participate in the selection of this year's winner. Unlike each of the other committee members, the appointee has a relative in the contest.
(E) Despite all the publicity, I am skeptical of the politician's claims of having just returned from the remote village. Just two days ago a reporter spoke with the villagers and said that not a single one reported seeing the politician in the past several months.

GO ON TO THE NEXT PAGE.

3. Nylon industry spokesperson: Even though cotton and nylon are used for similar purposes, some people have the mistaken notion that cotton is natural but nylon is not. However, nylon's main components come from petroleum and from the nitrogen in the atmosphere. Clearly the atmosphere is natural. And petroleum comes from oil, which in turn comes from ancient plants—a natural source.

Which one of the following principles, if valid, most helps to justify the nylon industry spokesperson's reasoning?

(A) A substance is unnatural only if the function it serves is unnatural.

(B) A substance is no less natural than the processes used in its production.

(C) A substance is no more natural than its least natural component.

(D) One substance can be more natural than another if only one is wholly derived from natural substances.

(E) A substance is natural if the origins of its main components are natural.

4. Computer manufacturers and retailers tell us that the complexity involved in connecting the various components of personal computers is not a widespread obstacle to their use, but this is wrong. Customers who install accessories to their personal computers have to take full responsibility for the setting of jumpers and switches to satisfy mysterious specifications. Many accessories require extra software that can cause other accessories to stop working; adding a modem, for instance, may disable a printer.

Which one of the following, if true, most seriously weakens the argument?

(A) Personal computer instruction manuals usually explain the purposes of the jumpers and switches.

(B) Software for accessories can often be obtained for free.

(C) Installing an accessory will become extremely easy in the foreseeable future.

(D) A personal computer is usually sold as part of a package that includes accessories and free installation.

(E) Computer manufacturers rarely take into account ease of installation when they are designing programs or accessories.

5. Rats fed high doses of the artificial sweetener saccharin develop silicate crystals that are toxic to cells lining the bladder. When the cells regenerate, some are cancerous and form tumors. Unlike rats, mice fed high doses of saccharin do not get bladder cancer.

Which one of the following, if true, does the most to resolve the apparent discrepancy in the information above?

(A) Urine proteins that react with saccharin to form silicate crystals are found in rats but not in mice.

(B) Cells in the bladder regenerate more quickly in mice than they do in rats.

(C) High doses of saccharin are much more likely to produce silicate crystals than lower doses are.

(D) The silicate crystals are toxic only to the cells lining the bladder and not to other bladder cells.

(E) High doses of other artificial sweeteners have been shown to produce silicate crystals in mice but not in rats.

6. Although we could replace the beautiful—but dilapidated—old bridge across Black River with a concrete skyway, we should instead replace it with a cable bridge even though this would be more expensive than building a concrete skyway. The extra cost is clearly justified by the importance of maintaining the beauty of our river crossing.

Which one of the following is an assumption on which the argument depends?

(A) It is no more costly to maintain a cable bridge than a concrete skyway.

(B) A concrete skyway would not have any practical advantages over a cable bridge.

(C) The beauty of the river crossing must be preserved.

(D) If the new cable bridge is built, most people who see it will think the extra money well spent.

(E) Building a cable bridge across Black River would produce a more aesthetically pleasing result than building a concrete skyway.

GO ON TO THE NEXT PAGE.

7. A typical gasoline-powered lawn mower emits about as much air-polluting material per hour of use as does an automobile. Collectively, such mowers contribute significantly to summer air pollution. Since electric mowers emit no air pollutants, people can help reduce air pollution by choosing electric mowers over gasoline ones whenever feasible.

    Which one of the following, if true, provides the most support for the argument?

    (A)   Lawns help to clean the air, replacing pollutants with oxygen.
    (B)   Electric lawn mowers are more expensive to purchase and maintain than are gasoline mowers.
    (C)   Producing the power to run an electric mower for an hour causes less air pollution than does running an automobile for an hour.
    (D)   Most manufacturers of gasoline lawn mowers are trying to redesign their mowers to reduce the emission of air pollutants.
    (E)   Lawn mowers are used for fewer hours per year than are automobiles.

8. Ariel: Government art subsidies never benefit art, for art's role is to challenge society's values. A society's values, however, are expressed by its government, and artists cannot challenge the very institution upon which they depend.

    Sasha: I agree that art should challenge society's values. However, by its very nature, a democratic government respects dissent and encourages challenges to its own values. Therefore, in a democratic society, government art subsidies ensure that artists can be fully committed to their work while expressing themselves freely.

    The dialogue most supports the claim that Ariel and Sasha disagree with each other about whether

    (A)   art's role is to challenge society's values
    (B)   a society's values are expressed by its government
    (C)   artists can express themselves freely in a nondemocratic society
    (D)   art subsidies provided by a democratic government benefit art
    (E)   only governments that respect dissent ensure that art subsidies are fairly distributed

9. Public health expert: Until recently people believed that applications of biochemical research would eventually achieve complete victory over the microorganisms that cause human disease. However, current medical research shows that those microorganisms reproduce so rapidly that medicines developed for killing one variety will only spur the evolution of other varieties that are immune to those medicines. The most rational public health strategy, therefore, would place much more emphasis than at present on fully informing people about the transmission of diseases caused by microorganisms, with a view to minimizing the incidence of such diseases.

    Of the following, which one most accurately expresses the conclusion drawn by the public health expert?

    (A)   A medicine that kills one variety of disease-causing microorganism can cause the evolution of a drug-resistant variety.
    (B)   A patient who contracts a disease caused by microorganisms cannot be effectively cured by present methods.
    (C)   There is good reason to make a particular change to public health policy.
    (D)   No one who is fully informed about the diseases caused by microorganisms will ever fall victim to those diseases.
    (E)   Some previous approaches to public health policy ignored the fact that disease-causing microorganisms reproduce at a rapid rate.

10. The enthusiastic acceptance of ascetic lifestyles evidenced in the surviving writings of monastic authors indicates that medieval societies were much less concerned with monetary gain than are contemporary Western cultures.

    The reasoning in the argument is most vulnerable to criticism on the grounds that the argument

    (A)   employs the imprecise term "ascetic"
    (B)   generalizes from a sample that is likely to be unrepresentative
    (C)   applies contemporary standards inappropriately to medieval societies
    (D)   inserts personal opinions into what purports to be a factual debate
    (E)   advances premises that are inconsistent

GO ON TO THE NEXT PAGE.

11. Between 1976 and 1985, chemical wastes were dumped into Cod Bay. Today, 3 percent of the bay's bluefin cod population have deformed fins, and wary consumers have stopped buying the fish. In seeking financial reparations from companies that dumped the chemicals, representatives of Cod Bay's fishing industry have claimed that since the chemicals are known to cause genetic mutations, the deformity in the bluefin cod must have been caused by the presence of those chemicals in Cod Bay.

The answer to each of the following questions would be helpful in evaluating the representatives' claim EXCEPT:

(A) What is the incidence of deformed fins in bluefin cod that are not exposed to chemicals such as those dumped into Cod Bay?

(B) What was the incidence of deformed fins in bluefin cod in Cod Bay before the chemical dumping began?

(C) Has the consumption of the bluefin cod from Cod Bay that have deformed fins caused any health problems in the people who ate them?

(D) Are bluefin cod prone to any naturally occurring diseases that can cause fin deformities of the same kind as those displayed by the bluefin cod of Cod Bay?

(E) Are there gene-altering pollutants present in Cod Bay other than the chemical wastes that were dumped by the companies?

12. Columnist: If you received an unsigned letter, you would likely have some doubts about the truth of its contents. But news stories often include statements from anonymous sources, and these are usually quoted with the utmost respect. It makes sense to be skeptical of these sources, for, as in the case of the writer of an unsigned letter, their anonymity makes it possible for them to plant inaccurate or slanted statements without ever having to answer for them.

The columnist's argument proceeds by

(A) pointing out that a certain attitude would presumably be adopted in one situation, in order to support the claim that a similar attitude would be justified in an analogous situation

(B) drawing an analogy between an attitude commonly adopted in one situation and a different attitude commonly adopted in another situation, and establishing that the latter attitude is better justified than the former

(C) inferring that an attitude would be justified in all situations of a given type on the grounds that this attitude is justified in a hypothetical situation of that type

(D) calling into question a certain type of evidence by drawing an analogy between that evidence and other evidence that the argument shows is usually false

(E) calling into question the motives of those presenting certain information, and concluding for this reason that the information is likely to be false

13. Art theft from museums is on the rise. Most stolen art is sold to wealthy private collectors. Consequently, since thieves steal what their customers are most interested in buying, museums ought to focus more of their security on their most valuable pieces.

The argument depends on assuming which one of the following?

(A) Art thieves steal both valuable and not-so-valuable art.

(B) Art pieces that are not very valuable are not very much in demand by wealthy private collectors.

(C) Art thieves steal primarily from museums that are poorly secured.

(D) Most museums provide the same amount of security for valuable and not-so-valuable art.

(E) Wealthy private collectors sometimes sell their stolen art to other wealthy private collectors.

GO ON TO THE NEXT PAGE.

14. Insufficient rain can cause crops to falter and agricultural prices to rise. Records indicate that during a certain nation's recent crisis, faltering crops and rising agricultural prices prompted the government to take over food distribution in an effort to prevent starvation. Thus, the weather must have played an important role in bringing about the crisis.

The argument's reasoning is most vulnerable to criticism on the grounds that the argument

(A) concludes, merely from the fact that the period of insufficient rain occurred before the nation's crisis, that insufficient rain caused the nation's crisis

(B) fails to take into account the possibility that the scarcity was not severe enough to justify the government's taking over food distribution

(C) uses the term "crisis" equivocally in the reasoning, referring to both a political crisis and an economic crisis

(D) infers, merely from the fact that one event could have caused a second event, that the first event in fact caused the second

(E) takes for granted that any condition that is necessary for an increase in agricultural prices is also sufficient for such an increase

15. The cost of a semester's tuition at a certain university is based on the number of courses in which a student enrolls that semester. Although the cost per course at that university has not risen in four years, many of its students who could afford the tuition when they first enrolled now claim they can no longer afford it.

Each of the following, if true, helps to resolve the apparent discrepancy above EXCEPT:

(A) Faculty salaries at the university have risen slightly over the past four years.

(B) The number of courses per semester for which full-time students are required to enroll is higher this year than any time in the past.

(C) The cost of living in the vicinity of the university has risen over the last two years.

(D) The university awards new students a large number of scholarships that are renewed each year for the students who maintain high grade averages.

(E) The university has turned many of its part-time office jobs, for which students had generally been hired, into full-time, nonstudent positions.

16. People are not happy unless they feel that they are needed by others. Most people in modern society, however, can achieve a feeling of indispensability only within the sphere of family and friendship, because almost everyone knows that his or her job could be done by any one of thousands of others.

The statements above most strongly support which one of the following?

(A) People who realize that others could fill their occupational roles as ably as they do themselves cannot achieve any happiness in their lives.

(B) The nature of modern society actually undermines the importance of family life to an individual's happiness.

(C) Most people in modern society are happy in their private lives even if they are not happy in their jobs.

(D) A majority of people in modern society do not appreciate having the jobs that they do have.

(E) Fewer than a majority of people in modern society can find happiness outside the sphere of private interpersonal relationships.

17. Art critic: Criticism focuses on two issues: first, whether the value of an artwork is intrinsic to the work; and second, whether judgments about an artwork's quality are objective rather than merely matters of taste. These issues are related, for if an artwork's value is not intrinsic, then it must be extrinsic, and thus judgments about the quality of the work can only be a matter of taste.

The art critic's reasoning is most vulnerable to the criticism that it takes for granted that

(A) judgments about the quality of an artwork are always a matter of taste

(B) people sometimes agree about judgments that are only matters of taste

(C) judgments about extrinsic value cannot be objective

(D) judgments about intrinsic value are always objective

(E) an artwork's value is sometimes intrinsic to it

GO ON TO THE NEXT PAGE.

18. Decentralization enables divisions of a large institution to function autonomously. This always permits more realistic planning and strongly encourages innovation, since the people responsible for decision making are directly involved in implementing the policies they design. Decentralization also permits the central administration to focus on institution-wide issues without being overwhelmed by the details of daily operations.

The statements above most strongly support which one of the following?

(A) In large institutions whose divisions do not function autonomously, planning is not maximally realistic.
(B) Innovation is not always encouraged in large centralized institutions.
(C) For large institutions the advantages of decentralization outweigh its disadvantages.
(D) The central administrations of large institutions are usually partially responsible for most of the details of daily operations.
(E) The people directly involved in implementing policies are always able to make innovative and realistic policy decisions.

19. According to some astronomers, Earth is struck by a meteorite large enough to cause an ice age on an average of once every 100 million years. The last such incident occurred nearly 100 million years ago, so we can expect that Earth will be struck by such a meteorite in the near future. This clearly warrants funding to determine whether there is a means to protect our planet from such meteorite strikes.

The reasoning in the argument is most subject to criticism on the grounds that the argument

(A) makes a bold prescription on the basis of evidence that establishes only a high probability for a disastrous event
(B) presumes, without providing justification, that the probability of a chance event's occurring is not affected by whether the event has occurred during a period in which it would be expected to occur
(C) moves from evidence about the average frequency of an event to a specific prediction about when the next such event will occur
(D) fails to specify the likelihood that, if such a meteorite should strike Earth, the meteorite would indeed cause an ice age
(E) presumes, without providing justification, that some feasible means can be found to deter large meteorite strikes

20. Polling data reveal that an overwhelming majority of nine-year-olds can correctly identify the logos of major cigarette brands. However, of those nine-year-olds who recognize such logos, less than 1 percent smoke. Therefore, there is little or no connection between recognition of cigarette brand logos and smoking.

Which one of the following uses flawed reasoning most similar to the flawed reasoning above?

(A) The concern about the long-term effect on dolphins of small quantities of mercury in the ocean is unfounded. During a three-month observation period, 1,000 dolphins were exposed to small quantities of mercury in seawater, with no effect on the animals.
(B) Many ten-year-olds dream of becoming actors. Yet it is not likely they will seriously consider becoming actors, because most parents discourage their children from pursuing such a highly competitive career.
(C) Most dentists recommend using fluoride to reduce the incidence of cavities, but few recommend giving up candy entirely; so, using fluoride is probably more effective in preventing cavities than is avoiding sweets.
(D) A large percentage of men exercise moderately throughout their lives, but the average life span of those who do so is not significantly greater than of those who get little or no exercise. So there is little or no correlation between moderate exercise and good health.
(E) Most people cannot name their legislative representatives. Nonetheless, this is insignificant, for when queried, most of them displayed an adequate command of current political issues.

GO ON TO THE NEXT PAGE.

21. Etiquette firmly opposes both obscene and malicious talk, but this does not imply that speech needs to be restricted by law. Etiquette does not necessarily even oppose the expression of offensive ideas. Rather, it dictates that there are situations in which the expression of potentially offensive, disturbing, or controversial ideas is inappropriate and that, where appropriate, the expression and discussion of such ideas is to be done in a civil manner.

Which one of the following judgments most closely corresponds to the principles of etiquette stated above?

(A)   Neighbors should not be gruff or unfriendly to one another when they meet on the street.

(B)   When prosecutors elicit testimony from a cooperative witness they should do so without intensive questioning.

(C)   There should be restrictions on speech only if a large majority of the population finds the speech offensive and hateful.

(D)   The journalists at a news conference should not ask a politician potentially embarrassing questions about a controversial policy issue.

(E)   The moderator of a panel discussion of a divisive moral issue should not allow participants to engage in name-calling.

22. The only preexisting recordings that are transferred onto compact disc are those that record companies believe will sell well enough on compact disc to be profitable. So, most classic jazz recordings will not be transferred onto compact disc, because few classic jazz recordings are played on the radio.

The conclusion above follows logically if which one of the following is assumed?

(A)   Few of the preexisting recordings that record companies believe can be profitably transferred to compact disc are classic jazz recordings.

(B)   Few compact discs featuring classic jazz recordings are played on the radio.

(C)   The only recordings that are played on the radio are ones that record companies believe can be profitably sold as compact discs.

(D)   Most record companies are less interested in preserving classic jazz recordings than in making a profit.

(E)   No recording that is not played on the radio is one that record companies believe would be profitable if transferred to compact disc.

23. Agricultural economist: Over the past several years, increases in worldwide grain production have virtually ceased. Further increases will be extremely difficult; most usable farmland is already being farmed with near-maximal efficiency. But worldwide demand for grain has been increasing steadily, due largely to continuing population growth. Hence, a severe worldwide grain shortage is likely.

Which one of the following most accurately describes the role played in the agricultural economist's argument by the claim that further increases in worldwide grain production will be extremely difficult?

(A)   It is one of the two conclusions drawn by the agricultural economist, neither of which is used to provide support for the other.

(B)   It is a description of a phenomenon, a causal explanation of which is the main conclusion of the argument.

(C)   It is the only premise offered in support of the argument's main conclusion.

(D)   It is a prediction for which the agricultural economist's first claim is offered as the primary justification.

(E)   It is an intermediate conclusion that is presented as evidence for the argument's main conclusion.

GO ON TO THE NEXT PAGE.

24. Bardis: Extensive research shows that television advertisements affect the buying habits of consumers. Some people conclude from this that violent television imagery sometimes causes violent behavior. But the effectiveness of television advertisements could be a result of those televised images being specifically designed to alter buying habits, whereas television violence is not designed to cause violent behavior. Hence we can safely conclude that violent television imagery does not cause violence.

The reasoning in Bardis's argument is flawed because that argument

(A) relies on an illegitimate inference from the fact that advertisements can change behavior to the claim that advertisements can cause violent behavior

(B) fails to distinguish a type of behavior from a type of stimulus that may or may not affect behavior

(C) undermines its own position by questioning the persuasive power of television advertising

(D) concludes that a claim is false on the basis of one purported fault in an argument in favor of that claim

(E) fails to consider the possibility that the argument it disputes is intended to address a separate issue

25. Sarah: Our regulations for staff review are vague and thus difficult to interpret. For instance, the regulations state that a staff member who is performing unsatisfactorily will face dismissal, but they fail to define unsatisfactory performance. Thus, some staff may be dismissed merely because their personal views conflict with those of their supervisors.

Which one of the following generalizations, if applicable to Sarah's company, most helps to justify her reasoning?

(A) Performance that falls only somewhat below expectations results in disciplinary measures short of dismissal.

(B) Interpreting regulations is a prerogative that belongs solely to supervisors.

(C) A vague regulation can be used to make those subject to it answer for their performance.

(D) A vague regulation can be used to keep those subject to it in subordinate positions.

(E) Employees usually consider specific regulations to be fairer than vague regulations.

STOP
IF YOU FINISH BEFORE TIME IS CALLED, YOU MAY CHECK YOUR WORK ON THIS SECTION ONLY.
DO NOT WORK ON ANY OTHER SECTION IN THE TEST.

ACKNOWLEDGMENTS

Acknowledgment is made to the following sources from which material has been adapted for use in this test booklet:

Ronald Dworkin, *Taking Rights Seriously.* ©1977 by Pantheon Books.

James H. March, ed., *The Canadian Encyclopedia.* ©1988 by Hurtig Publishers Ltd.

Christopher B. Ogden, "What Kinds of Help?" ©1993 by Time Inc.

Edmund D. Pellegrino, MD, "Ethics: Rethinking the Hippocratic Oath." ©1996 by the American Medical Association.

Norman Solomon, *Hidden Agenda.* ©1995 by San Francisco Bay Guardian Co., Inc.

Carol Kaesuk Yoon, "Pariahs of the Fungal World, Lichens Finally Get Some Respect." ©June 13, 1995 by The New York Times.

Wait for the supervisor's instructions before you open the page to the topic.
Please print and sign your name and write the date in the designated spaces below.

Time: 35 Minutes

General Directions

You will have 35 minutes in which to plan and write an essay on the topic inside. Read the topic and the accompanying directions carefully. You will probably find it best to spend a few minutes considering the topic and organizing your thoughts before you begin writing. In your essay, be sure to develop your ideas fully, leaving time, if possible, to review what you have written. **Do not write on a topic other than the one specified. Writing on a topic of your own choice is not acceptable.**

No special knowledge is required or expected for this writing exercise. Law schools are interested in the reasoning, clarity, organization, language usage, and writing mechanics displayed in your essay. How well you write is more important than how much you write.

Confine your essay to the blocked, lined area on the front and back of the separate Writing Sample Response Sheet. Only that area will be reproduced for law schools. Be sure that your writing is legible.

Both this topic sheet and your response sheet must be turned over to the testing staff before you leave the room.

Topic Code

Date
/   /

Print Your Full Name Here		
Last	First	M.I.

Sign Your Name Here

Scratch Paper
Do not write your essay in this space.

LSAT® Writing Sample Topic

Directions: The scenario presented below describes two choices, either one of which can be supported on the basis of the information given. Your essay should consider both choices and argue for one over the other, based on the two specified criteria and the facts provided. There is no "right" or "wrong" choice: a reasonable argument can be made for either.

An architectural firm is growing dramatically and needs additional space. The firm is deciding whether to expand and remodel its present building near the center of the city or to build a new building on the city's outskirts. Write an argument in favor of choosing one option over the other, based on the following considerations:

- The firm needs to economically provide functional, convenient, and comfortable workspace for its growing staff.
- The firm wants to create an architecturally noteworthy showplace building to make a statement to prospective clients and enhance its image and reputation.

The firm is presently housed in an architecturally important historic building that has become associated with the firm's image. The building is in a popular, historic neighborhood of the city near the business district and public transportation. However, parking is difficult and quite costly. Expansion and remodeling would have to meet the stringent restrictions of the historic district, limiting the design options and adding to the complexity of the construction. The project would spotlight two of the firm's strengths: designing building additions that aesthetically complement existing structures, and creating modern working spaces in older buildings. The firm has a strong reputation for such work and dominates that type of business in the city, which has a large stock of older buildings.

Alternatively, the firm can build a new building on the outskirts of the city in its own distinctive architectural style, which integrates a building with its landscape and surroundings. A new building would require purchasing land, but it would provide more space than the alternative, and the lack of architectural constraints would allow for more design freedom and greater efficiency in creating working space. However, the city's outskirts are not well served by public transportation and many employees who drive to work would face longer commutes as well. There would, however, be plenty of room for on-site parking. The firm believes that the majority of the future architectural work in the area will be new buildings outside the city.

WP-L025-A

Scratch Paper
Do not write your essay in this space.

COMPUTING YOUR SCORE

Directions:

1. Use the Answer Key on the next page to check your answers.

2. Use the Scoring Worksheet below to compute your raw score.

3. Use the Score Conversion Chart to convert your raw score into the 120-180 scale.

Scoring Worksheet

1. Enter the number of questions you answered correctly in each section.

   Number Correct

   SECTION I .... _____
   SECTION II .... _____
   SECTION III .... _____
   SECTION IV .... _____

2. Enter the sum here: _____

   This is your Raw Score.

Conversion Chart
For Converting Raw Score to the 120-180 LSAT Scaled Score
LSAT Form 5LSN64

Reported Score	Raw Score Lowest	Raw Score Highest
180	97	99
179	96	96
178	95	95
177	94	94
176	93	93
175	92	92
174	91	91
173	90	90
172	89	89
171	88	88
170	87	87
169	86	86
168	85	85
167	83	84
166	82	82
165	81	81
164	79	80
163	78	78
162	76	77
161	75	75
160	73	74
159	71	72
158	70	70
157	68	69
156	66	67
155	65	65
154	63	64
153	61	62
152	59	60
151	58	58
150	56	57
149	54	55
148	53	53
147	51	52
146	49	50
145	48	48
144	46	47
143	44	45
142	43	43
141	41	42
140	40	40
139	38	39
138	37	37
137	35	36
136	34	34
135	32	33
134	31	31
133	29	30
132	28	28
131	27	27
130	25	26
129	24	24
128	23	23
127	21	22
126	20	20
125	19	19
124	17	18
123	16	16
122	14	15
121	—*	—*
120	0	13

*There is no raw score that will produce this scaled score for this form.

ANSWER KEY

SECTION I

1.	A	8.	A	15.	E	22.	E
2.	C	9.	E	16.	C	23.	C
3.	B	10.	A	17.	B	24.	B
4.	C	11.	C	18.	D	25.	C
5.	*	12.	C	19.	A	26.	E
6.	D	13.	E	20.	D		
7.	B	14.	E	21.	A		

SECTION II

1.	D	8.	E	15.	D	22.	C
2.	B	9.	D	16.	B	23.	E
3.	D	10.	A	17.	C	24.	B
4.	C	11.	E	18.	A	25.	A
5.	A	12.	B	19.	E	26.	E
6.	E	13.	C	20.	C	27.	C
7.	B	14.	E	21.	B		

SECTION III

1.	E	8.	A	15.	D	22.	C
2.	B	9.	A	16.	B		
3.	C	10.	A	17.	A		
4.	D	11.	C	18.	A		
5.	B	12.	E	19.	A		
6.	E	13.	B	20.	E		
7.	A	14.	E	21.	C		

SECTION IV

1.	D	8.	D	15.	A	22.	E
2.	B	9.	C	16.	E	23.	E
3.	E	10.	B	17.	C	24.	D
4.	D	11.	C	18.	A	25.	B
5.	A	12.	A	19.	C		
6.	E	13.	B	20.	A		
7.	C	14.	D	21.	E		

*Item removed from scoring.

PREPTEST 46
JUNE 2005
FORM 6LSN68

SECTION I
Time—35 minutes
27 Questions

<u>Directions:</u> Each set of questions in this section is based on a single passage or a pair of passages. The questions are to be answered on the basis of what is <u>stated</u> or <u>implied</u> in the passage or pair of passages. For some of the questions, more than one of the choices could conceivably answer the question. However, you are to choose the <u>best</u> answer; that is, the response that most accurately and completely answers the question, and blacken the corresponding space on your answer sheet.

Economists have long defined prosperity in terms of monetary value, gauging a given nation's prosperity solely on the basis of the total monetary value of the goods and services produced annually.
(5) However, critics point out that defining prosperity solely as a function of monetary value is questionable since it fails to recognize other kinds of values, such as quality of life or environmental health, that contribute directly to prosperity in a broader sense.
(10) For example, as the earth's ozone layer weakens and loses its ability to protect people from ultraviolet radiation, sales of hats, sunglasses, and sunscreens are likely to skyrocket, all adding to the nation's total expenditures. In this way, troubling reductions in
(15) environmental health and quality of life may in fact initiate economic activity that, by the economists' measure, bolsters prosperity.

It can also happen that communities seeking to increase their prosperity as measured strictly in
(20) monetary terms may damage their quality of life and their environment. The situation of one rural community illustrates this point: residents of the community value the local timber industry as a primary source of income, and they vocally protested
(25) proposed limitations on timber harvests as a threat to their prosperity. Implicitly adopting the economists' point of view, the residents argued that the harvest limitations would lower their wages or even cause the loss of jobs.
(30) But critics of the economists' view argue that this view of the situation overlooks a crucial consideration. Without the harvest limitations, they say, the land on which the community depends would be seriously damaged. Moreover, they point out that the residents
(35) themselves cite the abundance of natural beauty as one of the features that make their community a highly desirable place to live. But it is also extremely poor, and the critics point out that the residents could double their incomes by moving only 150 kilometers
(40) away. From their decision not to do so, the critics conclude that their location has substantial monetary value to them. The community will thus lose much more—even understood in monetary terms—if the proposed harvest limits are not implemented.
(45) Economists respond by arguing that to be a useful concept, prosperity must be defined in easily quantifiable terms, and that prosperity thus should not include difficult-to-measure values such as happiness or environmental health. But this position dodges the
(50) issue—emphasizing ease of calculation causes one to disregard substantive issues that directly influence real prosperity. The economists' stance is rather like that of a literary critic who takes total sales to be the best measure of a book's value—true, the number of
(55) copies sold is a convenient and quantifiable measure, but it is a poor substitute for an accurate appraisal of literary merit.

1. Which one of the following most accurately states the main point of the passage?

(A) According to critics, communities that seek to increase their prosperity recognize the need to gauge the value and ensure the long-term health of their local environment.

(B) Economists' definition of prosperity strictly in terms of monetary value is too narrow to truly capture our ordinary conception of this notion.

(C) If economists were to alter and expand their definition of prosperity, it is likely that the economic and environmental health of most communities would appear worse under the new definition than under the old definition.

(D) In contrast with the views of economists, some critics believe that prosperity can be neither scientifically measured nor accurately defined, and as a concept is therefore of little use for economists.

(E) While they are generally an accurate and practical measure of current economic prosperity, figures for the total expenditures of a nation do not aid in providing an indication of that nation's future economic prospects.

GO ON TO THE NEXT PAGE.

2. The example in the passage of the timber industry and its effect on a poor rural community suggests that the critics would most likely agree with which one of the following statements?

(A)   Harvest limitations have little relationship to lower wages or fewer jobs in the community.

(B)   Harvest limitations should be imposed only when the limitations have wide public support in the community.

(C)   The advantages to the community that would be created by harvest limitations are likely to outweigh the disadvantages.

(D)   Communities protest harvest limitations primarily because they do not understand the long-term monetary impact of such regulation.

(E)   It is the arguments of economists that often cause residents of rural communities to view harvest limitations more negatively.

3. Based on the information in the passage, the author would be most likely to agree with which one of the following statements regarding the weakening of the earth's ozone layer?

(A)   Paradoxically, the weakening of the ozone layer actually contributes to environmental health and quality of life.

(B)   The environmental effects of this problem are likely to occur more gradually than the economic effects.

(C)   The appearance of prosperity that results from this problem has directed attention away from solving it.

(D)   This problem should be regarded primarily as threatening rather than contributing to true prosperity.

(E)   This problem has resulted in part from the failure of economists to recognize it in its formative stages.

4. According to the passage, economists defend their concept of prosperity in which one of the following ways?

(A)   by claiming that alternative definitions of the concept would not be easily quantifiable

(B)   by asserting that environmental preservation can cause the loss of jobs

(C)   by citing the relevance of nonmonetary values such as environmental health

(D)   by showing that the value of natural beauty can be understood in quantifiable terms

(E)   by detailing the historical development of their definition of the concept

5. The author compares the economists' position to that of a literary critic (lines 52–57) primarily to

(A)   introduce the idea that the assessment of worth is basically subjective

(B)   advocate an innovative method of measuring literary merit

(C)   suggest that quality of life is mainly an aesthetic issue

(D)   provide additional evidence that prosperity cannot be quantified

(E)   illustrate the limitations of the economists' position

6. In the passage, the author cites which one of the following claims?

(A)   that hats, sunglasses, and sunscreens provide an adequate substitute for the ozone layer

(B)   that environmental protection measures are unpopular and often rejected by communities

(C)   that the value of a locale's environment can be gauged by the incomes of its residents

(D)   that timber harvest limits are needed to save one area from environmental damage

(E)   that most nations measure their own prosperity in terms broader than monetary value

7. The primary purpose of the passage is to

(A)   argue that there is an inherent and potentially detrimental conflict between two schools of thought concerning a certain concept

(B)   summarize and illustrate the main points of the conflict between two schools of thought over the definition of a certain concept

(C)   question one school of thought's definition of a certain concept and suggest several possible alternative definitions

(D)   criticize one school of thought's definition of a certain concept by providing examples that illustrate the implications of adhering to this definition

(E)   bring one school of thought's perspective to bear on a concept traditionally considered to be the exclusive territory of another school of thought

GO ON TO THE NEXT PAGE.

Joy Kogawa's *Obasan* is an account of a Japanese-Canadian family's experiences during World War II. The events are seen from the viewpoint of a young girl who watches her family disintegrate as it
(5) undergoes the relocation that occurred in both Canada and the United States. Although the experience depicted in *Obasan* is mainly one of dislocation, Kogawa employs subtle techniques that serve to emphasize her major character's heroism and to
(10) critique the majority culture. The former end is achieved through the novel's form and the latter through the symbols it employs.

The form of the novel parallels the three-stage structure noted by anthropologists in their studies of
(15) rites of passage. According to these anthropologists, a rite of passage begins with separation from a position of security in a highly structured society; proceeds to alienation in a deathlike state where one is stripped of status, property, and rank; and concludes with
(20) reintegration into society accompanied by a heightened status gained as a result of the second stage. The process thus has the effect of transforming a society's victim into a hero. The first eleven chapters of *Obasan* situate the young protagonist
(25) Naomi Nakane in a close-knit, securely placed family within Vancouver society. Chapters 12–32 chronicle the fall into alienation, when Naomi's family is dislodged from its structured social niche and removed from the city into work camps or exile.
(30) Separated from her parents, Naomi follows her aunt Aya Obasan to the ghost town of Slocan, where Naomi joins the surrogate family of her uncle and aunt. In chapters 33–39 this surrogate family nurtures Naomi as she develops toward a final integration with
(35) the larger society and with herself: as an adult, when she receives a bundle of family documents and letters from her aunt, Naomi breaks through the personal and cultural screens of silence and secretiveness that have enshrouded her past, and reconciles herself with
(40) her history.

Kogawa's use of motifs drawn from Christian rituals and symbols forms a subtle critique of the professed ethics of the majority culture that has shunned Naomi. In one example of such symbolism,
(45) Naomi's reacquaintance with her past is compared with the biblical story of turning stone into bread. The bundle of documents—which Kogawa refers to as "stone-hard facts"—brings Naomi to the recognition of her country's abuse of her people. But
(50) implicit in these hard facts, Kogawa suggests, is also the "bread" of a spiritual sustenance that will allow Naomi to affirm the durability of her people and herself. Through the careful deployment of structure and symbol, Kogawa thus manages to turn Naomi's
(55) experience—and by extension the wartime experiences of many Japanese Canadians—into a journey of heroic transformation and a critique of the majority culture.

8. Which one of the following most accurately states the main idea of the passage?

(A) While telling a story of familial disruption, *Obasan* uses structure and symbolism to valorize its protagonist and critique the majority culture.

(B) By means of its structure and symbolism, *Obasan* mounts a harsh critique of a society that disrupts its citizens' lives.

(C) Although intended primarily as social criticism, given its structure *Obasan* can also be read as a tale of heroic transformation.

(D) With its three-part structure that parallels rites of passage, *Obasan* manages to valorize its protagonist in spite of her traumatic experiences.

(E) Although intended primarily as a story of heroic transformation, *Obasan* can also be read as a work of social criticism.

9. Item removed from scoring.

GO ON TO THE NEXT PAGE.

10. Which one of the following most accurately describes the organization of the passage?

(A) Two points are made about a novel, the first supported with a brief example, the second reasserted without support.

(B) Two points are made about a novel, the first supported with an extended analogy, the second reasserted without support.

(C) Two points are made about a novel, the first reasserted without support, the second supported with an extended analogy.

(D) Two points are made about a novel, the first supported with a brief example, the second supported with an extended analogy.

(E) Two points are made about a novel, the first supported with an extended analogy, the second supported with a brief example.

11. It can be inferred that the heroism Naomi gains in the course of *Obasan* is manifested in her

(A) reconciliation with her past
(B) careful deployment of structure and symbol
(C) relationship with her surrogate family
(D) renewal of her religious beliefs
(E) denunciation of the majority culture

12. According to the anthropologists cited by the author, rites of passage are best described by which one of the following sequences of stages?

(A) alienation, dislocation, integration
(B) separation, alienation, reintegration
(C) integration, alienation, disintegration
(D) dislocation, reconciliation, reintegration
(E) disintegration, transformation, reintegration

13. According to the passage, the agent of Naomi's reconciliation with her past is

(A) her reunion with her parents
(B) the exile of her parents
(C) her critique of the majority society
(D) her separation from her aunt and uncle
(E) her receipt of documents and letters

14. The passage suggests that Joy Kogawa believes which one of the following about the society that shuns Naomi?

(A) It discouraged its citizens from seeking out their heritage.

(B) It endeavored to thwart its citizens' attempts at heroic transformation.

(C) It violated its own supposed religious ethics by doing so.

(D) It prohibited its citizens from participating in rites of passage.

(E) It demanded that loyalty to the government replace loyalty to the family.

15. Based on the passage, which one of the following aspects of Kogawa's work does the author of the passage appear to value most highly?

(A) her willingness to make political statements
(B) her imaginative development of characters
(C) her subtle use of literary techniques
(D) her knowledge of Christian rituals and symbols
(E) her objectivity in describing Naomi's tragic life

GO ON TO THE NEXT PAGE.

The pronghorn, an antelope-like mammal that lives on the western plains of North America, is the continent's fastest land animal, capable of running 90 kilometers per hour and of doing so for several
(5) kilometers. Because no North American predator is nearly fast enough to chase it down, biologists have had difficulty explaining why the pronghorn developed its running prowess. One biologist, however, has recently claimed that pronghorns run as
(10) fast as they do because of adaptation to predators known from fossil records to have been extinct for 10,000 years, such as American cheetahs and long-legged hyenas, either of which, it is believed, were fast enough to run down the pronghorn.
(15) Like all explanations that posit what is called a relict behavior—a behavior that persists though its only evolutionary impetus comes from long-extinct environmental conditions—this one is likely to meet with skepticism. Most biologists distrust explanations positing relict
(20) behaviors, in part because testing these hypotheses is so difficult due to the extinction of a principal component. They typically consider such historical explanations only when a lack of alternatives forces them to do so. But present-day observations sometimes yield
(25) evidence that supports relict behavior hypotheses.
In the case of the pronghorn, researchers have identified much supporting evidence, as several aspects of pronghorn behavior appear to have been shaped by enemies that no longer exist. For example,
(30) pronghorns—like many other grazing animals—roam in herds, which allows more eyes to watch for predators and diminishes the chances of any particular animal being attacked but can also result in overcrowding and increased competition for food. But, since
(35) pronghorns have nothing to fear from present-day carnivores and thus have nothing to gain from herding, their herding behavior appears to be another adaptation to extinct threats. Similarly, if speed and endurance were once essential to survival, researchers would
(40) expect pronghorns to choose mates based on these athletic abilities, which they do—with female pronghorns, for example, choosing the victor after male pronghorns challenge each other in sprints and chases.
Relict behaviors appear to occur in other animals
(45) as well, increasing the general plausibility of such a theory. For example, one study reports relict behavior in stickleback fish belonging to populations that have long been free of a dangerous predator, the sculpin. In the study, when presented with sculpin, these
(50) stickleback fish immediately engaged in stereotypical antisculpin behavior, avoiding its mouth and swimming behind to bite it. Another study found that ground squirrels from populations that have been free from snakes for 70,000 to 300,000 years still clearly recognize
(55) rattlesnakes, displaying stereotypical antirattlesnake behavior in the presence of the snake. Such fear, however, apparently does not persist interminably. Arctic ground squirrels, free of snakes for about 3 million years, appear to be unable to recognize the
(60) threat of a rattlesnake, exhibiting only disorganized caution even after being bitten repeatedly.

16. Which one of the following most accurately states the main point of the passage?

(A) Evidence from present-day animal behaviors, together with the fossil record, supports the hypothesis that the pronghorn's ability to far outrun any predator currently on the North American continent is an adaptation to predators long extinct.

(B) Although some biologists believe that certain animal characteristics, such as the speed of the pronghorn, are explained by environmental conditions that have not existed for many years, recent data concerning arctic ground squirrels make this hypothesis doubtful.

(C) Research into animal behavior, particularly into that of the pronghorn, provides strong evidence that most present-day characteristics of animals are explained by environmental conditions that have not existed for many years.

(D) Even in those cases in which an animal species displays characteristics clearly explained by long-vanished environmental conditions, evidence concerning arctic ground squirrels suggests that those characteristics will eventually disappear.

(E) Although biologists are suspicious of hypotheses that are difficult to test, there is now widespread agreement among biologists that many types of animal characteristics are best explained as adaptations to long-extinct predators.

17. Based on the passage, the term "principal component" (line 21) most clearly refers to which one of the following?

(A) behavior that persists even though the conditions that provided its evolutionary impetus are extinct

(B) the original organism whose descendants' behavior is being investigated as relict behavior

(C) the pronghorn's ability to run 90 kilometers per hour over long distances

(D) the environmental conditions in response to which relict behaviors are thought to have developed

(E) an original behavior of an animal of which certain present-day behaviors are thought to be modifications

GO ON TO THE NEXT PAGE.

18. The last paragraph most strongly supports which one of the following statements?

(A) An absence of predators in an animal's environment can constitute just as much of a threat to the well-being of that animal as the presence of predators.

(B) Relict behaviors are found in most wild animals living today.

(C) If a behavior is an adaptation to environmental conditions, it may eventually disappear in the absence of those or similar conditions.

(D) Behavior patterns that originated as a way of protecting an organism against predators will persist interminably if they are periodically reinforced.

(E) Behavior patterns invariably take longer to develop than they do to disappear.

19. Which one of the following describes a benefit mentioned in the passage that grazing animals derive from roaming in herds?

(A) The greater density of animals tends to intimidate potential predators.

(B) The larger number of adults in a herd makes protection of the younger animals from predators much easier.

(C) With many animals searching it is easier for the herd to find food and water.

(D) The likelihood that any given individual will be attacked by a predator decreases.

(E) The most defenseless animals can achieve greater safety by remaining in the center of the herd.

20. The passage mentions each of the following as support for the explanation of the pronghorn's speed proposed by the biologist referred to in line 8 EXCEPT:

(A) fossils of extinct animals believed to have been able to run down a pronghorn

(B) the absence of carnivores in the pronghorn's present-day environment

(C) the present-day preference of pronghorns for athletic mates

(D) the apparent need for a similar explanation to account for the herding behavior pronghorns now display

(E) the occurrence of relict behavior in other species

21. The third paragraph of the passage provides the most support for which one of the following inferences?

(A) Predators do not attack grazing animals that are assembled into herds.

(B) Pronghorns tend to graze in herds only when they sense a threat from predators close by.

(C) If animals do not graze for their food, they do not roam in herds.

(D) Female pronghorns mate only with the fastest male pronghorn in the herd.

(E) If pronghorns did not herd, they would not face significantly greater danger from present-day carnivores.

GO ON TO THE NEXT PAGE.

Many legal theorists have argued that the only morally legitimate goal in imposing criminal penalties against certain behaviors is to prevent people from harming others. Clearly, such theorists would oppose (5) laws that force people to act purely for their own good or to refrain from certain harmless acts purely to ensure conformity to some social norm. But the goal of preventing harm to others would also justify legal sanctions against some forms of nonconforming (10) behavior to which this goal might at first seem not to apply.

In many situations it is in the interest of each member of a group to agree to behave in a certain way on the condition that the others similarly agree. (15) In the simplest cases, a mere coordination of activities is itself the good that results. For example, it is in no one's interest to lack a convention about which side of the road to drive on, and each person can agree to drive on one side assuming the others do (20) too. Any fair rule, then, would be better than no rule at all. On the assumption that all people would voluntarily agree to be subject to a coordination rule backed by criminal sanctions, if people could be assured that others would also agree, it is argued to (25) be legitimate for a legislature to impose such a rule. This is because prevention of harm underlies the rationale for the rule, though it applies to the problem of coordination less directly than to other problems, for the act that is forbidden (driving on the other side (30) of the road) is not inherently harm-producing, as are burglary and assault; instead, it is the lack of a coordinating rule that would be harmful.

In some other situations involving a need for legally enforced coordination, the harm to be averted (35) goes beyond the simple lack of coordination itself. This can be illustrated by an example of a coordination rule—instituted by a private athletic organization—which has analogies in criminal law. At issue is whether the use of anabolic steroids, which (40) build muscular strength but have serious negative side effects, should be prohibited. Each athlete has at stake both an interest in having a fair opportunity to win and an interest in good health. If some competitors use steroids, others have the option of either (45) endangering their health or losing their fair opportunity to win. Thus they would be harmed either way. A compulsory rule could prevent that harm and thus would be in the interest of all competitors. If they understand its function and trust the techniques (50) for its enforcement, they will gladly consent to it. So while it might appear that such a rule merely forces people to act for their own good, the deeper rationale for coercion here—as in the above example—is a somewhat complex appeal to the legitimacy of (55) enforcing a rule with the goal of preventing harm.

22. Which one of the following most accurately states the main point of the passage?

(A) In order to be morally justifiable, laws prohibiting activities that are not inherently harm-producing must apply equitably to everyone.

(B) It is justifiable to require social conformity where noncompliance would be harmful to either the nonconforming individual or the larger group.

(C) Achieving coordination can be argued to be a morally legitimate justification for rules that prevent directly harmful actions and others that prevent indirectly harmful actions.

(D) It is reasonable to hold that restricting individual liberty is always justified on the basis of mutually agreed-upon community standards.

(E) The principle of preventing harm to others can be used to justify laws that do not at first glance appear to be designed to prevent such harm.

23. It can be most reasonably inferred from the passage that the author considers which one of the following factors to be generally necessary for the justification of rules compelling coordination of people's activities?

(A) evidence that such rules do not force individuals to act for their own good

(B) enactment of such rules by a duly elected or appointed government lawmaking organization

(C) the assurance that criminal penalties are provided as a means of securing compliance with such rules

(D) some form of consent on the part of rational people who are subject to such rules

(E) a sense of community and cultural uniformity among those who are required to abide by such rules

GO ON TO THE NEXT PAGE.

24. It can be most reasonably inferred from the passage that the author would agree with which one of the following statements?

    (A)   In all situations in which compulsory rules are needed for the coordination of human activities, any uniformly enforced rule is as acceptable as any other.

    (B)   No private organizational rules designed to coordinate the activities of members have as complex a relation to the goal of preventing harm as have some criminal statutes.

    (C)   Every fair rule that could be effectively used to prescribe which side of the road to drive on is a rule whose implementation would likely cause less harm than it would prevent.

    (D)   There would be little need for formal regulation and enforcement of conventional driving patterns if all drivers understood and accepted the rationale behind such regulation and enforcement.

    (E)   Unlike rules forbidding such acts as burglary and assault, those that are designed primarily to prevent the inconvenience and chaos of uncoordinated activities should not involve criminal penalties.

25. The author distinguishes between two examples of coordinating rules on the basis of whether or not such rules

    (A)   prevent some harm beyond that which consists simply in a lack of coordination

    (B)   are intended to ensure conformity to a set of agreed-upon standards

    (C)   are voluntarily agreed upon by all those affected by such rules

    (D)   could be considered justifiable by the legal theorists discussed in the passage

    (E)   apply less directly to the problem of preventing harm than do rules against burglary and assault

26. Which one of the following is a rule that primarily addresses a problem of coordination most similar to that discussed in the second paragraph?

    (A)   a rule requiring that those who wish to dig for ancient artifacts secure the permission of relevant authorities and the owners of the proposed site before proceeding with their activities

    (B)   a rule requiring that pharmacists dispense certain kinds of medications only when directed to do so by physicians' prescriptions, rather than simply selling medicines at the customers' request

    (C)   a rule requiring that advertisers be able to substantiate the claims they make in advertisements, rather than simply saying whatever they think will help to attract customers

    (D)   a rule requiring that employees of a certain restaurant all wear identical uniforms during their hours of employment, rather than wearing whatever clothes they choose

    (E)   a rule requiring different aircraft to fly at different altitudes rather than flying at any altitude their pilots wish

27. In line 54, the author uses the expression "somewhat complex" primarily to describe reasoning that

    (A)   involves two layers of law, one governing the private sector and the other governing the public sector

    (B)   requires that those affected by the rule understand the motivation behind its imposition

    (C)   involves a case in which a harm to be prevented is indirectly related to the kind of act that is to be prohibited

    (D)   can convince athletes that their health is as important as their competitive success

    (E)   illustrates how appeals to the need for coordination can be used to justify many rules that do not involve coordination

S T O P

IF YOU FINISH BEFORE TIME IS CALLED, YOU MAY CHECK YOUR WORK ON THIS SECTION ONLY.
DO NOT WORK ON ANY OTHER SECTION IN THE TEST.

SECTION II
Time—35 minutes
25 Questions

Directions: The questions in this section are based on the reasoning contained in brief statements or passages. For some questions, more than one of the choices could conceivably answer the question. However, you are to choose the best answer; that is, the response that most accurately and completely answers the question. You should not make assumptions that are by commonsense standards implausible, superfluous, or incompatible with the passage. After you have chosen the best answer, blacken the corresponding space on your answer sheet.

1. Cox: The consumer council did not provide sufficient justification for its action when it required that Derma-35 be recalled from the market.

   Crockett: I disagree. Derma-35 in fact causes inflammation, but in citing only the side effect of blemishes as the justification for its decision, the council rightly acknowledged that blemishes are a legitimate health concern.

   Cox and Crockett disagree over whether

   (A) Derma-35 should remain on the market
   (B) blemishes are sometimes caused by inflammation
   (C) the council based its decision on the threat of inflammation or on the threat of blemishes
   (D) the council gave an adequate reason for its decision to recall Derma-35
   (E) inflammation is a serious health threat

2. Literary historian: William Shakespeare, a humble actor, could have written the love poetry attributed to him. But the dramas attributed to him evince such insight into the minds of powerful rulers that they could only have been written by one who had spent much time among them; Francis Bacon associated with rulers, but Shakespeare did not.

   Which one of the following logically follows from the literary historian's claims?

   (A) Bacon wrote the dramas attributed to Shakespeare, but could not have written the love poetry.
   (B) Bacon wrote both the love poetry and the dramas attributed to Shakespeare.
   (C) Shakespeare wrote neither the love poetry nor the dramas attributed to him.
   (D) One person could not have written both the love poetry and the dramas attributed to Shakespeare.
   (E) Shakespeare may have written the love poetry but did not write the dramas attributed to him.

3. Philosopher: Effective tests have recently been developed to predict fatal diseases having a largely genetic basis. Now, for the first time, a person can be warned well in advance of the possibility of such life-threatening conditions. However, medicine is not yet able to prevent most such conditions. Simply being informed that one will get a disease that is both fatal and incurable can itself be quite harmful to some people. This raises the question of whether such "early warning" tests should be made available at all.

   Which one of the following statements is best illustrated by the state of affairs described by the philosopher?

   (A) The advance of medicine fails to provide solutions to every problem.
   (B) The advance of medicine creates new contexts in which ethical dilemmas can arise.
   (C) Medical technologies continue to advance, increasing our knowledge and understanding of disease.
   (D) The more we come to learn, the more we realize how little we know.
   (E) The advance of technology is of questionable value.

GO ON TO THE NEXT PAGE.

4. Chapin: Commentators have noted with concern the recent electoral success by extremist parties in several democratic countries. But these successes pose no threat to democracy in those countries. The extremists have won pluralities, not majorities. Furthermore, they have won only when the moderate parties were preoccupied with arguing among themselves.

Which one of the following, if assumed, enables Chapin's conclusion to be properly drawn?

(A) Parties that win pluralities but not majorities never directly or indirectly effect changes in their country's political arrangements.

(B) Multiparty political systems are always more democratic than two-party political systems are.

(C) Countries in which extremist parties win pluralities sometimes have democratic governments as strong as those in countries that lack extremist parties.

(D) Members of moderate parties who consider extremist parties to be a serious threat to democracy will sometimes put aside their differences with each other to oppose them.

(E) People are not always supporting a move toward an extremist government when they vote for extremist parties in democratic elections.

5. Futurist: Artists in the next century will be supported largely by private patrons. Because these patrons will almost invariably be supporters of the social order—whatever it happens to be at the time—art in the next century will rarely express social and political doctrines that are perceived to be subversive of that social order.

Which one of the following principles, if valid, provides the most support for the futurist's inference?

(A) Art patrons tend not to support artists whose art expresses social and political views that are in opposition to their own.

(B) Art patrons tend to be more interested in formal artistic problems than in the social and political issues of their time.

(C) Artists are as prone to attack the contemporary social and political order in their work as they are to defend it.

(D) Artists tend to become more critical of contemporary social and political arrangements after they are freed of their dependency on private patrons.

(E) Art patrons tend to oppose all social change except that initiated by artists.

6. University budget committee: Athletes experience fewer injuries on artificial-turf athletic fields than on natural-grass fields. Additionally, natural-grass fields are more expensive to maintain than fields made of artificial turf. Nevertheless, this committee recommends replacing the university's current artificial-turf field with a natural-grass field.

Which one of the following, if true, most helps to resolve the apparent discrepancy in the committee's position?

(A) The university's current artificial-turf athletic field has required extensive maintenance since its original installation.

(B) Most injuries sustained on artificial-turf fields take longer to heal and require more expensive physical therapy than do injuries sustained on natural-grass fields.

(C) It is difficult for spectators at athletic events to determine whether an athletic field is artificial turf or natural grass.

(D) Maintaining artificial-turf fields involves the occasional replacement of damaged sections of turf, whereas natural-grass fields require daily watering and periodic fertilization.

(E) Athletes who have spent most of their playing time on natural-grass fields generally prefer not to play on artificial-turf fields.

7. Although instinct enables organisms to make complex responses to stimuli, instinctual behavior involves no reasoning and requires far fewer nerve cells than does noninstinctual (also called flexible) behavior. A brain mechanism capable of flexible behavior must have a large number of neurons, and no insect brain has yet reached a size capable of providing a sufficiently large number of neurons.

Which one of the following can be properly inferred from the statements above?

(A) The behavior of organisms with elaborate brain mechanisms is usually not instinctual.

(B) Insect behavior is exclusively instinctual.

(C) All organisms with brains larger than insects' brains are capable of some measure of flexible behavior.

(D) All organisms with large brains are biologically equipped for flexible behavior.

(E) Only organisms with brains of insect size or smaller engage in purely instinctual behavior.

GO ON TO THE NEXT PAGE.

8. The laboratory experiment, the most effective method for teaching science, is disappearing from most secondary school curricula, and students are now simulating experiments with computers. This trend should be stopped. It results in many students' completing secondary school and going on to a university without knowing how to work with laboratory equipment.

Which one of the following, if true, most weakens the argument?

(A) Scientific knowledge is changing so rapidly it is difficult for secondary schools to keep up without using computers.

(B) In some secondary schools, teachers conduct laboratory experiments while students observe.

(C) Computers have proven to be a valuable tool for teaching secondary school students scientific terminology.

(D) Secondary schools and universities across the nation have put a great deal of money into purchasing computers.

(E) University students can learn science effectively without having had experience in working with laboratory equipment.

9. Alice: In democracies, politicians garner support by emphasizing the differences between their opponents and themselves. Because they must rule in accord with their rhetoric, policies in democracies fluctuate wildly as one party succeeds another.

Elwell: But despite election rhetoric, to put together majority coalitions in democracies, politicians usually end up softening their stands on individual issues once they are elected.

The statements above provide the most support for the claim that Alice and Elwell disagree about whether

(A) politicians heighten the differences between themselves and their opponents during elections

(B) basic policies change drastically when one party succeeds another in a democracy

(C) in a democracy the best way of ensuring continuity in policies is to form a coalition government

(D) most voters stay loyal to a particular political party even as it changes its stand on particular issues

(E) the desire of parties to build majority coalitions tends to support democratic systems

10. Air traffic controllers and nuclear power plant operators are not allowed to work exceptionally long hours, because to do so would jeopardize lives. Yet physicians in residency training are typically required to work 80-hour weeks. The aforementioned restrictions on working exceptionally long hours should also be applied to resident physicians, since they too are engaged in work of a life-or-death nature.

Which one of the following is an assumption the argument depends on?

(A) There is no indispensable aspect of residency training that requires resident physicians to work exceptionally long hours.

(B) Resident physicians have a more direct effect on the lives of others than do air traffic controllers and nuclear power plant operators.

(C) The more hours one works in a week, the less satisfactorily one performs one's work.

(D) Those who are not engaged in work that has life-or-death consequences should only sometimes be allowed to work exceptionally long hours.

(E) Some resident physicians would like to complete their residency training without working exceptionally long hours.

11. Career consultant: The most popular career advice suggests emphasizing one's strengths to employers and downplaying one's weaknesses. Research shows this advice to be incorrect. A study of 314 managers shows that those who use self-deprecating humor in front of their employees are more likely to be seen by them as even-handed, thoughtful, and concerned than are those who do not.

The career consultant's reasoning is most vulnerable to criticism on the grounds that it

(A) bases a conclusion about how one group will respond to self-deprecation on information about how a different group responds to it

(B) ignores the possibility that what was viewed positively in the managers' self-deprecating humor was the self-deprecation and not its humor

(C) ignores the possibility that non-self-deprecating humor might have been viewed even more positively than self-deprecating humor

(D) infers from the fact that self-deprecating humor was viewed positively that nonhumorous self-deprecation would not be viewed positively

(E) bases a conclusion about certain popular career advice on a critique of only one part of that advice

12. Researcher: We studied two groups of subjects over a period of six months. Over this period, one of the groups had a daily routine of afternoon exercise. The other group, the control group, engaged in little or no exercise during the study. It was found that those in the exercise group got 33 percent more deep-sleep at night than did the control group. Exercising in the afternoon tends to raise body temperature slightly until after bedtime, and this extra heat induces deeper sleep.

The researcher's statements, if true, most strongly support which one of the following?

(A) Regular afternoon exercise is one of the things required for adequate deep-sleep.
(B) Exercise in the morning is almost as likely to have as many beneficial effects on sleep as is exercise in the afternoon.
(C) The best way to get increased deep-sleep is to induce a slight increase in body temperature just before bedtime.
(D) No one in the control group experienced a rise in body temperature just before bedtime.
(E) Raising body temperature slightly by taking a warm bath just before bedtime will likely result in increased deep-sleep.

13. Companies wishing to boost sales of merchandise should use in-store displays to catch customers' attention. According to a marketing study, today's busy shoppers have less time for coupon-clipping and pay little attention to direct-mail advertising; instead, they make two-thirds of their buying decisions on the spot at the store.

Which one of the following is an assumption that the argument requires?

(A) Companies are increasingly using in-store displays to catch customers' attention.
(B) Coupons and direct-mail advertising were at one time more effective means of boosting sales of merchandise than they are now.
(C) In-store displays are more likely to influence buying decisions made on the spot at the store than to influence other buying decisions.
(D) In-store displays that catch customers' attention increase the likelihood that customers will decide on the spot to buy the company's merchandise.
(E) Many of today's shoppers are too busy to pay careful attention to in-store displays.

14. Roger Bacon, the thirteenth-century scientist, is said to have made important discoveries in optics. He was an early advocate of hands-on experimentation, and as a teacher warned his students against relying uncritically on the opinions of authorities. Nevertheless, this did not stop Bacon himself from appealing to authority when it was expedient for his own argumentation. Thus, Bacon's work on optics should be generally disregarded, in view of the contradiction between his statements and his own behavior.

The reasoning in the argument is flawed because the argument

(A) presumes, without providing justification, that authority opinion is often incorrect
(B) attacks Bacon's uncritical reliance on authority opinion
(C) uses Bacon's remarks to his students as evidence of his opinions
(D) ignores the fact that thirteenth-century science may not hold up well today
(E) criticizes Bacon's character in order to question his scientific findings

15. One's palate is to a great extent socially determined: that is, if we notice that a lot of people enjoy consuming a certain type of food, we will eventually come to like the food as well, once we have become accustomed to the food.

Which one of the following most closely conforms to the principle above?

(A) Maxine spoke to her neighbor about the many different ways he prepared pasta, and after trying some of his recipes found out that she loves to eat pasta.
(B) Mike dislikes lima beans, due to his having parents who dislike them and few family members who enjoy them.
(C) All of George's Ukrainian relatives love to eat pierogies, and by staying with them for several summers, George has become very fond of pierogies as well.
(D) Yolanda dislikes pickles because she has observed that many of her relatives wince when eating pickles.
(E) Sally found jalapeño peppers to be too hot when she first tried them, but now she can eat them without discomfort, because her family members use them frequently in their cooking.

GO ON TO THE NEXT PAGE.

16. The ability to access information via computer is a tremendous resource for visually impaired people. Only a limited amount of printed information is accessible in braille, large type, or audiotape. But a person with the right hardware and software can access a large quantity of information from libraries and museums around the world, and can have the computer read the information aloud, display it in large type, or produce a braille version. Thus, visually impaired people can now access information from computers more easily than they can from most traditional sources.

Which one of the following, if true, most strengthens the argument?

(A) A computerized speech synthesizer is often less expensive than a complete library of audiotapes.

(B) Relatively easy-to-use computer systems that can read information aloud, display it in large type, or produce a braille version of it are widely available.

(C) Many visually impaired people prefer traditional sources of information to computers that can read information aloud, display it in large type, or produce a braille version of it.

(D) Most visually impaired people who have access to information via computer also have access to this same information via more traditional sources.

(E) The rate at which printed information is converted into formats easily accessible to visually impaired people will increase.

17. Legislator: The recently released crime statistics clearly show that the new laws requiring stiffer punishments for violators have reduced the crime rate. In the areas covered by those laws, the incidence of crime has decreased by one-fourth over the four years since the legislation was enacted.

Analyst: The statistics are welcome news, but they do not provide strong evidence that the new laws caused the drop in crime. Many comparable areas that lack such legislation have reported a similar drop in the crime rate during the same period.

Which one of the following most accurately describes the strategy used by the analyst to call into question the legislator's argument?

(A) pointing out that the legislator has provided no evidence of the reliability of the statistics on which the legislator's conclusion is based

(B) arguing that the legislator has unreasonably concluded that one event has caused another without ruling out the possibility that both events are effects of a common cause

(C) objecting that the statistics on which the legislator is basing his conclusion are drawn from a time period that is too short to yield a meaningful data sample

(D) claiming that the legislator has attempted to establish a particular conclusion because doing so is in the legislator's self-interest rather than because of any genuine concern for the truth of the matter

(E) implying that the legislator has drawn a conclusion about cause and effect without considering how often the alleged effect has occurred in the absence of the alleged cause

GO ON TO THE NEXT PAGE.

18. Many physicists claim that quantum mechanics may ultimately be able to explain all fundamental phenomena, and that, therefore, physical theory will soon be complete. However, every theory in the history of physics that was thought to be final eventually had to be rejected for failure to explain some new observation. For this reason, we can expect that quantum mechanics will not be the final theory.

Which one of the following arguments is most similar in its reasoning to the argument above?

(A) Only a few species of plants now grow in very dry climates; therefore, few species of animals can live in those climates.

(B) Four companies have marketed a new food processing product; therefore, a fifth company will not be able to market a similar product.

(C) Your sister is a very good chess player but she has never won a chess tournament; therefore, she will not win this chess tournament.

(D) A rare virus infected a group of people a decade ago; therefore, it will not reinfect the same population now.

(E) Each team member has failed to live up to people's expectations; therefore, the team will not live up to people's expectations.

19. In an experiment, researchers played a series of musical intervals—two-note sequences—to a large, diverse group of six-month-old babies. They found that the babies paid significantly more attention when the intervals were perfect octaves, fifths, or fourths than otherwise. These intervals are prevalent in the musical systems of most cultures around the world. Thus, humans probably have a biological predisposition to pay more attention to those intervals than to others.

Which one of the following, if true, most strengthens the argument?

(A) Several similar experiments using older children and adults found that these subjects, too, had a general tendency to pay more attention to octaves, fifths, and fourths than to other musical intervals.

(B) None of the babies in the experiment had previous exposure to music from any culture.

(C) All of the babies in the experiment had been exposed to music drawn equally from a wide variety of cultures around the world.

(D) In a second experiment, these same babies showed no clear tendency to notice primary colors more than other colors.

(E) Octaves, fifths, and fourths were played more frequently during the experiment than other musical intervals were.

20. Professor Donnelly's exams are always more difficult than Professor Curtis's exams. The question about dinosaurs was on Professor Donnelly's last exam. Therefore, the question must be difficult.

Which one of the following exhibits both of the logical flaws exhibited in the argument above?

(A) Lewis is a better baker than Stockman. Lewis made this cake. Therefore, it must be better than most of Stockman's cakes.

(B) Porter's new book of poetry is better than any of her other books of poetry. This poem is from Porter's new book, so it must be good.

(C) Professor Whitburn is teaching English this year and always assigns a lot of reading. Therefore, this year's English class will have to do more reading than last year's class.

(D) Shield's first novel has a more complicated plot than any other that she has written. Hence, that plot must be very complex.

(E) Mathematics is more difficult than history. Therefore, my calculus test will be more difficult than my history test.

GO ON TO THE NEXT PAGE.

21. Ethicist: As a function of one's job and societal role, one has various duties. There are situations where acting in accord with one of these duties has disastrous consequences, and thus the duties are not absolute. However, it is a principle of morality that if one does not have overwhelming evidence that fulfilling such a duty will have disastrous consequences, one ought to fulfill it.

Which one of the following most closely conforms to the principle of morality cited by the ethicist?

(A) A teacher thinks that a certain student has received the course grade merited by the quality of his work. The teacher should fulfill her duty not to raise the student's grade, even though the lower grade might harm the student's chance of obtaining an internship.

(B) A person should not fulfill his duty to tell his friend the truth about the friend's new haircut, because lying will make the friend happier than the truth would.

(C) A police investigator discovers that a contractor has slightly overcharged wealthy customers in order to lower rates for a charity. The investigator should not fulfill his duty to report the contractor provided that the contractor stops the practice.

(D) A psychiatrist's patient tells her about his recurring nightmares of having committed a terrible crime. The psychiatrist should fulfill her duty to report this to the authorities because the patient may have broken the law, even though the psychiatrist also has a duty of confidentiality to her patients.

(E) A journalist thinks there is a slight chance that a story about a developing crisis will endanger innocent lives. Therefore, the journalist should await further developments before fulfilling his duty to file the story.

22. Detective: Laser-printer drums are easily damaged, and any nick in a drum will produce a blemish of similar dimensions on each page produced by that printer. So in matching a blemish on a page with a nick on a drum, we can reliably trace a suspicious laser-printed document to the precise printer on which it was produced.

Which one of the following, if true, most weakens the detective's argument?

(A) Criminals are unlikely to use their own laser printers to produce suspicious documents.

(B) Drum nicks are usually so small that it requires skill to accurately determine their size and shape.

(C) The manufacturing process often produces the same nick on several drums.

(D) Blemishes on documents are sometimes totally concealed by characters that are printed over them.

(E) Most suspicious documents are not produced on laser printers.

23. Whoever is kind is loved by somebody or other, and whoever loves anyone is happy. It follows that whoever is kind is happy.

The conclusion follows logically if which one of the following is assumed?

(A) Whoever loves someone loves everyone.
(B) Whoever loves everyone loves someone.
(C) Whoever is happy loves everyone.
(D) Whoever loves no one is loved by no one.
(E) Whoever loves everyone is kind.

GO ON TO THE NEXT PAGE.

24. It is now clear that the ancient Egyptians were the first society to produce alcoholic beverages. It had been thought that the ancient Babylonians were the first; they had mastered the process of fermentation for making wine as early as 1500 B.C. However, archaeologists have discovered an Egyptian cup dating from 2000 B.C. whose sides depict what appears to be an Egyptian brewery, and whose chemical residue reveals that it contained a form of alcoholic beer.

The reasoning above is most vulnerable to criticism on which one of the following grounds?

(A) It makes a generalization about Egyptian society based on a sample so small that it is likely to be unrepresentative.

(B) It uses the term "alcoholic beverage" in a different sense in the premises than in the conclusion.

(C) It presumes, without providing justification, that because one society developed a technology before another, the development in the latter was dependent on the development in the former.

(D) It ignores the possibility that the first known instance of a kind is not the first instance of that kind.

(E) It provides no evidence for the claim that the Babylonians produced wine as early as 1500 B.C.

25. Studies have shown that specialty sports foods contain exactly the same nutrients in the same quantities as do common foods from the grocery store. Moreover, sports foods cost from two to three times more than regular foods. So very few athletes would buy sports foods were it not for expensive advertising campaigns.

Which one of the following, if true, most weakens the argument?

(A) Sports foods are occasionally used by world-famous athletes.

(B) Many grocery stores carry sports foods alongside traditional inventories.

(C) Sports foods are easier than regular foods to carry and consume during training and competition.

(D) Regular foods contain vitamins and minerals that are essential to developing strength and endurance.

(E) Sports foods can nutritionally substitute for regular meals.

STOP
IF YOU FINISH BEFORE TIME IS CALLED, YOU MAY CHECK YOUR WORK ON THIS SECTION ONLY.
DO NOT WORK ON ANY OTHER SECTION IN THE TEST.

SECTION III
Time—35 minutes
26 Questions

Directions: The questions in this section are based on the reasoning contained in brief statements or passages. For some questions, more than one of the choices could conceivably answer the question. However, you are to choose the best answer; that is, the response that most accurately and completely answers the question. You should not make assumptions that are by commonsense standards implausible, superfluous, or incompatible with the passage. After you have chosen the best answer, blacken the corresponding space on your answer sheet.

1. Sambar deer are physically incapable of digesting meat. Yet sambar deer have been reported feeding on box turtles after killing them.

   Which one of the following, if true, best resolves the discrepancy above?

   (A) Sambar deer eat only the bony shells of box turtles.
   (B) Sambar deer often kill box turtles by accident.
   (C) Sambar deer kill box turtles only occasionally.
   (D) Box turtles sometimes compete with sambar deer for food.
   (E) Box turtles are much slower and clumsier than are sambar deer.

2. Benson: In order to maintain the quality of life in our city, we need to restrict growth. That is why I support the new zoning regulations.

   Willett: I had heard such arguments ten years ago, and again five years ago. Each time the city council was justified in deciding not to restrict growth. Since there is nothing new in this idea of restricting growth, I oppose the regulations.

   Which one of the following most accurately describes a way in which Willett's reasoning is questionable?

   (A) It presumes that growth is necessarily good without offering support for that position.
   (B) It is based on attacking Benson personally rather than responding to Benson's reasoning.
   (C) It ignores the possibility that new reasons for restricting growth have arisen in the past five years.
   (D) It fails to take into account the variety of factors that contribute to the quality of life in a city.
   (E) It overlooks the possibility that the city council of ten years ago was poorly qualified to decide on zoning regulations.

3. A recent study involved feeding a high-salt diet to a rat colony. A few months after the experiment began, standard tests of the rats' blood pressure revealed that about 25 percent of the colony had normal, healthy blood pressure, about 70 percent of the colony had high blood pressure, and 5 percent of the colony had extremely high blood pressure. The conclusion from these results is that high-salt diets are linked to high blood pressure in rats.

   The answer to which one of the following questions is most relevant to evaluating the conclusion drawn above?

   (A) How much more salt than is contained in a rat's normal diet was there in the high-salt diet?
   (B) Did the high blood pressure have any adverse health effects on those rats that developed it?
   (C) What percentage of naturally occurring rat colonies feed on high-salt diets?
   (D) How many rats in the colony studied had abnormally high blood pressure before the study began?
   (E) Have other species of rodents been used in experiments of the same kind?

4. Detective: Bill has been accused of committing the burglary at the warehouse last night. But no one saw Bill in the vicinity of the warehouse. So we must conclude that Bill did not commit the burglary.

   The reasoning in the detective's argument is most vulnerable to criticism on the grounds that the argument

   (A) treats evidence that is irrelevant to the burglar's identity as if it were relevant
   (B) merely attacks the character of Bill's accusers
   (C) fails to provide independent evidence for the theory that Bill committed the burglary
   (D) treats a lack of evidence against Bill as if it exonerated Bill
   (E) fails to establish the true identity of the burglar

GO ON TO THE NEXT PAGE.

5. Psychologist: Because of a perceived social stigma against psychotherapy, and because of age discrimination on the part of some professionals, some elderly people feel discouraged about trying psychotherapy. They should not be, however, for many younger people have greatly benefited from it, and people in later life have certain advantages over the young—such as breadth of knowledge, emotional maturity, and interpersonal skills—that contribute to the likelihood of a positive outcome.

Which one of the following most accurately expresses the main conclusion of the psychologist's argument?

(A) Certain psychotherapists practice age discrimination.
(B) Elderly people are better able to benefit from psychotherapy than are younger people.
(C) Elderly people should not be reluctant to undergo psychotherapy.
(D) Characteristics associated with maturity are important factors in psychotherapy's success.
(E) Elderly people are less inclined to try psychotherapy than are younger people.

6. Heavy salting of Albritten's roads to melt winter ice and snow began about 20 years ago. The area's groundwater now contains approximately 100 milligrams of dissolved salt per liter. Groundwater in a nearby, less highly urbanized area, where little salt is used and where traffic patterns resemble those of Albritten 20 years ago, contains only about 10 milligrams of dissolved salt per liter. Since water that contains 250 or more milligrams of dissolved salt per liter tastes unacceptably salty, continuing the salting of Albritten's roads at its present rate will render Albritten's groundwater unpalatable within the next few decades.

Which one of the following, if true, most seriously weakens the argument?

(A) Even water that contains up to 5,000 milligrams of dissolved salt per liter is safe to drink.
(B) The concentration of dissolved salt in Albritten's groundwater is expected to reach 400 milligrams per liter within a few decades.
(C) Salting icy roads is the simplest way to prevent accidents on those roads.
(D) Albritten's groundwater contained roughly 90 milligrams of dissolved salt per liter 20 years ago.
(E) Salting of Albritten's roads is likely to decrease over the next few decades.

7. Numerous books describe the rules of etiquette. Usually the authors of such books merely codify standards of behavior by classifying various behaviors as polite or rude. However, this suggests that there is a single, objective standard of politeness. Clearly, standards of politeness vary from culture to culture, so it is absurd to label any one set of behaviors as correct and others as incorrect.

The reasoning in the argument is most vulnerable to criticism on the grounds that the argument

(A) reaches a conclusion about how people actually behave on the basis of assertions regarding how they ought to behave
(B) bases a generalization about all books of etiquette on the actions of a few authors
(C) fails to justify its presumption regarding the influence of rules of etiquette on individual behavior
(D) overlooks the possibility that authors of etiquette books are purporting to state what is correct behavior for one particular culture only
(E) attempts to lend itself credence by unfairly labeling the position of the authors of etiquette books "absurd"

8. In jazz history, there have been gifted pianists who, because they had no striking musical ideas, led no memorable recording sessions. But precisely because they lacked such ideas, they were able to respond quickly to the ideas of imaginative and difficult leaders. Thus, these pianists are often heard adding masterful touches to some of the greatest jazz recordings.

Which one of the following principles is best illustrated by the information above?

(A) The success of a group enterprise depends on the ability of the leader to recognize the weaknesses of others in the group.
(B) The production of any great work requires contributions from those who are unimaginative but technically skilled.
(C) People without forceful personalities cannot become great leaders in a field.
(D) A trait that is a weakness in some settings can contribute to greatness in other settings.
(E) No one can achieve great success without the help of others who are able to bring one's ideas to fruition.

GO ON TO THE NEXT PAGE.

9. Editorial: When legislators discover that some public service is not being adequately provided, their most common response is to boost the funding for that public service. Because of this, the least efficiently run government bureaucracies are the ones that most commonly receive an increase in funds.

The statements in the editorial, if true, most strongly support which one of the following?

(A) The least efficiently run government bureaucracies are the bureaucracies that legislators most commonly discover to be failing to provide some public service adequately.

(B) When legislators discover that a public service is not being adequately provided, they never respond to the problem by reducing the funding of the government bureaucracy providing that service.

(C) Throughout the time a government bureaucracy is run inefficiently, legislators repeatedly boost the funding for the public service that this bureaucracy provides.

(D) If legislators boost funding for a public service, the government bureaucracy providing that service will commonly become less efficient as a result.

(E) The most inefficiently run government bureaucracy receives the most funding of any government bureaucracy.

10. Fred argued that, since Kathleen is a successful film director, she has probably worked with famous actors. But, while Fred is right in supposing that most successful film directors work with famous actors, his conclusion is not warranted. For, as he knows, Kathleen works only on documentary films, and directors of documentaries rarely work with famous actors.

Which one of the following strategies is used above to criticize Fred's reasoning?

(A) maintaining that too little is known about Kathleen to justify any conclusion

(B) showing that Kathleen must not have worked with famous actors

(C) claiming that Fred has failed to take relevant information into account

(D) showing that Fred has mistakenly assumed that all successful film directors work with famous actors

(E) demonstrating that Fred has failed to show that most successful film directors work with famous actors

11. In early 1990, Queenston instituted a tax increase that gave its school system a larger operating budget. The school system used the larger budget to increase the total number of teachers in the system by 30 percent between 1990 and 1993. Nevertheless, there was no change in the average number of students per teacher between 1990 and 1993.

If the statements above are true, then on the basis of them which one of the following must also be true?

(A) No classes in Queenston's school system experienced an increase in enrollment between 1990 and 1993.

(B) The total number of students enrolled in Queenston's school system increased between 1990 and 1993.

(C) The operating budget of Queenston's school system increased by exactly 30 percent between 1990 and 1993.

(D) Most teachers who worked for Queenston's school system in 1990 were still working for the system in 1993.

(E) The quality of education in Queenston's school system improved between 1990 and 1993.

12. Our computer experts are asked from time to time to allocate funds for new hardware and software for our company. Unfortunately, these experts favor cutting-edge technologies, because that is what excites them, despite the fact that such experimental technologies are highly expensive, full of undiscovered "bugs," and thus are not the most profitable investments.

Of the following, which one conforms most closely to the principle illustrated by the situation described above?

(A) When senior executives choose to promote junior executives, they tend to favor those who share their professional interests, not those who have had the most education.

(B) When supermarkets choose foods, they choose the kinds that can be sold for the most profit, not the kinds of foods that are the most healthful for consumers.

(C) When librarians choose books for the library, they choose the kinds that they enjoy reading, not the kinds of books that serve the interests of the community.

(D) When students choose courses, they choose those that require the least amount of work, not those in which they might learn the most.

(E) When television executives choose programs to air, they choose the ones with the most sex and violence because that is what viewers want, not the shows with the highest artistic merit.

GO ON TO THE NEXT PAGE.

13. It is characteristic of great artists generally, and of great writers in particular, to have a discerning view of the basic social and political arrangements of the society in which they live. Therefore, the greater a writer one is, the more astute one will be in perceiving the basic social and political arrangements of one's society.

Which one of the following most accurately describes a flaw in the reasoning above?

(A) It assumes, without providing justification, that members of a group that is part of a larger group possess all of the characteristics possessed by members of the larger group.

(B) It assumes, without providing justification, that because something is sometimes the case it must always be the case.

(C) It assumes, without providing justification, that those artists with political insight do not have insight into matters outside of politics.

(D) It assumes, without providing justification, that only great individuals can make discerning criticisms of their societies.

(E) It assumes, without providing justification, that because people who have one quality tend to have a second quality, those who have more of the first quality will have more of the second.

14. Political scientist: The economies of a number of European countries are currently in severe difficulty. Germany is the only neighboring country that has the resources to resuscitate these economies. Therefore, Germany should begin aiding these economically troubled countries.

Which one of the following principles most helps to justify the political scientist's reasoning?

(A) Any nation that alone has an obligation to economically resuscitate neighboring countries ought to be the only nation to provide any economic aid.

(B) Any nation that alone has the capacity to economically resuscitate neighboring countries should exercise that capacity.

(C) Any nation that can afford to give economic aid to just a few other nations ought to aid just those few.

(D) Only nations that alone have the capacity to economically resuscitate neighboring countries should exercise that capacity.

(E) Only nations that can afford to give economic aid to just a few other nations ought to aid just those few.

15. Critic: Works of literature often present protagonists who scorn allegiance to their society and who advocate detachment rather than civic-mindedness. However, modern literature is distinguished from the literature of earlier eras in part because it more frequently treats such protagonists sympathetically. Sympathetic treatment of such characters suggests to readers that one should be unconcerned about contributing to societal good. Thus, modern literature can damage individuals who appropriate this attitude, as well as damage society at large.

Which one of the following is an assumption on which the critic's argument relies?

(A) Some individuals in earlier eras were more concerned about contributing to societal good than is any modern individual.

(B) It is to the advantage of some individuals that they be concerned with contributing to societal good.

(C) Some individuals must believe that their society is better than most before they can become concerned with benefiting it.

(D) The aesthetic merit of some literary works cannot be judged in complete independence of their moral effects.

(E) Modern literature is generally not as conducive to societal good as was the literature of earlier eras.

16. Psychologist: Some people contend that children should never be reprimanded. Any criticism, let alone punishment, they say, harms children's self-esteem. This view is laudable in its challenge to the belief that children should be punished whenever they misbehave, yet it gives a dangerous answer to the question of how often punishment should be inflicted. When parents never reprimand their children, they are in effect rewarding them for unacceptable behavior, and rewarded behavior tends to recur.

The view that children should never be reprimanded functions in the psychologist's argument as a statement of a position that the psychologist's argument

(A) is designed to discredit entirely

(B) is designed to establish as true

(C) is designed to establish as well intentioned

(D) claims has a serious flaw though is not without value

(E) claims is less reasonable than any other view mentioned

GO ON TO THE NEXT PAGE.

17. Traditionally, students at Kelly University have evaluated professors on the last day of class. But some professors at Kelly either do not distribute the paper evaluation forms or do so selectively, and many students cannot attend the last day of class. Soon, students will be able to use school computers to evaluate their professors at any time during the semester. Therefore, evaluations under the new system will accurately reflect the distribution of student opinion about teaching performance.

Which one of the following is an assumption required by the argument?

(A) Professors who distribute the paper evaluation forms selectively distribute them only to students they personally like.

(B) Students can wisely and insightfully assess a professor's performance before the end of the semester.

(C) The traditional system for evaluating teaching performance should not be used at any university.

(D) Nearly all professors who fail to distribute the paper evaluation forms do so because they believe the students will evaluate them unfavorably.

(E) Dissatisfied students are in general not more likely than satisfied students to submit a computerized evaluation.

18. A seriously maladaptive trait is unlikely to persist in a given animal population for long, since there is enough genetic variation in populations that some members will lack the trait. Those lacking the trait will compete more successfully for the available resources. Hence these members of the population survive and reproduce at a higher rate, crowding out those with the maladaptive trait.

The proposition that those lacking a maladaptive trait will compete more successfully for the available resources figures in the argument in which one of the following ways?

(A) It expresses a view that the argument as a whole is designed to discredit.

(B) It is the argument's main conclusion.

(C) It is a premise of the argument.

(D) It presents evidence that the argument attempts to undermine.

(E) It is an intermediate conclusion of the argument.

19. Tanya would refrain from littering if everyone else refrained from littering. None of her friends litter, and therefore she does not litter either.

Which one of the following uses flawed reasoning most similar to the flawed reasoning in the argument above?

(A) All residents of the same neighborhood have some goals in common. One group of neighborhood residents wants improvements made to a local park, so some other residents of that neighborhood must share this goal.

(B) If a talented artist is willing to starve for her career, then her friends should take her choice of profession seriously. Donna's friends take her choice of profession seriously, and she is willing to starve for her career, so she must be a talented artist.

(C) Herbert will stop selling office supplies in his store if none of his regular customers complains. Some of his regular customers never knew that Herbert sold office supplies, so those customers will not complain.

(D) If all whales need to surface for air, then whales must be easy to observe. Blue whales are easily observed, so they must surface for air.

(E) If all of a restaurant's customers like its food, it must be an exceptional restaurant. Everyone whom Sherryl consulted liked the food at Chez Louis, so it must be an exceptional restaurant.

GO ON TO THE NEXT PAGE.

20. Scientist: Genetic engineering has aided new developments in many different fields. But because these techniques require the manipulation of the genetic codes of organisms, they are said to be unethical. What the critics fail to realize is that this kind of manipulation has been going on for millennia; virtually every farm animal is the result of selective breeding for desired traits. Since selective breeding is genetic engineering of a crude sort, genetic engineering is not unethical.

Which one of the following is an assumption on which the scientist's argument depends?

(A) The manipulation of the genetic code of organisms is never unethical.
(B) Anything that is accomplished by nature is not unethical to accomplish with science.
(C) The manipulation of the genetic code through selective breeding for desired traits is not unethical.
(D) The manipulation of the genetic code through selective breeding for desired traits is important for human survival.
(E) Science can accomplish only what is already in some sense natural, and nothing natural is unethical.

21. Baumgartner's comparison of the environmental hazards of gasoline-powered cars with those of electric cars is misleading. He examines only production of the cars, whereas it is the product's total life cycle—production, use, and recycling—that matters in determining its environmental impact. A typical gasoline-powered car consumes 3 times more resources and produces 15 to 20 times more air pollution than a typical electric car.

Which one of the following most accurately expresses the conclusion of the argument?

(A) Baumgartner makes a deceptive comparison between the environmental hazards of gasoline-powered and electric cars.
(B) The use of a typical gasoline-powered car results in much greater resource depletion than does the use of a typical electric car.
(C) Baumgartner uses inaccurate data in his comparison of the environmental hazards of gasoline-powered and electric cars.
(D) The total life cycle of a product is what matters in assessing its environmental impact.
(E) The production of gasoline-powered cars creates more environmental hazards than does that of electric cars.

GO ON TO THE NEXT PAGE.

22. Over the last 10 years, there has been a dramatic increase in the number of people over the age of 65 living in this region. This is evident from the fact that during this time the average age of people living in this region has increased from approximately 52 to 57 years.

Which one of the following, if true, would most strengthen the argument?

(A) The number of people in the region under the age of 18 has increased over the last 10 years.

(B) The birth rate for the region decreased significantly over the last 10 years.

(C) The total number of people living in the region has decreased over the last 10 years.

(D) The number of people who moved into the region over the last 10 years is greater than the number of those who moved out.

(E) The average age for people in the region is higher than that for people in surrounding regions.

23. Editorial: A recently passed law limits freedom of speech in order to silence dissenters. It has been said that those who are ignorant of history will repeat its patterns. If this is true, then those responsible for passing the law must be ignorant of a great deal of history. Historically, silencing dissenters has tended to promote undemocratic policies and the establishment of authoritarian regimes.

The editorialist's reasoning is flawed in that it fails to take into account that

(A) the law may have other purposes in addition to silencing dissenters

(B) certain freedoms might sometimes need to be limited in order to ensure the protection of certain other freedoms

(C) some historical accounts report that legal restrictions on freedom of speech have occasionally undermined the establishment of authoritarian regimes

(D) many good laws have been passed by people who are largely ignorant of history

(E) even those who are not ignorant of history may repeat its patterns

24. Editorialist: Despite the importance it seems to have in our lives, money does not really exist. This is evident from the fact that all that would be needed to make money disappear would be a universal loss of belief in it. We witness this phenomenon on a small scale daily in the rises and falls of financial markets, whose fluctuations are often entirely independent of concrete causes and are the results of mere beliefs of investors.

The conclusion of the editorialist's argument can be properly drawn if which one of the following is assumed?

(A) Anything that exists would continue to exist even if everyone were to stop believing in it.

(B) Only if one can have mistaken beliefs about a thing does that thing exist, strictly speaking.

(C) In order to exist, an entity must have practical consequences for those who believe in it.

(D) If everyone believes in something, then that thing exists.

(E) Whatever is true of money is true of financial markets generally.

GO ON TO THE NEXT PAGE.

25. False chicory's taproot is always one half as long as the plant is tall. Furthermore, the more rain false chicory receives, the taller it tends to grow. In fact, false chicory plants that receive greater than twice the average rainfall of the species' usual habitat always reach above-average heights for false chicory.

If the statements above are true, then which one of the following must also be true?

(A) If two false chicory plants differ in height, then it is likely that the one with the shorter taproot has received less than twice the average rainfall of the species' usual habitat.

(B) If a false chicory plant has a longer-than-average taproot, then it is likely to have received more than twice the average rainfall of the species' usual habitat.

(C) It is not possible for a false chicory plant to receive only the average amount of rainfall of the species' usual habitat and be of above-average height.

(D) If the plants in one group of false chicory are not taller than those in another group of false chicory, then the two groups must have received the same amount of rainfall.

(E) If a false chicory plant receives greater than twice the average rainfall of the species' usual habitat, then it will have a longer taproot than that of an average-sized false chicory plant.

26. Fossilized teeth of an extinct species of herbivorous great ape have on them phytoliths, which are microscopic petrified remains of plants. Since only phytoliths from certain species of plants are found on the teeth, the apes' diet must have consisted only of those plants.

The argument assumes which one of the following?

(A) None of the plant species that left phytoliths on the apes' teeth has since become extinct.

(B) Plants of every type eaten by the apes left phytoliths on their teeth.

(C) Each of the teeth examined had phytoliths of the same plant species on it as all the other teeth.

(D) Phytoliths have also been found on the fossilized teeth of apes of other extinct species.

(E) Most species of great ape alive today have diets that consist of a fairly narrow range of plants.

S T O P
IF YOU FINISH BEFORE TIME IS CALLED, YOU MAY CHECK YOUR WORK ON THIS SECTION ONLY.
DO NOT WORK ON ANY OTHER SECTION IN THE TEST.

SECTION IV

Time—35 minutes

22 Questions

Directions: Each group of questions in this section is based on a set of conditions. In answering some of the questions, it may be useful to draw a rough diagram. Choose the response that most accurately and completely answers each question and blacken the corresponding space on your answer sheet.

Questions 1–6

Exactly six guideposts, numbered 1 through 6, mark a mountain trail. Each guidepost pictures a different one of six animals—fox, grizzly, hare, lynx, moose, or porcupine. The following conditions must apply:

The grizzly is pictured on either guidepost 3 or guidepost 4.
The moose guidepost is numbered lower than the hare guidepost.
The lynx guidepost is numbered lower than the moose guidepost but higher than the fox guidepost.

1. Which one of the following could be an accurate list of the animals pictured on the guideposts, listed in order from guidepost 1 through guidepost 6?

    (A)   fox, lynx, grizzly, porcupine, moose, hare
    (B)   fox, lynx, moose, hare, grizzly, porcupine
    (C)   fox, moose, grizzly, lynx, hare, porcupine
    (D)   lynx, fox, moose, grizzly, hare, porcupine
    (E)   porcupine, fox, hare, grizzly, lynx, moose

2. Which one of the following animals CANNOT be the one pictured on guidepost 3?

    (A)   fox
    (B)   grizzly
    (C)   lynx
    (D)   moose
    (E)   porcupine

3. If the moose is pictured on guidepost 3, then which one of the following is the lowest numbered guidepost that could picture the porcupine?

    (A)   guidepost 1
    (B)   guidepost 2
    (C)   guidepost 4
    (D)   guidepost 5
    (E)   guidepost 6

4. If guidepost 5 does not picture the moose, then which one of the following must be true?

    (A)   The lynx is pictured on guidepost 2.
    (B)   The moose is pictured on guidepost 3.
    (C)   The grizzly is pictured on guidepost 4.
    (D)   The porcupine is pictured on guidepost 5.
    (E)   The hare is pictured on guidepost 6.

5. Which one of the following animals could be pictured on any one of the six guideposts?

    (A)   fox
    (B)   hare
    (C)   lynx
    (D)   moose
    (E)   porcupine

6. If the moose guidepost is numbered exactly one higher than the lynx guidepost, then which one of the following could be true?

    (A)   Guidepost 5 pictures the hare.
    (B)   Guidepost 4 pictures the moose.
    (C)   Guidepost 4 pictures the porcupine.
    (D)   Guidepost 3 pictures the lynx.
    (E)   Guidepost 3 pictures the porcupine.

GO ON TO THE NEXT PAGE.

4 ⚫**4** ⚫**4** ⚫**4** ⚫**4** -211- **4**

Questions 7–11

Each side of four cassette tapes—Tapes 1 through 4—contains exactly one of the following four genres: folk, hip-hop, jazz, and rock. The following conditions must apply:

Each genre is found on exactly two of the eight sides.

Tape 1 has jazz on at least one side, but neither hip-hop nor rock.

Tape 2 has no jazz.

Folk is not on any tape numbered exactly one higher than a tape that has any rock on it.

7. Which one of the following could be an accurate matching of tapes with the musical genres found on them?

   (A) Tape 1: folk and jazz; Tape 2: folk and jazz; Tape 3: hip-hop and rock; Tape 4: hip-hop and rock
   (B) Tape 1: folk and jazz; Tape 2: folk and rock; Tape 3: hip-hop and jazz; Tape 4: hip-hop and rock
   (C) Tape 1: folk and jazz; Tape 2: folk and rock; Tape 3: two sides of jazz; Tape 4: two sides of hip-hop
   (D) Tape 1: hip-hop and jazz; Tape 2: folk and hip-hop; Tape 3: folk and jazz; Tape 4: two sides of rock
   (E) Tape 1: two sides of jazz; Tape 2: folk and rock; Tape 3: hip-hop and rock; Tape 4: folk and hip-hop

8. Which one of the following must be true?

   (A) If Tape 1 has two sides of jazz, Tape 4 has at least one side of rock.
   (B) If Tape 2 has two sides of folk, Tape 3 has at least one side of hip-hop.
   (C) If Tape 2 has two sides of rock, Tape 4 has at least one side of folk.
   (D) If Tape 3 has two sides of folk, Tape 2 has at least one side of jazz.
   (E) If Tape 4 has two sides of hip-hop, Tape 3 has at least one side of folk.

9. Which one of the following could be true?

   (A) Tape 1 has jazz on both sides while Tape 4 has folk and hip-hop.
   (B) Tape 2 has hip-hop on one side while Tape 3 has hip-hop and jazz.
   (C) Tape 3 has folk on both sides while Tape 4 has jazz and rock.
   (D) Tape 3 has jazz on one side while Tape 4 has folk on both sides.
   (E) Tapes 2 and 3 each have jazz on one side.

10. Which one of the following could be true?

    (A) Tape 1 has two sides of folk.
    (B) Tape 2 has both hip-hop and jazz.
    (C) Tape 4 has both folk and rock.
    (D) Tapes 1 and 4 each have a side of hip-hop.
    (E) Tapes 3 and 4 each have a side of folk.

11. Which one of the following CANNOT be true?

    (A) Tape 2 has rock on both sides while Tape 3 has hip-hop on both sides.
    (B) Tape 3 has rock on both sides while Tape 2 has hip-hop on both sides.
    (C) Tape 3 has rock on both sides while Tape 4 has hip-hop on both sides.
    (D) Tape 4 has rock on both sides while Tape 2 has hip-hop on both sides.
    (E) Tape 4 has rock on both sides while Tape 3 has hip-hop on both sides.

GO ON TO THE NEXT PAGE.

Questions 12–16

One afternoon, a single thunderstorm passes over exactly five towns—Jackson, Lofton, Nordique, Oceana, and Plattesville—dropping some form of precipitation on each. The storm is the only source of precipitation in the towns that afternoon. On some towns, it drops both hail and rain; on the remaining towns, it drops only rain. It passes over each town exactly once and does not pass over any two towns at the same time. The following must obtain:

The third town the storm passes over is Plattesville.

The storm drops hail and rain on the second town it passes over.

The storm drops only rain on both Lofton and Oceana.

The storm passes over Jackson at some time after it passes over Lofton and at some time after it passes over Nordique.

12. Which one of the following could be the order, from first to fifth, in which the storm passes over the towns?

(A) Lofton, Nordique, Plattesville, Oceana, Jackson
(B) Lofton, Oceana, Plattesville, Nordique, Jackson
(C) Nordique, Jackson, Plattesville, Oceana, Lofton
(D) Nordique, Lofton, Plattesville, Jackson, Oceana
(E) Nordique, Plattesville, Lofton, Oceana, Jackson

13. If the storm passes over Oceana at some time before it passes over Jackson, then each of the following could be true EXCEPT:

(A) The first town the storm passes over is Oceana.
(B) The fourth town the storm passes over is Lofton.
(C) The fourth town the storm passes over receives hail and rain.
(D) The fifth town the storm passes over is Jackson.
(E) The fifth town the storm passes over receives only rain.

14. If the storm drops only rain on each town it passes over after passing over Lofton, then which one of the following could be false?

(A) The first town the storm passes over is Oceana.
(B) The fourth town the storm passes over receives only rain.
(C) The fifth town the storm passes over is Jackson.
(D) Jackson receives only rain.
(E) Plattesville receives only rain.

15. If the storm passes over Jackson at some time before it passes over Oceana, then which one of the following could be false?

(A) The storm passes over Lofton at some time before it passes over Jackson.
(B) The storm passes over Lofton at some time before it passes over Oceana.
(C) The storm passes over Nordique at some time before it passes over Oceana.
(D) The fourth town the storm passes over receives only rain.
(E) The fifth town the storm passes over receives only rain.

16. If the storm passes over Oceana at some time before it passes over Lofton, then which one of the following must be true?

(A) The third town the storm passes over receives only rain.
(B) The fourth town the storm passes over receives only rain.
(C) The fourth town the storm passes over receives hail and rain.
(D) The fifth town the storm passes over receives only rain.
(E) The fifth town the storm passes over receives hail and rain.

GO ON TO THE NEXT PAGE.

Questions 17–22

A reporter is trying to uncover the workings of a secret committee. The committee has six members—French, Ghauri, Hsia, Irving, Magnus, and Pinsky—each of whom serves on at least one subcommittee. There are three subcommittees, each having three members, about which the following is known:

> One of the committee members serves on all three subcommittees.
> French does not serve on any subcommittee with Ghauri.
> Hsia does not serve on any subcommittee with Irving.

17. If French does not serve on any subcommittee with Magnus, which one of the following must be true?

   (A) French serves on a subcommittee with Hsia.
   (B) French serves on a subcommittee with Irving.
   (C) Irving serves on a subcommittee with Pinsky.
   (D) Magnus serves on a subcommittee with Ghauri.
   (E) Magnus serves on a subcommittee with Irving.

18. If Pinsky serves on every subcommittee on which French serves and every subcommittee on which Ghauri serves, then which one of the following could be true?

   (A) Magnus serves on every subcommittee on which French serves and every subcommittee on which Ghauri serves.
   (B) Magnus serves on every subcommittee on which Hsia serves and every subcommittee on which Irving serves.
   (C) Hsia serves on every subcommittee on which French serves and every subcommittee on which Ghauri serves.
   (D) French serves on every subcommittee on which Pinsky serves.
   (E) Hsia serves on every subcommittee on which Pinsky serves.

19. If Irving serves on every subcommittee on which Magnus serves, which one of the following could be true?

   (A) Magnus serves on all of the subcommittees.
   (B) Irving serves on more than one subcommittee.
   (C) Irving serves on every subcommittee on which Pinsky serves.
   (D) French serves on a subcommittee with Magnus.
   (E) Ghauri serves on a subcommittee with Magnus.

20. Which one of the following could be true?

   (A) French serves on all three subcommittees.
   (B) Hsia serves on all three subcommittees.
   (C) Ghauri serves on every subcommittee on which Magnus serves and every subcommittee on which Pinsky serves.
   (D) Pinsky serves on every subcommittee on which Irving serves and every subcommittee on which Magnus serves.
   (E) Magnus serves on every subcommittee on which Pinsky serves, and Pinsky serves on every subcommittee on which Magnus serves.

21. Which one of the following must be true?

   (A) Ghauri serves on at least two subcommittees.
   (B) Irving serves on only one subcommittee.
   (C) French serves on a subcommittee with Hsia.
   (D) Ghauri serves on a subcommittee with Irving.
   (E) Magnus serves on a subcommittee with Pinsky.

22. Which one of the following must be true?

   (A) Every subcommittee has either French or Ghauri as a member.
   (B) Every subcommittee has either Hsia or Irving as a member.
   (C) No subcommittee consists of French, Magnus, and Pinsky.
   (D) Some committee member serves on exactly two subcommittees.
   (E) Either Magnus or Pinsky serves on only one subcommittee.

S T O P

IF YOU FINISH BEFORE TIME IS CALLED, YOU MAY CHECK YOUR WORK ON THIS SECTION ONLY.
DO NOT WORK ON ANY OTHER SECTION IN THE TEST.

ACKNOWLEDGMENTS

Acknowledgment is made to the following sources from which material has been adapted for use in this test booklet:

Cheng Lok Chua, "Witnessing the Japanese Canadian Experience in World War II: Processual Structure, Symbolism, and Irony in Joy Kogawa's *Obasan*." ©1992 by Temple University.

Joel Feinberg, *The Moral Limits of the Criminal Law*. ©1988 by Oxford University Press.

Myrna I. Lewis, "What's So Bad about Feeling Good? How Psychotherapy Can Help You Find Peace of Mind." ©1993 by the American Association of Retired Persons.

William Bryant Logan, "What Is Prosperity?" ©1995 by POINT.

James Shreeve, "Music of the Hemispheres." ©October 1996 by Discover.

Carol Kaesuk Yoon, "Pronghorn's Speed May Be Legacy of Past Predators." ©1996 by The New York Times.

Wait for the supervisor's instructions before you open the page to the topic.
Please print and sign your name and write the date in the designated spaces below.

Time: 35 Minutes

General Directions

You will have 35 minutes in which to plan and write an essay on the topic inside. Read the topic and the accompanying directions carefully. You will probably find it best to spend a few minutes considering the topic and organizing your thoughts before you begin writing. In your essay, be sure to develop your ideas fully, leaving time, if possible, to review what you have written. **Do not write on a topic other than the one specified. Writing on a topic of your own choice is not acceptable.**

No special knowledge is required or expected for this writing exercise. Law schools are interested in the reasoning, clarity, organization, language usage, and writing mechanics displayed in your essay. How well you write is more important than how much you write.

Confine your essay to the blocked, lined area on the front and back of the separate Writing Sample Response Sheet. Only that area will be reproduced for law schools. Be sure that your writing is legible.

Both this topic sheet and your response sheet must be turned over to the testing staff before you leave the room.

Topic Code	Print Your Full Name Here		
	Last	First	M.I.

Date	Sign Your Name Here
/ /	

Scratch Paper
Do not write your essay in this space.

LSAT® Writing Sample Topic

Directions: The scenario presented below describes two choices, either one of which can be supported on the basis of the information given. Your essay should consider both choices and argue for one over the other, based on the two specified criteria and the facts provided. There is no "right" or "wrong" choice: a reasonable argument can be made for either.

The *Tribune*, a growing large-city newspaper with a civic-minded publisher, will be adding a new column to the Arts and Leisure section. The publisher must decide between a restaurant review and a theater review. Write an essay in which you argue for one proposal over the other, keeping in mind the following two criteria:

- The publisher wants to increase the paper's circulation, making it more attractive to advertisers.
- The publisher wants to contribute to the revitalization of the city's Lakewood district, which is a magnet for nightlife and is perceived as being crucial to the city's development.

The *Tribune*'s chief competitor, the *Standard*, publishes a restaurant review that is one of its most popular lifestyle features. Surveys indicate that readers of the *Tribune* would be receptive to a restaurant review in its pages. An established reviewer from an alternative newspaper in a larger city would write the column. He lacks the prestige of the *Standard*'s reviewer, but is less traditional and would probably appeal to a different audience. Several local restaurants have indicated that they would be more willing to advertise in the *Tribune* if it featured a restaurant review. Some of these are in the Lakewood district, whose already flourishing restaurant scene would likely improve with the interest another restaurant review column would generate.

If the *Tribune* were to publish a theater review, it would be the only one in the city, since the *Standard* does not publish one. The *Tribune* has the opportunity to hire a distinguished reviewer from a major metropolitan newspaper, who would like to return to her home city, where the *Tribune* is located. Her coming to the *Tribune* would be an event that would attract considerable publicity. The *Tribune*'s current readers express little demand for a theater column, but interest in theater in the city is growing, and with a distinguished theater critic on a city newspaper, it would be spurred considerably. All of the city's major theaters are located in the Lakewood district, which would therefore benefit from such a development. Currently, advertising by theaters is a significantly smaller source of revenue to newspapers than advertising by restaurants.

Scratch Paper
Do not write your essay in this space.

COMPUTING YOUR SCORE

Directions:

1. Use the Answer Key on the next page to check your answers.

2. Use the Scoring Worksheet below to compute your raw score.

3. Use the Score Conversion Chart to convert your raw score into the 120-180 scale.

Scoring Worksheet

1. Enter the number of questions you answered correctly in each section.

   Number Correct

   SECTION I .... _____
   SECTION II .... _____
   SECTION III .... _____
   SECTION IV .... _____

2. Enter the sum here: _____
   This is your Raw Score.

Conversion Chart
For Converting Raw Score to the 120-180 LSAT Scaled Score
LSAT Form 6LSN68

Reported Score	Raw Score Lowest	Raw Score Highest
180	98	99
179	97	97
178	96	96
177	—*	—*
176	95	95
175	94	94
174	—*	—*
173	93	93
172	92	92
171	91	91
170	90	90
169	89	89
168	88	88
167	87	87
166	85	86
165	84	84
164	83	83
163	81	82
162	80	80
161	78	79
160	77	77
159	75	76
158	74	74
157	72	73
156	71	71
155	69	70
154	67	68
153	66	66
152	64	65
151	62	63
150	61	61
149	59	60
148	57	58
147	56	56
146	54	55
145	52	53
144	51	51
143	49	50
142	47	48
141	46	46
140	44	45
139	42	43
138	41	41
137	39	40
136	37	38
135	36	36
134	34	35
133	32	33
132	31	31
131	29	30
130	28	28
129	26	27
128	24	25
127	23	23
126	21	22
125	20	20
124	18	19
123	17	17
122	15	16
121	14	14
120	0	13

*There is no raw score that will produce this scaled score for this form.

ANSWER KEY

SECTION I

1.	B	8.	A	15.	C	22.	E
2.	C	9.	*	16.	A	23.	D
3.	D	10.	E	17.	D	24.	C
4.	A	11.	A	18.	C	25.	A
5.	E	12.	B	19.	D	26.	E
6.	D	13.	E	20.	B	27.	C
7.	D	14.	C	21.	E		

SECTION II

1.	D	8.	E	15.	C	22.	C
2.	E	9.	B	16.	B	23.	D
3.	B	10.	A	17.	E	24.	D
4.	A	11.	A	18.	C	25.	C
5.	A	12.	E	19.	B		
6.	B	13.	D	20.	B		
7.	B	14.	E	21.	A		

SECTION III

1.	A	8.	D	15.	B	22.	A
2.	C	9.	A	16.	D	23.	E
3.	D	10.	C	17.	E	24.	A
4.	D	11.	B	18.	C	25.	E
5.	C	12.	C	19.	E	26.	B
6.	D	13.	E	20.	C		
7.	D	14.	B	21.	A		

SECTION IV

1.	A	8.	C	15.	D	22.	D
2.	A	9.	B	16.	B		
3.	D	10.	C	17.	C		
4.	A	11.	B	18.	C		
5.	E	12.	A	19.	B		
6.	A	13.	C	20.	D		
7.	B	14.	E	21.	E		

*Item removed from scoring.

PREPTEST 47
OCTOBER 2005
FORM 5LSN65

SECTION I
Time—35 minutes
26 Questions

Directions: The questions in this section are based on the reasoning contained in brief statements or passages. For some questions, more than one of the choices could conceivably answer the question. However, you are to choose the best answer; that is, the response that most accurately and completely answers the question. You should not make assumptions that are by commonsense standards implausible, superfluous, or incompatible with the passage. After you have chosen the best answer, blacken the corresponding space on your answer sheet.

1. While it might be expected that those neighborhoods most heavily patrolled by police have the least crime, the statistical evidence overwhelmingly supports the claim that such neighborhoods have the most crime. This shows that the presence of police does not decrease crime in a neighborhood.

The reasoning in the argument is flawed because the argument

(A) attempts to support its conclusion by making an appeal to emotions

(B) fails to consider the possibility that criminals may commit crimes in more than one neighborhood

(C) draws a general conclusion from too small a sample of data

(D) fails to consider the possibility that police presence in a particular area is often a response to the relatively high crime rate in that area

(E) takes for granted that public resources devoted to police presence could be allocated in another manner that would be a stronger deterrent to crime

2. Despite increasing international efforts to protect the natural habitats of endangered species of animals, the rate at which these species are becoming extinct continues to rise. It is clear that these efforts are wasted.

Which one of the following, if true, most weakens the argument?

(A) Scientists are better able to preserve the habitats of endangered species now than ever before.

(B) Species that would have become extinct have been saved due to the establishment of animal refuges.

(C) Scientists estimate that at least 2000 species become extinct every year.

(D) Many countries do not recognize the increased economic benefit of tourism associated with preserved natural habitats.

(E) Programs have been proposed that will transfer endangered species out of habitats that are in danger of being destroyed.

3. When a lawmaker spoke out against a research grant awarded to a professor in a university's psychology department as a foolish expenditure of public money, other professors in that department drafted a letter protesting the lawmaker's interference in a field in which he was not trained. The chair of the psychology department, while privately endorsing the project, refused to sign the protest letter on the ground that she had previously written a letter applauding the same legislator when he publicized a senseless expenditure by the country's military.

Which one of the following principles, if established, provides the strongest justification for the department chair's refusal, on the ground she gives, to sign the protest letter?

(A) A person should not publicly criticize the actions of a lawmaker in different cases without giving careful consideration to the circumstances of each particular case.

(B) The chair of an academic department has an obligation to ensure that public funds allocated to support projects within that department are spent wisely.

(C) A person who has praised a lawmaker for playing a watchdog role in one case should not criticize the lawmaker for attempting to play a watchdog role in another case that involves the person's professional interests.

(D) Since academic institutions accept public funds but do not pay taxes, a representative of an academic institution should not publicly pass judgment on the actions of government officials.

(E) Academic institutions have the same responsibility as military institutions have to spend public money wisely.

GO ON TO THE NEXT PAGE.

4. Aaron: A prominent judge, criticizing "famous lawyers who come before courts ill-prepared to argue their cases," recently said, "This sort of cavalier attitude offends the court and can do nothing but harm to the client's cause." I find the judge's remarks irresponsible.

Belinda: I find it natural and an admirable display of candor. Letting people know of the damage their negligence causes is responsible behavior.

The point at issue between Aaron and Belinda is whether

(A) ill-prepared lawyers damage their clients' causes

(B) the judge's criticism of lawyers is irresponsible

(C) a lawyer's being ill-prepared to argue a client's case constitutes negligence

(D) famous lawyers have a greater responsibility to be well prepared than do lawyers who are not famous

(E) it is to be expected that ill-prepared lawyers would offend the court in which they appear

5. The human emotional response presents an apparent paradox. People believe that they can be genuinely moved only by those things and events that they believe to be actual, yet they have genuine emotional responses to what they know to be fictional.

Which one of the following situations most closely conforms to the principle cited above?

(A) Fred was watching a horror movie. Although he did not expect to be bothered by make-believe monsters, he nonetheless felt frightened when they appeared on the screen.

(B) Tamara was reading *Hamlet*. Although she knew that it was a work of fiction, she still made statements such as "Hamlet was born in Denmark" and "Hamlet was a prince."

(C) Raheem thought that his sister was in the hospital. Although he was mistaken, he was nevertheless genuinely worried when he believed she was there.

(D) Jeremy was upset by the actions that a writer attributed to a secret organization, although he considered it unlikely that the writer's account was accurate.

(E) Sandy was watching a film about World War II. Although the film's details were accurate, it was nevertheless difficult for Sandy to maintain interest in the characters.

6. Recent investigations of earthquakes have turned up a previously unknown type of seismic shock, known as a displacement pulse, which is believed to be present in all earthquakes. Alarmingly, high-rise buildings are especially vulnerable to displacement pulses, according to computer models. Yet examination of high-rises within cities damaged by recent powerful earthquakes indicates little significant damage to these structures.

Which one of the following, if true, contributes to a resolution of the apparent paradox?

(A) Displacement pulses travel longer distances than other types of seismic shock.

(B) Scientific predictions based on computer models often fail when tested in the field.

(C) While displacement pulses have only recently been discovered, they have accompanied all earthquakes that have ever occurred.

(D) The displacement pulses made by low- and medium-intensity earthquakes are much less powerful than those made by the strongest earthquakes.

(E) Computer models have been very successful in predicting the effects of other types of seismic shock.

7. Terry: Months ago, I submitted a claim for my stolen bicycle to my insurance company. After hearing nothing for several weeks, I contacted the firm and found they had no record of my claim. Since then, I have resubmitted the claim twice and called the firm repeatedly, but I have yet to receive a settlement. Anyone can make mistakes, of course, but the persistence of the error makes me conclude that the company is deliberately avoiding paying up.

Which one of the following principles is violated by Terry's reasoning?

(A) Consumers should avoid attributing dishonesty to a corporation when the actions of the corporation might instead be explained by incompetence.

(B) Consumers should attempt to keep themselves informed of corporate behavior that directly affects their interests.

(C) In judging the quality of service of a corporation, a consumer should rely primarily on the consumer's own experience with the corporation.

(D) In judging the morality of a corporation's behavior, as opposed to that of an individual, mitigating circumstances are irrelevant.

(E) Corporations ought to make available to a customer any information the customer requests that is relevant to the customer's interests.

GO ON TO THE NEXT PAGE.

8. Fortune-teller: Admittedly, the claims of some self-proclaimed "psychics" have been shown to be fraudulent, but the exposure of a few charlatans cannot alter the fundamental fact that it has not been scientifically proven that there is no such thing as extrasensory perception (ESP). Furthermore, since the failed attempts to produce such a proof have been so numerous, one must conclude that some individuals do possess ESP.

The reasoning in the fortune-teller's argument is most vulnerable to criticism on the grounds that the argument

(A) takes for granted that proof that many people lack a characteristic does not establish that everyone lacks that characteristic

(B) takes for granted that the number of unsuccessful attempts to prove a claim is the only factor relevant to whether one should accept that claim

(C) overlooks the possibility that some of the scientific studies mentioned reached inaccurate conclusions about whether ESP exists

(D) takes for granted that there is no scientific way to determine whether some individuals possess ESP

(E) takes for granted that the fact that a claim has not been demonstrated to be false establishes that it is true

9. Film historians have made two major criticisms of Depression-era filmmakers: first, that they were too uncritical of the economic status quo; and second, that they self-indulgently created films reflecting their own dreams and desires. However, these filmmakers made their movies with an eye to profit, and so they provided what their audiences most wanted in a film: a chance to imagine being wealthy enough not to have a care in the world. Thus, the second criticism cannot be accurate.

The conclusion of the argument follows logically if which one of the following is assumed?

(A) To avoid self-indulgence, filmmakers should take a critical stance toward the existing economic system and should allow audiences to form their own personal aspirations.

(B) It is unjustified to demand of all filmmakers that their films engage in criticism of the economic status quo.

(C) The people who regularly went to movies during the Depression were those likely to have been most satisfied with the economic status quo.

(D) Depression-era filmmakers who did not make films for profit could not take radical critical stances toward then-current economic and political issues.

(E) It cannot be self-indulgent for a filmmaker to give an audience what it most wants.

10. Editorial: Many observers note with dismay the decline in the number of nongovernmental, voluntary community organizations. They argue that this decline is caused by the corresponding growth of government services once provided by these voluntary community groups. But this may not be true. The increase in government services may coincide with a decrease in volunteerism, but the former does not necessarily cause the latter; the latter may indeed cause the former.

The editorial undermines the conclusion of the causal argument by

(A) showing that there is no causality involved
(B) offering a counterexample to the alleged correlation
(C) proving that no generalization can properly be drawn about people's motives for volunteering
(D) offering an alternate explanation of the correlation cited
(E) proving that governments must do what community organizations fail to do

11. In contemplating major purchases, businesses often consider only whether there is enough money left from monthly revenues after paying monthly expenses to cover the cost of the purchase. But many expenses do not occur monthly; taking into account only monthly expenses can cause a business to overexpand. So the use of a cash-flow statement is critical for all businesses.

Which one of the following, if true, most strengthens the argument?

(A) Only a cash-flow statement can accurately document all monthly expenses.
(B) Any business that has overexpanded can benefit from the use of a cash-flow statement.
(C) When a business documents only monthly expenses it also documents only monthly revenue.
(D) A cash-flow statement is the only way to track both monthly expenses and expenses that are not monthly.
(E) When a business takes into account all expenses, not just monthly ones, it can make better decisions.

GO ON TO THE NEXT PAGE.

12. All known living things are made of the same basic kinds of matter, are carbon based, and are equipped with genetic codes. So human life has the same origin as all other known life.

The conclusion follows logically if which one of the following is assumed?

(A) Without the existence of other life forms, human life would never have come into existence.
(B) There are not any living beings that have genetic codes but are not carbon based.
(C) There can never be any living thing that does not have a genetic code.
(D) Many yet-to-be-discovered types of living things will also be carbon based.
(E) Any two living things made of the same basic kinds of matter have the same origin.

13. All societies recognize certain rules to be so crucial that they define those rules as duties, such as rules restricting violence and those requiring the keeping of agreements. Contained in the notion of a duty is the idea that its fulfillment is so fundamental to a properly functioning society that persons obligated by it cannot be excused on the ground that its fulfillment would be harmful to their self-interest. This shows that _____.

Which one of the following most reasonably completes the argument?

(A) all societies overrate the benefits of certain rules, such as those governing the keeping of agreements
(B) all societies have certain rules that no people are capable of following
(C) all societies recognize the possibility of clashes between individual self-interest and the performance of duty
(D) a properly functioning society will recognize that some duties take priority over others
(E) societies have no right to expect people always to perform their duties

14. Linguist: Regional dialects, many of which eventually become distinct languages, are responses by local populations to their own particular communicative needs. So even when the unification of the world economy forces the adoption of a universal language for use in international trade, this language itself will inevitably develop many regional dialects.

Which one of the following is an assumption that the linguist's argument requires?

(A) No two local populations have the same communicative needs as each other.
(B) In some regions of the world, at least some people will not engage in international trade after the unification of the world economy.
(C) A universal language for use in international trade will not arise unless the world economy is unified.
(D) When the unification of the world economy forces the adoption of a universal language for use in international trade, many regional dialects of other languages will be eradicated.
(E) After the unification of the world economy, there will be variation among many different local populations in their communicative needs in international trade.

GO ON TO THE NEXT PAGE.

15. Often, a product popularly believed to be the best of its type is no better than any other; rather, the product's reputation, which may be independent of its quality, provides its owner with status. Thus, although there is no harm in paying for status if that is what one wants, one should know that one is paying for prestige, not quality.

Which one of the following arguments is most similar in its reasoning to the argument above?

(A) Often, choosing the best job offer is a matter of comparing the undesirable features of the different jobs. Thus, those who choose a job because it has a desirable location should know that they might be unhappy with its hours.

(B) Most people have little tolerance for boastfulness. Thus, although one's friends may react positively when hearing the details of one's accomplishments, it is unlikely that their reactions are entirely honest.

(C) Those beginning a new hobby sometimes quit it because of the frustrations involved in learning a new skill. Thus, although it is fine to try to learn a skill quickly, one is more likely to learn a skill if one first learns to enjoy the process of acquiring it.

(D) Personal charm is often confused with virtue. Thus, while there is nothing wrong with befriending a charming person, anyone who does so should realize that a charming friend is not necessarily a good and loyal friend.

(E) Many theatrical actors cannot enjoy watching a play because when they watch others, they yearn to be on stage themselves. Thus, although there is no harm in yearning to perform, such performers should, for their own sakes, learn to suppress that yearning.

16. Essayist: Many people are hypocritical in that they often pretend to be more morally upright than they really are. When hypocrisy is exposed, hypocrites are embarrassed by their moral lapse, which motivates them and others to try to become better people. On the other hand, when hypocrisy persists without exposure, the belief that most people are good is fostered, which motivates most people to try to be good.

The essayist's statements, if true, most strongly support which one of the following?

(A) The existence of hypocrisy encourages people to believe that no one is morally blameless.

(B) The existence of hypocrisy encourages people to make efforts to live by moral standards.

(C) The existence of hypocrisy in some people encourages others to fall into moral lapses.

(D) The hiding of hypocrisy is a better way of motivating people to try to be good than is the exposing of it.

(E) There is no stronger motivator for people to try to be good than the exposing of hypocrisy.

17. "Multiple use" refers to the utilization of natural resources in combinations that will best meet the present and future needs of the public. Designating land as a wilderness area does not necessarily violate the multiple-use philosophy, for even when such use does not provide the greatest dollar return, it can provide the greatest overall benefit from that site.

Which one of the following is an assumption required by the argument?

(A) Natural resources should be used in combinations that will most greatly benefit present and future generations.

(B) Designating a wilderness area prevents any exploitation of natural resources in that area.

(C) The present and future needs of the public would best be met by designating greater numbers of wilderness areas.

(D) The multiple-use philosophy takes into account some nonfinancial needs of the public.

(E) The multiple-use philosophy holds that the future needs of the public are more important than the present ones.

GO ON TO THE NEXT PAGE.

18. In the troposphere, the lowest level of the earth's atmosphere, the temperature decreases as one progresses straight upward. At the top, the air temperature ranges from −50 degrees Celsius over the poles to −85 degrees Celsius over the equator. At that point the stratosphere begins, and the temperature stops decreasing and instead increases as one progresses straight upward through the stratosphere. The stratosphere is warmed by ozone. When an ozone particle absorbs a dose of ultraviolet sunlight, heat is generated.

If the statements above are true, which one of the following must also be true?

(A) The troposphere over the poles is thicker than the troposphere over the equator.

(B) It is warmer at the top of the stratosphere over the poles than it is at the top of the stratosphere over the equator.

(C) The temperature in the middle part of the stratosphere over the North Pole is at least as great as the temperature in the middle part of the stratosphere over the equator.

(D) The temperature at any point at the top of the stratosphere is at least as great as the temperature at the top of the troposphere directly beneath that point.

(E) Depletion of the earth's ozone layer would increase the air temperature in the stratosphere and decrease the air temperature in the troposphere.

19. There have been no new cases of naturally occurring polio in North America in recent years. Yet there are approximately 12 new cases of polio each year in North America, all caused by the commonly administered live oral polio vaccine (OPV). Substituting inactivated polio vaccine (IPV) for most childhood polio immunizations would cut the number of cases of vaccination-caused polio about in half. Clearly it is time to switch from OPV to IPV as the most commonly used polio vaccine for North American children.

Which one of the following, if true, most weakens the argument?

(A) If IPV replaces OPV as the most commonly used polio vaccine, at least a few new cases of naturally occurring polio in North America will result each year.

(B) The vast majority of cases of polio caused by OPV have occurred in children with preexisting but unsuspected immunodeficiency disorders.

(C) A child's risk of contracting polio from OPV has been estimated at 1 in 8.7 million, which is significantly less than the risk of being struck by lightning.

(D) Although IPV is preferred in some European nations, most countries with comprehensive child immunization programs use OPV.

(E) IPV, like most vaccines, carries a slight risk of inducing seizures in children with neurological diseases such as epilepsy.

20. Professor: Each government should do all that it can to improve the well-being of all the children in the society it governs. Therefore, governments should help finance high-quality day care since such day care will become available to families of all income levels if and only if it is subsidized.

Which one of the following is an assumption on which the professor's argument depends?

(A) Only governments that subsidize high-quality day care take an interest in the well-being of all the children in the societies they govern.

(B) Government subsidy of high-quality day care would not be so expensive that it would cause a government to eliminate benefits for adults.

(C) High-quality day care should be subsidized only for those who could not otherwise afford it.

(D) At least some children would benefit from high-quality day care.

(E) Government is a more efficient provider of certain services than is private enterprise.

GO ON TO THE NEXT PAGE.

21. Opposition leader: Our country has the least fair court system of any country on the continent and ought not to be the model for others. Thus, our highest court is the least fair of any on the continent and ought not to be emulated by other countries.

The flawed reasoning in which one of the following arguments is most similar to that in the opposition leader's argument?

(A) The residents of medium-sized towns are, on average, more highly educated than people who do not live in such towns. Therefore, Maureen, who was born in a medium-sized town, is more highly educated than Monica, who has just moved to such a town.

(B) At a certain college, either philosophy or engineering is the most demanding major. Therefore, either the introductory course in philosophy or the introductory course in engineering is the most demanding introductory-level course at that college.

(C) For many years its superior engineering has enabled the Lawson Automobile Company to make the best racing cars. Therefore, its passenger cars, which use many of the same parts, are unmatched by those of any other company.

(D) Domestic cats are closely related to tigers. Therefore, even though they are far smaller than tigers, their eating habits are almost the same as those of tigers.

(E) If a suit of questionable merit is brought in the first district rather than the second district, its chances of being immediately thrown out are greater. Therefore, to have the best chance of winning the case, the lawyers will bring the suit in the second district.

22. Columnist: There are certain pesticides that, even though they have been banned for use in the United States for nearly 30 years, are still manufactured there and exported to other countries. In addition to jeopardizing the health of people in these other countries, this practice greatly increases the health risk to U.S. consumers, for these pesticides are often used on agricultural products imported into the United States.

Which one of the following, if true, most seriously weakens the columnist's argument?

(A) Trace amounts of some of the pesticides banned for use in the United States can be detected in the soil where they were used 30 years ago.

(B) Most of the pesticides that are manufactured in the United States and exported are not among those banned for use in the United States.

(C) The United States is not the only country that manufactures and exports the pesticides that are banned for use in the United States.

(D) The banned pesticides pose a greater risk to people in the countries in which they are used than to U.S. consumers.

(E) There are many pesticides that are banned for use in other countries that are not banned for use in the United States.

23. Columnist: Neuroscientists have found that states of profound creativity are accompanied by an increase of theta brain waves, which occur in many regions of the brain, including the hippocampus. They also found that listening to music increases theta waves dramatically. Thus, one can attain a state of profound creativity merely by listening to a tape of recorded music.

The columnist's reasoning is most vulnerable to criticism on the grounds that it

(A) takes for granted that there is a causal connection between the hippocampus and being in a state of profound creativity

(B) fails to consider that music is not necessary for one to be in a state of profound creativity

(C) does not rule out the possibility that listening to music by means other than a tape recording also increases theta waves

(D) ignores the possibility that an increase in theta waves may not always be accompanied by a state of profound creativity

(E) provides insufficient reasons to believe that people who are not in states of profound creativity have low levels of theta brain waves

GO ON TO THE NEXT PAGE.

24. Consumer advocate: The manufacturer's instructions for assembling a product should be written in such a way that most consumers would find it much easier to put the product together if the instructions were available than if they were not.

Which one of the following, if true, would provide the strongest reason for thinking that the principle advanced by the consumer advocate cannot always be followed?

(A) The typical consumer who assembles a product does so using the manufacturer's instructions, but still has great difficulty.

(B) Often the store at which a consumer purchases an unassembled product will offer, for a fee, to assemble the product and deliver it.

(C) For the typical product, most consumers who assemble it do so very easily and without ever consulting the manufacturer's instructions.

(D) Usually a consumer who is trying to assemble a product using the manufacturer's instructions has no difficulty understanding the instructions.

(E) Some consumers refer to the manufacturer's instructions for assembling a product only if they have difficulty assembling the product.

25. Claude: Because of the relatively high number of middle-aged people in the workforce, there will be fewer opportunities for promotion into upper-management positions. Since this will decrease people's incentive to work hard, economic productivity and the quality of life will diminish.

Thelma: This glut of middle-aged workers will lead many people to form their own companies. They will work hard and thus increase economic productivity, improving the quality of life even if many of the companies ultimately fail.

On the basis of their statements, Claude and Thelma are committed to agreeing about which one of the following?

(A) The quality of life in a society affects that society's economic productivity.

(B) The failure of many companies will not necessarily have a negative effect on overall economic productivity.

(C) How hard a company's employees work is a function of what they think their chances for promotion are in that company.

(D) The number of middle-aged people in the workforce will increase in the coming years.

(E) Economic productivity will be affected by the number of middle-aged people in the workforce.

26. Researchers gave 100 first-graders after-school lessons in handwriting. They found that those whose composition skills had improved the most had learned to write letters the most automatically. This suggests that producing characters more automatically frees up mental resources for other activities.

Which one of the following, if true, most strengthens the argument?

(A) Among the first-graders who received the after-school lessons in handwriting, those who practiced the most learned to write letters the most automatically.

(B) The first-graders who wrote letters the most automatically before receiving the after-school lessons in handwriting showed the greatest improvement in their composition skills over the course of the lessons.

(C) Over the course of the lessons, the first-graders who showed greater improvement in their ability to write letters automatically also generally showed greater improvement in their composition skills.

(D) Before receiving the after-school lessons in handwriting, the 100 first-graders who received the lessons were representative of first-graders more generally, with respect to their skills in both handwriting and composition.

(E) Among the first-graders who received the lessons in handwriting, those who started out with strong composition skills showed substantial improvement in how automatically they could write letters.

STOP

IF YOU FINISH BEFORE TIME IS CALLED, YOU MAY CHECK YOUR WORK ON THIS SECTION ONLY.
DO NOT WORK ON ANY OTHER SECTION IN THE TEST.

SECTION II

Time—35 minutes

26 Questions

<u>Directions:</u> Each set of questions in this section is based on a single passage or a pair of passages. The questions are to be answered on the basis of what is <u>stated</u> or <u>implied</u> in the passage or pair of passages. For some of the questions, more than one of the choices could conceivably answer the question. However, you are to choose the <u>best</u> answer; that is, the response that most accurately and completely answers the question, and blacken the corresponding space on your answer sheet.

In 1963, a three-week-long demonstration for jobs at the construction site of the Downstate Medical Center in Brooklyn, New York, became one of the most significant and widely publicized campaigns of
(5) the civil rights movement in the United States. An interdenominational group made up mostly of locally based African American ministers, who had remained politically moderate until then, organized and led hundreds of people in an aggressive protest. Their
(10) efforts relied mainly on the participation and direct financial support of the ministers' own congregations and other congregations throughout Brooklyn. The goal of this campaign was to build a mass movement that would force changes in government policies as
(15) well as in trade union hiring practices, both of which they believed excluded African Americans from construction jobs.

Inspired by the emergence of African American religious leaders as key figures elsewhere in the civil
(20) rights movement, and reasoning that the ministers would be able to mobilize large numbers of people from their congregations and network effectively with other religious leaders throughout the city, the Congress of Racial Equality (CORE), a national civil
(25) rights organization, had decided to ask the ministers to lead the Downstate campaign. However, by organizing a civil disobedience campaign, the ministers were jeopardizing one of the very factors that had led CORE to seek their involvement: their
(30) positions as politically moderate community leaders. Urban African American ministers and churches had been working for decades with community and government organizations to address the social, political, and economic concerns of their
(35) communities, and ministers of African American congregations in Brooklyn had often acted as mediators between their communities and the government. Many of them also worked for major political parties and ran for political office themselves.
(40) By endorsing and leading the Downstate protest, the ministers were risking their political careers and their reputations within their communities for effecting change through established political channels.

The Downstate campaign ended with an
(45) agreement between the ministers and both government and union officials. This agreement did not include new legislation or a commitment to a specific numerical increase in jobs for African Americans, as the protestors had demanded. But even
(50) though some civil rights activists therefore considered the agreement incomplete, government officials did pledge to enforce existing antidiscrimination legislation. Moreover, the Downstate campaign effectively aroused public concern for the previously
(55) neglected problem of discrimination in the construction industry. It also drew public attention, which had hitherto focused on the progress of the civil rights movement primarily in the southern United States, to the additional need to alleviate
(60) discrimination in the North. Finally, throughout the campaign, the ministers managed to maintain their moderate political ties. The dual role played by the ministers—activists who nonetheless continued to work through established political channels—served
(65) as a model for future ministers who sought to initiate protest actions on behalf of their communities.

1. It can be reasonably inferred from the passage that the author's attitude is most favorable toward which one of the following?

(A) the ways in which the Downstate campaign altered the opinions of union leaders
(B) the impact that the Downstate campaign had on the implementation of new anti-discrimination legislation
(C) CORE's relationship to the demonstrators in the Downstate campaign
(D) the effects that the Downstate campaign had on public awareness
(E) the way in which the leaders of the Downstate campaign negotiated the agreement that ended the campaign

GO ON TO THE NEXT PAGE.

2. Which one of the following assertions about the results of the Downstate campaign does the author affirm in the passage?

   (A)   It achieved all of its participants' goals for changes in union policy but not all of its participants' goals for government action.
   (B)   It directly achieved neither all of its participants' goals for government action nor all of its participants' goals for changes in union hiring policies.
   (C)   It achieved all of its participants' goals for changes in government policies, but did not achieve all of its participants' goals for union commitment to hiring policies.
   (D)   It achieved all of its particular goals for government action immediately, but only gradually achieved some of its participants' desired effects on public opinion.
   (E)   It eventually achieved all of its participants' particular goals for both government action and establishment of union hiring policies, but only after extended effort and significant risk.

3. The primary function of the reference to past activities of ministers and churches (lines 31–38) is to

   (A)   demonstrate that the tactics used by the leaders of the Downstate campaign evolved naturally out of their previous political activities
   (B)   explain why the leaders of the Downstate campaign decided to conduct the protest in the way they did
   (C)   provide examples of the sorts of civil rights activities that the leaders of CORE had promoted
   (D)   indicate how the Downstate campaign could have accomplished its goals by means other than those used
   (E)   underscore the extent to which the Downstate campaign represented a change in approach for its leaders

4. Which one of the following does the author affirm in the passage?

   (A)   CORE was one of several civil rights organizations that challenged the hiring practices of the construction industry.
   (B)   The Downstate campaign relied primarily on CORE and other national civil rights organizations for most of its support.
   (C)   After the Downstate campaign, concern for discrimination in the construction industry was directed primarily toward the northern United States.
   (D)   Many ministers of African American congregations in Brooklyn had sought election to political office.
   (E)   In response to the Downstate campaign, union officials pledged to adopt specific numerical goals for the hiring of African Americans.

5. The passage most clearly suggests that which one of the following is true of the group of ministers who led the Downstate campaign?

   (A)   The Downstate campaign did not signal a significant change in their general political and social goals.
   (B)   After the Downstate campaign, they went on to organize various other similar campaigns.
   (C)   They had come together for the purpose of addressing problems in the construction industry well before CORE's involvement in the Downstate campaign.
   (D)   They were criticized both by CORE and by other concerned organizations for their incomplete success in the Downstate campaign.
   (E)   Prior to the Downstate campaign, many of them had not been directly involved in civil rights activities.

GO ON TO THE NEXT PAGE.

The Cultural Revolution of 1966 to 1976, initiated by Communist Party Chairman Mao Zedong in an attempt to reduce the influence of China's intellectual elite on the country's institutions, has had
(5) lasting repercussions on Chinese art. It intensified the absolutist mind-set of Maoist Revolutionary Realism, which had dictated the content and style of Chinese art even before 1966 by requiring that artists "truthfully" depict the realities of socialist life in
(10) China. Interest in nonsocial, nonpolitical subjects was strictly forbidden, and, during the Cultural Revolution, what constituted truth was entirely for revolutionary forces to decide—the only reality artists could portray was one that had been thoroughly
(15) colored and distorted by political ideology.

Ironically, the same set of requirements that constricted artistic expression during the Cultural Revolution has had the opposite effect since; many artistic movements have flourished in reaction to the
(20) monotony of Revolutionary Realism. One of these, the Scar Art movement of the 1980s, was spearheaded by a group of intellectual painters who had been trained in Maoist art schools and then exiled to rural areas during the Cultural Revolution.
(25) In exile, these painters were for perhaps the first time confronted with the harsh realities of rural poverty and misery—aspects of life in China that their Maoist mentors would probably have preferred they ignore. As a result of these experiences, they developed a
(30) radically new approach to realism. Instead of depicting the version of reality sanctioned by the government, the Scar Art painters chose to represent the "scarred reality" they had seen during their exile. Their version of realist painting emphasized the day-
(35) to-day hardships of rural life. While the principles of Revolutionary Realism had insisted that artists choose public, monumental, and universal subjects, the Scar artists chose instead to focus on the private, the mundane, and the particular; where the principles of
(40) Revolutionary Realism had demanded that they depict contemporary Chinese society as outstanding or perfect, the Scar artists chose instead to portray the bleak realities of modernization.

As the 1980s progressed, the Scar artists' radical
(45) approach to realism became increasingly co-opted for political purposes, and as this political cast became stronger and more obvious, many artists abandoned the movement. Yet a preoccupation with rural life persisted, giving rise to a related development known
(50) as the Native Soil movement, which focused on the native landscape and embodied a growing nostalgia for the charms of peasant society in the face of modernization. Where the Scar artists had reacted to the ideological rigidity of the Cultural Revolution by
(55) emphasizing the damage inflicted by modernization,

the Native Soil painters reacted instead by idealizing traditional peasant life. Unfortunately, in the end Native Soil painting was trivialized by a tendency to romanticize certain qualities of rural Chinese society
(60) in order to appeal to Western galleries and collectors.

6. Which one of the following titles most accurately captures the main point of the passage?

(A) "Painting and Politics: A Survey of Political Influences on Contemporary Chinese Art"
(B) "How Two Movements in Chinese Painting Transformed the Cultural Revolution"
(C) "Scarred Reality: A Look into Chinese Rural Life in the Late Twentieth Century"
(D) "The Rise of Realism in Post-Maoist Art in China"
(E) "The Unforeseen Artistic Legacy of China's Cultural Revolution"

7. Which one of the following works of art would be most compatible with the goals and interests of Scar Art as described in the passage?

(A) a painting of a village scene in which peasants commemorate a triumph over cruel political officials
(B) a painting symbolically representing the destruction caused by a large fire
(C) a painting depicting the weary face of a poorly clothed peasant toiling in a grain mill
(D) a painting caricaturing Mao Zedong as an overseer of farm workers
(E) a painting of two traditionally dressed peasant children walking in a summer wheat field

8. Which one of the following statements about realism in Chinese art can most reasonably be inferred from the passage?

(A) The artists who became leaders of the Native Soil movement practiced a modified form of realism in reaction against the styles and techniques of Scar Art.
(B) Chinese art has encompassed conflicting conceptions of realism derived from contrasting political and artistic purposes.
(C) The goals of realism in Chinese art have been effectively furthered by both the Scar Art movement and the Native Soil movement.
(D) Until the development of the Scar Art movement, interest in rural life had been absent from the types of art that prevailed among Chinese realist painters.
(E) Unlike the art that was predominant during the Cultural Revolution, Scar Art was not a type of realist art.

GO ON TO THE NEXT PAGE.

9. It can be inferred from the passage that the author would be LEAST likely to agree with which one of the following statements regarding the Cultural Revolution?

(A) It had the ironic effect of catalyzing art movements at odds with its policies.

(B) The art that was endorsed by its policies was less varied and interesting than Chinese art since the Cultural Revolution.

(C) Much of the art that it endorsed did not accurately depict the realities of life in China but rather a politically motivated idealization.

(D) Its effects demonstrate that restrictive policies generally foster artistic growth more than liberal policies do.

(E) Its impact has continued to be felt in the Chinese art world years after it ended.

10. The primary function of the first paragraph is to

(A) introduce the set of political and artistic ideas that spurred the development of two artistic movements described in the subsequent paragraphs

(B) acknowledge the inescapable melding of political ideas and artistic styles in China

(C) explain the transformation of Chinese society that came about as a result of the Cultural Revolution

(D) present a hypothesis about realism in Chinese art that is refuted by the ensuing discussion of two artistic movements

(E) show that the political realism practiced by the movements discussed in the ensuing paragraphs originated during the Cultural Revolution

11. It can be inferred from the passage that the author would be most likely to agree with which one of the following views of the Native Soil movement?

(A) Its development was the inevitable consequence of the Scar Art movement's increasing politicization.

(B) It failed to earn the wide recognition that Scar Art had achieved.

(C) The rural scenes it depicted were appealing to most people in China.

(D) Ironically, it had several key elements in common with Revolutionary Realism, in opposition to which it originally developed.

(E) Its nostalgic representation of rural life was the means by which it stood in opposition to Revolutionary Realism.

GO ON TO THE NEXT PAGE.

Individual family members have been assisted in resolving disputes arising from divorce or separation, property division, or financial arrangements, through court-connected family mediation programs, which
(5) differ significantly from court adjudication. When courts use their authority to resolve disputes by adjudicating matters in litigation, judges' decisions are binding, subject only to appeal. Formal rules govern the procedure followed, and the hearings are
(10) generally open to the public. In contrast, family mediation is usually conducted in private, the process is less formal, and mediators do not make binding decisions. Mediators help disputing parties arrive at a solution themselves through communication and
(15) cooperation by facilitating the process of negotiation that leads to agreement by the parties.

Supporters of court adjudication in resolving family disputes claim that it has numerous advantages over family mediation, and there is some validity to
(20) this claim. Judges' decisions, they argue, explicate and interpret the broader social values involved in family disputes, and family mediation can neglect those values. Advocates of court adjudication also argue that since the dynamics of power in disputes
(25) are not always well understood, mediation, which is based on the notion of relatively equal parties, would be inappropriate in many situations. The court system, on the other hand, attempts to protect those at a disadvantage because of imbalances in bargaining
(30) power. Family mediation does not guarantee the full protection of an individual's rights, whereas a goal of the court system is to ensure that lawyers can secure all that the law promises to their clients. Family mediation also does not provide a formal record of
(35) the facts and principles that influence the settlement of a dispute, so if a party to a mediated agreement subsequently seeks modification of the judgment, the task of reconstructing the mediation process is especially difficult. Finally, mediated settlements
(40) divert cases from judicial consideration, thus eliminating the opportunity for such cases to refine the law through the ongoing development of legal precedent.

But in the final analysis, family mediation is
(45) better suited to the unique needs of family law than is the traditional court system. Proponents of family mediation point out that it constitutes a more efficient and less damaging process than litigation. By working together in the mediation process, family members
(50) can enhance their personal autonomy and reduce government intervention, develop skills to resolve future disputes, and create a spirit of cooperation that can lead to greater compliance with their agreement. The family mediation process can assist in resolving
(55) emotional as well as legal issues and thus may reduce

stress in the long term. Studies of family mediation programs in several countries report that the majority of participants reach a full or partial agreement and express positive feelings about the process, perceiving
(60) it to be more rational and humane than the court system.

12. Which one of the following most accurately expresses the main point of the passage?

(A) Recent studies show that family mediation is preferred by family members for resolving family disputes because it is more rational and humane than the court adjudication process.

(B) Even though a majority of participants in family mediation programs are satisfied with the settlements they reach, the use of court adjudication in resolving family disputes has several advantages over the use of mediation.

(C) When given the option, family members involved in disputes have typically elected to use family mediation rather than court adjudication to settle their disputes.

(D) While court adjudication of family disputes has certain advantages, family mediation serves the needs of family members better because it enhances autonomy and encourages greater communication and cooperation in reaching an agreement.

(E) Although supporters of court adjudication argue that family mediation does not contribute to the development and refinement of legal precedent, they fail to recognize that most family disputes can be resolved without appeal to legal precedents.

13. Which one of the following most accurately expresses the primary purpose of the sentence at lines 30–33?

(A) to illustrate that court adjudication can have certain benefits that family mediation may lack

(B) to present material that reveals the inherent limitations of the court adjudication model

(C) to prove that the assumptions implicit in court adjudication and family mediation are irreconcilable

(D) to present an alternative judicial option that combines the benefits of both court adjudication and family mediation

(E) to suggest that lawyers are essential for the protection of individual rights during disputes

GO ON TO THE NEXT PAGE.

14. Based on the passage, which one of the following relationships is most analogous to that between the mediator and the family members involved in a dispute?

(A) A labor relations specialist assists a group of auto assembly workers and the plant's management in reaching an agreeable salary increase for the workers.

(B) A drama teacher decides on the school's annual production based on the outcome of a majority vote by the student body.

(C) A group director solicits feedback from staff prior to implementing a new computer system designed to be more efficient.

(D) An administrative assistant records the minutes of an office meeting in order to improve interoffice communications.

(E) A judge meets privately with the opposing counsel of two parties after rendering a decision in a case.

15. According to the passage, proponents of family mediation note that the family mediation process

(A) is more time-consuming than court adjudication

(B) almost always results in full agreement among the parties

(C) attempts to protect those at a disadvantage because of unequal bargaining power

(D) is most effective in resolving disputes involved in divorce and separation

(E) helps develop the conflict-resolving skills of the parties in a dispute

16. It can most reasonably be inferred from the passage that the author would agree with which one of the following statements regarding the differences between court adjudication and family mediation?

(A) The differences are minimal and would rarely lead to substantially different settlements of similar disputes.

(B) The two processes are so different that the attitudes of the participants toward the outcomes reached can vary significantly depending on which process is used.

(C) The main difference between family mediation and court adjudication is that while family mediation is less damaging, court adjudication is more efficient.

(D) Family mediation led by expert mediators differs much less from court adjudication than does mediation led by mediators who have less expertise.

(E) While family mediation differs significantly from court adjudication, these differences do not really make one or the other better suited to the needs of family law.

17. According to the passage, proponents of court adjudication of family disputes would be most likely to agree with which one of the following?

(A) Court adjudication of family disputes usually produces a decision that satisfies all parties to the dispute equally.

(B) Family mediation fails to address the underlying emotional issues in family disputes.

(C) Settlements of disputes reached through family mediation are not likely to guide the resolution of similar future disputes among other parties.

(D) Court adjudication presumes that the parties to a dispute have relatively equal bargaining power.

(E) Court adjudication hearings for family disputes should always be open to the public.

18. The author's primary purpose in the passage is to

(A) document the evolution of a particular body of law and its various conflict-resolution processes

(B) describe how societal values are embedded in and affect the outcome of two different processes for resolving disputes

(C) explain why one method of conflict resolution is preferable to another for a certain class of legal disputes

(D) show how and why legal precedents in a certain branch of the law can eventually alter the outcomes of future cases

(E) demonstrate that the court system too often disregards the needs of individuals involved in disputes

GO ON TO THE NEXT PAGE.

Until recently, biologists were unable to explain the fact that pathogens—disease-causing parasites—have evolved to incapacitate, and often overwhelm, their hosts. Such behavior is at odds with the
(5) prevailing view of host-parasite relations—that, in general, host and parasite ultimately develop a benign coexistence. This view is based on the idea that parasites that do not harm their hosts have the best chance for long-term survival: they thrive because
(10) their hosts thrive. Some biologists, however, recently have suggested that if a pathogen reproduced so extensively as to cause its host to become gravely sick, it could still achieve evolutionary success if its replication led to a level of transmission into new
(15) hosts that exceeded the loss of pathogens resulting from the host's incapacitation. This scenario suggests that even death-causing pathogens can achieve evolutionary success.

One implication of this perspective is that a
(20) pathogen's virulence—its capacity to overcome a host's defenses and incapacitate it—is a function of its mode of transmission. For example, rhinoviruses, which cause the common cold, require physical proximity for transmission to occur. If a rhinovirus
(25) reproduces so extensively in a solitary host that the host is too unwell to leave home for a day, the thousands of new rhinoviruses produced that day will die before they can be transmitted. So, because it is transmitted directly, the common cold is unlikely to
(30) disable its victims.

The opposite can occur when pathogens are transported by a vector—an organism that can carry and transmit an infectious agent. If, for example, a pathogen capable of being transported by a mosquito
(35) reproduces so extensively that its human host is immobilized, it can still pass along its genes if a mosquito bites the host and transmits this dose to the next human it bites. In such circumstances the virulence is likely to be more severe, because the
(40) pathogen has reproduced to such concentration in the host that the mosquito obtains a high dose of the pathogen, increasing the level of transmission to new hosts.

While medical literature generally supports the
(45) hypothesis that vector-borne pathogens tend to be more virulent than directly transmitted pathogens—witness the lethal nature of malaria, yellow fever, typhus, and sleeping sickness, all carried by biting insects—a few directly transmitted pathogens such as
(50) diphtheria and tuberculosis bacteria can be just as lethal. Scientists call these "sit and wait" pathogens, because they are able to remain alive outside their hosts until a new host comes along, without relying on a vector. Indeed, the endurance of these pathogens,
(55) many of which can survive externally for weeks or months before transmission into a new host—compared, for instance, to an average rhinovirus life span of hours—makes them among the most dangerous of all pathogens.

19. Which one of the following most accurately summarizes the main idea of the passage?

(A) A new hypothesis about the host-incapacitating behavior of some pathogens suggests that directly transmitted pathogens are just as virulent as vector-borne pathogens, due to the former's ability to survive outside a host for long periods of time.

(B) A new hypothesis about the host-incapacitating behavior of some pathogens suggests that, while most pathogens reproduce so extensively as to cause their hosts to become gravely sick or even to die, some eventually develop a benign coexistence with their hosts.

(C) A new hypothesis about the host-incapacitating behavior of some pathogens suggests that they are able to achieve reproductive success because they reproduce to a high level of concentration in their incapacitated hosts.

(D) A new hypothesis about the host-incapacitating behavior of some pathogens suggests that they are generally able to achieve reproductive success unless their reproduction causes the death of the host.

(E) A new hypothesis about the host-incapacitating behavior of some pathogens suggests that pathogen virulence is generally a function of their mode of transmission, with vector-borne pathogens usually more virulent than directly transmitted pathogens, except for those directly transmitted pathogens able to endure outside their hosts.

20. According to the passage, the prevailing view of the host-parasite relationship is that, in general,

(A) the host is ultimately harmed enough to prevent the parasite from thriving

(B) a thriving parasite will eventually incapacitate its host

(C) a parasite must eventually be transmitted to a new host in order to survive

(D) the parasite eventually thrives with no harm to its host

(E) ultimately the host thrives only if the parasite thrives

21. With which one of the following statements about the prevailing view of host-parasite relations would the biologists mentioned in line 10 be most likely to agree?

(A) The view contradicts most evidence of actual host-parasite relations.

(B) The view suggests that even death-causing pathogens can achieve evolutionary success.

(C) The view presumes the existence of a type of parasite behavior that does not exist.

(D) The view ignores the possibility that there is more than one way to achieve evolutionary success.

(E) The view erroneously assumes that hosts never harm the parasites that feed off them.

GO ON TO THE NEXT PAGE.

22. The examples of diphtheria and tuberculosis bacteria provide the most support for which one of the following conclusions about the dangerousness of pathogens?

   (A)   The most dangerous pathogens are those with the shortest life spans outside a host.

   (B)   Those pathogens with the greatest endurance outside a host are among the most dangerous.

   (C)   Those pathogens transported by vectors are always the most dangerous.

   (D)   The least dangerous pathogens are among those with the longest life spans outside a host.

   (E)   Those pathogens transmitted directly are always least dangerous.

23. Which one of the following, if true, would most seriously challenge the position of the biologists mentioned in line 10?

   (A)   Most pathogens capable of causing their hosts' deaths are able to achieve reproductive success.

   (B)   Most pathogens transmitted from incapacitated hosts into new hosts are unable to overwhelm the new hosts.

   (C)   Most pathogens that do not incapacitate their hosts are unable to achieve reproductive success.

   (D)   Most hosts that become gravely sick are infected by pathogens that reproduce to relatively high concentrations.

   (E)   Most pathogens transmitted from incapacitated hosts are unable to reproduce in their new hosts.

24. Which one of the following most accurately describes the organization of the passage?

   (A)   introduction of a scientific anomaly; presentation of an explanation for the anomaly; mention of an implication of the explanation; discussion of two examples illustrating the implication; discussion of exceptions to the implication

   (B)   introduction of a scientific anomaly; presentation of an explanation for the anomaly; discussion of two examples illustrating the explanation; discussion of exceptions to the explanation; mention of an implication of the explanation

   (C)   introduction of a scientific anomaly; presentation of an explanation for the anomaly; discussion of two examples illustrating the explanation; mention of an implication of the explanation; discussion of examples illustrating the implication

   (D)   introduction of a scientific anomaly; presentation of an implication of the anomaly; discussion of two examples illustrating the implication; discussion of exceptions to the implication

   (E)   introduction of a scientific anomaly; discussion of two examples illustrating the anomaly; presentation of an explanation for the anomaly; discussion of examples illustrating the explanation

25. The passage implies that which one of the following is a reason that rhinoviruses are unlikely to be especially virulent?

   (A)   They immobilize their hosts before they have a chance to reproduce extensively enough to pass directly to new hosts.

   (B)   They cannot survive outside their hosts long enough to be transmitted from incapacitated hosts to new hosts.

   (C)   They cannot reproduce in numbers sufficient to allow vectors to obtain high enough doses to pass to new hosts.

   (D)   They cannot survive long enough in an incapacitated host to be picked up by vectors.

   (E)   They produce thousands of new rhinoviruses each day.

26. The primary purpose of the passage is to

   (A)   compare examples challenging the prevailing view of host-parasite relations with examples supporting it

   (B)   argue that the prevailing view of host-parasite relations is correct but is based on a mistaken rationale

   (C)   offer a modification to the prevailing view of host-parasite relations

   (D)   attack evidence that supports the prevailing view of host-parasite relations

   (E)   examine the origins of the prevailing view of host-parasite relations

STOP

IF YOU FINISH BEFORE TIME IS CALLED, YOU MAY CHECK YOUR WORK ON THIS SECTION ONLY.
DO NOT WORK ON ANY OTHER SECTION IN THE TEST.

SECTION III
Time—35 minutes
26 Questions

Directions: The questions in this section are based on the reasoning contained in brief statements or passages. For some questions, more than one of the choices could conceivably answer the question. However, you are to choose the best answer; that is, the response that most accurately and completely answers the question. You should not make assumptions that are by commonsense standards implausible, superfluous, or incompatible with the passage. After you have chosen the best answer, blacken the corresponding space on your answer sheet.

1. Although fiber-optic telephone cable is more expensive to manufacture than copper telephone cable, a telephone network using fiber-optic cable is less expensive overall than a telephone network using copper cable. This is because copper cable requires frequent amplification of complex electrical signals to carry them for long distances, whereas the pulses of light that are transmitted along fiber-optic cable can travel much farther before amplification is needed.

   The above statements, if true, most strongly support which one of the following?

   (A) The material from which fiber-optic cable is manufactured is more expensive than the copper from which copper cable is made.
   (B) The increase in the number of transmissions of complex signals through telephone cables is straining those telephone networks that still use copper cable.
   (C) Fiber-optic cable can carry many more signals simultaneously than copper cable can.
   (D) Signals transmitted through fiber-optic cable travel at the same speed as signals transmitted through copper cable.
   (E) The cost associated with frequent amplification of signals traveling through copper cable exceeds the extra manufacturing cost of fiber-optic cable.

2. Being near woodlands, the natural habitat of bees, promotes the health of crops that depend on pollination. Bees, the most common pollinators, visit flowers far from woodlands less often than they visit flowers close to woodlands.

   Which one of the following, if true, most strengthens the argument?

   (A) The likelihood that a plant is pollinated increases as the number of visits from pollinators increases.
   (B) Many bees live in habitats other than woodlands.
   (C) Woodlands are not the natural habitat of all pollinators.
   (D) Some pollinators visit flowers far from their habitats more often than they visit flowers close to their habitats.
   (E) Many crops that are not near woodlands depend on pollination.

3. According to the rules of the university's housing lottery, the only students guaranteed dormitory rooms are fourth-year students. In addition, any fourth-year student on the dean's list can choose a dormitory room before anyone who is not a fourth-year student.

   Which one of the following inferences is most strongly supported by the rules described above?

   (A) Benizer is a fourth-year student who is not on the dean's list, so she is not guaranteed a dormitory room.
   (B) Ivan and Naomi are both fourth-year students but only Naomi is on the dean's list. Therefore, Ivan can choose a dormitory room before Naomi.
   (C) Halle, a third-year student, is on the dean's list. Thus, she is guaranteed a dormitory room.
   (D) Gerald and Katrina are both on the dean's list but only Gerald is a fourth-year student. Thus, Gerald can choose a dormitory room before Katrina.
   (E) Anissa is a fourth-year student who is on the dean's list. Thus, since Jehan is a second-year student who is also on the dean's list, he can choose a dormitory room before Anissa.

GO ON TO THE NEXT PAGE.

4. To the editor:

For generations, magnificent racehorses have been bred in our area. Our most valuable product, however, has been generations of children raised with the character that makes them winners in the contests of life. Gambling is wrong, and children raised in an atmosphere where the goal is to get something for nothing will not develop good character. Those who favor developing good character in children over gambling on horses should vote against allowing our first racetrack to be built.

L.E.

Which one of the following, if true, most weakens L.E.'s argument?

(A) If good character is developed in children early, the children continue to have good character in different environments.

(B) In other areas with gambling, parents are able to raise children of good character.

(C) In most areas with horse racing, the percentage of adults who gamble increases gradually from year to year.

(D) Children whose parents gamble do not necessarily gamble when they become adults.

(E) Where voters have had the opportunity to vote on horse racing, they have consistently approved it.

5. Azadeh: The recent increase in the amount of organically produced food indicates that consumers are taking a greater interest in the environment. Thus, there is new hope for a healthier planet.

Ben: No, Azadeh, if you interviewed people who buy organic produce, you'd see that they're actually as selfish as everyone else, since they're motivated only by worries about their own health.

Azadeh's and Ben's statements provide the most support for holding that they disagree about whether

(A) it is likely that a healthy planet can be maintained if most people continue in their present eating habits

(B) people can become healthier by increasing their consumption of organic foods

(C) people ought to be more concerned about the environment than they currently are

(D) the rise in organic food production shows people to have a greater concern for the environment than they had before

(E) people can be persuaded to have a greater concern for the environment than they now have

6. Citizen: The primary factor determining a dog's disposition is not its breed, but its home environment. A bad owner can undo generations of careful breeding. Legislation focusing on specific breeds of dogs would not address the effects of human behavior in raising and training animals. As a result, such breed-specific legislation could never effectively protect the public from vicious dogs. Moreover, in my view, the current laws are perfectly adequate.

Which one of the following most accurately expresses the conclusion drawn by the citizen?

(A) The public would not be effectively protected from violent dogs by breed-specific legislation.

(B) A good home environment is more important than breeding to a dog's disposition.

(C) The home environment of dogs would not be regulated by breed-specific legislation.

(D) Irresponsible dog owners are capable of producing dogs with bad dispositions regardless of generations of careful breeding.

(E) The vicious-dog laws that are currently in effect do not address the effects of human behavior in raising and training dogs.

7. Legislator: To keep our food safe, we must prohibit the use of any food additives that have been found to cause cancer.

Commentator: An absolute prohibition is excessive. Today's tests can detect a single molecule of potentially cancer-causing substances, but we know that consuming significantly larger amounts of such a chemical does not increase one's risk of getting cancer. Thus, we should instead set a maximum acceptable level for each problematic chemical, somewhat below the level at which the substance has been shown to lead to cancer but above zero.

Of the following, which one, if true, is the logically strongest counter the legislator can make to the commentator's argument?

(A) The level at which a given food additive has been shown to lead to cancer in children is generally about half the level at which it leads to cancer in adults.

(B) Consuming small amounts of several different cancer-causing chemicals can lead to cancer even if consuming such an amount of any one cancer-causing chemical would not.

(C) The law would prohibit only the deliberate addition of cancer-causing chemicals and would not require the removal of naturally occurring cancer-causing substances.

(D) For some food additives, the level at which the substance has been shown to lead to cancer is lower than the level at which the additive provides any benefit.

(E) All food additives have substitutes that can be used in their place.

GO ON TO THE NEXT PAGE.

8. Consumer advocate: There is ample evidence that the model of car one drives greatly affects the chances that one's car will be stolen. The model of car stolen most often in our country last year, for example, was also the model stolen most often in the preceding year.

The consumer advocate's reasoning is most vulnerable to criticism on the grounds that it

(A) fails to address adequately the possibility that the model of car that was stolen most often last year was the most common model of car in the consumer advocate's country

(B) fails to address adequately the possibility that the age of a car also greatly affects its chances of being stolen

(C) fails to address adequately the possibility that the car model that was stolen most often last year was stolen as often as it was because it has a very high resale value

(D) presumes, without providing justification, that someone considering whether or not to steal a particular car considers only what model the car is

(E) presumes, without providing justification, that the likelihood of a car's being stolen should override other considerations in deciding which car one should drive

9. Laird: Pure research provides us with new technologies that contribute to saving lives. Even more worthwhile than this, however, is its role in expanding our knowledge and providing new, unexplored ideas.

Kim: Your priorities are mistaken. Saving lives is what counts most of all. Without pure research, medicine would not be as advanced as it is.

Laird and Kim disagree on whether pure research

(A) derives its significance in part from its providing new technologies

(B) expands the boundaries of our knowledge of medicine

(C) should have the saving of human lives as an important goal

(D) has its most valuable achievements in medical applications

(E) has any value apart from its role in providing new technologies to save lives

10. Naturalist: To be dependable, the accounting framework used by national economists to advise the government must take into account all of our nation's assets; but the current accounting framework used by our national economists assigns no value to government-owned natural resources, which are clearly assets.

The naturalist's statements, if true, most strongly support which one of the following?

(A) Economists' indifference toward the destruction of natural resources will lead policymakers to make poor decisions.

(B) Naturalists and economists disagree about whether natural resources have value.

(C) The accounting framework used by national economists is not reliable.

(D) Natural resources are a vital economic asset for every nation.

(E) Changes in the environment have a value that is not represented in any accounting framework.

11. Carrots are known to be one of the best sources of naturally occurring vitamin A. However, although farmers in Canada and the United States report increasing demand for carrots over the last decade, the number of people diagnosed with vitamin A deficiency in these countries has also increased in that time.

Each of the following, if true of Canada and the United States over the last decade, helps to resolve the apparent discrepancy described above EXCEPT:

(A) The population has significantly increased in every age group.

(B) The purchase of peeled and chopped carrots has become very popular, though carrots are known to lose their vitamins quickly once peeled.

(C) Certain cuisines that have become popular use many more vegetable ingredients, including carrots, than most cuisines that were previously popular.

(D) Carrot consumption has increased only among those demographic groups that have historically had low vitamin A deficiency rates.

(E) Weather conditions have caused a decrease in the availability of carrots.

GO ON TO THE NEXT PAGE.

12. Critics have argued that because Freudianism holds that people have unconscious desires that can defeat their attempts to follow rational life plans, it is incompatible with the predominantly rationalistic spirit of Western philosophical and psychological thought. But it is a central tenet of Freudianism that through psychoanalysis one can become conscious of one's previously unconscious desires, enabling one to avoid being defeated by them. Therefore, _____.

Which one of the following most logically completes the argument?

(A) Freudianism does not run counter to the rationalistic mainstream of Western philosophical and psychological thought

(B) Freudianism holds that people can always achieve happiness through psychoanalysis

(C) Freudianism may be the beginning of a new trend in Western philosophical and psychological thought

(D) psychoanalysis provides one with a rational life plan

(E) Freudianism reflects the predominantly rationalistic spirit of Western philosophical and psychological thought more than any other psychological theory

13. Writer: In the diplomat's or lawyer's world, a misinterpreted statement can result in an international incident or an undeserved prison term. Thus, legal and diplomatic language is stilted and utterly without literary merit, since by design it prevents misinterpretation, which in these areas can have severe consequences.

The writer's argument requires assuming which one of the following?

(A) Language that has literary value is more likely to be misunderstood than language without literary value.

(B) Literary documents are generally less important than legal or diplomatic documents.

(C) Lawyers and diplomats are much less likely to be misunderstood than are novelists.

(D) The issues that are of interest to lawyers and diplomats are of little interest to others.

(E) People express themselves more cautiously when something important is at stake.

14. Overexposure to certain wavelengths of strong sunlight is the main cause of melanoma, a virulent form of skin cancer. For this reason, doctors now urge everyone to put adequate sunblock on skin exposed to strong sunlight. Adequate sunblock, according to doctors, is any preparation that prevents sunburn even if the person is exposed to strong sunlight for a significant length of time.

Which one of the following, if true, most weakens the recommendation that people wear adequate sunblock?

(A) There is no evidence that there are wavelengths of sunlight that lead to both sunburn and melanoma.

(B) There are people who have allergic reactions to certain chemicals found in many sunblocks.

(C) Many sunblocks need repeated applications to remain effective for a significant length of time.

(D) Toxins contained in certain chemical compounds also cause melanoma.

(E) Sunburns appear immediately after exposure to the sun but melanoma appears years after repeated exposures.

15. In a study, parents were asked to rate each television program that their children watched. The programs were rated for violent content on a scale of one to five, with "one" indicating no violence and "five" indicating a great deal. The number of times their children were disciplined in school was also recorded. Children who watched programs with an average violence rating of three or higher were 50 percent more likely to have been disciplined than other children.

Each of the following, if true, helps to explain the statistical relationship described above EXCEPT:

(A) Children who are excited by violent action programs on television tend to become bored with schoolwork and to express their boredom in an unacceptable fashion.

(B) When parents watch violent programs on television with their children, those children become more likely to regard antisocial behavior as legitimate.

(C) Parents who rated their children's television viewing low on violence had become desensitized to the violence on television by watching too much of it.

(D) Children learn from violent programs on television to disrespect society's prohibitions of violence and, as a result, are more likely than other children to disrespect the school disciplinary codes.

(E) Parents who do not allow their children to watch programs with a high level of violence are more likely than other parents to be careful about other aspects of their children's behavior.

GO ON TO THE NEXT PAGE.

16. In the last election, 89 percent of reporters voted for the incumbent. The content of news programs reveals that reporters allowed the personal biases reflected in this voting pattern to affect their news coverage: 54 percent of coverage concerning the challenger was negative, compared with only 30 percent of that concerning the incumbent.

The argument is logically most vulnerable to criticism on the grounds that it

(A) presumes, without providing justification, that both candidates received equal amounts of coverage overall

(B) ignores the possibility that there was more negative news worthy of reporting concerning the challenger than there was concerning the incumbent

(C) presumes, without providing justification, that allowing biases to influence reporting is always detrimental to the resulting news coverage

(D) ignores the possibility that the electorate's voting behavior is not significantly affected by the content of coverage of candidates

(E) ignores the possibility that reporters generally fear losing access to incumbents more than they fear losing access to challengers

17. Art critic: Abstract paintings are nonrepresentational, and so the only measure of their worth is their interplay of color, texture, and form. But for a painting to spur the viewer to political action, instances of social injustice must be not only represented, but also clearly comprehensible as such. Therefore, abstract painting can never be a politically significant art form.

Which one of the following is an assumption that is required by the art critic's argument?

(A) Abstract painting cannot stimulate people to act.

(B) Unless people view representations of social injustice, their political activity is insignificant.

(C) Only art that prompts people to counter social injustice is significant art.

(D) Paintings that fail to move a viewer to political action cannot be politically significant.

(E) The interplay of color, texture, and form is not a measure of the worth of representational paintings.

18. North Americans who travel to Europe for the first time should include significant time in Italy on their itinerary. To develop an appreciation of a continent that goes beyond the mere accumulation of impressions, one needs to acquire a thorough knowledge of at least one country, and North Americans seem to find it easier to get to know Italy than other European countries.

Which one of the following best illustrates the principle illustrated by the argument above?

(A) A person who wants to learn to play the piano should study classical music, because though it is more difficult to play than is popular music, mastery of its techniques enables one to quickly master popular pieces.

(B) To overcome a fear of water that prevents one from swimming, one should paddle about in shallow water with a trusted friend who is a good swimmer.

(C) Edith Wharton is the most accessible of the classical U.S. writers. So in order to provide a superb introduction to U.S. literature, a class should emphasize her work while also studying the works of others.

(D) One can appreciate Taiko-drumming only if one understands how physically demanding it is. Thus, one should see Taiko-drumming and not just hear it in order to appreciate it fully.

(E) One should travel through North America by train rather than by automobile, because train travel imparts the same sense of open space as does automobile travel, while also affording one the full leisure to attend to the scenery.

GO ON TO THE NEXT PAGE.

19. Although high cholesterol levels have been associated with the development of heart disease, many people with high cholesterol never develop heart disease, while many without high cholesterol do. Recently, above average concentrations of the blood particle lipoprotein(a) were found in the blood of many people whose heart disease was not attributable to other causes. Dietary changes that affect cholesterol levels have no effect on lipoprotein(a) levels. Hence, there is no reason for anyone to make dietary changes for the sake of preventing heart disease.

Which one of the following most accurately describes a flaw in the argument?

(A) It fails to consider the possibility that lipoprotein(a) raises cholesterol levels.
(B) It provides no evidence for a link between lipoprotein(a) and heart disease.
(C) It presents but ignores evidence that, for some people, high cholesterol contributes to heart disease.
(D) It fails to consider the possibility that poor diets cause some people to develop health problems other than heart disease.
(E) It offers no explanation for why some people with high cholesterol levels never develop heart disease.

20. Philosopher: It is absurd to argue that people are morally obligated to act in a certain way simply because not acting in that way would be unnatural. An unnatural action is either a violation of the laws of nature or a statistical anomaly. There is no possibility of acting as one cannot, nor does the mere fact that something is not usually done provide any good reason not to do it.

Which one of the following most accurately describes a technique used in the philosopher's argument?

(A) undermining a concept by showing that its acceptance would violate a law of nature
(B) stating the definition of a key term of the argument
(C) using statistical findings to dispute a claim
(D) undermining a claim by showing that the claim is self-contradictory
(E) using empirical evidence to support one definition of a key term of the argument over another

21. Clearly, fitness consultants who smoke cigarettes cannot help their clients become healthier. If they do not care about their own health, they cannot really care for their clients' health, and if they do not care for their clients' health, they cannot help them to become healthier.

The conclusion follows logically if which one of the following is assumed?

(A) Anyone who does not care for his or her own health cannot help others become healthier.
(B) Anyone who cares about the health of others can help others become healthier.
(C) Anyone who does not care for the health of others cannot help them become healthier.
(D) Anyone who does not smoke cares about the health of others.
(E) Anyone who cares about his or her own health does not smoke.

GO ON TO THE NEXT PAGE.

22. If one does not have enough information to make a well-informed decision, one should not make a decision solely on the basis of the information one does possess. Instead, one should continue to seek information until a well-informed decision can be made.

Of the following, which one most closely conforms to the principle stated above?

(A) Economists should not believe the predictions of an economic model simply because it is based on information about the current economy. Many conflicting models are based on such information, and they cannot all be accurate.

(B) When deciding which career to pursue, one needs to consider carefully all of the information one has. One should not choose a career solely on the basis of financial compensation; instead, one should consider other factors such as how likely one is to succeed at the career and how much one would enjoy it.

(C) Though a researcher may know a great deal about a topic, she or he should not assume that all information relevant to the research is already in her or his possession. A good researcher always looks for further relevant information.

(D) When one wants to buy a reliable car, one should not choose which car to buy just on the inadequate basis of one's personal experience with cars. Rather, one should study various models' reliability histories that summarize many owners' experiences.

(E) When there is not enough information available to determine the meaning of a line of poetry, one should not form an opinion based on the insufficient information. Instead, one should simply acknowledge that it is impossible to determine what the line means.

23. Television network executive: Some scientists have expressed concern about the numerous highly popular television programs that emphasize paranormal incidents, warning that these programs will encourage superstition and thereby impede the public's scientific understanding. But these predictions are baseless. Throughout recorded history, dramatists have relied on ghosts and spirits to enliven their stories, and yet the scientific understanding of the populace has steadily advanced.

The television network executive's argument is most vulnerable to criticism on which one of the following grounds?

(A) It fails to consider that one phenomenon can steadily advance even when it is being impeded by another phenomenon.

(B) It takes for granted that if a correlation has been observed between two phenomena, they must be causally connected.

(C) It fails to consider that the occurrence of one phenomenon can indirectly affect the pervasiveness of another even if the former does not impede the latter.

(D) It fails to consider that just because one phenomenon is known to affect another, the latter does not also affect the former.

(E) It takes for granted that the contention that one phenomenon causes another must be baseless if the latter phenomenon has persisted despite steady increases in the pervasiveness of the former.

24. Police commissioner: Last year our city experienced a 15 percent decrease in the rate of violent crime. At the beginning of that year a new mandatory sentencing law was enacted, which requires that all violent criminals serve time in prison. Since no other major policy changes were made last year, the drop in the crime rate must have been due to the new mandatory sentencing law.

Which one of the following, if true, most seriously weakens the police commissioner's argument?

(A) Studies of many other cities have shown a correlation between improving economic conditions and decreased crime rates.

(B) Prior to the enactment of the mandatory sentencing law, judges in the city had for many years already imposed unusually harsh penalties for some crimes.

(C) Last year, the city's overall crime rate decreased by only 5 percent.

(D) At the beginning of last year, the police department's definition of "violent crime" was broadened to include 2 crimes not previously classified as "violent."

(E) The city enacted a policy 2 years ago requiring that 100 new police officers be hired in each of the 3 subsequent years.

GO ON TO THE NEXT PAGE.

25. A corporation created a new division. To staff it, applicants were rigorously screened and interviewed. Those selected were among the most effective, efficient, and creative workers that the corporation had ever hired. Thus, the new division must have been among the most effective, efficient, and creative divisions the corporation had ever created.

The flawed pattern of reasoning in which one of the following is most similar to that in the argument above?

(A) In order to obtain the best players for its country's Olympic team, a committee reviewed the performance of its country's teams. After reviewing statistics and reading reports, the committee chose one player from each of the six best teams, thus assuring that the six best players in the country had been chosen.

(B) Several salespeople were given incentives to recruit the largest number of new customers in one month. To monitor the incentive program, the boss interviewed one of the salespeople and found that the salesperson had already exceeded the minimum goals of the program. Thus the incentive program was indeed effective.

(C) A law firm decided to add a department devoted to family law. To obtain the best employees it could, the firm studied the credentials and composition of several other firms well known to have successful staffs working in family law. Eventually, the firm hired a staff of new lawyers and support personnel having training and aptitudes as much like those of the studied firms as possible. Thus the law firm must have created one of the best family-law departments.

(D) To put together this year's two All-Star Teams, the best players in the league were selected. Half of them were put on Team One, and half were put on Team Two. Since each player on the two teams was one of the best players in the league this year, it follows that the two All-Star Teams are the two best teams this year.

(E) Various schools chose teams of students to compete in a debate tournament. Each school's team presented a position and rebutted the others' positions. After the initial scores were in, the ten top teams competed against each other. Since one team eventually emerged with the highest average score, it was clearly the best team.

26. Students in a college ethics class were asked to judge whether two magazines had been morally delinquent in publishing a particular classified advertisement that was highly offensive in its demeaning portrayal of some people. They were told only that the first magazine had undertaken to screen all classified advertisements and reject for publication those it found offensive, whereas the second magazine's policy was to publish any advertisement received from its subscribers. Most students judged the first magazine, but not the second, to have been morally delinquent in publishing the advertisement.

Which one of the following principles, if established, provides the strongest justification for the judgment that the first magazine and not the second was morally delinquent?

(A) It is wrong to publish messages that could cause direct or indirect harm to innocent people.

(B) Anyone regularly transmitting messages to the public has a moral responsibility to monitor the content of those messages.

(C) If two similar agents commit two similar actions, those agents should be held to the same standard of accountability.

(D) Failure to uphold a moral standard is not necessarily a moral failing except for those who have specifically committed themselves to upholding that standard.

(E) A magazine should not be considered at fault for publishing a classified advertisement if that advertisement would not be offensive to any of the magazine's subscribers.

S T O P
IF YOU FINISH BEFORE TIME IS CALLED, YOU MAY CHECK YOUR WORK ON THIS SECTION ONLY.
DO NOT WORK ON ANY OTHER SECTION IN THE TEST.

SECTION IV

Time—35 minutes

22 Questions

Directions: Each group of questions in this section is based on a set of conditions. In answering some of the questions, it may be useful to draw a rough diagram. Choose the response that most accurately and completely answers each question and blacken the corresponding space on your answer sheet.

Questions 1–5

Exactly seven products—P, Q, R, S, T, W, and X—are each to be advertised exactly once in a section of a catalog. The order in which they will be displayed is governed by the following conditions:

  Q must be displayed in some position before W.
  R must be displayed immediately before X.
  T cannot be displayed immediately before or immediately after W.
  S must be displayed either first or seventh.
  Either Q or T must be displayed fourth.

1. Which one of the following CANNOT be the product that is displayed first?

  (A) P
  (B) Q
  (C) R
  (D) T
  (E) X

2. If X is displayed immediately before Q, then which one of the following could be true?

  (A) T is displayed first.
  (B) R is displayed fifth.
  (C) Q is displayed last.
  (D) Q is displayed second.
  (E) P is displayed second.

3. If P is displayed second, then which one of the following could be displayed third?

  (A) R
  (B) S
  (C) T
  (D) W
  (E) X

4. Which one of the following could be true?

  (A) Q is displayed fifth.
  (B) Q is displayed seventh.
  (C) R is displayed third.
  (D) W is displayed third.
  (E) X is displayed fifth.

5. If R is displayed sixth, then which one of the following must be displayed fifth?

  (A) P
  (B) Q
  (C) T
  (D) W
  (E) X

GO ON TO THE NEXT PAGE.

Questions 6–11

A lighting control panel has exactly seven switches, numbered from 1 to 7. Each switch is either in the on position or in the off position. The circuit load of the panel is the total number of its switches that are on. The control panel must be configured in accordance with the following conditions:

If switch 1 is on, then switch 3 and switch 5 are off.
If switch 4 is on, then switch 2 and switch 5 are off.
The switch whose number corresponds to the circuit load of the panel is itself on.

6. Which one of the following could be a complete and accurate list of the switches that are on?

(A)   switch 2, switch 3, switch 4, switch 7
(B)   switch 3, switch 6, switch 7
(C)   switch 2, switch 5, switch 6
(D)   switch 1, switch 3, switch 4
(E)   switch 1, switch 5

7. If switch 1 and switch 3 are both off, then which one of the following could be two switches that are both on?

(A)   switch 2 and switch 7
(B)   switch 4 and switch 6
(C)   switch 4 and switch 7
(D)   switch 5 and switch 6
(E)   switch 6 and switch 7

8. If exactly two of the switches are on, then which one of the following switches must be off?

(A)   switch 3
(B)   switch 4
(C)   switch 5
(D)   switch 6
(E)   switch 7

9. If switch 6 and switch 7 are both off, then what is the maximum circuit load of the panel?

(A)   one
(B)   two
(C)   three
(D)   four
(E)   five

10. If switch 5 and switch 6 are both on, then which one of the following switches must be on?

(A)   switch 1
(B)   switch 2
(C)   switch 3
(D)   switch 4
(E)   switch 7

11. What is the maximum circuit load of the panel?

(A)   three
(B)   four
(C)   five
(D)   six
(E)   seven

GO ON TO THE NEXT PAGE.

Questions 12–17

In Crescentville there are exactly five record stores, whose names are abbreviated S, T, V, X, and Z. Each of the five stores carries at least one of four distinct types of music: folk, jazz, opera, and rock. None of the stores carries any other type of music. The following conditions must hold:

Exactly two of the five stores carry jazz.
T carries rock and opera but no other type of music.
S carries more types of music than T carries.
X carries more types of music than any other store in Crescentville carries.
Jazz is among the types of music S carries.
V does not carry any type of music that Z carries.

12. Which one of the following could be true?

   (A) S carries folk and rock but neither jazz nor opera.
   (B) T carries jazz but neither opera nor rock.
   (C) V carries folk, rock, and opera, but not jazz.
   (D) X carries folk, rock, and jazz, but not opera.
   (E) Z carries folk and opera but neither rock nor jazz.

13. Which one of the following could be true?

   (A) S, V, and Z all carry folk.
   (B) S, X, and Z all carry jazz.
   (C) Of the five stores, only S and V carry jazz.
   (D) Of the five stores, only T and X carry rock.
   (E) Of the five stores, only S, T, and V carry opera.

14. If exactly one of the stores carries folk, then which one of the following could be true?

   (A) S and V carry exactly two types of music in common.
   (B) T and S carry exactly two types of music in common.
   (C) T and V carry exactly two types of music in common.
   (D) V and X carry exactly two types of music in common.
   (E) X and Z carry exactly two types of music in common.

15. Which one of the following must be true?

   (A) T carries exactly the same number of types of music as V carries.
   (B) V carries exactly the same number of types of music as Z carries.
   (C) S carries at least one more type of music than Z carries.
   (D) Z carries at least one more type of music than T carries.
   (E) X carries exactly two more types of music than S carries.

16. If V is one of exactly three stores that carry rock, then which one of the following must be true?

   (A) S and Z carry no types of music in common.
   (B) S and V carry at least one type of music in common.
   (C) S and Z carry at least one type of music in common.
   (D) T and Z carry at least one type of music in common.
   (E) T and V carry at least two types of music in common.

17. If S and V both carry folk, then which one of the following could be true?

   (A) S and T carry no types of music in common.
   (B) S and Z carry no types of music in common.
   (C) T and Z carry no types of music in common.
   (D) S and Z carry two types of music in common.
   (E) T and V carry two types of music in common.

GO ON TO THE NEXT PAGE.

Questions 18–22

Maggie's Deli is open exactly five days every week: Monday through Friday. Its staff, each of whom works on at least one day each week, consists of exactly six people—Janice, Kevin, Nan, Ophelia, Paul, and Seymour. Exactly three of them—Janice, Nan, and Paul—are supervisors. The deli's staffing is consistent with the following:

    Each day's staff consists of exactly two people, at least one of whom is a supervisor.

    Tuesday's and Wednesday's staffs both include Ophelia.

    Of the days Nan works each week, at least two are consecutive.

    Seymour does not work on any day before the first day Paul works that week.

    Any day on which Kevin works is the first day during the week that some other staff member works.

18. Which one of the following could be an accurate staffing schedule?

(A) Monday: Janice, Kevin
    Tuesday: Nan, Ophelia
    Wednesday: Nan, Paul
    Thursday: Kevin, Paul
    Friday: Janice, Seymour

(B) Monday: Paul, Seymour
    Tuesday: Ophelia, Paul
    Wednesday: Nan, Ophelia
    Thursday: Kevin, Nan
    Friday: Janice, Seymour

(C) Monday: Janice, Kevin
    Tuesday: Nan, Ophelia
    Wednesday: Nan, Ophelia
    Thursday: Kevin, Paul
    Friday: Paul, Seymour

(D) Monday: Janice, Kevin
    Tuesday: Janice, Ophelia
    Wednesday: Nan, Ophelia
    Thursday: Nan, Seymour
    Friday: Kevin, Paul

(E) Monday: Paul, Seymour
    Tuesday: Ophelia, Paul
    Wednesday: Nan, Ophelia
    Thursday: Janice, Kevin
    Friday: Nan, Paul

19. If Kevin and Paul work Thursday, who must work Friday?

(A) Janice
(B) Kevin
(C) Nan
(D) Paul
(E) Seymour

20. Each of the following could be true EXCEPT:

(A) Janice works Monday and Tuesday.
(B) Kevin and Paul work Friday.
(C) Seymour works Monday and Friday.
(D) Janice and Kevin work Thursday.
(E) Paul works Monday and Friday.

21. Which one of the following CANNOT be the pair of staff that works Monday?

(A) Janice and Seymour
(B) Kevin and Paul
(C) Paul and Seymour
(D) Nan and Ophelia
(E) Janice and Nan

22. Which one of the following could be true?

(A) Nan works Wednesday and Friday only.
(B) Seymour works Monday and Paul works Tuesday.
(C) Kevin works Monday, Wednesday, and Friday.
(D) Nan works Wednesday with Ophelia and Thursday with Kevin.
(E) Ophelia and Kevin work Tuesday.

STOP
IF YOU FINISH BEFORE TIME IS CALLED, YOU MAY CHECK YOUR WORK ON THIS SECTION ONLY.
DO NOT WORK ON ANY OTHER SECTION IN THE TEST.

ACKNOWLEDGMENTS

Acknowledgment is made to the following sources from which material has been adapted for use in this test booklet:

"Court-Connected Family Mediation Programs in Canada." ©May 1994 by Alberta Law Reform Institute.

Paul W. Ewald, "The Evolution of Virulence." ©April 1993 by Scientific American, Inc.

Clarence Taylor, *The Black Churches of Brooklyn.* ©1994 by Columbia University Press.

Li Xianting, "Major Trends in the Development of Contemporary Chinese Art." tr. Valerie C. Doran. ©1993 by Hanart T Z Gallery.

Wait for the supervisor's instructions before you open the page to the topic.
Please print and sign your name and write the date in the designated spaces below.
Time: 35 Minutes

General Directions

You will have 35 minutes in which to plan and write an essay on the topic inside. Read the topic and the accompanying directions carefully. You will probably find it best to spend a few minutes considering the topic and organizing your thoughts before you begin writing. In your essay, be sure to develop your ideas fully, leaving time, if possible, to review what you have written. **Do not write on a topic other than the one specified. Writing on a topic of your own choice is not acceptable.**

No special knowledge is required or expected for this writing exercise. Law schools are interested in the reasoning, clarity, organization, language usage, and writing mechanics displayed in your essay. How well you write is more important than how much you write.

Confine your essay to the blocked, lined area on the front and back of the separate Writing Sample Response Sheet. Only that area will be reproduced for law schools. Be sure that your writing is legible.

Both this topic sheet and your response sheet must be turned over to the testing staff before you leave the room.

LSAC®

Topic Code

Print Your Full Name Here		
Last	First	M.I.

Date
/ /

Sign Your Name Here

LSAT® Writing Sample Topic

Directions: The scenario presented below describes two choices, either one of which can be supported on the basis of the information given. Your essay should consider both choices and argue for one over the other, based on the two specified criteria and the facts provided. There is no "right" or "wrong" choice: a reasonable argument can be made for either.

The Poplar Valley Civic Association (PVCA) needs to raise money to buy new playground equipment for the local park. Board members have narrowed their fundraising options to a raffle or a pancake breakfast. Write an essay in which you argue for one option over the other, keeping in mind the following two criteria:

- The PVCA wants to raise at least enough money to pay for the fundraiser itself and the new playground equipment.
- The PVCA wants to use the event to foster cohesion in the community.

If the PVCA holds a raffle, tickets will be sold by community volunteers for a drawing to be held at the town's annual picnic. PVCA board members will be charged with soliciting prize donations from local businesses. The town's bike shop has already pledged a pair of bikes if the raffle is held. A local travel agency donated a cruise for a similar raffle last year. Local restaurants are also likely prospects. The number of tickets sold will depend not only on the attractiveness of the prizes but on the diligence of volunteer ticket sellers, who will need to canvass the neighborhood and their workplaces systematically for buyers. The cost of printing tickets and holding the raffle will be nominal, so almost all of the money raised could be used to buy equipment.

If the PVCA opts for the pancake breakfast, printed invitations will be mailed to all households in the community. The mailing itself will be fairly expensive, given the cost of postage, but response rates for such solicitations are usually high, and many people end up donating more than the actual cost of tickets. The breakfast will be held on a weekend morning in the elementary school cafeteria, using community volunteers to do the cooking, serving, setup, and cleanup. The cafeteria's kitchen is fully equipped. A local caterer has already volunteered to donate the batter, syrup, and paper products; otherwise, the cost of supplies for the breakfast would be considerably higher than the minimal costs for the raffle.

Scratch Paper
Do not write your essay in this space.

LAST NAME (Print)

FIRST NAME (Print)

LAST 4 DIGITS OF SOCIAL SECURITY/SOCIAL INSURANCE NO.

L

MI

TEST CENTER NO.

SIGNATURE

M M D D Y Y

TEST DATE

LSAC ACCOUNT NO.

TOPIC CODE

Writing Sample Response Sheet

DO NOT WRITE IN THIS SPACE

Begin your essay in the lined area below.
Continue on the back if you need more space.

COMPUTING YOUR SCORE

Directions:

1. Use the Answer Key on the next page to check your answers.

2. Use the Scoring Worksheet below to compute your raw score.

3. Use the Score Conversion Chart to convert your raw score into the 120-180 scale.

Scoring Worksheet

1. Enter the number of questions you answered correctly in each section.

	Number Correct
SECTION I	_____
SECTION II	_____
SECTION III	_____
SECTION IV	_____

2. Enter the sum here: _____

   This is your Raw Score.

Conversion Chart
For Converting Raw Score to the 120-180 LSAT Scaled Score
LSAT Form 5LSN65

Reported Score	Raw Score Lowest	Raw Score Highest
180	99	100
179	98	98
178	97	97
177	96	96
176	—*	—*
175	95	95
174	94	94
173	93	93
172	92	92
171	91	91
170	90	90
169	89	89
168	88	88
167	87	87
166	85	86
165	84	84
164	83	83
163	81	82
162	80	80
161	78	79
160	77	77
159	75	76
158	73	74
157	72	72
156	70	71
155	68	69
154	66	67
153	65	65
152	63	64
151	61	62
150	59	60
149	57	58
148	55	56
147	54	54
146	52	53
145	50	51
144	48	49
143	46	47
142	45	45
141	43	44
140	41	42
139	40	40
138	38	39
137	36	37
136	35	35
135	33	34
134	32	32
133	30	31
132	29	29
131	27	28
130	26	26
129	25	25
128	24	24
127	22	23
126	21	21
125	20	20
124	19	19
123	18	18
122	17	17
121	16	16
120	0	15

*There is no raw score that will produce this scaled score for this form.

ANSWER KEY

SECTION I

1.	D	8.	E	15.	D	22.	C
2.	B	9.	E	16.	B	23.	D
3.	C	10.	D	17.	D	24.	C
4.	B	11.	D	18.	D	25.	E
5.	A	12.	E	19.	A	26.	C
6.	B	13.	C	20.	D		
7.	A	14.	E	21.	B		

SECTION II

1.	D	8.	B	15.	E	22.	B
2.	B	9.	D	16.	B	23.	E
3.	E	10.	A	17.	C	24.	A
4.	D	11.	E	18.	C	25.	B
5.	A	12.	D	19.	E	26.	C
6.	E	13.	A	20.	D		
7.	C	14.	A	21.	D		

SECTION III

1.	E	8.	A	15.	C	22.	D
2.	A	9.	D	16.	B	23.	A
3.	D	10.	C	17.	D	24.	E
4.	B	11.	C	18.	C	25.	D
5.	D	12.	A	19.	C	26.	D
6.	A	13.	A	20.	B		
7.	B	14.	A	21.	E		

SECTION IV

1.	E	8.	B	15.	C	22.	B
2.	A	9.	C	16.	C		
3.	C	10.	C	17.	B		
4.	A	11.	C	18.	C		
5.	D	12.	E	19.	E		
6.	B	13.	D	20.	B		
7.	A	14.	B	21.	A		

PREPTEST 48
DECEMBER 2005
FORM 5LSN66

SECTION I

Time—35 minutes

26 Questions

Directions: The questions in this section are based on the reasoning contained in brief statements or passages. For some questions, more than one of the choices could conceivably answer the question. However, you are to choose the <u>best</u> answer; that is, the response that most accurately and completely answers the question. You should not make assumptions that are by commonsense standards implausible, superfluous, or incompatible with the passage. After you have chosen the best answer, blacken the corresponding space on your answer sheet.

1. The effort involved in lying produces measurable physiological reactions such as a speedup of the heartbeat. Since lying is accompanied by physiological reactions, lie-detector tests that can detect these reactions are a sure way of determining when someone is lying.

   Which one of the following statements, if true, most seriously weakens the argument?

   (A) Lie-detector tests can measure only some of the physiological reactions that occur when someone is lying.

   (B) People are often unaware that they are having physiological reactions of the sort measured by lie-detector tests.

   (C) Lying about past criminal behavior does not necessarily produce stronger physiological reactions than does lying about other things.

   (D) For people who are not lying, the tension of taking a lie-detector test can produce physiological reactions identical to the ones that accompany the act of lying.

   (E) When employers use lie-detector tests as part of their preemployment screening, some candidates tested are highly motivated to lie.

2. Publishing executive: Our company must sell at least 100,000 books to make a profit this year. However, it is unlikely that we will sell that many, since of the twelve titles we will sell, the one with the best sales prospects, a novel, is unlikely to sell as many as 100,000 copies.

   The publishing executive's argument is most vulnerable to criticism because it overlooks the possibility that

   (A) the publishing company will sell considerably fewer than 100,000 copies of the novel

   (B) the publishing company will not make a profit even if it sells more than 100,000 books

   (C) what is true of the overall profitability of a publishing company is not true of its profitability in a particular year

   (D) what is true of the sales prospects of the publishing company's individual titles is not true of the sales prospects of the group of titles as a whole

   (E) the publishing company will sell even fewer books if it does not advertise its books efficiently

3. A recent study proves that at least some people possess an independent "sixth sense" that allows them to detect whether someone is watching them. In the study, subjects were seated one at a time in the center of a room facing away from a large window. On average, subjects decided correctly 60 percent of the time whether or not they were being watched through the window.

   Which one of the following, if true, most supports the conclusion drawn from the study mentioned above?

   (A) Most of the time, subjects said they were being watched.

   (B) The person recording the experimental results was careful not to interact with the subjects after the experiment ended.

   (C) A similar result was found when the subjects were watched from another room on a video monitor.

   (D) The room in which the subjects were seated was not soundproof.

   (E) The subjects were mostly graduate students in psychology from a nearby university.

GO ON TO THE NEXT PAGE.

4. Philosopher: We should not disapprove of the unearthing of truths that we would rather not acknowledge or that, by their dissemination, might influence society in pernicious ways.

Which one of the following conforms most closely to the principle stated by the philosopher?

(A) A law enforcement officer should not act upon illegally obtained information, even though such action might, in some cases, result in a benefit to society.

(B) Scientific research should not be restricted even if it could lead to harmful applications, such as the manufacture of sophisticated weapons.

(C) A physician should never withhold the truth from a patient, except in cases where depression induced by bad news might significantly affect the patient's recuperation.

(D) Investigative journalists who employ illegal means of obtaining information should not be subjected to moral disapproval, if the revelation of that information does more good for society than does its suppression.

(E) A poem need not adhere too strictly to the truth. Art is exempt from such requirements—it matters only that the poem provoke a response in the reader.

5. Compact discs (CDs) offer an improvement in artistic freedom over vinyl records. As the record needle moves in toward a vinyl record's center, it must fight centrifugal force. Wide, shallow, or jagged grooves will cause the needle to jump; consequently, the song nearest the center—the last song on the side—cannot have especially loud, high-pitched, or low-pitched passages. The CD suffers no such limitations, leaving artists free to end recordings with any song.

Which one of the following most accurately expresses the main conclusion of the argument?

(A) CDs provide greater artistic latitude than do vinyl records.

(B) On vinyl records, the song farthest from the center can have loud, high-pitched, or low-pitched passages.

(C) As the record needle moves in toward the vinyl record's center, the centrifugal force on the needle becomes stronger.

(D) CDs represent a considerable technological advance over vinyl records.

(E) CDs can have louder passages, as well as both higher- and lower-pitched passages, than can vinyl records.

6. The public interest comprises many interests and the broadcast media must serve all of them. Perhaps most television viewers would prefer an action show to an opera. But a constant stream of action shows on all channels is not in the public interest. Thus, _____.

Which one of the following most logically completes the argument?

(A) broadcasters' obligations are not satisfied if they look only to popularity to decide their programming schedules

(B) television networks should broadcast more artistic and cultural shows and fewer action shows

(C) the public interest should be considered whenever television producers develop a new program

(D) the popularity of a television program is a poor indicator of its artistic quality

(E) broadcast media could be rightly accused of neglecting the public interest only if all channels carried mostly action shows

7. Enthusiasm for the use of calculators in the learning of mathematics is misplaced. Teachers rightly observe that in some cases calculators enable students to focus on general principles rather than the tedious, largely rote calculations that constitute the application of these principles. But principles are more likely to be remembered when knowledge of them is grounded in habits ingrained by painstaking applications of those principles. The very fact that calculators make calculation easier, therefore, makes it reasonable to restrict their use.

Which one of the following, if true, most strengthens the argument?

(A) Some students who know how to use calculators also thoroughly understand the mathematical principles that calculators obey.

(B) Slide rules, which are less technologically sophisticated analogues of calculators, were widely used in the learning of mathematics several decades ago.

(C) It is much more important that students retain the knowledge of general principles than that this knowledge be easily acquired.

(D) Habits that are acquired by laborious and sometimes tedious practice are not as valuable as those that are painlessly mastered.

(E) Teachers' enthusiasm for new educational aids is often not proportional to the pedagogical effectiveness of those devices.

GO ON TO THE NEXT PAGE.

8. Commentator: Most journalists describe their individual political orientations as liberal, and it is often concluded that there is therefore a liberal bias in current journalism. This is not the case, however, because newspapers, magazines, radio, and television are all in the business of selling news and advertising, and therefore face market pressures that tend to keep them impartial, since in order to maximize profits they must target the broadest customer base possible.

Which one of the following most accurately expresses the main conclusion drawn by the commentator's argument?

(A) The individual political orientations of journalists do not constitute acceptable evidence regarding media bias.
(B) Major media face significant market pressures.
(C) Current journalism does not have a liberal political bias.
(D) Major media must target the broadest customer base possible in order to maximize profits.
(E) It is often maintained that current journalism has a liberal bias.

9. Theories generated by scientific research were used to develop several products that, although useful, damage the environment severely. The scientists who conducted the research, however, should not be held responsible for that damage, since they merely generated the theories and could neither foresee nor restrict the kinds of products that might be designed using those theories.

Which one of the following principles, if established, justifies the conclusion above?

(A) Individuals who develop something that has desirable characteristics should not be held responsible for any undesirable characteristics that the thing has if improperly used.
(B) Individuals are justified in performing an activity that has both desirable and undesirable foreseeable consequences only if they alone bear its undesirable consequences.
(C) Individuals should receive credit for the foreseeable desirable consequences of the activities they perform only if those individuals are to be held responsible for any unforeseeable undesirable consequences those activities might have.
(D) Individuals who perform an activity should not be held responsible for any unforeseen undesirable consequences that arise from the use to which others put the results of that activity.
(E) Individuals should be held responsible for the foreseeable undesirable consequences of the activities that they perform and receive credit for the foreseeable desirable consequences of those activities.

10. The administration at a certain university has explained this year's tuition increase by citing increased spending on faculty salaries and on need-based aid to students. However, this year's budget indicated that faculty salaries constitute a small part of the university's expenditure, and the only significant increases in scholarship aid have gone to academic scholarships awarded regardless of need. The administration's explanation is not believable.

Which one of the following, if true, most strengthens the argument that the administration's explanation is not believable?

(A) With this year's budget, the university has increased its total spending on scholarship aid by 5 percent.
(B) With this year's budget, the university increased the allotment for faculty salaries by 5 percent while tuition was increased by 6 percent.
(C) Faculty salaries at the university have increased in line with the national average, and substantial cuts in government student-loan programs have caused financial difficulties for many students at the university.
(D) Of the substantial items in the budget, the greatest increase was in administrative costs, facilities maintenance costs, and costs associated with the provision of athletic facilities.
(E) Because enrollment projections at the university are very unreliable, it is difficult to accurately estimate the amount of money the university will collect from tuition fees ahead of time.

11. Students asked by a psychologist to tell a lie before discussion groups vastly overestimated how many people in the discussion groups could tell they were lying. Other research has found that when volleyball players perform unusually poorly on the court, teammates notice this far less often than the players expect. Finally, in one research experiment a student wearing a funny T-shirt entered a room full of people. Questioning revealed that only a small fraction of the people in the room noticed the shirt, contrary to the student's expectations.

Which one of the following is best illustrated by the statements above?

(A) People tend to be far less aware of their own appearance and behavior than are other people.
(B) People tend not to notice the appearance or behavior of others.
(C) We are actually less observant of the appearance and behavior of others than we think ourselves to be.
(D) People will notice the appearance or behavior of others only if it is specifically highlighted in some way.
(E) People tend to believe their appearance and behavior are noticed by others more often than is actually the case.

GO ON TO THE NEXT PAGE.

12. Extinction is inevitable for all biological species. In fact, the vast majority of all species that have ever lived are now extinct. Since all species die out eventually, there is no justification for trying to protect species that are presently endangered, even those that can be saved from extinction now.

The reasoning in the argument above is most closely paralleled by the argument that there is no reason to

(A) look for a book in the library because it is sometimes checked out

(B) spend money on preventive maintenance of a car because no car can last indefinitely

(C) reinforce bridges against earthquakes in earthquake-prone areas because earthquakes occur only very infrequently

(D) take a route that will avoid the normal traffic jams because traffic jams can occur along any route

(E) plant a flower garden in soil that is not beneficial to plants because the plants are likely to die in such soil

13. Psychology professor: Applied statistics should be taught only by the various social science departments. These departments can best teach their respective students which statistical methodologies are most useful for their discipline, and how best to interpret collected data and the results of experiments.

Mathematics professor: I disagree. My applied statistics course covers much of the same material taught in the applied statistics courses in social science departments. In fact, my course uses exactly the same textbook as those courses!

Which one of the following most accurately describes a questionable aspect of the reasoning in the mathematics professor's response to the psychology professor?

(A) The response gives no evidence for its presumption that students willing to take a course in one department would choose a similar course in another.

(B) The response gives no evidence for its presumption that social science students should have the same competence in statistics as mathematics students.

(C) The response does not effectively address a key reason given in support of the psychology professor's position.

(D) The response depends for its plausibility on a personal attack made against the psychology professor.

(E) The response takes for granted that unless the course textbook is the same the course content will not be the same.

14. Among a sample of diverse coins from an unfamiliar country, each face of any coin portrays one of four things: a judge's head, an explorer's head, a building, or a tree. By examining the coins, a collector determines that none of them have heads on both sides and that all coins in the sample with a judge's head on one side have a tree on the other.

If the statements above are true, which one of the following must be true of the coins in the sample?

(A) All those with an explorer's head on one side have a building on the other.

(B) All those with a tree on one side have a judge's head on the other.

(C) None of those with a tree on one side have an explorer's head on the other.

(D) None of those with a building on one side have a judge's head on the other.

(E) None of those with an explorer's head on one side have a building on the other.

15. There are two supposedly conflicting hypotheses as to what makes for great national leaders: one is that such leaders successfully shape public opinion, and the other is that they are adept at reacting to it. However, treating these hypotheses as mutually exclusive is evidently a mistake. All leaders who have had success getting their programs passed by their country's legislature have been adroit both in shaping and reacting to public opinion.

Which one of the following is an assumption on which the argument depends?

(A) Having success getting programs passed by the legislature is indicative of being a great national leader.

(B) It is impossible to successfully shape public opinion without in some way reacting to it.

(C) To lead, one must either successfully shape public opinion or be adept at reacting to it, or both.

(D) Having a good rapport with the members of the legislature allows a leader to shape public opinion.

(E) To be a great leader one must not be swayed by public opinion.

GO ON TO THE NEXT PAGE.

16. Most business ethics courses and textbooks confine themselves to considering specific cases and principles. For example, students are often given lists of ethical rules for in-class discussion and role-playing. This approach fails to provide a framework for understanding specific principles and should thus be changed to include abstract ethical theory.

Which one of the following, if valid, most helps to justify the reasoning above?

(A) A moralizing approach that fails to recognize the diversity of the ethical rules in use is unacceptable.

(B) Courses that concentrate mainly on role-playing are undesirable because students must adopt alien personae.

(C) People have no obligation to always behave ethically unless they are acquainted with abstract ethical theory.

(D) Abstract ethical theory is the most appropriate of any context for understanding specific principles.

(E) An ethics course should acquaint students with a wide range of specific principles and appropriate applications.

17. Some classes of animal are so successful that they spread into virtually every ecosystem, whereas others gradually recede until they inhabit only small niches in geographically isolated areas and thereby become threatened. Insects are definitely of the former sort and ants are the most successful of these, ranging from the Arctic Circle to Tierra del Fuego. Hence, no species of ant is a threatened species.

The argument is flawed because it takes for granted that

(A) the Arctic Circle and Tierra del Fuego do not constitute geographically isolated areas

(B) because ants do not inhabit only a small niche in a geographically isolated area, they are unlike most other insects

(C) the only way a class of animal can avoid being threatened is to spread into virtually every ecosystem

(D) what is true of the constituent elements of a whole is also true of the whole

(E) what is true of a whole is also true of its constituent elements

18. Advocate: You claim that it is wrong to own gasoline-powered cars because they pollute too much; you have an electric car, which pollutes far less. But the company that made your car also makes millions of gasoline-powered vehicles, so your patronage benefits a producer of products to which you object. Thus, if you are right about gasoline-powered cars, you should not have your electric car either.

Which one of the following principles, if valid, would most help to justify the advocate's reasoning?

(A) An action can be wrong even if it has fewer negative consequences than another action.

(B) One should purchase a product only if it pollutes less than any competing product.

(C) One should purchase every product whose use has no negative consequences.

(D) One should not support an organization that does anything one believes to be wrong.

(E) One should not purchase products from companies that make no environmentally sound products.

19. Analyst: A recent survey showed that although professors of biology who teach but do not pursue research made up one-twentieth of all science professors, they were appointed to fewer than one-twentieth of all the scientific administrative positions in universities. We can conclude from this survey that failing to pursue research tends to bias university administrators against appointing these professors to scientific administrative positions.

Which one of the following, if true, most seriously weakens the support for the analyst's conclusion?

(A) In universities there are fewer scientific administrative positions than there are nonscientific administrative positions.

(B) Biologists who do research fill a disproportionately low number of scientific administrative positions in universities.

(C) Biology professors get more than one-twentieth of all the science grant money available.

(D) Conducting biological research tends to take significantly more time than does teaching biology.

(E) Biologists who hold scientific administrative positions in the university tend to hold those positions for a shorter time than do other science professors.

GO ON TO THE NEXT PAGE.

20. Researcher: We have found that some cases of high blood pressure can be treated effectively with medicine. Since it is generally accepted that any illness caused by stress is treatable only by the reduction of stress, some cases of high blood pressure must not be caused by stress.

Which one of the following is an assumption required by the researcher's argument?

(A) The correlation between stress and all cases of high blood pressure is merely coincidental.
(B) The reduction of stress in a person's life can at times lower that person's blood pressure.
(C) Reduced stress does not reduce a person's responsiveness to medicine used to treat high blood pressure.
(D) Some conditions that are treated effectively by medicines are not also treatable through the reduction of stress.
(E) Medicine used to treat high blood pressure does not itself reduce stress.

21. Catmull: Although historians consider themselves to be social scientists, different historians never arrive at the same conclusions about specific events of the past. Thus historians never determine what actually happened; like novelists, they merely create interesting fictional stories about the many different problems that people have faced.

The reasoning in Catmull's argument is flawed because the argument

(A) draws a conclusion that simply restates a claim presented in support of that conclusion
(B) concludes, solely on the basis of the claim that different people have reached different conclusions about a topic, that none of these conclusions is true
(C) presumes, without providing justification, that unless historians' conclusions are objectively true, they have no value whatsoever
(D) bases its conclusion on premises that contradict each other
(E) mistakes a necessary condition for the objective truth of historians' conclusions for a sufficient condition for the objective truth of those conclusions

22. In a poll conducted by interviewing eligible voters in their homes just before the recent election, incumbent candidate Kenner was significantly ahead of candidate Muratori. Nonetheless, Muratori won the recent election.

Which one of the following, if true, most helps to resolve the apparent discrepancy described by the statements above?

(A) The positions taken by Muratori and Kenner on many election issues were not very similar to each other.
(B) Kenner had held elected office for many years before the recent election.
(C) In the year leading up to the election, Kenner was implicated in a series of political scandals.
(D) Six months before the recent election, the voting age was lowered by three years.
(E) In the poll, supporters of Muratori were more likely than others to describe the election as important.

GO ON TO THE NEXT PAGE.

23. Statistical analysis is a common tool for explanation in the physical sciences. It can only be used, however, to explain events that can be replicated to the last detail. Since human mental events never precisely recur, statistical analysis cannot be employed to explain these events. Therefore, they cannot be explained by the physical sciences.

Which one of the following arguments is most similar in its flawed reasoning to the argument above?

(A) Computer modeling is used to try to explain the way in which wind resistance affects the movement of bicycles. To use computer modeling, the phenomenon being modeled must be predictable. But wind resistance is not predictable. Therefore, the way in which wind resistance affects the movement of bicycles cannot be explained by computer modeling.

(B) The only way to explain how music affects the emotional state of a person is to appeal to the psychology of emotion. The psychology of emotion can be applied only to cases involving human beings. But not all music is created by human beings; some music is computer generated. Therefore, the way in which music affects the emotional state of a person cannot be explained.

(C) The best way to explain why an object has a particular color is in terms of the interaction of light and matter. It is sometimes impossible to find out what kind of matter constitutes an object. Therefore, the color of such objects has nothing to do with the interaction of light and matter.

(D) To determine which explanation of the origin of the universe is correct, we would need to know about the first moments of the existence of the universe. Due to the immense time that has passed since the universe began, it is impossible to get such information. Therefore, none of the explanations of the origin of the universe is likely to be correct.

(E) A good way to explain historical events is to construct a coherent narrative about those events. In order to construct such a narrative, a great many details about the events must be known. Virtually no details can be known of certain very ancient historical events. Therefore, no historical explanation can be given for these events.

24. Journalist: Although a recent poll found that more than half of all eligible voters support the idea of a political party whose primary concern is education, only 26 percent would like to join it, and only 16 percent would be prepared to donate money to it. Furthermore, there is overwhelming historical evidence that only a party that has at least 30 percent of eligible voters prepared to support it by either joining it or donating money to it is viable in the long run. Therefore, it is unlikely that an education party is viable in the long run.

The reasoning in the journalist's argument is most vulnerable to criticism on the grounds that the argument fails to consider that

(A) some of those who said they were willing to donate money to an education party might not actually do so if such a party were formed

(B) an education party could possibly be viable with a smaller base than is customarily needed

(C) the 16 percent of eligible voters prepared to donate money to an education party might donate almost as much money as a party would ordinarily expect to get if 30 percent of eligible voters contributed

(D) a party needs the appropriate support of at least 30 percent of eligible voters in order to be viable and more than half of all eligible voters support the idea of an education party

(E) some of the eligible voters who would donate money to an education party might not be prepared to join such a party

GO ON TO THE NEXT PAGE.

25. Almost all microbe species live together in dense, interdependent communities, supporting the environment for each other, and regulating the population balances for their different species through a complex system of chemical signals. For this reason, it is currently impossible to cultivate any one such species in isolation. Thus, microbiologists lack complete knowledge of most microbe species.

Which one of the following, if assumed, enables the argument's conclusion to be properly drawn?

(A)   It is currently impossible for microbiologists to reproduce the complex systems of chemical signals with which microbe communities regulate the population balances for their different species.

(B)   If it is currently impossible to reproduce the environmental supports and chemical signals in dense, interdependent communities of microbe species, then it is also impossible to cultivate any microbe species from such a community in isolation.

(C)   No microbiologist can have complete knowledge of any species of organism unless that microbiologist can cultivate that species in isolation.

(D)   At least some microbiologists lack complete knowledge of any microbe species that live together in dense, interdependent communities.

(E)   No microbe species that normally lives together with other microbe species in dense, interdependent communities can survive outside such a community.

26. Reza: Language requires the use of verbal signs for objects as well as for feelings. Many animals can vocally express hunger, but only humans can ask for an egg or an apple by naming it. And using verbal signs for objects requires the ability to distinguish these objects from other objects, which in turn requires conceptual thought.

If all of Reza's statements are true, then which one of the following must also be true?

(A)   Conceptual thought is required for language.
(B)   Conceptual thought requires the use of verbal signs for objects.
(C)   It is not possible to think conceptually about feelings.
(D)   All humans are capable of conceptual thought.
(E)   The vocal expressions of animals other than humans do not require conceptual thought.

STOP
IF YOU FINISH BEFORE TIME IS CALLED, YOU MAY CHECK YOUR WORK ON THIS SECTION ONLY.
DO NOT WORK ON ANY OTHER SECTION IN THE TEST.

SECTION II

Time—35 minutes

22 Questions

Directions: Each group of questions in this section is based on a set of conditions. In answering some of the questions, it may be useful to draw a rough diagram. Choose the response that most accurately and completely answers each question and blacken the corresponding space on your answer sheet.

Questions 1–6

Henri has exactly five electrical appliances in his dormitory room: a hairdryer, a microwave oven, a razor, a television, and a vacuum. As a consequence of fire department regulations, Henri can use these appliances only in accordance with the following conditions:

Henri cannot use both the hairdryer and the razor simultaneously.

Henri cannot use both the hairdryer and the television simultaneously.

When Henri uses the vacuum, he cannot at the same time use any of the following: the hairdryer, the razor, and the television.

1. Which one of the following is a pair of appliances Henri could be using simultaneously?

   (A) the hairdryer and the razor
   (B) the hairdryer and the television
   (C) the razor and the television
   (D) the razor and the vacuum
   (E) the television and the vacuum

2. Assume that Henri is using exactly two appliances and is not using the microwave oven. Which one of the following is a list of all the appliances, other than the microwave oven, that Henri CANNOT be using?

   (A) hairdryer
   (B) razor
   (C) vacuum
   (D) hairdryer, razor
   (E) hairdryer, vacuum

3. Which one of the following CANNOT be true?

   (A) Henri uses the hairdryer while using the microwave oven.
   (B) Henri uses the microwave oven while using the razor.
   (C) Henri uses the microwave oven while using two other appliances.
   (D) Henri uses the television while using two other appliances.
   (E) Henri uses the vacuum while using two other appliances.

4. If Henri were to use exactly three appliances, then what is the total number of different groups of three appliances any one of which could be the group of appliances he is using?

   (A) one
   (B) two
   (C) three
   (D) four
   (E) five

5. Which one of the following statements, if true, guarantees that Henri is using no more than one of the following: the hairdryer, the razor, the television?

   (A) Henri is using the hairdryer.
   (B) Henri is using the television.
   (C) Henri is not using the hairdryer.
   (D) Henri is not using the microwave oven.
   (E) Henri is not using the vacuum.

6. Which one of the following must be true?

   (A) Henri uses at most three appliances simultaneously.
   (B) Henri uses at most four appliances simultaneously.
   (C) Henri uses at most one other appliance while using the microwave oven.
   (D) Henri uses at most one other appliance while using the razor.
   (E) Henri uses at least two other appliances while using the hairdryer.

GO ON TO THE NEXT PAGE.

Questions 7–12

A farmer harvests eight separate fields—G, H, J, K, L, M, P, and T. Each field is harvested exactly once, and no two fields are harvested simultaneously. Once the harvesting of a field begins, no other fields are harvested until the harvesting of that field is complete. The farmer harvests the fields in an order consistent with the following conditions:

Both P and G are harvested at some time before K.
Both H and L are harvested at some time before J.
K is harvested at some time before M but after L.
T is harvested at some time before M.

7. Which one of the following could be true?

   (A)　J is the first field harvested.
   (B)　K is the second field harvested.
   (C)　M is the sixth field harvested.
   (D)　G is the seventh field harvested.
   (E)　T is the eighth field harvested.

8. If M is the seventh field harvested, then any one of the following could be the fifth field harvested EXCEPT:

   (A)　H
   (B)　J
   (C)　K
   (D)　L
   (E)　P

9. Which one of the following CANNOT be the field that is harvested fifth?

   (A)　G
   (B)　J
   (C)　M
   (D)　P
   (E)　T

10. If J is the third field harvested, then which one of the following must be true?

   (A)　L is the first field harvested.
   (B)　H is the second field harvested.
   (C)　T is the fourth field harvested.
   (D)　K is the seventh field harvested.
   (E)　M is the eighth field harvested.

11. If H is the sixth field harvested, then which one of the following must be true?

   (A)　G is harvested at some time before T.
   (B)　H is harvested at some time before K.
   (C)　J is harvested at some time before M.
   (D)　K is harvested at some time before J.
   (E)　T is harvested at some time before K.

12. If L is the fifth field harvested, then which one of the following could be true?

   (A)　J is harvested at some time before G.
   (B)　J is harvested at some time before T.
   (C)　K is harvested at some time before T.
   (D)　M is harvested at some time before H.
   (E)　M is harvested at some time before J.

GO ON TO THE NEXT PAGE.

Questions 13–17

In a repair facility there are exactly six technicians: Stacy, Urma, Wim, Xena, Yolanda, and Zane. Each technician repairs machines of at least one of the following three types—radios, televisions, and VCRs—and no other types. The following conditions apply:

Xena and exactly three other technicians repair radios.
Yolanda repairs both televisions and VCRs.
Stacy does not repair any type of machine that Yolanda repairs.
Zane repairs more types of machines than Yolanda repairs.
Wim does not repair any type of machine that Stacy repairs.
Urma repairs exactly two types of machines.

13. For exactly how many of the six technicians is it possible to determine exactly which of the three types of machines each repairs?

(A) one
(B) two
(C) three
(D) four
(E) five

14. Which one of the following must be true?

(A) Of the types of machines repaired by Stacy there is exactly one type that Urma also repairs.
(B) Of the types of machines repaired by Yolanda there is exactly one type that Xena also repairs.
(C) Of the types of machines repaired by Wim there is exactly one type that Xena also repairs.
(D) There is more than one type of machine that both Wim and Yolanda repair.
(E) There is more than one type of machine that both Urma and Wim repair.

15. Which one of the following must be false?

(A) Exactly one of the six technicians repairs exactly one type of machine.
(B) Exactly two of the six technicians repair exactly one type of machine each.
(C) Exactly three of the six technicians repair exactly one type of machine each.
(D) Exactly one of the six technicians repairs exactly two types of machines.
(E) Exactly three of the six technicians repair exactly two types of machines each.

16. Which one of the following pairs of technicians could repair all and only the same types of machines as each other?

(A) Stacy and Urma
(B) Urma and Yolanda
(C) Urma and Xena
(D) Wim and Xena
(E) Xena and Yolanda

17. Which one of the following must be true?

(A) There is exactly one type of machine that both Urma and Wim repair.
(B) There is exactly one type of machine that both Urma and Xena repair.
(C) There is exactly one type of machine that both Urma and Yolanda repair.
(D) There is exactly one type of machine that both Wim and Yolanda repair.
(E) There is exactly one type of machine that both Xena and Yolanda repair.

GO ON TO THE NEXT PAGE.

Questions 18–22

Three folk groups—Glenside, Hilltopper, Levon—and three rock groups—Peasant, Query, Tinhead—each perform on one of two stages, north or south. Each stage has three two-hour performances: north at 6, 8, and 10; south at 8, 10, and 12. Each group performs individually and exactly once, consistent with the following conditions:

    Peasant performs at 6 or 12.

    Glenside performs at some time before Hilltopper.

    If any rock group performs at 10, no folk group does.

    Levon and Tinhead perform on different stages.

    Query performs immediately after a folk group, though not necessarily on the same stage.

18. Which one of the following could be a complete and accurate ordering of performances on the north stage, from first to last?

    (A)   Glenside, Levon, Query
    (B)   Glenside, Query, Hilltopper
    (C)   Hilltopper, Query, Peasant
    (D)   Peasant, Levon, Tinhead
    (E)   Peasant, Query, Levon

19. Which one of the following groups must perform earlier than 10?

    (A)   Glenside
    (B)   Hilltopper
    (C)   Levon
    (D)   Peasant
    (E)   Tinhead

20. Which one of the following groups could perform at 6?

    (A)   Glenside
    (B)   Hilltopper
    (C)   Levon
    (D)   Query
    (E)   Tinhead

21. If Query performs at 12, then which one of the following could be an accurate ordering of the performances on the north stage, from first to last?

    (A)   Glenside, Levon, Query
    (B)   Peasant, Hilltopper, Tinhead
    (C)   Peasant, Tinhead, Glenside
    (D)   Peasant, Tinhead, Hilltopper
    (E)   Peasant, Tinhead, Levon

22. If a rock group performs at 10, then which one of the following must be true?

    (A)   A folk group performs at 6.
    (B)   A folk group performs at 8.
    (C)   A folk group performs at 12.
    (D)   A rock group performs at 8.
    (E)   A rock group performs at 12.

STOP
IF YOU FINISH BEFORE TIME IS CALLED, YOU MAY CHECK YOUR WORK ON THIS SECTION ONLY.
DO NOT WORK ON ANY OTHER SECTION IN THE TEST.

SECTION III
Time—35 minutes
27 Questions

Directions: Each set of questions in this section is based on a single passage or a pair of passages. The questions are to be answered on the basis of what is <u>stated</u> or <u>implied</u> in the passage or pair of passages. For some of the questions, more than one of the choices could conceivably answer the question. However, you are to choose the <u>best</u> answer; that is, the response that most accurately and completely answers the question, and blacken the corresponding space on your answer sheet.

One of the intriguing questions considered by anthropologists concerns the purpose our early ancestors had in first creating images of the world around them. Among these images are 25,000-year-
(5) old cave paintings made by the Aurignacians, a people who supplanted the Neanderthals in Europe and who produced the earliest known examples of representational art. Some anthropologists see these paintings as evidence that the Aurignacians had a
(10) more secure life than the Neanderthals. No one under constant threat of starvation, the reasoning goes, could afford time for luxuries such as art; moreover, the art is, in its latter stages at least, so astonishingly well-executed by almost any standard of excellence
(15) that it is highly unlikely it was produced by people who had not spent a great deal of time perfecting their skills. In other words, the high level of quality suggests that Aurignacian art was created by a distinct group of artists, who would likely have spent
(20) most of their time practicing and passing on their skills while being supported by other members of their community.

Curiously, however, the paintings were usually placed in areas accessible only with extreme effort
(25) and completely unilluminated by natural light. This makes it unlikely that these representational cave paintings arose simply out of a love of beauty or pride in artistry—had aesthetic enjoyment been the sole purpose of the paintings, they would presumably
(30) have been located where they could have been easily seen and appreciated.

Given that the Aurignacians were hunter-gatherers and had to cope with the practical problems of extracting a living from a difficult environment, many
(35) anthropologists hypothesize that the paintings were also intended to provide a means of ensuring a steady supply of food. Since it was common among pretechnological societies to believe that one can gain power over an animal by making an image of it,
(40) these anthropologists maintain that the Aurignacian paintings were meant to grant magical power over the Aurignacians' prey—typically large, dangerous animals such as mammoths and bison. The images were probably intended to make these animals
(45) vulnerable to the weapons of the hunters, an explanation supported by the fact that many of the pictures show animals with their hearts outlined in red, or with bright, arrow-shaped lines tracing paths to vital organs. Other paintings clearly show some
(50) animals as pregnant, perhaps in an effort to assure

plentiful hunting grounds. There is also evidence that ceremonies of some sort were performed before these images. Well-worn footprints of dancers can still be discerned in the clay floors of some caves, and
(55) pictures of what appear to be shamans, or religious leaders, garbed in fantastic costumes, are found among the painted animals.

1. Which one of the following most accurately describes the author's position regarding the claims attributed to anthropologists in the third paragraph?

    (A) implicit acceptance
    (B) hesitant agreement
    (C) noncommittal curiosity
    (D) detached skepticism
    (E) broad disagreement

2. The passage provides information that answers which one of the following questions?

    (A) For how long a period did the Neanderthals occupy Europe?
    (B) How long did it take for the Aurignacians to supplant the Neanderthals?
    (C) Did the Aurignacians make their homes in caves?
    (D) What are some of the animals represented in Aurignacian cave paintings?
    (E) What other prehistoric groups aside from the Aurignacians produced representational art?

GO ON TO THE NEXT PAGE.

3. The author would be most likely to agree with which one of the following statements?

   (A) The cave paintings indicate that the Aurignacians lived a relatively secure life compared to most other hunter-gatherer cultures.
   (B) Skill in art was essential to becoming an Aurignacian shaman.
   (C) Prehistoric hunter-gatherers did not create any art solely for aesthetic purposes.
   (D) All art created by the Aurignacians was intended to grant magical power over other beings.
   (E) The Aurignacians sought to gain magical power over their prey by means of ceremonial acts in addition to painted images.

4. The author mentions the relative inaccessibility of the Aurignacian cave paintings primarily to

   (A) stress the importance of the cave paintings to the lives of the artists who painted them by indicating the difficulties they had to overcome to do so
   (B) lay the groundwork for a fuller explanation of the paintings' function
   (C) suggest that only a select portion of the Aurignacian community was permitted to view the paintings
   (D) help explain why the paintings are still well preserved
   (E) support the argument that Aurignacian artists were a distinct and highly skilled group

5. The passage suggests that the author would be most likely to agree with which one of the following claims about the Aurignacians?

   (A) They were technologically no more advanced than the Neanderthals they supplanted.
   (B) They were the first humans known to have worn costumes for ceremonial purposes.
   (C) They had established some highly specialized social roles.
   (D) They occupied a less hostile environment than the Neanderthals did.
   (E) They carved images of their intended prey on their weapons to increase the weapons' efficacy.

GO ON TO THE NEXT PAGE.

The poet Louise Glück has said that she feels comfortable writing within a tradition often characterized as belonging only to male poets. About her own experience reading poetry, Glück notes that
(5) her gender did not keep her from appreciating the poems of Shakespeare, Blake, Keats, and other male poets. Rather she believed this was the tradition of her language and that it was for this reason her poetic inheritance. She thus views the canon of poets in
(10) English as a literary family to which she clearly belongs. Whereas many contemporary women poets have rejected this tradition as historically exclusionary and rhetorically inadequate for women, Glück embraces it with respect and admiration.
(15) Glück's formative encounters with poetry also provided her with the theoretical underpinnings of her respect for this tradition; she notes that in her youth she could sense many of the great themes and subjects of poetry even before experiencing them in
(20) her own life. These subjects—loss, the passage of time, desire—are timeless, available to readers of any age, gender, or social background. Glück makes no distinction between these subjects as belonging to female or male poets alone, calling them "the great
(25) human subjects." If the aim of a poem is to explore the issue of human mortality, for example, then issues of gender distinction fade behind the presence of this universal reality.
Some of Glück's critics claim that this idea of the
(30) universal is suspect and that the idea that gender issues are transcended by addressing certain subjects may attribute to poetry an innocence that it does not have. They maintain that a female poet writing within a historically male-dominated tradition will on some
(35) level be unable to avoid accepting certain presuppositions, which, in the critics' view, are determined by a long-standing history of denigration and exclusion of female artists. Furthermore, they feel that this long-standing history cannot be confronted
(40) using tools—in Glück's case, poetic forms—forged by the traditions of this history. Instead critics insist that women poets should strive to create a uniquely female poetry by using new forms to develop a new voice.
(45) Glück, however, observes that this ambition, with its insistence on an essentially female perspective, is as limiting as her critics believe the historically male-dominated tradition to be. She holds that to the extent that there are some gender differences that have been
(50) shaped by history, they will emerge in the differing ways that women and men write about the world— indeed, these differences will be revealed with more authority in the absence of conscious intention. She points out that the universal subjects of literature do
(55) not make literature itself timeless and unchanging. Literature, she maintains, is inescapably historical, and every work, both in what it includes and in what it omits, inevitably speaks of its social and historical context.

6. Which one of the following most accurately expresses the main point of the passage?

(A) In response to her critics, Glück argues that the attempt to develop a uniquely female voice is as restrictive as they believe the male tradition in poetry to be.

(B) Although critics have taken Glück to task for writing poetry that is generic in subject rather than specifically aimed at addressing women's concerns, she believes that poetry must instead concern itself with certain universal themes.

(C) In spite of critics who attempt to limit art to expressing the unique perspectives of the artist's gender, Glück believes that art in fact represents a perspective on its subject matter that is equally male and female.

(D) In opposition to some critics, Glück writes on universal themes rather than striving for a uniquely female voice, believing that whatever gender differences are present will emerge unconsciously in any case.

(E) Aside from the power and accomplishment of her writing, Glück has yet to offer a completely satisfying response to the critics' demand that her work reflect the conflict between male and female perspectives on poetic subject matter.

7. Based on the passage, with which one of the following statements regarding the poetic tradition in English would Glück be most likely to agree?

(A) This tradition is somewhat diminished for its lack of recognized female poets.

(B) This tradition transcends its social and historical context.

(C) The male-dominated aspect of this tradition can be overcome only by developing a uniquely female voice in poetry.

(D) The view of this tradition as an inheritance is necessary for a poet to be successful.

(E) This tradition, though male dominated, addresses universal subjects.

GO ON TO THE NEXT PAGE.

8. As it is used in the passage, "inheritance" (line 9) refers most specifically to

(A) the burden that a historically male-dominated poetic canon places on a contemporary woman poet

(B) the set of poetic forms and techniques considered acceptable within a linguistic culture

(C) the poetry written in a particular language, whose achievement serves as a model for other poets writing in that language

(D) the presumption that contemporary poets can write only on subjects already explored by the poets in that language who are considered to be the most celebrated

(E) the imposition on a poet, based on the poetry of preceding generations in that language, of a particular writing style

9. Based on the description in the passage, a poem that reveals gender differences in the absence of any specific intention by the poet to do so is most like

(A) a bird's flight that exposes unseen air currents

(B) a ship's prow that indicates how strong a wave it is designed to withstand

(C) a building's facade that superficially embellishes an ordinary structure

(D) a railroad track, without which travel by train is impossible

(E) a novel that deliberately conceals the motives of its main character

10. According to the passage, Glück believes that art reveals gender differences with more authority when which one of the following is true?

(A) The artist refuses to accept certain presuppositions about gender.

(B) The artist uses the tools of that art's tradition.

(C) The artist does not consciously intend to reveal such differences.

(D) The artist comments on gender issues through the use of other subject matter.

(E) The artist embraces that art's tradition with respect.

11. Which one of the following statements about Glück is made in the passage?

(A) She objects to the use of traditional poetic forms to confront the history of the poetic tradition.

(B) She recognizes that the idea of the universal in poetry is questionable.

(C) She claims to accept only male poets as her literary family.

(D) She claims to write from a gender-neutral perspective.

(E) She claims to have sensed the great themes and subjects of poetry while in her youth.

12. Based on the passage, which one of the following most accurately characterizes the author's attitude toward Glück's view of poetry?

(A) respectful dismissal
(B) grudging acceptance
(C) detached indifference
(D) tacit endorsement
(E) enthusiastic acclaim

GO ON TO THE NEXT PAGE.

Although the rights of native peoples of Canada have yet to be comprehensively defined in Canadian law, most native Canadians assert that their rights include the right not only to govern themselves and
(5) their land, but also to exercise ownership rights over movable cultural property—artifacts ranging from domestic implements to ceremonial costumes. Assignment of such rights to native communities has been difficult to achieve, but while traditional
(10) Canadian statute and common law has placed ownership of movable property with current custodians such as museums, recent litigation by native Canadians has called such ownership into question.
(15) Canadian courts usually base decisions about ownership on a concept of private property, under which all forms of property are capable of being owned by individuals or by groups functioning legally as individuals. This system is based on a
(20) philosophy that encourages the right of owners to use their property as they see fit without outside interference. But litigation by native Canadians challenges courts to recognize a concept of property ownership that clashes with the private property
(25) concept. Although some tribes now recognize the notion of private property in their legal systems, they have traditionally employed a concept of collective ownership—and in all cases in which native Canadians have made legal claim to movable
(30) property they have done so by invoking this latter concept, which is based on the philosophy that each member should have an equal say regarding the use of the community's resources. Under this collective ideology, access to and use of resources is determined
(35) by the collective interests of the community. Furthermore, collective ownership casts an individual in the role of guardian or caretaker of property rather than as a titleholder; while every tribe member is an owner of the property, individual members cannot sell
(40) this right, nor does it pass to their heirs when they die. Nevertheless, their children will enjoy the same rights, not as heirs but as communal owners.

Because the concept of collective property assigns ownership to individuals simply because they are
(45) members of the community, native Canadians rarely possess the legal documents that the concept of private property requires to demonstrate ownership. Museums, which are likely to possess bills of sale or proof of prior possession to substantiate their claims
(50) of ownership, are thus likely to be recognized as legally entitled to the property they hold, even when such property originated with native Canadian communities. But as their awareness of the inappropriateness of applying the private property
(55) concept to all cultural groups grows, Canadian courts will gradually recognize that native Canadians, while they cannot demonstrate ownership as prescribed by the notion of private property, can clearly claim ownership as prescribed by the notion of collective
(60) property, and that their claims to movable cultural property should be honored.

13. Which one of the following most accurately expresses the main idea of the passage?

(A) Litigation by native Canadians to regain control of their movable cultural property illustrates how the concept of private ownership has become increasingly obsolete and demonstrates that this concept should be replaced by the more modern concept of collective ownership.

(B) Litigation by native Canadians to regain control of their movable cultural property is likely to succeed more frequently as courts begin to acknowledge that the concept of collective ownership is more appropriate than the concept of private ownership in such cases.

(C) The conflict between the concepts of collective and private ownership that has led to litigation by native Canadians to regain control of their movable cultural property is in reality a debate over whether individuals should act as titleholders or merely as caretakers with respect to their property.

(D) The conflict between the concepts of collective and private ownership that has led to litigation by native Canadians to regain control of their movable cultural property cannot be resolved until the rights of native Canadians have been comprehensively defined in Canadian law.

(E) The conflict between the concepts of collective and private ownership that has led to litigation by native Canadians to regain control of their movable cultural property illustrates the need to expand the concept of private property to include cases of joint ownership by a collection of individuals.

14. According to the concept of private property as presented in the passage, which one of the following most completely describes the meaning of the term "property owner"?

(A) one who possesses a bill of sale to substantiate his or her claims to property ownership

(B) one who possesses proof of prior possession to substantiate his or her claims to property ownership

(C) one who is allowed to make use of his or her property in whatever manner he or she wishes

(D) one who is allowed to transfer ownership rights to his or her children as heirs

(E) one who is allowed to exercise property rights because of his or her membership in a community

GO ON TO THE NEXT PAGE.

15. The author's attitude toward the possibility of courts increasingly assigning ownership rights to native communities is best described as which one of the following?

    (A) certain that it will never be realized and concerned that it should

    (B) concerned that it will never be realized but hopeful that it will

    (C) uncertain whether it will be realized but hopeful that it will

    (D) uncertain whether it will be realized but confident that it should

    (E) convinced that it will be realized and pleased that it will

16. The primary function of the first paragraph of the passage is to

    (A) identify some of the specific types of property at issue in litigation by native Canadians to regain control of their movable cultural property from museums

    (B) describe the role of the concept of property ownership in litigation by native Canadians to regain control of their movable cultural property from museums

    (C) summarize the difficulties that have been experienced in attempting to develop a comprehensive definition of the rights of native Canadians under the law

    (D) provide the context within which litigation by native Canadians to regain control of their movable cultural property is occurring

    (E) discuss the difficulty of deciding legal cases that rest on a clash between two cultures' differing definitions of a legal concept

17. Given the information in the passage, Canadian courts hearing a dispute over movable cultural property between a museum and a group of native Canadians will be increasingly unlikely to treat which one of the following as a compelling reason for deciding the case in the museum's favor?

    (A) The museum is able to produce evidence that the property did not originate in the native community.

    (B) The museum cannot produce written documentation of its claims to ownership of the property.

    (C) The group of native Canadians produces evidence that the property originated in their community.

    (D) The group of native Canadians cannot produce written documentation of their claims to ownership of the property.

    (E) The group of native Canadians do not belong to a tribe that employs a legal system that has adopted the concept of private property.

18. The passage suggests that the concepts of collective and private ownership differ in each of the following ways EXCEPT:

    (A) The collective concept allows groups of individuals to own property; the private concept does not.

    (B) The collective concept requires consideration of community interests; the private concept does not.

    (C) The collective concept assigns ownership on the basis of membership in a community; the private concept does not.

    (D) The private concept allows owners to function as titleholders to their property; the collective concept does not.

    (E) The private concept permits individuals to sell property; the collective concept does not.

19. The passage most supports which one of the following statements about the tribal legal systems mentioned in the second paragraph of the passage?

    (A) All tribes whose legal system employs the concept of collective property have engaged in litigation over control of movable cultural property.

    (B) Only tribes that have engaged in litigation over control of movable property have a legal system that employs the concept of collective property.

    (C) All tribes that have engaged in litigation over control of movable cultural property have a legal system that employs the concept of collective property.

    (D) All tribes whose legal system recognizes the concept of private property can expect to succeed in litigation over control of movable cultural property.

    (E) Only those tribes whose legal system recognizes the concept of private property can expect to succeed in litigation over control of movable cultural property.

GO ON TO THE NEXT PAGE.

The first thing any embryo must do before it can develop into an organism is establish early polarity—that is, it must set up a way to distinguish its top from its bottom and its back from its front. The
(5) mechanisms that establish the earliest spatial configurations in an embryo are far less similar across life forms than those relied on for later development, as in the formation of limbs or a nervous system: for example, the signals that the developing fruit fly uses
(10) to know its front end from its back end turn out to be radically different from those that the nematode, a type of worm, relies on, and both appear to be quite different from the polarity signals in the development of humans and other mammals.

(15) In the fruit fly, polarity is established by signals inscribed in the yolklike cytoplasm of the egg before fertilization, so that when the sperm contributes its genetic material, everything is already set to go. Given all the positional information that must be
(20) distributed throughout the cell, it takes a fruit fly a week to make an egg, but once that well-appointed egg is fertilized, it is transformed from a single cell into a crawling larva in a day. By contrast, in the embryonic development of certain nematodes, the
(25) point where the sperm enters the egg appears to provide crucial positional information. Once that information is present, little bundles of proteins called p-granules, initially distributed uniformly throughout the cytoplasm, begin to congregate at one end of the
(30) yolk; when the fertilized egg divides, one of the resulting cells gets all the p-granules. The presence or absence of these granules in cells appears to help determine whether their subsequent divisions will lead to the formation of the worm's front or back
(35) half. A similar sperm-driven mechanism is also thought to establish body orientation in some comparatively simple vertebrates such as frogs, though apparently not in more complex vertebrates such as mammals. Research indicates that in human
(40) and other mammalian embryos, polarity develops much later, as many stages of cell division occur with no apparent asymmetries among cells. Yet how polarity is established in mammals is currently a tempting mystery to researchers.

(45) Once an embryo establishes polarity, it relies on sets of essential genes that are remarkably similar among all life forms for elaboration of its parts. There is an astonishing conservation of mechanism in this process: the genes that help make eyes in flies
(50) are similar to the genes that make eyes in mice or humans. So a seeming paradox arises: when embryos of different species are at the one- or few-cell stage and still appear almost identical, the mechanisms of development they use are vastly different; yet when
(55) they start growing brains or extremities and become identifiable as distinct species, the developmental mechanisms they use are remarkably similar.

20. Which one of the following most accurately expresses the main point of the passage?

(A) Species differ more in the mechanisms that determine the spatial orientation in an embryo than they do in their overall genetic makeup.

(B) Embryos determine their front from their back and top from bottom by different methods, depending on whether the organism is simple or more complex.

(C) While very similar genes help determine the later embryonic development of all organisms, the genetic mechanisms by which embryos establish early polarity vary dramatically from one organism to the next.

(D) The mechanisms by which embryos establish early polarity differ depending on whether the signals by which polarity is achieved are inscribed in the cytoplasm of the egg or the p-granules of the sperm.

(E) Despite their apparent dissimilarity from species to species, the means by which organisms establish polarity rely on essentially the same genetic mechanisms.

21. The passage suggests that the author would be most likely to agree with which one of the following statements?

(A) The simpler the organism, the greater the speed at which it develops from fertilized egg to embryo.

(B) Scientists have determined how polarity is established in most simple vertebrates.

(C) Scientists will try to determine how polarity is established in humans.

(D) Very few observations of embryonic development after polarity is established are generalizable to more than a single species.

(E) Simpler organisms take longer to establish polarity than do more complex organisms.

GO ON TO THE NEXT PAGE.

22. The passage provides information to suggest that which one of the following relationships exists between the development of humans and the development of fruit flies?

  (A) Since humans and fruit flies use similar genetic material in their development, analogies from fruit fly behavior can be useful in explaining human behavior.

  (B) For the elaboration of parts, human development relies on genetic material quite different in nature, though not in quantity, from that of a fruit fly.

  (C) Positional information for establishing polarity in a human embryo, as in that of the fruit fly, is distributed throughout the egg prior to fertilization.

  (D) A study of the development of the fruit fly's visual system would more likely be applicable to questions of human development than would a study of the mechanisms that establish the fruit fly's polarity.

  (E) While the fruit fly egg becomes a larva in a single day, a human embryo takes significantly longer to develop because humans cannot develop limbs until they have established a nervous system.

23. According to the passage, polarity is established in a human embryo

  (A) after more stages of cell division than in frogs

  (B) before the sperm enters the egg

  (C) after positional information is provided by the massing of p-granules

  (D) by the same sperm-driven mechanism as in the nematode

  (E) in the same way as in simpler vertebrates

24. By "conservation of mechanism" (line 48) the author is probably referring to

  (A) how the same mechanism can be used to form different parts of the same organism

  (B) the fact that no genetic material is wasted in development

  (C) how few genes a given organism requires in order to elaborate its parts

  (D) a highly complex organism's requiring no more genetic material than a simpler one

  (E) the fact that analogous structures in different species are brought about by similar genetic means

25. Which one of the following most accurately states the main purpose of the second paragraph?

  (A) to illustrate the diversity of processes by which organisms establish early polarity

  (B) to elaborate on the differences between embryonic formation in the fruit fly and in the nematode

  (C) to suggest why the process of establishing early polarity in humans is not yet understood

  (D) to demonstrate the significance and necessity for genetic development of establishing polarity

  (E) to demonstrate that there are two main types of mechanism by which early polarity is established

26. According to the passage, which one of the following is a major difference between the establishment of polarity in the fruit fly and in the nematode?

  (A) The fruit fly embryo takes longer to establish polarity than does the nematode embryo.

  (B) The mechanisms that establish polarity are more easily identifiable in the nematode than in the fruit fly.

  (C) Polarity signals for the fruit fly embryo are inscribed entirely in the egg and these signals for the nematode embryo are inscribed entirely in the sperm.

  (D) Polarity in the fruit fly takes more stages of cell division to become established than in the nematode.

  (E) Polarity is established for the fruit fly before fertilization and for the nematode through fertilization.

27. The author's primary purpose in the passage is to

  (A) articulate a theory of how early polarity is established and support the theory by an analysis of data

  (B) describe a phase in the development of organisms in which the genetic mechanisms used are disparate and discuss why this disparity is surprising

  (C) provide a classification of the mechanisms by which different life forms establish early polarity

  (D) argue that a certain genetic process must occur in all life forms, regardless of their apparent dissimilarity

  (E) explain why an embryo must establish early polarity before it can develop into an organism

STOP
IF YOU FINISH BEFORE TIME IS CALLED, YOU MAY CHECK YOUR WORK ON THIS SECTION ONLY.
DO NOT WORK ON ANY OTHER SECTION IN THE TEST.

SECTION IV
Time—35 minutes
26 Questions

Directions: The questions in this section are based on the reasoning contained in brief statements or passages. For some questions, more than one of the choices could conceivably answer the question. However, you are to choose the best answer; that is, the response that most accurately and completely answers the question. You should not make assumptions that are by commonsense standards implausible, superfluous, or incompatible with the passage. After you have chosen the best answer, blacken the corresponding space on your answer sheet.

1. While 65 percent of the eligible voters who were recently polled favor Perkins over Samuels in the coming election, the results of that poll are dubious because it was not based on a representative sample. Given that Perkins predominantly advocates the interests of the upper-middle class and that the survey was conducted at high-priced shopping malls, it is quite probable that Perkins's supporters were overrepresented.

    Which one of the following statements most accurately expresses the main conclusion of the argument?

    (A)   The poll was intentionally designed to favor Perkins over Samuels.
    (B)   Samuels's supporters believe that they were probably not adequately represented in the poll.
    (C)   The poll's results probably do not accurately represent the opinions of the voters in the coming election.
    (D)   Samuels is quite likely to have a good chance of winning the coming election.
    (E)   Those who designed the poll should have considered more carefully where to conduct the survey.

2. Sleep research has demonstrated that sleep is characterized by periods of different levels of brain activity. People experience dreams during only one of these periods, known as REM (rapid eye movement) sleep. Test subjects who are chronically deprived of REM sleep become irritable during waking life. This shows that REM sleep relieves the stresses of waking life.

    Which one of the following, if true, most strengthens the argument?

    (A)   Test subjects who are chronically deprived of non-REM sleep also become irritable during waking life.
    (B)   Chronically having bad dreams can cause stress, but so can chronically having pleasant but exciting dreams.
    (C)   During times of increased stress, one's REM sleep is disturbed in a way that prevents one from dreaming.
    (D)   Only some people awakened during REM sleep can report the dreams they were having just before being awakened.
    (E)   Other factors being equal, people who normally have shorter periods of REM sleep tend to experience more stress.

GO ON TO THE NEXT PAGE.

3. Since 1989 the importation of ivory from African elephants into the United States and Canada has been illegal, but the importation of ivory from the excavated tusks of ancient mammoths remains legal in both countries. Following the ban, there was a sharp increase in the importation of ivory that importers identified as mammoth ivory. In 1989 customs officials lacked a technique for distinguishing elephant ivory from that of mammoths. Just after such a technique was invented and its use by customs officials became widely known, there was a dramatic decrease in the amount of ivory presented for importation into the U.S. and Canada that was identified by importers as mammoth ivory.

Which one of the following is most strongly supported by the information above?

(A) Customs officials still cannot reliably distinguish elephant ivory from mammoth ivory.

(B) Most of the ivory currently imported into the U.S. and Canada comes from neither African elephants nor mammoths.

(C) In the period since the technique for distinguishing elephant ivory from mammoth ivory was implemented, the population of African elephants has declined.

(D) Much of the ivory imported as mammoth ivory just after the ban on ivory from African elephants went into effect was actually elephant ivory.

(E) Shortly after the importation of ivory from African elephants was outlawed, there was a sharp increase in the total amount of all ivory presented for importation into the U.S. and Canada.

4. My suspicion that there is some truth to astrology has been confirmed. Most physicians I have talked to believe in it.

The flawed pattern of reasoning in the argument above is most similar to that in which one of the following?

(A) Professor Smith was convicted of tax evasion last year. So I certainly wouldn't give any credence to Smith's economic theories.

(B) I have come to the conclusion that several governmental social programs are wasteful. This is because most of the biology professors I have discussed this with think that this is true.

(C) Quantum mechanics seems to be emerging as the best physical theory we have today. Most prominent physicists subscribe to it.

(D) Most mechanical engineers I have talked to say that it is healthier to refrain from eating meat. So most mechanical engineers are vegetarians.

(E) For many years now, many people, some famous, have reported that they have seen or come in contact with unidentified flying objects. So there are probably extraterrestrial societies trying to contact us.

5. The best explanation for Mozart's death involves the recently detected fracture in his skull. The crack, most likely the result of an accident, could have easily torn veins in his brain, allowing blood to leak into his brain. When such bleeding occurs in the brain and the blood dries, many of the brain's faculties become damaged, commonly, though not immediately, leading to death. This explanation of Mozart's death is bolstered by the fact that the fracture shows signs of partial healing.

The claim that the fracture shows signs of partial healing figures in the argument in which one of the following ways?

(A) It shows that Mozart's death could have been avoided.

(B) It shows that the fracture did not occur after Mozart's death.

(C) It shows that the dried blood impaired Mozart's brain's faculties.

(D) It shows that Mozart's death occurred suddenly.

(E) It suggests that Mozart's death was accidental.

6. In the first phase of the Industrial Revolution, machines were invented whose main advantage was that they worked faster than human workers. This technology became widely used because it was economically attractive; many unskilled workers could be replaced by just a few skilled workers. Today managers are looking for technology that will allow them to replace highly paid skilled workers with a smaller number of less-skilled workers.

The examples presented above best illustrate which one of the following propositions?

(A) Employers utilize new technology because it allows them to reduce labor costs.

(B) Workers will need to acquire more education and skills to remain competitive in the labor market.

(C) In seeking employment, highly skilled workers no longer have an advantage over less-skilled workers.

(D) Technology eliminates many jobs but also creates just as many jobs.

(E) Whereas technological innovations were once concentrated in heavy industry, they now affect all industries.

GO ON TO THE NEXT PAGE.

7. For many types of crops, hybrid strains have been developed that have been found in test plantings to produce significantly higher yields than were produced by traditional nonhybrid strains of those crops planted alongside them. However, in many parts of the world where farmers have abandoned traditional nonhybrid strains in favor of the hybrid strains, crop yields have not increased.

Which one of the following, if true, most helps to resolve the apparent discrepancy?

(A) Most farmers who plant the hybrid strains of their crops have larger farms than do farmers who continue to plant traditional nonhybrid strains of the same crops.

(B) Hybrid strains of crops produced higher yields in some areas than did nonhybrid strains in those areas.

(C) The hybrid strains were tested under significantly better farming conditions than are found in most areas where farmers grow those strains.

(D) Many traditional nonhybrid strains of plants produce crops that taste better and thus sell better than the hybrid strains of those crops.

(E) Many governments subsidize farmers who plant only hybrid strains of staple crops.

8. This stamp is probably highly valuable, since it exhibits a printing error. The most important factors in determining a stamp's value, assuming it is in good condition, are its rarity and age. This is clearly a fine specimen, and it is quite old as well.

The conclusion is properly inferred if which one of the following is assumed?

(A) The older a stamp is, the more valuable it is.

(B) Printing errors are always confined to a few individual stamps.

(C) Most stamps with printing errors are already in the hands of collectors.

(D) Rarity and age are of equal importance to a stamp's value.

(E) Even old and rare stamps are usually not valuable if they are in poor condition.

9. A recent study of several hundred female physicians showed that their tendency to develop coronary disease was inversely proportional to their dietary intake of two vitamins, folate and B6. The researchers concluded that folate and B6 inhibit the development of heart disease in women.

Which one of the following would, if true, most weaken the researchers' conclusion?

(A) The foods that contain significant amounts of the vitamins folate and B6 also contain significant amounts of nonvitamin nutrients that inhibit heart disease.

(B) It is very unlikely that a chemical compound would inhibit coronary disease in women but not in men.

(C) Physicians are more likely than nonphysicians to know a great deal about the link between diet and health.

(D) The physicians in the study had not been screened in advance to ensure that none had preexisting heart conditions.

(E) The vitamins folate and B6 are present only in very small amounts in most foods.

10. The proposed coal-burning electric plant should be approved, since no good arguments have been offered against it. After all, all the arguments against it have been presented by competing electricity producers.

Which one of the following is an assumption on which the reasoning above depends?

(A) The competing electricity producers would stand to lose large amounts of revenue from the building of the coal-burning electric plant.

(B) If a person's arguments against a proposal are defective, then that person has a vested interest in seeing that the proposal is not implemented.

(C) Approval of the coal-burning electric plant would please coal suppliers more than disapproval would please suppliers of fuel to the competing electricity producers.

(D) If good arguments are presented for a proposal, then that proposal should be approved.

(E) Arguments made by those who have a vested interest in the outcome of a proposal are not good arguments.

GO ON TO THE NEXT PAGE.

11. Psychiatrist: While the first appearance of a phobia is usually preceded by a traumatizing event, not everyone who is traumatized by an event develops a phobia. Furthermore, many people with phobias have never been traumatized. These two considerations show that traumatizing events do not contribute to the occurrence of phobias.

The reasoning in the psychiatrist's argument is most vulnerable to criticism on the grounds that the argument

(A) treats the cause of the occurrence of a type of phenomenon as an effect of phenomena of that type
(B) presumes, without providing justification, that some psychological events have no causes that can be established by scientific investigation
(C) builds the conclusion drawn into the support cited for that conclusion
(D) takes for granted that a type of phenomenon contributes to the occurrence of another type of phenomenon only if phenomena of these two types are invariably associated
(E) derives a causal connection from mere association when there is no independent evidence of causal connection

12. Some species are called "indicator species" because the loss of a population of such a species serves as an early warning of problems arising from pollution. Environmentalists tracking the effects of pollution have increasingly paid heed to indicator species; yet environmentalists would be misguided if they attributed the loss of a population to pollution in all cases. Though declines in population often do signal environmental degradation, they are just as often a result of the natural evolution of an ecosystem. We must remember that, in nature, change is the status quo.

Which one of the following most accurately expresses the argument's conclusion?

(A) Environmentalists sometimes overreact to the loss of a specific population.
(B) The loss of a specific population should not always be interpreted as a sign of environmental degradation.
(C) Environmentalists' use of indicator species in tracking the effects of pollution is often problematic.
(D) The loss of a specific population is often the result of natural changes in an ecosystem and in such cases should not be resisted.
(E) The loss of a specific population as a result of pollution is simply part of nature's status quo.

13. Columnist: Tagowa's testimony in the Pemberton trial was not heard outside the courtroom, so we cannot be sure what she said. Afterward, however, she publicly affirmed her belief in Pemberton's guilt. Hence, since the jury found Pemberton not guilty, we can conclude that not all of the jury members believed Tagowa's testimony.

Which one of the following describes a flaw in the columnist's reasoning?

(A) It overlooks that a witness may think that a defendant is guilty even though that witness's testimony in no way implicates the defendant.
(B) It confuses facts about what certain people believe with facts about what ought to be the case.
(C) It presumes, without providing warrant, that juries find defendants guilty only if those defendants committed the crimes with which they are charged.
(D) It presumes, without providing warrant, that a jury's finding a defendant not guilty is evidence of dishonesty on the part of someone who testified against the defendant.
(E) It fails to consider that jury members sometimes disagree with each other about the significance of a particular person's testimony.

14. A new tax law aimed at encouraging the reforestation of cleared land in order to increase the amount of forested land in a particular region offers lumber companies tax incentives for each unit of cleared land they reforest. One lumber company has accordingly reduced its tax liability by purchasing a large tract of cleared land in the region and reforesting it. The company paid for the purchase by clearing a larger tract of land in the region, a tract that it had planned to hold in long-term reserve.

If the statements above are true, which one of the following must be true about the new tax law?

(A) It is a failure in encouraging the reforestation of cleared land in the region.
(B) It will have no immediate effect on the amount of forested land in the region.
(C) It will ultimately cause lumber companies to plant trees on approximately as much land as they harvest in the region.
(D) It can provide a motivation for companies to act in a manner contrary to the purpose of the law while taking advantage of the tax incentives.
(E) It will provide lumber companies with a tax incentive that will ultimately be responsible for a massive decrease in the number of mature forests in the region.

GO ON TO THE NEXT PAGE.

15. Trustee: The recent exhibit at the art museum was extensively covered by the local media, and this coverage seems to have contributed to the record-breaking attendance it drew. If the attendance at the exhibit had been low, the museum would have gone bankrupt and closed permanently, so the museum could not have remained open had it not been for the coverage from the local media.

The reasoning in the trustee's argument is most vulnerable to criticism on the grounds that the argument

(A) confuses a necessary condition for the museum's remaining open with a sufficient condition for the museum's remaining open

(B) takes for granted that no previous exhibit at the museum had received such extensive media coverage

(C) takes for granted that most people who read articles about the exhibit also attended the exhibit

(D) fails to address the possibility that the exhibit would have drawn enough visitors to prevent bankruptcy even without media coverage

(E) presupposes the very conclusion that it is trying to prove

16. Economist: A tax is effective if it raises revenue and burdens all and only those persons targeted by the tax. A tax is ineffective, however, if it does not raise revenue and it costs a significant amount of money to enforce.

Which one of the following inferences is most strongly supported by the principles stated by the economist?

(A) The tax on cigarettes burdens most, but not all, of the people targeted by it. Thus, if it raises revenue, the tax is effective.

(B) The tax on alcohol raises a modest amount of revenue, but it costs a significant amount of money to enforce. Thus, the tax is ineffective.

(C) The tax on gasoline costs a significant amount of money to enforce. Thus, if it does not raise revenue, the tax is ineffective.

(D) The tax on coal burdens all of the people targeted by it, and this tax does not burden anyone who is not targeted by it. Thus, the tax is effective.

(E) The tax on steel does not cost a significant amount of money to enforce, but it does not raise revenue either. Thus, the tax is ineffective.

17. A large amount of rainfall in April and May typically leads to an increase in the mosquito population and thus to an increased threat of encephalitis. People cannot change the weather. Thus people cannot decrease the threat of encephalitis.

The reasoning in the argument above is flawed in that the argument

(A) takes for granted that because one event precedes another the former must be the cause of the latter

(B) presumes, without providing justification, that a certain outcome would be desirable

(C) ignores the possibility that a certain type of outcome is dependent on more than one factor

(D) takes for granted that a threat that is aggravated by certain factors could not occur in the absence of those factors

(E) draws a conclusion about what is possible from a premise about what is actually the case

18. Leadership depends as much on making one's followers aware of their own importance as it does on conveying a vivid image of a collective goal. Only if they are convinced both that their efforts are necessary for the accomplishment of this goal, and that these efforts, if expended, will actually achieve it, will people follow a leader.

If all of the statements above are true, then which one of the following CANNOT be true?

(A) Some leaders who convince their followers of the necessity of their efforts in achieving a goal fail, nevertheless, to lead them to the attainment of that goal.

(B) One who succeeds in conveying to one's followers the relationship between their efforts and the attainment of a collective goal succeeds in leading these people to this goal.

(C) Only if one is a leader must one convince people of the necessity of their efforts for the attainment of a collective goal.

(D) Sometimes people succeed in achieving a collective goal without ever having been convinced that by trying to do so they would succeed.

(E) Sometimes people who remain unsure of whether their efforts are needed for the attainment of a collective goal nevertheless follow a leader.

GO ON TO THE NEXT PAGE.

19. Fifty chronic insomniacs participated in a one-month study conducted at an institute for sleep disorders. Half were given a dose of a new drug and the other half were given a placebo every night before going to bed at the institute. Approximately 80 percent of the participants in each group reported significant relief from insomnia during the first two weeks of the study. But in each group, approximately 90 percent of those who had reported relief claimed that their insomnia had returned during the third week of the study.

Which one of the following, if true, most helps to explain all the data from the study?

(A) Because it is easy to build up a tolerance to the new drug, most people will no longer experience its effects after taking it every night for two weeks.

(B) The psychological comfort afforded by the belief that one has taken a sleep-promoting drug is enough to prevent most episodes of insomnia.

(C) The new drug is very similar in chemical composition to another drug, large doses of which have turned out to be less effective than expected.

(D) Most insomniacs sleep better in a new environment, and the new drug has no effect on an insomniac's ability to sleep.

(E) Some insomniacs cannot reliably determine how much sleep they have had or how well they have slept.

20. Advertisement: The Country Classic is the only kind of car in its class that offers an antilock braking system that includes TrackAid. An antilock braking system keeps your wheels from locking up during hard braking, and TrackAid keeps your rear wheels from spinning on slippery surfaces. So if you are a safety-conscious person in the market for a car in this class, the Country Classic is the only car for you.

The advertisement is misleading if which one of the following is true?

(A) All of the cars that are in the same class as the Country Classic offer some kind of antilock braking system.

(B) Most kinds of cars that are in the same class as the Country Classic are manufactured by the same company that manufactures the Country Classic.

(C) Without an antilock braking system, the wheels of the Country Classic and other cars in its class are more likely to lock up during hard braking than they are to spin on slippery surfaces.

(D) Other cars in the same class as the Country Classic offer an antilock braking system that uses a method other than TrackAid to prevent rear wheels from spinning on slippery surfaces.

(E) The Country Classic is more expensive than any other car in its class.

21. Sociologist: Traditional norms in our society prevent sincerity by requiring one to ignore unpleasant realities and tell small lies. But a community whose members do not trust one another cannot succeed. So, if a community is to succeed, its members must be willing to face unpleasant realities and speak about them honestly.

The sociologist's conclusion follows logically if which one of the following is assumed?

(A) Sincerity is required if community members are to trust each other.

(B) The more sincere and open community members are, the more likely that community is to succeed.

(C) A community sometimes can succeed even if its members subscribe to traditional norms.

(D) Unless a community's members are willing to face unpleasant realities, they cannot be sincere.

(E) A community's failure is often caused by its members' unwillingness to face unpleasant realities and to discuss them honestly.

GO ON TO THE NEXT PAGE.

22. If there is an election, you can either vote or not. If you vote, you have the satisfaction of knowing you influenced the results of the election; if you do not vote, you have no right to complain about the results. So, following an election, either you will have the satisfaction of knowing you influenced its results or you will have no right to complain.

The reasoning in which one of the following most closely resembles that in the argument above?

(A) When you rent a car, you can either take out insurance or not. If you take out insurance you are covered, but if you are uninsured, you are personally liable for any costs incurred from an accident. So in case of an accident, you will be better off if you are insured.

(B) If you go for a walk, when you are finished either you will feel relaxed or you will not. If you feel relaxed, then your muscles will likely not be sore the next day, though your muscles will more likely become conditioned faster if they do feel sore. Therefore, either your muscles will feel sore, or they will become better conditioned.

(C) If you attend school, you will find the courses stimulating or you will not. If your teachers are motivated, you will find the courses stimulating. If your teachers are not motivated, you will not. So either your teachers are motivated, or their courses are not stimulating.

(D) If you use a computer, its messages are either easily readable or not. If the messages are easily readable, they are merely password protected. If they are not easily readable, they are electronically encrypted. So any message on the computer you use is either password protected or electronically encrypted.

(E) When manufacturers use a natural resource, they are either efficient or inefficient. If they are inefficient, the resource will be depleted quickly. If they are efficient, the resource will last much longer. So either manufacturers are efficient or they should be fined.

23. Company president: Our consultants report that, in general, the most efficient managers have excellent time management skills. Thus, to improve productivity I recommend that we make available to our middle-level managers a seminar to train them in techniques of time management.

Each of the following, if true, would weaken the support for the company president's recommendation EXCEPT:

(A) The consultants use the same criteria to evaluate managers' efficiency as they do to evaluate their time management skills.

(B) Successful time management is more dependent on motivation than on good technique.

(C) Most managers at other companies who have attended time management seminars are still unproductive.

(D) Most managers who are already efficient do not need to improve their productivity.

(E) Most managers who are efficient have never attended a time management seminar.

24. Many Seychelles warblers of breeding age forgo breeding, remaining instead with their parents and helping to raise their own siblings. This behavior, called cooperative breeding, results from the scarcity of nesting territory for the birds on the tiny island that, until recently, was home to the world's population of Seychelles warblers. Yet when healthy warblers were transplanted to a much larger neighboring island as part of an experiment, most of those warblers maintained a pattern of cooperative breeding.

Which one of the following, if true, most helps to explain the result of the experiment?

(A) Many of the Seychelles warblers that were transplanted to the neighboring island had not yet reached breeding age.

(B) The climate of the island to which Seychelles warblers were transplanted was the same as that of the warblers' native island.

(C) Most of the terrain on the neighboring island was not of the type in which Seychelles warblers generally build their nests.

(D) Cooperative breeding in species other than the Seychelles warbler often results when the environment cannot sustain a rise in the population.

(E) The Seychelles warblers had fewer competitors for nesting territory on the island to which they were transplanted than on their native island.

GO ON TO THE NEXT PAGE.

25. Therapist: In a recent study, researchers measured how quickly 60 different psychological problems waned as a large, diverse sample of people underwent weekly behavioral therapy sessions. About 75 percent of the 60 problems consistently cleared up within 50 weeks of therapy. This shows that 50 weekly behavioral therapy sessions are all that most people need.

The therapist's argument is logically most vulnerable to criticism on the grounds that it

(A) takes for granted that there are no psychological problems that usually take significantly longer to clear up than the 60 psychological problems studied

(B) fails to address the possibility that any given one of the 60 psychological problems studied might afflict most people

(C) takes for granted that no one suffers from more than one of the 60 psychological problems studied

(D) fails to address the possibility that some forms of therapy have never been proven to be effective as treatments for psychological problems

(E) takes for granted that the sample of people studied did not have significantly more psychological problems, on average, than the population as a whole

26. Researcher: It is commonly believed that species belonging to the same biological order, such as rodents, descended from a single common ancestor. However, I compared the genetic pattern in 3 rodent species—guinea pigs, rats, and mice—as well as in 13 nonrodent mammals, and found that while rats and mice are genetically quite similar, the genetic differences between guinea pigs and mice are as great as those between mice and some nonrodent species. Thus, despite their similar physical form, guinea pigs stem from a separate ancestor.

Which one of the following, if true, most seriously undermines the researcher's reasoning?

(A) The researcher examined the genetic material of only 3 of over 2,000 species of rodents.

(B) Some pairs of species not having a common ancestor are genetically more similar to each other than are some pairs that do have a common ancestor.

(C) The researcher selected nonrodent species that have the specific cell structures she wanted to analyze genetically, though many nonrodent mammals lack these cell structures.

(D) For some genuine biological orders, the most recent common ancestor dates from later epochs than does the most recent common ancestor of other biological orders.

(E) Peculiarities of body structure, such as distinctive teeth and olfactory structures, are shared by all rodents, including guinea pigs.

STOP
IF YOU FINISH BEFORE TIME IS CALLED, YOU MAY CHECK YOUR WORK ON THIS SECTION ONLY.
DO NOT WORK ON ANY OTHER SECTION IN THE TEST.

ACKNOWLEDGMENTS

Acknowledgment is made to the following sources from which material has been adapted for use in this test booklet:

Natalie Angier, "Heads or Tails? How Embryos Get It Right." ©1995 by The New York Times.

Catherine Bell, "Aboriginal Claims to Cultural Property in Canada: A Comparative Legal Analysis of the Repatriation Debate." ©1992 by the American Indian Law Review.

Louise Glück, *Proofs & Theories: Essays on Poetry.* ©1994 by Louise Glück.

"Why Bad Hair Days May Not Matter." ©1996 by Sussex Publishers Inc.

Wait for the supervisor's instructions before you open the page to the topic.
Please print and sign your name and write the date in the designated spaces below.

Time: 35 Minutes

General Directions

You will have 35 minutes in which to plan and write an essay on the topic inside. Read the topic and the accompanying directions carefully. You will probably find it best to spend a few minutes considering the topic and organizing your thoughts before you begin writing. In your essay, be sure to develop your ideas fully, leaving time, if possible, to review what you have written. **Do not write on a topic other than the one specified. Writing on a topic of your own choice is not acceptable.**

No special knowledge is required or expected for this writing exercise. Law schools are interested in the reasoning, clarity, organization, language usage, and writing mechanics displayed in your essay. How well you write is more important than how much you write.

Confine your essay to the blocked, lined area on the front and back of the separate Writing Sample Response Sheet. Only that area will be reproduced for law schools. Be sure that your writing is legible.

Both this topic sheet and your response sheet must be turned over to the testing staff before you leave the room.

Topic Code

Date
/ /

Print Your Full Name Here		
Last	First	M.I.

Sign Your Name Here

Scratch Paper
Do not write your essay in this space.

LSAT® Writing Sample Topic

Directions: The scenario presented below describes two choices, either one of which can be supported on the basis of the information given. Your essay should consider both choices and argue for one over the other, based on the two specified criteria and the facts provided. There is no "right" or "wrong" choice: a reasonable argument can be made for either.

The owner of Avanti Pizza, which currently makes pizzas for pickup or delivery only, is considering expanding his business. He can either purchase a brick pizza oven or he can add a small dining room to his restaurant. Write an essay in which you argue for one option over the other, keeping in mind the following two criteria:

- Avanti's owner wants to increase profits by offering customers something of value that Avanti does not currently provide.
- Avanti's owner wants to distinguish his restaurant from local competitors.

Brick-oven pizza has become extremely popular, and Avanti's owner estimates that including it on the menu would substantially increase takeout and delivery business. The profit margin on such pizzas is higher than that on conventional pizzas. In addition, Avanti's pizza chef could use the opportunity to introduce a selection of gourmet pizzas with creative toppings. Avanti's competitors consist of a well-established Italian restaurant, La Stella, and a franchisee of the large pizza delivery chain Pronto. Neither has a brick oven, although La Stella is rumored to be considering the option. The new oven could be up and running two weeks after the start of construction.

Avanti does not currently have space for a dining room, but the adjacent storefront property has recently become available on good lease terms. Obtaining permits and remodeling would take six months to a year, during which time the rest of the business could continue to operate. Avanti's chef would like to expand the menu to include dishes other than pizza, and with an eat-in option for customers she could easily do so. La Stella already offers sit-down dining, but in a relatively formal setting. Avanti could be more relaxed and family-friendly. In addition, Avanti could allow patrons to bring their own wine or beer, which would attract economy-minded customers. La Stella, which has a liquor license and a full bar, charges a substantial markup on all the alcoholic beverages it serves.

Scratch Paper
Do not write your essay in this space.

LAST NAME (Print)

FIRST NAME (Print)

LAST 4 DIGITS OF SOCIAL SECURITY/SOCIAL INSURANCE NO.

L

MI

TEST CENTER NO.

SIGNATURE

M M D D Y Y
TEST DATE

LSAC ACCOUNT NO.

TOPIC CODE

Writing Sample Response Sheet

DO NOT WRITE IN THIS SPACE

Begin your essay in the lined area below.
Continue on the back if you need more space.

COMPUTING YOUR SCORE

Directions:

1. Use the Answer Key on the next page to check your answers.

2. Use the Scoring Worksheet below to compute your raw score.

3. Use the Score Conversion Chart to convert your raw score into the 120-180 scale.

Scoring Worksheet

1. Enter the number of questions you answered correctly in each section.

   Number Correct

   SECTION I .... _____
   SECTION II .... _____
   SECTION III .... _____
   SECTION IV.............. _____

2. Enter the sum here: _____
   This is your Raw Score.

Conversion Chart
For Converting Raw Score to the 120-180 LSAT Scaled Score
LSAT Form 5LSN66

Reported Score	Raw Score Lowest	Raw Score Highest
180	100	101
179	—*	—*
178	99	99
177	98	98
176	—*	—*
175	97	97
174	96	96
173	—*	—*
172	95	95
171	94	94
170	93	93
169	92	92
168	90	91
167	89	89
166	88	88
165	86	87
164	85	85
163	83	84
162	81	82
161	80	80
160	78	79
159	76	77
158	74	75
157	72	73
156	70	71
155	68	69
154	66	67
153	64	65
152	62	63
151	60	61
150	58	59
149	56	57
148	54	55
147	52	53
146	50	51
145	49	49
144	47	48
143	45	46
142	43	44
141	41	42
140	39	40
139	38	38
138	36	37
137	34	35
136	33	33
135	31	32
134	30	30
133	29	29
132	27	28
131	26	26
130	25	25
129	23	24
128	22	22
127	21	21
126	20	20
125	19	19
124	18	18
123	17	17
122	16	16
121	15	15
120	0	14

*There is no raw score that will produce this scaled score for this form.

ANSWER KEY

SECTION I

1.	D	8.	C	15.	A	22.	E
2.	D	9.	D	16.	D	23.	E
3.	C	10.	D	17.	E	24.	E
4.	B	11.	E	18.	D	25.	C
5.	A	12.	B	19.	B	26.	A
6.	A	13.	C	20.	E		
7.	C	14.	D	21.	B		

SECTION II

1.	C	8.	B	15.	D	22.	B
2.	E	9.	C	16.	C		
3.	E	10.	E	17.	C		
4.	A	11.	D	18.	A		
5.	A	12.	E	19.	A		
6.	A	13.	C	20.	A		
7.	C	14.	A	21.	D		

SECTION III

1.	A	8.	C	15.	E	22.	D
2.	D	9.	A	16.	D	23.	A
3.	E	10.	C	17.	D	24.	E
4.	B	11.	E	18.	A	25.	A
5.	C	12.	D	19.	C	26.	E
6.	D	13.	B	20.	C	27.	B
7.	E	14.	C	21.	C		

SECTION IV

1.	C	8.	B	15.	D	22.	D
2.	E	9.	A	16.	C	23.	D
3.	D	10.	E	17.	C	24.	C
4.	B	11.	D	18.	E	25.	B
5.	B	12.	B	19.	D	26.	B
6.	A	13.	A	20.	D		
7.	C	14.	D	21.	A		

PREPTEST 49
JUNE 2006
FORM 7LSN72

SECTION I

Time—35 minutes

22 Questions

Directions: Each group of questions in this section is based on a set of conditions. In answering some of the questions, it may be useful to draw a rough diagram. Choose the response that most accurately and completely answers each question and blacken the corresponding space on your answer sheet.

Questions 1–7

During an international film retrospective lasting six consecutive days—day 1 through day 6—exactly six different films will be shown, one each day. Twelve films will be available for presentation, two each in French, Greek, Hungarian, Italian, Norwegian, and Turkish. The presentation of the films must conform to the following conditions:

    Neither day 2 nor day 4 is a day on which a film in Norwegian is shown.

    A film in Italian is not shown unless a film in Norwegian is going to be shown the next day.

    A film in Greek is not shown unless a film in Italian is going to be shown the next day.

1. Which one of the following is an acceptable order of films for the retrospective, listed by their language, from day 1 through day 6?

    (A)   French, Greek, Italian, Turkish, Norwegian, Hungarian

    (B)   French, Hungarian, Italian, Norwegian, French, Hungarian

    (C)   Hungarian, French, Norwegian, Greek, Norwegian, Italian

    (D)   Norwegian, Turkish, Hungarian, Italian, French, Turkish

    (E)   Turkish, French, Norwegian, Hungarian, French, Turkish

2. If two films in Italian are going to be shown, one on day 2 and one on day 5, then the film shown on day 1 could be in any one of the following languages EXCEPT:

    (A)   French
    (B)   Greek
    (C)   Hungarian
    (D)   Norwegian
    (E)   Turkish

3. If two films in Italian are shown during the retrospective, which one of the following must be false?

    (A)   A film in French is shown on day 3.
    (B)   A film in Greek is shown on day 1.
    (C)   A film in Hungarian is shown on day 6.
    (D)   A film in Norwegian is shown on day 5.
    (E)   A film in Turkish is shown on day 4.

4. Which one of the following is a complete and accurate list of the days, any one of which is a day on which a film in Italian could be shown?

    (A)   day 1, day 3, day 5
    (B)   day 2, day 4, day 5
    (C)   day 2, day 5, day 6
    (D)   day 1, day 3
    (E)   day 2, day 4

5. If two films in French are going to be shown, one on day 3 and one on day 5, which one of the following is a pair of films that could be shown on day 1 and day 6, respectively?

    (A)   a film in French, a film in Turkish
    (B)   a film in Greek, a film in Hungarian
    (C)   a film in Italian, a film in Norwegian
    (D)   a film in Norwegian, a film in Turkish
    (E)   a film in Turkish, a film in Greek

6. If neither a film in French nor a film in Italian is shown during the retrospective, which one of the following must be true?

    (A)   A film in Norwegian is shown on day 1.
    (B)   A film in Norwegian is shown on day 5.
    (C)   A film in Turkish is shown on day 4.
    (D)   A film in Hungarian or else a film in Norwegian is shown on day 3.
    (E)   A film in Hungarian or else a film in Turkish is shown on day 2.

7. If a film in Greek is going to be shown at some time after a film in Norwegian, then a film in Norwegian must be shown on

    (A)   day 1
    (B)   day 3
    (C)   day 5
    (D)   day 1 or else day 3
    (E)   day 3 or else day 5

GO ON TO THE NEXT PAGE.

Questions 8–12

There are exactly five pieces of mail in a mailbox: a flyer, a letter, a magazine, a postcard, and a survey. Each piece of mail is addressed to exactly one of three housemates: Georgette, Jana, or Rini. Each housemate has at least one of the pieces of mail addressed to her. The following conditions must apply:

    Neither the letter nor the magazine is addressed to Georgette.

    If the letter is addressed to Rini, then the postcard is addressed to Jana.

    The housemate to whom the flyer is addressed has at least one of the other pieces of mail addressed to her as well.

8. Which one of the following could be a complete and accurate matching of the pieces of mail to the housemates to whom they are addressed?

    (A)   Georgette: the flyer, the survey
             Jana: the letter
             Rini: the magazine
    (B)   Georgette: the flyer, the postcard
             Jana: the letter, the magazine
             Rini: the survey
    (C)   Georgette: the magazine, the survey
             Jana: the flyer, the letter
             Rini: the postcard
    (D)   Georgette: the survey
             Jana: the flyer, the magazine
             Rini: the letter, the postcard
    (E)   Georgette: the survey
             Jana: the letter, the magazine, the postcard
             Rini: the flyer

9. Which one of the following is a complete and accurate list of the pieces of mail, any one of which could be the only piece of mail addressed to Jana?

    (A)   the postcard
    (B)   the letter, the postcard
    (C)   the letter, the survey
    (D)   the magazine, the survey
    (E)   the letter, the magazine, the postcard

10. Which one of the following CANNOT be a complete and accurate list of the pieces of mail addressed to Jana?

    (A)   the flyer, the letter, the magazine
    (B)   the flyer, the letter, the postcard
    (C)   the flyer, the letter, the survey
    (D)   the flyer, the magazine, the postcard
    (E)   the flyer, the magazine, the survey

11. Which one of the following CANNOT be a complete and accurate list of the pieces of mail addressed to Rini?

    (A)   the magazine, the postcard
    (B)   the letter, the survey
    (C)   the letter, the magazine
    (D)   the flyer, the magazine
    (E)   the flyer, the letter

12. If the magazine and the survey are both addressed to the same housemate, then which one of the following could be true?

    (A)   The survey is addressed to Georgette.
    (B)   The postcard is addressed to Rini.
    (C)   The magazine is addressed to Jana.
    (D)   The letter is addressed to Rini.
    (E)   The flyer is addressed to Jana.

GO ON TO THE NEXT PAGE.

Questions 13–17

A summer program offers at least one of the following
seven courses: geography, history, literature, mathematics,
psychology, sociology, zoology. The following restrictions on
the program must apply:

If mathematics is offered, then either literature or sociology
(but not both) is offered.

If literature is offered, then geography is also offered but
psychology is not.

If sociology is offered, then psychology is also offered but
zoology is not.

If geography is offered, then both history and zoology are
also offered.

13. Which one of the following could be a complete and
accurate list of the courses offered by the summer
program?

(A) history, psychology
(B) geography, history, literature
(C) history, mathematics, psychology
(D) literature, mathematics, psychology
(E) history, literature, mathematics, sociology

14. If the summer program offers literature, then which one
of the following could be true?

(A) Sociology is offered.
(B) History is not offered.
(C) Mathematics is not offered.
(D) A total of two courses are offered.
(E) Zoology is not offered.

15. If history is not offered by the summer program, then
which one of the following is another course that
CANNOT be offered?

(A) literature
(B) mathematics
(C) psychology
(D) sociology
(E) zoology

16. If the summer program offers mathematics, then which
one of the following must be true?

(A) Literature is offered.
(B) Psychology is offered.
(C) Sociology is offered.
(D) At least three courses are offered.
(E) At most four courses are offered.

17. Which one of the following must be false of the summer
program?

(A) Both geography and psychology are offered.
(B) Both geography and mathematics are offered.
(C) Both psychology and mathematics are offered.
(D) Both history and mathematics are offered.
(E) Both geography and sociology are offered.

GO ON TO THE NEXT PAGE.

Questions 18–22

Exactly eight computer processor chips—F, G, H, J, K, L, M, and O—are ranked according to their speed from first (fastest) to eighth (slowest). The ranking must be consistent with the following:

>   There are no ties.
>   Either F or G is ranked first.
>   M is not the slowest.
>   H is faster than J, with exactly one chip intermediate in speed between them.
>   K is faster than L, with exactly two chips intermediate in speed between them.
>   O is slower than both J and L.

18.   Which one of the following could be true?

   (A)   F is ranked first and M is ranked eighth.
   (B)   G is ranked fifth and O is ranked eighth.
   (C)   J is ranked third and L is ranked seventh.
   (D)   K is ranked second and H is ranked third.
   (E)   M is ranked seventh and L is ranked eighth.

19.   H CANNOT be ranked

   (A)   second
   (B)   third
   (C)   fourth
   (D)   fifth
   (E)   sixth

20.   If O is faster than F, then which one of the following chips could be ranked second?

   (A)   G
   (B)   H
   (C)   M
   (D)   J
   (E)   L

21.   If M is faster than J, then the fastest ranking J could have is

   (A)   second
   (B)   third
   (C)   fourth
   (D)   fifth
   (E)   sixth

22.   Which one of the following must be true?

   (A)   J is ranked no faster than fifth.
   (B)   K is ranked no faster than third.
   (C)   L is ranked no faster than fifth.
   (D)   M is ranked no faster than third.
   (E)   O is ranked no faster than eighth.

S T O P
IF YOU FINISH BEFORE TIME IS CALLED, YOU MAY CHECK YOUR WORK ON THIS SECTION ONLY.
DO NOT WORK ON ANY OTHER SECTION IN THE TEST.

SECTION II

Time—35 minutes

26 Questions

Directions: The questions in this section are based on the reasoning contained in brief statements or passages. For some questions, more than one of the choices could conceivably answer the question. However, you are to choose the best answer; that is, the response that most accurately and completely answers the question. You should not make assumptions that are by commonsense standards implausible, superfluous, or incompatible with the passage. After you have chosen the best answer, blacken the corresponding space on your answer sheet.

1. Ilana: Carver's stories are somber and pessimistic, which is a sure sign of inferior writing. I have never read a single story of his that ends happily.

Gustav: Carver was one of the finest writers of the past 30 years. Granted, his stories are characterized by somberness and pessimism, but they are also wryly humorous, compassionate, and beautifully structured.

On the basis of their statements, Ilana and Gustav are committed to disagreeing over whether

(A)   Carver's stories are truly compassionate
(B)   Carver's stories are pessimistic in their vision
(C)   stories that are characterized by somberness and pessimism can appropriately be called humorous
(D)   stories that are well written can be somber and pessimistic
(E)   there are some characteristics of a story that are decisive in determining its aesthetic value

2. Statistical studies show that last year there was the greatest drop in the violent crime rate over the course of a year since such statistics were first gathered. But they also reveal that at the same time public anxiety about violent crime substantially increased.

Which one of the following, if true, most helps to resolve the apparent discrepancy described above?

(A)   Longer prison sentences were the primary cause of the decrease in the violent crime rate over the course of last year.
(B)   As in the past, last year's increase in public anxiety about violent crime has been consistently underreported in the news media.
(C)   Most people can realistically assess the likelihood that they will become victims of violent crime.
(D)   People who feel the most anxiety about violent crime usually live in areas with relatively high violent crime rates.
(E)   The proportion of violent crimes covered in the news media nearly doubled over the course of last year.

3. Most employees spend their time completing unimportant tasks for which they have been given firm schedules and deadlines. Efficient employees know how to ignore such demands and instead spend their time on projects that will yield big rewards for their employers if successful, even when such projects carry the risk of significant loss if unsuccessful.

Which one of the following is an example of efficiency as described above?

(A)   spending the entire afternoon working on a report that a supervisor has ordered completed by the following day
(B)   instead of working on a report that a supervisor has ordered completed by the following day, spending the entire afternoon completing routine correspondence that could be delayed
(C)   deciding to take an urgent call from a major customer instead of being punctual at a monthly sales meeting
(D)   meeting daily with other staff members to discuss workloads and schedules
(E)   spending time each morning scheduling tasks according to the most immediate deadlines

GO ON TO THE NEXT PAGE.

4. Child psychologist: Some studies in which children have been observed before and after playing video games with violent content have shown that young children tend to behave more aggressively immediately after playing the games. This suggests that the violence in such video games leads young children to believe that aggressive behavior is acceptable.

Each of the following, if true, strengthens the child psychologist's argument EXCEPT:

(A)   Young children tend to be more accepting of aggressive behavior in others immediately after playing video games with violent content.

(B)   Many young children who have never played video games with violent content believe that aggressive behavior is acceptable.

(C)   Other studies have shown no increase in aggressive behavior in young children who have just played nonviolent video games.

(D)   Older children are less likely before playing video games with violent content than they are afterwards to believe that aggressive behavior is acceptable.

(E)   Young children tend to behave more aggressively immediately after being told that aggressive behavior is acceptable than they did beforehand.

5. Letter to the editor: Middle-class families in wealthy nations are often criticized for the ecological damage resulting from their lifestyles. This criticism should not be taken too seriously, however, since its source is often a movie star or celebrity whose own lifestyle would, if widely adopted, destroy the environment and deplete our resources in a short time.

The reasoning in the letter to the editor is vulnerable to criticism in that it

(A)   criticizes a characteristic of the people giving an argument rather than criticizing the argument itself

(B)   takes failure to act consistently with a belief as an indication of the sincerity with which that belief is held

(C)   presumes that a viewpoint must be unreasonable to accept simply because some of the grounds advanced to support it do not adequately do so

(D)   fails to recognize that evidence advanced in support of a conclusion actually undermines that conclusion

(E)   generalizes about the behavior of all people on the basis of the behavior of a few

6. The cattle egret is a bird that lives around herds of cattle. The only available explanation of the fact that the cattle egret follows cattle herds is that the egrets consume the insects stirred up from the grasses as the cattle herds graze.

Which one of the following, if true, would most seriously undermine the claim that the explanation given above is the only available one?

(A)   Birds other than cattle egrets have been observed consuming insects stirred up by the movement of cattle.

(B)   Cattle egrets are known to follow other slow-moving animals, such as rhinoceroses and buffalo.

(C)   The presence of cattle dissuades many would-be predators of the cattle egret.

(D)   Cattle egrets are not generally known to live outside the range of large, slow-moving animals.

(E)   Forests are generally inhospitable to cattle egrets because of a lack of insects of the kind egrets can consume.

7. Any fruit that is infected is also rotten. No fruit that was inspected is infected. Therefore, any fruit that was inspected is safe to eat.

The conclusion of the argument follows logically if which one of the following is assumed?

(A)   It is not safe to eat any fruit that is rotten.
(B)   It is safe to eat any fruit that is not rotten.
(C)   It would have been safe to eat infected fruit if it had been inspected.
(D)   It is not safe to eat any fruit that is infected.
(E)   It is safe to eat any fruit that is uninfected.

8. 1990 editorial: Local pay phone calls have cost a quarter apiece ever since the 1970s, when a soft drink from a vending machine cost about the same. The price of a soft drink has more than doubled since, so phone companies should be allowed to raise the price of pay phone calls too.

Which one of the following, if true, most weakens the editorial's argument?

(A)   A pay phone typically cost less than a soft-drink machine in the 1970s.

(B)   Due to inflation, the prices of most goods more than doubled between the 1970s and 1990.

(C)   Government regulation of phone call prices did not become more stringent between the 1970s and 1990.

(D)   Between the 1970s and 1990 the cost of ingredients for soft drinks increased at a greater rate than the cost of telephone equipment.

(E)   Technological advances made telephone equipment more sophisticated between the 1970s and 1990.

GO ON TO THE NEXT PAGE.

9. Members of large-animal species must consume enormous amounts of food to survive. When climatic conditions in their environment deteriorate, such animals are often unable to find enough food. This fact helps make large-animal species more vulnerable to extinction than small-animal species, which can maintain greater populations on smaller amounts of food.

The statements above, if true, most support which one of the following?

(A) The maximum population size that an animal species could maintain on any given amount of food is the main factor determining whether that species will become extinct.

(B) The vulnerability of an animal species to extinction depends at least in part on how much food individuals of that species must consume to survive.

(C) When conditions deteriorate in a given environment, no small-animal species will become extinct unless some large-animal species also becomes extinct.

(D) Within any given species, the prospects for survival of any particular individual depend primarily on the amount of food that individual requires.

(E) Whenever climatic conditions in a given environment are bad enough to threaten large-animal species with extinction, small-animal species are able to find enough food to survive.

10. Megan: People pursue wealth beyond what their basic needs require only if they see it as a way of achieving high status or prestige.

Channen: Not everybody thinks that way. After all, money is the universal medium of exchange. So, if you have enough of it, you can exchange it for whatever other material goods you may need or want even if you are indifferent to what others think of you.

Megan and Channen disagree over whether

(A) people ever pursue wealth beyond what is required for their basic needs

(B) it is irrational to try to achieve high status or prestige in the eyes of one's society

(C) the pursuit of monetary wealth is irrational only when it has no further purpose

(D) it is rational to maximize one's ability to purchase whatever one wants only when the motive for doing so is something other than the desire for prestige

(E) the motive for pursuing wealth beyond what one's basic needs require is ever anything other than the desire for prestige or high status

11. Cholesterol, which is a known factor in coronary heart disease and stroke, needs a carrier, known as a lipoprotein, to transport it through the bloodstream. Low-density lipoproteins (LDLs) increase the risk of coronary heart disease and stroke, but we can tentatively conclude that high-density lipoproteins (HDLs) help prevent coronary heart disease and stroke. First, aerobic exercise increases one's level of HDLs. Second, HDL levels are higher in women than in men. And both aerobic exercise and being female are positively correlated with lower risk of coronary heart disease and stroke.

Each of the following, if true, strengthens the argument EXCEPT:

(A) HDLs, unlike LDLs, help the body excrete cholesterol.

(B) Persons who are overweight tend to have a higher risk of early death due to coronary heart disease and stroke, and tend to have low levels of HDLs.

(C) HDLs are less easily removed from the bloodstream than are LDLs.

(D) A high level of HDLs mitigates the increased health risks associated with LDLs.

(E) Men whose level of HDLs is equal to the average level for women have been found to have a lower risk of coronary heart disease and stroke than that of most men.

GO ON TO THE NEXT PAGE.

12. It is primarily by raising interest rates that central bankers curb inflation, but an increase in interest rates takes up to two years to affect inflation. Accordingly, central bankers usually try to raise interest rates before inflation becomes excessive, at which time inflation is not yet readily apparent either. But unless inflation is readily apparent, interest rate hikes generally will be perceived as needlessly restraining a growing economy. Thus, central bankers' success in temporarily restraining inflation may make it harder for them to ward off future inflation without incurring the public's wrath.

Which one of the following most accurately describes the role played in the argument by the claim that it is primarily by raising interest rates that central bankers curb inflation?

(A) It is presented as a complete explanation of the fact that central bankers' success in temporarily restraining inflation may make it harder for them to ward off future inflation without incurring the public's wrath.

(B) It is a description of a phenomenon for which the claim that an increase in interest rates takes up to two years to affect inflation is offered as an explanation.

(C) It is a premise offered in support of the conclusion that central bankers' success in temporarily restraining inflation may make it harder for them to ward off future inflation without incurring the public's wrath.

(D) It is a conclusion for which the statement that an increase in interest rates takes up to two years to affect inflation is offered as support.

(E) It is a premise offered in support of the conclusion that unless inflation is readily apparent, interest rate hikes generally will be perceived as needlessly restraining a growing economy.

13. A survey of clerical workers' attitudes toward their work identified a group of secretaries with very positive attitudes. They responded "Strongly agree" to such statements as "I enjoy word processing" and "I like learning new secretarial skills." These secretaries had been rated by their supervisors as excellent workers—far better than secretaries whose attitudes were identified as less positive. Clearly these secretaries' positive attitudes toward their work produced excellent job performance.

Which one of the following identifies a reasoning error in the argument?

(A) It attempts to prove a generalization about job performance by using the single example of clerical workers.

(B) It restates the claim that the secretaries' positive attitudes produced their excellent job performance instead of offering evidence for it.

(C) It does not consider the possibility that secretaries with very positive attitudes toward their work might also have had very positive attitudes toward other activities.

(D) It uses the term "positive attitudes" to mean two different things.

(E) It identifies the secretaries' positive attitudes as the cause of their excellent job performance although their attitudes might be an effect of their performance.

14. Scientist: A controversy in paleontology centers on the question of whether prehistoric human ancestors began to develop sophisticated tools before or after they came to stand upright. I argue that they stood upright first, simply because advanced toolmaking requires free use of the hands, and standing upright makes this possible.

Which one of the following statements, if true, most weakens the scientist's argument?

(A) Many animals that do not stand upright have learned to make basic tools.

(B) Advanced hunting weapons have been discovered among the artifacts belonging to prehistoric human ancestors who did not stand upright.

(C) Many prehistoric human ancestors who stood upright had no sophisticated tools.

(D) Those prehistoric human ancestors who first came to stand upright had no more dexterity with their hands than did those who did not stand upright.

(E) Many of the earliest sophisticated tools did not require their users to be able to stand upright.

GO ON TO THE NEXT PAGE.

15. The greater the number of people who regularly use a product, the greater the number whose health is potentially at risk due to that product. More people regularly use household maintenance products such as cleaning agents and lawn chemicals than regularly use prescription medicines. Therefore, it is even more important for such household products to be carefully tested to ensure their safety than it is for prescription medicines to be so tested.

Which one of the following principles, if valid, most helps to justify drawing the conclusion in the argument above?

(A) Whether or not it is important for a given product to be carefully tested depends mainly on the number of people who regularly use that product.

(B) It is very important for any product that is regularly used by a large number of people to be carefully tested to ensure its safety.

(C) The more people whose health might be at risk from the regular use of a particular product, the more important it is for that product to be carefully tested to ensure its safety.

(D) If one type of medicine must be taken in more frequent doses than another type of medicine, it is more important for the former to be carefully tested than for the latter.

(E) It is generally more important for a medicine than it is for a nonmedical product to be carefully tested to ensure its safety unless more people's health would be at risk from the nonmedical product than from the medicine.

16. Most successful entrepreneurs work at least 18 hours a day, and no one who works at least 18 hours a day has time for leisure activities. But all happy entrepreneurs have time for leisure activities.

If the statements above are true, each of the following could be true EXCEPT:

(A) Anyone who has no time for leisure activities works at least 18 hours a day.

(B) Some entrepreneurs who work at least 18 hours a day are successful.

(C) Some happy entrepreneurs are successful.

(D) Some entrepreneurs who work at least 18 hours a day are happy.

(E) Some successful entrepreneurs work less than 18 hours a day.

17. Human beings can exhibit complex, goal-oriented behavior without conscious awareness of what they are doing. Thus, merely establishing that nonhuman animals are intelligent will not establish that they have consciousness.

Which one of the following is an assumption on which the argument depends?

(A) Complex, goal-oriented behavior requires intelligence.

(B) The possession of consciousness does not imply the possession of intelligence.

(C) All forms of conscious behavior involve the exercise of intelligence.

(D) The possession of intelligence entails the possession of consciousness.

(E) Some intelligent human behavior is neither complex nor goal-oriented.

18. New Age philosopher: Nature evolves organically and nonlinearly. Furthermore, it can best be understood as a whole; its parts are so interconnected that none could exist without support from many others. Therefore, attaining the best possible understanding of nature requires an organic, holistic, nonlinear way of reasoning rather than the traditional linear reasoning of science, which proceeds through experiments on deliberately isolated parts of nature.

The reasoning in the New Age philosopher's argument is most vulnerable to criticism on the grounds that the argument

(A) takes for granted that if a statement must be true for the argument's conclusion to be true, then that statement's truth is sufficient for the truth of the conclusion

(B) overlooks the possibility that the overall structure of a phenomenon is not always identical to the overall structure of the reasoning that people do about that phenomenon

(C) fails to distinguish adequately between the characteristics of a phenomenon as a whole and those of the deliberately isolated parts of that phenomenon

(D) takes for granted that what is interconnected cannot, through abstraction, be thought of as separate

(E) takes for granted that a phenomenon that can best be understood as having certain properties can best be understood only through reasoning that shares those properties

GO ON TO THE NEXT PAGE.

19. Vanwilligan: Some have argued that professional
    athletes receive unfairly high salaries. But in
    an unrestricted free market, such as the market
    these athletes compete in, salaries are determined
    by what someone else is willing to pay for their
    services. These athletes make enormous profits for
    their teams' owners, and that is why owners are
    willing to pay them extraordinary salaries. Thus
    the salaries they receive are fair.

Vanwilligan's conclusion follows logically if which one
of the following is assumed?

(A)   The fairest economic system for a society is one
       in which the values of most goods and services
       are determined by the unrestricted free market.
(B)   If professional athletes were paid less for their
       services, then the teams for which they play
       would not make as much money.
(C)   The high level of competition in the marketplace
       forces the teams' owners to pay professional
       athletes high salaries.
(D)   Any salary that a team owner is willing to pay
       for the services of a professional athlete is a fair
       salary.
(E)   If a professional athlete's salary is fair, then that
       salary is determined by what an individual is
       willing to pay for the athlete's services in an
       unrestricted free market.

20. Environmentalist: Discarding old appliances
    can be dangerous: refrigerators contain
    chlorofluorocarbons; electronic circuit boards and
    cathode-ray tubes often contain heavy metals like
    lead; and old fluorescent bulbs contain mercury,
    another heavy metal. When landfills are operated
    properly, such materials pose no threat. However,
    when landfills are not operated properly, lead and
    mercury from them contaminate groundwater,
    for example. On the other hand, when trash is
    incinerated, heavy metals poison the ash and
    escape into the air.

The environmentalist's statements, if true, most strongly
support which one of the following inferences?

(A)   Old fluorescent bulbs should be recycled.
(B)   Appliances containing heavy metals should not
       be incinerated.
(C)   Chlorofluorocarbons are harmful to the
       atmosphere.
(D)   Newer appliances are more dangerous to the
       environment than older ones.
(E)   Appliances should be kept out of landfills.

21. Since the sweetness of sugared beverages makes athletes
    more likely to drink them, they can be helpful in avoiding
    dehydration. Furthermore, small amounts of sugar
    enhance the body's absorption of water and delay muscle
    fatigue by maintaining the body's glucose level. Still, one
    must use sugared beverages cautiously, for large amounts
    draw water from the blood to the stomach, thereby
    exacerbating the dehydration process.

If the statements above are true, then each of the
following could also be true EXCEPT:

(A)   Glucose is not the only type of sugar whose
       absence or scarcity in one's diet causes muscle
       fatigue.
(B)   Problems caused by dehydration are invariably
       exacerbated if substances that delay muscle
       fatigue are consumed.
(C)   Dehydrated athletes find beverages containing
       large amounts of sugar to be too sweet.
(D)   Some situations that exacerbate the problems
       caused by muscle fatigue do not exacerbate
       those caused by dehydration.
(E)   The rate at which the body absorbs water depends
       primarily on the amount of water already present
       in the blood.

22. A mathematical theorem proved by one mathematician
    should not be accepted until each step in its proof
    has been independently verified. Computer-assisted
    proofs generally proceed by conducting a vast number
    of calculations—surveying all the possible types of
    instances in which the theorem could apply and proving
    that the theorem holds for each type. In most computer-
    assisted proofs there are astronomically many types of
    instances to survey, and no human being could review
    every step in the proof. Hence, computer-assisted proofs
    involving astronomically many types of instances should
    not be accepted.

Which one of the following is an assumption on which
the argument relies?

(A)   The use of the computer to assist in the proof of
       mathematical theorems has greatly simplified
       the mathematician's task.
(B)   Most attempts to construct proofs of
       mathematical theorems do not result in
       demonstrations that the theorems are true.
(C)   Computers cannot be used to assist in generating
       proofs of mathematical theorems that involve
       only a very limited number of steps.
(D)   Any mathematical proof that does not rely on
       the computer cannot proceed by surveying
       all possible types of instances to which the
       candidate theorem might apply.
(E)   The use of an independent computer program
       does not satisfy the requirement for independent
       verification of each step in a proof that is
       extended enough to be otherwise unverifiable.

GO ON TO THE NEXT PAGE.

23. Commentator: Human behavior cannot be fully understood without inquiring into nonphysical aspects of persons. As evidence of this, I submit the following: suppose that we had a complete scientific account of the physical aspects of some particular human action—every neurological, physiological, and environmental event involved. Even with all that we would obviously still not truly comprehend the action or know why it occurred.

Which one of the following most accurately describes a flaw in the argument's reasoning?

(A) No support is offered for its conclusion other than an analogy that relates only superficially to the issue at hand.

(B) The purported evidence that it cites in support of its conclusion presumes that the conclusion is true.

(C) It concludes that a proposition must be true merely on the grounds that it has not been proven false.

(D) It fails to indicate whether the speaker is aware of any evidence that could undermine the conclusion.

(E) It presumes, without providing justification, that science can provide a complete account of any physical phenomenon.

24. Judicial punishment's power to deter people from committing crimes is a function of the severity of the penalty and the likelihood of one's actually receiving the penalty. Occasionally, juries decide that a crime's penalty is too severe and so refuse to convict a person they are convinced has committed that crime. Thus, increasing the penalty may decrease the deterrent power of judicial punishment.

The pattern of reasoning in which one of the following arguments is most similar to the pattern of reasoning in the argument above?

(A) Success in attaining one's first academic job depends on the quality of one's dissertation and the amount of time spent working on it in graduate school. But sometimes, so much time is spent on a dissertation that it becomes too lengthy to be coherent and its quality suffers. So spending more time working on a dissertation can lead to less success in attaining a first academic job.

(B) People who drive cars having many safety features are likely to drive more aggressively than do people who drive cars having few safety features. Thus, the people who drive the safest cars are likely to be the most dangerous drivers on the road.

(C) A new surgical technique is developed to treat a dangerous condition. This technique enables people to live longer than does an older form of surgery. But the new surgery's mortality rate is also slightly higher. Thus, if more people choose to undergo the new surgery, more people may die from the dangerous condition than previously.

(D) To be attractive to tourists, it is best for a city to have both wide appeal and sufficient hotel space. Though a sufficient number of hotel rooms alone cannot attract tourists, it is much harder for city governments to affect the appeal of their city than for them to affect its amount of hotel space. Thus, governments of cities that want to increase their attractiveness to tourists should put their energies into increasing their hotel space.

(E) Many young, talented artists, because they are unknown, decide to charge low prices for their work. As their reputations grow, the prices they can charge for their work increase. Thus, raising the price of an artist's work can improve that artist's reputation.

GO ON TO THE NEXT PAGE.

25. Cecile's association requires public disclosure of an officer's investments in two cases only: when an officer is authorized to disburse association funds, and when an officer sits on the board of a petrochemical company. Cecile, an officer who is not authorized to disburse funds, sits on the board of just one company, a small timber business. Therefore, there is no reason for Cecile to publicly disclose her investments at this time.

The conclusion of the argument follows logically if which one of the following is assumed?

(A) Cecile will not be appointed to a position in the association that authorizes her to disburse funds.
(B) Cecile's office and her position on the timber business's board create no conflicts of interest.
(C) The association's requirements provide the only reasons there might be for Cecile to disclose her investments.
(D) The timber business on whose board Cecile sits is owned by a petrochemical company.
(E) Cecile owns no investments in the petrochemical industry.

26. The obesity invariably associated with some high-fat diets is caused by an absence in these diets of certain nutrients that are necessary for an active metabolism, not by excessive caloric intake. Hence, people on these high-fat diets do not consume too many calories.

The questionable pattern of reasoning in the argument above is most similar to that in which one of the following?

(A) Electrical storms are strongly correlated with precipitous drops in barometric pressure. So, electrical storms are caused by such drops in pressure, rather than by air turbulence.
(B) The impression that most viewers of sports programming are beer drinkers is due not to mere stereotyping but to the vast number of beer commercials broadcast during televised sports. Hence, most beer drinkers are avid fans of sports programs.
(C) The disorientation observed in airline pilots after transoceanic flights is caused not by sleep deprivation but by disruption in their exposure to daylight. Hence, transoceanic pilots do not suffer from sleep deprivation.
(D) Stock market crashes are due, not to panic in the face of predicted economic downturns, but to mere rumormongering without any basis in fact. Hence, economic downturns cannot be accurately predicted.
(E) The preponderance of mathematics graduates among professional computer programmers is due not to the intelligence of mathematicians but to the appropriateness of mathematical training for computer programming. Hence, most computer programmers have mathematical training.

S T O P
IF YOU FINISH BEFORE TIME IS CALLED, YOU MAY CHECK YOUR WORK ON THIS SECTION ONLY.
DO NOT WORK ON ANY OTHER SECTION IN THE TEST.

SECTION III
Time—35 minutes
27 Questions

Directions: Each set of questions in this section is based on a single passage or a pair of passages. The questions are to be answered on the basis of what is <u>stated</u> or <u>implied</u> in the passage or pair of passages. For some of the questions, more than one of the choices could conceivably answer the question. However, you are to choose the <u>best</u> answer; that is, the response that most accurately and completely answers the question, and blacken the corresponding space on your answer sheet.

The use of computer-generated visual displays in courtrooms is growing as awareness of their ability to recreate crime scenes spreads. Displays currently in use range from still pictures in series that mimic
(5) simple movement to sophisticated simulations based on complex applications of rules of physics and mathematics. By making it possible to slow or stop action, to vary visual perspectives according to witnesses' vantage points, or to highlight or enlarge
(10) images, computer displays provide litigators with tremendous explanatory advantages. Soon, litigators may even have available graphic systems capable of simulating three dimensions, thus creating the illusion that viewers are at the scene of a crime or accident,
(15) directly experiencing its occurrence. The advantages of computer-generated displays derive from the greater psychological impact they have on juries as compared to purely verbal presentations; studies show that people generally retain about 85 percent of visual
(20) information but only 10 percent of aural information. This is especially valuable in complex or technical trials, where juror interest and comprehension are generally low. In addition, computers also allow litigators to integrate graphic aids seamlessly into
(25) their presentations.

Despite these benefits, however, some critics are urging caution in the use of these displays, pointing to a concomitant potential for abuse or unintentional misuse, such as the unfair manipulation of a juror's
(30) impression of an event. These critics argue further that the persuasive and richly communicative nature of the displays can mesmerize jurors and cause them to relax their normal critical faculties. This potential for distortion is compounded when one side in a trial
(35) does not use the technology—often because of the considerable expense involved—leaving the jury susceptible to prejudice in favor of the side employing computer displays. And aside from the risk of intentional manipulation of images or deceitful use
(40) of capacities such as stop-action and highlighting, there is also the possibility that computer displays can be inherently misleading. As an amalgamation of data collection, judgment, and speculation, the displays may in some instances constitute evidence unsuitable
(45) for use in a trial.

To avoid misuse of this technology in the courtroom, practical steps must be taken. First, counsel must be alert to the ever-present danger of its misuse; diligent analyses of the data that form the
(50) basis for computer displays should be routinely

performed and disclosed. Judges, who have the discretion to disallow displays that might unfairly prejudice one side, must also be vigilant in assessing the displays they do allow. Similarly, judges should
(55) forewarn jurors of the potentially biased nature of computer-generated evidence. Finally, steps should be taken to ensure that if one side utilizes computer technology, the opposing side will also have access to it. Granting financial aid in these circumstances
(60) would help create a more equitable legal arena in this respect.

1. Which one of the following most accurately states the main point of the passage?

(A) Those involved in court trials that take advantage of computer-generated displays as evidence need to take steps to prevent the misuse of this evidence.

(B) The use of computer-generated displays has grown dramatically in recent years because computer aids allow litigators to convey complex information more clearly.

(C) The persuasive nature of computer-generated displays requires that the rules governing the use of these displays be based on the most sophisticated principles of jurisprudence.

(D) Litigators' prudent use of computer-generated displays will result in heightened jury comprehension of complex legal issues and thus fairer trials.

(E) Any disadvantages of computer-generated visual displays can be eliminated by enacting a number of practical procedures to avoid their intentional misuse.

GO ON TO THE NEXT PAGE.

2. Which one of the following most accurately describes the organization of the passage?

   (A)   The popularity of a new technology is lamented; criticisms of the technology are voiced; corrective actions to stem its use are recommended.

   (B)   A new technology is endorsed; specific examples of its advantages are offered; ways to take further advantage of the technology are presented.

   (C)   A new technology is presented as problematic; specific problems associated with its use are discussed; alternative uses of the technology are proposed.

   (D)   A new technology is introduced as useful; potential problems associated with its use are identified; recommendations for preventing these problems are offered.

   (E)   A new technology is described in detail; arguments for and against its use are voiced; recommendations for promoting the widespread use of the technology are advanced.

3. As described in the passage, re-creating an accident with a computer-generated display is most similar to which one of the following?

   (A)   using several of a crime suspect's statements together to suggest that the suspect had a motive

   (B)   using an author's original manuscript to correct printing errors in the current edition of her novel

   (C)   using information gathered from satellite images to predict the development of a thunderstorm

   (D)   using a video camera to gather opinions of passersby for use in a candidate's political campaign advertisements

   (E)   using detailed geological evidence to design a museum exhibit depicting a recent volcanic eruption

4. Based on the passage, with which one of the following statements regarding the use of computer displays in courtroom proceedings would the author be most likely to agree?

   (A)   The courts should suspend the use of stop-action and highlighting techniques until an adequate financial aid program has been established.

   (B)   Computer-generated evidence should be scrutinized to ensure that it does not rely on excessive speculation in depicting the details of an event.

   (C)   Actual static photographs of a crime scene are generally more effective as displays than are computer displays.

   (D)   Verbal accounts by eyewitnesses to crimes should play a more vital role in the presentation of evidence than should computer displays.

   (E)   Computer displays based on insufficient or inaccurate input of data would not seem realistic and would generally not persuade jurors effectively.

5. The author states which one of the following about computer displays used in trial proceedings?

   (A)   Despite appearances, computer displays offer few practical advantages over conventional forms of evidence.

   (B)   Most critics of computer-generated evidence argue for banning such evidence in legal proceedings.

   (C)   Judges should forewarn jurors of the potentially biased nature of computer-generated displays.

   (D)   Computer displays are used primarily in technical trials, in which jury interest is naturally low.

   (E)   Litigators who utilize computer-generated displays must ensure that the opposing side has equal access to such technology.

6. The author mentions each of the following as an advantage of using computer displays in courtroom proceedings EXCEPT:

   (A)   They enable litigators to slow or stop action.

   (B)   They can aid jurors in understanding complex or technical information.

   (C)   They make it possible to vary visual perspectives.

   (D)   They allow litigators to integrate visual materials smoothly into their presentations.

   (E)   They prevent litigators from engaging in certain kinds of unjustified speculation.

GO ON TO THE NEXT PAGE.

Through the last half century, the techniques used by certain historians of African art for judging the precise tribal origins of African sculptures on the basis of style have been greatly refined. However, as (5) one recent critic of the historians' classificatory assumptions has put it, the idea that the distribution of a particular style is necessarily limited to the area populated by one tribe may be "a dreadful oversimplification … a decided falsification of the (10) very life of art in Africa."

Objects and styles have often been diffused through trade, most notably by workshops of artists who sell their work over a large geographical area. Styles cannot be narrowly defined as belonging (15) uniquely to a particular area; rather, there are important "centers of style" throughout Africa where families, clans, and workshops produce sculpture and other art that is dispersed over a large, multitribal geographical area. Thus, a family of artists belonging (20) to a single ethnic group may produce sculpture on commission for several neighboring tribes. While this practice contributes to a marked uniformity of styles across a large area, the commissioned works must nevertheless be done to some extent in the style of (25) the tribe commissioning the work. This leads to much confusion on the part of those art historians who attempt to assign particular objects to individual groups on the basis of style.

One such center of style is located in the village (30) of Ouri, in central Burkina Faso, where members of the Konaté family continue a long tradition of sculpture production not only for five major neighboring ethnic groups, but in recent times also for the tourist trade in Ouagadougou. The Konaté (35) sculptors are able to distinguish the characteristics of the five styles in which they carve, and will point to the foliate patterns that radiate from the eyes of a Nuna mask, or the diamond-shaped mouth of many Ko masks, as characteristics of a particular tribal style (40) that must be included to satisfy their clients. Nevertheless, their work is consistent in its proportions, composition, color, and technique. In fact, although the Konaté sculptors can identify the styles they carve, the characteristic patterns are so (45) subtly different that few people outside of the area can distinguish Nuna masks from Ko masks.

Perhaps historians of African art should ask if objects in similar styles were produced in centers of style, where artists belonging to one ethnic group (50) produced art for all of their neighbors. Perhaps it is even more important to cease attempting to break down large regional styles into finer and finer tribal styles and substyles, and to recognize that artists in Africa often do not produce work only in their own (55) narrowly defined ethnic contexts. As the case of the Konaté sculptors makes clear, one cannot readily tell which group produced an object by analyzing fine style characteristics.

7. Which one of the following titles most completely and accurately describes the contents of the passage?

(A) *African Centers of Style: Their Implications for Art Historians' Classifications of African Art*
(B) *African Art Redefined: The Impact of the Commercialization of Sculpture and the Tourist Demand on Style*
(C) *Characteristics of African Sculpture: Proportion, Composition, Color, and Technique*
(D) *Style Versus Technique: The Case Against Historians of African Art*
(E) *Konaté Sculptors: Pioneers of the African Art Trade*

8. Based on the passage, the art historians mentioned in line 2 would be most likely to agree with which one of the following statements?

(A) Understanding the nature of centers of style is a key to better classification of African art.
(B) Similarities among African masks can be due to standard techniques used in carving the eyes and mouths of the masks.
(C) Some subtly distinguished substyles should not be distinguished from large regional styles.
(D) It is a fairly recent practice for African mask sculptors to produce masks for tribes of which they are not members.
(E) The tribal origin of African sculptures is important to their classification.

9. According to the passage, which one of the following is a feature that Konaté sculptors can identify as a requirement of a particular tribal style?

(A) horizontal incisions
(B) eye position
(C) top attachments
(D) bottom decorations
(E) mouth shape

10. The author's primary purpose in the passage is to

(A) classify a set of artistic styles according to a newly proposed set of principles
(B) provide evidence that the elements of a particular group of artistic works have been misclassified
(C) explain the principles used by a group of historians to classify certain kinds of artistic works
(D) reveal the underlying assumptions of a traditional approach to the classification of certain kinds of artistic works
(E) argue that a particular approach to classifying certain kinds of artistic works is mistaken

GO ON TO THE NEXT PAGE.

11. The passage provides the most support for which one of the following inferences?

(A) Some of the sculptures that the Konaté family produces are practically indistinguishable from those produced by certain other sculptors far from Burkina Faso.

(B) The carving styles used by some members of the Konaté family are distinctly different from those used by other members.

(C) Other families of sculptors in Burkina Faso collaborate with the Konaté family in producing masks.

(D) The Konaté family produces masks for some African ethnic groups other than the Nuna and Ko groups.

(E) The village of Ouri where the Konaté family produces sculptures is the oldest center of style in Burkina Faso.

12. Which one of the following does the author attribute to the Konaté sculptors?

(A) use of nontraditional materials in sculptures

(B) production of sculptures in several distinct styles that are nevertheless very similar to one another

(C) stylistic innovations that have influenced the work of other sculptors in a large geographical area

(D) adoption of a carving style that was previously used only by members of a different tribe

(E) introduction of the practice of producing sculptures for neighboring groups

13. Which one of the following most accurately expresses what the author means by "centers of style" (line 16)?

(A) geographical areas in which masks and similar sculptures are for the most part interchangeable among a number of closely connected tribes who use them

(B) locations in which works of art are produced by sculptors using a particular style who then instruct other artists throughout large surrounding geographical areas

(C) locations in which stylistically consistent but subtly varied works of art are produced and distributed to ethnically varied surrounding areas

(D) large geographical areas throughout which the various tribes produce works of art that differ subtly along ethnic lines but are so similar that they are very difficult for outside observers to distinguish from one another

(E) locations in which sculptures and similar works of art are traditionally produced by a diverse community of artists who migrate in from various tribes of surrounding areas

GO ON TO THE NEXT PAGE.

Surviving sources of information about women doctors in ancient Greece and Rome are fragmentary: some passing mentions by classical authors, scattered references in medical works, and about 40

(5) inscriptions on tombs and monuments. Yet even from these fragments we can piece together a picture. The evidence shows that in ancient Greece and Rome there were, in fact, female medical personnel who were the ancient equivalent of what we now call

(10) medical doctors. So the history of women in medicine by no means begins in 1849 with Dr. Elizabeth Blackwell, the first woman to earn an M.D. in modern times, or even in 1321 with Francesca de Romana's licensure to practice general medicine, the

(15) earliest known officially recorded occurrence of this sort.

The very nature of the scant evidence tells us something. There is no list of women doctors in antiquity, no direct comment on the fact that there

(20) were such people. Instead, the scattering of references to them indicates that, although their numbers were probably small, women doctors were an unremarkable part of ancient life. For example, in *The Republic* (421 B.C.), the earliest known source attesting to the

(25) existence of women doctors in Greece, Plato argues that, for the good of the state, jobs should be assigned to people on the basis of natural aptitude, regardless of gender. To support his argument he offers the example that some women, as well as some

(30) men, are skilled in medicine, while others are not. Here, Plato is not trying to convince people that there ought to be women doctors. Rather, he is arguing for an ideal distribution of roles within the state by pointing to something that everyone could already

(35) see—that there were female doctors as well as male.

Moreover, despite evidence that some of these women doctors treated mainly female patients, their practice was clearly not limited to midwifery. Both Greek and Latin have distinct terms for midwife and

(40) doctor, and important texts and inscriptions refer to female practitioners as the latter. Other references provide evidence of a broad scope of practice for women doctors. The epitaph for one named Domnina reads: "You delivered your homeland from disease."

(45) A tribute to another describes her as "savior of all through her knowledge of medicine."

Also pointing to a wider medical practice are the references in various classical medical works to a great number of women's writings on medical

(50) subjects. Here, too, the very nature of the evidence tells us something, for Galen, Pliny the elder, and other ancient writers of encyclopedic medical works quote the opinions and prescriptions of male and female doctors indiscriminately, moving from one to

(55) the other and back again. As with the male doctors they cite, these works usually simply give excerpts from the female authority's writing without biographical information or special comment.

14. Which one of the following most accurately states the main point of the passage?

(A) There is a range of textual evidence indicating that the existence and professional activity of women doctors were an accepted part of everyday life in ancient Greece and Rome.

(B) Some scholars in ancient Greece and Rome made little distinction in their writings between learned women and learned men, as can especially be seen in those scholars' references to medical experts and practitioners.

(C) Although surviving ancient Greek and Roman texts about women doctors contain little biographical or technical data, important inferences can be drawn from the very fact that those texts pointedly comment on the existence of such doctors.

(D) Ancient texts indicate that various women doctors in Greece and Rome were not only practitioners but also researchers who contributed substantially to the development of medical science.

(E) Scholars who have argued that women did not practice medicine until relatively recently are mistaken, insofar as they have misinterpreted textual evidence from ancient Greece and Rome.

15. Which one of the following does the author mention in the passage?

(A) diseases that were not curable in ancient times but are readily cured by modern medicine

(B) a specialized field of medicine that was not practiced by women in ancient Greece and Rome

(C) a scholar who has argued that Francesca de Romana was the first female doctor in any Western society

(D) the extent to which medical doctors in ancient Greece and Rome were trained and educated

(E) ancient writers whose works refer explicitly to the writings of women

GO ON TO THE NEXT PAGE.

16. The primary function of the third paragraph of the passage is to

   (A) provide additional support for the argument presented in the first paragraph
   (B) suggest that the implications of the argument presented in the first paragraph are unnecessarily broad
   (C) acknowledge some exceptions to a conclusion defended in the second paragraph
   (D) emphasize the historical importance of the arguments presented in the first two paragraphs
   (E) describe the sources of evidence that are cited in the first two paragraphs in support of the author's main conclusion

17. Which one of the following could most logically be appended to the end of the final paragraph?

   (A) So it is only by combining the previously mentioned fragments of ancient writings that historians have been able to construct a fairly complete account of some of these women's lives.
   (B) That there were women doctors apparently seemed unremarkable to these writers who cited their works, just as it did to Plato.
   (C) Although the content of each of these excerpts is of limited informative value, the very range of topics that they cover suggests that Plato's claims about women doctors should be reevaluated.
   (D) These texts indicate that during a certain period of ancient Greek and Roman history there were female medical scholars, but it is unclear whether at that time there were also female medical practitioners.
   (E) Nevertheless, these writers' evenhanded treatment of male and female medical researchers must be interpreted partly in light of the conflicting picture of ancient medical practice that emerges from the fragmentary earlier writings.

18. Which one of the following most accurately describes the author's attitude toward the sources of information mentioned in lines 1–5?

   (A) wary that they might be misinterpreted due to their fragmentary nature
   (B) optimistic that with a more complete analysis they will yield answers to some crucial lingering questions
   (C) hopeful that they will come to be accepted generally by historians as authentic documents
   (D) confident that they are accurate enough to allow for reliable factual inferences
   (E) convinced of their appropriateness as test cases for the application of a new historical research methodology

19. The tribute quoted in lines 45–46 is offered primarily as evidence that at least some women doctors in ancient times were

   (A) acknowledged as authorities by other doctors
   (B) highly educated
   (C) very effective at treating illness
   (D) engaged in general medical practice
   (E) praised as highly as male doctors

20. The passage most strongly supports which one of the following inferences about women in ancient Greece and Rome?

   (A) Those who became doctors usually practiced medicine for only a short time.
   (B) Those who were not doctors were typically expected to practice medicine informally within their own families.
   (C) There is no known official record that any of them were licensed to practice general medicine.
   (D) There is no reliable evidence that any of them who practiced general medicine also worked as a midwife.
   (E) Some of those who practiced medicine were posthumously honored for nonmedical civic accomplishments.

GO ON TO THE NEXT PAGE.

Every culture that has adopted the cultivation of maize—also known as corn—has been radically changed by it. This crop reshaped the cultures of the Native Americans who first cultivated it, leading to
(5) such developments as the adoption of agrarian and in some cases urban lifestyles, and much of the explosion of European populations after the fifteenth century was driven by the introduction of maize together with another crop from the Americas,
(10) potatoes. The primary reason for this plant's profound influence is its sheer productivity. With maize, ancient agriculturalists could produce far more food per acre than with any other crop, and early Central Americans recognized and valued this characteristic
(15) of the plant. But why are maize and a few similar crops so much more bountiful than others? Modern biochemistry has revealed the physical mechanism underlying maize's impressive productivity.

To obtain the hydrogen they use in the production
(20) of carbohydrates through photosynthesis, all plants split water into its constituent elements, hydrogen and oxygen. They use the resultant hydrogen to form one of the molecules they need for energy, but the oxygen is released into the atmosphere. During
(25) photosynthesis, carbon dioxide that the plant takes in from the atmosphere is used to build sugars within the plant. An enzyme, rubisco, assists in the sugar-forming chemical reaction. Because of its importance in photosynthesis, rubisco is arguably the most
(30) significant enzyme in the world. Unfortunately, though, when the concentration of oxygen relative to carbon dioxide in a leaf rises to a certain level, as can happen in the presence of many common atmospheric conditions, oxygen begins to bind competitively to the enzyme,
(35) thus interfering with the photosynthetic reaction.

Some plants, however, have evolved a photosynthetic mechanism that prevents oxygen from impairing photosynthesis. These plants separate the places where they split water atoms into hydrogen
(40) and oxygen from the places where they build sugars from carbon dioxide. Water molecules are split, as in all plants, in specialized chlorophyll-containing structures in the green leaf cells, but the rubisco is sequestered within airtight tissues in the center of the
(45) leaf. The key to the process is that in these plants, oxygen and all other atmospheric gases are excluded from the cells containing rubisco. These cells, called the bundle sheath cells, surround the vascular structures of the leaf—structures that function
(50) analogously to human blood vessels. Carbon dioxide, which cannot enter these cells as a gas, first undergoes a series of reactions to form an intermediary, nongas molecule named C-4 for the four carbon atoms it contains. This molecule enters
(55) the bundle sheath cells and there undergoes reactions that release the carbon dioxide that will fuel the production of carbohydrates (e.g., sugars). Taking its name from the intermediary molecule, the entire process is called C-4 photosynthesis. Such C-4 plants
(60) as sugar cane, rice, and maize are among the world's most productive crops.

21. Which one of the following most accurately states the main point of the passage?

(A) The greater productivity of maize, as compared with many other crops, is due to its C-4 photosynthetic process, in which the reactions that build sugars are protected from the effects of excess oxygen.

(B) Because of their ability to produce greater quantities and higher qualities of nutrients, those plants, including maize, that use a C-4 photosynthetic process have helped to shape the development of many human cultures.

(C) C-4 photosynthesis, which occurs in maize, involves a complex sequence of chemical reactions that makes more efficient use of available atmospheric hydrogen than do photosynthetic reactions in non-C-4 plants.

(D) The presence of the enzyme rubisco is a key factor in the ability of C-4 plants, including maize, to circumvent the negative effects of gases such as oxygen on the production of sugars in photosynthesis.

(E) Some of the world's most productive crop plants, including maize, have evolved complex, effective mechanisms to prevent atmospheric gases that could bind competitively to rubisco from entering the plants' leaves.

22. Which one of the following most accurately describes the organization of the material presented in the second and third paragraphs of the passage?

(A) The author suggests that the widespread cultivation of a particular crop is due to its high yield, explains its high yield by describing the action of a particular enzyme in that crop, and then outlines the reasons for the evolution of that enzyme.

(B) The author explains some aspects of a biochemical process, describes a naturally occurring hindrance to that process, and then describes an evolutionary solution to that hindrance in order to explain the productivity of a particular crop.

(C) The author describes a problem inherent in certain biochemical processes, scientifically explains two ways in which organisms solve that problem, and then explains the evolutionary basis for one of those solutions.

(D) The author describes a widespread cultural phenomenon involving certain uses of a type of plant, explains the biochemical basis of the phenomenon, and then points out that certain other plants may be used for similar purposes.

(E) The author introduces a natural process, describes the biochemical reaction that is widely held to be the mechanism underlying the process, and then argues for an alternate evolutionary explanation of that process.

GO ON TO THE NEXT PAGE.

23. Assuming that all other relevant factors remained the same, which one of the following, if it developed in a species of plant that does not have C-4 photosynthesis, would most likely give that species an advantage similar to that which the author attributes to C-4 plants?

    (A) Water is split into its constituent elements in specialized chlorophyll-containing structures in the bundle sheath cells.

    (B) An enzyme with which oxygen cannot bind performs the role of rubisco.

    (C) The vascular structures of the leaf become impermeable to both carbon dioxide gas and oxygen gas.

    (D) The specialized chlorophyll-containing structures in which water is split surround the vascular structures of the leaf.

    (E) An enzyme that does not readily react with carbon dioxide performs the role of rubisco in the green leaf cells.

24. The author's reference to "all other atmospheric gases" in line 46 plays which one of the following roles in the passage?

    (A) It indicates why certain atmospheric conditions can cause excess oxygen to build up and thus hinder photosynthesis in non-C-4 plants as described in the previous paragraph.

    (B) It supports the claim advanced earlier in the paragraph that oxygen is not the only atmospheric gas whose presence in the leaf can interfere with photosynthesis.

    (C) It supports the conclusion that non-C-4 photosynthesis makes use of several atmospheric gases that C-4 photosynthesis does not use.

    (D) It explains why carbon dioxide molecules undergo the transformations described later in the paragraph before participating in photosynthesis in C-4 plants.

    (E) It advances a broader claim that oxygen levels remain constant in C-4 plants in spite of changes in atmospheric conditions.

25. The passage contains information sufficient to justify inferring which one of the following?

    (A) In rice plants, atmospheric gases are prevented from entering the structures in which water is split into its constituent elements.

    (B) In rice plants, oxygen produced from split water molecules binds to another type of molecule before being released into the atmosphere.

    (C) Rice is an extremely productive crop that nourishes large segments of the world's population and is cultivated by various widely separated cultures.

    (D) In rice plants, rubisco is isolated in the bundle sheath cells that surround the vascular structures of the leaves.

    (E) Although rice is similar to maize in productivity and nutritive value, maize is the more widely cultivated crop.

26. The author of the passage would be most likely to agree with which one of the following statements?

    (A) Maize's impressive productivity cannot be understood without an understanding of its cultural influences.

    (B) Maize is an example of a plant in which oxygen is not released as a by-product of photosynthesis.

    (C) Maize's high yields are due not only to its use of C-4 but also to its ability to produce large quantities of rubisco.

    (D) Until maize was introduced to Europeans by Native Americans, European populations lacked the agricultural techniques required for the cultivation of C-4 plants.

    (E) Maize's C-4 photosynthesis is an example of an effective evolutionary adaptation that has come to benefit humans.

27. The passage provides the most support for which one of the following statements?

    (A) In many plants, rubisco is not isolated in airtight tissues in the center of the leaf.

    (B) A rubisco molecule contains four carbon atoms.

    (C) Rubisco is needed in photosynthesis to convert carbon dioxide to a nongas molecule.

    (D) In maize, rubisco helps protect against the detrimental effects of oxygen buildup in the leaves.

    (E) Rubisco's role in the C-4 process is optimized when oxygen levels are high relative to carbon dioxide levels.

STOP
IF YOU FINISH BEFORE TIME IS CALLED, YOU MAY CHECK YOUR WORK ON THIS SECTION ONLY.
DO NOT WORK ON ANY OTHER SECTION IN THE TEST.

SECTION IV
Time—35 minutes
25 Questions

Directions: The questions in this section are based on the reasoning contained in brief statements or passages. For some questions, more than one of the choices could conceivably answer the question. However, you are to choose the best answer; that is, the response that most accurately and completely answers the question. You should not make assumptions that are by commonsense standards implausible, superfluous, or incompatible with the passage. After you have chosen the best answer, blacken the corresponding space on your answer sheet.

1. Editorial: Clearly, during the past two years, the unemployment situation in our city has been improving. Studies show that the number of unemployed people who are actively looking for jobs has steadily decreased during that period.

The editorial's reasoning is most vulnerable to criticism on the grounds that it

(A) presumes, without providing justification, that the government is at least partly responsible for the improvement in the employment situation

(B) relies on data from a period that is too short to justify an inference about a general trend

(C) fails to take into account the possibility that many unemployed workers who still desire jobs may have stopped looking for jobs

(D) fails to take into account that the sorts of governmental efforts that reduce unemployment may not be effective in creating more high-paying jobs

(E) ignores other economic indicators, which may not have improved during the past two years

2. Eating garlic reduces the levels of cholesterol and triglycerides in the blood and so helps reduce the risk of cardiovascular disease. Evidence that eating garlic reduces these levels is that a group of patients taking a garlic tablet each day for four months showed a 12 percent reduction in cholesterol and a 17 percent reduction in triglycerides; over the same period, a group of similar patients taking a medically inert tablet showed only a 2 percent reduction in triglycerides and a 3 percent reduction in cholesterol.

It would be most important to determine which one of the following in evaluating the argument?

(A) whether the garlic tablets are readily available to the public

(B) what the diets of the two groups were during the period

(C) what effect taking the garlic tablets each day for a period of less than four months had on the levels of cholesterol and triglycerides

(D) whether large amounts of garlic are well tolerated by all patients

(E) whether the manufacturer of the garlic tablets cites the study in its advertising

3. Educator: If there is a crisis in education today, it is one of maintaining quality. People love to reduce serious learning to degrees and certificates. But one also can obtain these credentials by plodding through courses without ever learning much of value. When that happens, the credentials one receives are almost meaningless.

If the educator's statements are true, then which one of the following must be true?

(A) Increasingly, institutions are granting meaningless degrees and certificates.

(B) It has become easier for students to complete their coursework without learning anything of importance.

(C) Educational institutions should cease to grant degrees and certificates.

(D) Degrees and certificates do not guarantee that a person has acquired much worthwhile knowledge.

(E) A person benefits from an education only to the extent that he or she invests effort in it.

GO ON TO THE NEXT PAGE.

4. Essayist: Politicians deserve protection from a prying press. No one wants his or her private life spread across the pages of the newspapers. Furthermore, the press's continual focus on politicians' private lives dissuades talented people from pursuing a career in politics and turns reporters into character cops who walk their beats looking for minute and inconsequential personality flaws in public servants. It is time to put a halt to this trivial journalism.

Each of the following, if true, strengthens the essayist's argument EXCEPT:

(A) The press is unusually inaccurate when it reports on people's private lives.

(B) Reporting on politicians' private lives distracts voters from more important issues in a campaign.

(C) Much writing on politicians' private lives consists of rumors circulated by opposing candidates.

(D) In recent elections, the best local politicians have refused to run for national office because of the intrusiveness of press coverage.

(E) Politicians' personality flaws often ultimately affect their performance on the job.

5. Most veterinarians, and especially those at university veterinary research centers, have a devoted interest in the biological sciences. But most veterinarians choose their profession primarily because they love animals. Among persons who are seriously interested in biological science but lack any special love for animals, one does not find any prominent veterinarians.

If all of the statements above are true, which one of the following CANNOT be true?

(A) Some veterinarians have a greater love for biological science than for individual animals.

(B) Most veterinarians love animals and have an interest in biological science.

(C) Prominent veterinarians at some veterinary research centers are intensely devoted to the biological sciences but do not feel any pronounced affection for animals.

(D) Few veterinarians at university research centers chose their profession primarily because they love animals.

(E) Most veterinarians who are not prominent regard an understanding of the biological sciences as the most important quality for success in their profession.

6. The simultaneous and apparently independent development in several ancient cultures of a myth of creatures who were half human and half horse parallels the increased use of horses in these cultures. But despite the nobility and gentleness traditionally ascribed to the horse, the mythical half-horse, half-humans were frequently portrayed as violent and savage. Many human cultures use myth to express unconscious thoughts, so these mythical creatures obviously reflect people's unconscious fear of the horse.

The reasoning in the argument is flawed because the argument

(A) fails to show that the mythical creature mentioned represents the horse in people's minds

(B) fails to consider that people might have good reason to fear horses

(C) confuses the expression of unconscious thoughts with the suppression of them

(D) fails to demonstrate that the myth was not borrowed from one of the cultures by the others

(E) fails to explain why people use myth for the expression of unconscious thoughts

7. Editorialist: There would seem to be little hazard for consumers associated with chemicals used in treated lumber because the lumber is used outside where fumes cannot accumulate. However, immediate steps should be taken to determine the safety of these chemicals since consumers could ingest them. If the lumber is used for children's playground equipment, youngsters could put their mouths on the wood, and if it is used to contain soil in a vegetable garden, the chemicals could leach into the soil.

Which one of the following most accurately expresses the main conclusion of the editorialist's argument?

(A) The chemicals used in treated lumber are apparently not dangerous to the consumer.

(B) Treated lumber is as dangerous when used outdoors as it is when used indoors.

(C) The effects on humans from the chemicals in treated lumber should be studied.

(D) Parents should not allow children to put their mouths on playground equipment.

(E) Treated lumber is more dangerous than was once believed.

GO ON TO THE NEXT PAGE.

8. One good clue as to which geographical regions an ancient relic was moved through in the past involves the analysis of pollen that clings to the surface of the relic. A relic is linked to a geographical area by the identification of pollen from plants that are known to have been unique to that area.

Which one of the following, if true, casts the most doubt on the reliability of the method described above?

(A) Pollens are often transported from one region to another by wind or human movement.

(B) There are several less complicated methods of determining the history of the movement of an object than the analysis and identification of pollen.

(C) Many types of pollen were common to several geographical regions in the ancient world.

(D) Data are scarce as to the geographical distribution of the pollens of many ancient plants.

(E) Pollen analysis is a painstaking process that is also expensive to conduct.

9. Executive: In order to add to our profits, I was planning to promote and distribute herbal tinctures. However, some members of my advisory staff questioned the medical efficacy of such products. So I have consulted a variety of reliable medical publications, and these likewise claim that herbal tinctures are ineffective. Therefore, I must conclude that marketing such products would not produce the result I intended.

The executive's reasoning most closely conforms to which one of the following generalizations?

(A) To be reliable, a medical publication that evaluates consumer products must include at least some independent evidence.

(B) If a majority of reliable sources conclude that a particular substance is medically ineffective, then that substance almost certainly is medically ineffective.

(C) Consulting reliable publications is not, by itself, a reliable basis for determining whether or not the promotion of a new line of products will be profitable.

(D) It would not be profitable to promote and distribute a new line of products if these products have adverse medical effects.

(E) The promotion and distribution of a new line of products will not prove profitable if a number of reliable authorities declare them to be ineffective.

10. To be great, an artwork must express a deep emotion, such as sorrow or love. But an artwork cannot express an emotion that the artwork's creator is incapable of experiencing.

Which one of the following can be properly inferred from the statements above?

(A) A computer can create an artwork that expresses sorrow or love only if it has actually experienced such an emotion.

(B) The greatest art is produced by those who have experienced the deepest emotions.

(C) An artwork that expresses a deep emotion of its creator is a great artwork.

(D) As long as computers are constructed so as to be incapable of experiencing emotions they will not create great artworks.

(E) Only artworks that succeed in expressing deep emotions are the products of great artists.

11. Consumer activist: When antilock brakes were first introduced, it was claimed that they would significantly reduce the incidence of multiple-car collisions, thereby saving lives. Indeed, antilock brakes have reduced the incidence of multiple-car collisions. I maintain, however, that to save lives, automobile manufacturers ought to stop equipping cars with them.

Which one of the following, if true, most helps to resolve the apparent conflict in the consumer activist's statements?

(A) Drivers and passengers in automobiles with antilock brakes feel less vulnerable, and are thus less likely to wear seat belts.

(B) Under some circumstances, automobiles with traditional brakes stop just as quickly as do automobiles with antilock brakes.

(C) For inexperienced drivers, antilock brakes are easier to use correctly than are traditional brakes.

(D) Antilock brakes are considerably more expensive to manufacture than are traditional brakes.

(E) Antilock brakes are no more effective in preventing multiple-car accidents than in preventing other kinds of traffic accidents.

GO ON TO THE NEXT PAGE.

12. Politician: The huge amounts of money earned by oil companies elicit the suspicion that the regulations designed to prevent collusion need to be tightened. But just the opposite is true. If the regulations designed to prevent collusion are not excessively burdensome, then oil companies will make profits sufficient to motivate the very risky investments associated with exploration that must be made if society is to have adequate oil supplies. But recent data show that the oil industry's profits are not the highest among all industries. Clearly, the regulatory burden on oil companies has become excessive.

The reasoning in the politician's argument is most vulnerable to criticism on the grounds that the argument

(A) fails to justify its presumption that profits sufficient to motivate very risky investments must be the highest among all industries

(B) attacks the character of the oil companies rather than the substance of their conduct

(C) fails to justify its presumption that two events that are correlated must also be causally related

(D) treats the absence of evidence that the oil industry has the highest profits among all industries as proof that the oil industry does not have the highest profits among all industries

(E) illicitly draws a general conclusion from a specific example that there is reason to think is atypical

13. It is due to a misunderstanding that most modern sculpture is monochromatic. When ancient sculptures were exhumed years ago, they were discovered to be uncolored. No one at the time had reason to believe, as we now do, that the sculptures had originally been colorfully painted, but that centuries of exposure to moisture washed away the paint.

Which one of the following is an assumption on which the argument depends?

(A) The natural beauty of the materials out of which modern sculptures are made plays a part in their effect.

(B) Modern sculpture has been influenced by beliefs about ancient sculpture.

(C) Ancient sculptures were more susceptible to moisture damage than are modern sculptures.

(D) Some ancient paintings known to early archaeologists depicted sculptures.

(E) As modern sculptors come to believe that ancient sculpture was painted, they will begin to create polychromatic works.

14. In older commercial airplanes, the design of the control panel allows any changes in flight controls made by one member of the flight crew to be immediately viewed by the other crew members. In recently manufactured aircraft, however, a crew member's flight control changes are harder to observe, thereby eliminating a routine means for performing valuable cross-checks. As a result, the flight crews operating recently manufactured airplanes must inform each other verbally about flight control changes much more frequently.

The statements above, if true, most strongly support which one of the following?

(A) How frequently an airplane's flight crew members will inform each other verbally about flight control changes depends in large part on how long it takes to perform those changes.

(B) In recently manufactured aircraft, the most valuable means available for performing cross-checks involves frequent verbal exchanges of information among the flight crew members.

(C) In older commercial airplanes, in contrast to recently manufactured airplanes, flight crew members have no need to exchange information verbally about flight control changes.

(D) The flight crew members operating a recently manufactured airplane cannot observe the flight control changes made by other crew members by viewing the control panel.

(E) How often flight crew members must share information verbally about flight control changes depends in part on what other means for performing cross-checks are available to the crew.

GO ON TO THE NEXT PAGE.

15. According to the proposed Factory Safety Act, a company may operate an automobile factory only if that factory is registered as a class B factory. In addressing whether a factory may postpone its safety inspections, this Act also stipulates that no factory can be class B without punctual inspections. Thus, under the Factory Safety Act, a factory that manufactures automobiles would not be able to postpone its safety inspections.

The argument proceeds by

(A) pointing out how two provisions of the proposed Factory Safety Act jointly entail the unacceptability of a certain state of affairs

(B) considering two possible interpretations of a proposed legal regulation and eliminating the less plausible one

(C) showing that the terms of the proposed Factory Safety Act are incompatible with existing legislation

(D) showing that two different provisions of the proposed Factory Safety Act conflict and thus cannot apply to a particular situation

(E) pointing out that if a provision applies in a specific situation, it must apply in any analogous situation

16. There is a difference between beauty and truth. After all, if there were no difference, then the most realistic pieces of art would be the best as well, since the most realistic pieces are the most truthful. But many of the most realistic artworks are not among the best.

Which one of the following is an assumption required by the argument?

(A) The most beautiful artworks are the best artworks.

(B) If an artwork contains nonrealistic elements, then it is not at all truthful.

(C) None of the best artworks are realistic.

(D) Only the best artworks are beautiful.

(E) An artwork's beauty is inherently subjective and depends on who is viewing it.

17. From the fact that people who studied music as children frequently are quite proficient at mathematics, it cannot be concluded that the skills required for mathematics are acquired by studying music: it is equally likely that proficiency in mathematics and studying music are both the result of growing up in a family that encourages its children to excel at all intellectual and artistic endeavors.

The pattern of reasoning in which one of the following arguments is most parallel to that in the argument above?

(A) Although children who fail to pay attention tend to perform poorly in school, it should not necessarily be thought that their poor performance is caused by their failure to pay attention, for it is always possible that their failure to pay attention is due to undiagnosed hearing problems that can also lead to poor performance in school.

(B) People who attend a university in a foreign country are usually among the top students from their native country. It would therefore be wrong to conclude from the fact that many foreign students perform better academically than others in this country that secondary schools in other countries are superior to those in this country; it may be that evaluation standards are different.

(C) People whose diet includes relatively large quantities of certain fruits and vegetables have a slightly lower than average incidence of heart disease. But it would be premature to conclude that consuming these fruits and vegetables prevents heart disease, for this correlation may be merely coincidental.

(D) Those who apply to medical school are required to study biology and chemistry. It would be a mistake, however, to conclude that those who have mastered chemistry and biology will succeed as physicians, for the practical application of knowledge is different from its acquisition.

(E) Those who engage in vigorous exercise tend to be very healthy. But it would be silly to conclude that vigorous exercise is healthful simply because people who are healthy exercise vigorously, since it is possible that exercise that is less vigorous also has beneficial results.

GO ON TO THE NEXT PAGE.

18. A physician has a duty to see to the health and best medical interests of the patient. On the other hand, the patient has a right to be fully informed about any negative findings concerning the patient's health. When this duty conflicts with this right, the right should prevail since it is a basic right. Anything else carries the risk of treating the patient as a mere object, not as a person.

The conclusion drawn above follows logically if which one of the following is assumed?

(A)   All persons have a right to accept or reject any medical procedures proposed by a physician.
(B)   Some actions are right independently of the consequences that might ensue.
(C)   Because only persons have rights, objects do not have rights.
(D)   A person's basic rights should never be violated.
(E)   In medicine, the patient's basic right to information is stronger than most other rights.

19. Forester: The great majority of the forests remaining in the world are only sickly fragments of the fully functioning ecosystems they once were. These fragmented forest ecosystems have typically lost their ability to sustain themselves in the long term, yet they include the last refuges for some of the world's most endangered species. To maintain its full complement of plant and animal species, a fragmented forest requires regular interventions by resource managers.

The forester's statements, if true, most strongly support which one of the following?

(A)   Most of the world's forests will lose at least some of their plant or animal species if no one intervenes.
(B)   Unless resource managers regularly intervene in most of the world's remaining forests, many of the world's most endangered species will not survive.
(C)   A fragmented forest ecosystem cannot sustain itself in the long term if it loses any of its plant or animal species.
(D)   A complete, fully functioning forest ecosystem can always maintain its full complement of plant and animal species even without interventions by resource managers.
(E)   At present, resource managers intervene regularly in only some of the world's fragmented forest ecosystems.

20. Magazine article: Sugar consumption may exacerbate attention deficit disorder (ADD) in children. A recent study found that children produce large amounts of adrenaline within hours after consuming large amounts of sugar. This increase in adrenaline is especially noticeable if the source of sugar is candy, in which case the sugar's effects are not ameliorated by the ingestion of other foodstuffs.

Which one of the following is an assumption on which the argument in the magazine article depends?

(A)   The adrenaline level of children who do not have ADD is not increased by excessive sugar consumption.
(B)   Overproduction of adrenaline causes ADD in children.
(C)   The most effective way to treat ADD in children is to restrict their intake of sugars.
(D)   Increased adrenaline production can make ADD more severe in children.
(E)   Sugar consumed with food substances other than candy does not substantially increase the level of adrenaline in the bloodstream of children with ADD.

GO ON TO THE NEXT PAGE.

21. Ethicist: People who avoid alcoholic beverages simply
       because they regard them as a luxury beyond their
       financial means should not be praised for their
       abstinence. Similarly, those who avoid alcohol
       simply because they lack the desire to partake
       should not be praised, unless this disinclination
       has somehow resulted from an arduous process
       of disciplining oneself to refrain from acting
       indiscriminately on one's desires.

Which one of the following principles, if valid, most
helps to justify the ethicist's claims?

   (A)   Whether behavior should be regarded as
          praiseworthy is a function of both its
          consequences and the social context in which
          the agent acts.
   (B)   A person should be blamed for an action only
          if that action was not motivated by a desire
          to be virtuous or if the person did not have to
          overcome any obstacles in order to perform that
          action.
   (C)   A person is praiseworthy for a particular behavior
          only if, in order to adopt that behavior, the
          person at some point had to overcome a desire
          to do something that she or he felt able to afford
          to do.
   (D)   The extent to which the process of acquiring self-
          discipline is arduous for a person is affected by
          that person's set of desires and aversions.
   (E)   The apportionment of praise and blame should be
          commensurate with the arduousness or ease of
          the lives of those who receive praise or blame.

22. Economist: Some people argue that when large countries
       split into several small countries, the world
       economy is harmed by increased barriers to
       free trade in the form of an increased number of
       national tariffs. But small countries do not think
       of themselves as economically self-sufficient.
       Therefore, such division of large countries does
       not increase barriers to free trade.

Which one of the following, if assumed, enables the
economist's conclusion to be properly drawn?

   (A)   A country has the right to split into smaller
          countries even if some of the economic
          consequences of division would harm the world
          economy.
   (B)   Increasing the number of countries in the world
          would strengthen rather than weaken the world
          economy.
   (C)   All countries that impose national tariffs or other
          barriers to free trade think of themselves as
          economically self-sufficient.
   (D)   There is strong evidence that national tariffs
          and other barriers to free trade harm the world
          economy.
   (E)   Large countries tend to be more economically
          self-sufficient than small countries.

23. Counselor: Constantly comparing oneself to those
       one sees as more able or more successful
       almost invariably leads to self-disparagement.
       Conversely, constantly comparing oneself to those
       one sees as less able or less successful almost
       invariably leads to being dismissive of others.
       So, those who for the most part refrain from
       comparing themselves to others will most likely
       be, on the whole, self-accepting and accepting of
       others.

The counselor's reasoning is most vulnerable to criticism
because it

   (A)   overlooks the possibility that one can compare
          oneself both to those one perceives to be more
          able and more successful than oneself and to
          those one perceives to be less able and less
          successful than oneself
   (B)   overlooks the possibility that constantly
          comparing oneself to others may have beneficial
          effects that those who refrain from making such
          comparisons are deprived of
   (C)   takes for granted that if one is both dismissive of
          others and self-disparaging, one will not be self-
          accepting and accepting of others
   (D)   overlooks the possibility that self-disparagement
          and being dismissive of others can result from
          something other than comparing oneself to
          others
   (E)   takes for granted that whenever one compares
          oneself to others one sees them as more
          successful and more able than oneself or less
          successful and less able than oneself

GO ON TO THE NEXT PAGE.

24. Most of the employees of the Compujack Corporation are computer programmers. Since most computer programmers receive excellent salaries from their employers, at least one Compujack employee must receive an excellent salary from Compujack.

Which one of the following arguments exhibits a flawed pattern of reasoning most similar to the flawed pattern of reasoning exhibited by the argument above?

(A) Most gardeners are people with a great deal of patience. Since most of Molly's classmates are gardeners, at least one of Molly's classmates must be a person with a great deal of patience.

(B) Most of Molly's classmates are gardeners. Since most gardeners are people with a great deal of patience, some of Molly's classmates could be people with a great deal of patience.

(C) Most gardeners are people with a great deal of patience. Since most of Molly's classmates are gardeners, at least one of Molly's classmates who is a gardener must be a person with a great deal of patience.

(D) Most gardeners are people with a great deal of patience. Since most of Molly's classmates who garden are women, at least one female classmate of Molly's must be a person with a great deal of patience.

(E) Most of Molly's classmates are gardeners with a great deal of patience. Since most of Molly's classmates are women, at least one female classmate of Molly's must be a gardener with a great deal of patience.

25. A study conducted over a 6-month period analyzed daily attendance and average length of visit at the local art museum. The results showed that when the museum was not featuring a special exhibition, attendance tended to be lower but patrons spent an average of 45 minutes longer in the museum than when it was featuring a special exhibition.

Each of the following, if true, could help to explain the differing average lengths of visits to the museum EXCEPT:

(A) Visitors to the museum during special exhibitions tend to have narrower artistic interests, and do not view as many different exhibits during their visit.

(B) A plan to extend normal museum hours during special exhibitions was considered but not enacted during the period studied.

(C) Many people who go to special exhibitions go simply for the prestige of having been there.

(D) Admission tickets to the special exhibitions at the museum are issued for a specific 1-hour period on a specific day.

(E) Many people who go to special exhibitions are on organized tours and do not have the opportunity to browse.

STOP
IF YOU FINISH BEFORE TIME IS CALLED, YOU MAY CHECK YOUR WORK ON THIS SECTION ONLY.
DO NOT WORK ON ANY OTHER SECTION IN THE TEST.

ACKNOWLEDGMENTS

Acknowledgment is made to the following sources from which material has been adapted for use in this test booklet:

Michael J. Balick, *Plants, People, and Culture: The Science of Ethnobotany.* ©1996 by Scientific American Library.

Declan O'Flaherty, "Computer-Generated Displays in the Courtroom: For Better or Worse?" ©1996 by Declan O'Flaherty.

Holt N. Parker, "Women Doctors in Greece, Rome, and the Byzantine Empire." ©1997-2000 by The University Press of Kentucky.

Christopher D. Roy, *Art and Life in Africa: Selections from the Stanley Collection, Exhibitions of 1985 and 1992.* ©1992 by the University of Iowa Museum of Art.

"Shooting at Inflation." ©1996 by The Economist Newspaper Limited.

Wait for the supervisor's instructions before you open the page to the topic.
Please print and sign your name and write the date in the designated spaces below.

Time: 35 Minutes

General Directions

You will have 35 minutes in which to plan and write an essay on the topic inside. Read the topic and the accompanying directions carefully. You will probably find it best to spend a few minutes considering the topic and organizing your thoughts before you begin writing. In your essay, be sure to develop your ideas fully, leaving time, if possible, to review what you have written. **Do not write on a topic other than the one specified. Writing on a topic of your own choice is not acceptable.**

No special knowledge is required or expected for this writing exercise. Law schools are interested in the reasoning, clarity, organization, language usage, and writing mechanics displayed in your essay. How well you write is more important than how much you write.

Confine your essay to the blocked, lined area on the front and back of the separate Writing Sample Response Sheet. Only that area will be reproduced for law schools. Be sure that your writing is legible.

Both this topic sheet and your response sheet must be turned over to the testing staff before you leave the room.

Topic Code	Print Your Full Name Here		
	Last	First	M.I.

Date	Sign Your Name Here
/ /	

LSAT® Writing Sample Topic

Directions: The scenario presented below describes two choices, either one of which can be supported on the basis of the information given. Your essay should consider both choices and argue for one over the other, based on the two specified criteria and the facts provided. There is no "right" or "wrong" choice: a reasonable argument can be made for either.

Curtaincall Theater in the town of Middleburg must choose one of two plays—a familiar classic drama or an original modern comedy—to inaugurate its first season. Write an essay in which you argue for one choice over the other, keeping in mind the following two criteria:

- Curtaincall seeks to establish a reputation for innovation and experimentation.
- To survive financially, Curtaincall needs to attract large local audiences.

The drama, if selected, would be staged by director Joanna Muller, who is famous for her experimental treatments of plays that are rarely presented in innovative, experimental ways. Choosing the drama would represent a bold move for Curtaincall, since most Middleburg theatergoers claim to have conventional tastes in theater. The costumes and stage sets of Muller's productions are invariably elaborate and strikingly unusual, often drawing people who come more for the costumes and sets than for the play itself. Although Muller has staged no plays recently, many of her previous productions attracted large audiences in major cities and won praise both from critics with conventional tastes and those who prefer theatrical innovation and experimentation. Muller says she will work with a large cast of local but relatively unknown actors.

Curtaincall's other option, the comedy, would be directed by Tim Williams, the work's playwright. Williams has won both popular and critical acclaim not only for his theater works but also for his action-movie screenplays, which critics have praised for their "breathtakingly experimental approach" to a genre that is sometimes regarded as mired in conventions. Williams would give several lectures about his film work while in town to direct the comedy. Choosing Williams's comedy would entail some risk for Curtaincall, as Williams insists on using a bare stage, minimal props, and only three actors for twelve different roles—an unusual and fairly experimental strategy for a comedy that, according to Williams, is thoroughly conventional in its plot and character development. Two of the actors slated for the play have performed in local productions of Williams's plays that received high critical praise in Middleburg's press. The Curtaincall production would be the play's world premiere.

Scratch Paper
Do not write your essay in this space.

LAST NAME (Print)

L

FIRST NAME (Print)

LAST 4 DIGITS OF SOCIAL SECURITY/SOCIAL INSURANCE NO.

MI

TEST CENTER NO.

SIGNATURE

M M D D Y Y
TEST DATE

LSAC ACCOUNT NO.

TOPIC CODE

Writing Sample Response Sheet

DO NOT WRITE IN THIS SPACE

**Begin your essay in the lined area below.
Continue on the back if you need more space.**

COMPUTING YOUR SCORE

Directions:

1. Use the Answer Key on the next page to check your answers.

2. Use the Scoring Worksheet below to compute your raw score.

3. Use the Score Conversion Chart to convert your raw score into the 120-180 scale.

Scoring Worksheet

1. Enter the number of questions you answered correctly in each section.

    Number Correct

    SECTION I .... _____
    SECTION II .... _____
    SECTION III .... _____
    SECTION IV.............. _____

2. Enter the sum here: _____

    This is your Raw Score.

Conversion Chart
For Converting Raw Score to the 120-180 LSAT Scaled Score
LSAT Form 7LSN72

Reported Score	Raw Score Lowest	Raw Score Highest
180	99	100
179	98	98
178	97	97
177	96	96
176	—*	—*
175	95	95
174	94	94
173	93	93
172	92	92
171	91	91
170	90	90
169	89	89
168	88	88
167	87	87
166	85	86
165	84	84
164	82	83
163	81	81
162	79	80
161	78	78
160	76	77
159	74	75
158	73	73
157	71	72
156	69	70
155	67	68
154	65	66
153	63	64
152	62	62
151	60	61
150	58	59
149	56	57
148	54	55
147	52	53
146	51	51
145	49	50
144	47	48
143	45	46
142	43	44
141	42	42
140	40	41
139	38	39
138	37	37
137	35	36
136	34	34
135	32	33
134	31	31
133	29	30
132	28	28
131	27	27
130	25	26
129	24	24
128	23	23
127	22	22
126	20	21
125	19	19
124	18	18
123	—*	—*
122	17	17
121	16	16
120	0	15

*There is no raw score that will produce this scaled score for this form.

ANSWER KEY

SECTION I

1.	E	8.	B	15.	A	22.	C
2.	D	9.	B	16.	D		
3.	A	10.	E	17.	E		
4.	B	11.	B	18.	B		
5.	D	12.	E	19.	E		
6.	E	13.	A	20.	B		
7.	D	14.	C	21.	D		

SECTION II

1.	D	8.	D	15.	C	22.	E
2.	E	9.	B	16.	D	23.	B
3.	C	10.	E	17.	A	24.	A
4.	B	11.	C	18.	E	25.	C
5.	A	12.	C	19.	D	26.	C
6.	C	13.	E	20.	B		
7.	E	14.	B	21.	B		

SECTION III

1.	A	8.	E	15.	E	22.	B
2.	D	9.	E	16.	A	23.	B
3.	E	10.	E	17.	B	24.	D
4.	B	11.	D	18.	D	25.	D
5.	C	12.	B	19.	D	26.	E
6.	E	13.	C	20.	C	27.	A
7.	A	14.	A	21.	A		

SECTION IV

1.	C	8.	A	15.	A	22.	C
2.	B	9.	E	16.	A	23.	D
3.	D	10.	D	17.	A	24.	A
4.	E	11.	A	18.	D	25.	B
5.	C	12.	A	19.	A		
6.	A	13.	B	20.	D		
7.	C	14.	E	21.	C		

PREPTEST 50
SEPTEMBER 2006
FORM 6LSN70

SECTION I
Time—35 minutes
28 Questions

Directions: Each set of questions in this section is based on a single passage or a pair of passages. The questions are to be answered on the basis of what is stated or implied in the passage or pair of passages. For some of the questions, more than one of the choices could conceivably answer the question. However, you are to choose the best answer; that is, the response that most accurately and completely answers the question, and blacken the corresponding space on your answer sheet.

One of the most prominent characteristics of the literature by United States citizens of Mexican descent is that it is frequently written in a combination of English and Spanish. By not limiting
(5) itself to one language, such writing resonates with its authors' bicultural experiences. Their work is largely Mexican in its sensibility, its traditions, and its myths, but its immediate geographical setting is the United States. And though Mexican American literature is
(10) solidly grounded in Mexican culture, it distinguishes itself from Mexican literature in its content and concerns.

Many Mexican Americans are only a generation away from the mostly agrarian culture of their
(15) ancestors, and the work of most Mexican American writers shows evidence of heavy influence from this culture. Their novels are often simple in structure, and some of the common themes in these novels include the struggle to overcome the agricultural
(20) adversity that caused their families to emigrate, and a feeling of being distanced from the traditions of rural Mexico and yet striving to hold on to them. These themes coexist with ever-present images of the land, which symbolizes the values of the characters'
(25) culture, such as the spiritual and religious benefits of working the land.

Much of Mexican writing, on the other hand, has been criticized for being dominated by the prominent literary establishment concentrated in Mexico City.
(30) Literary reputation and success in Mexico—including the attainment of publicly sponsored positions in the arts—are often bestowed or denied by this literary establishment. Moreover, the work of Mexican writers is often longer in form and marked by greater
(35) cosmopolitanism and interest in theoretical ideas and arguments than is Mexican American writing. Not surprisingly, the Mexican literary community views Mexican American literature as a variety of "regional" writing. But the apparent simplicity of
(40) what this community sees as parochial concerns belies the thematic richness of Mexican American writing.

The work of Mexican American writers can be richly textured in its complex mixture of concerns;
(45) among other things, their work is distinguished by an overarching concern with the complexities of cultural transition. Many Mexican American writers assert that rather than working to be absorbed into U.S. society, they are engaged in the process of creating a new
(50) identity. Physically distanced from Mexico and yet convinced of its importance, these writers depict a new reality by creating "in-between" characters. These characters inhabit a social and cultural milieu which is neither that of Mexico nor that of the U.S.
(55) And while this new setting reflects the contemporary social realities of both Mexico and the U.S., it also derives a great deal of emotional power from an evocation of a romanticized memory of Mexico. What results is an intermediate cultural borderland in
(60) which nostalgia and reality are combined in the service of forging a new identity.

1. Which one of the following most accurately states the main point of the passage?

(A) Mexican American literature is characterized by a strong sense of transition, which is due to its writers' physical distance from Mexico and their clear vision of the future of Mexican culture.

(B) Unlike Mexican writing, which is largely tied to an urban literary establishment, Mexican American writing is a movement that attempts through its works to develop a literary voice for agrarian workers.

(C) The work of Mexican American writers reflects Mexican Americans' bicultural experiences, both in its close links with the culture of rural Mexico and in its striving to develop a new identity out of elements of Mexican culture and U.S. culture.

(D) Mexican American literature, although unique in its content and concerns as well as in its stylistic innovations, has not yet achieved the prominence and reputation of Mexican literature.

(E) Many Mexican Americans are only a generation away from the culture of their ancestors and because of this, Mexican American literature is distinguished by the presence of powerful spiritual images, which are an organic part of the Mexican American agrarian culture.

GO ON TO THE NEXT PAGE.

2. It can most reasonably be inferred from the passage that the author would agree with which one of the following statements?

(A) While Mexican American writers are in the process of shaping their body of literature, one of their goals is to create a literary establishment in the U.S. essentially like the one concentrated in Mexico City.

(B) The use of a mixture of both Spanish and English in current Mexican American literature is evidence of a brief transitional period.

(C) The use of a romanticized Mexico in Mexican American literature is offensive to writers of the literary establishment of Mexico City, who find the images to be caricatures of their culture.

(D) Mexican American literature is noteworthy more for its thematic content than for its narrative structure.

(E) Mexican American writers are concerned that the importance of Mexico, currently central to their culture, will be diminished, and that Mexican American literature will be impoverished as a result.

3. It can most reasonably be inferred from the passage that many Mexican American writers tend to value which one of the following?

(A) stylistic innovations that distinguish their work from that of Mexican writers

(B) recognition from a U.S. literary establishment that is significantly different from that of Mexico

(C) an identity that resists absorption by U.S. culture

(D) critical acceptance of bilingual forms of literary expression

(E) the ability to express in their literature a more complex fabric of concerns than is found in most U.S. literature

4. To which one of the following questions does the passage most clearly provide an answer?

(A) What is an example of a specific literary work by a Mexican American writer?

(B) For what reason are many Mexican American writings concerned with agrarian themes or topics?

(C) What is the prevailing view of Mexican American literature among critics in the United States?

(D) How has the literature of the United States influenced Mexican American writers?

(E) Are the works of Mexican American writers written more in Spanish or in English?

5. It can most reasonably be inferred from the passage that the author holds which one of the following views?

(A) Mexican American literature advocates an agrarian way of life as a remedy for the alienation of modern culture.

(B) The Mexican American "in-between" character is an instance of a type found in the literature of immigrant groups in general.

(C) A predominant strength of Mexican American writers is that they are not tied to a major literary establishment and so are free to experiment in a way many Mexican writers are not.

(D) Writers of "regional" literature find it more difficult to attain reputation and success in Mexico than writers whose work is concerned with more urban themes.

(E) History has an importance in Mexican American culture that it does not have in Mexican culture because Mexican Americans have attached greater importance to their ancestry.

GO ON TO THE NEXT PAGE.

In many Western societies, modern bankruptcy laws have undergone a shift away from a focus on punishment and toward a focus on bankruptcy as a remedy for individuals and corporations in financial

(5) trouble—and, perhaps unexpectedly, for their creditors. This shift has coincided with an ever-increasing reliance on declarations of bankruptcy by individuals and corporations with excessive debt, a trend that has drawn widespread criticism. However,

(10) any measure seeking to make bankruptcy protection less available would run the risk of preventing continued economic activity of financially troubled individuals and institutions. It is for this reason that the temptation to return to a focus on punishment of

(15) individuals or corporations that become insolvent must be resisted. Modern bankruptcy laws, in serving the needs of an interdependent society, serve the varied interests of the greatest number of citizens.

The harsh punishment for insolvency in centuries

(20) past included imprisonment of individuals and dissolution of enterprises, and reflected societies' beliefs that the accumulation of excessive debt resulted either from debtors' unwillingness to meet obligations or from their negligence. Insolvent debtors

(25) were thought to be breaking sacrosanct social contracts; placing debtors in prison was considered necessary in order to remove from society those who would violate such contracts and thereby defraud creditors. But creditors derive little benefit from

(30) imprisoned debtors unable to repay even a portion of their debt. And if the entity to be punished is a large enterprise, for example, an auto manufacturer, its dissolution would cause significant unemployment and the disruption of much-needed services.

(35) Modern bankruptcy law has attempted to address the shortcomings of the punitive approach. Two beliefs underlie this shift: that the public good ought to be paramount in considering the financial insolvency of individuals and corporations; and that

(40) the public good is better served by allowing debt-heavy corporations to continue to operate, and indebted individuals to continue to earn wages, than by disabling insolvent economic entities. The mechanism for executing these goals is usually a

(45) court-directed reorganization of debtors' obligations to creditors. Such reorganizations typically comprise debt relief and plans for court-directed transfers of certain assets from debtor to creditor. Certain strictures connected to bankruptcy—such as the fact

(50) that bankruptcies become matters of public record and are reported to credit bureaus for a number of years—may still serve a punitive function, but not by denying absolution of debts or financial reorganization. Through these mechanisms, today's

(55) bankruptcy laws are designed primarily to assure continued engagement in productive economic activity, with the ultimate goal of restoring businesses and individuals to a degree of economic health and providing creditors with the best hope of collecting.

6. Which one of the following most accurately expresses the main point of the passage?

(A) The modern trend in bankruptcy law away from punishment and toward the maintenance of economic activity serves the best interests of society and should not be abandoned.

(B) Bankruptcy laws have evolved in order to meet the needs of creditors, who depend on the continued productive activity of private citizens and profit-making enterprises.

(C) Modern bankruptcy laws are justified on humanitarian grounds, even though the earlier punitive approach was more economically efficient.

(D) Punishment for debt no longer holds deterrent value for debtors and is therefore a concept that has been largely abandoned as ineffective.

(E) Greater economic interdependence has triggered the formation of bankruptcy laws that reflect a convergence of the interests of debtors and creditors.

7. In stating that bankruptcy laws have evolved "perhaps unexpectedly" (line 5) as a remedy for creditors, the author implies that creditors

(A) are often surprised to receive compensation in bankruptcy courts

(B) have unintentionally become the chief beneficiaries of bankruptcy laws

(C) were a consideration, though not a primary one, in the formulation of bankruptcy laws

(D) are better served than is immediately apparent by laws designed in the first instance to provide a remedy for debtors

(E) were themselves active in the formulation of modern bankruptcy laws

8. The author's attitude toward the evolution of bankruptcy law can most accurately be described as

(A) approval of changes that have been made to inefficient laws

(B) confidence that further changes to today's laws will be unnecessary

(C) neutrality toward laws that, while helpful to many, remain open to abuse

(D) skepticism regarding the possibility of solutions to the problem of insolvency

(E) concern that inefficient laws may have been replaced by legislation too lenient to debtors

GO ON TO THE NEXT PAGE.

9. The primary purpose of the passage is to

(A)   offer a critique of both past and present approaches to insolvency

(B)   compare the practices of bankruptcy courts of the past with those of bankruptcy courts of the present

(C)   criticize those who would change the bankruptcy laws of today

(D)   reexamine today's bankruptcy laws in an effort to point to further improvements

(E)   explain and defend contemporary bankruptcy laws

10. Which one of the following claims would a defender of the punitive theory of bankruptcy legislation be most likely to have made?

(A)   Debt that has become so great that repayment is impossible is ultimately a moral failing and thus a matter for which the law should provide punitive sanctions.

(B)   Because insolvency ultimately harms the entire economy, the law should provide a punitive deterrent to insolvency.

(C)   The insolvency of companies or individuals is tolerable if the debt is the result of risk-taking, profit-seeking ventures that might create considerable economic growth in the long run.

(D)   The dissolution of a large enterprise is costly to the economy as a whole and should not be allowed, even when that enterprise's insolvency is the result of its own fiscal irresponsibility.

(E)   The employees of a large bankrupt enterprise should be considered just as negligent as the owner of a bankrupt sole proprietorship.

11. Which one of the following sentences could most logically be appended to the end of the last paragraph of the passage?

(A)   Only when today's bankruptcy laws are ultimately seen as inadequate on a large scale will bankruptcy legislation return to its original intent.

(B)   Punishment is no longer the primary goal of bankruptcy law, even if some of its side effects still function punitively.

(C)   Since leniency serves the public interest in bankruptcy law, it is likely to do so in criminal law as well.

(D)   Future bankruptcy legislation could include punitive measures, but only if such measures ultimately benefit creditors.

(E)   Today's bankruptcy laws place the burden of insolvency squarely on the shoulders of creditors, in marked contrast to the antiquated laws that weighed heavily on debtors.

12. The information in the passage most strongly suggests which one of the following about changes in bankruptcy laws?

(A)   Bankruptcy laws always result from gradual changes in philosophy followed by sudden shifts in policy.

(B)   Changes in bankruptcy law were initiated by the courts and only grudgingly adopted by legislators.

(C)   The adjustment of bankruptcy laws away from a punitive focus was at first bitterly opposed by creditors.

(D)   Bankruptcy laws underwent change because the traditional approach proved inadequate and contrary to the needs of society.

(E)   The shift away from a punitive approach to insolvency was part of a more general trend in society toward rehabilitation and away from retribution.

13. Which one of the following, if true, would most weaken the author's argument against harsh punishment for debtors?

(A)   Extensive study of the economic and legal history of many countries has shown that most individuals who served prison time for bankruptcy subsequently exhibited greater economic responsibility.

(B)   The bankruptcy of a certain large company has had a significant negative impact on the local economy even though virtually all of the affected employees were able to obtain similar jobs within the community.

(C)   Once imprisonment was no longer a consequence of insolvency, bankruptcy filings increased dramatically, then leveled off before increasing again during the 1930s.

(D)   The court-ordered liquidation of a large and insolvent company's assets threw hundreds of people out of work, but the local economy nevertheless demonstrated robust growth in the immediate aftermath.

(E)   Countries that continue to imprison debtors enjoy greater economic health than do comparable countries that have ceased to do so.

GO ON TO THE NEXT PAGE.

As the twentieth century draws to a close, we are learning to see the extent to which accounts and definitions of cultures are influenced by human biases and purposes, benevolent in what they include,
(5) incorporate, and validate, less so in what they exclude and demote. A number of recent studies have argued that the anxieties and agendas of the present exert an extraordinary influence on the national identities we construct from the cultural past. For example, Greek
(10) civilization was known originally to have had roots in Egyptian and various other African and Eastern cultures, but some current scholars charge that its identity was revised during the course of the nineteenth century to support an image of European
(15) cultural dominance—its African and other cultural influences either actively purged or hidden from view by European scholars. Because ancient Greek writers themselves openly acknowledged their culture's hybrid past, nineteenth-century European
(20) commentators habitually passed over these acknowledgments without comment.

Another example is the use of "tradition" to determine national identity. Images of European authority over other cultures were shaped and
(25) reinforced during the nineteenth century, through the manufacture and reinterpretation of rituals, ceremonies, and traditions. At a time when many of the institutions that had helped maintain imperial societies were beginning to recede in influence, and
(30) when the pressures of administering numerous overseas territories and large new domestic constituencies mounted, the ruling elites of Europe felt the clear need to project their power backward in time, giving it a legitimacy that only longevity could
(35) impart. Thus in 1876, Queen Victoria of England was declared empress of India and was celebrated in numerous "traditional" jamborees, as if her rule were not mainly a matter of recent edict but of age-old custom.
(40) Similar constructions have also been made by native cultures about their precolonial past, as in the case of Algeria during its war of independence from France, when decolonization encouraged Algerians to create idealized images of what they believed their
(45) culture to have been prior to French occupation. This strategy is at work in what many revolutionary poets say and write during wars of independence elsewhere, giving their adherents something to revive and admire.
(50) Though for the most part colonized societies have won their independence, in many cultures the imperial attitudes of uniqueness and superiority underlying colonial conquest remain. There is in all nationally defined cultures an aspiration to
(55) sovereignty and dominance that expresses itself in definitions of cultural identity. At the same time, paradoxically, we have never been as aware as we are now of the fact that historical and cultural experiences partake of many social and cultural
(60) domains and even cross national boundaries,

despite the claims to the contrary made by purveyors of nationalist dogma. Far from being unitary, monolithic, or autonomous, cultures actually include more "foreign" elements than
(65) they consciously exclude.

14. Which one of the following statements most accurately expresses the main point of the passage?

(A) Either by ignoring a native culture's own self-understanding or by substituting fabricated traditions and rituals, imperial societies often obscure the heterogeneous cultures of the peoples they colonize.

(B) Attempts to reconstruct a native, precolonial culture by members of decolonized societies are essentially no different from European colonial creation of traditions and rituals to validate their authority.

(C) In attempting to impose a monolithic culture on the peoples they colonize, imperial societies adopt artifices very similar to the tactics employed by revisionist historians of ancient Greek culture.

(D) While most colonized societies have regained their independence, they retain trappings of imperial culture that will need to be discarded if they are to regain the traditions of their past.

(E) Despite nationalistic creation of images of cultures as unified and monolithic, we now more clearly understand the extent to which cultures are in fact made up of heterogeneous elements.

15. The passage provides information to answer all of the following questions EXCEPT:

(A) What kinds of influences affect the national identities people construct from their past?

(B) Why did nineteenth-century European commentators ignore some discussion of Greek culture by ancient Greek writers?

(C) In what ways did African cultural influence affect the culture of ancient Greece?

(D) Why was Queen Victoria of England declared empress of India in 1876?

(E) What is one reason why revolutionary poets speak and write as they do?

GO ON TO THE NEXT PAGE.

16. The author's attitude toward the studies mentioned in line 6 is most likely

(A) overall agreement with their conclusion about influences on cultural identity

(B) reservation over their preoccupation with colonialism

(C) skepticism toward the relevance of the examples they cite

(D) concern that they fail to explain ancient Greek culture

(E) unqualified disagreement with their insistence that cultures are monolithic

17. The author's use of the word "traditional" in line 37 is intended to indicate that the jamborees

(A) had been revived after centuries of neglect

(B) were legitimized by their historic use in the native culture

(C) exemplified the dominance of the imperial culture

(D) conferred spurious historical legitimacy upon colonial authority

(E) combined historic elements of imperial and native cultures

18. The "purveyors of nationalist dogma" mentioned in line 62 would be most likely to agree with which one of the following?

(A) Colonized nations should not attempt to regain their historical cultures.

(B) Imperial cultures should incorporate the traditions of their colonies.

(C) The cultural traditions of a nation should remain untainted by outside influences.

(D) A country's cultural identity partakes of many social and cultural domains.

(E) National histories are created to further aspirations to sovereignty and dominance.

19. Which one of the following would most likely be an example of one of the "rituals, ceremonies, and traditions" mentioned in lines 26–27?

(A) an annual ceremony held by an institution of the colonizing culture to honor the literary and theatrical achievements of members of the native culture

(B) a religious service of the colonizing culture that has been adapted to include elements of the native culture in order to gain converts

(C) a traditional play that is part of a colonized nation's original culture, but is highly popular among the leaders of the imperial culture

(D) a ritual dance, traditionally used to commemorate the union of two native deities, that is modified to depict the friendship between the colonial and native cultures

(E) a traditional village oratory competition in which members of the native culture endeavor to outdo one another in allegorical criticisms of the colonizing culture

20. In the context of the passage, the examples in the second and third paragraphs best exemplify which one of the following generalizations?

(A) Apparent traditions may be products of artifice.

(B) National identity generally requires cultural uniformity.

(C) Most colonial cultures are by nature artificial and contrived.

(D) Historical and cultural experiences may cross national boundaries.

(E) Revolutionary cultures are often more authentic than imperial cultures.

21. The primary purpose of the passage is to

(A) argue for the creation of a global culture made up of elements from many national cultures

(B) explain how the desire for cultural uniformity supports imperialist attitudes

(C) stress the importance of objectivity in studying the actual sources of cultural identity

(D) advance the claim that present concerns motivate the shaping of cultural identities

(E) reveal the imperialist motivations of some nineteenth-century scholarship

GO ON TO THE NEXT PAGE.

One of the foundations of scientific research is that an experimental result is credible only if it can be replicated—only if performing the experiment a second time leads to the same result. But physicists
(5) John Sommerer and Edward Ott have conceived of a physical system in which even the least change in the starting conditions—no matter how small, inadvertent, or undetectable—can alter results radically. The system is represented by a computer model of a
(10) mathematical equation describing the motion of a particle placed in a particular type of force field.

Sommerer and Ott based their system on an analogy with the phenomena known as riddled basins of attraction. If two bodies of water bound a large
(15) landmass and water is spilled somewhere on the land, the water will eventually make its way to one or the other body of water, its destination depending on such factors as where the water is spilled and the geographic features that shape the water's path and
(20) velocity. The basin of attraction for a body of water is the area of land that, whenever water is spilled on it, always directs the spilled water to that body.

In some geographical formations it is sometimes impossible to predict, not only the exact destination
(25) of the spilled water, but even which body of water it will end up in. This is because the boundary between one basin of attraction and another is riddled with fractal properties; in other words, the boundary is permeated by an extraordinarily high number of
(30) physical irregularities such as notches or zigzags. Along such a boundary, the only way to determine where spilled water will flow at any given point is actually to spill it and observe its motion; spilling the water at any immediately adjacent point could give
(35) the water an entirely different path, velocity, or destination.

In the system posited by the two physicists, this boundary expands to include the whole system: i.e., the entire force field is riddled with fractal properties,
(40) and it is impossible to predict even the general destination of the particle given its starting point. Sommerer and Ott make a distinction between this type of uncertainty and that known as "chaos"; under chaos, a particle's general destination would be
(45) predictable but its path and exact destination would not.

There are presumably other such systems because the equation the physicists used to construct the computer model was literally the first one they
(50) attempted, and the likelihood that they chose the only equation that would lead to an unstable system is small. If other such systems do exist, metaphorical examples of riddled basins of attraction may abound in the failed attempts of scientists to replicate
(55) previous experimental results—in which case, scientists would be forced to question one of the basic principles that guide their work.

22. Which one of the following most accurately expresses the main point of the passage?

(A) Sommerer and Ott's model suggests that many of the fundamental experimental results of science are unreliable because they are contaminated by riddled basins of attraction.

(B) Sommerer and Ott's model suggests that scientists who fail to replicate experimental results might be working within physical systems that make replication virtually impossible.

(C) Sommerer and Ott's model suggests that experimental results can never be truly replicated because the starting conditions of an experiment can never be re-created exactly.

(D) Sommerer and Ott's model suggests that most of the physical systems studied by scientists are in fact metaphorical examples of riddled basins of attraction.

(E) Sommerer and Ott's model suggests that an experimental result should not be treated as credible unless that result can be replicated.

23. The discussion of the chaos of physical systems is intended to perform which one of the following functions in the passage?

(A) emphasize the extraordinarily large number of physical irregularities in a riddled basin of attraction

(B) emphasize the unusual types of physical irregularities found in Sommerer and Ott's model

(C) emphasize the large percentage of a riddled basin of attraction that exhibits unpredictability

(D) emphasize the degree of unpredictability in Sommerer and Ott's model

(E) emphasize the number of fractal properties in a riddled basin of attraction

24. Given the information in the passage, Sommerer and Ott are most likely to agree with which one of the following?

(A) It is sometimes impossible to determine whether a particular region exhibits fractal properties.

(B) It is sometimes impossible to predict even the general destination of a particle placed in a chaotic system.

(C) It is sometimes impossible to re-create exactly the starting conditions of an experiment.

(D) It is usually possible to predict the exact path water will travel if it is spilled at a point not on the boundary between two basins of attraction.

(E) It is usually possible to determine the path by which a particle traveled given information about where it was placed and its eventual destination.

GO ON TO THE NEXT PAGE.

25. Which one of the following most accurately describes the author's attitude toward the work of Sommerer and Ott?

   (A)   skeptical of the possibility that numerous unstable systems exist but confident that the existence of numerous unstable systems would call into question one of the foundations of science

   (B)   convinced of the existence of numerous unstable systems and unsure if the existence of numerous unstable systems calls into question one of the foundations of science

   (C)   convinced of the existence of numerous unstable systems and confident that the existence of numerous unstable systems calls into question one of the foundations of science

   (D)   persuaded of the possibility that numerous unstable systems exist and unsure if the existence of numerous unstable systems would call into question one of the foundations of science

   (E)   persuaded of the possibility that numerous unstable systems exist and confident that the existence of numerous unstable systems would call into question one of the foundations of science

26. According to the passage, Sommerer and Ott's model differs from a riddled basin of attraction in which one of the following ways?

   (A)   In the model, the behavior of a particle placed at any point in the system is chaotic; in a riddled basin of attraction, only water spilled at some of the points behaves chaotically.

   (B)   In a riddled basin of attraction, the behavior of water spilled at any point is chaotic; in the model, only particles placed at some of the points in the system behave chaotically.

   (C)   In the model, it is impossible to predict the destination of a particle placed at any point in the system; in a riddled basin of attraction, only some points are such that it is impossible to predict the destination of water spilled at each of those points.

   (D)   In a riddled basin of attraction, water spilled at two adjacent points always makes its way to the same destination; in the model, it is possible for particles placed at two adjacent points to travel to different destinations.

   (E)   In the model, two particles placed successively at a given point always travel to the same destination; in a riddled basin of attraction, water spilled at the same point on different occasions may make its way to different destinations.

27. Which one of the following best defines the term "basin of attraction," as that term is used in the passage?

   (A)   the set of all points on an area of land for which it is possible to predict the destination, but not the path, of water spilled at that point

   (B)   the set of all points on an area of land for which it is possible to predict both the destination and the path of water spilled at that point

   (C)   the set of all points on an area of land that are free from physical irregularities such as notches and zigzags

   (D)   the set of all points on an area of land for which water spilled at each point will travel to a particular body of water

   (E)   the set of all points on an area of land for which water spilled at each point will travel to the same exact destination

28. Which one of the following is most clearly one of the "metaphorical examples of riddled basins of attraction" mentioned in lines 52–53?

   (A)   A scientist is unable to determine if mixing certain chemicals will result in a particular chemical reaction because the reaction cannot be consistently reproduced since sometimes the reaction occurs and other times it does not despite starting conditions that are in fact exactly the same in each experiment.

   (B)   A scientist is unable to determine if mixing certain chemicals will result in a particular chemical reaction because the reaction cannot be consistently reproduced since it is impossible to bring about starting conditions that are in fact exactly the same in each experiment.

   (C)   A scientist is unable to determine if mixing certain chemicals will result in a particular chemical reaction because the reaction cannot be consistently reproduced since it is impossible to produce starting conditions that are even approximately the same from one experiment to the next.

   (D)   A scientist is able to determine that mixing certain chemicals results in a particular chemical reaction because it is possible to consistently reproduce the reaction even though the starting conditions vary significantly from one experiment to the next.

   (E)   A scientist is able to determine that mixing certain chemicals results in a particular chemical reaction because it is possible to consistently reproduce the reaction despite the fact that the amount of time it takes for the reaction to occur varies significantly depending on the starting conditions of the experiment.

S T O P
IF YOU FINISH BEFORE TIME IS CALLED, YOU MAY CHECK YOUR WORK ON THIS SECTION ONLY.
DO NOT WORK ON ANY OTHER SECTION IN THE TEST.

SECTION II

Time—35 minutes

25 Questions

Directions: The questions in this section are based on the reasoning contained in brief statements or passages. For some questions, more than one of the choices could conceivably answer the question. However, you are to choose the <u>best</u> answer; that is, the response that most accurately and completely answers the question. You should not make assumptions that are by commonsense standards implausible, superfluous, or incompatible with the passage. After you have chosen the best answer, blacken the corresponding space on your answer sheet.

1. Extract from lease: The tenant should record all preexisting damage on the preexisting damage list, because the tenant need not pay for preexisting damage recorded there. The tenant must pay for damage that was not recorded on the preexisting damage list, except for any damage caused by a circumstance beyond the tenant's control.

In which one of the following instances does the extract from the lease most strongly support the view that the tenant is not required to pay for the damage?

(A) a hole in the wall that was not recorded on the preexisting damage list and that was the result of an event within the tenant's control

(B) a crack in a window caused by a factor beyond the tenant's control and not recorded on the preexisting damage list

(C) a tear in the linoleum that was not preexisting but that was caused by one of the tenant's children

(D) a missing light fixture that was present when the tenant moved in but was later removed by the tenant

(E) paint splatters on the carpet that should have been recorded on the preexisting damage list but were not

2. Randy: After Mega Cable Television Company refused to carry the competing Azco News Service alongside its own news channels, the mayor used her influence to get Azco time on a community channel, demonstrating her concern for keeping a diversity of news programming in the city.

Marion: The mayor's action is fully explained by cruder motives: she's rewarding Azco's owner, a political supporter of hers.

Of the following, which one, if true, is the logically strongest counter Randy can make to Marion's objection?

(A) The owner of Azco supported the mayor simply because he liked her political agenda, and not for any expected reward.

(B) The mayor also used her influence to get time on a community channel for another news service, whose owner supported the mayor's opponent in the last election.

(C) Azco's news coverage of the mayor has never been judged to be biased by an impartial, independent organization.

(D) The many people whose jobs depend on Azco's continued presence on a community channel are a potential source of political support for the mayor.

(E) The number of people who watch Mega Cable Television Company's programming has decreased during the mayor's term.

GO ON TO THE NEXT PAGE.

3. On the first day of trout season a team of biologists went with local trout anglers to the Macawber River. Each angler who caught at least 2 trout chose exactly 2 of these trout for the biologists to weigh. A total of 90 fish were weighed. The measurements show that at the beginning of this season the average trout in the Macawber River weighed approximately 1.6 kilograms.

The reasoning above is most vulnerable to criticism on the grounds that it

(A)   makes a generalization from a sample that is unlikely to be representative
(B)   relies on evidence that is anecdotal rather than scientific
(C)   ignores the variations in weight that are likely to occur over the whole season
(D)   fails to take into account measurements from the same time in previous seasons
(E)   does not consider whether any fish other than trout were caught

4. A strong correlation exists between what people value and the way they act. For example, those who value wealth tend to choose higher-paying jobs in undesirable locations over lower-paying jobs in desirable locations. Thus, knowing what people value can help one predict their actions.

Which one of the following most accurately expresses the conclusion of the argument?

(A)   Knowing how people behave allows one to infer what they value.
(B)   People's claims concerning what they value are symptomatic of their actions.
(C)   No two people who value different things act the same way in identical circumstances.
(D)   People who value wealth tend to allow their desire for it to outweigh other concerns.
(E)   What people value can be a reliable indicator of how they will act.

5. An analysis of the number and severity of health problems among the population of a certain community showed that elderly people who were born in the community and resided there all their lives had significantly worse health than elderly people who had moved there within the past five years.

Each of the following, if true, contributes to an explanation of the difference in health between these two groups EXCEPT:

(A)   People who have the means to relocate tend to be in better-than-average health.
(B)   Although most people who have moved into the community are young, most people who have lived in the community all their lives are elderly.
(C)   The quality of health care available to the community is lower than that for the rest of the country.
(D)   Changes in one's environment tend to have a beneficial effect on one's health.
(E)   People in good health are more likely to move to new communities than are people in poor health.

6. Classical Roman architecture is beautiful, primarily because of its use of rounded arches and its symmetry. Postmodern architecture is dramatic, primarily because of its creative use both of materials and of the surrounding environment. An architectural style that combines elements of both classical Roman and postmodern architecture would therefore be both beautiful and dramatic.

The reasoning in the argument is flawed in that it

(A)   presumes, without providing justification, that for an architectural style to have certain qualities, its components must have those qualities
(B)   fails to justify its presumption that because postmodern architecture is dramatic, that is its most salient feature
(C)   neglects to consider that an architectural style combining elements of two other architectural styles may lack certain qualities of one or both of those styles
(D)   neglects to specify how the drama of an architectural style contributes to its beauty
(E)   ignores the possibility that there are other architectural styles whose defining qualities include both drama and beauty

GO ON TO THE NEXT PAGE.

7. After being subjected to clinical tests like those used to evaluate the effectiveness of prescription drugs, a popular nonprescription herbal remedy was found to be as effective in treating painful joints as is a certain prescription drug that has been used successfully to treat this condition. The manufacturer of the herbal remedy cited the test results as proof that chemical agents are unnecessary for the successful treatment of painful joints.

The test results would provide the proof that the manufacturer claims they do if which one of the following is assumed?

(A) People are likely to switch from using prescription drugs to using herbal remedies if the herbal remedies are found to be as effective as the prescription drugs.

(B) The herbal remedy contains no chemical agents that are effective in treating painful joints.

(C) None of the people who participated in the test of the prescription drug had ever tried using an herbal remedy to treat painful joints.

(D) The researchers who analyzed the results of the clinical testing of the herbal remedy had also analyzed the results of the clinical testing of the prescription drug.

(E) The prescription drug treats the discomfort associated with painful joints without eliminating the cause of that condition.

8. When companies' profits would otherwise be reduced by an increase in the minimum wage (a wage rate set by the government as the lowest that companies are allowed to pay), the companies often reduce the number of workers they employ. Yet a recent increase in the minimum wage did not result in job cutbacks in the fast-food industry, where most workers are paid the minimum wage.

Which one of the following, if true, most helps to explain why the increase in the minimum wage did not affect the number of jobs in the fast-food industry?

(A) After the recent increase in the minimum wage, decreased job turnover in the fast-food industry allowed employers of fast-food workers to save enough on recruiting costs to cover the cost of the wage increase.

(B) If, in any industry, an increase in the minimum wage leads to the elimination of many jobs that pay the minimum wage, then higher-paying supervisory positions will also be eliminated in that industry.

(C) With respect to its response to increases in the minimum wage, the fast-food industry does not differ significantly from other industries that employ many workers at the minimum wage.

(D) A few employees in the fast-food industry were already earning more than the new, higher minimum wage before the new minimum wage was established.

(E) Sales of fast food to workers who are paid the minimum wage did not increase following the recent change in the minimum wage.

9. One should always capitalize the main words and the first and last words of a title. But one should never capitalize articles, or prepositions and conjunctions with fewer than five letters, when they occur in the middle of a title.

Which one of the following can be properly inferred from the statements above?

(A) If a word that is a preposition or conjunction should be capitalized, then it is the first or last word of the title.

(B) If a word in the middle of a title should be capitalized, then that word is neither an article nor a conjunction shorter than five letters.

(C) All prepositions and conjunctions with fewer than five letters should be uncapitalized in titles.

(D) If a word is neither a main word nor a first or last word of a title, then it should not be capitalized.

(E) Prepositions and conjunctions with five or more letters should be capitalized in any text.

10. Letter to the editor: Recently, the city council passed an ordinance that prohibits loitering at the local shopping mall. The council's declared goal was to eliminate overcrowding and alleviate pedestrian congestion, thereby improving the mall's business and restoring its family-oriented image. But despite these claims, reducing overcrowding and congestion cannot be the actual goals of this measure, because even when fully implemented, the ordinance would not accomplish them.

Which one of the following most accurately describes a flaw in the argument's reasoning?

(A) The argument ignores the possibility that an action may achieve its secondary goals even if it does not achieve its primary goals.

(B) The argument takes for granted that something cannot be the goal of an action performed unless the action will in fact achieve that goal.

(C) The argument dismisses a claim because of its source rather than because of its content.

(D) The argument takes for granted that an action that does not accomplish its stated goals will not have any beneficial effects.

(E) The argument treats a condition that is necessary for achieving an action's stated goals as if this condition were sufficient for achieving these goals.

GO ON TO THE NEXT PAGE.

11. Cynthia: Corporations amply fund research that generates marketable new technologies. But the fundamental goal of science is to achieve a comprehensive knowledge of the workings of the universe. The government should help fund those basic scientific research projects that seek to further our theoretical knowledge of nature.

Luis: The basic goal of government support of scientific research is to generate technological advances that will benefit society as a whole. So only research that is expected to yield practical applications in fields such as agriculture and medicine ought to be funded.

Cynthia's and Luis's statements provide the most support for the contention that they would disagree with each other about the truth of which one of the following statements?

(A) The government should help fund pure theoretical research because such research might have unforeseen practical applications in fields such as agriculture and medicine.

(B) A proposed study of the effects of chemical fertilizers on crops, for the purpose of developing more-resistant and higher-yielding breeds, should not receive government funding.

(C) Although some research projects in theoretical science yield practical benefits, most do not, and so no research projects in theoretical science should be funded by the government.

(D) Research for the sole purpose of developing new technologies ought to be financed exclusively by corporations.

(E) Knowledge gained through basic scientific research need not be expected to lead to new and useful technologies in order for the research to merit government funding.

12. One can never tell whether another person is acting from an ulterior motive; therefore, it is impossible to tell whether someone's action is moral, and so one should evaluate the consequences of an action rather than its morality.

Which one of the following principles, if valid, most helps to justify the reasoning above?

(A) The intention of an action is indispensable for an evaluation of its morality.

(B) The assigning of praise and blame is what is most important in the assessment of the value of human actions.

(C) One can sometimes know one's own motives for a particular action.

(D) There can be good actions that are not performed by a good person.

(E) One cannot know whether someone acted morally in a particular situation unless one knows what consequences that person's actions had.

13. Fossil-fuel producers say that it would be prohibitively expensive to reduce levels of carbon dioxide emitted by the use of fossil fuels enough to halt global warming. This claim is probably false. Several years ago, the chemical industry said that finding an economical alternative to the chlorofluorocarbons (CFCs) destroying the ozone layer would be impossible. Yet once the industry was forced, by international agreements, to find substitutes for CFCs, it managed to phase them out completely well before the mandated deadline, in many cases at a profit.

Which one of the following, if true, most strengthens the argument?

(A) In the time since the chemical industry phased out CFCs, the destruction of the ozone layer by CFCs has virtually halted, but the levels of carbon dioxide emitted by the use of fossil fuels have continued to increase.

(B) In some countries, the amount of carbon dioxide emitted by the use of fossil fuels has already been reduced without prohibitive expense, but at some cost in convenience to the users of such fuels.

(C) The use of CFCs never contributed as greatly to the destruction of the ozone layer as the carbon dioxide emitted by the use of fossil fuels currently contributes to global warming.

(D) There are ways of reducing carbon dioxide emissions that could halt global warming without hurting profits of fossil-fuel producers significantly more than phasing out CFCs hurt those of the chemical industry.

(E) If international agreements forced fossil-fuel producers to find ways to reduce carbon dioxide emissions enough to halt global warming, the fossil-fuel producers could find substitutes for fossil fuels.

GO ON TO THE NEXT PAGE.

14. If legislators are to enact laws that benefit constituents, they must be sure to consider what the consequences of enacting a proposed law will actually be. Contemporary legislatures fail to enact laws that benefit constituents. Concerned primarily with advancing their own political careers, legislators present legislation in polemical terms; this arouses in their colleagues either repugnance or enthusiasm for the legislation.

Which one of the following is an assumption on which the argument depends?

(A) Legislation will not benefit constituents unless legislators become less concerned with their own careers.

(B) Legislatures that enact laws that benefit constituents are successful legislatures.

(C) The passage of laws cannot benefit constituents unless constituents generally adhere to those laws.

(D) Legislators considering a proposed law for which they have repugnance or enthusiasm do not consider the consequences that it will actually have.

(E) The inability of legislators to consider the actual consequences of enacting a proposed law is due to their strong feelings about that law.

15. Anderson maintains that travel writing has diminished in quality over the last few decades. Although travel writing has changed in this time, Anderson is too harsh on contemporary travel writers. Today, when the general public is better traveled than in the past, travel writers face a challenge far greater than that of their predecessors: they must not only show their readers a place but also make them see it anew. That the genre has not only survived but also flourished shows the talent of today's practitioners.

Which one of the following most accurately describes the role played in the argument by the statement that the general public is better traveled today than in the past?

(A) It is claimed to be a result of good travel writing.

(B) It is cited as evidence that contemporary travel writing is intended for a wider readership.

(C) It is part of a purported explanation of why readers are disappointed with today's travel writers.

(D) It is cited as a reason that travel writing flourishes more today than it has in the past.

(E) It is cited as a condition that has transformed the task of the travel writer.

16. Among multiparty democracies, those with the fewest parties will have the most-productive legislatures. The fewer the number of parties in a democracy, the more issues each must take a stand on. A political party that must take stands on a wide variety of issues has to prioritize those issues; this promotes a tendency to compromise.

Which one of the following is an assumption required by the argument?

(A) The more political parties a nation has, the more likely it is that there will be disagreements within parties.

(B) The fewer the number of a nation's political parties, the more important it is that those parties can compromise with each other.

(C) The tendency to compromise makes the legislative process more productive.

(D) The legislatures of nondemocracies are less productive than are those of democracies.

(E) Legislators in a multiparty democracy never all agree on important issues.

GO ON TO THE NEXT PAGE.

17. Warm air tends to be humid, and as humidity of air increases, the amount of rainfall also increases. So, the fact that rainfall totals for most continents have been increasing over the past five years is strong evidence that the air temperature is increasing as well.

Which one of the following has a flawed pattern of reasoning most similar to the flawed pattern of reasoning in the argument above?

(A) Food that is fresh tends to be nutritious, and the more nutritious one's diet the healthier one is. People today are generally healthier than people were a century ago. So it is likely that people today eat food that is fresher than the food people ate a century ago.

(B) Your refusal to make public your personal finances indicates some sort of financial impropriety on your part, for people who do not reveal their personal finances generally are hiding some sort of financial impropriety.

(C) People tend not to want to travel on mass transit when they are carrying bags and packages, and the more bags and packages one carries, the more awkward travel on mass transit becomes. Therefore, people who carry bags and packages tend to use automobiles rather than mass transit.

(D) Statistics show that people are generally living longer and healthier lives than ever before. However, more people are overweight and fewer people exercise than ever before. Therefore, being lean and physically fit is essential neither to long life nor to good health.

(E) People tend to watch only those television programs that they enjoy and appreciate. Since there are more television viewers today than there were ten years ago, it must be the case that viewers today are satisfied with at least some of the programs shown on television.

18. Asked by researchers to sort objects by shape, most toddlers in a large study had no trouble doing so. When subsequently told to sort by color, the toddlers seemed to have difficulty following the new rule and almost invariably persisted with their first approach. The researchers suggest such failures to adapt to new rules often result from insufficient development of the prefrontal cortex in toddlers. The cortex is essential for functions like adapting to new rules, yet is slow to mature, continuing to develop right into adolescence.

Which one of the following is most supported by the information above?

(A) Toddlers unable to sort objects by color tend to have a less developed prefrontal cortex than other children of the same age.

(B) Only adolescents and adults can solve problems that require adapting to new rules.

(C) Certain kinds of behavior on the part of toddlers may not be willfully disobedient.

(D) The maturing of the prefrontal cortex is more important than upbringing in causing the development of adaptive behavior.

(E) Skill at adapting to new situations is roughly proportional to the level of development of the prefrontal cortex.

19. Dietitian: It is true that nutrients are most effective when provided by natural foods rather than artificial supplements. While it is also true that fat in one's diet is generally unhealthy, eating raw carrots (which are rich in beta carotene) by themselves is nonetheless not an effective means of obtaining vitamin A, since the body cannot transform beta carotene into vitamin A unless it is consumed with at least some fat.

The statement that fat in one's diet is generally unhealthy plays which one of the following roles in the dietitian's argument?

(A) It is mentioned as a reason for adopting a dietary practice that the dietitian provides a reason for not carrying to the extreme.

(B) It is mentioned as the reason that is least often cited by those who recommend a dietary practice the dietitian disfavors.

(C) It is mentioned as a generally accepted hypothesis that the dietitian attempts to undermine completely.

(D) It is attacked as inadequate evidence for the claim that nutrients are most effective when provided by natural foods rather than artificial supplements.

(E) It is cited as a bad reason for adopting a dietary habit that the dietitian recommends.

GO ON TO THE NEXT PAGE.

20. Industrial engineer: Some people have suggested that the problem of global warming should be addressed by pumping some of the carbon dioxide produced by the burning of fossil fuels into the deep ocean. Many environmentalists worry that this strategy would simply exchange one form of pollution for an equally destructive form. This worry is unfounded, however; much of the carbon dioxide now released into the atmosphere eventually ends up in the ocean anyway, where it does not cause environmental disturbances as destructive as global warming.

Which one of the following most accurately expresses the conclusion of the industrial engineer's argument as a whole?

(A) Global warming from the emission of carbon dioxide into the atmosphere could be reduced by pumping some of that carbon dioxide into the deep ocean.

(B) Environmentalists worry that the strategy of pumping carbon dioxide into the deep ocean to reduce global warming would simply exchange one form of pollution for another, equally destructive one.

(C) Worrying that pumping carbon dioxide into the deep ocean to reduce global warming would simply exchange one form of pollution for another, equally destructive, form is unfounded.

(D) Much of the carbon dioxide now released into the atmosphere ends up in the ocean where it does not cause environmental disturbances as destructive as global warming.

(E) To reduce global warming, the strategy of pumping into the deep ocean at least some of the carbon dioxide now released into the atmosphere should be considered.

21. Several people came down with an illness caused by a type of bacteria in seafood. Health officials traced the history of each person who became ill to the same restaurant and date. Careful testing showed that most people who ate seafood at the restaurant on that date had not come in contact with the bacteria in question. Despite this finding, health officials remained confident that contaminated seafood from this restaurant caused the cases of illness.

Which one of the following, if true, most helps to resolve the apparent discrepancy indicated above?

(A) Most people are immune to the effects of the bacteria in question.

(B) Those made ill by the bacteria had all been served by a waiter who subsequently became ill.

(C) All and only those who ate contaminated seafood at the restaurant on that date were allergic to the monosodium glutamate in a sauce that they used.

(D) The restaurant in question had recently been given a warning about violations of health regulations.

(E) All and only those who ate a particular seafood dish at the restaurant contracted the illness.

22. Economist: Real wages in this country will increase significantly only if productivity increases notably. Thus, it is unlikely that real wages will increase significantly in the near future, since this country's businesses are currently investing very little in new technology and this pattern is likely to continue for at least several more years.

Which one of the following, if assumed about the economist's country, allows the economist's conclusion to be properly drawn?

(A) Neither real wages nor productivity have increased in the last several years.

(B) Real wages will increase notably if a significant number of workers acquire the skills necessary to use new technology.

(C) Sooner or later real wages will increase significantly.

(D) Productivity will not increase if businesses do not make a substantial investment in new technology.

(E) The new technology in which businesses are currently investing is not contributing to an increase in productivity.

GO ON TO THE NEXT PAGE.

23. In scientific journals, authors and reviewers have praised companies in which they have substantial investments. These scientists, with their potential conflict of interest, call into question the integrity of scientific inquiry, so there should be full public disclosure of scientific authors' commercial holdings.

Which one of the following conforms most closely to the principle illustrated by the argument above?

(A) Managers within any corporation should not make investments in the companies for which they work.
(B) Claims about the effectiveness of pharmaceuticals should be based on scientific studies.
(C) People with access to otherwise private information regarding the value of stocks should not be allowed to sell or purchase those stocks.
(D) Magazine publishers should not be allowed to invest in the companies that advertise in their magazines.
(E) Financial advisers should inform their clients about any incentives the advisers receive for promoting investments in particular companies.

24. Columnist: The amount of acidic pollutants released into the air has decreased throughout the world over the last several decades. We can expect, then, an overall decrease in the negative environmental effects of acid rain, which is caused by these acidic pollutants.

Each of the following, if true, would weaken the columnist's argument EXCEPT:

(A) Some ecosystems have developed sophisticated mechanisms that reduce the negative effects of increased levels of acids in the environment.
(B) The amount of acid-neutralizing buffers released into the air has decreased in recent years.
(C) The current decrease in acidic pollutants is expected to end soon, as more countries turn to coal for the generation of electricity.
(D) The effects of acid rain are cumulative and largely independent of current acid rain levels.
(E) The soils of many ecosystems exposed to acid rain have been exhausted of minerals that help protect them from acid rain's harmful effects.

25. Columnist: It is sometimes claimed that the only factors relevant to determining moral guilt or innocence are the intentions of the person performing an action. However, external circumstances often play a crucial role in our moral judgment of an action. For example, a cook at a restaurant who absentmindedly put an ingredient in the stew that is not usually in the stew would ordinarily be regarded as forgetful, not immoral. If, however, someone eating at the restaurant happens to be severely allergic to that ingredient, eats the stew, and dies, many people would judge the cook to be guilty of serious moral negligence.

Which one of the following propositions is best illustrated by the columnist's statements?

(A) It is sometimes fair to judge the morality of others' actions even without considering all of the circumstances under which those actions were performed.
(B) We sometimes judge unfairly the morality of other people's actions.
(C) We should judge all negligent people to be equally morally blameworthy, regardless of the outcomes of their actions.
(D) People are sometimes held morally blameworthy as a result of circumstances some of which were outside their intentional control.
(E) The intentions of the person performing an action are rarely a decisive factor in making moral judgments about that action.

S T O P
IF YOU FINISH BEFORE TIME IS CALLED, YOU MAY CHECK YOUR WORK ON THIS SECTION ONLY.
DO NOT WORK ON ANY OTHER SECTION IN THE TEST.

SECTION III

Time—35 minutes

22 Questions

Directions: Each group of questions in this section is based on a set of conditions. In answering some of the questions, it may be useful to draw a rough diagram. Choose the response that most accurately and completely answers each question and blacken the corresponding space on your answer sheet.

Questions 1–5

At each of six consecutive stops—1, 2, 3, 4, 5, and 6—that a traveler must make in that order as part of a trip, she can choose one from among exactly four airlines—L, M, N, and O—on which to continue. Her choices must conform to the following constraints:

Whichever airline she chooses at a stop, she chooses one of the other airlines at the next stop.
She chooses the same airline at stop 1 as she does at stop 6.
She chooses the same airline at stop 2 as she does at stop 4.
Whenever she chooses either L or M at a stop, she does not choose N at the next stop.
At stop 5, she chooses N or O.

1. Which one of the following could be an accurate list of the airlines the traveler chooses at each stop, in order from 1 through 6?

    (A)   L, M, M, L, O, L
    (B)   M, L, O, M, O, M
    (C)   M, N, O, N, O, M
    (D)   M, O, N, O, N, M
    (E)   O, M, L, M, O, N

2. If the traveler chooses N at stop 5, which one of the following could be an accurate list of the airlines she chooses at stops 1, 2, and 3, respectively?

    (A)   L, M, N
    (B)   L, O, N
    (C)   M, L, N
    (D)   M, L, O
    (E)   N, O, N

3. If the only airlines the traveler chooses for the trip are M, N, and O, and she chooses O at stop 5, then the airlines she chooses at stops 1, 2, and 3, must be, respectively,

    (A)   M, O, and N
    (B)   M, N, and O
    (C)   N, M, and O
    (D)   N, O, and M
    (E)   O, M, and N

4. Which one of the following CANNOT be an accurate list of the airlines the traveler chooses at stops 1 and 2, respectively?

    (A)   L, M
    (B)   L, O
    (C)   M, L
    (D)   M, O
    (E)   O, N

5. If the traveler chooses O at stop 2, which one of the following could be an accurate list of the airlines she chooses at stops 5 and 6, respectively?

    (A)   M, N
    (B)   N, L
    (C)   N, O
    (D)   O, L
    (E)   O, N

GO ON TO THE NEXT PAGE.

Questions 6–11

The members of a five-person committee will be selected from among three parents—F, G, and H—three students—K, L, and M—and four teachers—U, W, X, and Z. The selection of committee members will meet the following conditions:

The committee must include exactly one student.
F and H cannot both be selected.
M and Z cannot both be selected.
U and W cannot both be selected.
F cannot be selected unless Z is also selected.
W cannot be selected unless H is also selected.

6. Which one of the following is an acceptable selection of committee members?

   (A)   F, G, K, L, Z
   (B)   F, G, K, U, X
   (C)   G, K, W, X, Z
   (D)   H, K, U, W, X
   (E)   H, L, W, X, Z

7. If W and Z are selected, which one of the following is a pair of people who could also be selected?

   (A)   U and X
   (B)   K and L
   (C)   G and M
   (D)   G and K
   (E)   F and G

8. Which one of the following is a pair of people who CANNOT both be selected?

   (A)   F and G
   (B)   F and M
   (C)   G and K
   (D)   H and L
   (E)   M and U

9. If W is selected, then any one of the following could also be selected EXCEPT:

   (A)   F
   (B)   G
   (C)   L
   (D)   M
   (E)   Z

10. If the committee is to include exactly one parent, which one of the following is a person who must also be selected?

   (A)   K
   (B)   L
   (C)   M
   (D)   U
   (E)   X

11. If M is selected, then the committee must also include both

   (A)   F and G
   (B)   G and H
   (C)   H and K
   (D)   K and U
   (E)   U and X

GO ON TO THE NEXT PAGE.

Questions 12–17

Within a five-year period from 1991 to 1995, each of three friends—Ramon, Sue, and Taylor—graduated. In that period, each bought his or her first car. The graduations and car purchases must be consistent with the following:

Ramon graduated in some year before the year in which Taylor graduated.

Taylor graduated in some year before the year in which he bought his first car.

Sue bought her first car in some year before the year in which she graduated.

Ramon and Sue graduated in the same year as each other.

At least one of the friends graduated in 1993.

12. Which one of the following could be an accurate matching of each friend and the year in which she or he graduated?

(A) Ramon: 1991; Sue: 1991; Taylor: 1993
(B) Ramon: 1992; Sue: 1992; Taylor: 1993
(C) Ramon: 1992; Sue: 1993; Taylor: 1994
(D) Ramon: 1993; Sue: 1993; Taylor: 1992
(E) Ramon: 1993; Sue: 1993; Taylor: 1995

13. Which one of the following could have taken place in 1995?

(A) Ramon graduated.
(B) Ramon bought his first car.
(C) Sue graduated.
(D) Sue bought her first car.
(E) Taylor graduated.

14. Which one of the following must be false?

(A) Two of the friends each bought his or her first car in 1991.
(B) Two of the friends each bought his or her first car in 1992.
(C) Two of the friends each bought his or her first car in 1993.
(D) Two of the friends each bought his or her first car in 1994.
(E) Two of the friends each bought his or her first car in 1995.

15. Which one of the following must be true?

(A) None of the three friends graduated in 1991.
(B) None of the three friends graduated in 1992.
(C) None of the three friends bought his or her first car in 1993.
(D) None of the three friends graduated in 1994.
(E) None of the three friends bought his or her first car in 1995.

16. If Taylor graduated in the same year that Ramon bought his first car, then each of the following could be true EXCEPT:

(A) Sue bought her first car in 1991.
(B) Ramon graduated in 1992.
(C) Taylor graduated in 1993.
(D) Taylor bought his first car in 1994.
(E) Ramon bought his first car in 1995.

17. If Sue graduated in 1993, then which one of the following must be true?

(A) Sue bought her first car in 1991.
(B) Ramon bought his first car in 1992.
(C) Ramon bought his first car in 1993.
(D) Taylor bought his first car in 1994.
(E) Taylor bought his first car in 1995.

GO ON TO THE NEXT PAGE.

3   -349- **3**

Questions 18–22

A child eating alphabet soup notices that the only letters left in her bowl are one each of these six letters: T, U, W, X, Y, and Z. She plays a game with the remaining letters, eating them in the next three spoonfuls in accord with certain rules. Each of the six letters must be in exactly one of the next three spoonfuls, and each of the spoonfuls must have at least one and at most three of the letters. In addition, she obeys the following restrictions:

The U is in a later spoonful than the T.
The U is not in a later spoonful than the X.
The Y is in a later spoonful than the W.
The U is in the same spoonful as either the Y or the Z, but not both.

18. Which one of the following could be an accurate list of the spoonfuls and the letters in each of them?

(A) first: Y
second: T, W
third: U, X, Z
(B) first: T, W
second: U, X, Y
third: Z
(C) first: T
second: U, Z
third: W, X, Y
(D) first: T, U, Z
second: W
third: X, Y
(E) first: W
second: T, X, Z
third: U, Y

19. If the Y is the only letter in one of the spoonfuls, then which one of the following could be true?

(A) The Y is in the first spoonful.
(B) The Z is in the first spoonful.
(C) The T is in the second spoonful.
(D) The X is in the second spoonful.
(E) The W is in the third spoonful.

20. If the Z is in the first spoonful, then which one of the following must be true?

(A) The T is in the second spoonful.
(B) The U is in the third spoonful.
(C) The W is in the first spoonful.
(D) The W is in the second spoonful.
(E) The X is in the third spoonful.

21. Which one of the following is a complete list of letters, any one of which could be the only letter in the first spoonful?

(A) T
(B) T, W
(C) T, X
(D) T, W, Z
(E) T, X, W, Z

22. If the T is in the second spoonful, then which one of the following could be true?

(A) Exactly two letters are in the first spoonful.
(B) Exactly three letters are in the first spoonful.
(C) Exactly three letters are in the second spoonful.
(D) Exactly one letter is in the third spoonful.
(E) Exactly two letters are in the third spoonful.

STOP
IF YOU FINISH BEFORE TIME IS CALLED, YOU MAY CHECK YOUR WORK ON THIS SECTION ONLY.
DO NOT WORK ON ANY OTHER SECTION IN THE TEST.

SECTION IV
Time—35 minutes
25 Questions

<u>Directions:</u> The questions in this section are based on the reasoning contained in brief statements or passages. For some questions, more than one of the choices could conceivably answer the question. However, you are to choose the <u>best</u> answer; that is, the response that most accurately and completely answers the question. You should not make assumptions that are by commonsense standards implausible, superfluous, or incompatible with the passage. After you have chosen the best answer, blacken the corresponding space on your answer sheet.

1. Students in a first-year undergraduate course were divided into two groups. All the students in both groups were given newspaper articles identical in every respect, except for the headline, which was different for each group. When the students were later asked questions about the contents of the article, the answers given by the two groups were markedly different, though within each group the answers were similar.

Which one of the following is most strongly supported by the information above?

(A) Readers base their impressions of what is in a newspaper on headlines alone.
(B) Newspaper headlines hamper a reader's ability to comprehend the corresponding articles.
(C) Careless reading is more common among first-year undergraduates than among more senior students.
(D) Newspaper headlines tend to be highly misleading.
(E) Newspaper headlines influence a reader's interpretation of the corresponding articles.

2. All works of art are beautiful and have something to teach us. Thus, since the natural world as a whole is both beautiful and instructive, it is a work of art.

The reasoning in the argument is flawed because the argument

(A) uses the inherently vague term "beautiful" without providing an explicit definition of that term
(B) attempts to establish an evaluative conclusion solely on the basis of claims about factual matters
(C) concludes, simply because an object possesses two qualities that are each common to all works of art, that the object is a work of art
(D) presumes, without providing justification, that only objects that are beautiful are instructive
(E) fails to consider the possibility that there are many things that are both beautiful and instructive but are not part of the natural world

3. When Copernicus changed the way we think about the solar system, he did so not by discovering new information, but by looking differently at information already available. Edward Jenner's discovery of a smallpox vaccine occurred when he shifted his focus to disease prevention from the then more common emphasis on cure. History is replete with breakthroughs of this sort.

The examples provided above illustrate which one of the following?

(A) Many valuable intellectual accomplishments occur by chance.
(B) Shifting from earlier modes of thought can result in important advances.
(C) The ability to look at information from a different point of view is rare.
(D) Understanding is advanced less often by better organization of available information than it is by the accumulation of new information.
(E) Dramatic intellectual breakthroughs are more easily accomplished in fields in which the amount of information available is relatively small.

4. Politician: Suppose censorship is wrong in itself, as modern liberals tend to believe. Then an actor's refusing a part in a film because the film glamorizes a point of view abhorrent to the actor would be morally wrong. But this conclusion is absurd. It follows that censorship is not, after all, wrong in itself.

The reasoning in the politician's argument is most vulnerable to criticism on the grounds that this argument

(A) presumes, without providing justification, that actors would subscribe to any tenet of modern liberalism
(B) uses the term "liberal" in order to discredit opponents' point of view
(C) takes for granted that there is a moral obligation to practice one's profession
(D) draws a conclusion that is inconsistent with a premise it accepts
(E) presumes, without providing justification, that declining a film role constitutes censorship in the relevant sense

GO ON TO THE NEXT PAGE.

5. Motor oil serves to lubricate engines and thus retard engine wear. A study was conducted to assess the effectiveness of various brands of motor oil by using them in taxicabs over a 6,000-mile test period. All the oils did equally well in retarding wear on pistons and cylinders, the relevant parts of the engine. Hence, cheaper brands of oil are the best buys.

Which one of the following, if true, most weakens the argument?

(A) Cheaper brands of motor oil are often used by knowledgeable automobile mechanics for their own cars.

(B) Tests other than of the ability to reduce engine wear also can reliably gauge the quality of motor oil.

(C) The lubricating properties of all motor oils deteriorate over time, and the rate of deterioration is accelerated by heat.

(D) The engines of some individual cars that have had their oil changed every 3,000 miles, using only a certain brand of oil, have lasted an extraordinarily long time.

(E) Ability to retard engine wear is not the only property of motor oil important to the running of an engine.

6. Elena: The best form of government is one that fosters the belief among its citizens that they have a say in how the government is run. Thus, democracy is the best form of government.

Marsha: But there are many forms of government under which citizens can be manipulated into believing they have a say when they don't.

Marsha's claim that it is possible for governments to manipulate people into thinking that they have a say when they do not is used to

(A) concur with Elena's claim that democracy is the best form of government

(B) support Marsha's unstated conclusion that the best form of government is one that appears to be democratic but really is not

(C) suggest that the premise Elena uses to support her conclusion could be used to support a conflicting conclusion

(D) support Marsha's unstated conclusion that most people seek only the appearance of democracy rather than democracy itself

(E) reject Elena's conclusion that the best form of government is democracy

7. Researcher: The use of the newest drug in treating this disease should be discontinued. The treatment usually wreaks havoc with the normal functioning of the human body, causing severe side effects such as total loss of hair, debilitating nausea, and intense pain in the joints.

The argument's reasoning is flawed because the argument

(A) fails to specify what is meant by "normal functioning of the human body"

(B) fails to consider the consequences of not administering the treatment

(C) presumes that every patient with the disease is treated with the drug

(D) does not consider the length of time needed for the treatment to begin taking effect

(E) does not acknowledge that the effects of the treatment may not be of the same severity in all cases

8. Otis: Aristotle's principle of justice says that we should treat relevantly similar cases similarly. Therefore, it is wrong for a dentist to schedule an after-hours appointment to suit a family friend but refuse to do it for anyone else.

Tyra: I accept Aristotle's principle of justice, but it's human nature to want to do special favors for friends. Indeed, that's what friends are—those for whom you would do special favors. It's not unjust for dentists to do that.

It can be inferred on the basis of their statements that Otis and Tyra disagree about whether

(A) Aristotle's principle of justice is widely applicable

(B) situations involving friends and situations involving others should be considered relevantly similar cases

(C) human nature makes it impossible to treat relevantly similar cases similarly

(D) dentists should be willing to schedule an after-hours appointment for anyone who asks

(E) Aristotle recognizes that friendship sometimes morally outweighs justice

GO ON TO THE NEXT PAGE.

9. Typically, people who have diets high in saturated fat have an increased risk of heart disease. Those who replace saturated fat in their diets with unsaturated fat decrease their risk of heart disease. Therefore, people who eat a lot of saturated fat can lower their risk of heart disease by increasing their intake of unsaturated fat.

Which one of the following, if assumed, most helps to justify the reasoning above?

(A) People who add unsaturated fat to their diets will eat less food that is high in saturated fat.

(B) Adding unsaturated fat to a diet brings health benefits other than a reduced risk of heart disease.

(C) Diet is the most important factor in a person's risk of heart disease.

(D) Taking steps to prevent heart disease is one of the most effective ways of increasing life expectancy.

(E) It is difficult to move from a diet that is high in saturated fat to a diet that includes very little fat.

10. Only people who are willing to compromise should undergo mediation to resolve their conflicts. Actual litigation should be pursued only when one is sure that one's position is correct. People whose conflicts are based on ideology are unwilling to compromise.

If the statements above are true, then which one of the following must be true?

(A) People who do not undergo mediation to resolve their conflicts should be sure that their positions are correct.

(B) People whose conflicts are not based on ideology should attempt to resolve their conflicts by means of litigation.

(C) People whose conflicts are based on ideology are not always sure that their positions are correct.

(D) People who are sure of the correctness of their positions are not people who should undergo mediation to resolve their conflicts.

(E) People whose conflicts are based on ideology are not people who should undergo mediation to resolve their conflicts.

11. Scientists have long thought that omega-3 fatty acids in fish oil tend to lower blood cholesterol and strongly suspected that a diet that includes a modest amount of fish would provide substantial health benefits. Now these views have acquired strong support from a recent study showing that middle-aged people who eat fish twice a week are nearly 30 percent less likely to develop heart disease than are those who do not eat fish.

Which one of the following is an assumption required by the argument?

(A) The test subjects in the recent study who did not eat fish were not vegetarians.

(B) The test subjects in the recent study who ate fish twice a week did not have a diet that was otherwise conducive to the development of heart disease.

(C) The test subjects in the recent study who did not eat fish were significantly more likely to eat red meat several times per week than were those who did eat fish.

(D) The test subjects in the recent study who ate fish twice a week were not significantly more likely than those who did not to engage regularly in activities known to augment cardiorespiratory health.

(E) The test subjects in the recent study who ate fish twice a week were no more likely than those who did not to have sedentary occupations.

GO ON TO THE NEXT PAGE.

12. Researcher: A number of studies have suggested that, on average, clients in short-term psychotherapy show similar levels of improvement regardless of the kind of psychotherapy they receive. So any client improvement in short-term psychotherapy must be the result of some aspect or aspects of therapy that are common to all psychotherapies—for example, the presence of someone who listens and gives attention to the client.

Which one of the following, if true, would most weaken the researcher's argument?

(A) The methods by which the studies measured whether clients improved primarily concerned immediate symptom relief and failed to address other important kinds of improvement.

(B) On average, clients improve more dramatically when they receive long-term psychotherapy, a year or longer in duration, than when clients receive short-term psychotherapy.

(C) The studies found that psychotherapy by a trained counselor does not result in any greater improvement, on average, among clients than does simple counseling by an untrained layperson.

(D) The specific techniques and interventions used by therapists practicing different kinds of psychotherapy differ dramatically.

(E) More-experienced therapists tend to use a wider range of techniques and interventions in psychotherapy than do inexperienced therapists.

13. Journalists sometimes use historical photographs to illustrate articles about current events. But this recycling of old photographs overstates the similarities between past and present, and thereby denies the individual significance of those current events. Hence, the use of historical photographs in this manner by journalists distorts public understanding of the present by presenting current events as mere repetitions of historical incidents.

Which one of the following, if assumed, enables the conclusion of the argument to be properly inferred?

(A) Any practice by which journalists present current events as mere repetitions of historical incidents overstates the similarities between past and present.

(B) If the work of a journalist overstates the similarities between past and present, then it distorts public understanding of the present by presenting current events as mere repetitions of historical incidents.

(C) If a journalistic practice distorts public understanding of the present by overstating the similarities between past and present, then it denies the individual significance of any articles about current events.

(D) No article about a current event treats that event as merely a repetition of historical incidents unless it uses historical photographs to illustrate that article.

(E) If journalists believe current events to be mere repetitions of historical incidents, then public understanding of the present will be distorted.

GO ON TO THE NEXT PAGE.

14. If Juan went to the party, it is highly unlikely that Maria would have enjoyed the party. But in fact it turned out that Maria did enjoy the party; therefore, it is highly unlikely that Juan was at the party.

The pattern of reasoning in the argument above is most similar to that in which one of the following?

(A) According to the newspaper, all eight teams in the soccer tournament have an equal chance of winning it. If so, then we will probably lose our goalie, since if we do lose our goalie we will probably not win the tournament.

(B) Kapinski, our new neighbor, is probably friendly, for Kapinski sells insurance and most people who sell insurance are friendly.

(C) If the lottery were fair, the person who won the lottery would not have been likely to win it. Thus, since this person would have been likely to win the lottery if it were unfair, the lottery was probably unfair.

(D) If Clarissa missed the bus today, it is quite unlikely that she would have gotten to work on time. So, it is quite unlikely that Clarissa missed the bus, since she actually was at work on time today.

(E) This year's election will probably be fair. But Popov probably will not win unless the election is unfair. So, Popov will not win the election.

15. Sonya: Anyone who lives without constant awareness of the fragility and precariousness of human life has a mind clouded by illusion. Yet those people who are perpetually cognizant of the fragility and precariousness of human life surely taint their emotional outlook on existence.

Sonya's statements, if true, most strongly support which one of the following?

(A) Anyone who places a higher priority on maintaining a positive emotional outlook than on dispelling illusion will be completely unaware of the fragility and precariousness of human life.

(B) Either no one has a tainted emotional outlook on existence, or no one has a mind clouded by illusion.

(C) It is impossible for anyone to live without some degree of self-deception.

(D) Everyone whose emotional outlook on existence is untainted has a mind clouded by illusion.

(E) It is better to be aware of the fragility and precariousness of human life than to have an untainted emotional outlook on existence.

16. In a study, shoppers who shopped in a grocery store without a shopping list and bought only items that were on sale for half price or less spent far more money on a comparable number of items than did shoppers in the same store who used a list and bought no sale items.

Which one of the following, if true, most helps to explain the apparent paradox in the study's results?

(A) Only the shoppers who used a list used a shopping cart.

(B) The shoppers who did not use lists bought many unnecessary items.

(C) Usually, only the most expensive items go on sale in grocery stores.

(D) The grocery store in the study carries many expensive items that few other grocery stores carry.

(E) The grocery store in the study places relatively few items on sale.

17. A group of mountain climbers was studied to determine how they were affected by diminished oxygen in the air at high altitudes. As they climbed past 6,100 meters above sea level, the climbers slurred words, took longer to understand simple sentences, and demonstrated poor judgment. This combination of worsened performances disproves the theory that the area of the brain controlling speech is distinct from that controlling other functions.

The argument is most vulnerable to criticism on the grounds that it overlooks the possibility that

(A) the climbers' performance in speech, comprehension, and reasoning was impaired because oxygen deprivation affected their entire brains

(B) the climbers' performance in speech, comprehension, and reasoning was better than average before they were studied

(C) the climbers showed different levels of impairment in their performance in speech, comprehension, and reasoning

(D) some of the effects described were apparent just before the climbers reached 6,100 meters

(E) many of the climbers had engaged in special training before the climb because they wanted to improve the efficiency with which their bodies use oxygen

GO ON TO THE NEXT PAGE.

18. It was once thought that pesticide TSX-400 was extremely harmful to the environment but that pesticides Envirochem and Zanar were environmentally harmless. TSX-400 was banned; Envirochem and Zanar were not. However, according to recent studies, Envirochem and Zanar each cause greater environmental harm than does TSX-400. If these studies are accurate, then either Envirochem and Zanar should be banned or TSX-400 should be legalized.

Which one of the following principles, if valid, most helps to justify the argumentation?

(A) Two pesticides should not both be legal if one is measurably more harmful to the environment than the other is.

(B) Two pesticides should both be legal only if neither is harmful to the environment.

(C) Two pesticides should both be illegal only if both are harmful to the environment.

(D) One pesticide should be legal and another illegal only if the former is less harmful to the environment than is the latter.

(E) One pesticide should be legal and another illegal if the former is harmless to the environment and the latter is harmful to it.

19. Recent studies have demonstrated that smokers are more likely than nonsmokers to develop heart disease. Other studies have established that smokers are more likely than others to drink caffeinated beverages. Therefore, even though drinking caffeinated beverages is not thought to be a cause of heart disease, there is a positive correlation between drinking caffeinated beverages and the development of heart disease.

The argument's reasoning is most vulnerable to criticism on the grounds that the argument fails to take into account the possibility that

(A) smokers who drink caffeinated beverages are less likely to develop heart disease than are smokers who do not drink caffeinated beverages

(B) something else, such as dietary fat intake, may be a more important factor in the development of heart disease than are the factors cited in the argument

(C) drinking caffeinated beverages is more strongly correlated with the development of heart disease than is smoking

(D) it is only among people who have a hereditary predisposition to heart disease that caffeine consumption is positively correlated with the development of heart disease

(E) there is a common cause of both the development of heart disease and behaviors such as drinking caffeinated beverages and smoking

20. The layouts of supermarkets are not accidental: they are part of a plan designed to make customers walk all the way to the back of the store just to pick up a loaf of bread, passing tempting displays the whole way. But supermarkets can alienate customers by placing popular items in the rear; surveys list inconvenience as shoppers' top reason for disliking supermarkets.

Which one of the following propositions does the passage most precisely illustrate?

(A) Supermarkets should focus on customers who want to purchase many items in a single trip.

(B) Alienation of customers is not good for business.

(C) Even well-thought-out plans can fail.

(D) Distracting customers is not good for business.

(E) Manipulation of people can have unwelcome consequences.

21. Doctor: Medication to reduce blood pressure often has unhealthy side effects. However, lifestyle changes such as exercising more and avoiding fatty foods reduce blood pressure just as effectively as taking medication does. Therefore, it is healthier to rely on these lifestyle changes than on medication to reduce blood pressure.

Which one of the following is an assumption that the doctor's argument requires?

(A) Other than medication, the only way to reduce blood pressure is by making lifestyle changes such as exercising more and avoiding fatty foods.

(B) If it is healthier to rely on a lifestyle change than on medication to reduce blood pressure, then that lifestyle change reduces blood pressure at least as effectively as medication does.

(C) The side effects, if any, of exercising more and avoiding fatty foods in order to reduce blood pressure are less unhealthy than those of taking medication to reduce blood pressure.

(D) If an alternative to medication relieves a medical condition just as effectively as medication does, then it is always healthier to rely on that alternative than on medication to relieve that medical condition.

(E) If two different methods of treating a medical condition have similar side effects, then it is healthier to rely on the more effective method.

GO ON TO THE NEXT PAGE.

22. Columnist: Several recent studies show, and insurance statistics confirm, that more pedestrians are killed every year in North American cities when crossing with the light than when crossing against it. Crossing against the light in North American cities is therefore less dangerous than crossing with the light.

The columnist's reasoning is most vulnerable to criticism on the grounds that it

(A) relies on sources that are likely to be biased in their reporting

(B) presumes, without providing justification, that because two things are correlated there must be a causal relationship between them

(C) does not adequately consider the possibility that a correlation between two events may be explained by a common cause

(D) ignores the possibility that the effects of the types of actions considered might be quite different in environments other than the ones studied

(E) ignores possible differences in the frequency of the two actions whose risk is being assessed

23. Many scientific studies have suggested that taking melatonin tablets can induce sleep. But this does not mean that melatonin is helpful in treating insomnia. Most of the studies examined only people without insomnia, and in many of the studies, only a few of the subjects given melatonin appeared to be significantly affected by it.

Which one of the following, if true, most strengthens the argument?

(A) A weaker correlation between taking melatonin and the inducement of sleep was found in the studies that included people with insomnia than in the studies that did not.

(B) None of the studies that suggested that taking melatonin tablets can induce sleep examined a fully representative sample of the human population.

(C) In the studies that included subjects with insomnia, only subjects without insomnia were significantly affected by doses of melatonin.

(D) Several people who were in control groups and only given placebos claimed that the tablets induced sleep.

(E) If melatonin were helpful in treating insomnia, then every person with insomnia who took doses of melatonin would appear to be significantly affected by it.

GO ON TO THE NEXT PAGE.

24. The asteroid that hit the Yucatán Peninsula 65 million years ago caused both long-term climatic change and a tremendous firestorm that swept across North America. We cannot show that it was this fire that caused the extinction of the triceratops, a North American dinosaur in existence at the time of the impact of the asteroid. Nor can we show that the triceratops became extinct due to the climatic changes resulting from the asteroid's impact. Hence, we cannot attribute the triceratops's extinction to the asteroid's impact.

Which one of the following has flawed reasoning most similar to the flawed reasoning in the argument above?

(A) I know that one cannot move this piano unless one can lift at least 150 kilograms. I doubt that either Leon or Pam can lift 150 kilograms alone. So I doubt that either Leon or Pam can move this piano alone. Thus, I doubt that Leon and Pam can move this piano together.

(B) Since we are quite sure that Cheng and Lin are the only candidates in the mayoral election, we can be quite sure that either Cheng or Lin will win the election. Therefore, either we know that Cheng will win or we know that Lin will win.

(C) It has not been conclusively proven that the accident was caused by John's driving at excessive speeds. Nor has it been conclusively proven that the accident was the result of John's weaving out of his lane. Hence, it has been conclusively proven that the cause of the accident was neither John's driving at excessive speeds nor John's weaving out of his lane.

(D) The flooding in the basement caused damage to the furnace and also caused a short in the electrical system. Fire investigators could not show that the damage to the furnace caused the fire that resulted shortly after the flooding, nor could they show that the fire was caused by the short in the electrical system. Therefore, we cannot claim that the flooding in the basement caused the fire.

(E) We have good reason to believe that the cause of the flooding along the coast was the unusually high tides. We also have good reason to believe that the cause of the unusually high tides was either the sun or the moon. So it is reasonable to maintain that the cause of the flooding was either the sun or the moon.

25. Economist: Although obviously cuts in personal income tax rates for the upper income brackets disproportionately benefit the wealthy, across-the-board cuts for all brackets tend to have a similar effect. Personal income tax rates are progressive (i.e., graduated), and if total revenue remains constant, then across-the-board cuts in these taxes require increasing the amount of revenue generated through nonprogressive taxes, thereby favoring the wealthy. Yet if nonprogressive taxes are not increased to compensate for the cuts, then the budget deficit will increase, requiring more government borrowing and driving up interest rates. This favors those who have money to lend, once again benefiting primarily the wealthy.

Which one of the following statements most accurately expresses the main conclusion of the economist's argument?

(A) Cuts in personal income tax rates for upper income brackets benefit the wealthy more than they benefit others.

(B) Across-the-board cuts in personal income tax rates do not generate enough additional economic activity to prevent a net loss of revenue.

(C) It is the wealthy who are favored by generating a high amount of revenue through nonprogressive taxes.

(D) It is primarily the wealthy who benefit from increases in the budget deficit, which drive up interest rates.

(E) Across-the-board personal income tax rate cuts generally benefit the wealthy more than they benefit others.

S T O P

IF YOU FINISH BEFORE TIME IS CALLED, YOU MAY CHECK YOUR WORK ON THIS SECTION ONLY.
DO NOT WORK ON ANY OTHER SECTION IN THE TEST.

ACKNOWLEDGMENTS

Acknowledgment is made to the following sources from which material has been adapted for use in this test booklet:

Elise Hancock, "Unpredictable Outcomes Could Be 'Poison' to Science." ©1994 by The Johns Hopkins University.

"Motor Oil: What's Best for Your Car?" ©1996 by Consumer Reports.

Angela Pirist, "Why Tots Can't Play by the Rules." ©1996 by Sussex Publishers Inc.

Martha Robles, "An Historical Adventure: Notes on Chicano Literature." ©1992 by TriQuarterly.

Edward W. Said, *Culture and Imperialism.* ©1993 by Edward W. Said.

Wait for the supervisor's instructions before you open the page to the topic.
Please print and sign your name and write the date in the designated spaces below.

Time: 35 Minutes

General Directions

You will have 35 minutes in which to plan and write an essay on the topic inside. Read the topic and the accompanying directions carefully. You will probably find it best to spend a few minutes considering the topic and organizing your thoughts before you begin writing. In your essay, be sure to develop your ideas fully, leaving time, if possible, to review what you have written. **Do not write on a topic other than the one specified. Writing on a topic of your own choice is not acceptable.**

No special knowledge is required or expected for this writing exercise. Law schools are interested in the reasoning, clarity, organization, language usage, and writing mechanics displayed in your essay. How well you write is more important than how much you write.

Confine your essay to the blocked, lined area on the front and back of the separate Writing Sample Response Sheet. Only that area will be reproduced for law schools. Be sure that your writing is legible.

Both this topic sheet and your response sheet must be turned over to the testing staff before you leave the room.

Topic Code

Date
/ /

Print Your Full Name Here		
Last	First	M.I.

Sign Your Name Here

Scratch Paper
Do not write your essay in this space.

LSAT® Writing Sample Topic

Directions: The scenario presented below describes two choices, either one of which can be supported on the basis of the information given. Your essay should consider both choices and argue for one over the other, based on the two specified criteria and the facts provided. There is no "right" or "wrong" choice: a reasonable argument can be made for either.

Calvin, the hiring manager for Ocean Blue Cruise Line, is seeking a permanent chef for a cruise ship. In the meantime, he has found someone who can commit to a three-month contract and someone else who can commit to a six-month contract. Calvin has decided that Ocean Blue should enter into one of the limited-term contracts. Write an essay in which you argue for choosing one chef over the other, keeping in mind the following two criteria:

- Ocean Blue would like to hire a chef who can take over management of the large galley staff.
- Ocean Blue would like to hire a permanent chef as soon as possible.

Marie, who has served as executive chef in a large resort kitchen for the past three years, is available for a three-month contract, with no possibility of her staying on permanently. She has earned a strong reputation for competence in kitchen organization and management. Her objective, should she be offered the contract, is to reorganize and streamline the galley operations to sustain a degree of efficiency and productivity even after she leaves. Because Marie is also affiliated with a cooking school, Calvin would have the opportunity to establish contacts that might lead to the permanent hire he desires to make.

Jared is available to take on a six-month contract. Early in his career, he served as an assistant pastry chef on a cruise ship in a nonmanagement role. He has since had a very successful fourteen-year career managing a small catering company, in which he was responsible for staffing, food planning, and quality control, but he has never managed a staff as large as the ship's galley staff and would have to learn on his feet. While the contract with Jared offers Ocean Blue a greater period of stability and security than the shorter three-month contract does, it takes the cruise line off the market for hiring a permanent employee for twice as long. However, Jared has indicated that he would probably be willing to accept the permanent position at the end of the contract.

Scratch Paper
Do not write your essay in this space.

Writing Sample Response Sheet

DO NOT WRITE IN THIS SPACE

Begin your essay in the lined area below.
Continue on the back if you need more space.

COMPUTING YOUR SCORE

Directions:

1. Use the Answer Key on the next page to check your answers.

2. Use the Scoring Worksheet below to compute your raw score.

3. Use the Score Conversion Chart to convert your raw score into the 120-180 scale.

Scoring Worksheet

1. Enter the number of questions you answered correctly in each section.

	Number Correct
SECTION I	_____
SECTION II	_____
SECTION III	_____
SECTION IV	_____

2. Enter the sum here: _____

This is your Raw Score.

Conversion Chart
For Converting Raw Score to the 120-180 LSAT Scaled Score
LSAT Form 6LSN70

Reported Score	Raw Score Lowest	Raw Score Highest
180	98	100
179	97	97
178	—*	—*
177	96	96
176	95	95
175	94	94
174	—*	—*
173	93	93
172	92	92
171	91	91
170	90	90
169	89	89
168	88	88
167	86	87
166	85	85
165	84	84
164	83	83
163	81	82
162	80	80
161	78	79
160	77	77
159	75	76
158	73	74
157	72	72
156	70	71
155	68	69
154	66	67
153	64	65
152	63	63
151	61	62
150	59	60
149	57	58
148	55	56
147	53	54
146	52	52
145	50	51
144	48	49
143	46	47
142	45	45
141	43	44
140	41	42
139	40	40
138	38	39
137	36	37
136	35	35
135	33	34
134	32	32
133	30	31
132	29	29
131	27	28
130	26	26
129	25	25
128	23	24
127	22	22
126	21	21
125	20	20
124	18	19
123	17	17
122	16	16
121	15	15
120	0	14

*There is no raw score that will produce this scaled score for this form.

ANSWER KEY

SECTION I

1.	C	8.	A	15.	C	22.	B
2.	D	9.	E	16.	A	23.	D
3.	C	10.	A	17.	D	24.	C
4.	B	11.	B	18.	C	25.	E
5.	D	12.	D	19.	D	26.	C
6.	A	13.	E	20.	A	27.	D
7.	D	14.	E	21.	D	28.	B

SECTION II

1.	B	8.	A	15.	E	22.	D
2.	B	9.	B	16.	C	23.	E
3.	A	10.	B	17.	A	24.	A
4.	E	11.	E	18.	C	25.	D
5.	B	12.	A	19.	A		
6.	C	13.	D	20.	C		
7.	B	14.	D	21.	E		

SECTION III

1.	D	7.	D	13.	B	19.	D
2.	B	8.	B	14.	C	20.	E
3.	C	9.	A	15.	A	21.	D
4.	E	10.	E	16.	E	22.	A
5.	B	11.	B	17.	E		
6.	E	12.	B	18.	B		

SECTION IV

1.	E	8.	B	15.	D	22.	E
2.	C	9.	A	16.	C	23.	C
3.	B	10.	E	17.	A	24.	D
4.	E	11.	D	18.	D	25.	E
5.	E	12.	A	19.	A		
6.	C	13.	B	20.	E		
7.	B	14.	D	21.	C		

ANSWER SHEETS

General Directions for the LSAT Answer Sheet

The actual testing time for this portion of the test will be 2 hours 55 minutes. There are five sections, each with a time limit of 35 minutes. The supervisor will tell you when to begin and end each section. If you finish a section before time is called, you may check your work on that section **only;** do not turn to any other section of the test book and do not work on any other section either in the test book or on the answer sheet.

There are several different types of questions on the test, and each question type has its own directions. **Be sure you understand the directions for each question type before attempting to answer any questions in that section.**

Not everyone will finish all the questions in the time allowed. Do not hurry, but work steadily and as quickly as you can without sacrificing accuracy. You are advised to use your time effectively. If a question seems too difficult, go on to the next one and return to the difficult question after completing the section. **MARK THE BEST ANSWER YOU CAN FOR EVERY QUESTION. NO DEDUCTIONS WILL BE MADE FOR WRONG ANSWERS. YOUR SCORE WILL BE BASED ONLY ON THE NUMBER OF QUESTIONS YOU ANSWER CORRECTLY.**

ALL YOUR ANSWERS MUST BE MARKED ON THE ANSWER SHEET. Answer spaces for each question are lettered to correspond with the letters of the potential answers to each question in the test book. After you have decided which of the answers is correct, blacken the corresponding space on the answer sheet. **BE SURE THAT EACH MARK IS BLACK AND COMPLETELY FILLS THE ANSWER SPACE.** Give only one answer to each question. If you change an answer, be sure that all previous marks are **erased completely.** Since the answer sheet is machine scored, incomplete erasures may be interpreted as intended answers. **ANSWERS RECORDED IN THE TEST BOOK WILL NOT BE SCORED.**

There may be more question numbers on this answer sheet than there are questions in a section. Do not be concerned, but be certain that the section and number of the question you are answering matches the answer sheet section and question number. Additional answer spaces in any answer sheet section should be left blank. Begin your next section in the number one answer space for that section.

LSAC takes various steps to ensure that answer sheets are returned from test centers in a timely manner for processing. In the unlikely event that an answer sheet is not received, LSAC will permit the examinee either to retest at no additional fee or to receive a refund of his or her LSAT fee. **THESE REMEDIES ARE THE ONLY REMEDIES AVAILABLE IN THE UNLIKELY EVENT THAT AN ANSWER SHEET IS NOT RECEIVED BY LSAC.**

Score Cancellation

Complete this section only if you are absolutely certain you want to cancel your score. **A CANCELLATION REQUEST CANNOT BE RESCINDED. IF YOU ARE AT ALL UNCERTAIN, YOU SHOULD NOT COMPLETE THIS SECTION.**

To cancel your score from this administration, you **must:**

A. fill in both ovals here ...... ◯ ◯
 AND
B. read the following statement. Then sign your name and enter the date.
 YOUR SIGNATURE ALONE IS NOT SUFFICIENT FOR SCORE CANCELLATION. BOTH OVALS ABOVE MUST BE FILLED IN FOR SCANNING EQUIPMENT TO RECOGNIZE YOUR REQUEST FOR SCORE CANCELLATION.

I certify that I wish to cancel my test score from this administration. I understand that my request is irreversible and that my score will not be sent to me or to the law schools to which I apply.

_____
Sign your name in full

_____
Date

FOR LSAC USE ONLY ●

HOW DID YOU PREPARE FOR THE LSAT?
(Select all that apply.)

Responses to this item are voluntary and will be used for statistical research purposes only.

◯ By studying the free sample questions available on LSAC's website.
◯ By taking the free sample LSAT available on LSAC's website.
◯ By working through official LSAT *PrepTests*, *ItemWise*, and/or other LSAC test prep products.
◯ By using LSAT prep books or software **not** published by LSAC.
◯ By attending a commercial test preparation or coaching course.
◯ By attending a test preparation or coaching course offered through an undergraduate institution.
◯ Self study.
◯ Other preparation.
◯ No preparation.

CERTIFYING STATEMENT

Please write the following statement. Sign and date.

I certify that I am the examinee whose name appears on this answer sheet and that I am here to take the LSAT for the sole purpose of being considered for admission to law school. I further certify that I will neither assist nor receive assistance from any other candidate, and I agree not to copy, retain, or transmit examination questions in any form or discuss them with any other person.

_____
_____
_____
_____
_____
_____
_____
_____
_____
_____

SIGNATURE: _____ TODAY'S DATE: ___/___/___
 MONTH DAY YEAR

INSTRUCTIONS FOR COMPLETING THE BIOGRAPHICAL AREA ARE ON THE BACK COVER OF YOUR TEST BOOKLET.
USE ONLY A NO. 2 OR HB PENCIL TO COMPLETE THIS ANSWER SHEET. DO NOT USE INK.

A

1 LAST NAME / FIRST NAME / MI

2 LAST 4 DIGITS OF SOCIAL SECURITY/ SOCIAL INSURANCE NO.

3 LSAC ACCOUNT NUMBER

4 CENTER NUMBER

5 DATE OF BIRTH
MONTH DAY YEAR
Jan, Feb, Mar, Apr, May, June, July, Aug, Sept, Oct, Nov, Dec

6 TEST FORM CODE

7 RACIAL/ETHNIC DESCRIPTION
Mark one or more
- 1 Amer. Indian/Alaska Native
- 2 Asian
- 3 Black/African American
- 4 Canadian Aboriginal
- 5 Caucasian/White
- 6 Hispanic/Latino
- 7 Native Hawaiian/ Other Pacific Islander
- 8 Puerto Rican
- 9 TSI/Aboriginal Australian

8 GENDER
- Male
- Female

9 DOMINANT LANGUAGE
- English
- Other

10 ENGLISH FLUENCY
- Yes
- No

11 TEST DATE
MONTH / DAY / YEAR

12 TEST FORM

13 TEST BOOK SERIAL NO.

14 PLEASE PRINT INFORMATION
LAST NAME
FIRST NAME
DATE OF BIRTH

=== **Law School Admission Test** ===

Mark one and only one answer to each question. Be sure to fill in completely the space for your intended answer choice. If you erase, do so completely. Make no stray marks.

SECTION 1, SECTION 2, SECTION 3, SECTION 4, SECTION 5 — questions 1–30, each A B C D E

SCANTRON® EliteView™ EM-290725-3:654321   **SIDE 1**

INSTRUCTIONS FOR COMPLETING THE BIOGRAPHICAL AREA ARE ON THE BACK COVER OF YOUR TEST BOOKLET.
USE ONLY A NO. 2 OR HB PENCIL TO COMPLETE THIS ANSWER SHEET. DO NOT USE INK.

A

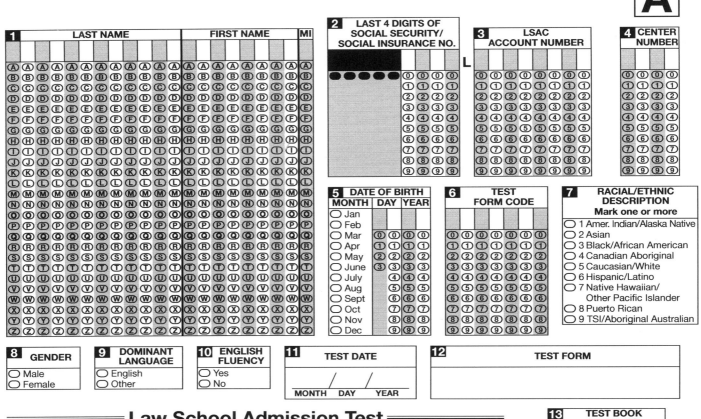

8 GENDER
- Male
- Female

9 DOMINANT LANGUAGE
- English
- Other

10 ENGLISH FLUENCY
- Yes
- No

11 TEST DATE
___ / ___ / ___
MONTH   DAY   YEAR

12 TEST FORM

Law School Admission Test

Mark one and only one answer to each question. Be sure to fill in completely the space for your intended answer choice. If you erase, do so completely. Make no stray marks.

13 TEST BOOK SERIAL NO.

SECTION 1	SECTION 2	SECTION 3	SECTION 4	SECTION 5
1 Ⓐ Ⓑ Ⓒ Ⓓ Ⓔ	1 Ⓐ Ⓑ Ⓒ Ⓓ Ⓔ	1 Ⓐ Ⓑ Ⓒ Ⓓ Ⓔ	1 Ⓐ Ⓑ Ⓒ Ⓓ Ⓔ	1 Ⓐ Ⓑ Ⓒ Ⓓ Ⓔ
2 Ⓐ Ⓑ Ⓒ Ⓓ Ⓔ	2 Ⓐ Ⓑ Ⓒ Ⓓ Ⓔ	2 Ⓐ Ⓑ Ⓒ Ⓓ Ⓔ	2 Ⓐ Ⓑ Ⓒ Ⓓ Ⓔ	2 Ⓐ Ⓑ Ⓒ Ⓓ Ⓔ
3 Ⓐ Ⓑ Ⓒ Ⓓ Ⓔ	3 Ⓐ Ⓑ Ⓒ Ⓓ Ⓔ	3 Ⓐ Ⓑ Ⓒ Ⓓ Ⓔ	3 Ⓐ Ⓑ Ⓒ Ⓓ Ⓔ	3 Ⓐ Ⓑ Ⓒ Ⓓ Ⓔ
4 Ⓐ Ⓑ Ⓒ Ⓓ Ⓔ	4 Ⓐ Ⓑ Ⓒ Ⓓ Ⓔ	4 Ⓐ Ⓑ Ⓒ Ⓓ Ⓔ	4 Ⓐ Ⓑ Ⓒ Ⓓ Ⓔ	4 Ⓐ Ⓑ Ⓒ Ⓓ Ⓔ
5 Ⓐ Ⓑ Ⓒ Ⓓ Ⓔ	5 Ⓐ Ⓑ Ⓒ Ⓓ Ⓔ	5 Ⓐ Ⓑ Ⓒ Ⓓ Ⓔ	5 Ⓐ Ⓑ Ⓒ Ⓓ Ⓔ	5 Ⓐ Ⓑ Ⓒ Ⓓ Ⓔ
6 Ⓐ Ⓑ Ⓒ Ⓓ Ⓔ	6 Ⓐ Ⓑ Ⓒ Ⓓ Ⓔ	6 Ⓐ Ⓑ Ⓒ Ⓓ Ⓔ	6 Ⓐ Ⓑ Ⓒ Ⓓ Ⓔ	6 Ⓐ Ⓑ Ⓒ Ⓓ Ⓔ
7 Ⓐ Ⓑ Ⓒ Ⓓ Ⓔ	7 Ⓐ Ⓑ Ⓒ Ⓓ Ⓔ	7 Ⓐ Ⓑ Ⓒ Ⓓ Ⓔ	7 Ⓐ Ⓑ Ⓒ Ⓓ Ⓔ	7 Ⓐ Ⓑ Ⓒ Ⓓ Ⓔ
8 Ⓐ Ⓑ Ⓒ Ⓓ Ⓔ	8 Ⓐ Ⓑ Ⓒ Ⓓ Ⓔ	8 Ⓐ Ⓑ Ⓒ Ⓓ Ⓔ	8 Ⓐ Ⓑ Ⓒ Ⓓ Ⓔ	8 Ⓐ Ⓑ Ⓒ Ⓓ Ⓔ
9 Ⓐ Ⓑ Ⓒ Ⓓ Ⓔ	9 Ⓐ Ⓑ Ⓒ Ⓓ Ⓔ	9 Ⓐ Ⓑ Ⓒ Ⓓ Ⓔ	9 Ⓐ Ⓑ Ⓒ Ⓓ Ⓔ	9 Ⓐ Ⓑ Ⓒ Ⓓ Ⓔ
10 Ⓐ Ⓑ Ⓒ Ⓓ Ⓔ	10 Ⓐ Ⓑ Ⓒ Ⓓ Ⓔ	10 Ⓐ Ⓑ Ⓒ Ⓓ Ⓔ	10 Ⓐ Ⓑ Ⓒ Ⓓ Ⓔ	10 Ⓐ Ⓑ Ⓒ Ⓓ Ⓔ
11 Ⓐ Ⓑ Ⓒ Ⓓ Ⓔ	11 Ⓐ Ⓑ Ⓒ Ⓓ Ⓔ	11 Ⓐ Ⓑ Ⓒ Ⓓ Ⓔ	11 Ⓐ Ⓑ Ⓒ Ⓓ Ⓔ	11 Ⓐ Ⓑ Ⓒ Ⓓ Ⓔ
12 Ⓐ Ⓑ Ⓒ Ⓓ Ⓔ	12 Ⓐ Ⓑ Ⓒ Ⓓ Ⓔ	12 Ⓐ Ⓑ Ⓒ Ⓓ Ⓔ	12 Ⓐ Ⓑ Ⓒ Ⓓ Ⓔ	12 Ⓐ Ⓑ Ⓒ Ⓓ Ⓔ
13 Ⓐ Ⓑ Ⓒ Ⓓ Ⓔ	13 Ⓐ Ⓑ Ⓒ Ⓓ Ⓔ	13 Ⓐ Ⓑ Ⓒ Ⓓ Ⓔ	13 Ⓐ Ⓑ Ⓒ Ⓓ Ⓔ	13 Ⓐ Ⓑ Ⓒ Ⓓ Ⓔ
14 Ⓐ Ⓑ Ⓒ Ⓓ Ⓔ	14 Ⓐ Ⓑ Ⓒ Ⓓ Ⓔ	14 Ⓐ Ⓑ Ⓒ Ⓓ Ⓔ	14 Ⓐ Ⓑ Ⓒ Ⓓ Ⓔ	14 Ⓐ Ⓑ Ⓒ Ⓓ Ⓔ
15 Ⓐ Ⓑ Ⓒ Ⓓ Ⓔ	15 Ⓐ Ⓑ Ⓒ Ⓓ Ⓔ	15 Ⓐ Ⓑ Ⓒ Ⓓ Ⓔ	15 Ⓐ Ⓑ Ⓒ Ⓓ Ⓔ	15 Ⓐ Ⓑ Ⓒ Ⓓ Ⓔ
16 Ⓐ Ⓑ Ⓒ Ⓓ Ⓔ	16 Ⓐ Ⓑ Ⓒ Ⓓ Ⓔ	16 Ⓐ Ⓑ Ⓒ Ⓓ Ⓔ	16 Ⓐ Ⓑ Ⓒ Ⓓ Ⓔ	16 Ⓐ Ⓑ Ⓒ Ⓓ Ⓔ
17 Ⓐ Ⓑ Ⓒ Ⓓ Ⓔ	17 Ⓐ Ⓑ Ⓒ Ⓓ Ⓔ	17 Ⓐ Ⓑ Ⓒ Ⓓ Ⓔ	17 Ⓐ Ⓑ Ⓒ Ⓓ Ⓔ	17 Ⓐ Ⓑ Ⓒ Ⓓ Ⓔ
18 Ⓐ Ⓑ Ⓒ Ⓓ Ⓔ	18 Ⓐ Ⓑ Ⓒ Ⓓ Ⓔ	18 Ⓐ Ⓑ Ⓒ Ⓓ Ⓔ	18 Ⓐ Ⓑ Ⓒ Ⓓ Ⓔ	18 Ⓐ Ⓑ Ⓒ Ⓓ Ⓔ
19 Ⓐ Ⓑ Ⓒ Ⓓ Ⓔ	19 Ⓐ Ⓑ Ⓒ Ⓓ Ⓔ	19 Ⓐ Ⓑ Ⓒ Ⓓ Ⓔ	19 Ⓐ Ⓑ Ⓒ Ⓓ Ⓔ	19 Ⓐ Ⓑ Ⓒ Ⓓ Ⓔ
20 Ⓐ Ⓑ Ⓒ Ⓓ Ⓔ	20 Ⓐ Ⓑ Ⓒ Ⓓ Ⓔ	20 Ⓐ Ⓑ Ⓒ Ⓓ Ⓔ	20 Ⓐ Ⓑ Ⓒ Ⓓ Ⓔ	20 Ⓐ Ⓑ Ⓒ Ⓓ Ⓔ
21 Ⓐ Ⓑ Ⓒ Ⓓ Ⓔ	21 Ⓐ Ⓑ Ⓒ Ⓓ Ⓔ	21 Ⓐ Ⓑ Ⓒ Ⓓ Ⓔ	21 Ⓐ Ⓑ Ⓒ Ⓓ Ⓔ	21 Ⓐ Ⓑ Ⓒ Ⓓ Ⓔ
22 Ⓐ Ⓑ Ⓒ Ⓓ Ⓔ	22 Ⓐ Ⓑ Ⓒ Ⓓ Ⓔ	22 Ⓐ Ⓑ Ⓒ Ⓓ Ⓔ	22 Ⓐ Ⓑ Ⓒ Ⓓ Ⓔ	22 Ⓐ Ⓑ Ⓒ Ⓓ Ⓔ
23 Ⓐ Ⓑ Ⓒ Ⓓ Ⓔ	23 Ⓐ Ⓑ Ⓒ Ⓓ Ⓔ	23 Ⓐ Ⓑ Ⓒ Ⓓ Ⓔ	23 Ⓐ Ⓑ Ⓒ Ⓓ Ⓔ	23 Ⓐ Ⓑ Ⓒ Ⓓ Ⓔ
24 Ⓐ Ⓑ Ⓒ Ⓓ Ⓔ	24 Ⓐ Ⓑ Ⓒ Ⓓ Ⓔ	24 Ⓐ Ⓑ Ⓒ Ⓓ Ⓔ	24 Ⓐ Ⓑ Ⓒ Ⓓ Ⓔ	24 Ⓐ Ⓑ Ⓒ Ⓓ Ⓔ
25 Ⓐ Ⓑ Ⓒ Ⓓ Ⓔ	25 Ⓐ Ⓑ Ⓒ Ⓓ Ⓔ	25 Ⓐ Ⓑ Ⓒ Ⓓ Ⓔ	25 Ⓐ Ⓑ Ⓒ Ⓓ Ⓔ	25 Ⓐ Ⓑ Ⓒ Ⓓ Ⓔ
26 Ⓐ Ⓑ Ⓒ Ⓓ Ⓔ	26 Ⓐ Ⓑ Ⓒ Ⓓ Ⓔ	26 Ⓐ Ⓑ Ⓒ Ⓓ Ⓔ	26 Ⓐ Ⓑ Ⓒ Ⓓ Ⓔ	26 Ⓐ Ⓑ Ⓒ Ⓓ Ⓔ
27 Ⓐ Ⓑ Ⓒ Ⓓ Ⓔ	27 Ⓐ Ⓑ Ⓒ Ⓓ Ⓔ	27 Ⓐ Ⓑ Ⓒ Ⓓ Ⓔ	27 Ⓐ Ⓑ Ⓒ Ⓓ Ⓔ	27 Ⓐ Ⓑ Ⓒ Ⓓ Ⓔ
28 Ⓐ Ⓑ Ⓒ Ⓓ Ⓔ	28 Ⓐ Ⓑ Ⓒ Ⓓ Ⓔ	28 Ⓐ Ⓑ Ⓒ Ⓓ Ⓔ	28 Ⓐ Ⓑ Ⓒ Ⓓ Ⓔ	28 Ⓐ Ⓑ Ⓒ Ⓓ Ⓔ
29 Ⓐ Ⓑ Ⓒ Ⓓ Ⓔ	29 Ⓐ Ⓑ Ⓒ Ⓓ Ⓔ	29 Ⓐ Ⓑ Ⓒ Ⓓ Ⓔ	29 Ⓐ Ⓑ Ⓒ Ⓓ Ⓔ	29 Ⓐ Ⓑ Ⓒ Ⓓ Ⓔ
30 Ⓐ Ⓑ Ⓒ Ⓓ Ⓔ	30 Ⓐ Ⓑ Ⓒ Ⓓ Ⓔ	30 Ⓐ Ⓑ Ⓒ Ⓓ Ⓔ	30 Ⓐ Ⓑ Ⓒ Ⓓ Ⓔ	30 Ⓐ Ⓑ Ⓒ Ⓓ Ⓔ

14 PLEASE PRINT INFORMATION

LAST NAME
_____

FIRST NAME
_____

DATE OF BIRTH
_____

● Ⓑ

A

INSTRUCTIONS FOR COMPLETING THE BIOGRAPHICAL AREA ARE ON THE BACK COVER OF YOUR TEST BOOKLET.
USE ONLY A NO. 2 OR HB PENCIL TO COMPLETE THIS ANSWER SHEET. DO NOT USE INK.

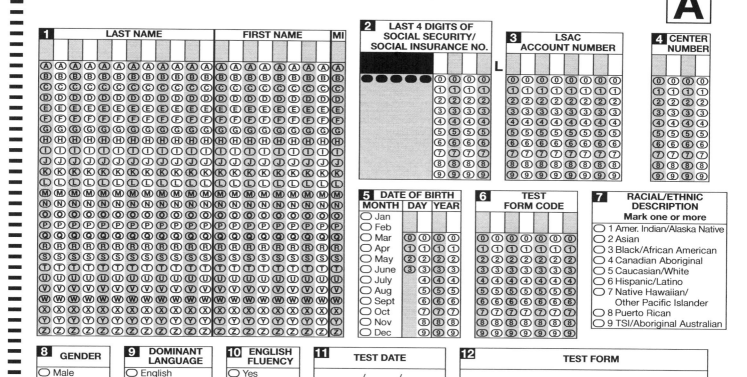

8 GENDER
- ○ Male
- ○ Female

9 DOMINANT LANGUAGE
- ○ English
- ○ Other

10 ENGLISH FLUENCY
- ○ Yes
- ○ No

11 TEST DATE
___ / ___ / ___
MONTH   DAY   YEAR

12 TEST FORM

Law School Admission Test

Mark one and only one answer to each question. Be sure to fill in completely the space for your intended answer choice. If you erase, do so completely. Make no stray marks.

13 TEST BOOK SERIAL NO.

SECTION 1	SECTION 2	SECTION 3	SECTION 4	SECTION 5
1 Ⓐ Ⓑ Ⓒ Ⓓ Ⓔ	1 Ⓐ Ⓑ Ⓒ Ⓓ Ⓔ	1 Ⓐ Ⓑ Ⓒ Ⓓ Ⓔ	1 Ⓐ Ⓑ Ⓒ Ⓓ Ⓔ	1 Ⓐ Ⓑ Ⓒ Ⓓ Ⓔ
2 Ⓐ Ⓑ Ⓒ Ⓓ Ⓔ	2 Ⓐ Ⓑ Ⓒ Ⓓ Ⓔ	2 Ⓐ Ⓑ Ⓒ Ⓓ Ⓔ	2 Ⓐ Ⓑ Ⓒ Ⓓ Ⓔ	2 Ⓐ Ⓑ Ⓒ Ⓓ Ⓔ
3 Ⓐ Ⓑ Ⓒ Ⓓ Ⓔ	3 Ⓐ Ⓑ Ⓒ Ⓓ Ⓔ	3 Ⓐ Ⓑ Ⓒ Ⓓ Ⓔ	3 Ⓐ Ⓑ Ⓒ Ⓓ Ⓔ	3 Ⓐ Ⓑ Ⓒ Ⓓ Ⓔ
4 Ⓐ Ⓑ Ⓒ Ⓓ Ⓔ	4 Ⓐ Ⓑ Ⓒ Ⓓ Ⓔ	4 Ⓐ Ⓑ Ⓒ Ⓓ Ⓔ	4 Ⓐ Ⓑ Ⓒ Ⓓ Ⓔ	4 Ⓐ Ⓑ Ⓒ Ⓓ Ⓔ
5 Ⓐ Ⓑ Ⓒ Ⓓ Ⓔ	5 Ⓐ Ⓑ Ⓒ Ⓓ Ⓔ	5 Ⓐ Ⓑ Ⓒ Ⓓ Ⓔ	5 Ⓐ Ⓑ Ⓒ Ⓓ Ⓔ	5 Ⓐ Ⓑ Ⓒ Ⓓ Ⓔ
6 Ⓐ Ⓑ Ⓒ Ⓓ Ⓔ	6 Ⓐ Ⓑ Ⓒ Ⓓ Ⓔ	6 Ⓐ Ⓑ Ⓒ Ⓓ Ⓔ	6 Ⓐ Ⓑ Ⓒ Ⓓ Ⓔ	6 Ⓐ Ⓑ Ⓒ Ⓓ Ⓔ
7 Ⓐ Ⓑ Ⓒ Ⓓ Ⓔ	7 Ⓐ Ⓑ Ⓒ Ⓓ Ⓔ	7 Ⓐ Ⓑ Ⓒ Ⓓ Ⓔ	7 Ⓐ Ⓑ Ⓒ Ⓓ Ⓔ	7 Ⓐ Ⓑ Ⓒ Ⓓ Ⓔ
8 Ⓐ Ⓑ Ⓒ Ⓓ Ⓔ	8 Ⓐ Ⓑ Ⓒ Ⓓ Ⓔ	8 Ⓐ Ⓑ Ⓒ Ⓓ Ⓔ	8 Ⓐ Ⓑ Ⓒ Ⓓ Ⓔ	8 Ⓐ Ⓑ Ⓒ Ⓓ Ⓔ
9 Ⓐ Ⓑ Ⓒ Ⓓ Ⓔ	9 Ⓐ Ⓑ Ⓒ Ⓓ Ⓔ	9 Ⓐ Ⓑ Ⓒ Ⓓ Ⓔ	9 Ⓐ Ⓑ Ⓒ Ⓓ Ⓔ	9 Ⓐ Ⓑ Ⓒ Ⓓ Ⓔ
10 Ⓐ Ⓑ Ⓒ Ⓓ Ⓔ	10 Ⓐ Ⓑ Ⓒ Ⓓ Ⓔ	10 Ⓐ Ⓑ Ⓒ Ⓓ Ⓔ	10 Ⓐ Ⓑ Ⓒ Ⓓ Ⓔ	10 Ⓐ Ⓑ Ⓒ Ⓓ Ⓔ
11 Ⓐ Ⓑ Ⓒ Ⓓ Ⓔ	11 Ⓐ Ⓑ Ⓒ Ⓓ Ⓔ	11 Ⓐ Ⓑ Ⓒ Ⓓ Ⓔ	11 Ⓐ Ⓑ Ⓒ Ⓓ Ⓔ	11 Ⓐ Ⓑ Ⓒ Ⓓ Ⓔ
12 Ⓐ Ⓑ Ⓒ Ⓓ Ⓔ	12 Ⓐ Ⓑ Ⓒ Ⓓ Ⓔ	12 Ⓐ Ⓑ Ⓒ Ⓓ Ⓔ	12 Ⓐ Ⓑ Ⓒ Ⓓ Ⓔ	12 Ⓐ Ⓑ Ⓒ Ⓓ Ⓔ
13 Ⓐ Ⓑ Ⓒ Ⓓ Ⓔ	13 Ⓐ Ⓑ Ⓒ Ⓓ Ⓔ	13 Ⓐ Ⓑ Ⓒ Ⓓ Ⓔ	13 Ⓐ Ⓑ Ⓒ Ⓓ Ⓔ	13 Ⓐ Ⓑ Ⓒ Ⓓ Ⓔ
14 Ⓐ Ⓑ Ⓒ Ⓓ Ⓔ	14 Ⓐ Ⓑ Ⓒ Ⓓ Ⓔ	14 Ⓐ Ⓑ Ⓒ Ⓓ Ⓔ	14 Ⓐ Ⓑ Ⓒ Ⓓ Ⓔ	14 Ⓐ Ⓑ Ⓒ Ⓓ Ⓔ
15 Ⓐ Ⓑ Ⓒ Ⓓ Ⓔ	15 Ⓐ Ⓑ Ⓒ Ⓓ Ⓔ	15 Ⓐ Ⓑ Ⓒ Ⓓ Ⓔ	15 Ⓐ Ⓑ Ⓒ Ⓓ Ⓔ	15 Ⓐ Ⓑ Ⓒ Ⓓ Ⓔ
16 Ⓐ Ⓑ Ⓒ Ⓓ Ⓔ	16 Ⓐ Ⓑ Ⓒ Ⓓ Ⓔ	16 Ⓐ Ⓑ Ⓒ Ⓓ Ⓔ	16 Ⓐ Ⓑ Ⓒ Ⓓ Ⓔ	16 Ⓐ Ⓑ Ⓒ Ⓓ Ⓔ
17 Ⓐ Ⓑ Ⓒ Ⓓ Ⓔ	17 Ⓐ Ⓑ Ⓒ Ⓓ Ⓔ	17 Ⓐ Ⓑ Ⓒ Ⓓ Ⓔ	17 Ⓐ Ⓑ Ⓒ Ⓓ Ⓔ	17 Ⓐ Ⓑ Ⓒ Ⓓ Ⓔ
18 Ⓐ Ⓑ Ⓒ Ⓓ Ⓔ	18 Ⓐ Ⓑ Ⓒ Ⓓ Ⓔ	18 Ⓐ Ⓑ Ⓒ Ⓓ Ⓔ	18 Ⓐ Ⓑ Ⓒ Ⓓ Ⓔ	18 Ⓐ Ⓑ Ⓒ Ⓓ Ⓔ
19 Ⓐ Ⓑ Ⓒ Ⓓ Ⓔ	19 Ⓐ Ⓑ Ⓒ Ⓓ Ⓔ	19 Ⓐ Ⓑ Ⓒ Ⓓ Ⓔ	19 Ⓐ Ⓑ Ⓒ Ⓓ Ⓔ	19 Ⓐ Ⓑ Ⓒ Ⓓ Ⓔ
20 Ⓐ Ⓑ Ⓒ Ⓓ Ⓔ	20 Ⓐ Ⓑ Ⓒ Ⓓ Ⓔ	20 Ⓐ Ⓑ Ⓒ Ⓓ Ⓔ	20 Ⓐ Ⓑ Ⓒ Ⓓ Ⓔ	20 Ⓐ Ⓑ Ⓒ Ⓓ Ⓔ
21 Ⓐ Ⓑ Ⓒ Ⓓ Ⓔ	21 Ⓐ Ⓑ Ⓒ Ⓓ Ⓔ	21 Ⓐ Ⓑ Ⓒ Ⓓ Ⓔ	21 Ⓐ Ⓑ Ⓒ Ⓓ Ⓔ	21 Ⓐ Ⓑ Ⓒ Ⓓ Ⓔ
22 Ⓐ Ⓑ Ⓒ Ⓓ Ⓔ	22 Ⓐ Ⓑ Ⓒ Ⓓ Ⓔ	22 Ⓐ Ⓑ Ⓒ Ⓓ Ⓔ	22 Ⓐ Ⓑ Ⓒ Ⓓ Ⓔ	22 Ⓐ Ⓑ Ⓒ Ⓓ Ⓔ
23 Ⓐ Ⓑ Ⓒ Ⓓ Ⓔ	23 Ⓐ Ⓑ Ⓒ Ⓓ Ⓔ	23 Ⓐ Ⓑ Ⓒ Ⓓ Ⓔ	23 Ⓐ Ⓑ Ⓒ Ⓓ Ⓔ	23 Ⓐ Ⓑ Ⓒ Ⓓ Ⓔ
24 Ⓐ Ⓑ Ⓒ Ⓓ Ⓔ	24 Ⓐ Ⓑ Ⓒ Ⓓ Ⓔ	24 Ⓐ Ⓑ Ⓒ Ⓓ Ⓔ	24 Ⓐ Ⓑ Ⓒ Ⓓ Ⓔ	24 Ⓐ Ⓑ Ⓒ Ⓓ Ⓔ
25 Ⓐ Ⓑ Ⓒ Ⓓ Ⓔ	25 Ⓐ Ⓑ Ⓒ Ⓓ Ⓔ	25 Ⓐ Ⓑ Ⓒ Ⓓ Ⓔ	25 Ⓐ Ⓑ Ⓒ Ⓓ Ⓔ	25 Ⓐ Ⓑ Ⓒ Ⓓ Ⓔ
26 Ⓐ Ⓑ Ⓒ Ⓓ Ⓔ	26 Ⓐ Ⓑ Ⓒ Ⓓ Ⓔ	26 Ⓐ Ⓑ Ⓒ Ⓓ Ⓔ	26 Ⓐ Ⓑ Ⓒ Ⓓ Ⓔ	26 Ⓐ Ⓑ Ⓒ Ⓓ Ⓔ
27 Ⓐ Ⓑ Ⓒ Ⓓ Ⓔ	27 Ⓐ Ⓑ Ⓒ Ⓓ Ⓔ	27 Ⓐ Ⓑ Ⓒ Ⓓ Ⓔ	27 Ⓐ Ⓑ Ⓒ Ⓓ Ⓔ	27 Ⓐ Ⓑ Ⓒ Ⓓ Ⓔ
28 Ⓐ Ⓑ Ⓒ Ⓓ Ⓔ	28 Ⓐ Ⓑ Ⓒ Ⓓ Ⓔ	28 Ⓐ Ⓑ Ⓒ Ⓓ Ⓔ	28 Ⓐ Ⓑ Ⓒ Ⓓ Ⓔ	28 Ⓐ Ⓑ Ⓒ Ⓓ Ⓔ
29 Ⓐ Ⓑ Ⓒ Ⓓ Ⓔ	29 Ⓐ Ⓑ Ⓒ Ⓓ Ⓔ	29 Ⓐ Ⓑ Ⓒ Ⓓ Ⓔ	29 Ⓐ Ⓑ Ⓒ Ⓓ Ⓔ	29 Ⓐ Ⓑ Ⓒ Ⓓ Ⓔ
30 Ⓐ Ⓑ Ⓒ Ⓓ Ⓔ	30 Ⓐ Ⓑ Ⓒ Ⓓ Ⓔ	30 Ⓐ Ⓑ Ⓒ Ⓓ Ⓔ	30 Ⓐ Ⓑ Ⓒ Ⓓ Ⓔ	30 Ⓐ Ⓑ Ⓒ Ⓓ Ⓔ

14 PLEASE PRINT INFORMATION

LAST NAME
_____

FIRST NAME
_____

DATE OF BIRTH
_____

INSTRUCTIONS FOR COMPLETING THE BIOGRAPHICAL AREA ARE ON THE BACK COVER OF YOUR TEST BOOKLET.
USE ONLY A NO. 2 OR HB PENCIL TO COMPLETE THIS ANSWER SHEET. DO NOT USE INK.

A

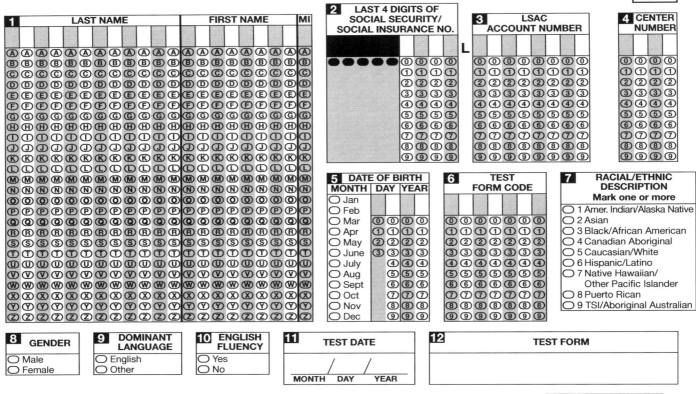

1 LAST NAME / FIRST NAME / MI

2 LAST 4 DIGITS OF SOCIAL SECURITY/ SOCIAL INSURANCE NO.

3 LSAC ACCOUNT NUMBER

4 CENTER NUMBER

5 DATE OF BIRTH — MONTH | DAY | YEAR
Jan, Feb, Mar, Apr, May, June, July, Aug, Sept, Oct, Nov, Dec

6 TEST FORM CODE

7 RACIAL/ETHNIC DESCRIPTION — Mark one or more
- 1 Amer. Indian/Alaska Native
- 2 Asian
- 3 Black/African American
- 4 Canadian Aboriginal
- 5 Caucasian/White
- 6 Hispanic/Latino
- 7 Native Hawaiian/ Other Pacific Islander
- 8 Puerto Rican
- 9 TSI/Aboriginal Australian

8 GENDER
- Male
- Female

9 DOMINANT LANGUAGE
- English
- Other

10 ENGLISH FLUENCY
- Yes
- No

11 TEST DATE — MONTH / DAY / YEAR

12 TEST FORM

Law School Admission Test

Mark one and only one answer to each question. Be sure to fill in completely the space for your intended answer choice. If you erase, do so completely. Make no stray marks.

13 TEST BOOK SERIAL NO.

SECTION 1	SECTION 2	SECTION 3	SECTION 4	SECTION 5
1 A B C D E	1 A B C D E	1 A B C D E	1 A B C D E	1 A B C D E
2 A B C D E	2 A B C D E	2 A B C D E	2 A B C D E	2 A B C D E
3 A B C D E	3 A B C D E	3 A B C D E	3 A B C D E	3 A B C D E
4 A B C D E	4 A B C D E	4 A B C D E	4 A B C D E	4 A B C D E
5 A B C D E	5 A B C D E	5 A B C D E	5 A B C D E	5 A B C D E
6 A B C D E	6 A B C D E	6 A B C D E	6 A B C D E	6 A B C D E
7 A B C D E	7 A B C D E	7 A B C D E	7 A B C D E	7 A B C D E
8 A B C D E	8 A B C D E	8 A B C D E	8 A B C D E	8 A B C D E
9 A B C D E	9 A B C D E	9 A B C D E	9 A B C D E	9 A B C D E
10 A B C D E	10 A B C D E	10 A B C D E	10 A B C D E	10 A B C D E
11 A B C D E	11 A B C D E	11 A B C D E	11 A B C D E	11 A B C D E
12 A B C D E	12 A B C D E	12 A B C D E	12 A B C D E	12 A B C D E
13 A B C D E	13 A B C D E	13 A B C D E	13 A B C D E	13 A B C D E
14 A B C D E	14 A B C D E	14 A B C D E	14 A B C D E	14 A B C D E
15 A B C D E	15 A B C D E	15 A B C D E	15 A B C D E	15 A B C D E
16 A B C D E	16 A B C D E	16 A B C D E	16 A B C D E	16 A B C D E
17 A B C D E	17 A B C D E	17 A B C D E	17 A B C D E	17 A B C D E
18 A B C D E	18 A B C D E	18 A B C D E	18 A B C D E	18 A B C D E
19 A B C D E	19 A B C D E	19 A B C D E	19 A B C D E	19 A B C D E
20 A B C D E	20 A B C D E	20 A B C D E	20 A B C D E	20 A B C D E
21 A B C D E	21 A B C D E	21 A B C D E	21 A B C D E	21 A B C D E
22 A B C D E	22 A B C D E	22 A B C D E	22 A B C D E	22 A B C D E
23 A B C D E	23 A B C D E	23 A B C D E	23 A B C D E	23 A B C D E
24 A B C D E	24 A B C D E	24 A B C D E	24 A B C D E	24 A B C D E
25 A B C D E	25 A B C D E	25 A B C D E	25 A B C D E	25 A B C D E
26 A B C D E	26 A B C D E	26 A B C D E	26 A B C D E	26 A B C D E
27 A B C D E	27 A B C D E	27 A B C D E	27 A B C D E	27 A B C D E
28 A B C D E	28 A B C D E	28 A B C D E	28 A B C D E	28 A B C D E
29 A B C D E	29 A B C D E	29 A B C D E	29 A B C D E	29 A B C D E
30 A B C D E	30 A B C D E	30 A B C D E	30 A B C D E	30 A B C D E

14 PLEASE PRINT INFORMATION

LAST NAME

FIRST NAME

DATE OF BIRTH

INSTRUCTIONS FOR COMPLETING THE BIOGRAPHICAL AREA ARE ON THE BACK COVER OF YOUR TEST BOOKLET.
USE ONLY A NO. 2 OR HB PENCIL TO COMPLETE THIS ANSWER SHEET. DO NOT USE INK.

A

1 LAST NAME — FIRST NAME — MI

2 LAST 4 DIGITS OF SOCIAL SECURITY/ SOCIAL INSURANCE NO.

3 LSAC ACCOUNT NUMBER

4 CENTER NUMBER

5 DATE OF BIRTH

MONTH	DAY	YEAR
Jan		
Feb		
Mar		
Apr		
May		
June		
July		
Aug		
Sept		
Oct		
Nov		
Dec		

6 TEST FORM CODE

7 RACIAL/ETHNIC DESCRIPTION
Mark one or more
1 Amer. Indian/Alaska Native
2 Asian
3 Black/African American
4 Canadian Aboriginal
5 Caucasian/White
6 Hispanic/Latino
7 Native Hawaiian/ Other Pacific Islander
8 Puerto Rican
9 TSI/Aboriginal Australian

8 GENDER
Male
Female

9 DOMINANT LANGUAGE
English
Other

10 ENGLISH FLUENCY
Yes
No

11 TEST DATE
____ / ____ / ____
MONTH   DAY   YEAR

12 TEST FORM

13 TEST BOOK SERIAL NO.

Law School Admission Test

Mark one and only one answer to each question. Be sure to fill in completely the space for your intended answer choice. If you erase, do so completely. Make no stray marks.

14 PLEASE PRINT INFORMATION
LAST NAME
FIRST NAME
DATE OF BIRTH

SECTION 1	SECTION 2	SECTION 3	SECTION 4	SECTION 5
1 A B C D E	1 A B C D E	1 A B C D E	1 A B C D E	1 A B C D E
2 A B C D E	2 A B C D E	2 A B C D E	2 A B C D E	2 A B C D E
3 A B C D E	3 A B C D E	3 A B C D E	3 A B C D E	3 A B C D E
4 A B C D E	4 A B C D E	4 A B C D E	4 A B C D E	4 A B C D E
5 A B C D E	5 A B C D E	5 A B C D E	5 A B C D E	5 A B C D E
6 A B C D E	6 A B C D E	6 A B C D E	6 A B C D E	6 A B C D E
7 A B C D E	7 A B C D E	7 A B C D E	7 A B C D E	7 A B C D E
8 A B C D E	8 A B C D E	8 A B C D E	8 A B C D E	8 A B C D E
9 A B C D E	9 A B C D E	9 A B C D E	9 A B C D E	9 A B C D E
10 A B C D E	10 A B C D E	10 A B C D E	10 A B C D E	10 A B C D E
11 A B C D E	11 A B C D E	11 A B C D E	11 A B C D E	11 A B C D E
12 A B C D E	12 A B C D E	12 A B C D E	12 A B C D E	12 A B C D E
13 A B C D E	13 A B C D E	13 A B C D E	13 A B C D E	13 A B C D E
14 A B C D E	14 A B C D E	14 A B C D E	14 A B C D E	14 A B C D E
15 A B C D E	15 A B C D E	15 A B C D E	15 A B C D E	15 A B C D E
16 A B C D E	16 A B C D E	16 A B C D E	16 A B C D E	16 A B C D E
17 A B C D E	17 A B C D E	17 A B C D E	17 A B C D E	17 A B C D E
18 A B C D E	18 A B C D E	18 A B C D E	18 A B C D E	18 A B C D E
19 A B C D E	19 A B C D E	19 A B C D E	19 A B C D E	19 A B C D E
20 A B C D E	20 A B C D E	20 A B C D E	20 A B C D E	20 A B C D E
21 A B C D E	21 A B C D E	21 A B C D E	21 A B C D E	21 A B C D E
22 A B C D E	22 A B C D E	22 A B C D E	22 A B C D E	22 A B C D E
23 A B C D E	23 A B C D E	23 A B C D E	23 A B C D E	23 A B C D E
24 A B C D E	24 A B C D E	24 A B C D E	24 A B C D E	24 A B C D E
25 A B C D E	25 A B C D E	25 A B C D E	25 A B C D E	25 A B C D E
26 A B C D E	26 A B C D E	26 A B C D E	26 A B C D E	26 A B C D E
27 A B C D E	27 A B C D E	27 A B C D E	27 A B C D E	27 A B C D E
28 A B C D E	28 A B C D E	28 A B C D E	28 A B C D E	28 A B C D E
29 A B C D E	29 A B C D E	29 A B C D E	29 A B C D E	29 A B C D E
30 A B C D E	30 A B C D E	30 A B C D E	30 A B C D E	30 A B C D E

INSTRUCTIONS FOR COMPLETING THE BIOGRAPHICAL AREA ARE ON THE BACK COVER OF YOUR TEST BOOKLET.
USE ONLY A NO. 2 OR HB PENCIL TO COMPLETE THIS ANSWER SHEET. DO NOT USE INK.

A

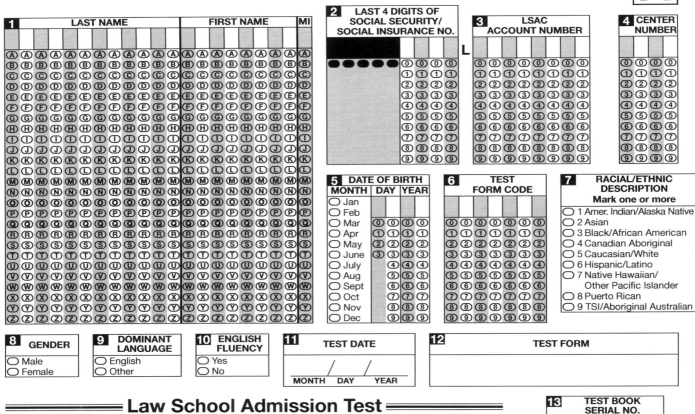

1 LAST NAME   FIRST NAME   MI

2 LAST 4 DIGITS OF SOCIAL SECURITY/ SOCIAL INSURANCE NO.

3 LSAC ACCOUNT NUMBER

4 CENTER NUMBER

5 DATE OF BIRTH — MONTH | DAY | YEAR
Jan, Feb, Mar, Apr, May, June, July, Aug, Sept, Oct, Nov, Dec

6 TEST FORM CODE

7 RACIAL/ETHNIC DESCRIPTION
Mark one or more
1 Amer. Indian/Alaska Native
2 Asian
3 Black/African American
4 Canadian Aboriginal
5 Caucasian/White
6 Hispanic/Latino
7 Native Hawaiian/ Other Pacific Islander
8 Puerto Rican
9 TSI/Aboriginal Australian

8 GENDER
Male
Female

9 DOMINANT LANGUAGE
English
Other

10 ENGLISH FLUENCY
Yes
No

11 TEST DATE
/ /
MONTH   DAY   YEAR

12 TEST FORM

Law School Admission Test

Mark one and only one answer to each question. Be sure to fill in completely the space for your intended answer choice. If you erase, do so completely. Make no stray marks.

13 TEST BOOK SERIAL NO.

SECTION 1	SECTION 2	SECTION 3	SECTION 4	SECTION 5
1 A B C D E	1 A B C D E	1 A B C D E	1 A B C D E	1 A B C D E
2 A B C D E	2 A B C D E	2 A B C D E	2 A B C D E	2 A B C D E
3 A B C D E	3 A B C D E	3 A B C D E	3 A B C D E	3 A B C D E
4 A B C D E	4 A B C D E	4 A B C D E	4 A B C D E	4 A B C D E
5 A B C D E	5 A B C D E	5 A B C D E	5 A B C D E	5 A B C D E
6 A B C D E	6 A B C D E	6 A B C D E	6 A B C D E	6 A B C D E
7 A B C D E	7 A B C D E	7 A B C D E	7 A B C D E	7 A B C D E
8 A B C D E	8 A B C D E	8 A B C D E	8 A B C D E	8 A B C D E
9 A B C D E	9 A B C D E	9 A B C D E	9 A B C D E	9 A B C D E
10 A B C D E	10 A B C D E	10 A B C D E	10 A B C D E	10 A B C D E
11 A B C D E	11 A B C D E	11 A B C D E	11 A B C D E	11 A B C D E
12 A B C D E	12 A B C D E	12 A B C D E	12 A B C D E	12 A B C D E
13 A B C D E	13 A B C D E	13 A B C D E	13 A B C D E	13 A B C D E
14 A B C D E	14 A B C D E	14 A B C D E	14 A B C D E	14 A B C D E
15 A B C D E	15 A B C D E	15 A B C D E	15 A B C D E	15 A B C D E
16 A B C D E	16 A B C D E	16 A B C D E	16 A B C D E	16 A B C D E
17 A B C D E	17 A B C D E	17 A B C D E	17 A B C D E	17 A B C D E
18 A B C D E	18 A B C D E	18 A B C D E	18 A B C D E	18 A B C D E
19 A B C D E	19 A B C D E	19 A B C D E	19 A B C D E	19 A B C D E
20 A B C D E	20 A B C D E	20 A B C D E	20 A B C D E	20 A B C D E
21 A B C D E	21 A B C D E	21 A B C D E	21 A B C D E	21 A B C D E
22 A B C D E	22 A B C D E	22 A B C D E	22 A B C D E	22 A B C D E
23 A B C D E	23 A B C D E	23 A B C D E	23 A B C D E	23 A B C D E
24 A B C D E	24 A B C D E	24 A B C D E	24 A B C D E	24 A B C D E
25 A B C D E	25 A B C D E	25 A B C D E	25 A B C D E	25 A B C D E
26 A B C D E	26 A B C D E	26 A B C D E	26 A B C D E	26 A B C D E
27 A B C D E	27 A B C D E	27 A B C D E	27 A B C D E	27 A B C D E
28 A B C D E	28 A B C D E	28 A B C D E	28 A B C D E	28 A B C D E
29 A B C D E	29 A B C D E	29 A B C D E	29 A B C D E	29 A B C D E
30 A B C D E	30 A B C D E	30 A B C D E	30 A B C D E	30 A B C D E

14 PLEASE PRINT INFORMATION
LAST NAME
FIRST NAME
DATE OF BIRTH

INSTRUCTIONS FOR COMPLETING THE BIOGRAPHICAL AREA ARE ON THE BACK COVER OF YOUR TEST BOOKLET.
USE ONLY A NO. 2 OR HB PENCIL TO COMPLETE THIS ANSWER SHEET. DO NOT USE INK.

A

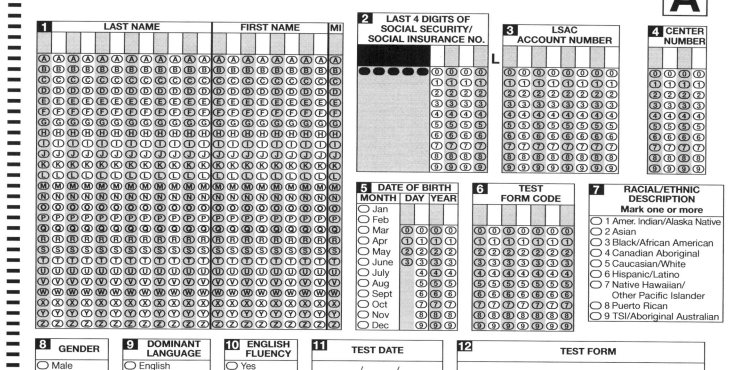

8 GENDER
○ Male
○ Female

9 DOMINANT LANGUAGE
○ English
○ Other

10 ENGLISH FLUENCY
○ Yes
○ No

11 TEST DATE
___ / ___ / ___
MONTH   DAY   YEAR

12 TEST FORM

Law School Admission Test

Mark one and only one answer to each question. Be sure to fill in completely the space for your intended answer choice. If you erase, do so completely. Make no stray marks.

13 TEST BOOK SERIAL NO.

14 PLEASE PRINT INFORMATION
LAST NAME
FIRST NAME
DATE OF BIRTH

SECTION 1	SECTION 2	SECTION 3	SECTION 4	SECTION 5
1 Ⓐ Ⓑ Ⓒ Ⓓ Ⓔ	1 Ⓐ Ⓑ Ⓒ Ⓓ Ⓔ	1 Ⓐ Ⓑ Ⓒ Ⓓ Ⓔ	1 Ⓐ Ⓑ Ⓒ Ⓓ Ⓔ	1 Ⓐ Ⓑ Ⓒ Ⓓ Ⓔ
2 Ⓐ Ⓑ Ⓒ Ⓓ Ⓔ	2 Ⓐ Ⓑ Ⓒ Ⓓ Ⓔ	2 Ⓐ Ⓑ Ⓒ Ⓓ Ⓔ	2 Ⓐ Ⓑ Ⓒ Ⓓ Ⓔ	2 Ⓐ Ⓑ Ⓒ Ⓓ Ⓔ
3 Ⓐ Ⓑ Ⓒ Ⓓ Ⓔ	3 Ⓐ Ⓑ Ⓒ Ⓓ Ⓔ	3 Ⓐ Ⓑ Ⓒ Ⓓ Ⓔ	3 Ⓐ Ⓑ Ⓒ Ⓓ Ⓔ	3 Ⓐ Ⓑ Ⓒ Ⓓ Ⓔ
4 Ⓐ Ⓑ Ⓒ Ⓓ Ⓔ	4 Ⓐ Ⓑ Ⓒ Ⓓ Ⓔ	4 Ⓐ Ⓑ Ⓒ Ⓓ Ⓔ	4 Ⓐ Ⓑ Ⓒ Ⓓ Ⓔ	4 Ⓐ Ⓑ Ⓒ Ⓓ Ⓔ
5 Ⓐ Ⓑ Ⓒ Ⓓ Ⓔ	5 Ⓐ Ⓑ Ⓒ Ⓓ Ⓔ	5 Ⓐ Ⓑ Ⓒ Ⓓ Ⓔ	5 Ⓐ Ⓑ Ⓒ Ⓓ Ⓔ	5 Ⓐ Ⓑ Ⓒ Ⓓ Ⓔ
6 Ⓐ Ⓑ Ⓒ Ⓓ Ⓔ	6 Ⓐ Ⓑ Ⓒ Ⓓ Ⓔ	6 Ⓐ Ⓑ Ⓒ Ⓓ Ⓔ	6 Ⓐ Ⓑ Ⓒ Ⓓ Ⓔ	6 Ⓐ Ⓑ Ⓒ Ⓓ Ⓔ
7 Ⓐ Ⓑ Ⓒ Ⓓ Ⓔ	7 Ⓐ Ⓑ Ⓒ Ⓓ Ⓔ	7 Ⓐ Ⓑ Ⓒ Ⓓ Ⓔ	7 Ⓐ Ⓑ Ⓒ Ⓓ Ⓔ	7 Ⓐ Ⓑ Ⓒ Ⓓ Ⓔ
8 Ⓐ Ⓑ Ⓒ Ⓓ Ⓔ	8 Ⓐ Ⓑ Ⓒ Ⓓ Ⓔ	8 Ⓐ Ⓑ Ⓒ Ⓓ Ⓔ	8 Ⓐ Ⓑ Ⓒ Ⓓ Ⓔ	8 Ⓐ Ⓑ Ⓒ Ⓓ Ⓔ
9 Ⓐ Ⓑ Ⓒ Ⓓ Ⓔ	9 Ⓐ Ⓑ Ⓒ Ⓓ Ⓔ	9 Ⓐ Ⓑ Ⓒ Ⓓ Ⓔ	9 Ⓐ Ⓑ Ⓒ Ⓓ Ⓔ	9 Ⓐ Ⓑ Ⓒ Ⓓ Ⓔ
10 Ⓐ Ⓑ Ⓒ Ⓓ Ⓔ	10 Ⓐ Ⓑ Ⓒ Ⓓ Ⓔ	10 Ⓐ Ⓑ Ⓒ Ⓓ Ⓔ	10 Ⓐ Ⓑ Ⓒ Ⓓ Ⓔ	10 Ⓐ Ⓑ Ⓒ Ⓓ Ⓔ
11 Ⓐ Ⓑ Ⓒ Ⓓ Ⓔ	11 Ⓐ Ⓑ Ⓒ Ⓓ Ⓔ	11 Ⓐ Ⓑ Ⓒ Ⓓ Ⓔ	11 Ⓐ Ⓑ Ⓒ Ⓓ Ⓔ	11 Ⓐ Ⓑ Ⓒ Ⓓ Ⓔ
12 Ⓐ Ⓑ Ⓒ Ⓓ Ⓔ	12 Ⓐ Ⓑ Ⓒ Ⓓ Ⓔ	12 Ⓐ Ⓑ Ⓒ Ⓓ Ⓔ	12 Ⓐ Ⓑ Ⓒ Ⓓ Ⓔ	12 Ⓐ Ⓑ Ⓒ Ⓓ Ⓔ
13 Ⓐ Ⓑ Ⓒ Ⓓ Ⓔ	13 Ⓐ Ⓑ Ⓒ Ⓓ Ⓔ	13 Ⓐ Ⓑ Ⓒ Ⓓ Ⓔ	13 Ⓐ Ⓑ Ⓒ Ⓓ Ⓔ	13 Ⓐ Ⓑ Ⓒ Ⓓ Ⓔ
14 Ⓐ Ⓑ Ⓒ Ⓓ Ⓔ	14 Ⓐ Ⓑ Ⓒ Ⓓ Ⓔ	14 Ⓐ Ⓑ Ⓒ Ⓓ Ⓔ	14 Ⓐ Ⓑ Ⓒ Ⓓ Ⓔ	14 Ⓐ Ⓑ Ⓒ Ⓓ Ⓔ
15 Ⓐ Ⓑ Ⓒ Ⓓ Ⓔ	15 Ⓐ Ⓑ Ⓒ Ⓓ Ⓔ	15 Ⓐ Ⓑ Ⓒ Ⓓ Ⓔ	15 Ⓐ Ⓑ Ⓒ Ⓓ Ⓔ	15 Ⓐ Ⓑ Ⓒ Ⓓ Ⓔ
16 Ⓐ Ⓑ Ⓒ Ⓓ Ⓔ	16 Ⓐ Ⓑ Ⓒ Ⓓ Ⓔ	16 Ⓐ Ⓑ Ⓒ Ⓓ Ⓔ	16 Ⓐ Ⓑ Ⓒ Ⓓ Ⓔ	16 Ⓐ Ⓑ Ⓒ Ⓓ Ⓔ
17 Ⓐ Ⓑ Ⓒ Ⓓ Ⓔ	17 Ⓐ Ⓑ Ⓒ Ⓓ Ⓔ	17 Ⓐ Ⓑ Ⓒ Ⓓ Ⓔ	17 Ⓐ Ⓑ Ⓒ Ⓓ Ⓔ	17 Ⓐ Ⓑ Ⓒ Ⓓ Ⓔ
18 Ⓐ Ⓑ Ⓒ Ⓓ Ⓔ	18 Ⓐ Ⓑ Ⓒ Ⓓ Ⓔ	18 Ⓐ Ⓑ Ⓒ Ⓓ Ⓔ	18 Ⓐ Ⓑ Ⓒ Ⓓ Ⓔ	18 Ⓐ Ⓑ Ⓒ Ⓓ Ⓔ
19 Ⓐ Ⓑ Ⓒ Ⓓ Ⓔ	19 Ⓐ Ⓑ Ⓒ Ⓓ Ⓔ	19 Ⓐ Ⓑ Ⓒ Ⓓ Ⓔ	19 Ⓐ Ⓑ Ⓒ Ⓓ Ⓔ	19 Ⓐ Ⓑ Ⓒ Ⓓ Ⓔ
20 Ⓐ Ⓑ Ⓒ Ⓓ Ⓔ	20 Ⓐ Ⓑ Ⓒ Ⓓ Ⓔ	20 Ⓐ Ⓑ Ⓒ Ⓓ Ⓔ	20 Ⓐ Ⓑ Ⓒ Ⓓ Ⓔ	20 Ⓐ Ⓑ Ⓒ Ⓓ Ⓔ
21 Ⓐ Ⓑ Ⓒ Ⓓ Ⓔ	21 Ⓐ Ⓑ Ⓒ Ⓓ Ⓔ	21 Ⓐ Ⓑ Ⓒ Ⓓ Ⓔ	21 Ⓐ Ⓑ Ⓒ Ⓓ Ⓔ	21 Ⓐ Ⓑ Ⓒ Ⓓ Ⓔ
22 Ⓐ Ⓑ Ⓒ Ⓓ Ⓔ	22 Ⓐ Ⓑ Ⓒ Ⓓ Ⓔ	22 Ⓐ Ⓑ Ⓒ Ⓓ Ⓔ	22 Ⓐ Ⓑ Ⓒ Ⓓ Ⓔ	22 Ⓐ Ⓑ Ⓒ Ⓓ Ⓔ
23 Ⓐ Ⓑ Ⓒ Ⓓ Ⓔ	23 Ⓐ Ⓑ Ⓒ Ⓓ Ⓔ	23 Ⓐ Ⓑ Ⓒ Ⓓ Ⓔ	23 Ⓐ Ⓑ Ⓒ Ⓓ Ⓔ	23 Ⓐ Ⓑ Ⓒ Ⓓ Ⓔ
24 Ⓐ Ⓑ Ⓒ Ⓓ Ⓔ	24 Ⓐ Ⓑ Ⓒ Ⓓ Ⓔ	24 Ⓐ Ⓑ Ⓒ Ⓓ Ⓔ	24 Ⓐ Ⓑ Ⓒ Ⓓ Ⓔ	24 Ⓐ Ⓑ Ⓒ Ⓓ Ⓔ
25 Ⓐ Ⓑ Ⓒ Ⓓ Ⓔ	25 Ⓐ Ⓑ Ⓒ Ⓓ Ⓔ	25 Ⓐ Ⓑ Ⓒ Ⓓ Ⓔ	25 Ⓐ Ⓑ Ⓒ Ⓓ Ⓔ	25 Ⓐ Ⓑ Ⓒ Ⓓ Ⓔ
26 Ⓐ Ⓑ Ⓒ Ⓓ Ⓔ	26 Ⓐ Ⓑ Ⓒ Ⓓ Ⓔ	26 Ⓐ Ⓑ Ⓒ Ⓓ Ⓔ	26 Ⓐ Ⓑ Ⓒ Ⓓ Ⓔ	26 Ⓐ Ⓑ Ⓒ Ⓓ Ⓔ
27 Ⓐ Ⓑ Ⓒ Ⓓ Ⓔ	27 Ⓐ Ⓑ Ⓒ Ⓓ Ⓔ	27 Ⓐ Ⓑ Ⓒ Ⓓ Ⓔ	27 Ⓐ Ⓑ Ⓒ Ⓓ Ⓔ	27 Ⓐ Ⓑ Ⓒ Ⓓ Ⓔ
28 Ⓐ Ⓑ Ⓒ Ⓓ Ⓔ	28 Ⓐ Ⓑ Ⓒ Ⓓ Ⓔ	28 Ⓐ Ⓑ Ⓒ Ⓓ Ⓔ	28 Ⓐ Ⓑ Ⓒ Ⓓ Ⓔ	28 Ⓐ Ⓑ Ⓒ Ⓓ Ⓔ
29 Ⓐ Ⓑ Ⓒ Ⓓ Ⓔ	29 Ⓐ Ⓑ Ⓒ Ⓓ Ⓔ	29 Ⓐ Ⓑ Ⓒ Ⓓ Ⓔ	29 Ⓐ Ⓑ Ⓒ Ⓓ Ⓔ	29 Ⓐ Ⓑ Ⓒ Ⓓ Ⓔ
30 Ⓐ Ⓑ Ⓒ Ⓓ Ⓔ	30 Ⓐ Ⓑ Ⓒ Ⓓ Ⓔ	30 Ⓐ Ⓑ Ⓒ Ⓓ Ⓔ	30 Ⓐ Ⓑ Ⓒ Ⓓ Ⓔ	30 Ⓐ Ⓑ Ⓒ Ⓓ Ⓔ

SCANTRON EliteView™ EM-290725-3:654321

INSTRUCTIONS FOR COMPLETING THE BIOGRAPHICAL AREA ARE ON THE BACK COVER OF YOUR TEST BOOKLET.
USE ONLY A NO. 2 OR HB PENCIL TO COMPLETE THIS ANSWER SHEET. DO NOT USE INK.

A

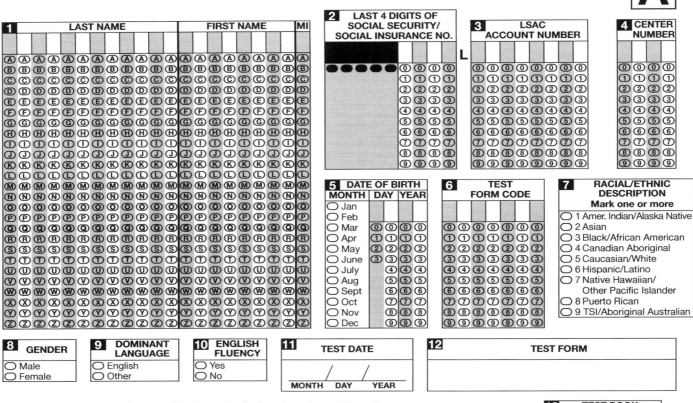

1 LAST NAME / FIRST NAME / MI

2 LAST 4 DIGITS OF SOCIAL SECURITY/SOCIAL INSURANCE NO.

3 LSAC ACCOUNT NUMBER

4 CENTER NUMBER

5 DATE OF BIRTH — MONTH DAY YEAR

6 TEST FORM CODE

7 RACIAL/ETHNIC DESCRIPTION
Mark one or more
- ○ 1 Amer. Indian/Alaska Native
- ○ 2 Asian
- ○ 3 Black/African American
- ○ 4 Canadian Aboriginal
- ○ 5 Caucasian/White
- ○ 6 Hispanic/Latino
- ○ 7 Native Hawaiian/ Other Pacific Islander
- ○ 8 Puerto Rican
- ○ 9 TSI/Aboriginal Australian

8 GENDER
- ○ Male
- ○ Female

9 DOMINANT LANGUAGE
- ○ English
- ○ Other

10 ENGLISH FLUENCY
- ○ Yes
- ○ No

11 TEST DATE
MONTH / DAY / YEAR

12 TEST FORM

13 TEST BOOK SERIAL NO.

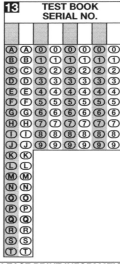

Law School Admission Test

Mark one and only one answer to each question. Be sure to fill in completely the space for your intended answer choice. If you erase, do so completely. Make no stray marks.

SECTION 1

1	Ⓐ Ⓑ Ⓒ Ⓓ Ⓔ
2	Ⓐ Ⓑ Ⓒ Ⓓ Ⓔ
3	Ⓐ Ⓑ Ⓒ Ⓓ Ⓔ
4	Ⓐ Ⓑ Ⓒ Ⓓ Ⓔ
5	Ⓐ Ⓑ Ⓒ Ⓓ Ⓔ
6	Ⓐ Ⓑ Ⓒ Ⓓ Ⓔ
7	Ⓐ Ⓑ Ⓒ Ⓓ Ⓔ
8	Ⓐ Ⓑ Ⓒ Ⓓ Ⓔ
9	Ⓐ Ⓑ Ⓒ Ⓓ Ⓔ
10	Ⓐ Ⓑ Ⓒ Ⓓ Ⓔ
11	Ⓐ Ⓑ Ⓒ Ⓓ Ⓔ
12	Ⓐ Ⓑ Ⓒ Ⓓ Ⓔ
13	Ⓐ Ⓑ Ⓒ Ⓓ Ⓔ
14	Ⓐ Ⓑ Ⓒ Ⓓ Ⓔ
15	Ⓐ Ⓑ Ⓒ Ⓓ Ⓔ
16	Ⓐ Ⓑ Ⓒ Ⓓ Ⓔ
17	Ⓐ Ⓑ Ⓒ Ⓓ Ⓔ
18	Ⓐ Ⓑ Ⓒ Ⓓ Ⓔ
19	Ⓐ Ⓑ Ⓒ Ⓓ Ⓔ
20	Ⓐ Ⓑ Ⓒ Ⓓ Ⓔ
21	Ⓐ Ⓑ Ⓒ Ⓓ Ⓔ
22	Ⓐ Ⓑ Ⓒ Ⓓ Ⓔ
23	Ⓐ Ⓑ Ⓒ Ⓓ Ⓔ
24	Ⓐ Ⓑ Ⓒ Ⓓ Ⓔ
25	Ⓐ Ⓑ Ⓒ Ⓓ Ⓔ
26	Ⓐ Ⓑ Ⓒ Ⓓ Ⓔ
27	Ⓐ Ⓑ Ⓒ Ⓓ Ⓔ
28	Ⓐ Ⓑ Ⓒ Ⓓ Ⓔ
29	Ⓐ Ⓑ Ⓒ Ⓓ Ⓔ
30	Ⓐ Ⓑ Ⓒ Ⓓ Ⓔ

SECTION 2 (questions 1–30, each Ⓐ Ⓑ Ⓒ Ⓓ Ⓔ)

SECTION 3 (questions 1–30, each Ⓐ Ⓑ Ⓒ Ⓓ Ⓔ)

SECTION 4 (questions 1–30, each Ⓐ Ⓑ Ⓒ Ⓓ Ⓔ)

SECTION 5 (questions 1–30, each Ⓐ Ⓑ Ⓒ Ⓓ Ⓔ)

14 PLEASE PRINT INFORMATION

LAST NAME

FIRST NAME

DATE OF BIRTH

● Ⓑ

SIDE 1

A

INSTRUCTIONS FOR COMPLETING THE BIOGRAPHICAL AREA ARE ON THE BACK COVER OF YOUR TEST BOOKLET.
USE ONLY A NO. 2 OR HB PENCIL TO COMPLETE THIS ANSWER SHEET. DO NOT USE INK.

1 LAST NAME | FIRST NAME | MI

2 LAST 4 DIGITS OF SOCIAL SECURITY/ SOCIAL INSURANCE NO.

L

3 LSAC ACCOUNT NUMBER

4 CENTER NUMBER

5 DATE OF BIRTH

MONTH	DAY	YEAR
Jan		
Feb		
Mar		
Apr		
May		
June		
July		
Aug		
Sept		
Oct		
Nov		
Dec		

6 TEST FORM CODE

7 RACIAL/ETHNIC DESCRIPTION
Mark one or more

- 1 Amer. Indian/Alaska Native
- 2 Asian
- 3 Black/African American
- 4 Canadian Aboriginal
- 5 Caucasian/White
- 6 Hispanic/Latino
- 7 Native Hawaiian/ Other Pacific Islander
- 8 Puerto Rican
- 9 TSI/Aboriginal Australian

8 GENDER
- Male
- Female

9 DOMINANT LANGUAGE
- English
- Other

10 ENGLISH FLUENCY
- Yes
- No

11 TEST DATE
/ /
MONTH DAY YEAR

12 TEST FORM

Law School Admission Test

Mark one and only one answer to each question. Be sure to fill in completely the space for your intended answer choice. If you erase, do so completely. Make no stray marks.

13 TEST BOOK SERIAL NO.

SECTION 1	SECTION 2	SECTION 3	SECTION 4	SECTION 5
1 A B C D E	1 A B C D E	1 A B C D E	1 A B C D E	1 A B C D E
2 A B C D E	2 A B C D E	2 A B C D E	2 A B C D E	2 A B C D E
3 A B C D E	3 A B C D E	3 A B C D E	3 A B C D E	3 A B C D E
4 A B C D E	4 A B C D E	4 A B C D E	4 A B C D E	4 A B C D E
5 A B C D E	5 A B C D E	5 A B C D E	5 A B C D E	5 A B C D E
6 A B C D E	6 A B C D E	6 A B C D E	6 A B C D E	6 A B C D E
7 A B C D E	7 A B C D E	7 A B C D E	7 A B C D E	7 A B C D E
8 A B C D E	8 A B C D E	8 A B C D E	8 A B C D E	8 A B C D E
9 A B C D E	9 A B C D E	9 A B C D E	9 A B C D E	9 A B C D E
10 A B C D E	10 A B C D E	10 A B C D E	10 A B C D E	10 A B C D E
11 A B C D E	11 A B C D E	11 A B C D E	11 A B C D E	11 A B C D E
12 A B C D E	12 A B C D E	12 A B C D E	12 A B C D E	12 A B C D E
13 A B C D E	13 A B C D E	13 A B C D E	13 A B C D E	13 A B C D E
14 A B C D E	14 A B C D E	14 A B C D E	14 A B C D E	14 A B C D E
15 A B C D E	15 A B C D E	15 A B C D E	15 A B C D E	15 A B C D E
16 A B C D E	16 A B C D E	16 A B C D E	16 A B C D E	16 A B C D E
17 A B C D E	17 A B C D E	17 A B C D E	17 A B C D E	17 A B C D E
18 A B C D E	18 A B C D E	18 A B C D E	18 A B C D E	18 A B C D E
19 A B C D E	19 A B C D E	19 A B C D E	19 A B C D E	19 A B C D E
20 A B C D E	20 A B C D E	20 A B C D E	20 A B C D E	20 A B C D E
21 A B C D E	21 A B C D E	21 A B C D E	21 A B C D E	21 A B C D E
22 A B C D E	22 A B C D E	22 A B C D E	22 A B C D E	22 A B C D E
23 A B C D E	23 A B C D E	23 A B C D E	23 A B C D E	23 A B C D E
24 A B C D E	24 A B C D E	24 A B C D E	24 A B C D E	24 A B C D E
25 A B C D E	25 A B C D E	25 A B C D E	25 A B C D E	25 A B C D E
26 A B C D E	26 A B C D E	26 A B C D E	26 A B C D E	26 A B C D E
27 A B C D E	27 A B C D E	27 A B C D E	27 A B C D E	27 A B C D E
28 A B C D E	28 A B C D E	28 A B C D E	28 A B C D E	28 A B C D E
29 A B C D E	29 A B C D E	29 A B C D E	29 A B C D E	29 A B C D E
30 A B C D E	30 A B C D E	30 A B C D E	30 A B C D E	30 A B C D E

14 PLEASE PRINT INFORMATION

LAST NAME

FIRST NAME

DATE OF BIRTH

A

INSTRUCTIONS FOR COMPLETING THE BIOGRAPHICAL AREA ARE ON THE BACK COVER OF YOUR TEST BOOKLET.
USE ONLY A NO. 2 OR HB PENCIL TO COMPLETE THIS ANSWER SHEET. DO NOT USE INK.

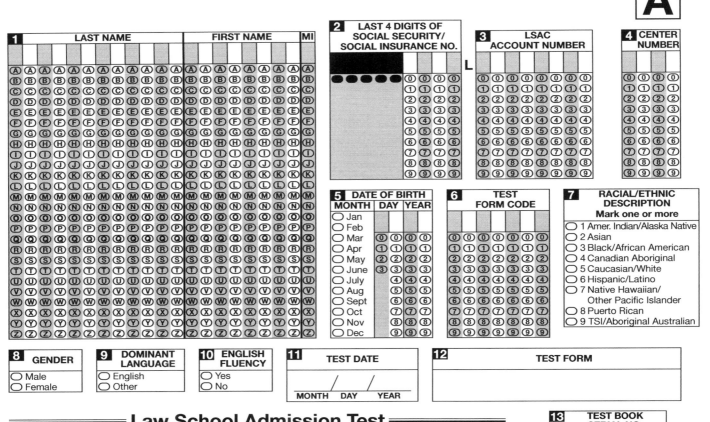

1 LAST NAME · FIRST NAME · MI

2 LAST 4 DIGITS OF SOCIAL SECURITY/ SOCIAL INSURANCE NO.

3 LSAC ACCOUNT NUMBER

4 CENTER NUMBER

5 DATE OF BIRTH — MONTH DAY YEAR
Jan, Feb, Mar, Apr, May, June, July, Aug, Sept, Oct, Nov, Dec

6 TEST FORM CODE

7 RACIAL/ETHNIC DESCRIPTION — Mark one or more
1 Amer. Indian/Alaska Native
2 Asian
3 Black/African American
4 Canadian Aboriginal
5 Caucasian/White
6 Hispanic/Latino
7 Native Hawaiian/ Other Pacific Islander
8 Puerto Rican
9 TSI/Aboriginal Australian

8 GENDER — Male / Female

9 DOMINANT LANGUAGE — English / Other

10 ENGLISH FLUENCY — Yes / No

11 TEST DATE — MONTH / DAY / YEAR

12 TEST FORM

Law School Admission Test

Mark one and only one answer to each question. Be sure to fill in completely the space for your intended answer choice. If you erase, do so completely. Make no stray marks.

SECTION 1 — questions 1–30, answer choices (A)(B)(C)(D)(E)
SECTION 2 — questions 1–30, answer choices (A)(B)(C)(D)(E)
SECTION 3 — questions 1–30, answer choices (A)(B)(C)(D)(E)
SECTION 4 — questions 1–30, answer choices (A)(B)(C)(D)(E)
SECTION 5 — questions 1–30, answer choices (A)(B)(C)(D)(E)

13 TEST BOOK SERIAL NO.

14 PLEASE PRINT INFORMATION
LAST NAME
FIRST NAME
DATE OF BIRTH

31045206R10215

Made in the USA
Charleston, SC
08 July 2014